Europe in the Middle Age

EUROPE IN THE MIDDLE AGE

BY

OLIVER J. THATCHER, PH.D.

AND

EDGAR HOLMES McNEAL, PH.D.

PROFESSOR OF EUROPEAN HISTORY IN THE OHIO STATE UNIVERSITY

WITH MAPS, CHARTS, AND ILLUSTRATIONS

CHARLES SCRIBNER'S SONS

NEW YORK CHICAGO BOSTON

A

To

THE MEMORY OF

HENRY HARRISON BROWN

1840-1917

"From all Life's grapes he pressed sweet wine."

PREFACE

The greatest factor in the progress of man has been his ability to use the experience—the achievements, the successes, and even the failures—of the generations that have preceded him. One generation stands on the shoulders of that which went before. It does not have to puzzle over the problems which its predecessor has solved. It need not follow the tortuous path of effort and failure which its predecessor followed. It need not expend its energy in inventing what has already been invented, in discovering what has already been discovered. The hard-won achievements of the past become stepping-stones to something greater and better. Every age builds on, and with, the yesterdays of the race. Of all creatures man alone is able to appropriate and to profit by the experiences of his kind. Else he would be as the beasts of the field, and progress would be impossible for him. The knowledge and appreciation of the best things that have been said and done should not only make a man cultured; they should also give him the best preparation for a life of higher and greater achievement. Does the study of history need any further justification? Does the twentieth century have less need of a knowledge of the Middle Age than of the nineteenth century? Indeed the nineteenth century gets its true perspective only when seen in its proper relation with the precedent centuries.

Of the utmost importance is it, therefore, that the achievements—intellectual, moral, spiritual, and material—the legacy, of an age should be passed on without diminution to its successor. For only when an age enters fully and freely on its heritage can it carry on the work of civilization at an accelerated speed. Failing of this, it must retrograde, and then slowly and with great effort find a new way over the lost course which its predecessor has travelled. Such a catastrophe serves to produce a marked contrast between what has gone before and what follows, and justifies us in making the convenient, though somewhat arbitrary, division of history into periods.

Now, just such a catastrophe in the fourth and fifth centuries ushered in the long period which we call the Middle Age. There is no doubt that, as will be clear from the first chapter of this book, there were many agencies at work to cause the people of the Roman empire to retrograde. But the crowning disaster, which cut nearly all of the western empire off from the legacy of the past, was the invasions of the barbarians. Their coming virtually destroyed existing government, both local and central; wiped out the schools, one of the chief instruments for passing on the achievements of one age to the next; weakened the administration of justice; and lowered almost to their own level the whole tone of society. We are fully justified, therefore, in regarding the invasions of the barbarians as the beginning of the Middle Age.

Why, it may be asked, did not the empire, reinforced with the high ideals and transforming power of the church, lift the barbarians up to its level instead of being brought down to theirs? The answer is plain: the more exalted an idea, the more difficult for a people that is low in the scale of civilization to adopt it. A barbarian people is not civilized by putting on civilization as a garment. A people must be fitted by nature and by training to appropriate fully—to make completely its own—the advanced ideas of a higher civilization. These ideas must wait for their complete reception until the whole nature of the people has been improved by long, continuous discipline.

The history of the Middle Age furnishes abundant proof of the truth of these statements. The legacy of the Roman empire, cut off by the coming of the barbarians, was not wholly destroyed but continued to exist, organized in the form of literature, law, ideas, and institutions.

The end of the Middle Age, not less than its beginning, is marked by a catastrophe. For, more than a hundred years of blighting, ruinous international, civil, and religious wars followed upon that stirring period which we call the Renaissance —a period, as we shall see, of voyage and discovery, of epoch-making inventions, of the keenest intellectual life, and of the most pronounced individualism, a period so full of life and energy that it seemed to promise a great acceleration in the process of civilization. So we conveniently end the Middle Age and begin the Modern Period with the commencement of those wars, which cut off the peoples of Europe from the beautiful and inspiring legacy of the Renaissance.

For another reason we are justified in fixing the beginning of the Middle Age at about 350 and the ending at about 1500. Changes in the conditions of living produce corresponding changes in a people. What were some of the important changes in the conditions of living that justify the limits assigned to the period?

1. As we have already said, the invasions of the barbarians virtually destroyed the existing machinery of government, both local and imperial, crippled the administration of justice, and wiped out the schools. Their wars and ravages were an attack on civilization and shook the civilized world on its foundations (Chapters II to IV).

2. At the same time commerce and industry were destroyed and almost every community was thereby made dependent on itself to supply its wants. The result was a rapid declension in the practical arts and the people generally were plunged into poverty (Chapter XXIV). In its organization the church was, as we shall see, modelled after the empire, and from the general wreckage saved all that it could. The church was essentially a reorganization of the forces of civilization, and in the course of the next thousand years transmitted, gradually and piecemeal, much of the legacy of Rome to the barbarians whom she slowly Christianized and civilized. There was a revival of learning among the Franks in the time of Charlemagne, which recovered a part of the legacy of Rome. Another revival in the twelfth century recovered a much larger part of it in the form of Roman law and literature. And the

Renaissance of the fourteenth and fifteenth centuries was a frank attempt to restore and enter again upon the civilization that had been Rome's.

3. This poverty, coupled with heavy taxation and with insecurity of life and justice, brought about a great social change and a new type of social organization. The middle class tended to disappear and there arose a large unfree class, the serfs (Chapters I, II, VII, and XXIV).

4. At the same time the church, with her vast system of ideas and practices, became powerful (Chapter VIII).

5. Asceticism in the form of monasticism became extremely popular (Chapter IX).

With these changed conditions the life of the people was profoundly modified and came into strong contrast with the life of the preceding centuries.

At the close of the Middle Age the changes in the conditions of living were perhaps even more marked.

1. The great plague known as the Black Death, which repeatedly ravaged Europe in the fourteenth century, led to a profound change in economic and social conditions and relations. It diminished serfdom and created a new social type, the free day-laborer (Chapter XIX).

2. Cities had become increasingly numerous and important because of their development in industry and commerce, and in their rich and powerful population we have a new type of social organization, the middle class or third estate (Chapter XXIV).

3. The empire and the papacy, the standard-bearers of the idea of world-wide empire, had become decadent (Chapters XXI and XXII), and in their place we find strong national governments ruled by kings who were ambitious to increase their authority at home and their power by conquest abroad. The feeling of nationalism was strong (Chapters XVI to XX).

4. Dissatisfaction with the papacy, which had been growing in volume and in intensity (Chapter XXI), culminated in the Protestant revolt (1517), which led to more than a century of ruinous war.

5. The ascetic ideal had lost its power to attract and monasticism had declined, and there was a more general feeling of joy and delight in this life (Chapter XXVI).

6. The discovery of America and of sea routes to India were only a part of a great period of voyage and discovery which opened up new fields of opportunity and endeavor (Chapter XXVI).

7. The Renaissance brought in new ideals in education and in art (Chapter XXVI).

8. And, finally, there were a few epoch-making inventions, such as gunpowder, the compass, paper, and movable type (Chapter XXVI).

In writing a brief history of the Middle Age the writer's most serious problem is connected with the choice of materials. It is impossible always to select out of the immense mass of historical materials of the period just those which will meet with the approval of his readers, much less that of his fellow historians. Each one will be influenced by the peculiar bent of his own mind, and by the line which his particular studies have taken. In general, I have been interested in explaining the genesis, the origins, of a movement, rather than in giving a detailed history of it. I thought it advisable to describe at some length the Roman empire because it is generally slighted in text-books, and especially because the Middle Age was developed on its ruins and drew from it both materials and inspiration. I have sketched rapidly and broadly the invasions of the barbarians and the kingdoms which they established within the empire, emphasizing only those details which seemed to me of special importance. The beginnings of the Franks, on the other hand, seemed to deserve a fuller treatment because of the great rôle which they were destined to play. I have written at some length about the imperial coronation of Charlemagne, not only because of the far-reaching effect of it but also because the character of it has, I think, generally been misunderstood.

In the chapter called "The Dissolution of the Empire" I have aimed merely to show the great lines of cleavage between the fragments into which the empire broke. To do this it seemed impossible not to introduce a large number of facts and names. Surely no teacher will require his students to commit these to memory. Their only purpose is to create in the mind a vivid and deep impression of the chaotic political conditions that existed in Europe about the year 900, and to indicate the lines along which some of the nascent states of western Europe were to develop.

The chapter on the development of the papacy also contains a large number of facts which are not meant to be committed to memory. They merely illustrate the lines along which the power of the bishop of Rome was growing and the conditions which made that growth possible and even inevitable. Most text-books slur over this subject and the student is generally left with the idea that somehow the papacy was either the miraculous creation of God or the work of scheming, ambitious, and unscrupulous bishops of Rome. I have shown the illustrative character of much of this material by the free use of foot-notes.

Monasticism is so foreign to the spirit of to-day that students have great difficulty in understanding it. Seen, however, in the light of the mental and the material state of the people of the third century, monasticism becomes explicable and natural. I have therefore spent more time in explaining the origins of the movement than in detailing its history.

In treating the struggle between the empire and the papacy I may have been influenced too much by the dramatic character of some of its episodes and by the fascination exercised on me by bold and effective personalities. I confess my sympathetic admiration for the three great popes and the three great emperors who played the leading rôles in that gigantic struggle. The struggle, however, had a tremendous influence on the political history of Germany and Italy.

From another point of view also that struggle is especially interesting. From the time of Alexander to the present there has appeared, at different times and under somewhat different forms, the idea of world domination. Nations and individuals have dreamed of reducing the whole world to subjection, of increasing their own glory and power by making the whole world subject to them. They have sought a place so high in the sun as to be able to overshadow all other peoples and individuals. Such an ideal is for many reasons alluring. Now, in the struggle between papacy and empire we have two aspirants to universal power, for the papacy claimed jurisdiction over the whole world and the empire had inherited Rome's pretensions to universal sway. The course of events in the world's history, however, has been away from autocracy toward democracy, from world empire toward national self-determination. That struggle claims our interest if only for the bigness of the ideals and interests involved.

I admit that the life of Mohammed, viewed narrowly, lies outside the field of European history. But in a larger, truer sense it may properly find a place there, because for centuries there has been a contest between Christian and Mohammedan peoples. It began with the attempt of the Mohammedans to establish themselves in Europe. The influence of Mohammedans on Europe has been considerable and, many times, good. The contest is far from being ended to-day. There are millions of Mohammedans in Europe, Asia, Africa, and the islands of the Pacific, and America is in many ways brought into contact with them. I have tried therefore to explain Mohammedanism by describing its founder. If I have succeeded in humanizing him, I am content.

The romantic character of the crusades is no doubt responsible for the extended treatment which they have heretofore received in text-books on mediæval history. The first edition of this book was the first text-book in English, I believe, to strip Peter the Hermit of his false honors and to portray the first crusade in its true character. The futility of the crusades as an effort to regain the Holy Land has led me to give them a brief treatment at the cost, perhaps, of much material that is romantic and full of color. I have not, however, slighted the effects of the crusades on Europe, although I have not followed those undiscriminating historians who have attributed every important change in Europe after 1100 to the influence of the crusades.

The remaining chapters will, I think, require no further explanation or apology.

I consider myself extremely fortunate in having had the help of Professor Edgar Holmes McNeal, of the Ohio State University. He has written the chapter on feudalism and the several chapters on France and England, as well as some pages of the chapter on "Civilization and Culture." Although he is in no way responsible for the shortcomings of the chapters which I have written, his criticisms and suggestions have been extremely helpful to me.

A feature of the book which I believe will be very helpful to both teachers and students, and also to the general reader, will be found in the copious marginal references to available source-books. S. B. refers to Thatcher and McNeal's *Source Book for Mediæval History;* R. refers to Robinson's *Readings;* O. refers to Ogg's *Source Book*, and M. refers to Munro's *Source Book for Roman History;* A. and S., to Adams and Stephens, *Select Documents of English Constitutional History;* L., to Lee's *Source Book of English History;* Ch., to Cheyney's *Selections from the Sources of English History.* The references are made to the numbers of the selections, and not to the pages.

Oliver J. Thatcher.

Beaumont, California.

CONTENTS

ILLUSTRATIONS

MAPS

EUROPE IN THE MIDDLE AGE

INTRODUCTION

THE earth is not merely the scene or stage on which history has been enacted, but by its physical forms and climate it has also affected the course of history. It is, therefore, necessary to keep in mind the physical geography of Europe, and to be constantly on the watch for its effects on the development of the peoples and states of Europe. Keeping in view the general character of this book, it would be out of place to do more than call attention to its mountain systems, its plains, its coast, its river systems, and its climate, and the effects which they tend to have on the life of its peoples.

Because of its varied natural conditions Europe is better fitted than any other continent to develop a high civilization. It has the advantage of size because it and Asia are so joined that they form but one great land mass and are, therefore, but one continent; it is fortunate in its zonal situation, for, although it extends from the tropical to the arctic, the most of it lies in the temperate zone; it has a great variety of relief and contour, being rich in mountains, valleys, and plains; it has a varied climate; its river systems are admirably arranged to promote travel and commerce; its rainfall is abundant and fairly well distributed; its flora and fauna are richly diversified; it has, in proportion to its area, the greatest length of coastline, with a large number of good harbors, and, on the whole, an excellent coastal zone.

Mountains act as natural barriers to communication between peoples separated by them, and tend to prevent war and to hinder commerce, the interchange of ideas, and the spread of civilization. Their effectiveness as barriers depends on the length of their chain, their height, their abruptness, and the number and character of their passes. They are likely to become permanent boundaries between states, races, and languages. Although they protect, they also isolate, and isolation may cause lethargy in a people. An isolated people must of itself develop its own resources and powers if it will keep pace with other nations. The greater the contact between two peoples, the more stimulating it is likely to be to both.

The influence of mountains on historical development may be illustrated by a brief statement of some of the effects which they have had on certain countries of Europe. Thus, the

The Pyrenees.

Pyrenees have protected Spain against successful aggression from Europe, but at the same time its people show the effects of isolation and the lack of stimulating contact with other peoples. The presence of Mohammedans in Spain from 711 to 1492 offset the ill effects of isolation by furnishing a strong internal stimulus to the Spaniards, which since then has been lacking. And, since the Pyrenees and the sea have together shut out foreign stimulus also, Spain has declined in the last four hundred years.

Again, although the Alps have not prevented northern powers from attempting to conquer and rule Italy, they have, in the long run, made all such attempts futile. Of all the countries bordered by the Alps Italy is the most unfortunate, because (1) the Alps are much more abrupt on the south than elsewhere, thus giving a northern invader the strategic advantage of a swift and sudden descent, and (2) all the passes, of which there are many, converge on the plain of the Po, enabling an enemy to invade the country by several passes at the same time, yet promptly unite all his troops as soon as they emerge from the mountains.

The Balkans are a continuation of the Alps, separating the Balkan peninsula from the valley of the lower Danube. The Balkan peninsula is extremely mountainous, and the segregating influence of mountains is seen in the formation of so many little Balkan states, such as Bosnia, Herzegovina, Servia, Montenegro, Bulgaria, and Greece.

The series of mountain chains and groups which surround

Bohemia on all sides except the south had the effect, during the Middle Age, of preserving the Bohemians against the influences which the Germans brought to bear upon them from the west and north. But for the existence of these mountains it is probable that the Germans, who were vigorously pushing their conquests to the east, would have conquered and germanized the Bohemians, as they did all their Slavic neighbors on the north between the Elbe and Vistula. Similarly the Hungarians have been protected from aggression on three sides by the Carpathians, which, like the mountains around Bohemia, put an effectual barrier in the way of German expansion. And now, after centuries of foreign domination and bitter struggle to preserve their nationality, these little nations are to profit by the modern principle of "self-determination," and are to have an opportunity to develop themselves freely along their peculiar national lines.

The Caucasus and the Ural Mountains make a natural boundary between Europe and Asia, forming a barrier to easy communication between the two continents and forcing travel and commerce, as well as invading peoples and armies, to follow certain well-defined routes.

Let us return to the Alps and look at their influence in other directions. Because they were an effective barrier to the spread of Roman civilization toward the north, central Europe received it, in a roundabout way and second-hand, from the Gauls and the peoples living along the Danube. The influence of the Alps as a barrier is well illustrated by the fact that the Germans received Christianity by way of the Rhône and the Danube.

Switzerland furnishes a fine example of the protecting and segregating influence of mountains. The cantons (counties) that were situated in the deep, retired valleys of the Alps were so secure and so isolated in their mountain fastnesses that they felt little or no need of a strong central government. Almost every valley in the Alps has sought independence. The segregating environment of the mountains which shut them in has caused political dismemberment and a lack of cohesion in the cantons. Nothing but the danger of being conquered by a common foe has been able to bring the cantons together. Threatened encroachments by their stronger neighbors have forced them to unite to form the Swiss republic. The mountain cantons have yielded grudgingly to the necessity of a central government and still oppose every attempt to strengthen it.

The history of Scotland shows constant feuds between Highlanders and Lowlanders, tribes and clans. These petty divisions among the people, so deep-seated in the Scotchman's heart, are due to the segregating environment of mountains, gorges, and deep inlets.

In mountainous countries agriculture offers scant returns. Short summers and long, cold winters add to the difficulties of making a living, and so in virtually all mountains we find various "winter" industries practised "on the side," in order to supplement the meagre income obtained from the soil during the summer. These winter industries vary from one region to another. Thus the Swiss peasants spend their winters in making wood carvings, watches, clocks, and lace; lace is made also in some of the mountains of Germany and of Italy; peasants of the Black Forest are famous for their clocks; other mountain regions are noted for the manufacture of dolls and toys.

Because it is so difficult to make a living in the Alps the women of Switzerland have, for some centuries, done nearly all the work in the fields, and the young men have sought a livelihood in foreign lands. They became famous as mercenary troops in many European countries, but after the abolition of mercenary armies in the nineteenth century they sought more peaceable forms of employment and became hotel managers, couriers, and waiters. Thousands of them spend the winters in the "winter" resorts around the Mediterranean, and the summers in Switzerland, which is usually filled at that season with tourists.

In modern times, however, mountains have been found to possess new sources of wealth, since they are frequently rich in mineral deposits, and their streams and waterfalls furnish an almost unlimited amount of electrical power.

Note to Map I.—Use this map to illustrate the points made in the introductory chapter. The important principle to be observed is the influence of physical or natural geography upon political and social history. Notice the extensive coast line of the continent, made by deep inlets, such as the Baltic, the Gulf of Finland, the Adriatic, the Ægean, and the Black Sea. Observe the effect of the mountain systems on political boundaries, etc. Note the important cities on the coast: Calais, Lübeck, Danzig, Marseilles, Genoa, Venice, and the very advantageous position of Constantinople, commanding the only waterway to the Black Sea and its shores. The river systems are great natural highways, especially in a time in which roads are not well maintained or policed because of disorderly political conditions; see how completely Europe is provided with such systems. Note also the fact that nearly all the important cities are on or near main river routes.

I

PHYSICAL MAP OF EUROPE AND THE MEDITERRANEAN BASIN

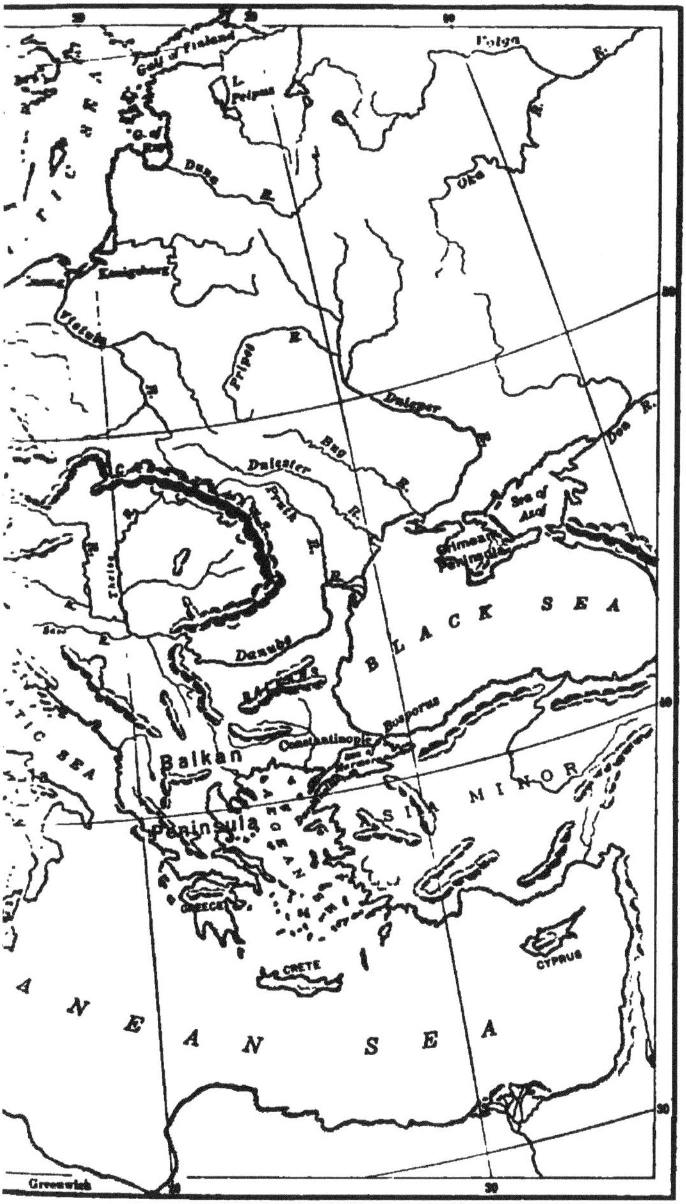

Gulf of Finland
L. Peipus
Volga
Dvina R.
Oka
Königsberg
Vistula
Pripet
Dnieper
Bug
Dniester
Pruth
Don R.
Sea of Azof
Crimean Peninsula
BLACK SEA
Theiss
Danube
Bosporus
Constantinople
Balkan Peninsula
ASIA MINOR
GREECE
CRETE
CYPRUS
ANEAN SEA
Greenwich

For travel, trade, and war mountain passes are important because they furnish the only direct means of communication between the countries which the mountains separate. In ancient times they offered the only favorable sites for the construction of connecting roads, and in modern times they are generally followed by the railroads. Because of the traffic that passes over them settlements are formed near their ends, which often grow into cities. This will be apparent if you will consult your map and locate the chief passes of the Alps, such as the Brenner, the St. Gothard, the Simplon, and the Mt. Genèvre, and observe the cities that are grouped about their ends.

On the other hand, great plains offer every opportunity for the development of peoples into homogeneity, and for the formation of governments with extensive sway. That explains, in part at least, why a single government has for many centuries been able to embrace the great plain of eastern Europe, although in the early Middle Age it, like western Europe, was the home of many independent tribes and races. A government resting on arms, such as has existed in Russia, finds it comparatively easy to extend its sway by the conquest of peoples that, living in a great plain and lacking the natural protection which is furnished by mountains, are easily overcome by superior numbers, no matter how brave and liberty-loving they are. The fate of the many peoples of Russia is in strong contrast with that of the peoples of Switzerland, who, under the protecting shadow of their mountains, have been able to beat off all aggressors and to maintain their liberty and independence.

Plains Unite.

Extensive plains seem to invite their inhabitants to expand politically. The valleys of the Seine and the Loire are essentially one, and it is a noteworthy fact, as we shall see in Chapter XVI, that on them was based the royal power which expanded to take in all France. They formed the centre about which all the rest of France was centralized.

In the same way Prussia, beginning with the flat plain of Brandenburg, has expanded to take in all the low plains lying south of the Baltic. Prussian statesmen followed the policy of absorbing the little principalities that lay helpless around them, and the logic of events demanded that eventually Holland, Luxemburg, and at least a part of Belgium be added to the territory of Prussia, had not the war of 1914–1918 resulted in the breaking of Prussian power. Now it seems that these countries are to have a safe and independent existence through the principle of "self-determination," a principle that bids fair soon to have universal application, even to the backward, uncivilized peoples of Africa, and to stop the exploitation of the weaker peoples by the stronger.

A nation or state occupying a plain may of course become great in spite of its lack of natural boundaries, but only on condition that its people are held together and possess great prowess in war. Poland, once a great state, had no natural frontiers, and its downfall was greatly facilitated by its lack of a protecting boundary.

The Sea Protects and Isolates.

Like mountains, the sea protects and isolates. By developing an extensive naval commerce a people may make use of the sea to overcome the injurious effects of their isolation by it. Of this England furnishes a fine example. Naval commerce, however, depends largely on the existence of good harbors, and of these some countries have many, while others, with a much longer coast-line, may have none. Isolation may be either a source of strength or a cause of weakness. Thus Spain and England are much alike in their isolation; but Spain has suffered from its isolation, because the Spaniards have neither developed the natural resources of their country nor built up a great naval commerce, while England, under the protection of its isolation, has grown great by doing both. Europe is fortunate in possessing more coast-line in proportion to its area than any other continent. This is due to the fact that it is essentially a peninsula, merely an extension of Asia, and is composed of peninsulas, being deeply indented by arms of the sea. In comparison with other continents it is rich in harbors. Its great inland seas offer excellent opportunities for the pursuit of commerce. It is not accidental that European commerce developed first on and around the Mediterranean and then the Baltic, and that the chief commercial cities were in those regions.

The Mediterranean has played an important rôle in history. Three continents meet around it, and, since it offers an easy means of communication, it has aided in the spread of civilization. The peoples on its shores have easily assimilated the culture of each other. Because of the mountains on the north of it and the desert on the south, it does not receive many important rivers, so that its tributary territory is comparatively small. In this respect the Baltic is far more fortunate, since it receives many large rivers; and even the Black Sea, which receives some important rivers, surpasses it in the extent and importance of its tributary territory.

Rivers are not good barriers and therefore are not effective frontiers. On the contrary, since they are convenient and ready-made highways, they serve rather to connect than to separate. In its river systems also Europe is more fortunate than other continents. Its numerous rivers could hardly be arranged so as to make travel and commerce easier. They rise, generally speaking, in the central part of the continent, so that the sources of those flowing north are near the sources of others flowing south. By a short portage the Rhine and the rivers of France are connected with one another and with the Rhône and its tributaries; in the same way the Rhine, the Main, the Elbe, and the Oder are connected with the Danube; and the Vistula, the Niemen, and the Duna, with the Dniester, the Dnieper, the Don, and the Volga. The importance of rivers as highways may be seen in the fact that those inland cities of Europe that have flourished have been, almost without exception, situated on a river. Furthermore, we know that the rivers of Europe have from the earliest times been used as highways by merchants and travellers. Long before Christ the Greeks, who bought tin in Cornwall, found that the easiest way to England was by boat across the Mediterranean and up the Rhône, then afoot to the Loire or Seine, and again by boat to the shores of Cornwall. We know also that during the Middle Age Scandinavian merchants

Rivers are Highways.

sailed across the Baltic, crossed the land to the Volga, down which they sailed to the Caspian, and carried on a brisk trade with the peoples around that sea, because large numbers of coins made by those peoples have been found along the Volga and in the lands around the Baltic. And pilgrims from Scandinavia preferred to go to the Holy Land by way of the Baltic, the Dnieper, the Black Sea, and the Mediterranean rather than by the land route through France, Germany, and the Balkan peninsula.

The most important factors in climate are heat and cold, moisture and aridity, the distribution of rainfall, and the prevailing winds. Although the influence of climate on a people is, in some respects, less tangible than that of mountains and rivers, it is not less real. It is indeed difficult to measure the varied yet subtle influence of climate on the temperament of a people. It is easy, however, to see that in the cold zones conditions would make the struggle for existence hard and unremitting, while in the warmer regions the prodigality of nature might easily beget slothfulness. Climate alone determines the fauna and flora of a country, which are matters of decisive importance to its inhabitants. Climate affects a people's dress, occupations, social life and habits, and its architecture, both public and private. Climate may also be a protection against foreign aggression. Thus, throughout the Middle Age the Italian climate did more than Italian arms to protect the freedom of the Italian cities against the imperial pretensions of the German emperors, because no German army was able to withstand Italian fevers. Europe is fortunate in that, although its climate ranges from the subtropical to the arctic, by far the larger part of it has a temperate climate, due in a measure to the Gulf Stream or the warm waters of the north Atlantic drift. And it is a fact that man has made the most progress in the temperate zone.

Climate.

Italian Fever.

No one can deny the great and varied influence of these factors which made up the physical environment of the peoples whose history we are about to study. But of far greater importance in this history are the psychical factors, for

> "Man is not dust, man is not dust, I say!
> A lightning substance thro' his being runs.
> A flame he knows not of illumes his clay—
> The cosmic fire that feeds the swarming suns."

Man is mind, and mind is master over matter. Through the power of his mind man has achieved whatever supremacy he enjoys. Under the overmastering urge of ideas and ideals he has won a substantial and ever-increasing domination over his physical environment; he has spanned the rivers, pierced the mountains with tunnels, wrested a livelihood from the trackless waste of the sea and the scarcely less inhospitable regions of the frozen north and the arid desert; he has made wind and wave serve him; by his means of rapid transit he has brought the ends of the earth together, and by his command of electricity he has annihilated space; he competes even with the fish of the sea and with the birds of the air for supremacy in their domains. The measure of the superiority of mind over matter may be gauged by the conquest which man has achieved over nature. History, in the truest sense, is the record of man's conquest of nature and of himself. That is, it is the record of the mind of man. "The history of the state sketches in coarse outline the progress of thought, and follows at a distance the delicacy of culture and of aspiration." The great factors of civilization are psychic and not material.

CHAPTER I

THE ROMAN EMPIRE TO 476 A. D.

UNDER a republican form of government the city of Rome had made extensive conquests in Europe, Asia, and Africa. It seemed, however, unequal to the task of governing its wide realm, partly because it had extended its sway faster than it had developed the structure of its government. The conqueror had outrun the statesman. Taking advantage of opportunities, Octavian (31 B. C.–14 A. D.) cleverly acquired control and gradually changed the republic to an empire. In doing this, however, he prudently made concessions to the sentiments of the people by observing and preserving as far as possible the existing political forms of the republic. Fearing to usurp authority, he had it conferred on him in due form by the senate. He did not destroy the high offices of the state, but caused himself to be elected to all of them, either for many years or for life. These offices had been so arranged that their holders would act as a check on each other, but now, since Octavian held them all, there was no one who had the authority to call him to account. His grip on the state was so firm that no one dared oppose his re-election, and consequently he held all the high offices so long that the Romans became accustomed to their union in one person. Thus these various offices fused to make one—that of emperor.

Octavian Becomes Emperor by Holding All the High Offices.

These offices conferred on Octavian extensive powers which under his successors tended to become absolute. By virtue of his tribunician power (*potestas tribunicia*) he exercised supreme authority in civil affairs, could veto the action of all magistrates, and convoke the senate and the popular assembly for the transaction of business. By virtue of his proconsular power (*imperium proconsulare*) he controlled the army, the navy, and those provinces which, being

Tends to Become Absolute.

still in an unsettled state, required the presence of troops. By a special act of the senate his proconsular power was extended to Rome. As high priest (*pontifex maximus*) he exercised authority over all religious matters. His pre-eminence in the state was indicated by two titles, *Augustus* (imperial majesty), and *princeps* (foremost citizen, hence, ruler). As the magistrate of the people he conducted all negotiations with foreign powers, and declared war and made peace. He had a large and increasing influence in jurisdiction in both civil and criminal cases. Indirectly he influenced the courts and controlled the senate when it sat as a court. The legislative power was under his control. The early emperors did not assume the lawmaking power, but of course prepared bills for the senate and popular assemblies to adopt. The emperor had the coinage of gold and silver, and he controlled taxation and deposed and created senators. His actual power effectually awed the senate and the popular assembly, and, no matter how great his vices or excesses, there was no effective means of removing him from office. The high position of an emperor did not, however, protect him against rebellion and the assassin's dagger.

Even in the days of the republic the sovereign authority of the state was absolute. The state demanded unqualified obedience and submission from all. In theory the people were sovereign, but they had delegated their sovereignty to the state, that is, to the officials whom they had chosen. Augustus merely took the place of all the magistrates, and hence acquired all the sovereignty that had been vested in them. He became the state, which was the visible form of the majesty and sovereignty of the Roman people. Roman sovereignty in the hands of the emperor did not become more imperious or absolute than it had been in the hands of the magistrates of the republic. Hence, in the absolutism of Augustus there was nothing new except that it was centralized in the hands of one man and was no longer in the hands of a number of magistrates.

The change from a republic to an empire was in many respects beneficial. It put an end to the disorders and lawlessness caused by the civil strife of the last years of the republic.

By an efficient police system the emperors put down brigandage and cleared the roads of robbers and the sea of pirates. They gave a new impetus to the construction of roads and to the erection of temples and baths both in Rome and in other cities. Most of them encouraged the cities by giving them the Latin law (*ius Latii*), in accordance with which they governed themselves much after the model of Rome. Generally each municipality had (1) a popular assembly, (2) a senate, and (3) two bodies of magistrates, one of which administered justice and convoked the senate, while the other controlled the police and other matters. The emperors exercised a wise oversight over the provinces and secured good government for them. They attempted to increase the free population of Italy (which had been diminishing for some time) by legislating against divorce, by making gifts to the parents of large families, and by creating a fund for the care of poor children and orphans, to prevent them from becoming slaves or *coloni* (an unfree, perpetual renter class), and for making loans to farmers at a low rate of interest—activities that are comparable to some modern legislation that is considered radical, and in some quarters even dangerous, such as providing for orphans through mothers' pensions, and the system of rural credits and farm loans. In their effort to produce a revival in religion they restored old temples, built new ones, and frequented them, taking a personal part in the various religious cults which were practised. In imperial legislation there appeared a new spirit of humaneness, due in large measure to the spread of the idea of the brotherhood of man (*ius naturale*), which was promulgated by Seneca, Epictetus, and other Stoic philosophers. Above all, the provinces outside of Italy profited by the change in the form of government. Under the republic they had suffered much at the hands of corrupt governors, tax-gatherers, and capitalists, but the emperor showed that he had their welfare at heart by putting over them honest, capable, well-trained governors, with long tenure of office, and making them responsible directly to himself. Consequently the provinces entered on an era of prosperity, and progressed

The Emperors Advance Civilization.

Note to Map II.—Note the location of races in Europe. The descendants of the Roman provincials make the "Latin peoples" of to-day in France, Spain, and Italy. The small part of the Celts that never came under Roman influence were in the remote corners, Wales, Ireland, and Scotland. Central Europe east of the Rhine and north of the Danube, as far as the Vistula, was occupied by German tribes, without definite boundaries and often shifting. Note the location of those tribes that were later to pour into the Roman Empire: East Goths, West Goths, Vandals, Burgundians, Lombards, Franks. East of the German tribes were the Slavs; they were to advance westward over lands left vacant by the Germans when the latter invaded the empire (see Map III). The Huns at this time were advancing from Asia across southern Russia; they were to penetrate to the middle Danube, and then recede without leaving permanent traces.

NORWAY
SWEDEN
Caledonia
BRITAIN
GERMAN SEA
IRELAND
Hibernia
ATLANTIC OCEAN
Jutes
Elbe
Saxons
Lombards
Ripuarian Franks
River
Burgundians
Marcomanni
London
Lutetia (Paris)
R.
Alamanni
VINDELICIA
Cantabrian Sea
GAUL
Milano
Rhone
ROMAN
Ravenna
PYRENEES
Ebro R.
Douro R.
SPAIN
CORSICA
Rome
Tagus R.
SARDINIA
MEDITERR
SICILY
MALTA
Strait Gibraltar
MAURETANIA
NUMIDIA
GAETULIA
RIC
L.L. POATES CO., N.Y.
Longitude West 0 Longitude East 10 from
10
0
10
50
40
30

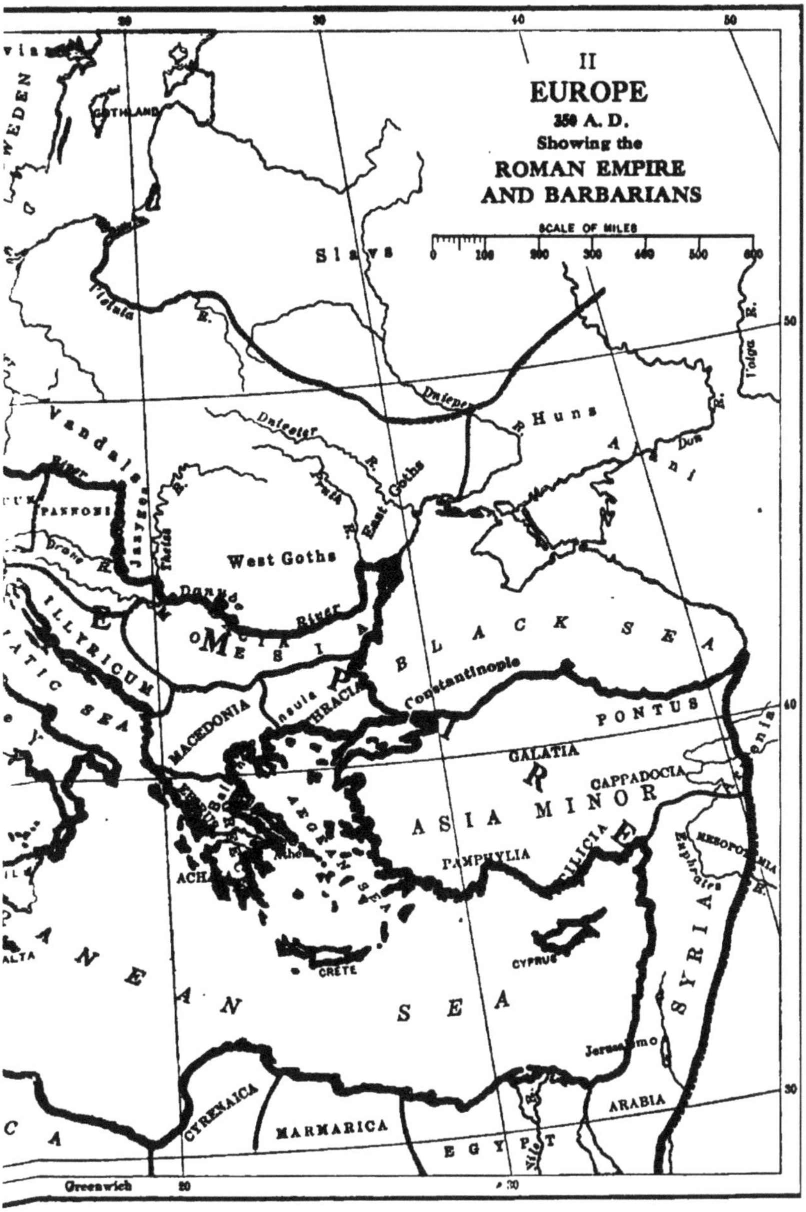
II
EUROPE
350 A. D.
Showing the
ROMAN EMPIRE
AND BARBARIANS
SCALE OF MILES
0 100 200 300 400 500 600
Slavs
Huns
Vandals
West Goths
East Goths
Alani
Dnieper R.
Dniester R.
Pruth R.
Danube River
Volga R.
Don
Vistula R.
Drave R.
Theiss R.
Jazyges
PANNONIA
GOTHLAND
SWEDEN
ILLYRICUM
ADRIATIC SEA
MACEDONIA
THRACIA
MOESIA
DACIA
BLACK SEA
Constantinople
PONTUS
GALATIA
CAPPADOCIA
ASIA MINOR
PAMPHYLIA
CILICIA
MESOPOTAMIA
Euphrates R.
Armenia
SYRIA
CYPRUS
CRETE
AEGEAN SEA
ACHAIA
EPIRUS
MEDITERRANEAN SEA
Jerusalem
ARABIA
EGYPT
Nile R.
MARMARICA
CYRENAICA
MALTA
Greenwich
ROMAN EMPIRE

in civilization more rapidly than ever before. Furthermore, the emperors encouraged the provincials, as all the free people outside of Italy were called, by liberally conferring Roman citizenship upon them. So great was the progress made in this direction that in 212 A. D. the emperor, Caracalla, recognized the fact that the provincials were virtually on the same plane of civilization as the Romans by conferring Roman citizenship on all the free inhabitants of the empire. He did this, however, in order that he might tax them.

Although the emperor's power was actually almost absolute, it must be said that from the time of Octavian to Diocletian (31 B. C.–284 A. D.) the government was technically and theoretically a diarchy; that is, the emperor shared the authority with the senate. In practice, however, the senate was dependent on imperial favor. Some of the emperors treated it with outward deference at least, and permitted it to preserve a show of its authority, while others treated it with supreme contempt and trampled on all its rights. The emperor kept control of the army, for in the division of territory between him and the senate the latter received only those provinces in which, peace having been established, the presence of troops was not necessary. The emperor also controlled the appointment of the governors of the senatorial provinces, and every senatorial province in which a disturbance arose passed at once from the control of the senate into his hands. He could reduce the senate to subjection by deposing all its members who opposed him or who were in any way obnoxious to him, or by bringing a charge of treason (*crimen maiestatis*) against them. By conferring senatorial rank on provincials he changed the character of the senate; from an aristocracy of Rome it became an aristocracy of the empire.

A Nominal Diarchy.

This change, however, did not increase its influence on the government. Its legislative powers, which had originally been very broad, dwindled steadily because of imperial encroachments. The senate, which had acquired the right to elect all magistrates, continued to exercise that right, but even here its power was formal because the

Senate's Power Declines.

emperor nominated all candidates. Perhaps the most important power of the senate was that of electing the emperor and of conferring his constitutional powers on him. Its right to elect the emperor was, however, soon curtailed. For the emperor usually succeeded in naming his successor and so made the office hereditary, while the army (either the pretorian guard at Rome or the legions in the provinces) frequently usurped authority in the matter and created an emperor of its own choice.

Matters went well enough till the third century, when the whole imperial system seemed to be breaking down. The chief trouble arose from the fact that not only the whole army but even a single legion, as well as the pretorian guard, assumed the right to create and depose the emperor. From 180 to 284, although there were more than thirty actual emperors, they were outnumbered by the usurpers. The soldiers sometimes put to death one emperor and elected another merely for the gifts which the newly elected emperor must give them; on one occasion they even sold the crown to the highest bidder. Usurpers appeared in many provinces, and because of their distance from Rome were able to maintain themselves for some time. Disastrous wars with the Parthians (their territory was about the same as the modern Kohistan) also caused the loss of the eastern provinces, and, to add to the confusion, German tribes dwelling beyond the Danube and the Rhine made numerous incursions into the empire, ravaging and devastating it. To the general dissolution of the empire many other causes—some of them both cause and effect—contributed. Here we can mention only a few of them: heavy and unwise taxation, extravagant expenditure of the state's funds, depreciation and debasement of the currency, the too rapid growth of imperialism at the expense of local autonomy and the feeling of nationality, pauperizing, free-corn laws, the lack of a system of credits, or banking system, able to support the industrial and commercial life of the empire, the decline of agriculture, and the increasing degeneracy of the Italian stock.

The Election Law Breaks Down.

Causes of Decline.

Of this list the last two items deserve a word of explanation. For some centuries there had been in progress a ruinous economic change. The land was passing into the hands of a few great landholders, and the small, free landholder was disappearing. These immense farms, or estates (*latifundia*), were tilled by an unfree class of perpetual renters, or lease-holders, called *coloni*, who were attached by law to the soil, and hence could never migrate from it. The burdens of taxation fell on them, because they were the producing class. Their landlords exacted more and more from them until they sank into a state of wretched poverty. Their power of production steadily diminished. When they could no longer produce enough to meet the taxes demanded of them, the landlords were, of course, held responsible for the payment, and so they also were ruined. Consequently, much of the land that had been under cultivation was in time abandoned and became waste. Probably no other cause contributed more to the general decline of the Roman empire than this system of land-tenure and agriculture, so disastrous and far-reaching were its effects. Indirectly it led the emperors, who were compelled to seek an income from other sources, to introduce burdensome monopolies, and it put upon the government the almost impossible task of finding a sufficient supply of food for the cities. Furthermore, it brought about the ruin of the industrial class in the cities because they could no longer sell the output of their factories to a people that had become impoverished.

Coloni and Land-Tenure.

Fortunately for the empire, a succession of able and determined emperors checked the threatened dissolution by destroying the usurpers and repelling for a while the barbarian invaders. Diocletian (284-305), the real founder of the later Roman empire, reorganized the whole administrative system and made the government a monarchy by stripping the senate of even its show of power and by concentrating all authority in the hands of the emperor. Experience had shown that the task of governing so extensive an empire exceeded the powers of one man. Diocletian determined that there should be two emperors, both called Augustus,

Diocletian's Reform.

M., 204.

one of them in the east, the other in the west; each should appoint an assistant, at the same time adopting him and conferring on him the title of Cæsar, a name which, since the time of Hadrian (117–138), had been given by the emperor to the man whom he had adopted and named as his successor. In case of the death of an emperor his Cæsar should succeed him at once, and, in any event, at the end of twenty years the emperors should resign and be succeeded by their respective Cæsars, who were then to create and adopt two new Cæsars.

The emperor was further protected by being declared to be a god; he was surrounded by a court and an elaborate system of etiquette so that those who approached him had to observe a fixed ceremonial, as if they were entering the presence of a god. He wore an imperial diadem and was clothed in a magnificent purple robe made gorgeous with gems and precious stones. Not only was his person sacred, but his palace, his treasury, his bedchamber, and his government (*imperium*) were called sacred (*sacer*). He himself was called master and god (*dominus ac deus*), and divine honors were paid him even during his lifetime.

Diocletian increased the authority of his office, for in all that he did he disregarded the senate. He vested in the emperors all power to legislate for the empire. The senate, being thus deprived of its two most important powers—the electoral and the legislative—could no longer be considered an imperial body. Thereafter its activities hardly extended beyond local Roman affairs. The ancient magistracies had already lost their importance for the empire and had become merely municipal offices of Rome. One of the essential features of Diocletian's system was the complete separation of the civil and military systems, each of which was organized in a bureaucratic way under a head who was responsible to the emperor. For the purposes of administration Diocletian divided the empire into four prefectures, putting a pretorian prefect over each; he divided each prefecture into dioceses, each under a governor, and each diocese into provinces, each under a provincial gov-

The Senate without Power.

Civil and Military Divided.

ernor. Diocletian took the prefecture of the east (Thrace, Asia Minor, Syria, and Egypt), with his residence at Nicomedia; his Cæsar, Galerius, exercised authority in the prefecture of Illyricum (the rest of the Balkan peninsula and the provinces of the lower Danube), with his residence at Sirmium (now Metrovitz, on the Save River); Maximian, the other emperor, took the prefecture of Italy (Italy, the provinces of the middle Danube, and Africa), with his residence at Milan; to his Cæsar, Constantius, he assigned the prefecture of Gaul (Gaul, Spain, and Britain), with his residence at Treves. Over each prefecture there was a pretorian prefect, with extensive powers over civil matters; he heard appeals, managed the imperial finances, and controlled the governors of the dioceses and of the provinces. Diocletian put the administration of military matters in each prefecture in the hands of a number of officials (*magistri militum*), and further subdivided the prefectures into military districts, each under a duke or count. Both administrations were organized bureaucratically, the officials rising in dignity and importance from the lowest to the highest.

Prefectures, Dioceses, Provinces.

The social classification of the inhabitants of the empire was also gradually modified. At the bottom of the social scale there was a constantly increasing servile class, among which there were many gradations in the degree of servitude. In the country slavery was changed into serfdom because, in order that the number of the tillers of the soil might not be diminished, masters were forbidden to sell their slaves, who were then entered on the tax-lists with the soil, and hence became attached to it, and were bought and sold with it. The *coloni* should be ranked with the unfree class, for, although they were personally free, they were attached to the soil. Their ranks were recruited by freedmen, by perpetual renters, and by small proprietors who found it necessary to surrender their lands to some nobleman in order to secure protection against violence. The *plebs* (freemen, small proprietors, laborers, artisans, shopkeepers, the population of the small towns) tended to lose their freedom, being forbidden

The Unfree.

Plebs.

to remove or to change their occupation. The class of *curiales* was composed of the well-to-do inhabitants of the country and of the cities. All who possessed a certain amount of wealth were ranked with this class. The burden of the government was put on them, and they were also made responsible for the payment of the imperial taxes—a burden which they tried to escape by sinking into a lower class or rising into a higher. Heavy taxation was rapidly ruining them. The nobility was composed of the former senatorial order, *i. e.*, of those who had obtained a magistracy or had received the rank of senator from the emperor, and of the equestrian order. There were gradations of rank among them (*illustres clarissimi, spectabiles*). They were the proprietors of the great estates (*latifundia*). "Senator" had become a mere title, conferred by the emperor. Many of those who bore the title had never been in Rome. Although subject to a land tax they had several special privileges, chiefly in the form of exemptions from the ordinary taxes, which were levied on the *curiales*.

Curiales.

Nobility.

The emperor needed immense sums of money for the support of his army, and the host of clerks employed in the bureaus of the government. For such purposes a generous outlay was both unavoidable and justifiable. But he squandered larger sums on the pompous ceremonial and splendor of his court, on the crowd of showy but useless functionaries with which he surrounded himself, on the immense and frequent largesses of grain and bread to the idle and pauperized population of the chief cities, and on the elaborate free games and shows which he provided for their entertainment. The ordinary income of the emperor was wholly inadequate to meet these expenses. Consequently he was compelled to levy numerous and heavy taxes. There were taxes on lands and persons, on manufactures, on inheritances, on sales made by merchants; tolls were collected on the highways and at bridges, and duties at the city gates and in the harbors; the people could be called on to furnish food and clothing for the army,

Burdensome Taxes.

Taxes, Tolls, and Service.

horses and wagons for the transportation of the emperor and his troops, lodgings for imperial officials, and to labor in the construction or repairing of roads and bridges. Taxation was, in fact, at the discretion of the emperor. Even in times of prosperity the people would have found the imperial taxation very burdensome, to say the least; they were crushed and ruined by it under the existing system of land-tenure and agriculture, and under the extraordinary calamities—the civil wars and the invasions of the barbarians—which befell the empire in the third and succeeding centuries.

Against oppressive taxation the tax-ridden population could obtain little relief. (1) To be sure, every fifteen years, beginning with the year 312 A. D., their property was revalued or assessed for the purpose of fixing the amount of their taxation for that period (the so-called indiction). But the assessors, or fiscal agents, deaf to the entreaties of the people and regardless of the true value of the property, strove to increase rather than to diminish the valuation. (2) Toward the middle of the fourth century, in response to the loud and frequent complaints of the people, the emperors permitted each province to have a "defender" to protect the inhabitants against oppressive taxation. It was his duty "to act as a father for the people of both country and city, to prevent them from being burdened with taxes, and to protect them against the arrogance of the imperial officials and the shamelessness of judges" (*Codex Just.*, I, 55. 4). These "defenders," however, were often powerless to help, and the only effective relief was given by the emperor himself, who, moved to pity by the distress of his subjects, frequently remitted the taxes of a province for a few years in order to enable its inhabitants to recover a little of their lost prosperity.

The Indiction.

Defensores.

Sensible as Diocletian's scheme of having two emperors and two Cæsars seemed, it was not long in force. It turned out to be neither practicable nor effective, for, after the resignation of the two emperors, Diocletian and Maximian, in 305, usurpers appeared and dissensions arose between the Augusti and the

Cæsars. Long civil wars ensued, out of which Constantine eventually emerged victor and sole emperor. He divided the empire among his three sons, but after the death of two of them it was reunited. Succeeding emperors, however, found it necessary to have an assistant, and so during the last quarter of the century there were generally two emperors. At the death of Theodosius (395), he named one of his sons, Arcadius, emperor in the east, and the other, Honorius, emperor in the west—an arrangement which continued in force under their successors till 476. Yet, although there were two emperors, the idea of the unity of the empire did not suffer in the least. In 476 Odovacer, an ambitious German, put himself at the head of the German troops, of which the army was chiefly composed, and demanded lands of the emperor. His demand was refused, whereupon he resorted to force. He seized the emperor, Romulus Augustulus, a mere boy, and killed his father, Orestes, in whose hands the actual authority had been. He then deposed the boy emperor, and in the name of the senate sent the imperial insignia to Zeno, the emperor at Constantinople, and begged him to assume the imperial sway over the whole empire, and to recognize Odovacer as governor of the diocese of Italy. Technically the change in 476 was merely from two emperors to one, but, as a matter of fact, the imperial authority disappeared in the west, which was already for the most part occupied by barbarian invaders.

Failure of Diocletian's Scheme.

One Emperor Residing at Constantinople.

There is no doubt that the empire had for some time been declining in many ways. We are justified in believing that there had been an intellectual decline, because after 150 A. D. no great writers or philosophers appeared. We infer that the spirit of commercial enterprise weakened, because the important trade of the empire with India almost ceased in the third century. In no other field is the decline more apparent than in that of art. In both the fine and practical arts the products of the fourth century after Christ are so far inferior to those of the first that the

Proofs of General Decline.

deterioration can be explained only on the supposition of a general decline in the whole people. They had lost the power of initiative—that strong, undertaking spirit—that had characterized the early Romans.

Free Population Diminished.

The empire had been growing steadily weaker in a military way, because its free population had been constantly diminishing. Those of them who became *coloni* lost the ability even to defend themselves. They could no longer fight. It is probable, though not certain, that they had actually diminished in numbers. The important fact is that their spirit was gone. They were of no value to the empire in its wars, whether of offense or defense. It seems certain that the free population had been further diminished by civil wars and rebellions, and by the marauding incursions of the barbarians. Furthermore, a plague in the time of Aurelian (270–275) was especially mortal, decimating the population of the empire. The oppressive taxation which was begun by Diocletian also prevented an increase of the population. Moreover, pagan philosophies and the teachings of the church fathers begot an indifference, and even a repugnance, to the married state, and after the third century the extraordinary religious value attaching to celibacy and the rapid growth of monasticism probably caused a further decrease in the population. In the absence of all statistics, however, we can make no positive statement about the increase or decrease of the population.

Barbarians are Imported.

Whether or not there had been a loss in population, the emperors resorted to the questionable expedient of importing barbarians. They did this sometimes in order to obtain recruits for the army, or to relieve the pressure of the barbarians on the frontier. By fallacious reasoning they persuaded themselves that these barbarians would cease to be dangerous to the empire when they were once settled in it. After the middle of the third century barbarians in ever-increasing numbers were brought in. They were established in various parts of Asia Minor; more than 100,000 were settled in Thrace at one time; the valleys of the Po, the Danube, and the Rhine were repeopled with them; and large colonies of Franks were placed in central Gaul. Generally the government paid these barbarian settlers a tribute in grain, in return for which they were expected to protect the country against invaders. In this way the population of whole provinces had become barbarian. By the fifth century not only was the army composed of barbarians, it was even commanded by them. Barbarians, especially Germans, were often the trusted counsellors of emperors; some had been made senators and consuls, and others had even been raised to the highest magistracies. Whatever advantages were gained by this wholesale importation of barbarians were counterbalanced by the damage they did in their frequent revolts. And it is highly probable that their prosperity within the empire exercised a considerable attraction on the barbarians beyond the frontier, and so helped cause the great invasions which resulted in severing the west from the empire. These numerous settlements of barbarians within the empire may be regarded as a kind of prelude to the great invasions.

The Army was German.

In these first five centuries of the empire the city of Rome had lost everything politically except the memory of its greatness. Twice it had been humiliated by falling a prey to barbarian invaders: Alaric and the West Goths sacked it and burnt a part of it in 410, and Gaiseric, king of the Vandals, put the same indignity upon it in 455. It was no longer the residence of the emperor; its senate and magistrates had only local influence; its popular assembly had no authority; the city had lost the right to elect the emperor and to invest him with his office; it did not in any way control the conduct or policy of the emperor; and it had no influence over the imperial officials or the administration of the government. The emperor had long since ceased to live at Rome. The imperial residence was first removed to Milan that the emperor might be nearer the frontier provinces, which required most of his attention. Then, when the barbarian invasions began in earnest, the emperor removed to Ravenna, where, behind its walls and marshes, he hoped to find security.

Rome Declines.

Rome's greatness seemed at an end in 476 when Zeno became sole emperor, with his residence at Constantinople. The Persian wars and the troubles on the frontier, as well as a desire to perpetuate his name, had influenced Constantine in choosing Byzantium for the site of a new city. Situated on the confines of Europe and Asia it was convenient to both continents; it commanded the sea for both war and commerce; and the configuration of its site made it a natural stronghold. History has given abundant evidence that Constantine's choice of it was wise.

The New Capital.

M., 205.

Constantinople soon took on a Greek character. The government, however, continued for some time to use Latin as its official language. Theodosius II (408–450) is generally regarded as the first Greek emperor. He issued some decrees in Greek, and established in Constantinople a university in which the professors who instructed in Greek slightly outnumbered those who instructed in Latin. From that time Latin declined. It should be remembered, however, that even to the fall of Constantinople (1453) the empire was still called Roman, and its subjects Romans. It is, however, customary to speak of it as the Greek, or the Byzantine, empire, to distinguish it from the western.

Peoples Outside the Empire

Outside the empire there were other peoples who were yet to become important factors in the history of Europe, and hence deserve a word of introduction. The inhabitants of Gaul, Britain, Scotland, and Ireland were called Celts, and all of them spoke Celtic dialects. The Celts of Gaul and Britain, however, had been conquered by the Romans, and their territory made Roman provinces. The inhabitants of Gaul had adopted the civilization of Rome and had made considerable progress in it. Southern Gaul especially was the seat of a flourishing civilization. On the other hand, the Celts of Britain had made much less progress in the acquisition of Roman civilization, and those of Scotland and Ireland, being unconquered, had not yet felt the influence of Rome, and were

The Celts.

still barbarians. They (as well as the Celts of Gaul and Britain before their conquest by Rome) were divided into a large number of tribes, each independent of the others. It was a peculiarity of all the Celts that their tribal government was an aristocracy, being in the hands of the nobility. The common people had no share in it, and, as Cæsar says, in matters of government were treated by the nobility as slaves. The Celts were brave, dashing warriors, but their ardor was easily quenched by disaster. As a people they were fond of shrill, martial music, and of bright, gay colors; they were peculiarly sensitive to eloquent speech, and their orators and poets had great power over them. They were noted for the liveliness rather than for the persistency of their feelings and emotions, and Gallic fickleness was proverbial.*

The Germans.

S. B., 1. O., 1, 2.

East of the continental Celts were the Germans—a numerous people, who occupied a vast territory which extended from the Black Sea far up into Norway and Sweden. Like the Celts, they were separated into a large number of independent tribes, each speaking a dialect of its own. From some unknown cause, however, they passed through a unifying process, during which many of the small tribes mentioned by Cæsar and Tacitus disappeared, and a few great groups or tribes were formed, chief of which were the East Goths, West Goths, Vandals, Alamanni (Suevi), Burgundians, Lombards, Bavarians, Franks, Saxons, and Angles. The Germanic peoples of Denmark, Norway, and Sweden are called Northmen, and among them the unifying process did not take place till much later (800–1000). Their government was essentially democratic in principle. For, although they had a nobility, and some tribes even had kings, whose opinions and advice were respected, the common freeman had a voice in the management of all the affairs of the

* To-day the people of France, Ireland, Wales, and the highlands of Scotland are called Celts. Celtic languages are still spoken in Wales, parts of Ireland, the Isle of Man, in the highlands of Scotland, and in parts of Brittany. The people of Portugal, Spain, France, Roumania, and southern Switzerland speak Romance languages; that is, languages derived from the spoken Latin.

tribe. Their organization was simple; in each small tribe all the freemen met once or twice a year to decide important matters concerning the whole tribe. The tribe was divided into districts called hundreds. The name hundred probably meant originally a group of one hundred warriors, a primitive division of the tribe for war, but in historical times it always means a district. The assembly of all the freemen of the hundred was the hundred-court, the regular court in which their crude and primitive justice was administered according to tribal law; this court met perhaps every month. The smallest division was the village, but this was primarily a social and economic group—a farming village community—and not a political or administrative division. After the amalgamation referred to the small tribe became, of course, a district of the new and larger tribe, and the former meeting of the freemen of the small tribe was replaced by the meeting of all the freemen of the large tribe. Thus a new division is created, standing between the tribe and the hundred; this is called the *Gau*, or county, or shire, but there is no assembly of the freemen of the *Gau*, except in England, where we find a shire-court.

Three Stages in Land-Ownership.

From a very early time the Germans practised agriculture. At first the whole tribe possessed the land and tilled it in common, putting all that was produced into a common store, from which each family was supplied as it had need. In the next stage of their development the whole tribe still possessed all the land but parcelled it out to each family, which tilled it and kept for its own use all that it produced. The tribe redistributed the lands every year, so that no family received the same fields to till for two years in succession. Slowly this arrangement gave way to individual and perpetual possession of the tillable land—the third stage—each head of a family receiving enough of the tillable land for the support of a family. The quantity of land necessary for such a purpose the Germans called a *Hufe*, the English a "hide." It was, of course, variable in size, according to the quality of the soil. The meadows, pasture-lands, and woods were still held as a common possession of the whole tribe, to be used by all. The men were occupied with fighting, hunting, and gambling; they regarded work as ignoble and proper only for women and slaves. It was customary for the young men to join some chieftain and accompany him in his expeditions. They fought for him, and in return he was bound to feed and clothe them, supply them with arms, and give them a share of the booty taken in war. The relation existing between the chieftain and his "following" (*Gefolge, comitatus*) was an honorable one and could be severed only by the consent of both parties.*

East of the Germans were the Slavs, who were also divided into tribes, and who were still barbarian. It was a long time before these Slavic peoples began to unite to form greater groups and to play any important part in the history of Europe. Their modern divisions are the western Russians, the Lithuanians, Poles, Bohemians, Servians, Bulgarians, and the other Slavic peoples occupying a number of provinces in the Balkan peninsula. They have always shown a fatal inability to work together, to make the individual concessions that are necessary in the formation of a successful government. The individual Slav has been unable to submit to the will of the majority. There have been, at different times, several promising Slavic states in Europe, but all (except Russia) have been absorbed by their neighbors, largely because they could not work together harmoniously. The outcome of the recent war has given them another chance, and a number of Slavics tates have been formed. It remains to be seen, however, whether the Slavs have learned the art of submitting to the will of the majority.

The Slavs.

Beyond the Slavs were other peoples, such as the Finns, Lapps, and Huns, known as Ural-Altaic or Turanian peoples.

* The following modern peoples are Germanic: the German population of Austria (chiefly in the grand duchy of Austria), of Switzerland, and of Germany; the inhabitants of Holland, Denmark, Norway, and Sweden; the Flemings of Belgium; and the Anglo-Saxons of Great Britain and America. The languages spoken by all these peoples are related, being derived from a common stock, and form a group of the so-called Indo-European languages.

Their migratory habits make their movements and location during the early Middle Age uncertain and unimportant. To-day they are represented in Europe by the Hungarians, Turks, Finns, and Lapps. Up to the present they have not made any important contribution to the civilization of Europe.*

Turanian Peoples.

The Rising Church

In contrast to the decaying empire was the new vigorous religion, Christianity, that was destined in the course of the Middle Age to play a leading rôle in the affairs of Europe. At first despised and persecuted, then tolerated, it was finally made the only religion of the state. It built up a far-reaching and powerful organization, and in its ideals and ambitions came into conflict with the empire. In the long, fierce ensuing struggle between them the church was victorious. It broke down the empire and sought to take its place as ruler of the world, and, in its attempt to obtain the universal sway that had been the empire's boast, it almost acquired the world-wide domination that had been the dream of the greatest emperors. To its development in the first centuries we must now direct our attention.

Under the republic as well as under the empire the state

* Sanscrit, Persian, Armenian, Greek, Latin, Celtic, German (including English, Dutch, Danish, Norwegian, Swedish, and Flemish), and Slavic are related, having many words in common and following the same general grammatical principles. Because of this relation these languages are grouped together and called Indo-European. It must not, however, be inferred that the peoples who spoke them were on that account necessarily related racially, although they are generally spoken of as Indo-European peoples. This classification concerns only the languages, not the peoples themselves. The languages spoken by Ural-Altaic peoples are called agglutinative, because of the peculiar way in which words are joined to express relations and ideas. For example, in Hungarian: név = name; nevem = my name; nevemben = in my name; penz = money; penzert = for the sake of money; atya = father; atyam = my father; atyamnal = with my father. In Turkish: tép = to kick; tepish = to kick one another; tepeme = to be unable to kick; tepdir = to cause a person to kick; tepdireme = to be unable to cause a person to kick.

controlled religion and all religious matters. The state assumed the right to say what religions its citizens might practise, what gods they might worship, and in what ways. This was an important principle because it governed the relations between church and state till far into modern times. The state might punish the Christians for various plausible reasons. It based its opposition to them on certain matters which we, however, know were not in the least criminal or dangerous either to society or to the state.

The State Controlled Religion.

(1) Rome had forbidden all eastern or Asiatic religions, except Judaism, to be practised in the west. Christianity was therefore a prohibited religion merely because it had arisen in Asia; hence, merely to be a Christian was a crime.

Persecuted the Christians.

(2) Since Christianity was forbidden, its adherents met secretly, thus arousing the suspicions of the police, who came to regard the church as a secret society which ought to be suppressed. Under the empire secret societies and all secret meetings were forbidden, because they gave opportunities to plot against the government.

(3) By refusing to worship the emperor* Christians exposed themselves to the charge of treason, or lese-majesty, the punishment for which was death.

(4) Christians could not serve the state because of the idolatrous character of many of the duties which rested on every state official. Neither could they freely share the social life of their pagan neighbors because of the numerous idolatrous practices and rites which custom and etiquette prescribed. In order to shun the guilt of idolatry Christians withdrew as much as possible from social

The State Lenient.

* The custom of worshipping the emperor as a god was borrowed from Parthia. It was practised in the eastern provinces during the reign of Augustus, and soon spread throughout the empire. Temples were built and altars erected in his honor. So popular did the worship of the emperor become, especially in the army, that it threatened to supersede all other forms of worship. The author of Revelation speaks of this emperor-worship in a veiled way, calling it the "worship of the beast and his image" (*cf.* Rev. 13: 11–15; 14: 9–11; 15: 2; 16: 2; 19: 20; 20: 4).

as well as from public life. For withdrawing from the service of the state they were regarded as rebels, and for withdrawing from social life they got the reputation of hating the human race. For all these offenses the state might punish. As a matter of fact, however, the Roman government was pacific, having learned the wisdom of leniency, and, in order not to embitter its subjects, took notice of only the most flagrant offenses. Except in times of persecution the government did not seek to enforce the law against Christians and did not arrest them except under strong provocation. The populace, however, was not so forbearing, but punished the refusal of the Christians to take part in the worship of the gods, to serve the state, and to share the social life of the community, by many acts of mob violence. All events of a calamitous nature, such as pests, storms, failure of crops, and famine, were popularly attributed to the anger of the gods, who were offended at the presence of those who refused to worship them. Consequently the Christians were constantly exposed to the unlicensed attacks of the mob, who greeted them with the oft-repeated shout "*Ad bestias*" (that is, let the Christians be thrown to the wild beasts in the amphitheatre). Against such attacks of the mob the Christians could have neither protection nor legal redress. The persecution of the Christians for their heresy in religious belief and for the eccentricity of their behavior grew out of the strong sense of corporate responsibility which animated the Romans. To their way of thinking, society formed such a corporation as must necessarily hold itself responsible for the words and acts of all its members. They were beset by the anxiety lest an individual offense should bring down a corporate punishment on the whole community.

The Mob Violent.

Christians complained bitterly of the form of the trial to which they were subjected when arrested on the charge of being Christians. It was conducted in such a way as to discover merely whether the accused was a Christian, and not whether he was guilty of some real crime, such as theft or murder. No matter how upright and honest a man was, if he was proved to be a

The Form of Trial.

M., 103.

Christian the law punished him as if he were a real malefactor. Ordinarily the accused was brought before a statue of the emperor and ordered to burn incense and to pour out a libation to it. If he refused to perform these acts he was declared guilty. The punishment was death by beheading, or by crucifixion, or by being thrown to the wild beasts in the amphitheatre as a show for the populace. Sometimes they were condemned to penal servitude in the state mines or to exile.

The First General Persecution, 249.

M., 123-130.

The first persecutions which the Christians suffered were either local or confined to a single province. In 249, however, the emperor Decius ordered a general persecution of the Christians throughout the empire, with the purpose of completely destroying them. The persecution lasted but a short time, and for about fifty years thereafter the Christians were not seriously molested. In 303, however, Diocletian, at the instigation of his Cæsar, Galerius, who was a fanatical pagan, issued in rapid succession three sweeping edicts against them: all officials who were Christian should resign; all Christians must sacrifice to the gods under pain of death; their churches were everywhere to be destroyed and their holy books seized and burned. For eight years persecution raged, but under its fury the number of Christians seemed to increase rather than diminish. In 311 Galerius, seeing the futility of the efforts of the state to destroy the new religion, issued an edict of toleration, which was re-enacted by Constantine in 312, and again in 313. In the struggle between opposing emperors two parties were formed, one reactionary, in favor of paganism and the old gods of the state; the other Christian. Constantine, with great political foresight, associated himself with the Christian party and thereby came out victorious.

The Diocletian Persecution, 303.

M., 132.

Christianity Legalized, 311.

R., 6.
M., 134.

After his victory over his last opponent, the emperor Licinius, in 323, Constantine openly espoused the Christian faith, although he postponed his baptism till shortly before his death (337). The edicts of toleration, however, it should be noted, merely made Christianity a legal religion by putting it on the same plane as the worship of all the other gods recognized by the state. Constantine made no attempt to diminish or to prevent the worship of the pagan divinities, although he removed their images from his coins (323). He bestowed such favors on Christianity as were already enjoyed by other religions. He released the Christian clergy from the burdensome duty of serving in municipal offices (312); he made valid the manumission of slaves which took place in churches; he permitted churches to hold property and receive inheritances. He himself contributed liberally to the building of churches and to the support of the clergy. He caused his children to be taught the Christian doctrines. He protected the Christians against the persecutions of the Jews. Out of deference to Christians he ordered that Sunday be observed by the closing of all courts and by the cessation from labor on that day. In fact, much of his legislation was permeated with a spirit of humaneness that should undoubtedly be attributed to the influence of Christianity upon him.*

The State Controls the Church.

When Constantine made Christianity a legal religion he assumed the same authority over it as he already exercised over all other religions in the empire. He regarded the Christian clergy as officials of the state. He called the council of Nicæa (325), presided over it, and made its decrees valid by ratifying them. Without actually dictating what the creed should be, he attempted to prevent heresy in the church by compelling the universal acceptance of a single creed.

Christianity the only Legal Religion in the Empire.

Constantine had merely made Christianity a legal religion, but the emperors Gratian (375–383) and Theodosius (379–395) issued a series of laws for the purpose of making the orthodox form of Christianity the religion of the state and the only legal religion in the empire. They confiscated the temple property and withdrew state support from the pagan priests and the vestal virgins. They forbade the worship of the pagan

* See *Vita Constantini*, IV, 26, for his legislation.

gods and prohibited all heresies, as the variations from the orthodox creed were called. Although these laws were not strictly enforced, both pagans and heretics were thereafter in danger of persecution.

Let us now stop a moment and ask: What were the essential elements of unity in this great Roman empire? What held the peoples in it together? What did they have in common?

Essential Elements of Unity.

1. Latin a Common Language.

First, they had a common language, for Latin was spoken at least in all the empire west of the Balkan peninsula. Out of that spoken Latin have been developed the modern languages of Portugal, Spain, France, Italy, Roumania, and some parts of Switzerland, and because they are derived from the language of Rome they are called Romance languages.

2. The Roman Law.

The second element of unity was the Roman law, the principles of which were the same throughout the empire, although the laws of one province might differ from those of another.

3. The Imperial Administration.

The third essential element of unity was the imperial administration, which was an organized scheme of absolute government. As the emperors extended their sway all local independence had disappeared. A new, imperial nationality had grown up, and the people, even of the remotest provinces, forgot their tribal names and called themselves Roman. They regarded themselves as citizens of Rome, just as though the walls of the city had been expanded to take in the whole empire. And, to give this element greater strength, the people believed that the Roman empire was never to end or to be divided. Territory that had once become a part of the empire must always remain a part of it, even though an enemy might get possession of it. In the Æneid Vergil expressed the popular belief in the words of Jupiter to Venus: "To the Romans I set no limits either in space or time; I have given them dominion without end" (Book II, lines 278–9).

The fourth essential element of unity was the Christian religion, for the minds of the people were dominated by the idea of one Roman Catholic church, with a uniform creed, from which no deviation was to be permitted. It was called Catholic because it claimed to be universal, and it was called Roman because it had identified itself with the Roman empire; Roman and Christian had come, in the fifth century, to have the same meaning.

4. The Church.

CHAPTER II

THE INVASIONS OF THE GERMANS AND THE ESTABLISHMENT OF GERMAN KINGDOMS ON ROMAN SOIL

THE protection of the frontier along the Danube and Rhine was, even in the second century, one of the hardest tasks of the emperor. Its difficulty increased continually, because the barbarians beyond those rivers showed a growing inclination to break into the empire. In this they seem to have been influenced by hunger, the desire for plunder, the pressure of other tribes that were attacking them in the rear, and perhaps by the longing to have a share in a superior civilization. It should be recalled that large numbers of barbarians had improved their condition by settling within the empire, and the Germans outside the empire were no doubt desirous of doing the same thing. During the two centuries preceding the invasion of the West Goths (160–376) these barbarians repeatedly invaded the empire (even Africa and Asia Minor were not spared), but withdrew after sacking and ravaging its richest provinces.

Sporadic Invasions.

The great migrations began in the latter half of the fourth century. Whole tribes, taking their meagre belongings with them, forcibly entered the empire and compelled the emperor to grant them large tracts of land. There they set up their own government under their kings, lived according to their own laws, and reduced the provincials to subjection. For the German tribes concerned, this movement was a migration; for the provincials affected by it and for the empire, it was a forcible invasion and occupation of various provinces of the empire by barbarians. It is true, however, that sooner or later the invaders made terms with the

The Great Migrations.

emperor, who, yielding to necessity, assigned certain lands to them. This cession of lands was but the continuation of the compromise between the empire and the Germans, which for two centuries had been steadily growing more serious. The emperors were generally unable to make a vigorous resistance against them because of the numerous usurpers who arose in various parts of the empire during those times.

The West Goths.

S. B., 2.
O., 3, 4.
R., 10–13.

In 376 the West Goths, who for more than two centuries had occupied an extensive territory north of the lower Danube, yielded to the pressure of the East Goths and of the Huns, who had attacked them in the rear, crossed the Danube, and were settled by the emperor in the lands south of that river. In 378 they rebelled, and after devastating the surrounding territory were pacified by the emperor only with the greatest difficulty. Toward the end of the century they grew restive and determined to migrate. Under the leadership of their young and ambitious king, Alaric, they set out rather blindly, without any definite destination in view. After ravaging a good part of the Balkan peninsula they were met in the western Peloponnesus by the imperial army under Stilicho, himself a German and an able general. Now, at both Rome and Constantinople there was a powerful patriotic party that was trying to rid the empire of barbarians. Stilicho, although his daughter was the wife of the emperor Honorius, knew that his position was precarious because of the opposition of this party. It was plainly not to his interest to destroy the West Goths and thus further the policy of his opponents. The sources are silent about what took place between Stilicho and Alaric, but it has been conjectured that Stilicho wished to make his son emperor, and in order to secure the aid of Alaric made terms with him. At any rate, Stilicho returned to Italy without striking a blow, and Alaric proceeded into Illyricum, ravaging the country as he went. There he established his people on the boundary between the prefectures of Illyricum (east of the upper Adriatic) and Italy. He then again entered into relations with the eastern emperor, from whom he received the title of

Alaric and Stilicho.

commander of the troops in Illyricum (*magister militum per Illyricum*). There his stay was short; in 401 he invaded Italy, but meeting only with defeat he withdrew his people into southern Noricum (corresponding to a part of Bavaria and Austria) and northern Illyricum (403).

Scarcely was Italy free of the West Goths when it was invaded by an immense army of East Goths under their king, Ratiger. To meet them Stilicho made extraordinary efforts to increase the number of his troops and called the distant legions on the Rhine to his aid. He was completely successful in battle, destroying the whole force of Ratiger (404-405). In 408 the national party caused the downfall of Stilicho; the emperor, listening to their charges of treason, put him to death. Alaric took advantage of the death of Stilicho to demand of the emperor a large sum of money, an exchange of hostages, and the cession of Pannonia (a part of Austria and Hungary) for his people. On the emperor's refusal he led his people into Italy. They marched directly against Rome, which, after fruitless negotiations with the emperor, they finally took and sacked (410). They passed the next winter in southern Italy, where Alaric died. Under his successor, Athaulf, the West Goths, slowly moving to the north, continued their depredations. In 412 they entered Gaul. In 414 Athaulf tried to assume a more authoritative position by marrying the emperor's sister, Gallia Placidia, whom Alaric had taken prisoner in the sack of Rome. Honorius, however, was offended by the marriage of his sister to a barbarian, and refused to be conciliated. Athaulf was soon afterward murdered (415), and his successor, Walia, surrendered the royal captive to Honorius and entered his service. He served the emperor faithfully, and was rewarded in 419 by the grant of northeastern Spain and southern Gaul. The West Goths were soon in possession of a kingdom which included a large part of Spain and southern Gaul as far as the Loire. During the sixth century, however, they were driven out of Gaul by the victorious Franks, but indemnified themselves for this

The Unprotected Rhine.

Sack of Rome, 410 R., 11.

The West Goth Kingdom.

loss by acquiring all of Spain. They began, however, to decline in vigor and warlike prowess, and in the eighth century fell an easy prey to the Mohammedans (711).

While Stilicho was destroying the East Goths under Ratiger, a usurper who had arisen in Britain was preparing to invade Gaul. Stilicho, unable to meet him, resorted to the questionable expedient of asking several German tribes which were along the upper Danube to enter Gaul (406-407). He expected them to come into conflict with the usurper, and thought that, no matter who was victorious, he would later find it easy to overcome the victor. In this he was disappointed, for, although the usurper gained an advantage over the invading Germans, he did not prosecute it, but sought to establish himself in southeastern Gaul. The invading Germans, chief of whom were the Suevi and Vandals, slowly passed through Gaul to the south, leaving desolation and ruin behind them. When the West Goths entered Gaul they found these Germans there and made war on them. The Suevi retreated before the West Goths into northwestern Spain and took possession of that part of the country. There they established a kingdom, which, however, was never powerful. The West Goths had little difficulty in overcoming them and annexing their territory (585). The Vandals withdrew into southern Spain, which they held for a few years. They were soon attracted into Africa, which offered them easy booty because its governor was in rebellion against the emperor. They were successful from the first, and in the course of ten years (429-439) took possession of the whole province and established their kingdom there. Led by their cunning, treacherous, and cruel king, Gaiseric, the Vandals, because of their ravaging expeditions, were a scourge to the civilized world about them. Under his weak successors, however, their power declined, and the army of Justinian had little difficulty in destroying their kingdom (533-534).

Suevi and Vandals.

S. B., 2.

Kingdom of the Suevi.

Kingdom of the Vandals.

Early in the fifth century the Burgundians entered the empire and were given lands in the neighborhood of Worms.

About 443 they obtained the permission of the emperor to remove into the valley of the upper Rhône. There

Kingdom of the Burgundians.

they flourished, and slowly extended their kingdom toward the south until they reached the Mediterranean. Their promising kingdom, however, was brought to an end by the Franks, who conquered them and annexed their territory (532).

The Alamanni were composed of many tribes who had formerly been known as Suevi, or Suabians. At first a loose confederation of tribes, they were united during the fifth century under a king. They took possession of some of the

The Alamanni.

lands of the empire, and enlarged their territory by conquest until their kingdom extended from the Main River to the Bernese Alps, and from the Vosges Mountains to the Lech River (including the modern kingdom of Würtemberg, the northern part of Switzerland, the Grand Duchy of Baden, Alsace, and Rhenish Franken). As they extended westward they came into conflict with the Franks, who conquered them and made an end of their kingdom by annexing a part of their territory.

After the deposition of Romulus Augustulus (476), Odovacer called himself king, and was, in fact, king over the combined German mercenaries in whose name and with whose aid he had acted. He made no use of the imperial insignia,

Odovacer King in Italy.

S. B., 2.

although he acted as an emperor in taking possession of the imperial domain and of the mines. The emperor and the people of Italy, however, regarded him merely as the governor of the diocese of Italy, with the title "patrician." He maintained the Roman administrative system as he found it, and the government proceeded with no essential change except that in place of an idle, worthless emperor a vigorous, able man was at the head of affairs. He established peace, administered the government ably, and defended the frontier against attacks of barbarians. Under his wise rule Italy began to enjoy an unwonted prosperity.

The rule of Odovacer was, however, soon cut short by the invasion of the East Goths, a powerful tribe which had been troubling the Danube frontier for about a hundred years, although for a large part of that time they had been tributary to S. B., 3. the Huns. After taking possession of southeastern The Huns. Europe in the last quarter of the fourth century, the O., 5. course of the Huns to the west was temporarily R., 14-16. checked. Their domination extended from the upper Danube to the Caspian Sea, and their ravages ranged from the Rhine to the Euphrates. During the first half of the fifth century there arose among them a great leader and conqueror, Attila by name. With an army composed of Huns and Germans he more than once ravaged the eastern empire. In 450 he attempted to conquer the West, but, after devastating northern Gaul, he was defeated by an army gathered from all quarters (451, in the "Catalaunian fields," the location of which is not certainly known), and compelled to withdraw. After his death (453) his great empire fell to pieces. The East Goths, having thus become free, entered into relations with the eastern emperor. Although they became subject to him, they did not hesitate to make war on him. Since they were a constant menace to the empire, the emperor gladly gave his consent when their king, Theodoric, asked for permission to invade Italy and wrest it from Odovacer. Two considerations seem to have determined Theodoric to invade Italy. (1) The East Goths were really in want, because the imperial government did not supply them with sufficient grain, and the whole territory of the Danube, having been devastated through years of constant pillaging and warfare, did not produce enough for their sustenance. (2) Odovacer had attacked and almost annihilated the Rugians, a German tribe that was friendly to the East Goths, and their king, after his defeat, had fled to Theodoric and begged him to avenge the injury. In 488 the East Goths, accompanied by Kingdom of the East Goths. the remnant of the Rugians, set out for Italy, which they reached the next year. After four years of fighting, Odovacer and Theodoric agreed to rule S. B., 3. the country together. Theodoric, however, having discovered, as it was said, that Odovacer was plotting against him, soon put him to death and became sole ruler.

The kingdom of the East Goths included the whole diocese of Italy. Although nominally subject to the emperor, Theodoric took possession of the imperial domain and of the mines and ruled as an independent king.

Theodoric the Great.

Theodoric gave Italy a remarkable rule. Perhaps the country had never before experienced so just, unerring, and impartial an administration of justice as his was. Through his efficient police protection life and property everywhere in his realm enjoyed a security which had long been unknown. Throughout Italy he restored the aqueducts, most of which were in a dilapidated condition, thus giving the cities an adequate supply of pure water. He provided for the defense of the cities by rebuilding their walls or raising new ones. He exhibited a keen appreciation of Roman civilization by preserving and restoring temples, monuments, and works of art, and he added to the beauty of many of the cities by erecting new palaces and baths. He repaired the roads, and by draining marshes recovered a large tract of land for cultivation. Under his reign agriculture so flourished that Italy, which for centuries had been compelled to import grain, was able to export it. He showed a statesmanlike sense and insight by preserving unchanged the imperial system of administering the government. He reopened the gold mines in Calabria and the iron mines in Dalmatia, encouraged commerce, and fostered industries and manufactures throughout his kingdom.

Seeks to Ally the Germans.

In his relations with the other German kingdoms which had been established within the empire Theodoric showed a remarkably clear political vision. Foreseeing that their continued existence depended on their union, he sought to bind them all together and to prevent them from destroying one another. By intermarriages he made alliances with most of their royal families: he gave his sister in marriage to the king of the Vandals, one of his daughters to the king of the Burgundians, another to the king of the West Goths, and a niece to the king of the Thuringians; he himself married a sister of Chlodovech, the king of the Franks.

Note to Map III.—After the end of the line of emperors in the year 476, the whole empire was supposed to be united under one ruler, the emperor at Constantinople. In fact, his authority was limited to the Balkan peninsula and the eastern Mediterranean lands (Asia Minor, Syria, and Egypt). Virtually all of the western empire was occupied by Germanic tribal kings established by the invasions. In some cases (West Goths, East Goths, Vandals) these tribes had been invited in by Roman officials or given permission to settle, under the name of "allies"; in fact, however, the German kings ruled over these lands and the people (both Roman and German) and the Roman emperor had no authority over them. Note how the Slavs had advanced westward as far as the Elbe River, occupying lands left vacant by the migrating German tribes (compare Map II).

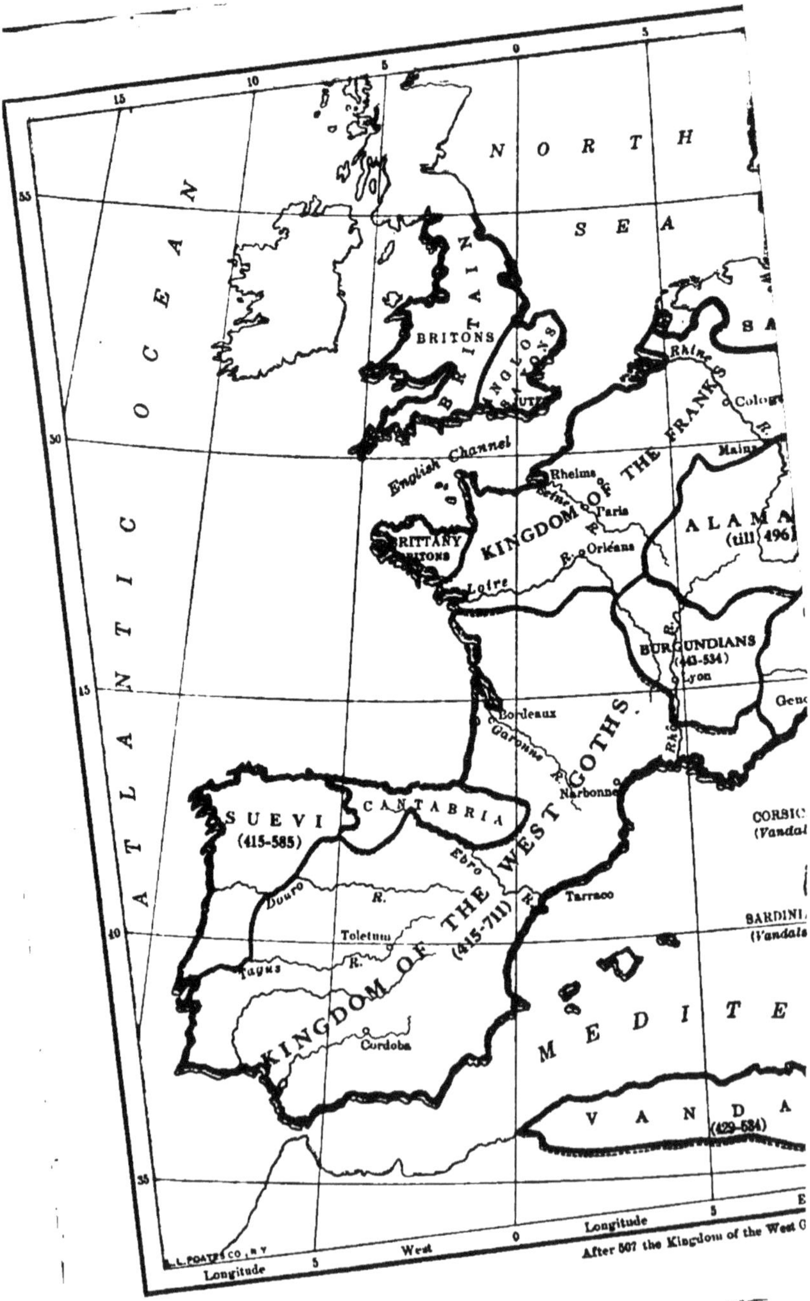

NORTH SEA
ATLANTIC OCEAN
BRITAIN
BRITONS
ANGLO SAXONS
JUTES
English Channel
BRITTANY
BRITONS
KINGDOM OF THE FRANKS
Rhine R.
Cologne
Main R.
Rheims
Seine R.
Paris
Orléans
Loire
ALAMA
(till 496)
BURGUNDIANS
(443-534)
Lyon
Bordeaux
Garonne R.
Rhône
Narbonne
KINGDOM OF THE WEST GOTHS
(415-711)
SUEVI
(415-585)
CANTABRIA
Ebro
Douro R.
Tagus R.
Toletum
Cordoba
Tarraco
CORSIC
(Vandal
SARDINI
(Vandals
MEDITE
VANDA
(429-534)
Longitude West
Longitude
After 507 the Kingdom of the West G

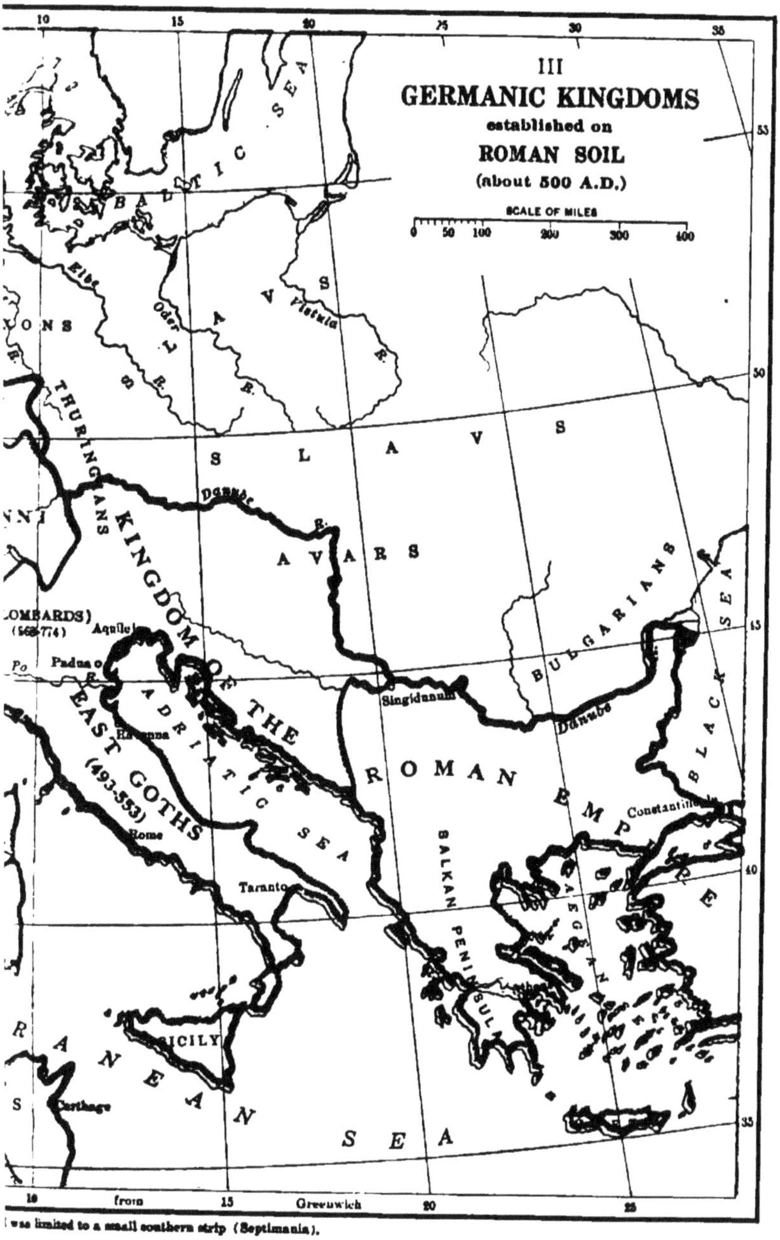

was limited to a small southern strip (Septimania).

He granted religious liberty in the most enlightened way, declaring that there ought to be no compulsion in matters of faith, and that the individual was accountable for his belief and conscience to God alone. The last years of his reign were embittered by the ingratitude and treasonable conduct of some of his trusted friends and officials, among whom were the famous Boëthius, the author of *The Consolations of Philosophy*, and Symmachus. Enraged at their unfaithfulness, he lost perhaps some of his fine self-control and his calm judgment and put them to death, thereby exposing himself to the charge of injustice and persecution. In spite of this, the character of his long reign justly entitled him to the surname Great. At his death (525) only a daughter was left to succeed him, and his kingdom began to go to pieces. In 534 the emperor Justinian attacked the East Goths, and, after a war which, with interruptions, lasted for nearly twenty years, conquered them, and Italy, ruined by this wretched war, was again reduced nominally to the rank of a province of the empire (553).

Religious Freedom.

There were several German tribes still outside the empire, and a word about them is necessary. Beyond the Danube were the Lombards and the Gepidæ, of which the latter were to be completely destroyed in the sixth century. In the course of the fifth century fragments of several tribes (Quadi, Marcomanni, Rugii, etc.), who were located in Bohemia, united to form a new tribe. From the country they came to be called Bavarians (men of Bohemia). Early in the sixth century they migrated and settled in Noricum, which was soon called Bavaria. Between the Bavarians and the Alamanni were the Suevi. The Franks, who were composed of many tribes, each under its own king, occupied both banks of the lower Rhine, and were gradually spreading over northern Gaul. As yet they had given little indication of the great rôle which they were to play in the history of Europe. To the northeast of the Franks were the Saxons, who extended to the Elbe. East of the Franks and south of the Saxons were the Thuringians, the descendants of the ancient Hermunduri.

Other German Tribes.

Their name is perpetuated in that of the Thuringian Forest. Angles, Jutes, and Danes occupied what is now known as Denmark, and the inhabitants of Norway and Sweden, consisting of many tribes, were called Northmen. About the middle of the fifth century various bands of Angles, Saxons, and Jutes migrated to Britain, where they established several little kingdoms, out of which the kingdom of England was to be evolved.

O., 8.

When the Germans moved into the empire they left vacant a large territory which was soon occupied by Slavs. Following close on the heels of the withdrawing Germans the Slavs took possession of the territory north of the lower Danube, of the region called Bohemia, and of all the land east of the Elbe (what is now Prussia). One of the most interesting and important chapters of German history in the Middle Age deals with the reconquest of this territory and the expansion of Germany to the east.

The Invaders Take a Part of the Land.

S. B., 3.

An important feature of the invasion was the seizure of land by the Germans. Indeed, their first demand was that farming land be given them. The fact that these Germans were invaders was cloaked under the name of allies (*fæderati*). As allies they had a right to a share of the land. Until the division could be made they quartered themselves on the provincials. Because of the scant information which the sources give us, the exact manner in which they dispossessed the provincials cannot be determined. It is certain, however, that the division was not made once for all, but that, as the Germans had need, they spread over new provinces, in each one demanding land. The divisions varied also from province to province. Of the Burgundians we know that they generally received half of everything, the houses and buildings, gardens, orchards, ploughlands, meadows, woodlands, and serfs (*coloni*), although in some provinces they took two-thirds of the ploughlands and one-third of the serfs. The king took all the lands which belonged to the emperor (crown lands), and may have seized others also. The rank of an individual determined the amount of land he received: the small proprietors were compelled to share their land with the freemen, while the great landlords divided their estates with the nobles. In this way the nobles acquired a solid advantage over the common freemen. The Germans under Odovacer took only one-third of the land. They were already quartered on the inhabitants. That is, they occupied one-third of the house of the man on whom they had been quartered. This seems to have determined their request for one-third of the land. The East Goths took the lands which Odovacer had given his people, and probably also some of the waste lands. The West Goths generally took two-thirds of the ploughlands and one-half of the woods. The Vandals were conquerors in Africa, and hence were never quartered on the inhabitants, as all the other Germans were. They actually took all the land about Carthage, dispossessing all the provincials. These they either killed, or expelled, or reduced to slavery, compelling them to till the soil for their new masters. Two whole provinces Gaiseric took for himself, and others he divided among his "followers" (*Gefolge*). Although it was a hardship to many of the provincials to be deprived of half of their possessions, yet the general effect of the division was probably good. For, as the formation of great estates caused in part the decline in agriculture and the increase in poverty, so the division of them had, in reality, a beneficial effect.

Nobles Become Rich in Land.

Since the Germans were invaders there could, of course, be no friendly relations between them and the people among whom they settled. There were also other causes operating to increase their mutual ill-will. The provincials looked down on the Germans as barbarians, and the Germans despised the provincials for their cowardice and their inability to defend themselves. The resentment of the provincials was further increased by the fact that the Germans seized so much of their land. Furthermore, the two peoples, though living side by side, were separated by their radically different legal conceptions and methods of legal procedure. In the early days of Rome Roman law was re-

Hostility between Romans and Germans.

garded as a personal possession, the possessor of which carried it with him wherever he went. But after the edict of Caracalla (212) conferring citizenship on all the free inhabitants of the empire, law had come to be regarded as territorial rather than personal. With the Germans law was still a private possession. A German was born into the rights which his father possessed, and these he took with him in all his wanderings; he demanded that he be tried, not according to the laws of the country in which he was, but according to his own tribal law. In their methods of legal procedure the differences were great. While the Roman left everything to the state and its officials, and the whole procedure was conducted in court, the German did everything himself out of court, and left to the court nothing except the rendering of the decision. The objection, common among uncivilized peoples, to the state's interference with the private affairs of the individual, operated among the Germans to restrict the function of the court to the simple decision of the case. The man who won his case put the decision into effect privately, without any further aid of the state. The Roman proved his guilt or innocence by means of the testimony of witnesses; the German did not seek the aid of witnesses, but relied on a certain number of his friends as compurgators to swear that they believed that he was telling the truth. In certain cases the trial took the form of an ordeal, or appeal to divine judgment. With the spread of Christianity among the Germans the clergy conducted these ordeals and invented others, surrounding them all with impressive religious ceremonies which were meant to inspire awe in the minds of those making use of them, and to insure their value as proofs of the guilt or innocence of those undergoing them.

Personal Law of the Germans.

Ordeals.

S. B., 234–239.

At the time of the invasions the laws of the Germans were still unwritten, the knowledge of them being kept alive by oral tradition. It was inevitable that their laws and legal forms should be affected by the legal customs of the people among whom they settled. When they observed that changes and un-

certainty were stealing into their legal practices and principles, they attempted to fix and preserve their ancient laws by re-
Laws of the Germans. ducing them to writing. The codes thus produced are called the "laws of the barbarians" ("*Leges*
S. B., 4. 7: 29. O., 7. *Barbarorum*"), and are an important source of our knowledge of the conditions that prevailed among the Germans. Of the Frankish laws there are two important collections, the *lex Salica* and the *lex Ripuariorum;* the code of the West Goths is called the *lex Wisigothorum*, that of the Burgundians the *lex Burgundionum*, and that of the Saxons the *lex Saxonum*. That the Germans on the continent were yielding to the influence of the empire is shown by the fact that all these codes were written in Latin. On the other hand, the Anglo-Saxons, who were in Britain, remaining for some centuries essentially unaffected by Roman influence, reduced their laws to writing in their mother tongue. In spite of their written codes, the laws of the Germans on the continent were increasingly influenced by Roman law, and their actual methods of legal procedure represented a fusion of Roman and German forms.

There was between the two peoples also a religious difference which, so long as it continued, made their fusion impossible. With the exception of the Angles, Saxons, Jutes, and
Arius. Franks, all the Germans were already Christian when they entered the empire. Unfortunately for them, they had accepted the Arian creed, which was soon afterward displaced in the empire by the Athanasian. The difference between the two creeds concerned the deity of Jesus. Arius, a priest of Alexandria, declared that, although Jesus was far above man, and was indeed the creator of the world, he was nevertheless himself a created being, and therefore not truly God in the same sense that God the Father was
Athanasius. God. His great opponent, Athanasius, was also a member of the church at Alexandria, in which he had the rank of archdeacon. He taught that Jesus was himself God, not created but of the same substance as the Father, and that in him God was incarnate. While the creed

of Arius might be called unitarian, that of Athanasius was trinitarian, and because of its ultimate acceptance by the church it is generally called the orthodox creed. It was not, however, immediately accepted. The struggle between the two creeds passed through several phases and lasted for some three centuries.

Now, missionary work among the Germans was begun while the Arian creed was in the ascendancy, and by those who were Arian in their belief. The Goths first learned of Christianity from Christian prisoners whom they had captured in their raids into the empire. Ulfilas, however, who devoted himself to the work of converting them, has won the title of "apostle of the Goths." He was a descendant of a Christian whom the Goths had carried away as a prisoner from Asia Minor. Although the chronology of his life cannot be fixed, it is certain that he labored to convert the West Goths, and that soon after 340 he was made a bishop over them. His zeal and success brought upon him the persecution of a determined pagan party among the Goths, and he and his followers were compelled to flee. About 348 they withdrew into the empire, and the emperor gave them lands on the northern slope of the Hæmus Mountains, in Mœsia (now the Balkans in Bulgaria). Some time after 370 Ulfilas translated nearly all the Bible into Gothic, for that purpose inventing a Gothic alphabet.* He died about 381. Not all the Christian Goths went into exile in 348, and from those who were left Christianity continued to spread.

Ulfilas.

The Gothic Bible.

In the course of the fourth century nearly all the German tribes accepted the Arian form of Christianity. When they settled in the empire they had their own ecclesiastical organization, their own churches, and their own clergy. Generally they did not seriously persecute the orthodox provincials, although the Vandals were an exception to this rule. Gradually, however, through the efforts of the orthodox clergy, all these Germans were converted from Arianism to the orthodox faith, and there-

* A part of this translation is still extant, and is the oldest example of ancient German, of which there were many dialects.

after intermarriages between them and the provincials were more numerous and the fusion of the two races was accelerated.

The Emperor Has No Authority in the West.

All these German kingdoms were established within the empire half by force and half with the consent of the imperial government. Making a virtue out of necessity, the emperor conferred upon them (except the Vandals, who were, and remained, hostile to the emperor) the title of allies (*fœderati*), sanctioned their occupation of the provinces of the empire, and made the empty stipulation that they should defend the frontier against further invasions. Technically, therefore, all these kingdoms (except that of the Vandals) and their kings were subject to the emperor. Practically, however, these kings governed their kingdoms independently and without any regard to him. Although they were pleased with titles and other empty honors and forms of recognition which the emperor occasionally bestowed upon them, they were really kings in their own right, and in no way answerable to him. The effect of the invasions was, therefore, the virtual loss of all the western provinces of the empire, for the emperor was never again able to make his authority felt throughout the west. It must be remembered, however, that the people in the west still thought of themselves as subjects of the emperor, and of their land as a part of the empire, for, to their way of thinking, the empire was both indivisible and indestructible.

Germans in Constantinople.

Although the Germans established their kingdoms only in the western provinces of the empire, it must not be supposed that they did not threaten the east also. Toward the end of the fourth century their influence in Constantinople itself was so great that it seemed they might be able to germanize the whole government. The army was composed chiefly of German mercenaries, and there was a large colony of Germans in Constantinople itself. The emperor Arcadius was married to the daughter of a Frank, Bauto by name, who had been the commander of the army in the east (*magister militum per orientem*). At the death of Bauto he was succeeded by Gainas, a Goth. The conduct of Gainas brought about a situation in Constantinople similar to that in Rome in 476, and which might easily have been as disastrous to the imperial government there as it was to that at Rome. The national or patriotic party, mention of which has already been made, was composed of senators and officials who resented the intrusion of barbarians into high and important offices, and the consequent barbarizing of the government as well as of the empire. Religious hatred added bitterness to the struggle, because the Germans were Arians and the Greeks orthodox. This anti-German party demanded that the barbarians be put under certain heavy disabilities, with the purpose of eventually driving them out of the empire.

Gainas.

Gainas, the leader of the Germans, was conscious of the gravity of the situation, and perceived that it was a struggle for existence. In 399 the Germans whom Theodosius had settled in Phrygia (in 386) revolted, and Gainas treacherously aided them in the hope of being able to frighten Arcadius into making concessions to him. In this he was successful; at his demand the emperor not only confirmed him in his position as commander of the army but also put to death one of his most powerful personal enemies. Emboldened by this success, Gainas demanded that the Arians be relieved of all the disabilities that had been placed upon them, and that they be permitted to worship freely. The patriarch and the emperor, however, stubbornly refused to grant his demands. His failure to obtain these concessions marks the decline of his power, and his position in Constantinople became more and more precarious. In the desperate hope of recovering his power he attempted to seize the imperial palace and to loot the imperial treasury. Failing in both these undertakings, he fled from the city with a part of his troops. An infuriated mob put to death all the Germans whom it could find in the city. Gainas ravaged Thrace without being able to take a single stronghold where he could intrench himself and prolong the struggle. He then determined to enter Asia Minor, but while crossing the Hellespont his troops were destroyed by the imperial army, also under a Goth, named Fravitta. Gainas fled beyond the Danube, where he was captured by the king of the Huns, who cut off his head and sent it as a present to Arcadius. With the downfall of Gainas the power of the German party in Constantinople was permanently weakened, and, although occasionally an able German leader appeared, none was ever again dangerously near overthrowing the government. Leo I (457-474) put an effective check on the Germans by enrolling other barbarians, the Isaurians, in the army. The cure, however, was as bad as the disease, for the Isaurians were quite as barbarous, turbulent, and ambitious as the Germans. They soon acquired a controlling influence over affairs, and even furnished several emperors. They repeated the rebellions of the Germans, and their power was broken only after a long war by deporting them to Thrace.

CHAPTER III

JUSTINIAN AND THE REACTION AGAINST THE GERMANS

In the fifth century the emperors were powerless before the invading barbarians, who, as we have seen, forcibly occupied nearly all the western part of the empire. Weak and helpless, these emperors gave a grudging and forced recognition to the governments which the German tribes established, but it was never forgotten that they were invaders and unwelcome guests. A series of able emperors so revived the empire in the sixth century that one of them, Justinian (527–565), was able to dream of driving out the hated Germans and of restoring the empire to its original boundaries. Under Zeno (474–491), Anastasius I (491–518), and Justin I (518–527), the empire was wisely administered, the treasury replenished, the army made more effective, and thus a good foundation was laid for the many-sided activity of Justinian.*

The Empire Revives.

Justinian (527–565) learned statecraft under his uncle, Justin I, who, being illiterate and deficient in knowledge of the practical workings of the government, depended on him to conduct the affairs of state. Justinian had an amazing capacity for mastering details and was an effective administrator. During his long service under his uncle he obtained a thorough knowledge of the machinery of government. When he came to the throne he had a well-defined ambition to rule in a grand manner—to be absolute in every way. He had already matured plans for various courses of action which would require the expenditure of large sums of money. He found in John of Cappadocia, the pretorian prefect, a successful and unscrupulous tax-collector, who kept him supplied with the money necessary to carry out his great plans.

Justinian, 527–565.

* *Cf.* J. B. Bury, *The Later Roman Empire*, 2 vols.

John not only collected with rigorous exactitude the old accustomed taxes, which were already heavy, but also invented new ones, by means of which he extorted immense sums from the people. He sold justice in so shameless a manner "that men would not go into court and the business of advocates declined."

"Greens" and "Blues."

The population of Constantinople, as well as that of the other large cities of the empire, was divided into two political parties, known as the "greens" and the "blues." These names, originally connected with the circus at Rome (their exact origin and character are unknown), had extended to all parts of the empire and had come to stand for different policies, for different theological doctrines, and for different candidates for the imperial throne. The blues supported Justinian, and in return for their support demanded immunity from the laws. They not only prevented the punishment of criminals who were of their party, but maltreated their opponents, the greens, who were without redress for all the indignities and wrongs done them. The blues became so domineering and turbulent that Justinian finally (532) determined to break their power and to make himself independent of them. In the circus the greens complained to the emperor that they were oppressed without redress, and the blues, resenting the charges, attacked them in the street. After some bloodshed seven offenders—some of whom were greens and some blues—were seized and condemned to death. Five of them were executed, but the remaining two were rescued and carried to a place of safety. The blues and greens, seeing that the emperor threatened the existence of both parties, united to resist him. They set fire to the city in several places and blood was freely shed in the streets. The numerous adherents of the family of Anastasius cleverly fomented the dissatisfaction, and finally succeeded in having Hypatius, the nephew of Anastasius, crowned emperor. At this Justinian, who was supported by only a small body of troops, was advised by his counsellors to flee. But Theodora, his wife, overruled them by declaring that death was preferable to flight, and that she would rather die an empress than live in exile. Justinian determined to fight, and sent out Belisarius at the head of his troops to attack the mob gathered in the circus to greet Hypatius. Taken at a disadvantage, the mob could neither resist nor escape, and the troops slaughtered about 35,000 of them. The factions, overwhelmed by this disaster, were for years rendered powerless to hamper the emperor, who was now left free to devote himself to the larger undertakings on which he had set his heart.

Justinian, fired with the ambition to destroy the Germans who had settled in the west and to restore the empire to its former boundaries, waited only for an opportunity to attack them. Such an opportunity came in 531, when the king of the Vandals was dethroned by a usurper and cast into prison. Justinian seized this as a pretext, and in 533 sent a large army under Belisarius to attack the Vandals. Belisarius was successful and before the end of the year was in possession of their kingdom, which was again made a province of the empire. Italy next claimed his attention.

Justinian's Anti-German Policy.

Destroys the Vandals.

Amalasuntha, queen of the East Goths, when her only son died, married her cousin, Theodahad, who soon imprisoned and then basely murdered her (535). Her murder served Justinian as a pretext for invading the kingdom of the East Goths. In 535 Belisarius was sent with an army into Italy. He landed first in Sicily, and the whole island submitted to him. During the next five years he overran Italy and got possession of all of it except a small part of the valley of the Po. In their extremity the East Goths sent ambassadors to the king of Persia and persuaded him to attack the empire on the east. Justinian was therefore compelled to recall Belisarius when the work of conquest was all but completed (540). Belisarius left a few troops in Italy to complete its subjugation, but made the mistake of dividing the command among several generals instead of putting the authority in the hands of one of them; the soldiers were dissatisfied because they were not properly paid, and consequently, after the departure of Belisarius, the campaign was conducted in a negligent manner.

The East Goths.

The country had been terribly harried during the five years

of war, and the people were in distress. Nevertheless Justinian's tax-collectors did not spare them, but assessed them so heavily as to cause the Italians to regret the easy rule of the East Goths, who had never burdened them with taxes. At the same time the East Goths elected an able man king and renewed the war. Success attended them, and by 544 they had retaken nearly all of Italy. In that year Belisarius returned to Italy, but, as he was not supplied with efficient troops, he was unable to repeat his successes of the first years of the war and so was recalled (548). The war was carried on in a desultory manner till 551, when Justinian sent Narses with a large force to Italy to complete, if possible, its conquest. He prosecuted the war with great vigor, and in 553 he destroyed the East Gothic army and put an end to all effective resistance on their part, although a few towns were not immediately taken (Verona and Brescia did not surrender till 562). Scarcely had Narses defeated the East Goths when a Frankish army appeared in Lombardy to dispute its possession with him, but he repulsed them with great loss. Italy, including Istria and Illyria (a large territory north and east of the Adriatic) was again made a province of the empire and put under an exarch, a kind of governor who exercised authority over all matters, civil, fiscal, and military. This exarch took up his residence at Ravenna.

Spain.

Justinian next attempted to recover Spain. The West Goths under rival kings were divided by civil war. One of the factions asked aid of the imperial governor of Africa, who took advantage of the situation to conquer a good part of the southeastern coast of Spain (Cordova, Carthagena, Malaga) for the emperor. But again Justinian's tax-collectors undid the work of his armies, and so oppressed the people with taxes that they welcomed the West Goths, who gradually reconquered the lost territory. In 623 the last Greek troops were driven out and Spain was then wholly in the hands of the West Goths.

Justinian had now reconquered northern Africa, Italy, and southeastern Spain, but with these successes he was compelled to be content. He was not able to prosecute further his ambitious plan of recovering all the western provinces which were then in the possession of the Germans, because he was frequently called on to resist some enemy in the east.

His Persian Wars.

It cannot be denied that Justinian courted trouble in many quarters, because, having a consuming ambition to enlarge the boundaries of his empire, he not only offended Persia by intriguing with the small independent states which lay on the frontier of the two empires but even carried on long and exhausting wars with that country for the possession of worthless tracts, merely because of his unreasoning pride in the size of his empire. Immediately after his accession to the throne he challenged Persia by beginning to erect a great fortress on the Persian frontier near Nisibis. The Persians accepted the challenge, and a war ensued, which was ended in 532 to the advantage of Persia, for Justinian agreed to pay a large sum of money, cede certain places, and remove his eastern military headquarters farther from the Persian frontier. Two other wars (540–545 and 549–556) followed, and both ended disastrously for Justinian. They interest us here only because they kept him from pursuing his policy of destroying the Germans and of recovering the west from them.

It has already been said that as the German tribes moved into the empire Slavs followed at their heels and took possession of the lands which they vacated. In this way various Slavic tribes had reached the frontier of the empire, and were now devastating the outlying provinces, much as the Germans before them had done.

Slavs Invade the Empire.

As early as 300, Slavs, singly or in small groups, began to pass quietly across the Danube and settle in the empire, so that by 500 there was a considerable Slavic population in the Balkan peninsula. Those who still lived beyond the Danube gave Justinian a great deal of trouble by their invasions. Year after year, in company with Bulgarians, a Tatar people, they crossed the Danube and ravaged the empire. In 540 they even reached the Isthmus of Corinth, but, being prevented from entering the Peloponnesus, they crossed to Asia Minor, which they devastated, and returned to their homes, laden with spoil.

About 558 the Avars, probably akin to the Huns of Attila, made their appearance on the Danube. They had been subject to the Turks in Asia, but, rebelling against them, had moved westward into Europe. They demanded and received tribute from Justinian, and in 562 invaded and harried Thrace. Although they caused Justinian some trouble, they expended most of their warlike energy in fighting the Slavs.

The Avars.

Toward the end of his reign the Cotrigur Huns and the Utrigur Huns, who occupied the territory north of the Black Sea, troubled the empire, but Justinian, unable to chastise them, cleverly set them each against the other. He followed the same policy with the Lombards and Gepidæ, two formidable German tribes on the middle Danube. In the end this policy was only partially successful; the Gepidæ were destroyed by the combined forces of the Lombards and Avars; but the Lombards then invaded Italy, while the Avars took possession of the lands which had been occupied by both the Lombards and Gepidæ, and at intervals continued their depredations in the empire.

The Huns.

Not only was Justinian prevented by his Persian wars and his struggles with these barbarian invaders from prosecuting his plan to recover all the empire, but even his success in recovering a part of Spain was to be undone, for the West Goths gradually reconquered all that they had lost. At the same time the Germanic element in the empire was strongly reinforced by the rapid development of the Franks. By conquering all of Gaul, Burgundy, and Batavia they became so powerful that no Greek emperor could ever hope to recover those lands. The Germans were then so firmly intrenched in the empire that the anti-German policy of Justinian could never be carried out. Moreover, this policy was soon abandoned because the development of affairs in the Greek empire was such that his successors were compelled to expend all their energies nearer home; succeeding emperors were so occupied in the east that they could never again effectively interfere in the affairs of the west —not even in Italy and those provinces which were nearest at hand. No emperor arose possessing the vaulting ambition of Justinian and no conquering general with the military skill of Belisarius. The territorial development of the Franks made permanent the loss of the west to the Greek emperor, and rendered futile any hope of reuniting east and west.

Justinian's reign was characterized by great activity in building, in which he spent vast sums of money. The constant invasions of the barbarians compelled him to restore the existing fortresses, and to build new ones, to fortify many cities with walls and towers, and even to found new cities in strategic positions. The burning of much of Constantinople in the sedition of 532 gave him the opportunity to rebuild many of its churches with great magnificence. His building operations were not confined to Constantinople; his interest in the church as well as in architecture led him to promote the erection of fine churches in all parts of his empire. In this he was aided by the most able Greek architect of the Middle Age, Anthemius of Tralles, immortal as the creator of the church of St. Sophia, now the chief mosque of Constantinople. This church had a wide influence on architecture throughout the empire, since, for several centuries, it served as a model which was copied with greater or less exactness by the architects of all the provincial cities. The style of architecture then in vogue in Constantinople is called Byzantine, and is characterized chiefly by the cupola, by the round arch, and by a lavish use of mosaics for decorative purposes. Byzantine art reached its highest development and originality in the age of Justinian, after which it became stereotyped and formal.

Justinian as Builder.

Byzantine Art.

Justinian's interest in the church manifested itself in various ways. Heathenism had still many adherents, especially among the philosophers and peasants—the extremes of learning and ignorance. Justinian was eager to destroy heathenism and heresy and to establish a uniform faith. He forbade the further teaching of heathen philosophy and closed the University of Athens because its teachers were heathen. He directed the labors of what may be called home missionaries in various parts of the empire,

Justinian and the Church.

especially among the peasants and mountaineers of Asia Minor. He displayed not less zeal for the conversion of the heathen peoples on his frontiers, to whom he sent missionaries to instruct them in the Christian faith. He assumed absolute authority over the church, confirming the election of bishops and controlling the formulation of the creed. In 555 he confirmed the election of Pelagius, bishop of Rome, whose predecessor, Vigilius, he had for some years held a prisoner in Constantinople because he opposed certain ecclesiastical measures of the emperor. After the Nicene Council (325) had declared for the complete deity of Jesus, it took more than 300 years to establish the doctrine of his complete humanity and to define their relation. The question turned on whether Jesus had two natures, the divine and the human, or one, and the relation of the one to the other, and on whether he had two wills, the divine and the human, or one, and the relation of the one to the other. In the sixth century the discussion concerned the question of the two natures of Christ, and its settlement was due in some measure to Justinian, who called the fifth ecumenical council at Constantinople (553), directed its discussions, and dictated its conclusions and its statement of the creed.

Under the imperial form of government the legislative power passed from the people to the emperor, whose *placita* (constitutions or decrees) took the place of the *leges* (laws), which were passed by the people in the *comitia* (popular assemblies). These imperial constitutions had at various times been collected and published; the last collection was that of Theodosius, published in 438. Since that time the emperors had issued many new constitutions, some of which had radically modified previous ones, but which had not been collected in a convenient form. To remedy this, Justinian appointed a commission of ten men, with the eminent jurisconsult, Tribonian, at its head, to make a complete collection of all the constitutions, to harmonize, clarify, and simplify them, and to state them as briefly as possible—in a word, to codify them. In 529 the commission published the result of its labors in the collection which is known as the *Codex* (code) of Justinian.

Justinian Codifies the Law.

The *Codex*.

In 530 Justinian appointed a second commission of seventeen eminent lawyers, again with Tribonian at its head, to collect the *responsa prudentium*, that is, the answers, decisions, or interpretations, of famous lawyers, who had come to be regarded as authorities in legal matters. They were to read all the "books pertaining to Roman law, written by those lawyers who had been licensed by imperial authority to interpret the law," collect their decisions, harmonize them, and present them in a kind of abstract form. This stupendous task they completed in three years, and published the result of their labors in a work of many volumes, which is known as the *Digest*, or *Pandects*. It is a comprehensive commentary on the whole body of Roman law, which had been about 1,300 years in forming.

The *Pandects*.

For the use of law students Justinian had a text-book on Roman law prepared. It is called the *Institutes*, or *Principles of Roman Law*, and is a discussion of legal principles. Without attempting to pursue the history of Roman law, it may be said that the study of it was revived in the early Middle Age at Bologna, and it soon came to form a part of the curriculum of study in other Italian universities. When Frederick Barbarossa went into Italy he met lawyers who were versed in the code of Justinian, and they profoundly influenced his conception of the imperial office. Then, in the thirteenth century, it became known in France, where it had a large influence on the formation of the absolute kingship of the Capetians and their successors. The present law of France, Germany, Scotland, French Canada, Mexico, and the civil law of Louisiana may be said to be descended from, or based on, the code of Justinian.

The *Institutes*.

Justinian appeared to foster industry and commerce, yet he was interested in them not so much because of their influence on the general welfare of the country as because he could make them a source of revenue to himself. In taxing industries and granting monopolies for the manufacture and sale of various articles he was guided, not by a statesmanlike knowledge of economic principles, but

The Work of Justinian.

merely by the desire to increase his revenues. The culture of silk was introduced into Europe during his reign by some monks who brought the eggs of silkworms from China. (According to another story a Persian brought the eggs concealed in a hollow wand.)

The reign of Justinian was a brilliant one from many points of view, yet there is hardly a doubt that the empire was in a less prosperous condition at the close of his reign than at its beginning. The decline of the empire may safely be attributed to oppressive taxation, to unwise governmental control of commerce and industries, and to constant wars, some of them useless and all of them ruinous.

From the time of Justinian the empire was no longer either "universal," as the Romans proudly called it, or even Roman. The western provinces were in the hands of Germans, and the population of the rest of the empire, for the most part, spoke Greek. During Justinian's reign Latin was superseded by Greek as the official language of the empire. Yet so long as there was an imperial government at Constantinople (to 1453) it continued to call itself the Roman empire. We are compelled, however, to speak of it as the Greek empire, to distinguish it from Charlemagne's empire, which was renewed in the west in 800, and which also called itself Roman. It will be quite impossible for us to follow even in outline the history of this Greek empire, and it will hardly be mentioned except as it occasionally became involved in the politics and struggles of western Europe. It must not, however, be supposed that the Greek empire had no history worth recording. One needs only to follow its fortunes and misfortunes in the stately periods of Gibbon, or in the not less interesting pages of Finlay, to discover that the Greek empire had an important place to fill. It was a mighty bulwark against the barbarians of the east, and especially against the Mohammedan hordes which at various times made Herculean efforts to break into Europe by way of the Balkan peninsula. It would be impossible to calculate the loss in civilization if either the barbarians, or the Arabs, or the Turks had taken possession

The "Greek" Empire.

of Constantinople in the early Middle Age. As it was, Constantinople kept alive Greek and Roman culture, and in the course of centuries transmitted a part of it to the west through one channel or another. Greek missionaries carried Christianity and the beginnings of culture to the barbarians beyond the Danube and brought them within the pale of civilization. Constantinople was a kind of gateway to the Orient, and during a large part of the Middle Age it was the leading commercial city of Europe, maintaining active commercial relations with Asia as well as Europe.

CHAPTER IV

THE FRANKS

About the middle of the third century the Germans along the middle and lower Rhine came to be called by a new collective name, the Franks. They were divided by their location into three great groups, the Salian, the Ripuarian, and the "Upper" Franks. Salian (the name appears first in 358) was applied to certain tribes who lived along the sea, and probably means "dwellers by the salt water." Their chief tribe was the *Batavi*, to whom were united the *Caninefates* and other tribes (about 350). About the same time they began to colonize the territory south of them, between the Scheldt and the Meuse (Maas). At first they met little or no opposition from the Roman government, because much of the territory which they occupied was waste, swampy, and thinly populated. Within the next century and a half they reached the Seine, and even made some settlements south of it. The middle group of the Franks, called Ripuarians (the name appears about 450 and means "dwellers on the banks of the Rhine"), came to include the *Chamavi*, the *Chasuarii*, the *Bructeri*, the *Ampsivarii*, and others. When they attempted to move into the empire they met with a long and stubborn resistance from the government. In the course of the fifth century, however, they broke down all opposition and took possession of the territory between the Meuse and the Moselle. Their chief towns were Cologne (which they took and lost several times), Aix-la-Chapelle, and Bonn. The "Upper" Franks occupied the territory between the Lahn and Main Rivers. Their principal tribe was the *Chatti*, the ancestors of the modern Hessians. Like the other Franks, they forced their way

Salian, "Upper," and Ripuarian Franks.

S. B., 5.

Their Expansion.

into the empire, and after a long struggle took possession of the valley of the Moselle. They took Treves four times before they were able to retain possession of it. They also took possession of the territory about Worms which was vacated by the Burgundians (443).

When the Franks began to invade the empire they had no kings, but each tribe elected its duke or leader in war. Among them, as among all other German tribes, migration or a considerable expansion by means of conquest was accompanied by the development of a royal power. The duration of the struggle which took place in connection with the advance of the Franks into the empire gave their duke (elected leader in war) an opportunity to make his office permanent, and he soon came to be called king. About 430 a tribe of Salian Franks was governed by a king named Chlodio, the first of the Merovingian family of whom there is any sure knowledge. He was followed a little later by Childerich (457–481), who had his residence at Tournai. He was on good terms with the Romans, and aided Ægidius, the Roman governor of Gaul, and his son Syagrius (464–486) in their wars with the West Goths. He was succeeded by his son Chlodovech* (481–511), famous for his conquests and for his subjugation and union of all the Franks.

Development of the Kingship.

His first conquest was toward the south. After Odovacer removed the emperor Romulus Augustulus (476), Syagrius (son of Ægidius), the governor of Gaul, continued to administer the government of that territory on his own responsibility. The Germans were pressing upon him from all sides, however, and his authority extended merely from the Somme to the Loire. In 486 Chlodovech made war on him and, after defeating him, took possession of his territory. Chlodovech apparently understood the possibilities which the situation offered him. He usurped the office which Syagrius had held, assumed the government of the conquered territory, and conducted it as if

Chlodovech, 481–511.

S. B., 5.
O., 6.
R., 17.

* Ludovic, Ludwig, Clovis, and Louis are modern forms of Chlodovech.

he were sovereign in his own right. The inhabitants merely changed governors and suffered no disabilities by the change. It was inevitable that Chlodovech's position as independent governor of this conquered territory would strengthen his kingship, because his authority there was greater than his authority over his Franks. The Franks did not migrate in large numbers into the newly acquired province, and hence the inhabitants, more fortunate than those of other provinces which were conquered by Germans, were not compelled to divide their lands with unwelcome guests. There was, however, a slow and peaceable colonization of the waste and unoccupied lands of the territory. Very few Franks ever settled south of the Loire.

As the Franks extended their sway to the south they came into conflict with the Alamanni, who from their seat on the upper Rhine were spreading westward into Gaul. Hostilities between them began in 496. Chlodovech was victorious and compelled the Alamanni to agree to pay him tribute. In the first years of the sixth century the Alamanni broke the treaty, and Chlodovech was completely successful in his effort to punish them. He was not permitted, however, to obtain the full reward of his victory because of the interference of Theodoric the Great, king of the East Goths. True to his "German" policy of preserving all the German peoples who had established themselves in the empire, Theodoric prevented the extinction of the Alamanni. They ceded the northwestern part of their kingdom to Chlodovech, and, retaining their territory on the upper Rhine and Danube (Suabia and Switzerland), continued to exist as a duchy under the protection of the East Goths. The Alamanni withdrew to a great extent from the territory ceded to Chlodovech, and, as it was soon colonized by Franks, the northern part of it came to be called Franconia.

Conquers the Alamanni, 496.

Unlike all other German tribes which had entered the empire, the Franks were still pagan. The conversion of Chlodovech to the orthodox form of Christianity is connected by tradition with his first encounter with the Alamanni (496). Although the story is not impossible, it is by no means above suspicion, and, furthermore, it is unnecessary to explain his adoption of the new faith. His wife, an earnest, orthodox Christian, was unceasing in her efforts to bring about the change; with his consent the two children which she had already borne him had received Christian baptism; for some time he had been familiarly associated with orthodox bishops, who frequented his court and who diligently improved every opportunity to recommend their faith to him. It was due to the persistent efforts of the bishop of Rheims that Chlodovech, with a large number of his warriors, finally yielded and accepted baptism at his hands. In honor of the occasion houses and churches were decorated as if for a great celebration. Some of his Franks were displeased with the change in religion and withdrew to neighboring Frankish tribes that were still pagan. A large majority of his people, however, made no objection, and eventually entered the church. Although Chlodovech built churches and monasteries, the conversion of both him and his people was merely formal and had little immediate effect on their morals and conduct.*

The Franks Become Orthodox Christians.

S. B., 5:30–31.

Chlodovech's adoption of orthodox Christianity had two important political effects: (1) In the eyes of the orthodox inhabitants of all the territory which he had conquered it supplied what was lacking in the legitimacy of his kingship, and consequently they now joyfully submitted to him; the clergy especially became devoted to him, and the kingdom of the Franks was fortunate that its German and Roman subjects were united in their creed. (2) It led to extensive conquests, for, both Burgundians and West Goths being Arian, their Roman subjects turned to Chlodovech as to a deliverer, and intrigued with him for the overthrow of their heretical masters. Such was apparently the cause of Chlodovech's war with the West Goths (507–509). At

Effects of the Change.

* The two accounts of the conversion of Chlodovech are found in Gregory of Tours' *History of the Franks*, bk. II, chaps. XXX and XXXI. A comparison of these two chapters is sufficient to discredit the story of his vow in battle.

any rate no other cause is assigned, and at least one bishop in the kingdom of the West Goths (Quintian of Rhodez) was charged with intriguing with Chlodovech, and with urging him to make the war. And another (Galactorius of Béarn) armed the people of his diocese and put himself at their head for the purpose of aiding the Franks. Chlodovech secured the help of the Burgundians in this war by promising them a part of the territory which he hoped to conquer. The war lasted for three years, and was ended by the interference of Theodoric the Great, who, by rendering timely assistance to the West Goths, prevented them from being driven out of Gaul. Peace was established by the cession of the territory between the Loire and the Garonne to the Franks.

Chlodovech Unites the Franks.

S. B., 5.

Not the least important work of Chlodovech was his union of all the Franks. It should be remembered that when he became king each tribe of the Franks, under its own king or duke, was independent of all the others. In one way or another Chlodovech removed all these rulers and united these tribes under his sceptre. Bishop Gregory of Tours (died 594), the historian of the Franks for this early period, has preserved some remarkable stories of the cunning, treacherous, and cruel manner in which Chlodovech destroyed king after king. His narrative, however, seems to be little more than the naïve accounts which were in circulation among the people, and can hardly be trusted in all its details. But it is safe to infer that Chlodovech made use of both fraud and force to accomplish his purpose. At any rate, there is no question about the important fact that he had, before his death, united all the Franks from the Main to the sea into one kingdom.

His Kingdom Divided.

Chlodovech died in 511, at the early age of forty-five, without having made any provision for the succession. His sons treated the kingdom as a private possession, dividing it among themselves. The age of each probably determined the size of his share: Theuderich, the oldest, received the largest portion, while Chlothar, the youngest, received the smallest. It may also be significant that each received a part of the territory conquered in 485, for it was in this territory that each took up his residence (the four capitals being Metz, Orleans, Paris, and Soissons). This division was merely a private arrangement in which the people were not consulted. The kingdom belonged to the family, consequently only its members were concerned in its partition. Although there were four kings, each exercising authority in a clearly defined territory, there was but one kingdom of the Franks, and one people of the Franks. Actual division did not destroy the ideal unity of kingdom and people. It was as a family that the four sons succeeded their father. While this presupposed that they would render one another mutual aid, it did not preclude the possibility of unbrotherly intrigues and even of fratricidal wars. Neither did it prevent the brothers, when one of them died, from putting to death his children and seizing his territory.

Conquest of the Thuringians, 531.

Of the Burgundians, 532–534.

Of Provence.

Of Bavaria.

The unity of the family showed itself most markedly in the common policy of foreign conquest which the brothers adopted, and in the partition of the spoils. In 531 Theuderich, with the aid of the neighboring Saxons, attacked and easily conquered the Thuringians. The Franks colonized the southern part of the newly conquered territory (between the Main and the Thuringian Forest), while the Saxons colonized the northern part (the Harz Mountains). After two unsuccessful attacks on the Burgundians, the Franks conquered them (532–534) and annexed their territory. In 536 Witiges, king of the East Goths, ceded Provence and the duchy of the Alamanni to the Franks, in return for which they promised to aid him in his war with the emperor. At the same time they accepted money from the emperor and promised to aid him against the East Goths. With characteristic treachery they helped neither, but invaded Italy for the purpose of securing a part of it for themselves (538). A little later (probably between 540 and 550) the Franks got possession of Bavaria, although nothing is known of the manner in which they did this. In neither Alamannia nor Bavaria did

Note to Map IV.—This shows the conquests of Chlodovech (Clovis) and his successors (the Merovingian line of Frankish kings). The figures in parentheses give the approximate dates of the successive conquests. The Pyrenees set a natural limit to their conquests on the southwest. The Lombards, protected by the Alps, a part of the Thuringians, by their forests, and the Saxons, by their swamps, were able to maintain their independence to the time of Charlemagne. Compare this with Map III, which shows the lands occupied by the Franks about 500, before the conquests of Clovis.

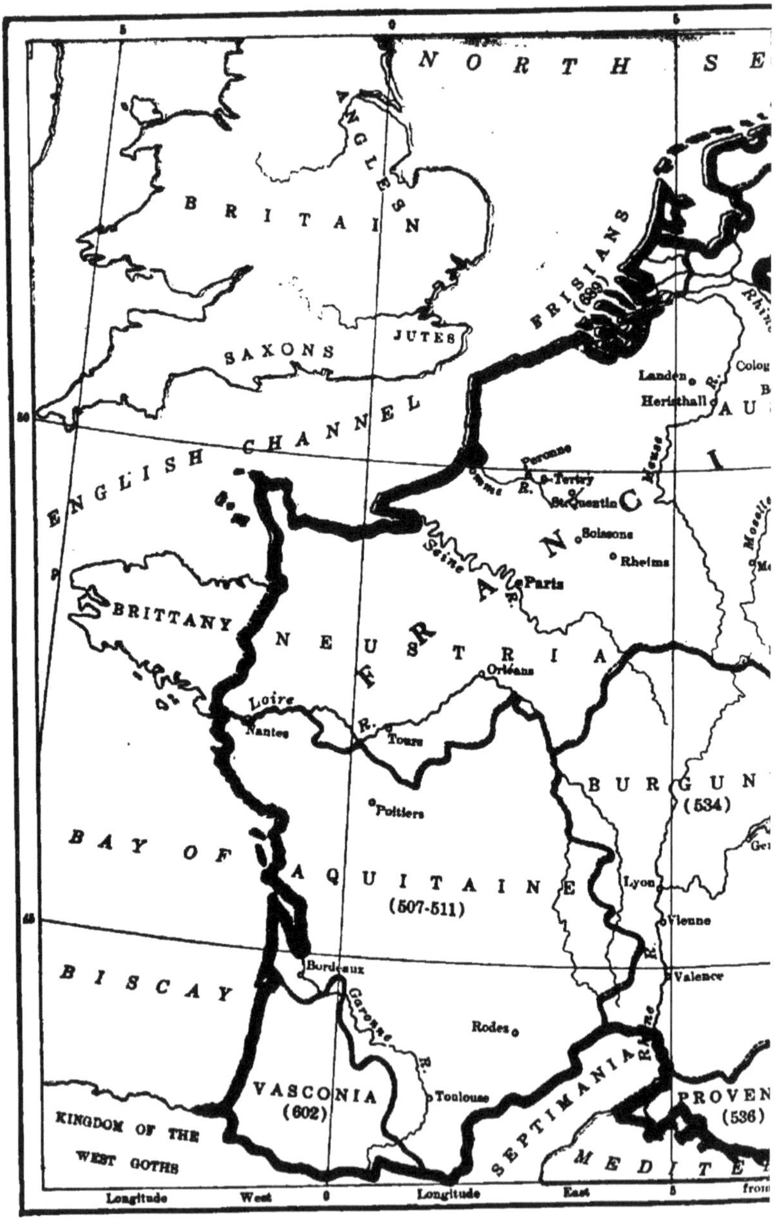
NORTH SE
ANGLES
BRITAIN
SAXONS
JUTES
FRISIANS (689)
ENGLISH CHANNEL
Landen
Heristhall
Colog
Peronne
Somme R.
S. Terry
St. Quentin
Soissons
Rheims
Meuse
Moselle
Seine R.
Paris
FRANCI
BRITTANY
NEUSTRIA
Orléans
Loire R.
Nantes
Tours
Poitiers
BURGUN
(534)
BAY OF BISCAY
AQUITAINE
(507-511)
Lyon
Vienne
Valence
Bordeaux
Garonne R.
Rodez
Toulouse
Rhone
VASCONIA
(602)
SEPTIMANIA
PROVEN
(536)
KINGDOM OF THE
WEST GOTHS
MEDITE
Longitude
West
Longitude
East
from

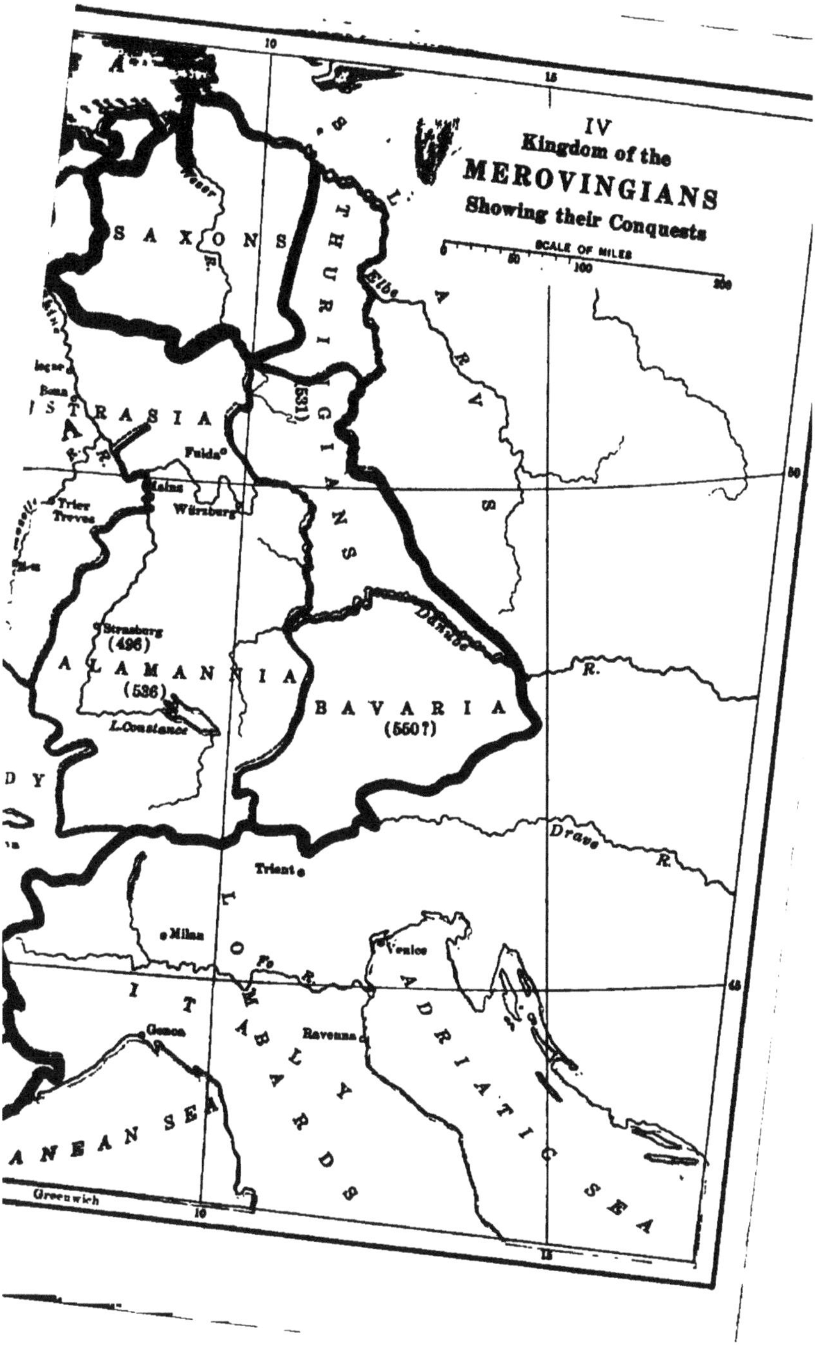
IV
Kingdom of the
MEROVINGIANS
Showing their Conquests
SCALE OF MILES
0
50
100
200
10
15
S A X O N S
Weser R.
Elbe
T H U R I N G I A N S
(531)
S L A V S
S T R A S I A
Fulda
Mainz
Würzburg
Trier
Treves
Strasburg
(496)
A L A M A N N I A
(536)
L.Constance
B A V A R I A
(550?)
Danube R.
Drave R.
Trient
Milan
Venice
Po R.
Genoa
Ravenna
L O M B A R D S
I T A L Y
A D R I A T I C S E A
A N E A N S E A
Greenwich

they disturb the government, but left each people with a large measure of independence under a native duke. Throughout the sixth century the Franks continued with unabated vigor their attacks on neighboring peoples. They made frequent campaigns against the Avars, Saxons, Lombards, Bretons, and Basques, although they often met with indifferent success.

"Emperor" Theudebert.

When Theuderich died he was succeeded by his son Theudebert (533–548), not only the most ambitious but also the ablest of all the Merovingian kings. His conduct was determined by the fact that he had a consuming desire to possess the title emperor. This ambition showed itself in his coinage; he not only stamped his own image on his coins, a practice hitherto unknown to the Merovingians, but also added *Augustus* to his name, thus attributing to himself imperial dignity. He made strenuous efforts to get possession of Italy, as if he were conscious that his imperial pretensions would be strengthened if he should become lord of that land. He is said to have harbored the somewhat extravagant plan of extending his conquests down the Danube to the frontier of the empire in order to be able to attack the emperor in his capital and wrest from him the imperial title.

Growth of the Royal Power.

A profound political change accompanied the territorial expansion of the Franks—their simple democracy was displaced by a monarchy more or less absolute. Whereas originally the people were sovereign, the king was now sovereign, and exercised all the powers of the state without any constitutional check. The king was no longer subject to the people; the people were subject to the king. He alone declared war and made peace, sent and received foreign ambassadors, and made treaties and alliances. He called the army into the field, and either led it in person or named its leader. All freemen were subject to military service, and must come at the king's summons. He made laws and enforced them through his officials, who were his servants. The state was so completely a private possession of the king that he made no distinction between the government of it and the management of his household, using his servants indiscriminately in both;

he administered justice through judges of his appointing, being himself the highest court of appeal and answerable to no court for his actions. All that had once been the common property of the tribe was now his, for he made no distinction between fiscal and personal possessions. All public revenues, such as taxes, fines, customs, and tolls, he regarded as his private and personal income. He possessed a formidable and lucrative list of crown rights, including the right to coin money, to establish markets, and the possession of all mines (minerals and salt). And finally he exercised complete authority over the church, appointing and deposing bishops, calling ecclesiastical councils, and rendering their actions valid by his sanction.

The Marchfield.

Although the king was under no constitutional check, there were two bodies that were in a position to influence him, namely, the army and his council. (1) The kingdom had grown so large that it was impossible to hold a meeting of the whole tribe, so that this, the most important feature of their early political life, had been discontinued. The nearest approach to it was the meeting of the army, which took place at the beginning of a campaign. Since there was usually a campaign every year, and the troops were called to meet in the month of March (later in May), this meeting was called the Marchfield (later the Mayfield). The king utilized these gatherings to publish his edicts, while the army took advantage of them to express their desires. Their wishes were by no means binding on the king, but he might find it wise to yield to their requests. (2) The king kept in his presence a large number of officials—bishops, abbots, and noblemen of various ranks—to assist him in the administration of the government. It was only natural that he should consult them on all important matters. They formed a kind of king's council, but were without authority. This body of councillors, a common feature of the governments established by Germans, may be regarded as the germ from which the three important departments of the government—the legislative, the judicial, and the financial—were eventually developed. For the discussion of the most im-

The King's Council.

portant questions the king might call them all together in a formal way. From this custom was developed the diet, which offered the nobility an opportunity by combining to influence, if not to control, the policy of the king.

Why the King's Power Grew.

The chief causes of the growth of the king's power are easily discovered. In the first place, his position at the head of his people during a long period of conquest gave him many opportunities which he industriously used to his own advantage. The conquests which they made he turned to his own profit rather than to that of the people. Acting in his own interests, he created monarchical institutions, and exercised authority not in the name of the people but in his own right. As the Franks became peasants and practised agriculture, it was of the highest importance to them that violence should cease and that peace should reign among them. Without foreseeing the result the people were more than content that the king should assume the protection of the peace, and establish a police and police regulations for the purpose of punishing all who should disturb it. In the same way, since their old law did not apply perfectly to their changed conditions, he assumed the right to make new and fitting laws. And to secure the observance of them he also assumed the right to impose a heavy fine—the king's ban—on all who should transgress them.

The King Takes All Conquered Land.

In the second place, it was of fundamental importance for the growth of the royal power that Chlodovech and his successors treated all conquests of both Germans and Romans as personal rather than national. They assumed the right to govern directly and absolutely all the conquered territories. Two considerations justified them in this: in the first place, they believed that conquest gave them the broadest sovereignty over the conquered; and, secondly, they believed that they succeeded to the place of the imperial government and inherited, in a way, the absolute authority of the emperor. Chlodovech was confirmed in such a view of his new powers in 508, when the emperor, Anastasius, sent an embassy to confer on him the title of consul, and to congratulate him on his success in the war with the West Goths. Both as a conqueror, therefore, and as the successor and representative of the emperor, Chlodovech could regard his power as virtually absolute. It was inevitable that his position as absolute ruler of both Germans and Romans, whom he had conquered, should affect his relation as tribal king, and, although his Franks offered stubborn resistance at first, they were unable to prevent him from extending his absolute power over them.

Secures Much Land and a Large Income.

And, lastly, an important effect of his conquests was to put great riches in both money and land into his hands, and these he used to increase his power. He not only inherited the imperial financial system in existence in the conquered provinces, the revenues of which he appropriated, but he also extended this system over the Germans whom he conquered and even over his Franks. He thus became possessed of an enormous income from taxation and from the administration of justice (fines). In the conquered provinces he also claimed as his personal possession all the lands of the imperial domain and all public, waste, or unclaimed lands. He thus became the largest landholder in the kingdom. He was in a position, therefore, to carry on an absolute government because he was abundantly able to reward his faithful officials by grants of both land and money. It seems superfluous to add that, having once acquired great power, the king could with impunity disregard law and custom, usurp further authority, and make his will law, simply because there was no one in a position to oppose him.

The King Creates a Nobility.

The absolutism of the Merovingian kings was, however, of short duration. By gifts of land and office the king had created a large class of nobles, who engaged in a struggle with the crown, and in the end were enabled by circumstances to set limits to the royal power. This nobility was formed of three classes: the great landed proprietors, the king's officials (dukes, counts), and the high clergy (bishops, abbots). (1) The king rewarded his chief warriors and his "followers" (*Gefolge*) by giving them large estates. In this way there were established a number of great landholding families, who, because of their wealth, were superior to the rest of the people and came to form a superior class—a landed aristocracy. (2) The king's officials, being his personal representatives, shared in a way his dignity and honor. Theoretically they held office at the will of the king, but practically their tenure was for life. Furthermore, they naturally strove to pass their office on to their sons, so that it soon came to be regarded as hereditary, the son always succeeding to the office which his father had held. The longer the tenure of such an office, the more firmly would its honor become attached to its holder and his family. Thus there came to be an aristocracy of officials, deriving its superiority or nobility from the fact that it held office from the king. These two classes, the landed aristocracy and the "official" aristocracy, soon fused, because the king enriched his officials with grants of land and also conferred office on the large landholders. Landed proprietorship and office-holding, at first entirely distinct the one from the other, soon came to be synonymous, because they were always found united in the same person. This was not, however, a nobility of a hard-and-fast type, because it was not entirely hereditary; nor was it exclusive, since those who newly acquired wealth or office were freely admitted to its ranks. (3) The high clergy formed a nobility because of their great spiritual prerogatives and their wealth in land, acquired through the gifts of the faithful. Furthermore, most of them were taken from the families of the landed and office-holding aristocracy, for the king rewarded his officials by appointing their younger sons to bishoprics and abbacies. These three classes, being bound together by common ties of blood and interests, might at any time become an effective check on the king's power.

Great Landlords.

Officials.

The High Clergy.

From the point of view of the royal power it was unfortunate that Chlodovech did not fix the succession by establishing the law of primogeniture instead of leaving the kingdom to be divided among his sons. During the next eighty years his descendants made various divisions of the kingdom along different lines. Toward the end of the sixth century there appeared a threefold division into Burgundy, Austrasia, and Neustria, which, in spite of all further divisions, tended to become fixed. Each of these sub-kingdoms possessed an administrative system of its own, which was kept intact even when they were all three held by one king. The fact that frequently the kings were mere boys made it easier for the nobles to obtain a preponderating influence in the direction of affairs. The great opportunity of the nobility, however, came in the latter part of the sixth century, when the royal family was divided into warring factions under the leadership of two bitterly hostile queens, Fredegonda and Brunhilda.

Three Sub-kingdoms.

In 567 Sigibert of Austrasia married Brunhilda, a daughter of the king of the West Goths, and Chilperich of Neustria married her sister, Galswintha. Chilperich, however, soon had Galswintha put to death and married Fredegonda, one of his former concubines. From this time to the death of Fredegonda (597) there was an inextinguishable feud between Brunhilda and Fredegonda, which involved the families of both, and led to the degradation of the royal power. Fredegonda did not hesitate to use the vilest means to accomplish her ends; she resorted to treachery, to the dagger, and to poison. The situation was complicated by the efforts of the nobles to increase their power at the expense of that of the king. They frequently plotted against his life and raised the standard of rebellion. Fredegonda even compromised with them and assisted them in their rebellion, so blind was her rage against Brunhilda; but the latter, true to her instincts as a royal princess by birth, defended the rights of the crown against the ambitious nobles, while waging a determined war against Fredegonda.

Opposition of the Nobles.

The death of Fredegonda (597) simplified matters somewhat for Brunhilda, who was then able to devote herself to the struggle between the crown and the nobles. With keen political sense she spent the rest of her life in the effort to break the power of the nobles and to unite all Frankland under one king.

More than once she seemed about to succeed, but at the critical moment fortune always deserted her; the death of a king whom she supported or a victory of the nobles would undo her work of union, and put each kingdom again under a king of its own. Her downfall and death were brought about by a league of the nobles of Austrasia (under the lead of Pippin and Bishop Arnulf of Metz, the ancestors of Charlemagne), of Neustria, and of Burgundy. They defeated her troops, took her and all her family prisoners, and put them to death (613–614). To be sure the unity for which she had striven was formally attained, for Chlothar II was recognized as king of all three kingdoms. This, however, was without significance, as he was helpless in the hands of the nobles. In 614 a diet was held at Paris, which put certain restrictions on the crown: (1) The legislative power of the crown was curtailed by the provision that royal enactments which conflicted with existing law should be null and void. (2) The king should no longer compel widows, maidens, and nuns to marry against their will. (3) If any one should die intestate the king should not prevent his relations from inheriting his property. (4) The king should be powerless to revoke gifts and grants made by his predecessors. (5) New and burdensome taxes and recently established tolls were to be abolished. (6) Only local landholders should be appointed to the office of count. (7) No one should be condemned without a trial. (8) And the high clergy were given a large measure of jurisdiction over their subordinate clergy. From this action of the diet we may, with a good deal of assurance, infer how great the abuses were which the king had practised on his people.

Brunhilda.

The Nobles Win.

The action of the diet at Paris gives overwhelming proof that the nobles had won the victory over the crown. They prevented Chlothar II from perfecting the union of the three kingdoms by compelling him to establish a *major domus* (mayor of the palace) in each of them. Soon the Austrasian nobles demanded a king of their own, and Chlothar put over them his son Dagobert (622). After the

The Kings Lose Power.

death of his father Dagobert made an unsuccessful attempt to become sole ruler. After his death (639) no Merovingian king was ever allowed to exercise any authority. The government was administered by the nobility through the *major domus*. The king was kept in retirement and shown to the people occasionally as a mere figurehead ("do-nothing kings"). Although the government was conducted in his name, he had no share in it.

The *Major Domus* Rules.

The latter part of the seventh century was filled with struggles between rival candidates for the office of *major domus*. In Austrasia a nobleman, called Pippin "of Landen," had been made *major domus*. He is supposed to have had an estate called Landen, now a village in Belgium, but this addition to his name was not made till about 1300. When he died (640) his son Grimoald put forth a hereditary claim to his office. Other nobles resisted this claim, but Grimoald, after a hard struggle, was successful, and for a short time was the sole *major domus* of the whole kingdom. In 656 he attempted to put his son Childebert on the throne in place of a Merovingian prince. Against this the nobles rebelled, and in the struggle that ensued both Grimoald and his son were slain. Years of civil strife followed, out of which a certain Ebroin emerged as victor and sole *major domus* of the whole kingdom (680). His murder the next year caused a renewal of the strife, which ended in the victory of Pippin, a nephew of Grimoald, in the battle of Tertry (687). He became sole *major domus* and began a policy which tended to strengthen his power, and which resulted in putting his grandson, Pippin, on the throne, with the title of king (751).

We have come at last to a fitting place for explaining the office of *major domus*. In order to understand its origin and character, it is necessary to describe the king's household and its relation to the administration of the government. Since the kingdom was regarded as a private possession of the king, its government would also be regarded as a private matter of the king. That is, the kingdom was merely an extension of his household, and was to be governed in the same way. That this was the king's view is clear

Rise of the *Major Domus*.

from the fact that he used the servants of his household to carry on the government of his kingdom. The administration of his household was divided into a few departments, chief of which were (1) the household servants, (2) the house or palace, with the treasury, (3) the royal stables, (4) the royal cellars (wine and provisions), (5) the secretariat, (6) the royal court for the administration of justice, and (7) the administration of the provinces. The servants were under a seneschal (chief servant); the palace and treasury were under a chamberlain or treasurer (*camerarius*, *thesaurarius*); the royal stables were under a marshall (*mariskalk*); the royal cellars were under a cupbearer (*pincerna*); the secretariat was under a secretary (*referendarius*); the royal court of justice was presided over by a count palatine (*comes palatii*, count of the palace); and the provincial administration was conducted by counts and dukes appointed by the king. In the first years of the kingdom the king no doubt received reports from, and gave orders to, the heads of all these departments directly. But in the course of time, as the work of each department increased and his duties as king multiplied, he found it expedient to establish one head over them all, who should serve as the channel of communication between him and them. This head, who was called the *major domus*, "the chief servant of the house," made his appearance among the Franks toward the middle of the sixth century. His position was naturally one of great influence and offered many opportunities for personal aggrandizement. Brunhilda, during her struggle with the nobles, was compelled to depend on this officer. In fact, she put the direction of affairs into his hands, and, owing to the youth and weakness of later kings, he was able to retain it. As soon as this office became of supreme importance the nobility got control of it and determined who should fill it. For some time, therefore (in the early part of the seventh century), the *major domus* appeared as the tool of the nobility through which they ruled the king and the state. The *major domus*, however, soon tried to free himself from the control of the nobility, to make his office hereditary, and to rule

The Tool of the Nobility; then Acquires the Power.

independently of both king and nobility. This was the position which Ebroin had attained at the time of his death (681) and which Pippin reached by his victory at Tertry (687). As *major domus* he was thereafter the actual ruler of the kingdom of the Franks.

The Border Provinces Revolt.

The long civil wars between Brunhilda and Fredegonda and the nobles resulted not only in weakening the crown, in advancing the nobility, and in developing the office of the *major domus*, but they also gave the border provinces an opportunity to separate themselves from the central government. When Pippin obtained the power (687), Aquitaine, Gascony, Brittany, Thuringia, Bavaria, Alamannia (the upper Danube and Rhine), and Alsace were to all intents and purposes independent sovereign states under their own dukes. The reunion of these provinces to the central government was to be the chief work of Pippin and his successors.

CHAPTER V

THE HOUSE OF CHARLEMAGNE

THE success of Pippin at Tertry (687) was the beginning of the greatness of the Karlings (Carolingians), as his family is generally called. The nobility threatened to strip his victory of much of its importance by compelling him to appoint a *major domus* for Neustria. His power, however, did not thereby suffer, because the man whom he named for the office remained faithful to him and soon gave way to one of Pippin's sons. The office, although divided, was thus kept in the family. For the next half-century the chief work of the Karlings was to restore the kingdom to its former limits—a task which Pippin merely began. In 689 he reconquered the Frisians. He also made a few campaigns against the Alamanni, or, as they were still called, the Suevi. He died, however, in 714, leaving the greater part of the work to be done by his successors.

Rise of the Karlings.

Plectrude, the widow of Pippin, almost wrecked the fortunes of his house. The two legitimate sons of Pippin had already died, leaving only young children to succeed to the office of *major domus*. Pippin left also an illegitimate son Charles Martel, who aspired to succeed his father, but Plectrude had him seized and imprisoned, and assumed the regency in the name of her grandchildren. The nobles immediately took advantage of her weak rule to recover the power. During the struggle that ensued Charles Martel, escaping from his prison, put himself at the head of the Austrasian nobles who were displeased with the rule of Plectrude, and with their help he soon became *major domus* of the whole kingdom. He made a good beginning of the unification of the realm by making a few campaigns against the duke of Aquitaine, the Frisians, the Bavarians, and the Suevi. He even ex-

Charles Martel, 714–741.

tended his boundaries by conquering some of the Saxons. In 732 he won the admiration and gratitude of all Christendom by repelling the Mohammedans, who, after conquering Spain, had crossed the Pyrenees (720) and were seeking to subject the Franks. Charles met them in battle northeast of Poitiers (the so-called battle of Tours, 732), and, after a severe struggle, overcame them. During the next years the Franks were able to drive them back over the Pyrenees, and thus they freed Europe from the Mohammedan peril which had threatened it.

Martel Aids Boniface.

Martel supported the missionary Boniface in his efforts to reform the church in east Frankland and to convert the German tribes which were still pagan (Frisians, Thuringians, Bavarians, and Saxons). "Without the protection of the prince of the Franks," wrote Boniface, "I can neither rule the Christian people nor protect the clergy, monks, and nuns. Nor could I destroy the existing heathen practices and idolatry were it not for his support and the fear which his name inspires in the people." Charles's interest in the reform of the church was, however, not very deep, for he made no effort to extend it to the clergy in the western part of his realm, although they were extremely lax in morals and discipline. In fact, he pursued a policy toward the land and offices of the church which tended to demoralize the clergy still more. His warriors had to be paid, and he proposed to pay them in church offices and church lands. This policy was forced upon him by the changed conditions, which require a word of explanation. While the Germans were still half-nomadic, and the work of cultivating the soil was done by their women and slaves, the men did not regard military service as burdensome, for fighting and booty were alike dear to them. But, as the Franks had become farmers, the majority of them, being without slaves, were compelled to take an active part in tilling their own soil. Consequently, during their absence on a campaign their farms were not properly cultivated. They were also bound to equip and support them-

Gives Church Lands and Church Offices to His Warriors

S. B., 197, and note.

selves in the field. For this military service they neither received pay from the state nor were the campaigns productive of much booty, especially those against the invading Mohammedans, which gave scant opportunity for spoils. Under these circumstances it is not strange that the people generally tried to escape military service or demanded some kind of pay. In order to raise an army Martel had to secure the help of the nobility by paying them. Being without sufficient means in either land or money, he turned for aid to the church and asked that some of its fat offices and broad lands be conferred on his warriors in return for their great service in driving out the Mohammedans.

The church was abundantly able to help him, for at that time it had in its possession probably one-fourth of all the land in the kingdom. Both monasteries and bishoprics had, through the gifts of the faithful and through purchase, become great landholders. Toward the end of the eighth century St. Denis, St. Martin of Tours, and Luxeuil, probably the three richest monasteries in the realm, each possessed about 2,000,000 acres, and some of the bishoprics were almost as rich. The honor, wealth, and power attaching to the office of bishop or abbot, made such positions very attractive, and the nobility coveted them. Their cupidity was aroused by the great wealth of the church, and they sought to obtain possession of it. In their efforts to do so Charles came to their aid. He had a plausible argument. Although the church has always held that property given to it for pious purposes should never be diverted to secular ends, it has more than once freely contributed large sums to the state in time of need. The common danger arising from the invasion of the Mohammedans was regarded by the church as a sufficient reason for yielding to the request of Charles. His chief warriors received temporary grants of church lands on the condition of paying a fixed annual rental to the church, and of rendering homage and military service to Charles. It was agreed that these lands still belonged to the church, and that they should eventually revert to it. In this the church should suffer no

Great Wealth of the Church.

loss. But after a few years the nobles ceased to pay the rental, yet refused to restore the lands to the church. For the next fifty years the church did not cease to appeal to the government for justice in this matter. Charlemagne finally ended the controversy, but some of the lands were never restored.

More baneful to the character of the clergy was Martel's practice of appointing his warriors themselves, who of course remained laymen, to the richest bishoprics and abbacies.

Lay Bishops and Abbots.

Sometimes such a lay bishop or abbot held the office alone and received all its income; sometimes he held it in connection with the real bishop or abbot, so that there were two bishops or abbots in the same office, one a clergyman, the other a layman, who divided its income.

When Martel came to die he disposed of his office of *major domus* as if it were a private possession, dividing it equally between his two sons, Pippin and Karlmann. Nevertheless,

Pippin Becomes King, 751.

S. B., 6.
O., 14.
R., 49-51.

since the two brothers acted for some time in complete harmony, the kingdom did not suffer from the division. Their accession, however, was the signal for uprisings in many parts of the realm. The Aquitanians, the Alamanni, the Bavarians, and the Saxons rebelled, and the brothers subdued them only after four or five years of vigorous fighting. Scarcely had order been restored when Karlmann, for some unknown reason, resigned his office, commended his children to the care of Pippin, and, after visiting the pope, retired to a monastery in the neighborhood of Rome (747). Pippin, being now sole *major domus*, and having the kingdom well in hand, determined to make himself king. His plan met with no opposition on the part of the Frankish nobles; so he sent messengers to Rome to consult the pope about the proposed change and to secure the papal influence for it. When his ambassadors returned with the answer of the pope (Zacharias), to the effect that it would be better that he who actually had the power should also have the title, Pippin summoned a diet to meet at Soissons (751). There the last of the Merovingian kings was deposed and sent into a monastery, and Pippin was elected in his place. Boniface anointed him with consecrated oil, and the nobles, in imitation of the ancient custom of elevating their chosen leader on a shield, raised him bodily and seated him on the throne.

In the end Pippin had to pay dearly for the papal influence which he had so easily obtained, for it involved him in the affairs of Italy. The pope, although subject to the emperor, had become the actual ruler of Rome and of the surrounding territory (the duchy of Rome). His independence, however, was threatened by a new foe, the Lombards, another German tribe, which, accompanied by fragments of other tribes, had invaded Italy in 568, and taken possession of the Po valley (which came to be called after them Lombardy), and the exarchate (the territory about Ravenna). Their king, Alboin, did not attempt to extend his conquests further, but some of his nobles went on to the south and, finding most of the cities in a defenseless condition, easily took them. The territory which they conquered was divided into the duchies of Benevento and Spoleto. The Lombards had not been accustomed to the absolute rule of a king and so were unwilling to submit to a strong central government. Alboin was murdered in 573, and his successor met the same fate. The Lombards then reverted to the political organization which they had had beyond the Danube; their tribe was broken into several groups, each of which was governed by a duke. A danger from without reunited them. The Franks invaded their territory in 584, and, feeling the necessity of uniting, they chose a new king. He was, however, unable to develop a strong kingship because the dukes gave him only a very unwilling obedience; those of Benevento and Spoleto even remained independent of him. Slowly the Lombards added to their territory by conquest until their king could fairly hope to unite all Italy under his sway.

The Pope Calls Pippin into Italy.

Lombards Invade Italy, 568.

For some years the popes had been able to check their advances, but in 752 Aistulf, king of the Lombards, invaded the duchy of Rome, threatened the city with siege, and demanded the submission of the Romans to Lombard rule. The pope, Stephen III, unable to secure aid from any other source, bethought himself of Pippin's debt of gratitude to the papacy. Accordingly, in 753, he set out for Frankland. Pippin received him with demonstrations of great respect, but hesitated to make war on the Lombards, with whom the Franks were at peace. Perhaps he would have refused the pope's request had not his brother, Karlmann, who had resigned his crown in 747, reappeared on the scene as the ambassador of Aistulf. Karlmann not only begged Pippin not to attack the Lombards, but probably also demanded his share of the Frankish realm for his sons. This seems to have decided Pippin; at any rate, he deprived Karlmann of his liberty and, after making monks of his (Karlmann's) sons, shut them up in a monastery. In order to make the position of his family secure, he had himself and his sons anointed by the pope, who strictly commanded the Franks never to elect their king from any other family. Pippin's obligations to the pope were thereby increased. In the light of what has been said, we can understand why Pippin had made two important concessions to Stephen. (1) He had agreed to make a campaign against the Lombards on behalf of the papacy, and (2) he had promised to give the pope Venice, Istria, and the territory of the exarchate. He had been led to make these promises not merely out of his sense of gratitude, but also because the pope had conferred upon him the title of *patricius* of the Romans. The approximate meaning of this title may be discovered from the fact that it was the official title of the exarch of Ravenna, the representative of the emperor in the "province Italy," as the territory in which the exarch exercised jurisdiction was called. Pippin was thereby made the protector and lord of Rome. The title brought with it certain rights and duties, but the pope emphasized the duties, and the distance of Rome from Frankland would prevent its king from exercising his rights to any great extent.

Attack the Pope.

Pope Appeals to Pippin.

The Frankish nobles showed great reluctance to promise the Italian campaign, but finally yielded to Pippin's solicitations. Two campaigns were necessary, however—one in 754, the other in 756. When the Frankish army reappeared in Italy (756), Aistulf surrendered without resistance, and made his kingdom tributary to the Franks. Pippin did not give to the pope all that he had promised; in fact, he left much of it in the possession of the Lombards. Nevertheless he did give him about twenty cities of the exarchate.

Pippin's Italian Campaigns.

R., 52.

S. B., 45.

During the last years of his reign Pippin had a dominant position in western Europe, although he was not able to reduce Aquitaine and Bavaria to complete subjection. At his death in 768 he divided his kingdom between his two sons, Karlmann and Charles, afterward called Charlemagne (*Carolus Magnus*). This division threatened to wreck the kingdom because the two brothers were bitter personal enemies, and civil war between them was prevented only by the constant intercession of their mother. She was also determined that friendly relations should be re-established between the Franks and the Lombards, and to this end brought about the marriage of Charles to the daughter of Desiderius, king of the Lombards. To this the pope objected, but, on being assured that Desiderius would satisfy all the papal demands in regard to the restitution of certain cities, he withdrew his opposition. Desiderius, however, then renewed the policy of his predecessors to get possession of the rest of Italy. Fearing that he was too weak to accomplish this by force of arms, he resorted to diplomacy. He felt that he must first secure Rome. So he went to the city, made a friend of the pope, and created a party of supporters there. His influence in Rome was rapidly becoming supreme, much to the displeasure of Charles, who felt that Desiderius was acquiring the position in Rome which belonged by right to himself as the *patricius* of the Romans. It was probably due to this that the friendly relations between Charles and Desiderius lasted

Pippin's Sons, Karlmann and Charles (Charlemagne).

but a short time. Charles divorced his wife within a year and sent her home, thus mortally offending Desiderius. Karlmann died in 771 and Charles, disregarding the rights of his infant nephews, took possession of the whole realm. Karlmann's widow fled with her children to Desiderius, and begged him to avenge at the same time the injustice that had been done her sons and the insult offered his daughter.

Charles the Great Sole King.

S. B., 7.
O., 15.
R., 53.

Just then the position of Desiderius in Rome was endangered; Stephen IV discovered the cunning of Desiderius, and learned that he was scheming to get control of Rome. The death of Stephen soon followed, and the next pope, Adrian I, an aristocratic Roman, was hostile to Lombard influence in Rome. Desiderius felt that he must strike at once. He first sought a quarrel with Adrian I by calling on him to come to Lombardy and anoint the sons of Karlmann as kings. The pope not only refused to do this, but demanded that Desiderius hand over the cities which he had long ago promised to surrender to the pope. Desiderius in turn resisted the pope's demand, attacked the papal territory, and took possession of some of its cities. Adrian I appealed to Charles for help (January, 773). The appeal was most unwelcome to both Charles and his nobles, but they felt that they could not refuse. By embassies Charles tried to settle the difficulties between the pope and the Lombards, but Desiderius was unyielding. Accordingly Charles set out for Italy with his army (773). The Lombards were no match for the Franks. Desiderius fled to Pavia, which the Franks besieged. All the other Lombard cities soon surrendered and the whole country was overrun. Karlmann's widow and children were taken prisoners and disappeared. They were probably immured in monasteries. Leaving his army before Pavia, Charles spent Easter at Rome, where, at the earnest solicitation of the pope, he renewed the promised "donation of Pippin." In May (774) Pavia surrendered, and Desiderius with all his family, including the divorced wife of Charles, fell into Charles's hands. They too ended their lives in monasteries. A bitter

Conquers the Lombards.

S B., 7:6.

disappointment was in store for the pope, in that Charles refused to keep his oath in regard to the "donation of Pippin," because he had determined to make himself king of the Lombards. This he now did, thereby inheriting all the political interests of Desiderius, whom he had just deposed. So long as Charles had been merely the overlord of the Lombards and the *patricius* of the Romans he was willing to increase the power of the pope that he might act as a check upon the king of the Lombards. But since he had become king of the Lombards his point of view had changed, and he no longer desired an increase in the power of the pope. It was to his interest to prevent the formation of a strong political power in Rome. Accordingly he broke his oath and refused to "restore" all that he had promised. Adrian was deeply offended at this, and for some time his relations with Charles were strained. Charles finally relented somewhat, and by way of compromise gave him certain Tuscan cities and some taxes from the rest of Tuscany and from Spoleto.

Becomes King of the Lombards.

Charles assumed the position, title, rights, and possessions of the king of the Lombards, and the territory, although still called the kingdom of the Lombards, became a part of the kingdom of the Franks. Charles left its government about as it was, but put Franks over some of its counties. As in Frankland so in Lombardy, he used bishops and abbots as counts, and entrusted them with the administration of secular matters in their territories. In 781 he took a step which emphasized the fact that Lombardy was really a separate kingdom; he made his son Pippin, a child of four years, king of the Lombards, and left him in Italy to grow up among his subjects.*

Time was to show that the conquest of Italy was a political mistake, because it disregarded the barriers which nature had established between the two countries. The Alps alone, to say nothing of the differences in race, would prevent the union of

* Spoleto and Benevento were not included in the first conquest (774), but in 776 the duke of Spoleto submitted to Charles; the duke of Benevento, however, would do nothing more than acknowledge Charles as his overlord. Charles sent several expeditions against him, but never succeeded in reducing him to subjection.

the two countries from ever becoming more than nominal. Only on the east was the way open to the Franks for successful territorial expansion. No mountains impeded the march in that direction, and pagan peoples had no recognized rights. In fact, it was regarded as the duty of a Christian sovereign to conquer and Christianize them. Charles's first war of consequence was against the Saxons, whose conquest was important because it expanded Frankland to the east, Christianized a large population that had hitherto been pagan, and reinforced the German element in his kingdom by the addition of a hardy people that was still uninfluenced by Rome and Roman institutions. The war with the Saxons dragged on for more than thirty years; Charles made his first campaign against them in 772 and his last one in 804. At the approach of the Frankish army the Saxons would flee; if overtaken, they would submit to the terms imposed upon them, but would rebel as soon as the Frankish troops were withdrawn. The Franks charged them with being "faithless" and "rebellious," but it should be remembered that they were fighting to preserve their religion and their liberty. Annual campaigns against them, severe punishments for their rebellions, the presence of Frankish troops, officials, and clergy, and stringent laws failed to subdue them, and Charles was able to break their spirit only by deporting thousands of them into Frankland and settling Franks in their place. Their territory was divided into counties, and put under Frankish counts. After Christianity had made a beginning among them, their ecclesiastical organization was completed by the erection of bishoprics (Münster, 804; Bremen, 805; Paderborn, 805 or 806; Halberstadt, Osnabrück, and Verden, whose exact dates are unknown). Scarcely had the Saxons been reduced and Christianized when they began to work for the expansion of Germany to the east by conquering and Christianizing the pagan Slavs east of them.

The Saxon Wars.

S. B., 7:7.
O., 16, 17, 22.
R., 54, 55.

Later generations invented so many stories about Charles's victories over the Mohammedans that it is worth while to give an account of his relations with them. In 777 the Mohammedan governors of a few cities in northern Spain, who were in rebellion against their lord, the Mohammedan ruler of Spain, came to Charles while he was in Saxony. They offered their allegiance to him as their lord and promised to surrender their cities to him if he would send an army to their aid. In the hope of extending his sway over Spain he eagerly consented. His motive was purely one of conquest. One division of his army, passing through the west Pyrenees, stormed Pampeluna, a Christian (Basque) city, and endeavored to conquer the Basques of the surrounding country. His troops all reached Saragossa, but its governor, who was one of those who had visited him, was not able to deliver it to him, nor was the Frankish army able to take it. So Charles soon had to raise the siege and begin to retreat. When he reached Pampeluna he ordered its walls to be torn down in order "that its inhabitants might not be able to rebel again." In the mountain passes the Basques attacked his army and inflicted some loss on it—an incident which gave rise to a series of legends which were incorporated in the epic poem, "The Song of Roland." This first expedition against the Mohammedans failed utterly.

Campaigns in Spain.

S. B., 7:9.

In order to strengthen the frontier against both the rebellious Basques in the Pyrenees and the Mohammedans in Spain, Charles, in 781, united Septimania and Aquitaine and put as king over them his infant son, afterward known as Ludwig the Pious. He also appointed an energetic regency with instructions to move against the Mohammedans as vigorously as possible. It was some time, however, before an advance could be made. In 785 the Franks got possession of Gerona and a few other cities, and a part of the Mediterranean coast. In 795 Charles constructed a line of forts and towers along the frontier (about half-way between the Ebro and the Pyrenees), and put the whole district under a count. This was the creation of the Spanish mark ("borderland"). Its inhabitants were constantly engaged in a kind of guerilla warfare and occasionally they made a real campaign against the Mohammedans. By the year 811 they had pushed

The Spanish Mark (March).

their frontier forward to the Ebro, although a few cities to the north of it were still in the hands of the Mohammedans. The mark rendered an important service to the little kingdom of Asturias and Galicia (that part of Spain which had never been conquered by the Mohammedans), by protecting it on the east. At that time the Mohammedan fleets were attacking the islands in the Mediterranean. Mallorca and Minorca (the Balearic Islands) obtained help from the Franks, successfully resisted the Mohammedans, and put themselves under Charles's protection (799). As he possessed no fleet he could give no aid to the more distant islands, Corsica, Sardinia, and Sicily, which were unable to defend themselves and so passed under Mohammedan sway.

Bavaria Reduced.

S. B., 7:11.

Bavaria, having been permitted to go its way during the struggles of the sixth century, was virtually independent. Although its duke, Tassilo, had taken an oath to be faithful to the king, he seldom appeared at court. For some unknown reason trouble arose between him and Charles in 785. This increased until 787, when the king sent his troops against him. Tassilo submitted without resistance and Charles restored his duchy to him as a fief. But the next year, while Tassilo was planning a revolt, Charles called him to a diet and seized him. Treasonable charges were made against him and he was condemned to death by the nobles. Charles, however, commuted the punishment to seclusion for life in a monastery. He then annexed Bavaria and appointed royal counts to administer its government (788).

The Avars Destroyed.

S. B., 7:13.

The Avars, who had come into Europe during the last years of the reign of Justinian, had established themselves on the middle Danube, where they held sway over an extensive territory. Their invasion of Bavaria in 788 (due, it was said, to the treacherous invitation of Tassilo) led to their ruin. After some ineffectual attempts to chastise them, Charles's armies finally defeated and subjected them (795, 796). They later made some feeble attempts to rebel, but were overcome in a few campaigns (802, 803), and were soon absorbed in the Slavic and Germanic peo-

Note to Map V.—This map shows the territory of the Franks at the accession of Charlemagne (768) and the additions which he made to it by conquest. Certain points should be noticed about these conquests, to explain their significance for later history. (1) The Spanish mark was the origin of the Spanish kingdom of Aragon, which was to have an important part in the reconquest of Spain from the Mohammedans in the later Middle Age. (2) The annexation of Lombardy led to the coronation of Charlemagne as emperor at Rome; this connection between Italy and Germany was perpetuated by the formation of the "Holy Roman Empire" in the time of Otto the Great, and that connection was to have disastrous consequences for the political development of both countries. (3) The annexation of the Saxons reinforced the German element in Charlemagne's empire by the addition of a vigorous stock untouched by Roman influence, and so checked the Romanizing of the German race. The Franks in what is now northern France were already partly Romanized and were to form part of the French nation; the rest of the Franks in the Rhine valley, along with the Alemanni, Bavarians, Thuringians, and Saxons, retained their German language and customs and constitute the German nation. (4) The marks along the eastern frontier were created from Slavic territory and prepared the way for the later expansion of the Germans eastward.

N O R T H
S E A
A T L A N T I C O C E A N
Irish Sea
ANGLO-
SAXON
KINGDOMS
London
English Channel
BRITTANY
NEUSTRIA
Paris
Orleans
Loire
Seine
Verdun
Trier
Metz
Strasburg
Mainz
Cologne
Aix-la-Chapelle
(Aachen)
Louvain
Rhine
BAY OF
BISCAY
AQUITAINE
Bordeaux
Garonne
GASCONY
Toulouse
Vienne
L. of Geneva
SPANISH MARCH
Ebro
Douro
Tagus
EMIRATE OF
CORDOVA
(Mohammedan)
Lisbon
Cordova
Guadiana
Guadalquivir
BALEARIC IS.
M E D I T E
West
Longitude
A. L. POATES CO., N.Y.

V
THE
EMPIRE OF CHARLEMAGNE,
AT HIS DEATH (814),
SHOWING HIS CONQUESTS
The area inside the dotted line represents the Kingdom of Charlemagne at his accession in 768; the area between this and the outer black line, the territory added by his conquests
BALTIC SEA
Hamburg
Bremen
Elbe
Slavs
Slavic Peoples
Vistula
Oder R.
Fulda
Prague
Würzburg
BOHEMIA
MORAVIA
Danube
BAVARIA
(Avars)
PANNONIAN
MARK
Drave
CROATIA
Theiss
Dniester
Dnieper
Hungarians
Bulgarians
Danube
BLACK SEA
Constantinople
Milan
Ravenna
ADRIATIC SEA
Rome
AEGEAN
SEA
EASTERN EMPIRE
SICILY
SEA
from
Greenwich

ples who came in and settled in their territory. Charles's interest in the expansion of the church showed itself here. He raised the bishop of Salzburg to the rank of archbishop, and commanded him to prosecute missionary work among the mixed population of the conquered territory. The archbishop sent out monks and priests as missionaries, and the work of Christianizing them was hastened by the numerous German colonists who settled in the lands north of the Drave.

For some thirty years Charles had scarcely sheathed his sword, but his wars were now nearly over. Extraordinary success had attended his arms. He had not only subdued the rebellious provinces of the Frankish kingdom, but he had also enlarged his realm by the conquest of new peoples. To the kingdom which he had inherited he had added a part of Spain, nearly all of Italy, and a broad territory running from the Baltic to the Adriatic. With so vast a domain in his possession it was only natural that he should covet the more pretentious title of emperor. For the same reason his subjects would quite as naturally regard him as emperor in fact, and be eager for him to secure the title which corresponded to his actual power. Hence it is evident that his coronation as emperor, on Christmas, 800, came as a recognition of his power and as the culmination of his glory. (1) His wide sway, embracing, as it did, all of western Europe that was still Christian; (2) his authority over Rome, the ancient capital of the empire, and (3) his protection of the church and his zealous extension of Christianity naturally led to the observation that in reality he occupied the position which the emperor had once held. It was not mere flattery that Alcuin, the great scholar of his court, referred to his kingdom as "imperial" (796–797). When the pope was driven out of Rome (799), and the emperor at Constantinople was deposed and the government seized by a woman, Alcuin in his letters declared that Charles was the ruler of the whole Christian empire, which God had committed to him to be ruled, and that his power was greater than that of both pope and emperor, and his position more exalted than theirs. It is not strange, therefore, that many persons thought

His "Imperial" Position.

that the time had come to elevate him to the rank which corresponded to his power, and to give him a title which would more adequately express the dignity of his actual position. At that time there were good grounds either for holding that the throne was vacant or for setting up an anti-emperor, and Charles was, in the opinion of all the west, the only worthy candidate for the place.

Certain other ideas must also be taken into account in order to explain the coronation of Charles as emperor.

(1) Although there had been no emperor in the west since 476, the people there still generally regarded themselves as a part of the empire. To them the empire, being divinely ordained for the government of the world, was both indivisible and indestructible. The fact that they were under kings who were actually independent of the government at Constantinople did not affect their idea of the unity of the empire or their relation to it. Consequently they were immediately concerned in the deposition of the emperor and the usurpation of power by a woman.

The Empire Indivisible and Indestructible.

(2) The inhabitants of Rome, after having been excluded for centuries from the management of the government, had just begun to remember that once the people of Rome had ruled the world, and that they had elected the emperor and conferred his power upon him. The recollection of their former greatness stirred them to the effort to recover it. This led to the formation of what may be called an "ancient republican" party in Rome, which for several centuries tried to restore the city to the political position which it had held under the republic. This party undoubtedly exercised a certain influence on the coronation of Charles by reasserting at this moment the ancient supremacy of the people of Rome.

Rome to Rule the World Again.

(3) It was not necessary, however, for the inhabitants of Rome to base their right to elect an emperor or to set up an anti-emperor on the authority which they had possessed under the ancient republic. Rebellion was so common that the people might claim it as their right; it was indeed the estab-

lished way of getting rid of an objectionable or inefficient emperor. In practice, the army, the senators, and the people had, either singly or combined, chosen emperors and deposed them. Hence the participation of one or all of these three groups in such an action was sufficient. Nor was it necessary that such an election should be held in any particular place. There is no question that the people everywhere throughout the empire acted upon what seemed to them their inalienable right to set up an anti-emperor whenever, in their opinion, their welfare justified it. For, after all, everything depended on whether the one whom they elected was able to establish himself in power. Toward the end of the pontificate of Gregory II (715-731) the people of Italy, the Romans at their head, angered by imperial taxation and the imperial opposition to the use of images in the churches, threatened to set up an anti-emperor. They were deterred from doing so merely by questions of expediency and not by constitutional considerations. The election of an anti-emperor was a theoretical deposition of the actual emperor, and it was left to the newly elected one to secure himself by destroying the other. The question of supremacy had always to be settled by force. Numerous precedents not only justified the election of Charles as an anti-emperor but also bound him to establish his power by destroying the line of emperors at Constantinople.

The People's Right to Rebel.

Let us now look at the events that led directly to the coronation of Charles as emperor. The ancient republican party in Rome was under the leadership of the aristocratic Roman family of which the deceased pope, Adrian I, had been a member. Pope Leo III had attempted to exclude them from all share in the government of the city, thereby incurring their hostility. The bitterness between him and them was increased by mutual charges and recriminations till 799, when the party rebelled against him. They attacked him while he was making a solemn procession through the city, and, after beating and wounding him, imprisoned him in a monastery. He soon escaped to Spoleto and sent word to Charles to come to his

The Pope in Trouble Asks Help of Charles.

S. B., 7:28.

aid. Charles was at that moment engaged in a campaign against the Saxons, and hence could not go at once to Rome. He sent ambassadors to conduct Leo into Frankland. Roman ambassadors also appeared before him and made serious charges against Leo, which, if true, would have made it scandalous for him to continue in the highest office of the church.

Charles was placed in a dilemma, because the leading churchmen of the day declared that the pope, being the head of the church, was not subject to any court and hence could not be tried. Charles yielded to these so far as to send his ambassadors with Leo to Rome, with the command to restore him to his office, but nevertheless to inquire into the charges which had been made against him. The ambassadors were unable either to prove or to disprove the charges, but seized some of the pope's opponents and sent them as prisoners to Frankland. Since they were unable to end the controversy between the pope and his opponents or to restore order in the city, Charles himself came. He first undertook to investigate the charges which had been made against Leo, but could make no progress, because the pope's accusers refused to swear to the truth of their charges. Finally Leo, in order to clear his good name, mounted the pulpit in St. Peter's and took a public oath that he was innocent of all the crimes laid to his charge* (December 23, 800).

S. B., 48, 49.

The Coronation.

O., 20.
R., 56.
S. B., 7:28.

On Christmas Charles attended the services in St. Peter's, and as he was rising from his knees beside the grave of St. Peter the pope crowned him, and the Romans who were present shouted: "Long life and victory to Charles, Augustus, crowned of God, the great and peace-bringing emperor of the Romans." There is convincing evidence here that the act of the pope had been planned; he must have prepared the crown; the Romans must

* In spite of the assertions of the clergy that the pope could not be tried by any court, Charles's investigation of the charges against Leo was in reality a trial. It is impossible to suppose that Charles would have permitted Leo to continue in the office if the charges against him had been proved. Yet we can only surmise what steps would have been taken to remove him from the office. In 555 Pope Pelagius I had similarly, by a voluntary oath, cleared himself of unproved charges.

have known what was going to take place in order to know that it was the imperial crown which was placed on his head; and they must have been taught the formula with which they in unison greeted the new emperor. The leading men of the city were present, and it is not to be supposed that they merely obeyed the pope's orders in greeting Charles as they did; they must have had some share in the plans: that is, they must have held a meeting in which they actually elected Charles, and his coronation by Leo was merely the publication of that fact. Although the chronicles of the time are somewhat obscure and brief in their narratives of this event, some of them either state or imply that such a meeting had been held, in which Charles had been elected emperor. After electing him they proceeded to crown him in the manner customary in Constantinople. That is, as, in Constantinople, the patriarch was called on to anoint and crown the newly elected emperor, so the Romans called on the pope to anoint and crown Charles. Neither the patriarch nor the pope created the emperor; each acted as the agent of those who had elected him. As the patriarch often took an active part in the election as a partisan of one or the other candidate, so Leo evidently had a share in the election of Charles.

Charles Displeased Because it Made Him a Rebel.

S. B., 7:28.

Einhard, the intimate friend and biographer of Charles, has made the surprising statement that Charles was unwilling to accept the imperial title, and that he afterward declared that he did not know that the pope was intending to crown him, and that if he had known it he would not have gone into the church that day. From this it can only be inferred that, if Charles was informed of his election, he refused to accept the title, and that the pope and the Romans, determined to make him emperor, proceeded to crown him, even against his will, in the hope that he would accept it after the coronation had become an accomplished fact. The reason of his reluctance to accept the election is indicated by Einhard, for, after reporting what Charles had said about it, he proceeds: "The emperors [at Constantinople] were very angry because he accepted the title of emperor, but Charles bore their hostility with great patience, and with his magnanimity overcame their ill-will and hostility, and sent them frequent embassies and called them brothers." That is, he hesitated to accept the title because its acceptance would make him a usurper in the eyes of the existing line of emperors at Constantinople. He knew that his acceptance of the election would put him on a hostile footing with the emperor and he was unwilling to make a war for the title.

In Constantinople it was confidently expected that Charles would resort to arms and endeavor to extend his sway over the whole empire, as usurpers before him had done. They regarded his acceptance of the title as a declaration of war. The crown, which was thrust upon him, he finally accepted, and, although that act was a declaration of war against Irene, who was then empress, he refused to appeal to arms. He proposed that there should be two emperors over the empire, for the existence of two emperors and the actual division of the government would not destroy the ideal unity of the empire. He was already in diplomatic communication with Irene (the object of the negotiations is not certainly known), and this he continued, with the purpose of securing the mutual recognition each of the other as emperor. It was reported in Constantinople that his embassy was prepared to ask Irene to confer her hand in marriage upon him. The embassy to which this matter was entrusted reached Constantinople at the moment of her downfall and deposition. Her successor, whose election was scarcely more "regular" than that of Charles, refused to acknowledge him. All of Charles's efforts to obtain recognition from him were unavailing. Finally war was actually begun between them for the possession of Venice. In 810 the Franks besieged it and compelled it to surrender. The Greek emperor then sued for peace, and Charles offered to restore Venice to him on condition that he himself be recognized as emperor. Peace was established on these terms, and Charles's joy over the recognition of himself as emperor and the ending of his hostile relations to the Greek emperor was unbounded. He was no longer a usurper, but a legally recognized emperor.

Charles did not Fight for Title.

S. B., 13, 14.

Although the imperial crown neither brought an actual increase of power to Charles, nor added to his resources, it nevertheless gave him a new basis for the conduct of his government.

A New Duty.

As emperor he believed that he was directly responsible to God for the Christian living of his subjects. Accordingly he ordered all his subjects between the ages of twelve and seventy to take an oath to be obedient and true to him as emperor, and to serve God and obey his commands according to their knowledge and strength.

After the imperial coronation Charles was seldom involved in serious wars, and hence was able to devote himself to the work of governing his wide realm. Each tribe within his empire had its own body of customs which were still in force. He took measures to preserve the laws of the Saxons, Frisians, and Thuringians, by having them reduced to writing. All these laws, having been made to fit conditions prevailing in a primitive community, were inadequate to meet the requirements of a more complicated society. The advancement of the Germans in civilization made a great deal of new legislation necessary. A distinction was made between these bodies of tribal law, which were fundamental and could not be changed except by the whole people, and the king's law, which concerned those things that were not determined by the tribal law. The king could enact only supplementary legislation. Charles made no attempt to make a harmonious code of laws for the whole empire, but was content to legislate for each particular case or need as it arose. Although the legislative authority was in his hands, his laws were enacted "with the advice and consent" of the nobles and high clergy who surrounded him as a body of counsellors.

Charles Preserves the "Laws."

S. B., 7:29.

New Legislation.

For the purpose of administering the government he divided his empire into small divisions called "counties," over each of which he placed an official called a "count." It was the duty of the count to carry on the government in the name of the emperor, to administer justice, to act as his financial agent, and to lead the troops of his county in time of

Counts.

war. The great extent of the empire and the consequent number of counts made it impossible for Charles to exercise an efficient control over them. There is abundant evidence that the counts took advantage of this lack of supervision to abuse their power; they sold justice, oppressed the weak, favored the rich and powerful, and enriched themselves at Charles's expense by fraudulently retaining money which they had collected for him. The task of looking after so many counts was beyond the ability of one man. It was a fatal weakness in the government that the counties were not grouped in provinces, with a man at the head of each, charged with the control of all the counts in his district. Such a position had been that of the dukes, but Charles removed all the dukes in his empire (with one or two exceptions), because they regarded themselves not as the officials of the emperor but as the representatives of the people, and the champions of local liberty. They regarded all action of the central government as "interference," and were prompt to rebel on the least provocation. Hence he destroyed them and their office, too.

Dukes.

Missi Dominici.

S. B., 9.
O., 21.
R., 62.

That Charles perceived the weakness of his government is proved by the fact that he sent out royal messengers (*missi dominici*) to inquire into the conduct of the counts. For this purpose he joined a layman to a high clergyman and sent them out together, assigning them a fixed district. They were instructed to investigate the whole administration of the counts, to examine the life of the clergy and monks, to right all wrongs, to hear appeals, and to refer doubtful or important cases to the emperor. The creation of the *missi* was a step in the right direction, but there were not enough of them, and the territory assigned them was so large that they were not able to perform their duties thoroughly and efficiently. Charles added his own efforts to those of his *missi*, and by his unceasing activity tried to make good the lack of organization.

Owing to the number and importance of Charles's wars, the army was the object of his special attention. Because of the size of the empire the principle that military service was obligatory on all freemen could no longer be carried out. The emperor was slow to admit this, and called on the Lombards to fight in Spain and beyond the Danube, the Aquitanians beyond the Rhine and in southern Italy, and the Franks in Spain, in Italy, and on the middle Danube. These long and distant campaigns were ruinous to the common freemen, who not only received no pay but were even compelled to bear their own expenses throughout the war. Added to this was the fact that their lands were poorly cultivated during their absence. Either the system had to be modified or the common people would be ruined. (1) Charles attempted to provide relief by decreeing that only those who possessed a certain amount of land were bound to serve when called upon, and that all others, divided into groups of two, three, four, five, or six, should contribute according to the amount of their possessions to the support of one of their number who should take the field while the others remained at home. (2) Many freemen commended themselves to some rich nobleman, or to the king, and became vassals, and agreed to render service in return for support. The *Gefolge* of the ancient German kings, the *antrustiones* of the Merovingians, became the vassals of the Karlings. In such cases their lords were expected either to aid them in escaping military service, or to supply them with arms as well as with all the necessities of life. (3) Sometimes the lord provided for such support by giving his vassals a sufficient amount of land to supply them with the means of existence and of equipping themselves for war. The effect of all this was seen in the increasing disappearance of the class of freemen and the formation of a dependent class of vassals. In other words, the burdensome character of Charles's wars hastened the development of feudalism.

Limited Military Service.

R., 57–60.

Freemen Become Unfree.

Freemen Become Vassals.

Charles acted as protector and ruler of the church in his empire in the most thorough-going manner. He disregarded the law of the church which prescribed that all elections of the clergy should be canonical, and appointed both bishops and abbots. The clergy were, in fact, state officials, differing in no important respect from the counts, for Charles appointed them, controlled them while in office, and used them in the administration of secular matters. He followed the practice of his ancestors in giving church property as fiefs to his warriors and in naming laymen as abbots. So free was he in using the lands of the church in this way that he seems to have made little or no distinction between them and the crown lands. Einhard, his biographer, was a layman, yet he was the abbot of four monasteries and besides held a "living" in the church of Pavia. Certain monasteries which were put under Charles's special protection were called "royal," and were controlled by him almost as if they were his private possession. He alone made laws for the church, and there was nothing either important or trivial that was not touched on in his legislation. Much of his legislation, in fact, concerned ecclesiastical matters, and it furnishes convincing proof that he controlled the church in all respects.

Charles Controls the Church and the Pope.

Charles had three sons, among whom, following the established custom, he divided his empire. In 806 he fixed the boundaries of the kingdom of each of them, and prescribed the principles which should govern them in their attitude and conduct to one another. Unfortunately, his two oldest sons, both of whom had shown excellent ability, died, thus leaving the empire to the youngest, Ludwig, who had given evidence of nothing but incompetency. In 813 Charles, warned by severe illness of his approaching end, summoned a general diet at Aix-la-Chapelle (Aachen) and, with the consent of all present, conferred the imperial title on Ludwig, who nevertheless, as long as Charles lived, occupied a subordinate position. The coronation of Ludwig as emperor took place with great ceremony in the cathedral at Aachen (813). Clothed in his imperial robes and wearing his imperial crown, Charles first knelt with Ludwig in prayer before the high altar. He then addressed his son at some length on the duties of his office, and, after Ludwig had promised to heed his

Provides for the Succession.

advice and obey his commands, Charles ordered him to take from the altar a golden crown, which had been placed there, and crown himself. This Ludwig did, and the people shouted "Long life to Emperor Ludwig."

A Decline in the Government.

It is impossible not to see a decline in Charles's government during the last years of his reign. He was unable to prevent his officials and great landholders—counts, bishops, and abbots alike—from oppressing the large middle class of small landholders and the poor freemen, and reducing them to vassalage. The central government was weak in organization and was unable to protect its subjects, who were fast losing their relation as subjects to the government and sinking into the relationship of vassalage, or dependence, on the nobles. Charles perceived the injurious effects of the changes that were going on, but was powerless to prevent them. His health was broken by his many hard campaigns and by the heavy labors which his office imposed upon him. He was deeply depressed by the death of his two sons, which crushed his hopes, for he was well aware of the unfitness of Ludwig to rule. For the last year or two of his life the state of his health made it impossible for him to take an active part in the government. He spent much of the time at Aachen, where he died, January 28, 814, in consequence of an attack of pleurisy. On the evening of the same day his body was placed in a marble sarcophagus of ancient Roman workmanship, and buried with simple ceremony in the cathedral which he had built at Aachen. The whole empire was overwhelmed with sorrow, for all loved him as a father. His greatness outlived him and grew with the centuries, and popular imagination never wearied of inventing new deeds of valor to increase the glory of his name.

Death of Charles, 814.

S. B., 7:30–31.

CHAPTER VI

THE DISSOLUTION OF THE EMPIRE OF CHARLEMAGNE

By the coronation of Charles in 800 the imperial line, which had been lacking in the west since 476, was renewed. On the face of it his coronation looked like a renewal of the old empire, yet it might be pointed out that there were many important points of difference between his empire and that of Constantine or Justinian—a difference in extent, in the machinery of government, in race, in language, and in the general degree of culture. In spite of such differences, however, Charles was really carrying on the work which Rome, first as a republic and then as an empire, had been doing. That is, he was civilizing all the peoples of his vast realm and raising them to the same plane of culture, and even extending the boundaries of the civilized world by conquering barbarians and subjecting them to the civilizing influence of Rome. The political, religious, and intellectual unity of western Europe appeared likely to be attained if his work were continued long enough. After his death this appearance was seen to be deceitful; his government, which had been unifying the peoples of his empire, was followed by a period of political chaos during which his empire broke up into a number of small independent kingdoms which then gradually came together in new groupings to form the chief states of Europe. Charles had extended his empire in spite of racial differences and natural boundaries. After his death the influence of natural obstacles to unity, such as mountain ranges and differences in race and language, again made itself felt, and the states of Europe began to take shape somewhat in accordance with the existing racial conditions and the boundaries which nature had prescribed.

The Work of the Empire.

The chief causes of the dissolution of the empire are easily discovered. The essential elements of unity which had once existed in the empire had either disappeared or had been profoundly modified. The spoken Latin was already developing into separate languages, such as Italian, Spanish, and French; in many regions German law had either displaced or modified the law of Justinian; and the imperial administration had broken down completely. In fact, the empire had been dismembered, for the Moors had conquered Africa and Spain, and Britain was occupied by Germans who paid no allegiance to the emperor. And in the territory added to the empire by conquest, the Latin language, Roman law, and the imperial administration were unknown, and hence it was already foreign in character to the rest of the empire. The Christian church, however, still held to the idea of unity, and during the four troubled centuries of invasions and disorder (400–800) had helped keep alive the idea of a world-wide Roman empire.

Essential Elements of Unity Disappear.

There were also other causes of the dissolution. The different peoples had not forgotten that they had been conquered, and they were only waiting for an opportunity to assert their independence. Each of these peoples, conscious of itself, felt that it had the right of self-determination, a principle which is directly opposed to that on which the world empire was built. So the old tribal feeling of separation and desire for freedom reappeared as soon as the force which had held them together was removed, and it was soon apparent that the various parts of the empire were far from being homogeneous, and that the differences in race, tribe, temperament, customs, and language had not been removed. Furthermore, the rulers themselves destroyed the unity of the empire by dividing it among their sons. And lastly, the family of Charles rapidly degenerated, his descendants being, with few exceptions, weaklings, unfit to rule and incapable of comprehending the task which devolved upon them with the title of king or emperor. Having no conception of the duties of their office they conducted themselves in such a manner as to strengthen and abet the forces which were tending toward the

Other Causes of Dissolution.

dissolution of the empire. Not one of them devoted himself intelligently and wisely to the work of governing the territory which he possessed. The history of the ninth century is a luminous commentary on these causes of dissolution.

Ludwig the Pious, 814-840.

The reign of Ludwig the Pious (814-840. The French call him Louis le Débonnaire) was a long series of blunders which degraded the empire, opened the way for foreign invaders, caused ruinous civil wars among his sons, and led to the final and permanent division of the empire. He lacked all the qualities of a ruler, and was better fitted to be a monk than an emperor. Lacking intelligence and being without will, he was the slave and tool in turn of the clergy, his sons, and his wife. Sluggish and indifferent to the affairs of state, he deserted his post at the most critical moments to spend weeks in hunting and fishing. He did little for the defense of the frontier, and during his reign Northmen ravaged his northern provinces and Mohammedans plundered the Mediterranean coast.

Division of the Empire, 817.

In 817 he narrowly escaped death by an accident, and in consequence determined to fix the succession. He accordingly divided his empire among his three sons and yet retained the imperial authority until his death. To the younger sons, Pippin, who received Aquitaine, and Ludwig the German, who received Bavaria, the title of king was given, while Lothar, the eldest, received all the rest of the territory, and was crowned emperor. Yet the unity of the realm was to be preserved, for Lothar was to have supreme authority in all foreign relations—declaring war, making peace, and receiving and sending embassies. This division was destined never to be put into effect. Ludwig the Pious, after the death of his wife (818), was determined to retire to a monastery, but unfortunately his counsellors persuaded him to take a second wife instead. His choice fell on Judith, a daughter of Count Welf, whose ancestral possessions were in Suabia. To the still greater misfortune of the empire she bore him a son, who is known as Charles the Bald. For this son she was determined to secure a kingdom and, since all the territory of the empire had been divided among the older sons, she sought to annul the settlement of 817. In 829 she began her machinations, and till the death of the emperor (840) intrigues, divisions of the empire, and civil wars followed each other in bewildering succession. It would be idle to recount them, futile as they all were and barren of results. Judith's insane ambition for her son grew till she finally boldly planned to dispossess all the other sons of Ludwig the Pious and to have all their territory conferred on Charles. To add to the confusion, Lothar was eager to rid himself of all his brothers, and even of his father, and to acquire the whole empire for himself. In the midst of civil war Ludwig the Pious died (840), leaving the question as far from solution as it had been in the beginning.

Intrigues of Judith.

Lothar, greedy as ever, tried to secure the whole empire. He attacked both Ludwig the German* and Charles without being able to overcome either. They finally united against him and defeated him (841). In 842 Ludwig and Charles met at Strasburg, and after taking oaths of mutual fidelity renewed the campaign against Lothar, who soon offered to make terms with them. A preliminary peace was made (842), and a commission sent out to make a description of the various provinces of the empire in order that a just division of it might be made. The commission made its report, and the three brothers concluded a treaty at Verdun (843). By the terms of this treaty Lothar, as the oldest, received the imperial title with Italy and a strip of territory extending from Italy along the Rhône and Rhine to the North Sea. The territory east of this strip (East Frankland, or Germany) was ceded to Ludwig, who was called the German because his subjects were chiefly Germans. The land west of this strip (West Frankland, or France) went to Charles the Bald. It must be remembered that nationality did not cause the division, nor was it taken into account in fixing the boundaries.

The Strasburg Oaths.

S. B., 16.
O., 24.
R., 68.

Treaty of Verdun, 843.

S. B., 17, 18.
O., 25.

France, Germany, and Lotharingia.

* As a mnemonic aid I have used the German form of the names of those who were king in East Frankland (Germany), and the French form of the name of those who ruled in West Frankland (France).

In this division Ludwig and Charles were far more fortunate than Lothar, because each was ruler of a compact territory, with natural boundaries more or less clearly marked, and occupied by peoples more nearly homogeneous than were Lothar's subjects, who were composed of Italians, Celts, and Germans. The kingdom of Lothar was unfortunate geographically as well as racially. It was a long narrow strip with no natural boundaries, and it was broken into two parts by the Alps. It could not possibly be made into a nation, and soon broke into many fragments. Ludwig was fortunate because his subjects were for the most part Germans, and because to the east of them there were barbarous peoples, by the conquest of which he could enlarge his territory. Although the population of Charles's kingdom belonged to different races, they were all more or less Romanized and, like the subjects of Ludwig, they formed at least the basis for the development of a nation.

For the next hundred years the history of these divisions is extremely confusing and barren of interest. It is necessary, however, to relate certain facts, unattractive as they may be, in order that the reader may understand the origin of some of the most important institutions of the Middle Age. Let us therefore take in order the three divisions—the imperial crown and Italy, which were inseparably connected, France, and Germany.

So long as Lothar remained emperor (843–855) the brothers preserved a kind of unity in the empire by holding diets together, and for the most part maintaining friendly relations with one another. It was assumed that all the territory which had once belonged to Charlemagne still belonged to his descendants; although divided, it was still a family possession. Lothar's territory was sadly troubled in the north by the Northmen, who invaded it yearly, and in the south by Mohammedans, who were making desperate efforts to conquer all southern Italy. Lothar remained in the north without, however, doing anything of importance to resist the invasions of the Northmen. In 844 he associated his son, Ludwig II, with him in the government and sent him into

Italy and the Empire.

Note to Map VI.—This shows the division of the empire between the three sons of Louis the Pious. The youngest son, Charles, took the western part, which corresponds pretty closely to modern France; its population comprised Romanized Gauls and that part of the Franks which had also become fairly well Romanized by this time; the language was a corrupt Latin, which was to develop into French. Note that the Franks, who were Germans, gave their name to the country. The next older son, Ludwig, took the eastern part, comprising the bulk of the German tribes and the conquered Slavs; the Roman influence was slight in this territory. Lothar, the oldest brother, had the title of emperor, and received a long narrow strip of land including the two capitals of Rome and Aachen (Aix-la-Chapelle). North of Italy this strip consisted of two parts, the Rhône valley and the valley of the Meuse and Rhine. The Rhône valley was Roman in population (including Romanized Burgundians) and most of it is to-day within the boundaries of France. The northern part was partly Roman and partly Germanic, and has been fought over through the centuries by France and Germany.

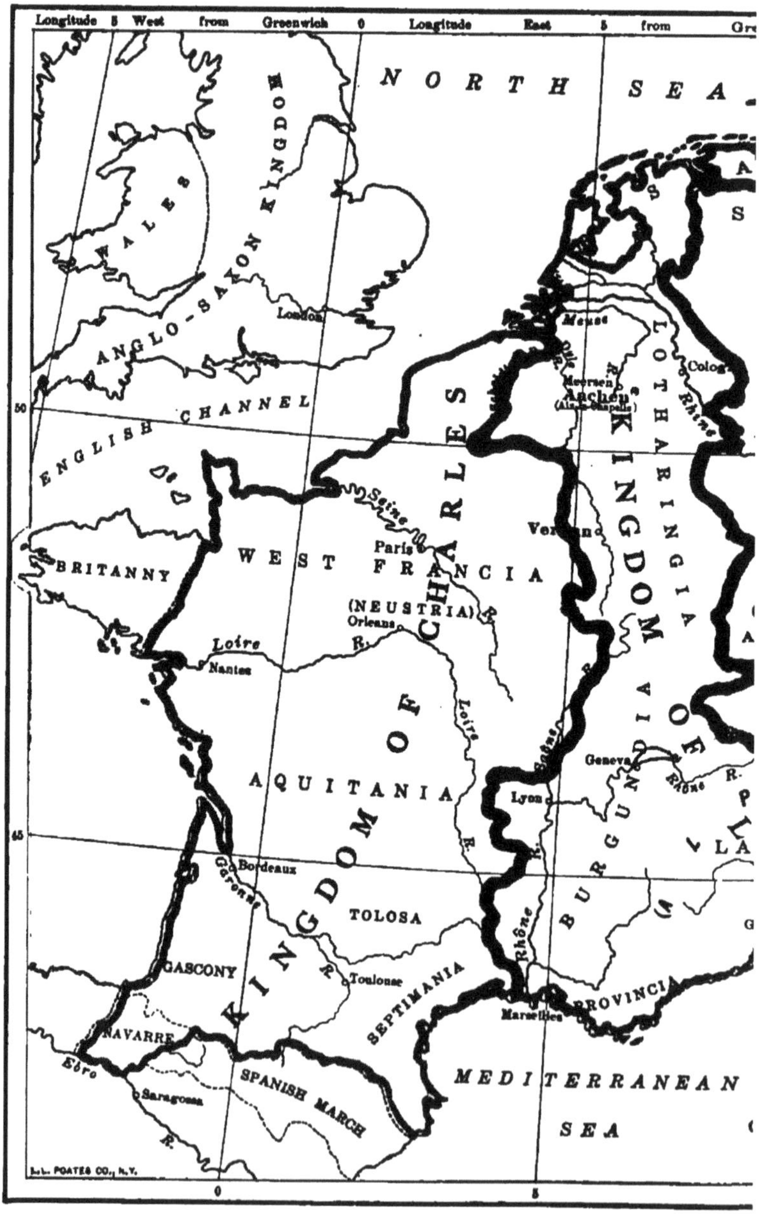
Longitude 5 West from Greenwich 0 Longitude East 5 from
NORTH SEA
ANGLO-SAXON KINGDOM
WALES
London
ENGLISH CHANNEL
50
BRITANNY
WEST FRANCIA
(NEUSTRIA)
Paris
Seine
Orleans
Loire R.
Nantes
KINGDOM OF CHARLES
AQUITANIA
45
Bordeaux
Garonne
TOLOSA
GASCONY
Toulouse
SEPTIMANIA
NAVARRE
Ebro
Saragossa
SPANISH MARCH
MEDITERRANEAN SEA
Marseilles
PROVINCIA
Rhône
Lyon
Geneva
BURGUNDIA
LOTHARINGIA
Meuse
Meersen
Aachen
Loire
Rhine
L. L. POATES CO., N.Y.
0
5

VI
THE DIVISION OF VERDUN, 843,
Showing the Beginning of France and Germany
SCALE OF MILES
RUGEN
Bremen
Elbe
Oder
SORABIANS (SORBES)
SLAVS
KINGDOM OF LUDWIG
EAST FRANCIA (FRANCONIA)
Prague
BOHEMIA
Regensburg (Ratisbon)
Danube
Altheim
BAVARIA
MORAVIA
Inn
CARINTHIA
PANNONIAN MARK
Drave
Save
Danube
CROATIA
Legnano
Milan
Padua
Venice
BARDY)
Po
Roncaglia
Canossa
Ravenna
SERVIA
ADRIATIC SEA
BYZANTINE EMPIRE
Assisi
Tiber
Rome
BENEVENTUM

Italy to rule. Ludwig II was crowned by the pope as king of the Lombards (844) and as emperor (850). He exerted himself to the utmost against the Mohammedans, but, as they received constant reinforcements from Africa, he was not able to master them.*

When a fatal illness overtook Lothar he divided his empire among his three sons and retired to a monastery, where he died within a few days (855). Ludwig II (855–875) received the imperial title with Italy; the kingdom of Burgundy fell to Charles (855–863); and Lothar II (855–869) obtained the rest. From this Lothar II his territory received the name of Lotharingia, which is still perpetuated in Lothringen (Lorraine), a province which Germany wrested from France in the Franco-Prussian War (1870–1871) and which has now been restored to France. Charles died in 863, and his brothers divided his kingdom. At the death of Lothar II, in 869, his land should have gone to his brother Ludwig II, but his uncles, Ludwig the German and Charles the Bald, seized it, and by the treaty of Meersen (870) divided it between them. Lothar II, during the last twelve years of his reign, had been so engrossed with an infamous attempt to divorce his wife that he had paid little attention to the affairs of state. The emperor, Ludwig II, the last of the three brothers, died in 875, and with him his family line became extinct.

France and Germany Divide Lotharingia. Treaty of Meersen, 870.

S. B., 19.

At the death of Ludwig II Italy entered on a troubled period. For some years it was the scene of bloody struggles between rival candidates for the crown of Lombardy as well as between those for the imperial crown. One candidate after another appeared and compelled the pope to crown him, but all displayed their weakness rather than their strength. Finally, in 891, Guido, duke of Spoleto, obtained

Troubles in Italy.

* In 846 they even attacked Rome, and plundered the churches of St. Peter and St. Paul, both of which were outside the city's walls. To prevent the recurrence of this Lothar ordered the pope to build a wall around St. Peter's and the houses which had sprung up about it. Pope Leo IV (847–855) put the order into effect, and that quarter of the city has ever since been called after him the Leonine quarter.

the crown, and the next year he associated his son Lambert with him in the office. Their rule was so oppressive that both the pope and the Italian nobles besought Arnulf, king of the East Franks, to come and deliver them from Guido and his son. Arnulf came into Lombardy, but, meeting with opposition, was soon compelled to return to Germany. In response to a second urgent invitation from the pope, Arnulf went to Italy again (896), and was crowned king. He then proceeded to Rome, which he took by storm, and was there crowned emperor by the pope (896). But as Lambert was still alive Arnulf's imperial title was not above dispute. He was taken ill, however, and had to withdraw to Germany without in any way improving conditions in Italy. On the contrary, for the next fifty years they grew worse, if that were possible. In 950, Adelaide of Burgundy was, by the death of her husband, left empress. One of the rival candidates for the throne, hoping to secure the crown for his family, seized her for the purpose of compelling her to marry his son.

Emperor Arnulf.

S. B., 23.

Adelaide Appeals to Otto I of Germany.

In her distress Adelaide appealed to the dukes of Bavaria and Suabia as well as to Otto I, king of Germany. Both dukes were willing to help her, because they coveted Italian territory, but Otto I forestalled them. He came into Italy, freed her from her captor, married her, and assumed the crown of Italy. He also negotiated with the pope for the imperial crown, but the pope refused it. Otto recognized Berengar, marquis of Friuli, as his vassal king in Italy, and went back to Germany. Berengar promptly rebelled against him and sought to increase his power in central Italy. In this he came into conflict with the pope, John XII. About 932 a certain Alberic had driven the emperor out of Rome, and had assumed the government of the city with the title "Prince and Senator of the Romans." Unscrupulous and efficient, he was able to keep the factions in the city as well as the successive popes in subjection until his death (954). His son Octavian succeeded him in the government of Rome, and in 955 was elected pope, assuming the title John XII (955–964). He sought to make his family supreme in central Italy, and so came into conflict with Berengar, who was supported by a faction in Rome itself. Remembering that Otto I had once desired the imperial crown, John now offered to crown him emperor if he would come and destroy Berengar. Otto came and was crowned emperor (962). For the next three centuries Italy and Germany were united because it was believed that the king of Germany had a right to the crown of Italy and to the imperial crown.*

Italy Dismembered.

The political dismemberment of Italy, already far advanced, made giant strides during the one hundred and fifty years after the death of Charlemagne. In the south, owing to the weak government of the Greek emperors, who still held nominal sway there, many cities had become independent, and Mohammedans were making determined efforts to get possession of all the southern part of the

* Nothing could be more dreary than the narrative of the dissolution of the empire, but a recital of the facts seems necessary, if only to give the reader an impression of the chaotic condition of political affairs and to show how the family of Charlemagne had degenerated, and how low the title of emperor had sunk. The following list of those who, from 800 to 962, received the imperial crown, may be of service:

Charlemagne, 800–814.
Ludwig the Pious, 814–840: crowned 813 by himself, and 817 by the pope.
Lothar I, 840–855: crowned emperor 817 by his father or by himself, 823 by the pope.
Ludwig II, 855–875: crowned by the pope as king of the Lombards 844, and as emperor 850.
Charles the Bald, 875–877.
Karl the Fat, 881–887: died 888.
Guido, duke of Spoleto, 891–894.
Lambert, his son, 892–899.
Arnulf, 896–899.
Louis III of Provence: 901, king in Pavia; 902, emperor; driven out 902; died 928.
Berengar: 888, king of Italy; 915, emperor; murdered 924.
Rudolf II of Upper Burgundy: king of Italy, 924–934; withdrew from Italy and united the two Burgundies 934.
Hugo of Arles, 926–947, but driven out of Rome by Alberic II.
Lothar II, 947–950.
Berengar II, vassal king of Otto I, 951–961.
Adalbert.
Otto I: king of Italy 951; emperor 962.

peninsula; in the central part the power was divided among the pope and the dukes of Benevento, Spoleto, and Tuscany; in the north there was a nominal king of the Lombards or of Italy. From the death of Lothar I (855) to the coronation of Otto I (962) no less than eight men were crowned emperor, and thirteen bore the title of king of Italy. Owing to the rivalries and inefficiency of these would-be kings and emperors an important political change had been going on in Italy. As the central government which had been established by Charlemagne broke down and disappeared, the bishops in the cities, who were also the imperial counts or governors, gradually came to exercise an independent political authority over their dioceses. By successive grants of immunity and jurisdiction from the emperors and by usurpations, in accordance with the general feudal tendency of the times, the bishops obtained a new relation to their dioceses; from officials of the emperor they had become lords of their counties. That is, each city with the territory about it had become a little city-state which, for the present, was ruled in an autocratic way by its bishop as its lord. But the inhabitants of the cities were beginning to grow restive under this arbitrary rule, and were preparing to rebel, to drive out their lord, and to establish a communal form of government. This spirit manifested itself first in Rome, where, as in every other city, the bishop had become the lord of the city. We have already seen that in 800 the people of Rome rebelled against the government of Leo III and expelled him from the city. More than once during the ninth and tenth centuries the pope was forced to choose between the curtailment of his political authority in Rome and the total loss of it.

Bishops Become Temporal Rulers.

Beginning of the Communal Movement.

Having traced the fortunes of the imperial crown, let us now turn to West Frankland, or France. Many parts of it, like the cities of Italy, were tending toward independence. The disintegration of the kingdom was hastened by the foolish actions of Charles the Bald, who, in his craze to acquire more territory, neglected to govern what he had. He made several wars against his brothers and nephews simply for the purpose of conquest, but paid no attention to his officials, who now held office at their own pleasure and administered the government as they pleased. He did nothing to check the Northmen who, year after year, ravaged the kingdom. He died in 877, leaving his kingdom to his three sons. The two oldest soon died, and the nobles refused to submit to the third, who was a mere child, known afterward as Charles the Simple. They elected Karl the Fat, who was already king of the East Franks and emperor. For three years he was the nominal ruler of virtually all the territory which Charlemagne had held. But a chronic illness rendered him unfit to govern and, matters going from bad to worse, the nobles deposed him (887). The unity of the West Frankish realm now disappeared for a while. The nobles north of the Loire elected Odo, count of Paris, king, but the duke of Aquitaine refused to acknowledge him and ruled his duchy quite independently. Brittany was left to itself, and Burgundy was divided into two little kingdoms. In 879 Count Boso of Vienne had usurped the royal title and made himself master of Lower Burgundy (Arles), and a little later (888) another count, Rudolf, seized Upper Burgundy and was crowned king. The formation of these two Burgundian kingdoms resulted in the loss of their territory to France for several centuries. They united in 934 to form the kingdom of Arles, or Burgundy, which passed in 1032 into the possession of the king of Germany, thus becoming a part of the empire.

France Dismembered.

S. B., 20. O., 26, 27. R., 65, 66, 69–71.

North France, Aquitaine, Brittany.

Lower Burgundy.

Upper Burgundy.

S. B., 22.

The condition of France in the ninth and tenth centuries was wretched in the extreme. For more than a hundred years marauding bands of Northmen ravaged the country and devastated it with fire and sword. The kings did little or nothing to resist their invasions, but left the work of defense to the nobles and bishops. The Northmen became bolder and bolder, and finally a large colony of them took possession of the valley of the lower Seine. Their

Northmen.

duke, Rolf (called Robert after his baptism), accepted Christianity and became the vassal of Charles the Simple, whose daughter he received as his wife. Under the strong rule of Robert and his successors his duchy became one of the most important provinces of France. His people were called Normans and his duchy Normandy.

Duchy of Normandy.

O., 27.

Since the death of Charlemagne feudalism had been taking on a definite form; that is, the royal officials had been steadily increasing their power at the expense of that of the crown, and the counts had made their offices hereditary and were governing their territories virtually as independent lords. They were often able to resist the king and did not hesitate to make war on him. The chief of these were now known as the great vassals, and their territories as the great fiefs, the principal ones of which were Flanders, Poitou, Anjou, Gascony, Aquitaine, and Normandy. The holders of these great fiefs were turbulent and rebellious. Since each one of them alone was almost a match for the king, when they combined their forces he was helpless before them.

Growth of Feudalism.

Odo (888–898) endeavored to make his position as king more secure by acknowledging Arnulf, a Carolingian who was king of the East Franks, as his lord. This vassal relation, however, was merely nominal, and probably had no effect on his rebellious barons. His reign was troubled by annual invasions of Northmen, and by the intrigues and rebellions of his great vassals, who tried to restore Charles the Simple to the throne. Charles was actually crowned at Rheims (893), but Odo maintained himself till his death. When Odo came to die he designated as his successor not his brother Robert, duke of Francia, who was his heir, but Charles the Simple (898–929). He was accepted by the barons, but was no more successful in restoring and maintaining order than Odo had been. In 923 Robert, duke of France, regretting that he had not seized the crown at the death of his brother Odo, rebelled and usurped the title of king. His troops met those of the king near Sois-

Odo.

S. B., 22.
O., 27.

Charles the Simple.

sons (923) and gained a victory, but Robert himself was slain. His son Hugo refused to be elected, so the nobles elected his son-in-law, Rudolf, king of Upper Burgundy. France was again divided till the death of Charles the Simple in 929, when Rudolf was acknowledged throughout France. At his death (936) the nobles recalled from over the sea (d'Outremer) the son of Charles the Simple, Louis IV, who had been taken for safety to the court of his grandfather, king Edward of England. After a stormy reign (936–954) Louis IV was succeeded by his son Lothaire (954–986), who was only eight years of age. Under this child-king matters grew worse; he was involved in quarrels with his clergy as well as with his nobles. He left the country ripe for revolt. His son Louis V (986–987) succeeded him, but died the next year. There was but one Carolingian left, Charles, duke of Lower Lotharingia. He was, however, without power, and could not hope to obtain the votes of the great vassals. The choice of the nobles fell on the strongest of them all, Hugh Capet, duke of Francia. Hugh had been following an ambitious policy, and had succeeded in getting possession of a good deal of land. He had become the feudal lord of several important fiefs, among them the counties of Blois, Champagne, Chartres, and Anjou, and the duchies of Burgundy and Aquitaine. He had made friends of the clergy too, and so when the royal family became extinct he was unanimously elected king. He was crowned with the high-sounding title, king of the Gauls, Bretons, Danes (Normans), Aquitanians, Goths, Spaniards, and Gascons. His actual authority, however, was slight, his great vassals being able to maintain a large degree of independence.

End of the Karlings in France.

Hugh Capet Elected King, 987.

O., 29.

Of the empire of Charlemagne there still remains Germany, the affairs of which we must now consider. There we find much the same state of affairs as in Italy and France—everything was tending toward political dissolution. Ludwig the German (843–876), although one of the most sensible of the descendants of Charlemagne, was not equal to his task. Moreover, his realm suffered much from

Dissolution in Germany.

invasions by the Northmen; he was compelled to make many campaigns against the Slavs, who frequently ravaged his eastern provinces; and the last fifteen years of his reign were troubled by rebellions of his three sons. He was, on the whole, successful in resisting the barbarian invaders, and he even extended his boundaries toward the east by conquering and subjecting several Slavic tribes. He dealt wisely with his rebellious sons, displayed a good sense of justice toward his people, and gave intelligent support to mission work among the barbarians outside his realm. When compared with his brothers, sons, and nephews, he seems worthy of praise. At his death he divided his kingdom among his three sons, but after the death of two of them it was reunited in 884 under the third, Karl the Fat, who had already been crowned emperor by the pope (881). At the same time he was chosen king of the West Franks, so that he was now the nominal ruler of all the lands which Charlemagne had once held. As his powers increased his inefficiency became more and more apparent, and, as matters went steadily from bad to worse, the nobles of Germany deposed him and chose his nephew, Arnulf, in his place (887–899).

Karl the Fat, 884–887.

Arnulf, although king only of the East Franks, felt that since he was a Karling all the empire belonged of right to him. But instead of attempting to get possession of it all, he contented himself with assuming merely the overlordship of all the little kingdoms into which the empire had been dissolved. Odo, when elected king of the West Franks, appealed to Arnulf and recognized him as his overlord. In return Arnulf sent him a crown and recognized him as king of the West Franks. In the same way the kings of both Upper and Lower Burgundy, and Berengar of Italy recognized Arnulf as their overlord. His reign was occupied with wars against invading barbarians. In the battle on the Dyle (891) he defeated the Northmen and inflicted such losses on them that they did not attempt a further invasion of Germany. In his wars with the Slavs, although meeting with some reverses, he was eventually successful in bringing the Slavs on

Arnulf, 887–899.

his eastern frontier to recognize his overlordship. Unfortunately for Germany he was troubled with the ambition to imitate his famous ancestor, Charlemagne, and coveted the empty title of emperor. In 894, in response to an embassy from the pope and some of the nobles of Rome, he went into Italy to attack Guido of Spoleto. After he had taken Bergamo by storm northern Italy submitted to him. He assumed the government of the country and dated his documents "in the first year of my reign in Italy," but at the same time he left Berengar as his vassal king. Since Arnulf was recalled to Germany, he was unable to proceed to Rome then, but two years later the pope again besought his aid, promising him in return the imperial crown. To this call Arnulf responded. He first deposed Berengar and made himself sole king of Italy. He then went to Rome, where he was refused admission by the widow of Guido, who was holding the city for her son Lambert. Arnulf stormed the city and was crowned emperor by the pope, Formosus. After compelling the Romans to swear that they would be true to him he set out for the north to punish Berengar, who had reasserted himself as king. On the way to the north he was taken ill and was compelled to return to Germany. At his departure the Italians, offended at his assumption of power, rebelled against him and undid everything that he had done.

Emperor Arnulf, 896.

S. B., 23.

Arnulf made one of his illegitimate sons, Zwentibold, king of Lorraine, and arranged that his legitimate son, Ludwig IV, commonly called Ludwig the Child, should succeed him in the rest of his kingdom. Ludwig the Child was only six years old at Arnulf's death, but the nobles accepted him as king. No regency was appointed, but a kind of council, consisting of many bishops and nobles, directed affairs. They rewarded themselves by ceding to themselves large tracts of the crown lands, and in general it may be said that they regarded rather their own advantage than the interests of the realm. Fortunately for the unity of the kingdom, Zwentibold governed Lorraine so tyrannically that the people rebelled against him, slew him, and acknowl-

Ludwig the Child, 899–911.

edged Ludwig the Child as king. During the reign of this child-king both Germany and Italy were invaded by the Hungarians, or Magyars, as they called themselves. Almost every year they invaded one or more of the German provinces, burning the towns and villages, killing the men, and carrying away the women and children. Mounted on swift horses, they passed like a destructive whirlwind over the country, and the Germans, who fought on foot, were helpless before them.

Invasions of the Magyars.

As if the woes of the land were not already great enough, the nobles, knowing the weakness of the government, engaged in destructive feuds. Violence and lawlessness, which had been on the increase since the death of Charlemagne, culminated in this reign. The strong oppressed the weak and the nobles fought one another. The weakness of the government led to the establishment of a duke in each of the five large divisions of Germany—Franconia, Suabia, Bavaria, Saxony, and Lotharingia. In Saxony the ducal title was usurped by a member of the family of Count Liudolf; in Franconia by a member of the family of Count Conrad; in Lorraine by Count Reginar, who had fought against Zwentibold; in Alamannia (Suabia) first by Count Burchard and then by Count Erchanger; and in Bavaria by Arnulf, son of the Marquis Liutbold. These usurpers were easily successful, not only because of the weak rule of the child-king, but also because they appealed to the latent tribal feeling and local desire for independence. Thus, the duke of Bavaria was, in a way, the symbol of Bavarian unity and freedom. In the same way and for the same reasons the dukes of the other duchies were hailed with satisfaction by their respective peoples. The duke was a centre about which his people could rally, and as each duchy now had an organization of its own, its tribal and temperamental differences were perpetuated. The dukes in Germany correspond to the great vassals in France and to the city-states in Italy, and were quite as turbulent and rebellious against their kings. Although in Italy independent city-states

Feuds of the Nobles.

Five Duchies Established: Saxony, Franconia, Lorraine, Suabia, Bavaria.

S. B., 24, 25.

were formed, and in France several independent kingdoms were established, in Germany the process of disintegration did not proceed so far. Although the country was divided into five great duchies the dukes of which exercised certain sovereign or crown rights, the principle of unity was maintained by the king.

With the death of Ludwig the Child the family of Charlemagne came to an end in Germany and a new king had to be chosen. The honor fell on Conrad, duke of Franconia. Conrad I (911–918) had an old-fashioned conception of the office of king, and was not willing to accept the situation which had been brought about by the development of feudalism and the growth of local independence in the duchies. He was able, active, brave, and ambitious to rule as a king of the old school, regardless of the rights which his great vassals, the dukes, were now in the habit of exercising. His reign was spent in the vain endeavor to make good the traditional authority of the king over the dukes, who stubbornly resisted him at every turn. He allied himself closely with the clergy, who, at a council at Altheim (916), attempted to coerce the dukes by threatening with the ban all who should resist the will of the king. But even with this aid of the clergy Conrad could not reduce the dukes to subjection. He grew weary of the unsuccessful struggle, and at his death designated as his successor his most powerful rival, Henry, duke of Saxony. With the accession of the Saxon family Germany entered on a new period of its history.

Conrad I, 911–918.

Fails in His Policy.

CHAPTER VII

FEUDALISM

Society in Mediæval States Unlike Modern Society.

Before we take up the history of the separate states of western Europe which emerged after the dissolution of the empire of Charlemagne, it will be helpful to consider the peculiar structure of society which prevailed among them. Conditions of life (social, political, economic, and cultural) were so different from those with which we are familiar, that without this preliminary survey we should miss the meaning of historical events.

Feudalism: a Society Based on Private and Personal Relations.

The form of society which prevailed in the mediæval states is known as "feudalism," or the "feudal system."* If we seek the quality in the feudal state which distinguishes it most essentially from the modern state, we shall find it in the fact that the bonds which held society together were the personal and private relations of men to one another, rather than the obedience of men to public law and government. In every age and every state both kinds of relations exist side by side. On the one hand are the private and personal relations between employer and employed, master and servant, landlord and tenant, leader and follower, patron and client—relations in which the superior exercises considerable influence over the lives and actions of the inferior. On the other hand are the public institutions—the central government, the public officials, the law, and the courts of justice, which have coercive power over the

* In reality this general name covers two distinguishable systems. Strictly speaking, feudal relations are the relations between members of the ruling class, based on the holding of a "fief" (Latin *feudum*). The relations of the mass of the people to the upper landowning class constitute the "manorial" system, a name taken from the small farming communities, or manors, in which the agricultural laborers lived under complete subjection to their landlord.

actions of citizens. According to our idea of a well-organized society (and it was also the Roman idea), public authority is superior to private authority. Men must obey the laws of the state, must be prevented by courts and public officials from pursuing their own interests to the injury of others or to the disturbance of the peace, must support the government by paying taxes. And because of the powers exercised by the state the citizens are enabled to live in peace, to hold their possessions in security, to act together in large ways (such as intercourse and trade) to their common advantage.

Effects of Weak Government on Private Relations.

In a state of society in which the government is so ineffective that strong and powerful persons are not made to obey, and weak and poor persons are not given protection and security, the comparative position of public and private authority is reversed. When the government cannot keep order or defend the territory, powerful individuals are likely to take authority into their own hands, defend their own possessions, fight out their own quarrels, and control their own followers; on the other hand, the weak and unprotected are forced into dependence upon their powerful neighbors. Under these conditions, private and personal relations become the important factors in determining the actions of men and constitute the real bonds of society.

No Real Public Government in Western Europe during Early Middle Age.

There had been no effective government in western Europe during most of the time since the collapse of the Roman empire. The invasions brought about the decline of the Roman government, and the Germanic tribal kings who then assumed control over the parts of the empire in the west were incapable of maintaining the machinery of the Roman state or of building up an effective rule of their own. Chlodovech, by his conquests, brought a considerable part of the west into a single state, the kingdom of the Franks, but he was only a barbarian warrior and not an organizer, and after his death there was almost constant war and confusion. The predecessors of Charlemagne, such as Pippin and Charles Martel, ruled with strong hands and restored order, while Charlemagne himself organized a government for his whole empire. His government, however, broke down completely under his successors, and there was another period of disorder, marked by civil wars and invasions. So, during most of the five or six centuries from the break-down of the Roman empire to the appearance of the feudal states, conditions favored the growth of private and personal relations at the expense of public authority.

Having made out the general nature of the new relations and the general causes of their growth, we must examine the principal forms under which they appeared and which were to give rise to the institutions of feudal society. There are three essential features: (1) the division of society into a small upper landlord class and the great mass of the laborers, who were tenants and subjects of this class; (2) the exercise of public powers and functions by local lords instead of by officials of the public government; (3) the bond of personal allegiance which bound the smaller landlords to the greater and which served as almost the only tie to hold together the society of the ruling class.

Three Essential Features of the Feudal System.

1. The division of society into wealthy landlords and poor peasants was already familiar in the Roman empire, where the small, independent farmer class had almost utterly disappeared, and where lands were held in large estates by the upper class and cultivated by dependent tenants and slaves. A similar class of great landlords developed among the Germans after the invasions. Those tribes which penetrated far within the empire (like the West Goths or Burgundians) were absorbed in the Roman system of landholding; the fortunate and successful ones became landed proprietors, the rest sank to the level of the Roman tenants. Among the Germans in northern Gaul and Germany (like the Franks, Alamanni, Bavarians) a class of powerful landlords developed. The kings, the tribal leaders and their followers, and the successful warriors, acquired large estates from the waste or ownerless lands, as did also by gift the churches and monasteries. In the times of violence and disorder, the former freemen of the German tribes found it

1. Division of Society into Landlord Class and Dependent Cultivators.

safer to live and easier to gain a livelihood by becoming tenants on the estates of such landlords or by giving over to them their former freeholds and receiving them back as tenant holdings. The distinctions between cultivators of different rank and different origin (Roman tenants, Roman slaves, German free farmers) lost their meaning; all of the cultivating class was assimilated to the one general status, that of tenants on the estates of a landlord, subject to his management and control.

2. Another important feature of the development of the feudal system was the exercise of public powers and authority by private lords. This was a natural result of the failure of an effective government during all these centuries. The first way in which this appeared was in the form of private jurisdiction; that is, the tenants and servants of a landlord obeyed him and looked to him to settle their disputes, instead of resorting to the local courts. This practice developed very rapidly in the Frankish kingdom; in the case of lands held by monasteries it was even legalized by "grants of immunity," charters by which the king freed these lands and their inhabitants from the control of local officials and the jurisdiction of local courts. Secular landlords sometimes secured such grants of immunity; more often they simply assumed the right to try the cases and control the actions of their peasants and retainers. During the centuries that followed, this became so general that the public courts of justice virtually disappeared, and law and justice for the common man was a matter not of state control but of the private authority of his lord.

2. Public Powers Exercised by Private Lords.

(a) Private Jurisdiction.

Immunity.

S. B., 192, 193, 194. R., I, 72, 73.

It was not only local jurisdiction which passed out of the control of the government; even larger public powers tended more and more to become matters of private authority. This, of course, was also a result of the absence of any effective rule during centuries. Take, for example, the case of the counts in the Frankish kingdom and empire. As we have seen, the count in each county was the representative of the king. He controlled

(b) Public Powers Exercised by Landlords.

the administration of justice in the hundred-courts of his county, executed the laws made by the central government, and saw to it that the obligations of serving in the army were observed and the taxes and payments due to the king were paid. Now, when we remember that the counts were great landlords and usually held their office by hereditary right, and further that during most of this time, except for the brief period of Charlemagne's rule, there was no effective control over them from the central government, we can see how they would tend to become independent and also how they would come to regard these large public powers as being part of their personal authority. In the ninth century the Carolingian government failed utterly, and the counts became virtually independent lords of their counties, exercising in their own right such important powers as they had formerly exercised in the name of the king or emperor.

Position of the Counts an Illustration.

S. B., 195, 196.

3. The third factor in the development of feudal society was the bond of personal allegiance which regulated the relations of members of the ruling class to one another. It was an essential feature of the holding of land; the smaller landlord held his estates from a greater lord, whose personal authority he recognized and to whom he rendered allegiance. The historical process by which this developed is worth tracing. In the period after the invasions the Germanic tribal kings gave out large tracts of land to their followers and to those who served them as agents or officials. These lands became the hereditary possessions of the holders, but the idea of a personal attachment to and a personal dependence upon the king persisted. During the Merovingian and Carolingian periods such landlords constituted a class bound to the king or emperor in a closer relation than that which affected the rest of the subjects.

3. Personal Allegiance among the Landlords.

Historical Origin.

With the breaking down of the Carolingian empire, classes or ranks of lords developed, among whom this personal relationship was established. As we have seen, the count became virtually hereditary lord of the county; the landlords of the county, instead of being directly bound to the king, were bound to the count, and held their lands from him. Below the large landlords of the county a smaller class arose. The retainers and followers of the landlords received from him small estates; or former free landowners entered into personal dependence on the greater landlord in order to secure protection. During this period of violence and confusion, when the successors of Charlemagne were almost powerless as rulers, a class of lords above that of the counts emerged. To resist the attacks of Northmen or Slavs or Hungarians, the counts of a whole region, as northern France, or Saxony, or Bavaria, combined under the leadership of some powerful member of their own class and recognized him as their overlord, paying him personal allegiance and holding their lands from him.

In the Late Carolingian Period.

Military service was a regular feature of personal allegiance and landholding. After the mass of the freemen had sunk into the position of dependent tenants, the duty and privilege of fighting became a monopoly of the landholding class. This was a result partly of the change in the manner of fighting. Since their contact with the Moorish invaders from Spain, the Franks had come to depend more and more upon mounted warriors; after the ninth century most of the fighting in western Europe was done by horsemen. Warriors were drawn necessarily from the class able to equip and maintain horses and able to devote their time to fighting. The chief service which the follower paid to his lord for the land which he held from him was to follow him on horseback to war. Lands were held, therefore, in the feudal system on terms of personal allegiance and military service to a superior.

Military Service a Feature of Personal Allegiance and Landholding.

The final step in the formation of a political society based on the personal allegiance of the landed aristocracy to their immediate superiors was taken when in the main divisions of the Carolingian empire the greatest lords chose one of their own number as hereditary leader and king. This step was taken in

France when, in 987, the last direct Carolingian in the western part of the empire died, and the lords chose Hugh, duke of Francia (Paris and the region around it), as king of France; it was taken in Germany when Henry, duke of Saxony, in 919, was recognized by the other great dukes as king of Germany. This, in fact, is the actual process by which the empire of Charlemagne was replaced by the separate kingdoms of medieval history.

System Completed; King at the Head.

In the preceding paragraphs we have traced the historical origin of those grades or ranks of nobles which, in the feudal age, were indicated by the titles of nobility. Titles once assumed became hereditary along with the lands; they differed in different countries, and included many varieties and grades. There were, however, four principal grades below that of king: namely, duke, count, baron, knight. The origin and meaning of these names will illustrate the process by which these classes arose. The powerful local landlord, holder of a considerable estate with several villages of peasants on it and able to build and defend a castle, was the *baron* (late Latin *baro*, warrior). He had retainers and followers, some of whom lived at his castle as part of his household; others of whom held small estates from the gift of the baron, for which they paid in military service. These latter are the *knights*. By derivation the English word knight means servant; it suggests the fact that this class sprang from the followers of the higher noble. The French word for the same class, *chevalier*, and the German, *Ritter*, mean horseman or rider, and indicate the essential duty of the knight, which was attendance on the lord from whom he held his small fief. The title *count* indicated originally the lord in whose family the former public office of governing the county had become hereditary and personal, and the one to whom the landlords of the county, the barons, paid allegiance. The overlord of the counts, the lord of a large geographical division, usually bore the title of *duke*. This is derived from the Latin *dux*, military leader, suggesting the original function of the duke, which was to command the armed forces of his province.

Origin and Meaning of Titles of Nobility.

The Baron.

The Knight.

The Count.

The Duke.

Sometimes, as in France, the leading count who made himself head of the larger district by becoming overlord of the counts in it, retained his original title, as the count of Flanders, or the count of Toulouse. Such counts were on a level with the dukes. There are all sorts of intermediate grades and varieties of titles, but these four represent the essential classes.

Summing up the study of the origins of feudalism, it may be said in general that it was the natural result of the centuries of disorder and weak government following the collapse of the Roman empire. The particular tendencies which were at work during these centuries were: (1) the mass of the people ceased to be freemen, and became, as cultivators of the soil, subject completely to the landlord class; (2) political authority was exercised, not by public officials, but by powerful private lords; (3) the strongest bond was not obedience to the government but personal allegiance to superiors, this allegiance being regularly associated with the holding of land and the performance of military service.

General Cause: Absence of Effective Public Government.

It was at the end of the tenth century, after the complete collapse of the Carolingian government, that these tendencies triumphed so completely as to constitute a new form of society. This form of society, feudalism, prevailed during the rest of the Middle Age, in the states which grew out of the empire of Charlemagne. It was also carried to England by the Norman conquest, although the essential elements were already present there; it spread to the states which later grew up around the old empire of Charlemagne, such as the small Christian kingdoms in Spain and the kingdoms on the eastern frontier of Germany (Bohemia, Poland, and Hungary); it was even transplanted for a time into Syria, when the western nobles established states there after the first crusade.

Extent of Feudal System in Western Europe and Beyond.

Having now traced its development, let us study the actual operations of the system. We can best do this by examining it in its important aspects: (1) as a form of government; (2) as an economic system; and (3) as to the manners of life and the culture which characterized it.

Three Aspects of the Feudal System:

In the feudal state public government scarcely existed. In the first place, authority over men was a personal and private affair. Every landlord was virtually the ruler of the peasants who cultivated his lands. The landlord himself was bound as vassal by ties of personal allegiance to a higher lord. This tie, however, was very different from that which bound the peasant to his landlord, since the vassal himself was a noble, possessed of independent power and resources. According to feudal custom the vassals were subject in certain matters to their lords, but a subject who had armed retainers and lived in a fortified castle, would be hard to control. And if a dispute arose between two nobles they would be more likely to fight it out than to submit to the decision of their overlord. Private wars of this sort were, in fact, a constant feature of the feudal age.

1. As a Form of Government.

Authority is a Matter of Personal Relations.

Law ordinarily was a matter of custom, not enacted by a public legislative body nor enforced by public officials. The law which regulated the relations of the peasants to one another and to their landlord was the local custom of the village. It determined the procedure and the amounts of fines and damages in cases arising between the villagers; it dealt also with disputes arising between the peasants and the landlord as to rents and other obligations. The provisions of the law were the outgrowth of local custom and differed in different villages. The test of the validity of a particular law was long usage; if the question were raised, it was usually settled by taking the testimony of the oldest and most respectable inhabitants as to what had been the custom within their memory. The agent of the landlord administered justice to the peasants according to this customary law in the local court of each village.

Law is Custom.

Manorial Law.

The life of the feudal nobles, as we have seen, was under the reign of might rather than the reign of law; nevertheless, they were more or less subject to "feudal law." This was not law in the modern sense; it was the body of customs which had grown up out of the conditions of

Feudal Law.

life in the noble class and the relations among the nobles. Now the most important factor in the position of the noble in society was his possession of a fief, that is, of a larger or smaller territory, held from a greater lord on terms of personal allegiance. Feudal law, therefore, had to do largely with the fief and the terms on which it was held.

The relationship of lesser lords to greater lords, connected with the holding of a fief, was known as vassalage. Every noble (except the very highest, the feudal king) was the vassal of a higher lord. The relationship was legally established when the vassal performed the act of homage and the lord invested him with the fief. The usual occasion was the inheritance of a fief by the son of a vassal on his father's death; for the relationship, in the ordinary course of events, was hereditary. In such a case the heir presented himself at the court of his lord and did him homage; that is, knelt before him and swore to be faithful to him. Then the lord invested him with the fief.

Vassalage.

S. B., 226.

Homage.

S. B., 209–214.
R., I, 83, 84, 85.
O., 36.

The act of homage and the oath of allegiance constituted a promise to perform faithfully the obligations inherent in the relation of vassalage. The vassal usually owed his lord military service of an amount and character fixed by custom; for the lower nobility (the knights) this was ordinarily forty days' service a year and a certain amount of guard duty in the lord's castle. The vassal also was bound to appear at his lord's court on certain occasions, to give him advice or to add to the dignity of his assemblage. Disputes among the vassals were supposed to be settled by a court of justice, held at the lord's castle and comprising all his vassals; as a matter of fact, such disputes were often fought out in private war between the opponents.

Duties Implied in Act of Homage.

R., I, 87

The obligations of the vassal to his lord were personal and honorable; he did not usually buy his fief or pay rent for it, but made his payment in personal services of a dignified sort. There were, however, certain occasions when, according to feudal custom, the lord could demand money from his vassals: when the lord was made prisoner in battle the vassals were bound to contribute to pay his ransom; when the lord's son was knighted or his daughter married the vassals helped defray the expenses. If the heir to the fief were a minor, the lord managed the fief until he came of age; if the fief fell to a woman, the lord's consent was necessary for her marriage, since her husband would become the actual holder and vassal. In general, however, we may say that the vassal, on being invested with his fief, became its lord and the ruler of the land and people comprised in it.

Customary Payments of Vassal to Lord.

S. B., 215–217. O., 38.

Other Powers of Lord over Vassal.

So much for law and authority over persons in the feudal system. Larger powers, such as the coinage of money, the control of highways and rivers, were exercised only by the greater lord, the count or duke, whose fief constituted a considerable district or province. The greatest public powers, taxation, legislation, maintaining the peace, were virtually in abeyance. This means that the feudal system scarcely constituted a government, in the modern sense. The great sovereign powers of a state did not exist, smaller public powers were exercised by private lords, custom was law, authority over men was a matter of private relations.

Larger Public Powers.

In fact, however, this absence of government was never complete. That is, there never was a time when the king of the feudal state did not try, in some measure, to assert an authority superior in character to that of the feudal lords. The political history of the feudal age, indeed, is the record of a conflict between the feudal nobility, trying to maintain its private sovereignty, and the king trying to create a royal government over his country. How and in what different ways this conflict was worked out in the various countries of western Europe, we shall study in succeeding chapters.

Inevitable Conflict between Feudal Lords and King over Sovereignty.

The position of the church in the feudal system deserves particular notice. By grants from kings and princes, and gifts of wealthy individuals, the church had acquired immense holdings of land. As we have seen, landholding in the feudal system carried with it certain powers and certain obligations: the landholder must be the vassal of some superior lord from whom he received the lands as a fief and to whom he rendered homage and allegiance; on the other hand, the landholder was himself the overlord of lesser vassals who held fiefs from him, and also the landlord of the peasants who cultivated the soil. Since this was the only recognized form of landholding, the lands of the church had to be fitted into this system. The ruling clergy (abbots, bishops, and archbishops) were recognized as the responsible lords of the great estates belonging to their monasteries or churches. As such they were the vassals of the king or dukes and were bound to do homage for their fiefs, and render either in person or through substitutes the military and other services regularly owed by a vassal to his lord. They were also great feudal lords, with vassals under them; they possessed the sovereign powers and exercised the private jurisdiction which were the prerogatives of the greater lords. In their interests and activities the great ecclesiastics were not very different from the dukes and counts. And yet at the same time, of course, they were officials in a great international religious system; they received their spiritual offices by canonical election, they were subject to the authority of the pope, their essential functions were spiritual and religious. This double position of the higher clergy was a source of trouble. Their interests were divided and conflicting; bishops and abbots were often more occupied with their secular interests than with their spiritual. Church offices were sought because of the wealth and power attached to them. Moreover, the great churchman owed a double allegiance. As a lord he was the vassal and subject of the king or duke from whom he held his fiefs, and these secular rulers often controlled the ecclesiastical elections in order to have their own followers put in control of the office. Bishops and abbots were used by the rulers as advisers and officials in secular government. On the other hand, as an ecclesiastic, the great churchman was subject to the authority of the pope from whom he received his spiritual powers and whom he was bound to obey. This double allegiance made difficulty, especially when there was a conflict between the pope and the secular ruler, and such conflicts were frequent from the eleventh century on. Illustrations of this occur in later chapters, for example, the "Investiture Conflict" and the dispute between Henry II of England and Thomas Becket, archbishop of Canterbury.

2. As an Economic System

Based on Agriculture.

In the foregoing paragraphs feudalism has been considered in its political aspect, as a form of government. No less important (indeed from the modern view, perhaps, even more important) is an understanding of the economic aspect. For we have come to realize that economic forces are often more decisive factors in shaping historical events than the purely political. The economic basis of feudal society was agriculture. As we have seen, this form of society developed in a time when there was almost no commerce or organized industry or city life. The wealth of the feudal noble consisted of land, and it was by exploiting the agricultural labor of his peasants that the lord derived the income necessary to maintain his position and exercise his powers as a member of the ruling class.

Sources of Revenue of the Landlord: Rents, Forced Labor, Market Privilege.

S. B., 228. R., I, 157.

Let us see what sources of revenue the lord possessed in the village. In the first place, the farm lands were cultivated by tenants who paid him rent in money or in produce. Then the landlord usually had a farm of his own in each village, and the work on this was done by some of the tenants who were bound by custom to perform such labor without pay. The produce which he received as rents and from his own farms supplied the needs of the lord's household; the surplus he sold in the local market. And the lord enjoyed by custom a special advantage in disposing of his crops—he had the right to sell his grain or wine a certain number of days before the peasants could sell theirs, which enabled him to get the top price of the market.

The necessary local industries of the village—the blacksmith-shop, the mill, the bake-oven, the wine-press—were usually established and controlled by the lord. They furnished a considerable revenue, since the peasants were compelled to use them and to pay for the service. The lord frequently let out the smithy or bake-oven or mill to one of the peasants for a yearly rent.* If the village were a local trading-centre, the lord got an income from the market rights, the rents of stalls, and the tolls on roads and at the gates of the town.

Tolls from Mill, etc.

The lord also derived an important part of his revenue from his right of private jurisdiction. The local court which tried the cases of the peasants was established and maintained by the lord. The penalties for violations of the customary law were mostly in the form of fines, which went to the lord. The authority of the lord over the peasants in other matters yielded him a revenue. The rights of the peasant to marry, to inherit, or dispose of his land or other property, were subject to restrictions from which he could be relieved by paying a customary charge.

Fines from Village Courts.

Restrictions on Freedom of Peasants.

To look after all these complicated rights the lord usually had an agent or manager in each village. It was the agent who saw to it that the peasants paid their rents and performed their enforced labor, and made their other customary payments to the lord. He was also the judge in the local court, and collected the fines that should go to the lord. In fact, the peasants had little to do directly with the lord and came in contact with him usually only through the local agent.

Position of the Lord's Agent in the Village.

So far we have looked at this system from the point of view of the landlord; let us now regard it from the peasant's side. Not all of the peasants, it should be noted, were on the same level. Some of them occupied a superior position, holding larger

* The position of village smith or baker or miller was usually handed on from father to son, and so produced those familiar family names. This is true not only in the English language, but also in French and German.

lands on easier terms and possessing greater personal liberties. The great body of peasants, however, was of that peculiar half-free, half-slave status which is known as serfdom. They were not slaves owned by the lord; on the other hand, they were not free to go where they wished or to dispose of their labor and possessions. The serf was born into his position; he was bound by his birth to cultivate a certain piece of ground, to pay certain rents and obligations, and to perform certain labor for his lord without pay. He could not sell or leave his land, nor hire himself out as a laborer. The most burdensome of his obligations, and the one that we may regard as the distinctive mark of the servile condition was the necessity of working on the lord's own land a certain number of days a week or a year. In many cases this amounted to as much as three days a week.

Most Peasants were Serfs.

Status of the Serf.

It is apparent, then, that mediæval society rested upon a foundation of serfdom; upon a system in which the great body of the population labored under hard and oppressive conditions, without political liberties or political rights. One of the most interesting movements to study in European history is the gradual process of improvement in the condition of the serfs. In the more progressive western countries, there was a marked improvement within the period of the Middle Age, due principally to changes in economic conditions. The revival of commerce and industries, with the consequent growth of towns, offered an outlet to a part of the laboring population. Since these towns grew out of manors or villages, the original population was made up of peasants and serfs of the landlord on whose estates the town was located. As the towns increased in population, and the industries and trade grew in importance, the inhabitants tended to become more independent. The artisans and traders formed associations (guilds) and became conscious of their united strength. They were able to drive bargains with their lord and induce him to relinquish his personal rights over them. In many towns, in the twelfth century, the inhabitants, by com-

Feudal Structure Based on Inequality.

Slow Progress toward Equality.

Improvement in Economic Status.

bining together, were able to secure charters which freed them from the lord's jurisdiction and enabled them to set up a government of their own. Serfs often fled to these towns to escape from their hard conditions, and the townsmen resisted the attempts of the landlord to recover them by force. In general, it came to be a recognized custom that an escaped serf who lived in a town "a year and a day" became a free resident. Thus the growth of towns enabled a part of the servile population to acquire the status of freemen.

Even more important in the breaking-down of serfdom was the increase in the use of money, which was greatly hastened by the growth of commerce and business. In the early feudal age, exchange was largely in the form of barter; the serf paid for his piece of land with bodily service and part of his produce. With the increase of money as a medium of exchange, the landlord sought to turn his rights over lands and tenants into a money income; he remitted to the tenants the services and restrictions and obligations in return for a money rental. The more fortunate serfs were able to acquire the status of free tenants, holding their farms for a fixed money rent, and free to leave or dispose of them. Some of the serfs became hired laborers, working for the landlords for a definite wage, which was determined, not by custom but by the "law of supply and demand." They approached the status of the free laborer, able to dispose of his labor where he could get the best price. By the end of the fifteenth century the worst features of serfdom had disappeared in England and France; in more eastern countries this advance was made much later.*

Movement toward Political Equality.

This improvement in the economic condition of the peasant class opened the way for that political advance which is an important feature of modern democracy. This, however, is a very recent advance, not yet everywhere fully achieved. It has aimed at securing to all men equality of opportunity, individual liberty, and a

* The disturbances connected with the transition from serfdom to free status are discussed in the chapters on England and France in the Hundred Years' War, pp. 376–378.

participation in government. At the end of the eighteenth century the peasant class was still deprived of these rights, and the French Revolution, in insisting on them as the "natural rights of man," started the movement for democracy in Europe.

3. As a Cultural System.

We have still to look at the cultural aspect of feudalism, for that too is necessary for an understanding of mediæval life. Certain features of feudal culture will be discussed in a later chapter on medieval civilization; we shall consider here those features which are most directly the outgrowth of feudal conditions, and which may, therefore, serve to throw an additional light on the real character of the feudal age.

The Castle.

Perhaps the most important factor in the life of the feudal noble was the fact that he lived in a castle. The essence of the castle is the combination of a private fortress and a residence. The general reason for the type is to be found, of course, in the character of the feudal age: the castle was a symbol both of the insecurity of the time and of the independent power of the individual noble. To maintain his independence he had to be able to defend himself; possessed of a castle, he could hold his own with his equals, lord it over his weaker neighbors, and even defy his superiors.

Sources of Castle-Building

The principles and methods of construction and plan were derived from several sources: from the fortified camp of the Roman legions, from the fortified manor-house of the Germanic chieftain after the invasions, from the intrenched camps constructed by the Northmen when they landed and harried a region. From these and other sources was derived in northern France and England a type of castle which we may take as characteristic of the feudal residence. This type developed and improved in the course of the Middle Age. About the beginning of the twelfth century the builders began to use stone in place of wood for walls and towers. At the end of that century the kings and greater nobles had developed and organized their revenues so that they could build the massive and complicated structures the ruins of

THE CASTLE OF ARQUES IN NORMANDY.

From Viollet-le-Duc, Dictionnaire raisonné de l'architecture française.

Notice the wide moat with a palisade outside, the approach across drawbridges, the strongly defended gateway, the walls with loopholes and battlements and a wide walk around the top, and the numerous wall-towers which project beyond the face of the wall. The principal structure is the massive rectangular keep at the farther end of the enclosure; the other buildings are of wood—stables, sheds, and lodgings for the garrison.

which still stand to impress us with their strength. In the later centuries the improvement in order and peace made the castle more of a fine residence and less of a fortress. We may not follow these changes, but will note the general features of the castle as it would appear at the height of the feudal age, around 1200.

General Features: Walls, Wall Towers, Moat, Main Tower (Keep).

The castle was built on a site that was easily defendable, as a hill or cliff or plateau. The area, of larger or smaller extent according to the resources of the builder, was surrounded with high stone walls, very wide at the base and wide enough even at the top to allow the besieged, in case of attack, to man the ramparts. At certain points in its circuit the surrounding wall bulged out in round towers, giving the defenders command of the whole of its surface. Beyond the wall a deep moat or ditch was dug around the whole circumference; this was sometimes filled with water. Within the walls the principal structure, the heart of the castle, was the great tower, called in English the "keep," in French the *donjon* (dungeon). This was not placed in the centre of the area but at one corner, usually the one most remote from the gateway, and close to the outer wall, so that the defenders on the walls could retreat to it and so that at the last they could escape by a secret outlet in the walls. This tower (which in the older castles was usually rectangular, in the later ones frequently round) contained three or four stories. The ground floor had no entrance from the level of the courtyard, and was occupied by store-rooms and cells. The first story above this was the main apartment; it contained the lord's hall and private quarters of his family. Above were other rooms for members of the household and for the guard. Entrance to the tower was gained by an external stairway to the main floor, which could be removed in time of danger. Entrance could also be gained to an upper story by a foot-bridge thrown from the outer wall.

Approach to the castle was by a single practicable road. This led across the moat by a drawbridge, which was kept raised in time of danger. The main entrance was through a strong gate-tower, with enormous wooden or iron doors, a falling grill or portcullis, and other ingenious barriers. The gate-tower was occupied at all times by the warder, and in time of danger by a corps of defenders. If a surprise attack on the gateway failed, the favorite form of assault was by sapping or mining the base of the wall. Mediæval chronicles are full of stories of attack and defense of castles, as features of private feuds or wars between princes.

Entrance.

Such was the ordinary castle of the twelfth century; it must have been wanting as a residence in many of the comforts and conveniences, to say nothing of the luxuries, of life. In the thirteenth century, when some degree of order had been introduced into feudal relations, the greater lords were able to pay more attention to these matters. The most marked improvement was the building of a hall apart from the donjon, with larger and more commodious quarters, in which the lord and his household lived in peaceful times. The finer castles of this sort became the real centres of culture and of court life, in which the civilization of the feudal age came to flower.

Improvements in Castle.

To illustrate this let us examine one of the actual castles of the thirteenth century. It was built by a powerful noble of northern France, Lord Enguerrand de Coucy, about 1225. Its massive tower, one of the best examples that had survived, was still standing until the spring of 1917, when the German army on its retreat from this occupied region razed it to the ground. Referring to the illustration and description on the opposite page, and comparing it with the rude castle of the eleventh century [opposite page 132] we can measure the advance, not only in the system of defense but also in the arrangements for a lordly and dignified life. The immense round tower, built in this case so as to dominate the outer court and the entrance, is about 180 feet high and 100 feet in diameter. It contains, including a sunken ground floor, four stories and is large enough to house a garrison in time of siege. Quite at the opposite end, however, is a structure built into the outer wall, with two stories

Castle of Coucy.

THE CASTLE OF COUCY, ABOUT 1225.

From Viollet-le-Duc, Dictionnaire raisonné de l'architecture française.

Notice the lower wall which surrounds an outer court, and the elaborately protected bridge over the moat. *A*, the great tower or donjon; just beyond is seen the east end of the chapel; *B*, the large hall used for assemblies; *C*, the dwelling of the lord and his household.

above the ground floor, containing the more commodious quarters for the lord and his household in ordinary times; its large windows and wide veranda open onto the courtyard, and a fine winding stairway enclosed in a tower gives access to the apartments. All along one side of the courtyard extends the great hall, whose upper story is a vast assembly-room where the lord holds his feudal court and council with his vassals. Projecting into the courtyard from this side is the fine Gothic chapel. The castle of Coucy was not only a powerful fortress; it was also a courtly residence and the political centre of a great landed domain.

Feudal Warfare.

Armor.

Fighting occupied a large share of the time and interest of the feudal noble. The battles of the feudal age were fought mainly by knights in armor and on horseback; the infantry in the form of pikemen, crossbowmen, and archers, played a subordinate rôle. The armor of the noble warrior, before the thirteenth century, was mainly of chain mail; that is, of links of iron or steel, welded together to form coat and leggings. The head was covered with an iron or steel helmet. Exposed parts (the shoulders, breast, elbows, knees) were often protected by plates of iron or steel fastened onto the chain mail. In time these developed into the "plate armor," in which the whole body was encased in jointed plates of iron or steel. The simpler chain mail of earlier times passed out of use, and most of the specimens of armor now preserved in museums and family collections are of the later sort. As an additional defense the knight carried a long, narrow shield on his left arm, which he could swing around to cover his body crouched on the horse for the charge. (The term "squire," in French *écuyer*, commonly used for a lower rank of nobles, had its origin in the fact that the follower or attendant of the knight carried the shield (*écu*) and handed it to him when the battle began.)

Shield.

Weapons.

The weapons of attack were the long lance, with which the knight charged at his enemy, and the sword, swung at his left side by a girdle. The sword was the nobler weapon, and the one upon which the warrior most depended; for when, as usually happened, the lances were shattered in the charge, the combatants drew their heavy swords and hewed at one another in close, hand-to-hand combat.

Feudal Customs: Tournaments, Knighthood, Heraldry, etc.

The customs of the feudal age which give to it its picturesqueness and romance are very largely connected with fighting. Tournaments developed out of mock combats and trials of skill which were part of the training of the young noble. The ceremony of knighting, which became so elaborate in the later age, had its origin in the practice of conferring arms and armor upon the young noble when he came of age and was prepared to participate in what that period and society considered the serious business of life. Heraldry probably developed from the practice of painting or fastening a design on the face of the shield; such marks served to distinguish knights from one another when they were hidden by helmet and armor. They were handed on from father to son and became family "coats of arms."

Ideals of Chivalry.

Not only the customs but the virtues and manners of the noble were largely those of a warrior class. Personal strength and skill in arms, bravery, and a strong sense of personal worth and honor were the most highly prized virtues. Gentler qualities held in esteem were fidelity to the pledged word, courtesy to equals, and respect for women (though the last was confined to women of the noble class, and was more apparent in the romantic literature of the age than in the practice of the nobles). The combination of these qualities constitutes what we call "chivalry." They had their defects: strength and courage might appear as brutality, the sense of personal honor as quarrelsomeness and arrogance. Nevertheless, the feudal age has bequeathed to modern times two fine conceptions: namely, romance and chivalry, without which our own civilization would be much poorer.

By its demands and the ability to pay for having its demands supplied feudal society fostered many important arts. Chief of these was architecture; in the development of that art the building of feudal castles stands close in importance to the build-

SECTION OF THE BAYEUX TAPESTRY.

The Bayeux Tapestry was made to record the Norman invasion of England of 1066. It is attributed to Matilda, wife of William the Conqueror. Note the chain-mail armor, the simple form of the helmet, the long triangular shield. This represents an early stage of arms and armor.

EFFIGY OF AN ENGLISH NOBLE.
From a tombstone dated 1277.

WARRIOR KNEELING.

Illustration of a manuscript. Note the coat of mail with sleeves, hand-covering and hood all of one piece, and the more elaborate helmet lying on the ground. The legs are given additional protection by what appear to be leather guards studded with metal rings. The cloth coat over the coat of mail is decorated with the same design as the pennant; this is the "arms," or armorial design, of the knight.

From Quicherat, Histoire de Costume en France.

ing of cathedrals. To supply his material needs the feudal noble required the work of the smith, the cabinet-maker, the carver, the weaver, and the dyer; and these artisans produced for him beautiful specimens of their handiwork, some of which are still preserved—steel blades and armor, carved furniture, tapestries, and gorgeous cloths. The books he owned were few, but the work of adorning them with colored drawings had a considerable part in the development of modern art.

Arts and Crafts of the Feudal Age.

One of the chief contributions of feudal society to the body of culture which we have inherited was the literature produced by poets to satisfy the intellectual and spiritual needs of the noble class. The favorite type was the long narrative poem, reciting the adventures and heroic deeds of legendary figures, such as Roland and the other warriors of Charlemagne's army, King Arthur and his knights, and the Greek and Trojan heroes of the Trojan war. The poets pictured these legendary heroes as feudal nobles of their own age, and embellished their stories with incidents and descriptions which would appeal to their noble audiences. The type of literature which we call the romance was very largely the product of this literary movement of the feudal age.

Literature of the Feudal Age.

In summing up the discussion of feudalism as a historical movement, we may say that it was essentially a makeshift. In the period between the collapse of the public government of the Roman empire and the formation of the strong national monarchies of the later Middle Age, society grouped itself about private leaders of the land-holding class. It served an important purpose, however, in holding men together in some sort of order during this period of transition, and it left indelible marks on the later life of western European peoples. Changing conditions in the later Middle Age deprived it of its dominating position in government and society. The relative importance of the feudal noble steadily declined before the growth of public royal governments, which took from him his political supremacy; before the growth of cities and of a power-

Feudalism a Transitory Form of Society.

Causes of its Decline.

ful middle class of traders, manufacturers, and bankers, which deprived him of his economic supremacy; before the development of national armies equipped with firearms, which deprived him of his military supremacy. To the development of these new forces feudalism stood as a barrier which was doomed to be swept away.

Survivals of Feudal Elements in Modern Society

While feudalism as a system passed away, it left on European society an imprint which is easily recognized to-day. Noble titles are still used and imply a superior position in the social scale, not only above that of the common people but above that also of the wealthy and influential class of merchants and capitalists. Members of the aristocracy affect an attitude of superiority toward those engaged in "trade." This attitude, it may be noticed, is much less general in England to-day than it was in the age of Thackeray. Lands are still held in the form of large estates, belonging to the titled class and cultivated by tenants, whose rents furnish the revenues of their lords. The military character of feudal society has been transmitted to modern times to a certain extent. In the period before the French Revolution, the armies were officered entirely by members of the titled class; and even in recent times, when armies are based on the duty of every citizen to serve, the officers are largely drawn from that class because of its traditions. Hence the "militaristic" sentiment, the belief in war as a noble pursuit, is a survival of feudal ideals.

CHAPTER VIII

THE DEVELOPMENT OF THE PAPACY

THE papacy can boast of being the oldest institution of Europe. Beginning with St. Peter and including the present pope, Benedict XV, it counts an unbroken line of two hundred and sixty-five rulers, some of them the most remarkable men of their age. At one time the bishop of Rome was (and still is for the Catholic world) the supreme authority in all matters pertaining to doctrine and morals. Even kings and emperors have humbled themselves before him and done penance at his command. As early as the sixth century he was already a temporal ruler, being really, if not technically, the lord and governor of Rome and the territory immediately about it. This position he held for about thirteen hundred years, losing it only in 1870, when the Italians took Rome by force and made it the capital of united Italy. For some hundreds of years he was, or strove to be, the overlord of all Christian countries, claiming the divine right to dispose of crowns and kingdoms, to make and unmake emperors, and to dictate in matters of government in each country. As a consequence of this, he was an international, or rather "supernational," political power in Europe, interfering at will in the internal as well as in the external affairs of every nation. So completely was the world subject to papal domination during the Middle Age that a knowledge of papal history is necessary for understanding the period.

Importance of the Papacy.

We must at the outset have a clear idea of the various offices and powers which the pope has at different times held. On the spiritual side he is (1) the bishop of Rome, and exercises his episcopal authority in his diocese as any other bishop does. (2) He has the position of an archbishop, having six (formerly seven) suffragan bishops under him. (3) He was also for a while called patriarch. (4) He is also the universal bishop, having the whole world for his diocese, and possessing authority superior to that of the local bishop. (5) As to his temporal power, he was the sovereign of Rome and the territory about it (the so-called papal states), governing it in his own right (to 1870). (6) Lastly, he was the lord of the whole Christian world, responsible to God for the good government of it, with the right and duty to control all temporal rulers and to depose all those who did not govern in a Christian manner. It must not, however, be supposed that the bishop of Rome from the first exercised all these powers. On the contrary, his claims were developed slowly, and often encountered stubborn resistance. In fact, the Greek part of the church never recognized the bishop of Rome as the bishop of the whole church, and the chief governments of Europe resisted the papal claims to temporal sovereignty over them, and submitted only when the force of circumstances compelled them to do so.

Sixfold Office of the Pope.

By way of introduction, as well as to explain the character and origin of the first three offices named, a brief account of the way in which the government of the church was developed is here in place. During the first three centuries of the existence of the church, an increasing honor was attached to the bishops of those congregations which had been founded by an apostle. Chief of these "apostolic" churches were those of Jerusalem, Antioch, Ephesus, Cæsarea, Corinth, Rome, and Alexandria, whose church was believed to have been founded by St. Mark the Evangelist, the companion of St. Peter. The chief reason of their importance and honor was the fact that the successive bishops of such a church were supposed to have preserved in a pure form the "tradition," that is, the oral teachings, of the apostle who had preached there. The high rank of the bishops of these cities, however, rested on sentiment and was not fixed by any official action.

"Apostolic" Churches.

R., 18, 19.

"Tradition."

This so-called "apostolic" principle was an impracticable as well as an inadequate basis on which to build a great institution, such as the government of the church was, and consequently the advancing organization of the church during the fourth century was carried out on a different plan. In working out its organization—a process which lasted some centuries—the church naturally used the government of the empire as its model. That is, the earliest ecclesiastical divisions coincided with existing political divisions, and the rank of an ecclesiastic was determined by the political rank of his city. There was the same lack of system, therefore, in the organization of the church as was found in that of the empire. Diocletian introduced system into the political organization by dividing the whole empire into four prefectures, each prefecture into a number of dioceses, and each diocese into a number of provinces. This organization the church adopted in some degree of completeness only in the prefecture of the east; at the head of each of its five dioceses (whose capitals were Antioch, Alexandria, Ephesus, Cæsarea, and Heraclea) there was an ecclesiastical head, called a patriarch; over each of the provinces of these dioceses there was an archbishop (also called metropolitan), and over each city there was a bishop. In the east, therefore, where the organization of the church had gone farthest, the offices in the order of their rank in an ascending scale were parish priest, bishop, archbishop (metropolitan), and patriarch. There the church made no attempt to develop an official over the whole prefecture, who should be superior to the patriarchs. In the other three prefectures of the empire the ecclesiastical organization was not completed on these lines. There the chief bishop of each province came to be an archbishop, but no ecclesiastical head corresponding to the patriarch in the east was developed over the dioceses, except, of course, in that of Italy. This may be explained (1) by the fact that the dioceses of the west did not generally have as capitals large and ancient cities, such as Ephesus, Antioch, and Alexandria were. (2) Nor could the churches of the cities

Organization of Church Follows Organization of Empire.

Patriarch, Archbishop, Bishop.

No Patriarch in the West except at Rome.

R., 21.

in the west boast that they had been founded by apostles. (3) The organization of the church in the west was arrested by the invasions of the barbarians and other serious political disturbances.

S. B., 33.

(4) And the bishop of Rome early put forth the claim to ecclesiastical supremacy, and was able to overcome the "patriarchal" aspirations of all other bishops. Consequently, no other patriarch was developed in the west. There the offices in the order of their rank were parish priest, bishop, archbishop (metropolitan), and pope.*

As local bishop, archbishop, and patriarch, the bishop of Rome does not differ in any respect from other bishops, archbishops, and patriarchs. We may therefore proceed at once to discuss the manner in which he became universal bishop, with the whole world for his diocese.

The Struggle.

R., 20, 22, 23, 25.

The claim of the bishop of Rome to the supreme headship of the church, as it became more and more clearly defined, met with increasing opposition. It is an admitted fact that the bishop of Rome never actually exercised any real authority over the church in the east. It is equally certain that his authority was not from the first recognized in all the west. The more distant archbishops and bishops, and even some of the archbishops of Italy (Ravenna, Milan, Aquileia), continued for some centuries to maintain their independence of Rome, and acted to all intents and purposes as patriarchs, though not possessing that title. After a long struggle, however, the bishop of Rome came out victorious, and was accepted throughout the west as the head of the church.

To this victory certain factors contributed materially, though in various degrees. (1) Rome had an important advantage

* Although the title "patriarch" did not secure a fixed place in the scale of offices in the Catholic church, it is not unknown there. In accordance with its historical origin, its holder outranks archbishops. There are at present ten patriarchates: Venice, Lisbon, Alexandria, Antioch, Jerusalem, Constantinople, Cilicia, the East Indies, the West Indies, and Babylon. The bishop of Rome ceased to call himself patriarch because that name seemed to put him on the same plane as the other patriarchs. He adopted the title of pope (a Greek word meaning father) and, in order that it might indicate his unique position, he appropriated it to his exclusive use.

over all other capitals of dioceses in that it had been the capital of the empire and the chief city of the west. Its ancient rank no doubt still had some influence on the minds of men, and caused greater honor to be paid to its bishop than to any other ecclesiastic in the west.

Influence of Rome.

(2) During the persecutions as well as during the invasions of the barbarians, the bishop of Rome zealously interfered on behalf of all the oppressed, and generously contributed money to the relief of the distressed. Everywhere in the west he boldly interceded with barbarian kings on behalf of the conquered and suffering orthodox provincials, whose grateful affection he thereby won.

Pope Aids the Distressed.

(3) He was especially fortunate in being the only patriarch in the west except that of Venice. Certain other bishops and archbishops held for a time an independent position, but they had no special title which indicated or justified their independence.

The Only Patriarch in the West

(4) During the long and intricate theological discussions (300–800), the bishop of Rome was always on that side of every question which eventually came to be regarded as orthodox. He could therefore convincingly point to his record, and declare that the Roman church had never erred.*

Always Orthodox.

(5) The legislation of some of the great church councils† led the bishop of Rome to assert his headship of the whole church more vigorously than ever, basing his claim on what is called the Petrine theory. Because Constantinople had become the

* It is frequently said that the council of Sardica (now Sofia, in Bulgaria), 343, recognized the pope as the supreme head of the church by enacting that appeals might be made to him. This council was, in fact, attended only by westerners, and its decrees were never accepted by the Greeks. It enacted that any bishop who felt that he had been wrongfully deposed might appeal to Julian (who was then bishop of Rome), who might either ratify the deposition or summon a new council for the purpose of rehearing the case.

† The councils of Nicæa, 325, Constantinople, 381, Ephesus, 431, Chalcedon, 451, Constantinople, 553, Constantinople, 680, and Nicæa, 787, are known as the seven ecumenical (*i. e.*, universal) councils, whose decrees are accepted by Greeks, Roman Catholics, and Protestants alike.

residence of one of the emperors, the council which was held there in 381, acting on the principle that the political rank of a city determined the ecclesiastical rank of its bishop, made the bishop of Constantinople a patriarch. It further enacted that because Rome was the ancient capital, and therefore more honorable, its patriarch should have the first place of honor; and that because Constantinople was the younger capital its patriarch should have the second place of honor. The council of Chalcedon, however, in 451 decreed that because Rome and Constantinople were the two capitals of the empire their patriarchs should have the same rank and honor, and should be equal in position, power, and authority, and should enjoy the same degree of superiority over all the other clergy.

Action of Councils.

To this action of the council Leo the Great (440–461), who was then bishop of Rome, objected. He refused to recognize the patriarch of Constantinople as his equal in authority, and declared that the fact that Rome was a capital of the empire had nothing whatever to do with his supremacy over the church. Freely admitting that Constantinople was one of the capitals of the empire, he declared that not the political rank of a city but the apostolic origin of its church determined the ecclesiastical rank of its bishop. Accordingly, the bishops of churches which had been founded by apostles enjoyed a higher rank than all other bishops. And of all the churches founded by apostles, that of Rome was supreme, because St. Peter, the prince of the apostles, had not only established it but had also been its first bishop; and, although he had established other congregations, he had been bishop in Rome, and had attached all his rights, dignity, and supremacy to the office of bishop of Rome in such a way that all his successors in that office inherited them, and thus became rulers of the whole church and endued with supreme power over it.*

The Petrine Theory.

S B., 35.
O., 10.
R., 24.

* The supremacy of St. Peter is based on the words of Jesus to him: "Thou art Peter, and upon this rock I will build my church; and the gates of hell shall not prevail against it. And I will give unto thee the keys of the kingdom of heaven: and whatsoever thou shalt bind on

The east, however, refused to accept this theory, and it is still one of the chief differences between the Greek and Roman churches. Even in the west Leo's authority was at that time far from being everywhere recognized. The Germans, who had taken possession of nearly all the west, were heretics and of course refused to acknowledge the pope's authority over them. In this way his influence had been destroyed in Africa by the Vandals, in Spain and southern Gaul by the West Goths and Suevi, and in the Rhône valley by the Burgundians. And his position was to become even worse, for a few years later the East Goths took possession of a large part of Italy (488–553), and they were followed by the Lombards (568–774), a still more vigorous people, who were not only heretics but, in their ambition to rule all Italy, made war on the pope and threatened to deprive him of the city of Rome and of all his lands. The permanent establishment of a Lombard kingdom with its capital at Rome would have made impossible the development of the medieval papacy as we know it.

The Pope Won the West by Mission Work.

From this critical situation the papacy was rescued by a broad and energetic mission work, coupled with a few events which, in their nature, seemed accidental. Among the latter may be classed the conversion of the Franks to the orthodox faith. In 496 Chlodovech, king of the Franks, accepted the orthodox form of Christianity, and soon set himself to destroy his heretical neighbors. By driving the West Goths over the Pyrenees and conquering the Burgundians he made all Gaul orthodox. Thanks to the persistent efforts of the pope and the Catholic clergy, the West Goths in Spain and the Lombards in Italy were gradually converted from their heresy and brought into subjection to the pope. A most important step was taken in 596, when Gregory I

earth shall be bound in heaven: and whatsoever thou shalt loose on earth shall be loosed in heaven" (Matt. 16 : 18*f*.). This passage was further reinforced by the words: "Feed my sheep" (John 21 : 15*ff*.), and "When thou art converted strengthen thy brethren" (Luke 22 : 32). From these and similar passages Leo inferred that to Peter was committed the supreme power over the church. The keys, which symbolized this supreme authority, had been intrusted to him in a special manner.

sent St. Augustine with some forty monks as missionaries to the pagan Angles, Saxons, and Jutes, who had taken possession of Britain. Since they were Roman monks sent out as missionaries by the bishop of Rome, they carried with them as a part of their faith the Petrine theory of the universal supremacy of the pope. They landed in Kent, whose king received them kindly and gave them permission to establish themselves in Canterbury. They met with success and soon extended their labors beyond the boundaries of Kent. Before the end of the seventh century all the little kingdoms of Angles and Saxons had accepted Christianity, and with it the tenet of papal supremacy. Roman Catholic England then furnished the man who was to reorganize the church among the Franks, to convert the more distant tribes, which had still remained independent and heathen, and to establish the authority of the pope over all Frankland. This was the work of Boniface.

St. Augustine and the English.

S. B., 39. O., 9. R., 27–31, 39–42.

Winfred, or Boniface, as he is generally called, was a West Saxon, born toward the end of the seventh century. He became a Benedictine monk and chose to become a missionary among the Franks. Although they had been nominally converted, Boniface in his letters gives a gloomy picture of the state of their religion and morals. Heathen beliefs and practices were mingled with their Christianity, and the clergy were ignorant and undisciplined. Worse than that in his eyes was the fact that they did not recognize the headship of the pope. Boniface carried with him as an article of his faith the tenet of papal supremacy, and this he taught to the Franks and to all the tribes which he converted. He visited Rome several times and secured the papal blessing on his work. The pope, perceiving the immense advantages which he might derive from the work of Boniface, made him a missionary bishop to the Germans, and showed that he regarded Germany as his diocese by requiring Boniface to take the same oath of obedience and faithfulness to him as he required of the bishops in the diocese of Rome. With the support of the Frankish government Boniface overcame the

Boniface and the Germans.

S. B., 40. R., 43–47.

difficulties in his way. He reformed the church in all the kingdom of the Franks, and completed its organization by the establishment of new bishoprics (Wuerzburg, Erfurt, Buraburg near Fritzlar). Boniface himself was made archbishop of Mainz. So well did he do his work that he deserved to be called the apostle of Germany. His missionary zeal led him to resign his archbishopric in 753 and to go with a large number of helpers as a missionary to the Frisians, at whose hands he met a martyr's death (754). The far-reaching effects of his work could not then be foreseen, but it resulted in the subjection of the west to papal authority. For it was from this church of Germany, now thoroughly dependent on the pope and holding to the dogma of his headship of the church, that Christianity was to be carried to the remaining German tribes (such as the Saxons and Scandinavians), and to the Slavic peoples east of the Germans. Unfortunately for the papacy, missionaries of the Greek church found their way among the Russians, and thereby set a limit to the extension of the papal church toward the east. But the west now acknowledged the supremacy of the pope. It was his by right of a bloodless conquest that reflects great honor on him and his devoted missionaries. It remained only for him to confirm his possession of it, and Gregory VII (1073–1085) did this by means of his legates.

Sacerdotal Character of Clergy.

The increasing separation of the clergy from the laity and their development into a priestly class had some influence on the growth of the ecclesiastical power of the pope, for it gave him an opportunity to put himself at the head of the clergy. The sacerdotal character of the clergy was the basis for their separation from the laity. All clergymen by their ordination received the priestly or sacerdotal character which expressed itself in their dress, their higher morals, and their manner of living; and, most important of all, it gave them the exclusive right and power to administer the sacraments. Now, it seemed to them that, possessing this priestly character and being intrusted with the administration of divine things, they ought to be exempt from the laws governing ordinary men. So for some centuries the clergy worked to secure privileges for themselves as a class and finally to free themselves entirely from the authority of the state. Their desire to escape from all secular control was probably increased by the fact that the emperor attempted to dictate the creed, that he made and deposed bishops, and that even the heretical kings of the Germans (East Goths, West Goths, Burgundians, Lombards) did the same. The clergy had very early been freed from taxes and certain public duties which were burdensome. Then they sought to be freed from the law of the state, declaring that only the clergy were competent to sit in judgment on the clergy, and demanding that all clergymen who were accused of a crime should be tried by their fellow clergymen and not by laymen. In this they were successful, and so the clergy came to form "a state within a state." They became, in fact, a great international state or organization, with the pope at their head. They were subject neither to the king nor to the law of the land in which they lived, but they naturally looked to the pope as their ruler, and in all struggles with the secular government they sought his aid.*

The Clergy Free from Law of the State.

In order to understand the origin of the temporal power of the pope it is necessary to begin with the relation between the state and religion in the Roman empire. According to Roman principles (both republican and imperial), religion and its min-

* This desire to free themselves from the law of the state led to a series of forgeries which culminated in the famous collection known as the Pseudo-Isidorean Decretals. The collection consists of some three hundred documents (chiefly acts of councils, letters, and decrees of popes, ranging from the fourth pope, Clement I, to the sixty-sixth, Gregory the Great, 590–604), many of which are spurious. The chief purpose of most of these forgeries was to show that the law of the church, as found in the decrees of both popes and councils, was superior to the law of the state, and that the clergy were subject only to the law of the church; anathema and excommunication should fall on all who violated the law of the church, and where the two bodies of law conflicted, that of the church always had the precedence. All this tended to the establishment of ecclesiastical courts and the formation of a body of law (canon law) applicable only to the clergy. In time a large body of ecclesiastical law was developed (canon law, *corpus juris canonici*) by which the clergy were governed.

isters were under the control of the government. Rome had a state religion, and all priests were state officials. When Constantine made the practice of Christianity legal he took the same attitude toward the new religion that he had had toward the old. He and his successors assumed authority over the church and the clergy; they called the church councils, presided over them, and made their decrees valid by imperial sanction. They controlled and confirmed the election of bishops, and deposed them at pleasure. Even the bishop of Rome was not an exception to this rule, for he could not be consecrated until his election had been confirmed by the emperor, and in the sixth and seventh centuries the emperors deposed and punished various popes who refused to obey them.* Some of the emperors attempted to dictate even in matters of doctrine. In a word, Christianity was the state religion and the Christian clergy were officials of the state.

The Roman Empire Controlled Religion.

S. B., 37, 38.

Since the clergy were officials of the state, the emperor felt that he had a right to their services in other than ecclesiastical matters. Relying on the uprightness and fairness of the clergy, the emperors intrusted them, especially the bishops, with an oversight over various secular officials and matters. In the midst of the violence of the times (350–600) the emperor gladly made use of the clergy to assist in the preservation of order and in the administration of justice. At the same time, in the general paralysis or destruction of government which was caused by the invasions of the barbarians (375–600), the clergy were confronted with the duty of resisting the violence of the invaders and of performing the functions of the civil government. The bishops did not shrink from these new and important duties which circumstances thrust upon them, but met them in a commendable spirit of helpfulness and self-sacrifice. They justified their

Emperors Used the Clergy in Secular Affairs.

* Thus Justinian I (527–565) deposed Pope Vigilius (537–555), and exiled him because he (with some hesitation) refused to accept the imperial statement of a certain doctrine. For a like reason Constans II seized the pope Martin I (649–655), and deposed and exiled him (653).

exercise of secular functions by declaring that their office bound them to protect the weak and defenseless, and to prevent injustice and oppression. So by the end of the sixth century the bishops throughout the west were performing certain secular functions, assumed sometimes at the command of the emperor, but more often under the pressure of circumstances.

This, which is true of bishops in general in the west, is especially true of the bishop of Rome, and may be regarded as one of the roots from which sprang his temporal sovereignty.

The Pope as Landlord.

It had another root also in the power which the pope exercised as a great landlord. In 321 Constantine issued a decree giving the Christian church the right to hold property. From that time the bishop of Rome as the representative of St. Peter received large and numerous gifts of land, chiefly from the emperors and from rich and noble families. All these lands taken together were known as the "patrimony* of St. Peter." It was also popularly called the "possession of the poor," and the popes managed it in a manner worthy of the purpose for which it had been given to St. Peter. They were solicitous that the serfs and slaves who tilled it should neither be overworked nor harshly dealt with, and that they should not be oppressed by the exorbitant demands of the papal overseers. The large income from the patrimony was wisely spent.† Now, since the

The Patrimony of St. Peter.

* After 600 this patrimony was not materially enlarged by further gifts, because (1) the liberality of the emperors, who lived then in the east, ceased entirely, and (2) the rich families of Italy had been either ruined or destroyed by wars and the invasions of the barbarians, especially of the Lombards. The lands of the patrimony were widely scattered; they were found in all parts of Italy and in the neighboring islands, in Gaul, in Africa, in Dalmatia, and even in the Greek part of the empire. For the purpose of managing them they were united into groups: a number of farms (*fundi*) formed a *massa*, and a number of *massæ* were called a *patrimony*, and designated by the name of the province in which the lands were situated. The patrimony of Sicily was probably the richest of all because of the great quantities of grain which it produced, while the patrimony of southern Italy was important for its forests, which supplied the popes with building-materials.

† (1) A part of it went to support the papal household, the clergy, and the officials who managed the patrimony. (2) The popes used some of it to keep churches in repair and to build new ones, to found

pope was dependent on the patrimony for means to carry on the work of the church, he was deeply and directly interested in everything that concerned it. Everything that affected the patrimony affected him, and all who were in any way dependent on him. On this account there grew up a community of interest between the pope and the people of all the provinces in which he had large possessions.*

Pope and People Have Common Interests.

and support monasteries, hospitals, orphan asylums, hospices for pilgrims and travellers, and homes for the poor. (3) Some of it they used for the purchase of freedom for Christian slaves, and for the ransom of prisoners of war. (4) And lastly, they had to expend a considerable part of it in feeding the people of Rome, who had been pauperized by the free distribution of grain by the emperors and rich Romans. In this important respect the pope early took the place of the emperor, and probably nothing else that he did brought him greater popularity in Rome.

* The growth of this feeling of solidarity between the pope and the people of Italy, and his consequent representation of them in political matters may be traced in the following incidents—a few selected from the many. Since there was no emperor in Rome (after 476 there was none in Italy) when the barbarians invaded Italy, both because of his landed interests and his ecclesiastical position it fell to him to represent the people against the invaders. When Alaric besieged Rome (410) the pope acted as the intermediary between him and the emperor, who was living in Ravenna. Leo I is said to have met Attila and turned him back from Rome, and it is certain that by his entreaties he mitigated to some extent the ferocity of the Vandals when they sacked Rome (455). During the rule of the East Goths in Italy the pope frequently appeared before Theodoric the Great in Ravenna to present appeals, or to represent the interests of the people of various parts of Italy, and he excused himself to Theodoric for mingling in secular matters by declaring that it was the duty of his office to champion the cause of the weak and oppressed. When the emperor was persecuting the Arians in the east Theodoric used the pope as his ambassador to the emperor to demand that he accord the Arians better treatment. A few years later Theodohat, king of the East Goths, sent the pope to Constantinople to beg the emperor to cease from his war against the East Goths. Justinian, in the pragmatic sanction by which he regulated the affairs of Italy (554), recognized the high position of the pope and of bishops in general, and assigned them definite secular duties. He gave all bishops a voice in the election of officials, with the authority to oversee their conduct in office. And he also deposited standard weights and measures with the pope and commanded him in conjunction with the senate to see that these were used throughout Italy.

S. B., 36.

Because of this solidarity between the pope and the people of Rome his secular duties and political activity rapidly increased after the Lombards entered Italy (568). He acted as the intermediary between the emperor and the exarch on the one hand and the Lombards on the other. Rome itself was in danger, and Gregory I was compelled to take upon himself the defense of the city. He begged both the emperor and the exarch for help. When he found that neither could protect him he made peace with the Lombards on his own responsibility. He had to furnish the money to carry on the government of Rome; he resisted the decisions of the imperial officials, and even opposed the emperor himself on behalf of some people who had been falsely accused; the people turned naturally to him and begged him to lay their appeals before the emperor or the king of the Lombards; the oversight of the defense of the city fell upon him and he reproved or praised the leaders of the troops; when the troops in Naples were without a leader, he appointed one for them; and when Nepi was without a governor, he appointed one for that city. Gregory I (590–604) said that his political duties were so absorbing and numerous that he could hardly tell whether he was an ecclesiastical or secular official.

The Pope Improves All Opportunities.

This solidarity showed itself in a striking manner when the growing dissatisfaction of the Italians with the imperial (Greek) government caused them to rally around the pope, who was the only part of the government that was still Italian. Of the former government of Rome the pope was all that was left. The senate* was no longer of importance; the prefect of the city, who had once been the governor, the mayor, the police director, and the judge of the city, was now merely a judge, and all his other functions had passed into the hands of the pope. Since 553 Greek officials had taken the place of

Italians Support the Pope against the Emperor.

The Pope's Power in Rome Increases.

* It is generally believed that the senate ceased to exist, since it is not mentioned after 603. Yet the senatorial class, the nobility, still existed, and about 750 the "holy senate" wrote a letter to Pippin (See M. G. Epp, III, 510).

Italians in all the government offices, and both as foreigners and as merciless tax-collectors they were hated by the people. These Greek officials were no doubt often guilty of injustice and oppression. Now, the pope was the only one who was in a position to interfere with them on behalf of the Italians. Community of interests, racial feeling, and Roman pride in the pope as an Italian and as the last relic of their old government, all combined to unite the Italians to the pope in such a way as to form something like a state. As the bonds of this union grew stronger the pope began to act with more independence. The time came when, backed by the arms of the Italians, he was able to resist the commands of the emperor, and even to free himself to a great extent from imperial domination. The power of the pope was daily growing into a state with all of sovereignty except the name.

The Pope Controls the Militia of Rome.

The pope acquired an important sovereign power when he got possession of the military forces of Rome. Toward the middle of the seventh century mention is made of a military organization of the Italians, which seems to have been much like what we call militia, or home guards. The frequent inroads of the Lombards had no doubt led the people to organize for their protection. This militia put itself under the command of the pope, and chiefly through its support he was enabled to resist successfully the emperor's commands.* In resisting the emperors the popes were struggling not only for themselves but also for the freedom of Italy. This the Italians understood, and the time came when they took up arms to defend their pope against their emperor.†

* The troops of Rome passed completely into the pope's hands. Thus, in 730 he put his generals and a part of his troops at the disposal of the exarch to quell a rebellion in Tuscany. In 778 Adrian I spoke of them as "our general army."

† In 692 a council held in Constantinople formulated doctrines in accordance with the command of the emperor. These doctrines Pope Sergius I (687–701) rejected, and the emperor sent a high official to Rome to take him and bring him a prisoner to Constantinople. Hearing of this, the militia of Ravenna and of the Pentapolis hastened to Rome, surrounded the papal palace, demanded to see the pope, and

Papal independence and resistance to the emperor became pronounced under Gregory II (715–731). The emperor, Leo III (716–741), attempted to levy a tax on Italy, including the patrimony of St. Peter. To this Gregory II objected and the militia of Italy supported him. In 727 the emperor forbade the religious use of images and ordered them to be removed from the churches. The pope opposed this also, and published the statement that the emperor's command was heretical. When the exarch and the imperial officials (dukes) attempted to enforce it the people rebelled against them in support of the pope. The militia even killed the exarch and various other officials who tried to carry out the decree. Gregory II then took a step hitherto unheard of. In a vigorous letter he condemned the imperial action and excommunicated the emperor. He declared in the plainest terms that matters of faith and worship concerned not the emperor but the pope. His successor, Gregory III (731–741), excommunicated in a formal way all who opposed images. The emperor was unable to send troops into Italy to punish the pope and his supporters, but he confiscated the rich patrimony of St. Peter in Sicily and southern Italy. Although this quarrel was very bitter, it did not signify that Italy freed itself from imperial rule. Imperial officials were still in Italy and even in Rome, and friendly relations between the pope and emperor were later renewed (after 741).

The Pope Excommunicates the Emperor.

S. B., 41, 42.

The policy of the Lombards had so important an influence on the development of the secular power of the pope that it is necessary to recount their history, dull though it be, at some length. The coming of the Lombards (568) and their desire to rule all Italy rendered the position of the pope precarious. He was threatened with the domination of a heretical king, and was therefore forced into greater political activity in order to maintain

The Pope Heads the Opposition to the Lombards.

refused to go away until the imperial official had withdrawn from the city, leaving the pope in security. A few years later the militia of all Italy came to Rome to protect the pope, John VI (701–705), when it was reported that the emperor was going to seize him.

the freedom which he had won. About 700 the provinces of Italy which were under the rule of the exarch were (1) Istria, (2) Venice, (3) Ravenna, (4) the Pentapolis, (5) Perugia, (6) Rome, (7) Naples, and (8) Calabria. Although the exarch was the nominal ruler of these duchies, as they were all called, the pope's authority in them was actually greater than his. The pope had a large income and could count on the arms of the militia, while the exarch had but meagre financial resources and few troops on whom he could rely. The task of holding all these duchies together and preserving them against the attacks of the Lombards devolved, therefore, upon the pope. He assumed the task for two special reasons: (1) The Lombards did not spare his patrimony, and (2) as they were several times on the point of conquering all Italy the pope's position of untrammelled freedom depended on his maintaining the political unity of the provinces of central Italy with himself at their head.* To this end he adopted the policy of allying himself

* The pope's first care was to prevent the Lombards from getting possession of the roads which connected these duchies. In 717 the duke of Benevento took Cumæ and cut off the free communication between Rome and Naples. Gregory II paid the Neapolitan militia seventy pounds to retake it. In 728 Liutprand, king of the Lombards, seized Sutri, and thus cut off communication between Rome and Perugia. In order to secure its restoration the pope made use of an argument which was later to become the basis for the founding of an ecclesiastical state. Wishing to produce an overwhelming effect on Liutprand, the pope declared that Rome and all its possessions were under the special protection of St. Peter, and any violation of his rights would bring down a severe penalty upon the offender; violence against the lands of St. Peter was sacrilege and would be punished accordingly; Liutprand might, however, gain the favor and blessing of the prince of the apostles by restoring his possessions to him. This produced the desired effect, and he restored Sutri.

In 728 the exarch made a determined effort to enforce the decree against the use of images and to compel the pope to accept it. To this end he secured the aid of Liutprand by agreeing first to aid him in reducing the rebellious Lombard dukes of Spoleto and Benevento to subjection. Their expedition against Spoleto and Benevento was successful, and Liutprand received the submission of their dukes, but when they appeared before Rome to besiege it, the pope so impressed Liutprand with the danger of attacking St. Peter's possessions that he refused to aid the exarch against Rome and withdrew. Sometime between 731 and 735 Liutprand attacked the exarch and took Ravenna for a short time. The pope, who did not wish to see the power of with the dukes of Benevento and Spoleto, who had, in the hope of re-establishing their independence, rebelled against Liutprand, the king of the Lombards. Liutprand, however, drove out the duke of Spoleto, who then fled to Rome. When Liutprand appeared before the city and demanded the surrender of his rebellious vassal, both the pope and the people of Rome refused. Liutprand besieged Rome in vain, because the popes (Sisinnius, Gregory II, and Gregory III) had repaired its walls and put it in a good state of defense. In his distress the pope appealed to Charles Martel, but in vain. Fortunately, Liutprand, finding that he could not take the city, gave up the siege and withdrew, although he devastated the duchy and seized some of the papal castles. In 742 Liutprand again besieged Ravenna, but yielded to the pope's entreaties and withdrew. The pope then had a short respite.

The Lombards Besiege Rome.

S. B., 43.

Liutprand had felt that his people must possess all Italy, but every time he had tried to advance his boundaries the pope had blocked him. His death in 744 was followed by a struggle for the crown, during which the rival candidates had no leisure for conquest. The successful one, Rachis, had at first no desire to break with the pope. But he too soon felt that the existence of the Lombards was bound up with the possession of all Italy, and in 749 he began the advance by taking forcible possession of Perugia. Again the pope held up before him the heinousness of his sin in attacking the lands of St. Peter, and Rachis was so impressed that he resigned his crown and went into a monastery to spend the rest of his life in penance. This, however, was the last time that the entreaties of the pope and the fear of St. Peter were effectual. The new king, Aistulf, renewed the policy of his predecessors, and tried to unite all Italy under Lombard sway. In 751 he seized the exarchate, the Pentapolis,

Rachis.

Aistulf.

the Lombards increased, did all he could to recover the city for the exarch. In 738 the duke of Spoleto seized Gallese, a papal castle protecting the road from Rome to Ravenna. After trying all other means in vain to recover it the pope paid a heavy ransom for it.

and Perugia, and at least threatened Venice and Istria. He took everything, in fact, up to the duchy of Rome. With this the Greek rule in northern Italy was at an end. Deaf to all expostulations and threats, Aistulf refused to restore any of his conquests, but was willing to make a treaty with the pope for forty years and to promise not to attack the duchy of Rome. He broke the treaty, however, within four months and invaded the duchy of Rome. He demanded (1) a poll tax from every Roman, and (2) complete jurisdiction in the duchy. These demands the pope must resist by force, for if he did not the papal government would come to an end. But where was he to find the necessary aid? Just then imperial ambassadors appeared at Rome, bringing a command from the emperor to the effect that the pope should aid in recovering all the imperial possessions in Italy. This the pope, Stephen III, was willing and anxious to do, but he knew that it could be done only by force. Accordingly, he demanded troops of the emperor. Again imperial ambassadors came, bringing in the place of troops a command that the pope should proceed to Aistulf and demand the restoration of the Greek lands which he had conquered. In the meantime, the pope, foreseeing that he could have no help from Constantinople, had sent ambassadors to Pippin, king of the Franks, and had secured from him an invitation to visit him in Frankland. In company with the ambassadors of both the emperor and Pippin, the pope went to see Aistulf and laid before him the demand of the emperor. Aistulf refused it, and the pope proceeded to Frankland, where he spent several months, the guest of the Frankish king.

The Pope Appeals to Pippin.

Cf. S. B., 41–46.

Stephen III besought Pippin to assume the protection of the cause of St. Peter and of the "state of the Romans" (it is uncertain whether this expression means the empire or the duchy of Rome, though probably the latter), and to bring about a permanent peace between them (*i. e.*, St. Peter and the "state of the Romans") and the Lombards. This he should do peaceably, if possible; otherwise through armed intervention. Stephen asked

The Pope in Frankland.

S. B., 44, 45.

that peace be re-established not on the basis of the existing holdings of the Lombards, but that they should surrender to him as the representative of the interests of the "state of the Romans" all their recent conquests. That is, he named a boundary line running across Italy, to the north of which the Lombards should be compelled to withdraw, thus vacating all their conquests made since about 590. This line had for a few years (about 590–600) been approximately the boundary between the Lombards and the provinces which were under the exarch. Owing to the fact that it consisted of mountains and a number of strongly fortified cities, it might well have served as a boundary between two states.* Pippin called his nobles to a diet and persuaded them to confirm the agreement which he had just made with the pope. That is, they agreed to interfere in Italy in favor of the pope against the Lombards, and, by force of arms if necessary, to compel them to restore to the pope the provinces in question. As a result of two campaigns into Italy Pippin was able to take from the Lombards about twenty cities (by no means all that were included in his promise) and hand them over to the pope. Although he had demanded much more territory, the pope nevertheless made peace with the Lombards, but continued, however, to make further territorial acquisitions from them whenever he could do so. We have already learned that Desiderius, the successor of Aistulf, finally renewed the war on the pope, and that Charlemagne, at the appeal of the pope, came into Italy, defeated Desiderius, and took possession of the kingdom of the Lombards (774). Although Charlemagne had taken an oath to fulfil the promise of his father, Pippin, he nevertheless broke it and as king of the Lombards retained possession of the territory which the pope

Pippin's "Promise" Partially Fulfilled.

* The provinces which the pope asked for were described in a document which took the form of a promise of Pippin to restore them to the pope. The description is as follows: "From Luna (the island of Corsica being included), to Suriano, thence over the Apennines to Berceto, thence to Parma, thence to Reggio, and thence to Mantua and Monselice; that is, the whole exarchate of Ravenna, as it had been of old, with the provinces of Istria and Venice; and, besides, the duchies of Benevento and Spoleto."

claimed. As a compromise, however, he later granted Adrian certain cities in Tuscany and the royal taxes from Tuscany and Spoleto.* In undisputed possession, however, of certain lands and cities, the pope was, from that time, in fact a temporal ruler.

The Pope Still Subject to the Emperor.

What was the relation of the pope to the new possessions? To answer this controverted question, certain considerations must be taken into account. (1) The pope was under the government of the Greek emperor at that time, and remained under it for many years. To be sure, the pope had gradually come to rule Rome, and the Greek dukes in the duchy of Rome were without actual power.† (2) At the time when Stephen went into Frankland (753-754) he was on good terms with the emperor. Two embassies from Constantinople had recently come to him, and it was in obedience to the emperor's command that he undertook the journey to Aistulf on his way to Frankland. Furthermore, these friendly relations between popes and emperors continued to exist for a long time. (3) Not only did the relations between pope and emperor continue to be friendly; they were also such as exist between a sovereign and his subject. The emperors continued to possess the sovereign right of coinage in Italy, and till 774 coins minted by the pope in Rome bore the imperial likeness. In official documents the popes still called the emperor "our lord," and dated their writings according to the year of his reign. From this we must infer that in theory the emperor was still sovereign over the pope, although it is evident from many other facts that the pope was exercising a power that approximated actual sovereignty. The

* The "promise" of Pippin was, therefore, not entirely fulfilled either by himself or his son Charlemagne. It remained, nevertheless, as an ideal ever before the popes, toward the realization of which they could work. This "promise" was one of the documents laid before Otto I for the purpose of securing his confirmation of the papal possessions (962). S. B., 54.

† The last of these Greek dukes of whom we have any record was a certain Stephen, during the pontificate of Zacharias (741-752); all later dukes, it is said, were appointed by the popes. Yet merely from the silence of our meagre sources we dare not infer that there were no longer Greek officials in Rome.

heresy of the Greeks (their prohibition of the use of images in the churches) gave Adrian I (772–795) good ground for enlarging his actual authority. Refusing to recognize a heretical emperor, he began to coin money in his own name and to omit the year of the emperor's reign from his documents. Even with these changes Adrian I neither claimed nor possessed absolute sovereignty over his lands. The idea that the empire was universal and indivisible still prevailed, and Adrian I did not even dream of saying that his lands were not a part of the empire. He had rebelled against a heretical emperor; as soon as the emperor became orthodox the pope recognized him again. So in 787 Adrian wrote to the emperor, Constantine, and his mother Irene: "May the Lord preserve our unconquered princes and great emperors." We must therefore conclude that the pope was merely the governor, not the absolute sovereign, of the lands which he held. His position was similar to that of many other bishops who held the office of count or duke.

Charlemagne Exercised Sovereignty in Rome.

S. B., 48.

Of their actual power the popes were very jealous, and resisted all interference from whatever quarter. They were not able, however, for some centuries to convert it immediately into constitutional sovereignty, nor did they attempt to do so. In fact their relations with the kings of the Franks for some time diminished their actual power. In conferring the title of *patricius* of the Romans on Pippin, and again on Charlemagne, the pope created another ruler over himself. Pippin did not attempt to exercise the rights of his office, but Charlemagne, after conquering the Lombards, took his office seriously and assumed sovereignty over the pope. He rebuked Adrian I for publishing the decrees of the council of Nicæa (787) without first receiving the royal permission to do so, and informed Leo III that he should devote himself strictly to the spiritual duties of his office. The establishment of an imperial line in the west (800) revived to a certain extent the sovereign rights of the emperor, and so put limits to the actual power of the pope. Thus (1) the German emperor assumed jurisdiction in Rome, even over papal officials, and his

S. B., 47.

representatives were the highest court of justice in Rome. (2) The emperor demanded that the people of Rome take an oath of fidelity to him. (3) In the matter of papal elections, the emperor required that an account of the election be sent to him, and forbade the newly elected pope to be invested with his office until he had received the imperial confirmation of his election. It is evident, therefore, that in the ninth century the pope, although the temporal ruler of Rome, was nevertheless not sovereign, but was subject to the emperor. The time was to come, however, when he was to assert his sovereignty not only over Rome but even over the whole world. Let us now sketch the origin of this stupendous claim.*

* The feeling that the pope's sovereignty in Rome was actual and the wish to make it constitutional led to the famous forgery called the "donation of Constantine." The date of its fabrication cannot be definitely determined, but it probably falls in the latter half of the eighth century (about 772). It relates that the emperor Constantine was afflicted with leprosy and, after physicians had failed to cure him, St. Peter and St. Paul appeared to him in a dream and told him to call Pope Silvester, who was then in hiding because of the persecutions of Christians. Constantine did so, and Silvester, after instructing him in the doctrine of the Trinity, baptized him. When Constantine came up out of the font he found that his leprosy was healed. Out of gratitude he established a church in the Lateran palace as the head of all the churches of the world, and built churches in honor of the two apostles who had appeared to him. For the support of the lamps in these churches Constantine endowed them with lands and possessions "in the east as well as in the west, and even in the north and in the south, namely: in Judæa, Greece, Asia, Thrace, Africa, and Italy, and in various islands."

To Silvester and to all his successors Constantine gave the Lateran palace, and the right to wear all the imperial ornaments and articles of dress—diadem, robe, mantle, collar, tunic, the imperial sceptre, and, in short, everything that indicated the imperial rank. The emperor also conferred upon him and his successors "the city of Rome, and the provinces, places, and cities of the western regions." That is, the emperor gave the pope constitutional sovereignty over all the west. Furthermore, because it was not proper that the earthly emperor should have authority where the heavenly emperor had established the head of the Christian religion and the priestly rule, Constantine withdrew from Rome and established the seat of his empire at Byzantium, which was called after him Constantinople. It is unnecessary to say that this is all pure invention. Constantine never had leprosy, he was not baptized till near the end of his life, and his baptism did not take place at Rome.

The rise of the papal claim of universal temporal sovereignty can be easily traced. At the beginning of the Middle Age it was the common belief that God had foreordained that the empire should never pass away; and that He had appointed the emperor to rule over the world, giving him supreme authority over it. The emperor, therefore, based his authority on "divine right." In opposition to this imperial theory, the pope, Gregory VII (1073-1085), formulated the papal theory by which he claimed supreme temporal authority over the whole world, declaring that "our Lord Jesus Christ has made the blessed St. Peter ruler over the kingdoms of this world"; in place of the empire the church was to be eternal; in place of the emperor the pope was, by divine right, the ruler of the world, having the right to make and depose emperors and kings. A few popes, such as Gregory VII, Alexander III, and Innocent III, were able to realize approximately their ideal of temporal supremacy over the Christian world.

Gregory VII, 1073-1085, Claims Universal Temporal Sovereignty.

R., 115.

A variety of causes aided the popes in the development and realization of their theory. (1) It needed no proof that the soul was more important than the body, and that the spiritual interests of man were superior to his temporal interests. From this it seemed to follow logically that the pope, who was intrusted with things spiritual, should be superior to the emperor, who was intrusted with things temporal. (2) The donation of Constantine no doubt contributed its share, although its influence cannot be traced in detail. (3) The popes made use of the authority of the Bible, many passages of which they quoted to enforce their claims. In that age these lines of argument were convincing, and would of themselves have done much to bring about papal supremacy. (4) The popes owed their success in realizing their claims to world sovereignty chiefly, however, to the embryonic stage in which the governments of Europe were during the early centuries of the Middle Age. The lack of unity, of compactness, of efficiency, and of strength in these governments has often been shown. Everywhere the crown

Aids to Papal Success.

R., 26.

was in a struggle with its vassals, and often enough was defeated by them. Feudalism at its height marks the degree of this impotence of the central governments. In their weakness emperors and kings did not hesitate to call on the pope for help against their subjects. They also sought the consent and approval of the pope for their most important undertakings. In this way they assisted in creating a series of papal acts which served as precedents and the basis for a large theory of papal authority.

A brief recital of a few of these acts will show their importance in the development of the papal theory. (1) In 751, when Pippin, mayor of the palace, desired to be made king of the Franks he sought to make the change more acceptable to them by first securing from the pope a statement that the change seemed a desirable one. In 754 the pope went to visit Pippin and set the approval of the church on the change in dynasty by solemnly recrowning Pippin and anointing him and his family with holy oil. Although the change was really made by the Frankish nobles, a few centuries later it was commonly believed that the pope had deposed the "do-nothing" king and put Pippin into his place.

Important Acts.

S. B., 6.

(2) In the ninth century the pope, by crowning three successive emperors, established the theory that he alone had the right to crown the emperor. In the first place he crowned Charlemagne, in the name, as we have seen, of the people who elected him. That Charlemagne did not regard the imperial crown as within the gift of the pope is shown by the fact that he caused his son, Ludwig the Pious, to crown himself (813). After the death of his father Ludwig recrowned himself, but made the mistake of permitting the pope to recrown him again in 817. At the time the pope did not claim that he was conferring the crown, but only that as the head of the church he should crown the emperor who was the head of the Christian world. When Ludwig the Pious divided his realm among his sons (817) he crowned Lothar emperor. But in 824 Lothar permitted himself to be recrowned by the

S. B., 51.

pope. Thereafter it was believed that the pope alone had the right to perform the coronation act. Although it was generally held, in Germany at least, that the king of the Germans had a right to the imperial crown, some popes denied this, and declared that they might confer the crown on whom they would.

(3) Toward the end of the tenth century the pope acted as if he were the source of all political authority. About 990 the ruler of the Poles put his territory "under the protection of St. Peter," and the pope agreed to give him the royal title. For some unknown reason the plan was not carried out. A few years later, however, Stephen, the ruler of the Hungarians, offered himself, his people, his kingdom, and all his possessions to the pope as the vicar of St. Peter, and begged to be made a king. The pope accepted the gift, conferred the title of king upon him, sent him the crown which he had prepared for the duke of the Poles, and assumed the protection and a sort of proprietorship over him and his kingdom (1000).

S. B., 56.

(4) In 1059 Nicholas II conferred the title of duke on Robert Guiscard, and confirmed him in the possession of southern Italy, which he had conquered, and conferred on him Sicily, which he was yet to conquer.

S. B., 58.

(5) Both Innocent II (1130–1143) and the antipope Anaclete II (1130–1138) conferred the title of king on duke Roger of Sicily, and raised the duchy to the rank of a kingdom.

(6) In 1066 William the Conqueror sought and obtained the papal sanction and blessing for his proposed invasion of England.

These examples show how general the belief was that the pope's authority extended over political matters, and with so many important precedents it is not strange that Gregory VII should have formulated the broadest claims to temporal sovereignty over all the Christian world.

CHAPTER IX

MONASTICISM

Asceticism, on which monasticism is based, is the practice of extreme self-denial in food, drink, dress, sleep, and in the necessities as well as in the comforts of life; it is the withdrawing from the world, the self-infliction of pain, excessive devotion to prayer and other pious duties and works, in the belief that whatever abases, pains, or does violence to the body produces a corresponding purification of soul and assists in atoning for sin. But how did such an idea gain so large a place in the Christian church, whose founder was not ascetic, and who exhibited a calm, deep-seated joy in life, and was even called a wine-bibber and a friend of publicans and sinners?

Asceticism.

The answer to this question is found in the fact that the thought of the whole civilized world of that day was permeated with asceticism. During the first three centuries of our era there were several popular, wide-spread systems of philosophy flourishing in the empire. All of them were ascetic in character, and by their teachings they paved the way for the monasticism of the church. In these popular systems of philosophy, chief of which were cynicism, stoicism, neo-Pythagoreanism, gnosticism, and neo-Platonism,* we find the philosophic basis for the asceticism which was organized in the church under the name of monasticism. Each of these systems made an important contribution to the monastic ideal, and all helped prepare the minds of the people for the ready acceptance of it.

Ascetic Philosophies.

These popular philosophies had all been developed from the

* The reader should by all means consult some history of philosophy, or some encyclopedia for a more complete statement of the principles and practices of these philosophies.

teaching of Socrates that the chief end of man was self-knowledge and the practice of virtue. Philosophers and moralists had developed this idea and had tried to define self-knowledge and virtue, and to determine the best method of acquiring them. Even Plato and Aristotle taught that the highest life was one of pure, serene contemplation. Their successors in the field of philosophy had agreed with them, and furthermore they had formulated many rules for the guidance of those who were seeking to attain it. They were essentially agreed that the man who wished to know himself and to practise the highest virtue should withdraw as far as possible from the duties, distractions, and cares which beset him in the family, in society, and in the state, and should live in quiet seclusion, with his eyes turned inward in solemn contemplation of his soul—of himself. They taught that a man who was thus poised upon himself, indifferent to all external things, rich in the contemplation of himself, and feeling no need of the things of this world, was approaching the loftiest ideal and acquiring the highest wisdom. And this idea was, in one way or another, embodied in the popular philosophies of the day, which were therefore religious and ascetic rather than speculative. They disparaged the world and tended to fill their adherents with dissatisfaction with it. They sought to estrange the soul from all surrounding objects. A brief statement about some of these systems of philosophy will help us understand the origin of monasticism.

Cynicism.

Cynicism, a popular philosophy with a considerable following, declared that the highest good consisted in the practice of virtue, and that virtue consisted in despising pleasures, knowledge, family, friends, wealth, culture, in a word, everything that the world esteems; and that the man who, scorning the world, was independent of all outward circumstances, had attained the highest good. In practice, cynicism was the glorification of poverty, filth, and ignorance —the negation of culture.

Stoicism, which also had a numerous following, especially among the cultured class, was essentially a system of ethical culture. It taught that virtue, that is, proper conduct, was the sole end to be sought in life, and that it could be attained without learning and knowledge. For the stoic, virtue consisted in a freedom from all desires, of whatever kind, and from all external wants, and in the destruction of all disturbing emotions. He strove to be superior to poverty and to wealth, to sorrow and to joy, to pain and to pleasure—in short, to all external conditions and circumstances. Complete self-renunciation and complete self-control formed his ideal.

Stoicism.

Gnosticism taught the dualism of spirit and matter; its fundamental idea was that matter is evil and the seat of evil, while spirit is good and becomes contaminated only when it is brought into contact with matter; every soul was pure until it was joined to a body, by contact with which it was rendered impure. From this body, sinful because composed of matter, the soul should be freed and purified by all kinds of ascetic exercises. To this end gnostics made specific rules of conduct: they forbade the use of certain meats and drinks, and sought to shun as far as possible all contact with the material elements of this world. "Touch not, taste not, handle not" (Col. 2 : 21) was the guiding principle of their conduct, by observing which they hoped to redeem the soul from its corrupting union with the body. They made use of certain technical terms to which they attached peculiar importance, among which were "fulness" (πλήρωμα), "wisdom" (σοφία), and "knowledge" (γνῶσις, whence the name of their system, gnosticism).

Gnosticism Ascetic.

Their conception of evil grew out of the gnostic theory of the origin of evil which was a part of their theory of creation. They believed that there was first of all an original spirit so pure and fine that he could have nothing to do with matter, not even in its creation. He was so fine in his essence that he could not even reveal himself in any way. Hence he was declared to be an "unfathomable abyss," "indefinable," "indescribable," "unnamable," and "unknowable." From him, the first spirit, there emanated a second spirit a little less fine than he, and from this second

Origin of Evil.

spirit a third, and so on through an infinite series of emanations until finally a spirit was produced which was so coarse that he was capable of creating matter. In this fantastic way gnostics bridged the infinite gulf which existed between spirit and matter. For this last and lowest of emanations created matter as an act of malice toward the purer spirits above him. This creation of matter was the creation of evil. Gnostics indulged in the wildest speculation about these myriads of spirits which formed the scale between pure spirit and matter, classifying them, defining their activities, and ranking them according to their powers. They gave them names which are obscure to us, such as "æons," "demiurges," "thrones," "dominions," "principalities," and "powers" (*cf.* Col. 1 : 16).

Many of the converts to Christianity during the first centuries were imbued with these ideas and sought in Christianity merely a more perfect ascetic system than they already possessed in their gnostic philosophy. They were still gnostics, but with a Christian bias. St. Paul came into frequent conflict with gnostics and gnostic ideas, and refuted them in some of his letters, declaring that all such gnostic practices were opposed to the principles of Christ's teachings.* The presence of so many gnostic Christians in the church led in the second century to a serious struggle. Many of them, unable to divest themselves of their philosophic theories, either denied the biblical account of creation, because it differed from their theory of it, or identified the God of the Old Testament with the evil spirit who had created matter. Consequently

Gnostic Christians.

St. Paul Refutes Gnostic Ideas.

Struggle and Compromise.

* In his letter to the Colossians he often refers to gnostic teachings, and uses their technical terms. The "invisible" God, he says, is not "unknowable," for he has revealed himself in Jesus, who is his image; the world was not created by an evil spirit, for Christ created all things that are in heaven and earth, "visible and invisible, whether they be thrones, or dominions, or principalities"; in Christ are all "fulness," and "all the treasures of wisdom and knowledge," and not in any of the emanations, as the gnostics declare; Christ was greater than all these emanations, by whatever name they are called, for he had triumphed over them; Christians should not worship these emanations (which Paul calls angels, Col. 2 : 18); matter—the material world is

they rejected the Old Testament entirely, and forbade Christians to read it. The question was argued with great bitterness, and the contest ended in a compromise. The church retained the Old Testament as a revelation of the true God, rejected the gnostic theory of creation, and expelled the gnostics as heretics. But the church partially accepted the gnostic ideas about the evil character of matter, and began to assert that the world is wholly given over to the devil; all nature, the handiwork of God who had declared it to be very good, was, as a consequence of this compromise, regarded as sinful and contaminating. Such was the view that prevailed generally during the Middle Age, and that controlled the attitude of men toward nature. It was an unfortunate compromise that opened the door for the introduction of a formal asceticism into the church.

Neo-Platonism, the last great system of heathen philosophy, claimed to be an absolute religion. Its theory of the origin of evil and of matter was similar to that of gnosticism. It taught the utter vanity of all earthly things. The one thing needful was a state of inward peace and repose of soul, and consequently its teachers developed a system of ascetic rules and practices by which this state could be attained and maintained. They taught that by renunciation, by asceticism, the soul should be raised far above the things of this life.

Neo-Platonism.

Now, owing to the wide diffusion and great popularity of these systems of philosophy, society in general, in the third century of our era, was permeated from top to bottom with ascetic ideas. So completely was philosophy identified with

not evil, for it was created by Christ, and hence Christians should not obey the prohibitions of gnostics—"Touch not, taste not, handle not"; nor should they suffer any one to prescribe what they should eat or drink, or compel them to observe any day as holy, not even the sabbath. All these ascetic practices punish the body, indeed, but are of no value to the soul, for the kingdom of God consists not in the observance of such external things. Instead of observing them Christians should shun all evil desires, covetousness, anger, malice, blasphemy, and other vices, and should practise mercy, kindness, humility, charity, and all Christian and humane virtues (*cf.* Col. 1 : 15–19; 2 : 3, 15–23; 3 : 5–8).

asceticism that the ascetic life was called the philosophic life and a hermit was regarded as the true philosopher. The world was in an ascetic mood, and thousands were ready to take to the desert if the way thither were but once pointed out to them. In the third and fourth centuries Christianity rapidly became popular, and it was inevitable that many of its converts would be imbued with ascetic ideas from which they could not, of course, at once free themselves. They carried them into the church and sought to reconcile them with their new faith. These ascetic ideas and practices were found not only among the laymen, for even Christian teachers, especially those in the east, were deeply influenced by these philosophies. They taught that the highest Christian ideal of life consisted in dying daily to the world, in separation from it, in losing oneself in the contemplation of God; and that the man who so lost himself in the contemplation of God that he forgot himself and his very existence would be freed from the material world, and finally be accounted worthy to obtain the beatific vision of the invisible God.

Philosophy Identified with Asceticism.

Christian Teachers Affected by Pagan Philosophies.

Thus pagan philosophers and moralists and Christian teachers united in recommending an ascetic ideal of life in which there was no place for the acquisition of wealth, for the enjoyment of possessions, for the practice of civic virtues, or even for marriage. And, since the people were saturated with these ideas, it could have been foreseen that asceticism would become a large factor in the life of the church. Monasticism was inevitable.

All Classes Ascetic in Third Century.

The increasing worldliness in the church—a phrase that covers a great many things—caused the asceticism in the church to take the particular form which is called monasticism, which may be defined as organized asceticism. The church had undergone a profound change in the two hundred years of its existence. At first the Christian converts had before them an ideal of perfect holiness; they sought to keep themselves "unspotted from the world." Now, idolatry was so woven into the warp and

The Devout Flee from Worldliness in the Church.

woof of daily life that no Christian could be an active member of society and of the state without incurring the guilt of idolatry in an infinite number of ways. This state of affairs tended to make the Christians a quiet sect, a group of holy people living quite outside of the great world. But such a position could not be maintained. Christians found that in order to gain a livelihood it was necessary to compromise with the world; a Christian artisan must ply his trade, even though it brought him into contact with idolatrous objects. So, imperceptibly, the church changed from a small band of holy enthusiasts, who separated themselves from the world at any cost, to a people living in the world, Christian in name but sinners in fact, possessing the high ideals of the early Christians but practising many of the vices of the heathen world. The church discovered that its members needed the most patient and considerate education in Christian living. With the recognition of this change in its members the church became an institution in the world, existing for the religious training and eventual salvation of its people. The church was no longer a body of saints, but a school for the training of its sinful members. All the time, however, there was a strict party in the church which opposed this change and insisted that all Christians should be holy, and that they should separate themselves completely from the world. They lamented what they considered the degeneracy of the church and did their utmost to keep Christianity within the narrow bounds of a quiet and passive sect removed from the life of the world. Among the sects of this character were the Encratites, the Ebionites, the Marcionists, and the Montanists. This party was in the minority, fortunately, for if Christianity was to become an effective civilizing factor in the world—in the education and training of nations—it could not remain a holy and separated sect but must be in the world as a leaven leavening the whole mass. In this compromise the church may have lost something in enthusiasm and earnestness, but it gained immensely in that it became an educational and uplifting power in the lives of whole nations. By making this compro-

Saints and Sinners.

mise Christianity became a world religion instead of a separatist sect without influence on the life of the world.

This change from a band of holy enthusiasts to an institution for the religious training and education of sinning humanity was, as has been said, accompanied by a loss in earnestness and also by an increase in formalism.

Real Christianity Not Understood.

Christianity as a filial attitude of mind toward God, which accepts with humility and gratitude whatever he may send; Christianity as a simplicity and purity of mind, which remain the same whether in poverty or wealth, in prosperity or misfortune; Christianity as a life of love and service, and of "being a neighbor" to all who are in need—this Christianity was not understood by the masses, who looked upon all religion as forms rather than life, as particular actions rather than a principle of conduct. The great majority of those who came from heathenism into the church were ignorant and incapable of rising to so high a conception of religion; they had to be educated by forms and symbols. Worse than that, they were not all serious about the matter, but manifested a thoughtless and worldly spirit which shocked the sterner members of the church, who in their zeal even courted martyrdom as the highest good that they could attain. A church in which the lax and worldly were in a rapidly increasing majority could not satisfy those who were so bitterly in earnest. For all such there was but one way of escape—flight from the world, flight from the church.

The Hermit Ideal.

So in the third century the monastic movement began, when large numbers of those earnest Christians fled into the desert and sought salvation in a life of solitude, of contemplation, of silence, of privation, of fasting, of prayer, of poverty, of chastity—in a word, in a life of the most rigorous asceticism. They believed that the highest Christian ideal could be realized only outside of society. This was the negation of all that is human, for it took into account only the duty of man to God. They made the attempt to flee from everything that could in any way occasion sin—a hopeless attempt, for what is there which may not occasion sin? Their mechanical isolation from the world might be virtually complete, but would that insure their spiritual isolation and its attendant elevation of soul?

Ascetic Excesses.

The eagerness with which thousands embraced this hermit life shows how thoroughly the minds of men were imbued with the ascetic philosophies of the time, and how deep and widespread was the dissatisfaction of soul among the more thoughtful. The hermit life came to them as a great and joyful deliverance. It seemed so simple and sure a cure for all the ills of the soul that it became immensely popular. Although some of these hermits, rejoicing in the freedom from the distractions and burdens of society, found the desired relief in quiet contemplation and shared in the peace of nature about them, others indulged in the wildest excesses of self-torture. Some exposed themselves to the bite and sting of insects; some wallowed in mire and filth; some fasted until they died of hunger; some beat themselves with stones and whips, or lay naked on thorns and briars until their bodies were horrid with cuts, bruises, and sores; and others reached the limit of self-torture by spending years on the top of lofty pillars where there was not even room for them to lie down, and where, half-naked, they were exposed to the sun, rain, and wind. They exhausted human invention in discovering new and original ways of doing violence to their bodies.

At First "Monk" Meant Hermit.

We do not know who the first monks were, because the beginnings of monasticism are lost in obscurity and overgrown with a tangle of improbable and contradictory legends. We do know, however, that about the middle of the third century the movement began in Egypt and western Asia, where the climate was such that those who lived out of doors suffered little from the inclemency of the weather. In those countries the monks needed protection chiefly against the heat of the sun, and this could be furnished by a tree, an overhanging rock, a cave, or a roof of palm leaves or reeds. At first they were true hermits, as the name monk indicates, each one living entirely alone. Sometimes they built their little cells near one another so that they formed a kind of colony of hermits. In countries where the climate was more rigorous their manner of life was modified; they found it necessary to live together in houses. At the same time, however, they tried to preserve the essential features of the hermit life; each one had his own room or cell, prepared his own food, and ate and lived alone.

Origin of the Rule.

S. B., 251 : 1.

The presence of impostors—false monks—among them, and the mere fact that they were under the same roof made some kind of regulations necessary, and some one had to be chosen to see that they were observed. So, in a natural way, every monastery came to have its "rule," and head or abbot to enforce it. Basil the Great (died 379) brought about uniformity in the Greek monasteries by making a rule which was eventually adopted by them all. He did not, however, essentially modify their established manner of life, for he provided that each monk should live alone in his cell and have little in common with his fellow monks except certain religious services.

Monasticism in the West.

R., 32, 33.

Monasticism was first made known in the west about 340, and the movement soon assumed vast proportions. St. Jerome (died 419) and St. Augustine (354–430) displayed the greatest enthusiasm for it, and recommended it to popular favor by their example and writings. It spread with amazing rapidity to the remotest corners of Christendom. People of all ranks were fascinated by the monkish ideal. The monastery offered a retreat where, freed from all cares and responsibilities of daily life, men could devote themselves to prayer, meditation, and holy association with those who were seeking the same high ends. The communistic life has always possessed strong attractions for persons of a certain type, and the conditions prevailing at that time made the monk's life very desirable. For just then life in the world was not altogether delightful. The imperial government was extremely oppressive, the cities were declining, a large class of the population was being impoverished, and the invasions of barbarians were bringing in their train an increasing amount of violence, injustice, oppression, and suffering. The monastery must have seemed to many a happy escape from a world where violence was on the increase and life had lost its security and joy. The monastery offered an escape from the material, social, and political shipwreck that had come upon the world.

As in the east so also in the west each monastery was independent of all others and made its own rule. This freedom and lack of common standards gave rise to various abuses.

Monastic Abuses.

S. B., 251 : 1.

Many monks, disappointed in not obtaining the inner peace which they sought, or finding the seclusion and discipline unbearable, grew tired of the life. Others, having embraced the monastic life without due deliberation, returned to the world after the first fit of enthusiasm was past, as if their monastic vows were not perpetually binding ("instability"). Some of those who deserted the monastery retained the monk's robe because of the deference and regard which it secured for them. Wearing the monk's dress but without the monk's morals, they roved about the country, leading dissolute lives and bringing reproach on the name. Others did not feel themselves bound to remain forever in the same monastery, but wandered from one to another. In various ways those who were not in earnest found a way to escape the rigors of the rule and to avoid all discipline. There was no organization to punish such, and no means of subjecting them to discipline.

All these abuses St. Benedict (died about 543) set himself to correct in the monastery of Monte Cassino (situated midway between Rome and Naples). He believed that the fundamental error was the "instability" of the monks.

St. Benedict.

Features of the Rule.

S. B., 251.

He therefore laid down the principle, "Once a monk, always a monk." He required the monk to take perpetual vows never to leave the monastery nor to forsake the monastic life ("stability"), to give up all secular and worldly practices and to conform to the ideals and standards of the monastic life, to observe the rule in every particular, to obey all his superiors as well as his abbot, and to lead a life of chastity and poverty. The life of a monk was therefore limited to a very narrow field. Monasticism was the negation of all duties to the state and to society. The vow of obedience was the negation of all individuality; the vow of chastity was the negation of the family; and the vow of poverty was the negation of all industry and cut the nerve of personal endeavor.

To prevent any one from too hastily becoming a monk each candidate had to undergo a novitiate, or period of probation, which would test him and give him the opportunity to discover in time whether he was really fitted for the life or not. St. Benedict fixed the occupations of the monks for every hour of the day and night. He appointed periods for prayer, reading, study, contemplation, and work. Idleness was to be shunned as in itself a most dangerous vice, and as rendering the monk accessible to all kinds of temptations. Instead of the solitary life of the monks of the east, St. Benedict provided that his monks should live in common. They ate in a common refectory, slept in a common dormitory, and passed all their time in the company of their fellow monks, so that privacy was unknown to them. No monk was allowed to possess property; when he entered the monastery he generally gave all his possessions to it. The strictest communism was practised, and no monk had the right even to the robe which he wore, since at the will of the abbot it might be taken from him and given to another.

St. Benedict understood the human character and had a patient sympathy for its weaknesses and faults. His rule, like himself, was sane, sensible, and moderate. It sets forth lofty Christian ideals in an attractive way. A kindly and charitable tone pervades it. The broad provision that the monk should work was probably the most important of its regulations, for it made the monks a great factor in the development of the west. Wherever they settled they began to till the soil and to introduce a better method of agriculture. They planted orchards, vineyards, and gardens. They taught the barbarians of Europe agriculture and the industrial arts as well as Christian doctrines. But not all their work was manual. They were required also to read

Monks must Work.

and study, and this kind of work was of even greater importance for the culture of Europe. St. Benedict was not the first one to prescribe reading and study for the monks, but through his rule learning found a home in the monasteries. In every monastery there was a school. For nearly six hundred years the monks were the schoolmasters of Europe; they wrote histories, chronicles, and biographies, from which we derive much of our knowledge of the period; and through their labors in copying manuscripts they preserved for us nearly all the literary treasures of Rome which we possess.

Learning in Monasteries.

The original ideal of the monks was a selfish one. They wished to separate themselves entirely from the world and to devote themselves to saving their own souls. Greek monks have been true to this ideal, and have, in fact, kept themselves separated from the world. Consequently Greek monasticism has remained unchanged for fifteen hundred years, and has exercised only a reactionary influence on the life of the Greek church. There, as everywhere else, fixation means stagnation. In the west, however, the Roman spirit of organization, of conquest, and of activity would not allow this ideal to prevail. The monks had fled from the world, but the papacy used them to conquer and rule it. In the hands of popes, emperors, and kings they became the most effective tools for Christianizing and civilizing the barbarians, and for extending the boundaries of both state and church. Abbots, like bishops, when found to possess ability, were used as the counsellors and helpers of kings, and monks were found to be the most efficient missionaries. For some centuries monks had a large share in the work of taming the forces of barbarism and enlisting them on the side of civilization. It was largely through their missionary labors that the remoter barbarian tribes were Christianized and the supremacy of the pope as head of the church established.

Kings and Popes Use Monks.

St. Benedict made his rule merely for the monastery of Monte Cassino about 530. By a series of fortuitous circumstances, however, it came to be accepted everywhere in the west, displacing all others. Its spread was due in the first place to a great misfortune which befell the monastery of Monte Cassino, in its destruction by the Lombards (about 580). The monks, being forced to find another home, went to Rome and established a monastery there. Pope Gregory the Great (590–604), being a Benedictine monk, naturally recommended its rule to other monasteries, and its spread was favored by his great personal popularity. He himself founded a number of monasteries, into all of which he introduced the Benedictine rule. Owing to papal support and to the superiority of the rule, it was gradually accepted by all the monasteries of Rome, and from there found its way into all parts of Italy. Augustine, whom Gregory sent to England, was a Benedictine monk, and of course took the rule with him. In this way it became the rule of all English monasteries. In the eighth century Boniface, an English monk, introduced it into the monasteries of the Franks and of the other Germans among whom he labored. So, within three hundred years after its composition, the rule had become recognized as the best and was in force in all the monasteries in the west.

Spread of Rule of St. Benedict.

S. B., 251 to 264.
O., 11.

The history of monasticism in the west does not, however, show the monks always living on the spiritual heights indicated by the rule. Their piety brought them popular favor; favor brought them wealth; and wealth too often brought leisure, idleness, and profligacy. They had periods of backsliding and worldliness, which were followed by periods of revival and renewed effort, during which the rigor of the original rule was increased and every effort made to prevent the possibility of another relapse. The most famous of all such revivals is connected with the monastery of Cluny, which was established (910) in the hills west of Mâcon, above the Rhône. Under the headship of a series of capable and earnest abbots, Cluny won a reputation far and wide for piety. With its growing fame the number of its monks increased until it could no longer accommodate all who sought admission. The

Relapses and Reforms.

Cf. S. B., 267, 268.

Cluny and Its Reform.

O., 42–44.

abbot then began to send out colonies of monks to establish new monasteries, the control of which he kept in his own hands. As the spirit of reform awoke elsewhere, other monasteries voluntarily put themselves under the control of the abbot of Cluny and asked him to send them one or more monks to introduce the reformed rule and discipline. In this way some two thousand monasteries were bound to Cluny and shared in its spiritual life and ideals. The result was a powerful religious revival which affected all Europe.

The Cluniac Programme.

It is difficult to state adequately the whole reform programme of Cluny, especially since it was developed slowly in the course of a hundred and fifty years or more. Perhaps it will be sufficient to note that the monastic rule was made more rigorous and was to be more vigorously enforced; the sacerdotal character of the clergy was to be emphasized, and they were to be separated more completely from the world; they were to be forbidden to marry, and were to be put under strict discipline by being compelled to live together in monasteries, subject to a rule, with their bishop as their head. The clergy, with whom the monks were now reckoned, were to form a spiritual aristocracy, freed from all secular control, from secular law and judges, with a law of their own which they alone administered. The laity were to be excluded from all share in the management of church affairs, and should no longer control the election and investiture of bishops or the choice of the parish priests. Because of their priestly character the clergy were superior to the laity, and were to have complete authority over them, at least in all ecclesiastical and religious matters. Owing to the greater importance of spiritual things, they had no doubt that whenever there was a conflict between the two, it was the temporal which should always give way. Gregory VII, having been a monk at Cluny, was imbued with its spirit and ideas, and when he came to the papal throne (1073) he claimed not only the spiritual authority over the whole Christian world but also the political authority. The tenth and eleventh centuries were largely dominated by the Cluniac movement.

The growth of the monastic spirit under the influence of Cluny led to the establishment of several new orders, with more severe rules. Many of these won only local fame and need not be named. But the Carthusians, founded in 1084, the Cistercians, in 1098, and the Carmelites, in 1156, became large and powerful orders, and were diffused throughout Europe. Their asceticism was extreme. The Carthusians and Cistercians may be said to have revived some of the original features of monasticism, inasmuch as they imposed a stricter silence on their members and abolished the common life of the Benedictines, each monk being restricted to his little cell, passing his time there as if in solitary confinement.

New Orders.

Monasticism, as we have been studying it, concerned only the monks and not the clergy. For monks, we must understand, were not necessarily clergymen. At first, indeed, they were all laymen, and they were rather doubtful about admitting clergymen to membership in their houses. But, as they needed the services of clergymen for the administration of the sacraments, it soon became customary for them to require a few of their number to take priestly orders. Nevertheless, the majority of the monks throughout the Middle Age were undoubtedly laymen. The ordinary clergy of the church, however, were also affected by the monastic movement. St. Augustine, bishop of Hippo in Africa (died 430), it is said, brought all the clergy of his diocese together and had them live in common with him under a rule which was essentially monastic. His example, while not imitated, was held in great esteem. In the eighth century St. Chrodegang, bishop of Metz, wishing to reform and improve his clergy, assembled them about him, made a rule for them, and instituted the common life. The clergy belonging to the cathedral, and thus living together, formed the "chapter" of the cathedral, and generally had the management of its affairs and the election of the bishop in their hands. St. Chrodegang found imitators, and the clergy not only of the cathedrals but

The Clergy Live according to a Monastic Rule.

Chrodegang of Metz.

S. B., 265.

also of many parish churches soon began to live in the same way. It was one of the articles of the Cluniac programme that the clergy should be compelled to live in this monastic fashion, and under the influence of this reform party the movement took on large proportions. They imitated the monks also in forming many orders, the most famous of which was that of the Premonstratensians. This order was founded about 1120 by St. Norbert, who soon became archbishop of Magdeburg, and who used the members of his order as missionaries among the Slavs to the east. All the clergy living thus according to a rule were called "regulars" (*regula*), "canons," or "regular canons" (*canon*, a Greek work meaning a "rule"), and as a body were known as the "regular clergy," a term which was sometimes used to include the monks. There were many clergymen whose parishes were so remote from the cathedral or other large church that it was impossible for them to live in the houses of the "regular clergy" and attend to their parish duties. Since they lived in the world (*in sæculo*) they were called by way of distinction the "secular clergy."

The Premonstratensians.

CHAPTER X

GERMANY AND THE EMPIRE, 919–1056

THE efforts of Conrad I (911–918) to produce unity in Germany by making the royal power supreme had by their failure rather tended to make the disunion greater. The dukes, who were essentially tribal kings, had successfully resisted him and were exercising the chief crown rights (*regalia*). Both Bavarians and Suabians seemed bent on securing complete independence, for, after Conrad's death, they would apparently have been content to let the office of king die out. At any rate they took no part in the election of his successor and were prepared to resist him, whoever he might be. Only two duchies, Franconia and Saxony, were represented in the election, which, according to the advice of Conrad, fell on Henry, duke of Saxony (called the "Fowler" and the "Builder of Cities," 919–936). Henry accepted the honor, but, as if to rebuke the clergy for their action at the council of Altheim (916), he refused to be anointed and crowned. His refusal was indicative of his conception of his office and of the attitude which he was going to assume toward his fellow dukes. He recognized that he was only a feudal king, chosen by his peers to be their overlord. He first led an army into Suabia and compelled its duke, Burchard, to become his vassal, but left in Burchard's hands the government of the duchy. He then proceeded against the duke of Bavaria, who was not willing to cede so much as had the duke of Suabia. Rather than engage in war with him Henry left him in possession of actual power, in return for which the duke took the oath of homage to Henry as overlord.

Henry, the City Builder, 919–936.

S. B., 26.
R., 102.

A Feudal King.

Content with the somewhat equivocal position of a feudal

king, Henry returned to Saxony and devoted himself to the government of his own duchy. The fact that in his numerous wars he received no help from his vassal dukes is evidence that his control over them was very slight; but by his conciliatory policy toward them he disarmed their fears and so eventually established friendly relations with them. Certain circumstances enabled him to increase his influence over them. He gave his daughter in marriage to the duke of Lotharingia, and, on the death of the duke of Suabia without heirs, he assumed the right to dispose of the vacant duchy and conferred it on one of his friends. Thus the dissolution of Germany into independent kingdoms, which was threatened under Ludwig the Child and Conrad I, was averted.

For some years the Hungarians, or Magyars, a nomadic people occupying a vast stretch of territory southeast of Bohemia, had been ravaging neighboring lands almost at will.

Magyars.

They invaded Saxony, too, and compelled Henry to make a nine years' truce with them, and to agree to pay them an annual tribute. The Saxons, who still fought on foot, were unable to compete with a mounted enemy. And, as they were generally accustomed to live in open villages, they had few places of refuge and their country was at the mercy of an invading army of excellent horsemen. Some of the bishops, however, had built walls about the towns that had grown up around their cathedrals, and monasteries were usually protected with walls. But these were not sufficiently numerous, nor were they within easy reach of all the people when attacked.

Fortified Places.

S. B., 26.

Henry not only ordered some of the towns (Merseburg, Gandersheim, Essen, Goslar) to be surrounded with walls, but also raised a levy by taking one of every nine men and setting them at work upon the construction of fortified places at convenient distances from one another. He caused these places to be well stocked with provisions to withstand a siege, and, in order to accustom the people to them, he ordered that courts and public gatherings should be held in them. At the same time Henry, by training his Saxons to fight on horseback, was able to put an efficient body of cavalry into the field and so to meet the invaders on equal terms.

The wisdom of this change was soon apparent. At the expiration of the truce with the Hungarians they renewed their invasions, but Henry repulsed them with heavy losses. He also made some successful campaigns against the Slavs on the east, in consequence of which many tribes, including the Bohemians, became tributary to him.* It can hardly be said that Henry established a system of marches, or marks, between the Saxons and the Slavs, although he organized the defense of the country by placing some counts on the frontier whose special duty it was to protect the country against Slavic invasions.

At the death of Henry (936) the nobles of Franconia and Saxony came together and elected his oldest son, Otto (936–973). With this election Otto was not content. He caused the nobles of all Germany, both lay and ecclesiastical, to be summoned to a general diet at Aachen, for the purpose of electing a king. There the nobles, who were present in great numbers, unanimously elected Otto, raised him to the throne, did him homage, and swore to be faithful to him and to aid him against all his enemies. He was then anointed and crowned with elaborate ceremony by the archbishops of Mainz, Cologne, and Treves. Otto's pride and love of pomp showed themselves in the coronation dinner. In order to heighten the dignity of the occasion, he revived the four chief offices of the royal household (chamberlain, seneschal, cup-bearer, marshal), and had their duties performed by the four dukes of Lotharingia, Franconia, Suabia, and Bavaria. This was merely a matter of etiquette and had no political significance whatever. Three hundred years later the right to vote for the king was limited to the three archbishops above named and to the four men who held these offices, but until

Otto I, 936–973.

S. B., 27. R., 103.

* Our word "slave" is derived from Slav, and got its meaning from the fact that so many Slavs were taken prisoners by the Germans and reduced to bondage that their racial name came to be applied to all bondmen.

that time they were sinecures; except on rare state occasions the duties connected with them were always performed by others.

The harmony exhibited at Aachen was of short duration. In all parts of the empire the nobles, regardless of their oaths of fidelity, rebelled and plotted against their overlord. Chief of these conspirators were Otto's brothers and the four dukes. Even his brothers tried to take his life, and for some time his position was insecure. He took advantage of vacancies in some of the duchies to put members of his family into them, and he sought to bind the other dukes to himself by marriages. But this policy can hardly be said to have been successful, since members of his own family were quite as faithless to him as were others. It would be idle to attempt to follow in detail all the local rebellions and conspiracies with which he had to contend during his reign. He was universally successful in suppressing them, although he was never able to bring his vassals to such a degree of submission that they did not dare renew their rebellion.

Opposition of the Nobles.

"Palatine" Count.

In order to keep a check on the dukes Otto established in each duchy a royal official, who was known as a "count of the palace" (palatine count) to safeguard all the king's interests. However, as the king paid him in land, he soon became a great landholder and vassal, bent on his own aggrandizement at the expense of the king. It was characteristic of the Middle Age that no ruler was able to retain the faithful and unselfish service of his officials and vassals.

The King's Income.

The king's income was derived from a great variety of sources. From his family (ducal) lands in Saxony, and from the crown lands, which were extensive but scattered throughout the kingdom, he received a large income, chiefly in the natural products of the soil. As king he possessed certain crown rights (*regalia*) which were important though subsidiary sources of revenue; thus, he received a share of, and in some cases all, the fines that were assessed in the administration of justice; the same is true of the tolls that were levied in various parts of the kingdom; the right of coinage was his; all mines were the property of the king (during the eleventh century salt-works were included with the mines); he had a right to a tax on the goods sold in all the markets or fairs of the kingdom, and of the fines assessed on all offenders during the continuance of the markets. In addition to these regalian rights, it was the custom for the nobles to give him valuable gifts whenever they came to him. These, with the ordinary feudal dues which he might collect from his vassals, and the annual tribute paid by peoples who had been conquered, amounted altogether to a considerable sum. His numerous campaigns cost him little, because his vassals were bound to support themselves in the field; it was for this that they had received their lands from the king.

The presence of barbarian peoples along the whole eastern frontier was a constant menace to the kingdom. Danes, Slavs (Poles, Bohemians, and many others), and Hungarians, made frequent invasions, during which they sacked and burned churches, monasteries, and villages, and carried off a great many prisoners. Otto recognized it as his first duty to conquer these pagan neighbors, to subject them to Germany, and to Christianize them. To this end he made many campaigns against them, established in suitable places archbishops, bishops, and colonies of monks, who should act as missionaries to the pagan peoples in question, and organized a defense which is generally known as a "mark" system.

Expansion of Germany.

He divided the debatable land between them and the Germans into districts which were called marches or marks (*i. e.*, border-lands), and put over each of them an official called a margrave (marquis, border count). To the margrave was intrusted the protection of the kingdom against invasions and the extension of its frontier to the east by conquest. By the time of Otto's death (973) the whole eastern frontier had been organized into a system of marks, which extended from the North Sea to the Adriatic. Against the Danes he erected the mark of Holstein, and established bishops at Schleswig, Ripen, and Aarhus, putting them under

The "Mark" System.

the archbishop of Bremen-Hamburg.* Sclavania, the borderland between the Germans and Slavs north of the Bohemians, he divided into six marks: the mark of Hermann Billung (along the Baltic), the north mark, the mark of Lausitz, and the marks of Merseburg, Zeitz, and Meissen. For conducting missionary work among the Slavs Otto established an archbishop at Magdeburg† (968), and bishops at Brandenburg, Havelberg, Merseburg, Zeitz, and Meissen. He conquered the Bohemians and reduced their duke to vassalage. Against the Hungarians, upon whom he inflicted an overwhelming defeat on the Lechfeld (a plain on the Lech River, near Augsburg, 955), he created the east mark, which eventually became Austria. And finally, against the Slavs on the upper waters of the Drave and Save Rivers, and against Italy, there were the marks of Carinthia (Kaernthen) and Friuli. Through these marks the forces of barbarism were gradually won over to the cause of civilization.

S. B., 28.

Toward the middle of the tenth century Otto held the central position on the political stage of Europe. His friendship was sought by the king of the West Franks as well as by Hugh Capet, the chief of the rebellious Frankish nobles. The young king of Burgundy fled to Otto to escape the machinations of his enemies, and after he returned to his kingdom in security (943) he retained a grateful remembrance of Otto's goodness to him. In like manner, Berengar, who had a hereditary claim on the Italian crown, fled for refuge to Otto (940), at whose court he spent the next

Otto I in Italy.

* In 983 Hamburg was destroyed by the Slavs, and its archbishop was driven out. Since the city remained desolate for some time, he could not return thither. In the meantime he established himself at Bremen. Hence writers sometimes call him the archbishop of Bremen. To avoid confusion we have combined the names.

† About 954 Otto had proposed to raise Magdeburg to an archbishopric, but was unable to do so because of the opposition of the archbishop of Mainz, in whose archdiocese Magdeburg was situated. Although Otto twice secured the consent of the pope to this arrangement, the resistance of the archbishop of Mainz prevented him from carrying it into effect. The death of the archbishop in 968 gave Otto the opportunity which he had so long desired, and the change was made before another archbishop was appointed.

five years. And both the pope and the Italian nobles, when endangered, naturally turned to Otto for help. The manner in which Otto was drawn into the affairs of Italy has already been narrated in connection with the account of the dissolution of the empire of Charlemagne. Berengar, the king of Italy, took Spoleto and threatened to deprive the pope, John XII, of his independence.* Consequently, John appealed to Otto for protection, and in return promised him the imperial crown. At the same time some Italian nobles, offended at the vigorous manner in which Berengar was exercising his royal authority, also called upon Otto for aid. Inasmuch as Otto desired the imperial title, he gladly accepted the invitation to interfere in Italian affairs. He was received in Rome with great joy and crowned emperor (962). When he attempted, however, to exercise the authority of his new office, he offended both the pope and the nobles. In the end Otto deposed John XII and put another pope, Leo VIII, in his place. He also compelled the Romans to swear that they would not elect and consecrate a pope without first obtaining his consent. Since Berengar possessed the dangerous ambition of ruling all Italy and refused to submit, Otto seized him and carried him off to Germany, where he was kept a prisoner to the time of his death.

Crowned Emperor, 962.

S. B., 29. R., 104.

A rebellion in Rome against the pope (967) recalled Otto to Italy, where he spent the next five years in a serious effort to establish his authority in southern Italy, which, he contended, was a part of his empire. He made several campaigns against the Greeks, who still held all of the peninsula south of Benevento and Capua. Unfortunately, he had conceived the idea that it would increase the prestige of his family and be more in keeping with his position as emperor if he should marry his son to a Greek princess. At first his proposal was rejected, but in 969 a rebellion in the Greek palace at Constantinople was successful, and the new emperor was more condescending. Knowing how eager Otto

Imperial Ideas.

* The position of Berengar in 961 was much like that of Aistulf in 750 and that of Desiderius in 773.

Note to Map VII.—By the coronation of Otto the Great as emperor (962), the empire of Lothar (with the exception of the Rhône valley) and the kingdom of Ludwig the German (see Map VI) were reunited. The two kingdoms of Upper and Lower Burgundy, which occupied the Rhône valley, united in 934 to form the kingdom of Arles or Burgundy (see Map VIII), which in turn was united to the empire in 1032. Otto I labored to extend his realm at the expense of the barbarians on the east, who were now forming states. The territory between the Elbe and the Oder was organized into marks (mark of the Billunger, as the family of the Billungs was called, north mark, and the marks of Lausitz, Meissen, and Zeitz) and slowly germanized and christianized. The east mark was enlarged. After his imperial coronation Otto assumed that southern Italy belonged to him and tried to exercise authority over it. In this he was only partially successful, for the extreme southern part still remained subject to the Greek emperor.

The Slavs are just beginning to have a sort of political existence in the states of Pomerania, Prussia, Poland, Croatia, Servia, and Bulgaria, all of which states had a very primitive, simple, and loosely organized government. The Hungarians were taking their first lessons in civilization, having just abandoned their nomadic life.

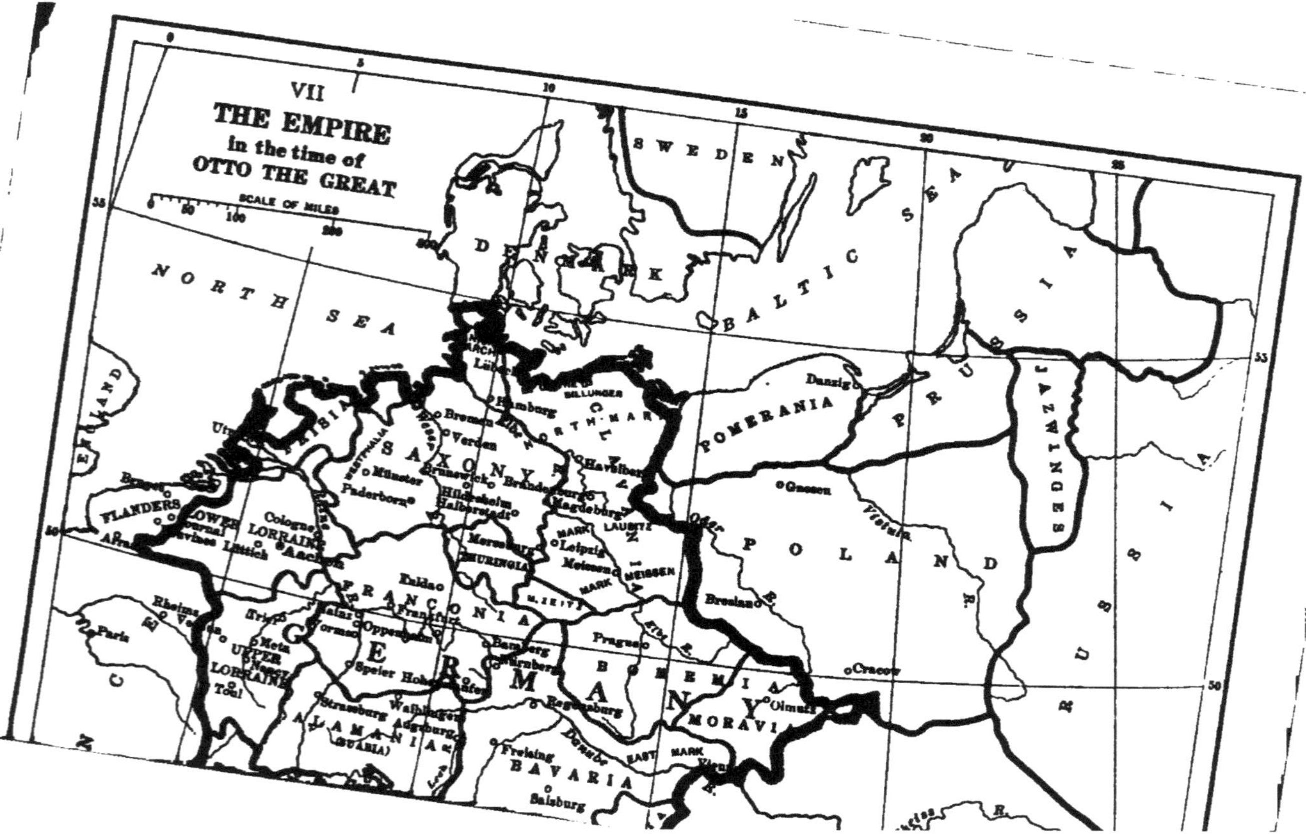
VII
THE EMPIRE
in the time of
OTTO THE GREAT
SCALE OF MILES
0
50
100
200
300
NORTH SEA
BALTIC SEA
SWEDEN
DENMARK
PRUSSIA
JAZWINGES
RUSSIA
POMERANIA
POLAND
SAXONY
FRANCONIA
GERMANY
BOHEMIA
MORAVIA
BAVARIA
ALAMANIA
(SUABIA)
THURINGIA
FLANDERS
LOWER LORRAINE
UPPER LORRAINE
WESTPHALIA
FRISIA
ENGLAND
BILLUNGER
NORTH MARK
MARK
LAUSITZ
MEISSEN
M. ZEITZ
EAST MARK
Danzig
Gnesen
Vistula
Oder
Breslau
Cracow
Prague
Olmutz
Elbe R.
Hamburg
Bremen
Verden
Münster
Paderborn
Brunswick
Brandenburg
Havelberg
Magdeburg
Hildesheim
Halberstadt
Merseburg
Leipzig
Meissen
Fulda
Cologne
Aachen
Lüttich
Bruges
Arras
Tournai
Cambrai
Nivelles
Utrecht
Rheims
Verdun
Paris
Trier
Metz
Nancy
Toul
Mainz
Worms
Frankfurt
Oppenheim
Speier
Strassburg
Augsburg
Bamberg
Nürnberg
Regensburg
Freising
Salzburg
Danube
Vienna
Lübeck
Rhine
0
5
10
15
20
25
55
50

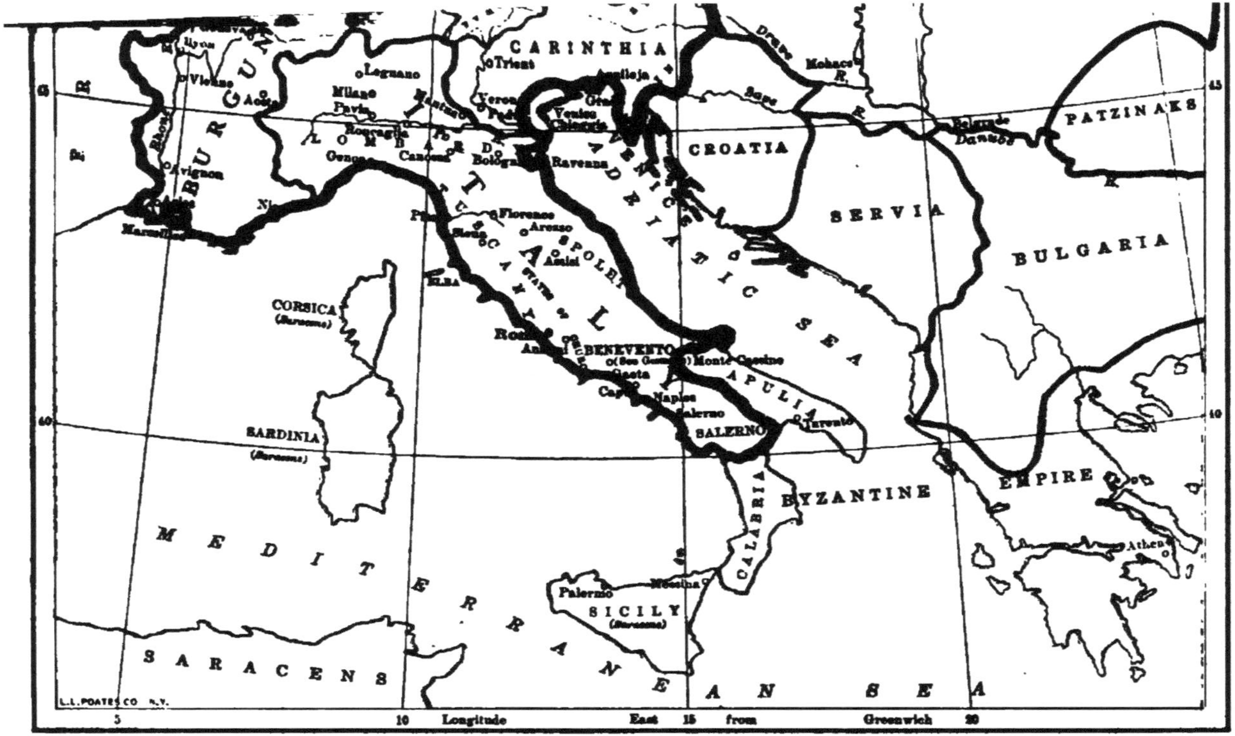

Burgundy was a Vassal-State of the Empire until 1032, when it was incorporated under Conrad II.

was for the alliance, he demanded the cession of all southern Italy in return for the princess. Otto was willing to pay the price, and the contract was concluded on these terms. The princess, Theophano, was sent to Italy and was married to the young prince, Otto II, in St. Peter's (972).

Long befor: his death Otto had aken care to secure the succession for his family. In 961 he had caused his first son, Otto II, to be crowned king of Germany, and in 967 he was equally successful in having the pope crown him as emperor. The death of Otto in 973 caused no interruption, therefore, in the administration of the government. The history of the emperors* for the next hundred years may be treated in a summary manner. In Germany there was an unceasing round of plots and rebellions on the part of the nobles, which prevented the country from arriving at the full benefits of peace. The king could maintain his authority only by constant fighting. The resentful attitude of the people toward the central government was invincible, and encouraged the nobles, whose ambition needed no stimulus, to renew their efforts to throw off the king's yoke. The king's work was never done, because the rebels, when defeated, yielded only for the moment, and at the first opportunity sought more powerful allies for their next uprising. On the whole, however, it can be said that toward the end of this period the power of the king increased, and that the rebellions diminished in both frequency and strength. It was a misfortune for Germany that its king was also emperor, because the duties of his office frequently called him to Italy and the nobles invariably took advantage of his absence to rebel.

Frequent Rebellions of the Nobles.

The numerous journeys of the German kings into Italy

* Otto II, 973-983, Otto III, 983-1002. Since Otto III died childless, the direct Saxon line ended with him. Civil war broke out between opposing candidates, but in the end Henry II (1002-1024, duke of Bavaria, and a distant relative of Otto III) secured the election and overcame all who opposed him. He also died childless. Conrad II (1024-1039) of Franconia was then elected, and he was succeeded by his son, Henry III (1039-1056). Under his son and successor, Henry IV (1056-1106), the great struggle between the empire and the papacy began.

brought heavy disasters to Germany on the eastern frontier, where both Slavs and Hungarians were eagerly watching for an opportunity to throw off the German yoke.

Germany Suffers when the Emperors go to Italy.

S. B., 32.

While Otto II was chasing the shadow of imperial sovereignty in Italy, the Slavs revolted and invaded Germany with overwhelming forces. The German nobles, weakened by feuds and the absence of many of their number, who had accompanied the emperor into Italy, were unable to stand before them. The whole border-land was devastated, the bishops driven from their seats, churches and monasteries destroyed, the German colonists either killed or expelled, and the mark system inaugurated by Otto I swept away. The German frontier, which had been advanced by the arms of Henry I and Otto I and by the missionary labors of bishops and monks, receded, and the most zealous efforts of all the kings for more than a hundred years were hardly sufficient to recover the ground lost during the reign of Otto II. The expansion of Germany to the east, thus temporarily checked, was rendered almost impossible for some time to come by two events which must now be described: the Poles acquired ecclesiastical independence, and the Hungarians, breaking the ties that bound them to the empire, became subject to the pope.

The Polish Church Independent of German Influence, 1000.

In the first place Otto III, in the year 1000, went to Gnesen in Poland, on a pilgrimage to the grave of his friend, Adalbert of Prague, who had suffered martyrdom as a missionary among the Poles. At that time, Otto III, under the stress of extravagant ideas, had lost his mental equilibrium, and with it a sane view and judgment of political matters. Incapable of foreseeing the consequences of his act, he made Gnesen the seat of an archbishop and established seven suffragan bishops in its archdiocese, which was made at the expense of the archbishop of Magdeburg. The German clergy who had begun the work of Christianizing the Poles were displaced by Polish clergy, and Poland, having an ecclesiastical organization of its own, was freed from German influence and its independent national existence was thereby secured. The duke of Poland remained nominally the vassal of Otto III, but, backed by the church and by the growing racial sentiment of the Poles, he inevitably tended toward independence. The process of Germanizing the Poles was stopped, and Poland, instead of being made a part of Germany, became merely a vassal state, the complete independence of which could not long be prevented.

The Hungarians Subject to the Pope.

S. B., 56, 32.

After the decisive defeat of the Hungarians by Otto I (955), they retired to the territory which they still occupy and gradually gave up their nomadic habits. German missionaries planted Christianity among them, and at the same time German colonists settled among them. Their territory was regarded as a part of the archdiocese of the archbishop of Salzburg, and their ecclesiastical dependence on Germany was naturally bringing about their political dependence too. They, like the Poles, were beginning to be Germanized. In the year 1000, however, their duke offered his territory to the pope as the representative of St. Peter, and received it back as a papal fief, and with it the title of king. At the same time the pope gave Hungary an independent ecclesiastical organization by establishing an archbishop in Gran. Ecclesiastical independence and the royal title together put an end to German influence. Successive kings of Germany made war on Hungary, and more than once compelled its king to take the oath of vassalage. But this was contrary to the papal claims, and Hungary, in fact, maintained its independence of Germany.

Independence of Poland and of Hungary, and the Mountains around Bohemia Check German Expansion.

The events of the year 1000 put an effectual barrier in the way of the conquest and Germanizing of Poland and Hungary. The mountains which surround Bohemia checked the advance of the Germans in that direction also. The duke of the Bohemians frequently took the oath of vassalage to the German king, but was practically independent of him. Only along the Baltic there was no barrier to German expansion, but during this period little or nothing was done there. The kings of Germany, having become involved in struggles with the Hungarians, Bohemians, and Poles, expended all their energies there, leaving the conquest of the north Slavs to later generations. If Otto III had acted with a wise and intelligent regard for the political interests of Germany, he would not have permitted the Poles and Hungarians to free themselves from German influence, and the expansion of Germany to the east might have gone on for some centuries.

On the southwest Germany received a large and important addition in the kingdom of Burgundy. Its last king, Rudolf III, being childless, made his friend, Henry II of Germany, his heir. After Henry's death (1024) Rudolf continued his friendly relations with Conrad II. Consequently when Rudolf died (1032) Conrad II claimed the kingdom. He was successful in causing himself to be elected by some of the nobles and crowned king of Burgundy, but he had to fight for the possession of the kingdom. A certain Burgundian count, Odo, coveted the crown, and many of the nobles supported him. Two vigorous campaigns were necessary to reduce the nobles to subjection and to establish Conrad II securely in possession of the land.

Burgundy Added to the Empire, 1032.

S. B., 30, 31.

Especially in Italy did the German emperor encounter difficulties, for, after asserting his authority over the Italian nobles and cities, he had also to contend with the Greeks. In spite of the fact that Otto I had surrendered the imperial claim to southern Italy (972), his successors renewed it. In support of it they were compelled to make frequent campaigns into that part of the peninsula, most of which were disastrous failures. They clashed there also with the Mohammedans, who, after taking possession of the islands, had established themselves in various places on the mainland. Greeks and Mohammedans even united to resist the Germans, their common foe. Under these circumstances the cities of southern Italy frequently changed their overlords. If the Greeks were successful, the cities obeyed them; if the Mohammedans were victorious, the cities paid them tribute; and wherever the German emperor appeared, the cities acknowledged him.

Wars with the Greeks in Southern Italy.

While Germans, Greeks, and Mohammedans were battling for the possession of southern Italy, a few hardy soldiers of fortune appeared on the scene, and in a short time cleared the

Note to Map VIII.—This map shows the kingdom of Burgundy as it was in 1032, when it was annexed to the empire. Geographically and linguistically it belonged to France, to which most of it eventually came; the rest of it went to Switzerland (compare this map with a map of modern France and Switzerland). It is worthy of note that Cluny, the home of the Cluniac revival, and the "Grande Chartreuse," the monastery in which the Carthusian Order had its origin, were in Burgundy, while Citeaux, the mother monastery of the Cistercian Order, was just beyond its boundary, only a few miles from Cluny. The northern part of the kingdom came to be called the free county of Burgundy (Franche Comté, see Map XV), and formed a part of the possessions of Charles the Bold of Burgundy (see Map XVI). For the various meanings of the word Burgundy in the Middle Age, see Bryce, *The Holy Roman Empire*, Appendix A.

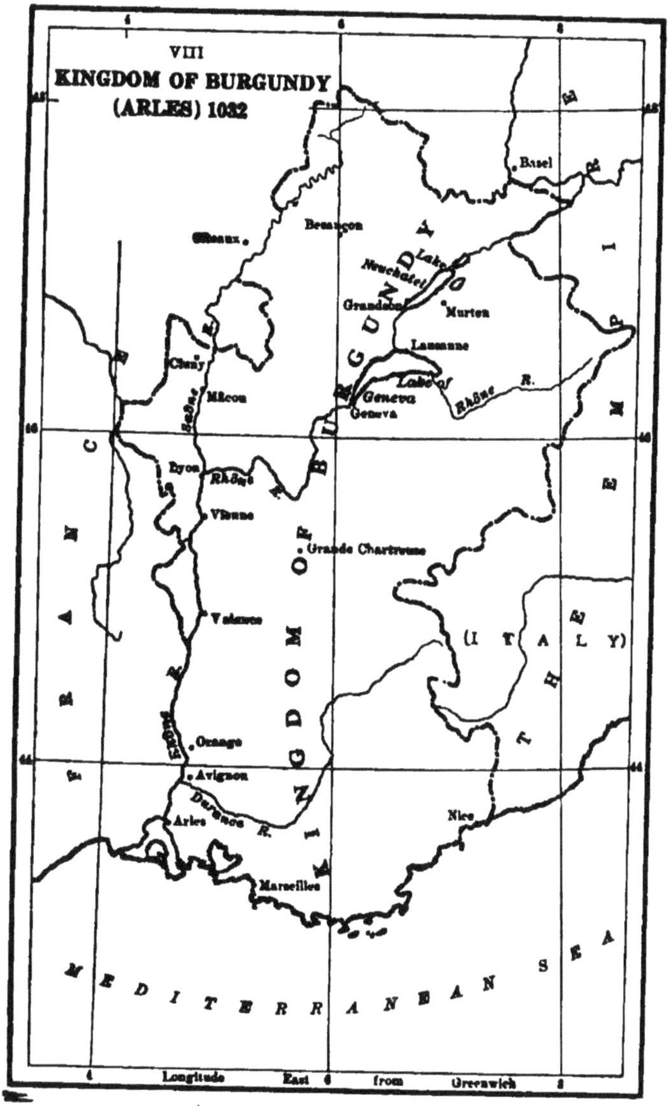
VIII
KINGDOM OF BURGUNDY
(ARLES) 1032
Basel
Besançon
Cîteaux
Lake of Neuchâtel
Grandson
Murten
Lausanne
Cluny
Mâcon
Saône
Lake of Geneva
Geneva
Rhône R.
Lyon
Rhône
Vienne
Grande Chartreuse
Valence
(ITALY)
Rhône
Orange
Avignon
Durance R.
Arles
Nice
Marseilles
KINGDOM OF BURGUNDY
FRANCE
EMPIRE
THE
MEDITERRANEAN SEA
Longitude East from Greenwich
4
6
8
46
44

field of all contestants and made themselves master of it. The romantic story of the establishment of a Norman state in southern Italy has often been told. In 1016 a band of about forty Norman knights, returning from a pilgrimage to Jerusalem, landed at Salerno, which was at that time besieged by Mohammedans. With the help of the Normans, Waimar, the prince of Salerno, defeated the Mohammedans and drove them off. Waimar tried in vain to engage these knights to remain with him, and, when they set out for Normandy, he sent ambassadors with them, who persuaded other Normans to enter his service. In return for their help Waimar invested one of them with Aversa and the title of count. Other Normans, seeking their fortune, also came. Some of them became vassals of Conrad II and agreed to defend the frontier of the empire. In 1041 they joined a certain Arduin —a Lombard count who wished to avenge himself on the Greeks for an injury they had done him—in a successful war on the Greek possessions in Apulia. Arduin kept half of the conquered territory and divided the rest into twelve counties, which he gave to the Normans for their pay. To these possessions they added by conquest until they held about all of southern Italy. They even submitted temporarily to the German emperor, for in 1047 Count Drogo did homage to Henry III and received from him Apulia as a fief. Nothing seems to have come of this, however, for there is no evidence that Drogo performed the duties incumbent on him as a vassal of the empire. With reckless disregard of the rights of others the Normans continued, like true soldiers of fortune, to make themselves master of all the cities and territories of southern Italy. Soon they attacked the lands of the pope. In 1053 Leo IX, with the help of German troops, made a campaign against them, but was defeated and made prisoner by them. They treated him with the greatest respect, however, fell at his feet, and begged him to accept them as vassals. This Leo refused to do, but in 1059 Pope Nicholas II yielded and conferred upon their count, Robert Guiscard, the title of duke of Apulia, Calabria, and "Sicily, if he should by the grace of God get possession of it,"

Normans in Italy.

Robert Guiscard Becomes a Duke, 1059.

S. B., 58.

and received his homage. The pope had no legal claim to all the lands which he thus gave away, but, as the emperor was a mere child, there was no one to oppose his action. Southern Italy had been so often conquered and lost that all legal claims on it seemed to have been destroyed; it was only a bit of prey, belonging to any one who was lucky enough to get it. At the moment it belonged to the Normans by the right of conquest, and, as neither the Greeks nor the Germans were able to substantiate their claims, the pope no doubt felt himself justified in assuming the overlordship of it and in saving as much as possible from the general wreckage caused by the long wars among the Greeks, Germans, Mohammedans, and Normans.*

The emperors of this period, without exception, exercised the same unlimited control of the pope and papacy as had Otto I. And, like him, they were frequently called on to free the pope

* The following details may throw some light on the conflicting imperial and papal claims in southern Italy. In 1050 it is said that Leo IX went into southern Italy and persuaded some cities to render him an oath of homage. This of course did not interfere with the fact that the pope was subject to the German emperor. In 1051 the people of Benevento expelled their duke and offered to submit to Leo IX. He accordingly went to Benevento and received their submission. Since their duke was a vassal of the German emperor and their city an imperial fief, it would logically follow that the pope merely took the place of their duke, and was, therefore, subject to the emperor. Henry III was not inclined to leave Benevento in the hands of Leo, because it was an imperial fief. However, in 1053 Henry yielded and granted Benevento to the pope in exchange for some papal possessions in Germany. The emperor, of course, still possessed imperial sovereignty over Benevento. Henry III was a warm personal friend of Pope Victor II (1054–1057), and granted him for his lifetime the duchy of Spoleto and the county of Fermo. At the death of Victor these should have reverted to the emperor, but, in the disorders attending the regency of Henry IV, the imperial claims to them were not pressed and, the popes retaining them, the papal claim to them was soon established. These facts give some basis for the action of Nicholas II in 1059. On the other hand, Henry III in 1047 became the feudal lord of the Norman count, Drogo, and invested him with Apulia; and at the same time he enfeoffed Waimar of Salerno with his lands; and, as the Normans were the vassals of Waimar, they would be the subvassals of the emperor. Out of these relations the emperor could claim that the lands which the pope received in 1059 were really his own, because he had once possessed them and had never alienated them.

IX

THE NORMAN KINGDOM OF SICILY

Established 1130

Note to Map IX.—The kingdom of the Normans was named after Sicily, although their possessions on the mainland were greater in extent than Sicily. It is an excellent example of a kingdom built up by conquest. The Normans conquered the independent cities in southern Italy as well as those provinces which were still subject to the Greek emperor, and then took Sicily from the Mohammedans. Both the Greek and German emperors claimed all this territory and refused to recognize the validity of the Norman title. Henry VI of Germany (1190–1197) got possession of it by marriage and conquest. Toward the end of the thirteenth century Sicily was separated from the mainland, but both parts were still called the "kingdom of Sicily." When they were reunited they were generally spoken of as the "kingdom of the two Sicilies."

from the tyranny of some Roman faction. Both Otto III and Henry II had to use force against the Crescentius family, which for several years was dominant in Rome. The head of this family controlled the successive popes and filled the office with his supporters. The papacy suffered still more when another powerful family arose in Rome, and factions were formed which fought for the control of the office. In 1046 there were three popes contending for the place, and Henry III was called into Italy to put an end to this scandalous state of affairs. The Romans, offended by the vices of Benedict IX, a creature of the Tusculan family, expelled him from the city, and elected another pope, Silvester III. Benedict IX was restored by force for a while, but sold the office to another member of his family, who took the title Gregory VI. Benedict still called himself pope, however.

The Emperors and the Popes.

S. B., 52, 55.

The Papacy a Local Office.

Three Popes.

Henry III held councils at Sutri and Rome (1046), in which he deposed all three claimants and then appointed a worthy man to the office. So long as Henry III lived the Romans did not attempt to elect a pope without first consulting him, and he named not less than four popes. Europe was, however, at that time becoming imbued with the spirit of Cluny, and already there were heard voices of protest against the influence of laymen in filling ecclesiastical offices.

Henry III Deposes and Appoints Popes.

S. B., 57.

The action of Leo IX (1048-1054) was indicative of the change that was going on. He refused the appointment at the hands of Henry III, but said that he was willing to accept a canonical election at the hands of the Romans. He entered the city in the garb of a penitent and was hailed with joy by the Romans, who unanimously elected him. With him the papacy—for some time a local political office, whose power was scarcely felt beyond the walls of Rome—again became a universal office, conscious of its world-wide authority and its duties to the whole church. He travelled through Italy, France, and Germany, holding councils and regulating ecclesiastical matters. Every-

Leo IX (1048-1054) a Universal Pope.

where he successfully asserted his authority and broke down the independence of the high clergy, who had almost forgotten that the headship of the church belonged to the pope. He made Hildebrand, a monk of Cluny and the embodiment of its spirit, his chief adviser. And under his successors Hildebrand continued to be the power behind the papal throne, until he himself was raised to the chair of St. Peter as Gregory VII (1073).

Election Decree of Nicholas II, 1059.

S. B., 59.

The danger which threatened the papal office from the factions in Rome was not yet entirely removed. At the death of Pope Stephen IX (1058) the Tusculan party took advantage of the absence of Hildebrand from the city—he was still in Germany, whither he had gone to secure the sanction of the empress for the election of Stephen IX—to elect one of their own number. On hearing of this Hildebrand returned in great haste, called a few of the cardinals together, elected another pope, Nicholas II, and succeeded in having him universally recognized. In order to free the papacy from this danger, Hildebrand saw that it was necessary to deprive all laymen of a share in the papal election. Accordingly, in 1059, Nicholas II published a papal election decree, which took the election of the pope from the clergy and people of Rome, and put it wholly into the hands of the cardinal clergy of the city. By the terms of this decree the seven cardinal bishops should choose the pope, and the rest of the cardinal clergy should confirm their election.*

* The term "cardinal" (chief, or principal) was early applied to the parish priests and to a few deacons connected with ancient ecclesiastical establishments in Rome, and to seven bishops in the neighborhood of the city (Palæstrina, Porto, Ostia, Tusculum, Silva Candida, Albano, and the Sabine territory). These seven bishops aided the bishop of Rome, representing him in his absence and assisting him in all important functions, such as the coronation of the emperor (*cf.* S. B., 34). The election decree of Nicholas greatly increased the honor of their title and the importance of their position. Their influence was still further enhanced by Gregory VII, who used them constantly as his legates to all parts of the Christian world. The title "cardinal," because of the honor attaching to it, was soon sought after by other clergymen. Pope Alexander III (1159-1181) is said to have been the first to confer it on one who did not live in Rome, and it then became an important

The election decree of 1059 met with sharp opposition in Germany. The empress, Agnes, who was regent for her little son, Henry IV, was offended by it as well as by the fact that Nicholas II had become the feudal lord of southern Italy and Sicily, thus infringing upon the rights of the emperor. She called together the German bishops, who not only rejected the decree but even declared Nicholas deposed. They took no steps, however, to make their deposition effective. In a short time Nicholas died, and Hildebrand, without consulting the empress, brought about the election of Alexander II. Angered by this, Agnes refused to recognize Alexander and set up an antipope. Although she soon deserted him, he continued, nevertheless, for some years to bear the papal title. This heated but brief quarrel was only a prelude to the great struggle that was soon to begin. For the papacy, so long subject to the emperors and a prey to the factions in Rome, was now in a position to dispute with the emperors for the supremacy of the world. The Cluniac reform had prepared the mind of Europe to welcome the theory of papal supremacy and all the corollaries that could be drawn from it. The "empire of souls" was undoubtedly superior to the "empire of bodies," and hence the pope was superior to the emperor. To most people such reasoning seemed incontrovertible. For the first time in its history the papacy was free from lay interference. The pope, who was the temporal lord of central and southern Italy, was in possession of strong temporal forces with which to support his claims. His Norman vassals, though turbulent and often rebellious, were nevertheless to be his best supporters in his struggle with the emperors. On the other hand, the

German Opposition to the Decree.

The Situation Favorable to the Papacy.

way of recognizing pre-eminent worth in a clergyman to confer upon him the title of cardinal, connecting him nominally with one of the parish churches of Rome. Thus the present Cardinal Archbishop Gibbons, of Baltimore, is the cardinal priest of St. Mary's beyond the Tiber, one of the oldest and most interesting churches of Rome. In 1586 it was decreed that the number of cardinal titles should not exceed seventy, of which six might be bishops, fifty priests, and fourteen deacons. But this decree is not now strictly observed, for in 1902 the college of cardinals consisted of six bishops, fifty-two priests, and eight deacons.

position of the king in Germany was weak, because Henry III had enriched the high clergy but had offended them by his strict control of them, the nobles were rebellious, and the Saxons were, as usual, disaffected, and hence could easily be drawn to the side of the pope. To make matters worse for the empire, Henry III had died at the height of his power (1056), leaving his son six years old to succeed him. The situation was in every way favorable to the papacy.

CHAPTER XI

THE STRUGGLE BETWEEN PAPACY AND EMPIRE. THE FIRST PERIOD (1073 TO 1152)

HENRY III, at his death (1056), left his little son, Henry IV, in an unfortunate position. The nobles of Germany, offended by the strong and independent rule of Henry III, longed for an opportunity to exercise their lawless and predatory instincts. Consequently the accession of a child under the regency of his mother, Agnes, a weak and vacillating woman, was the signal for the beginning of feuds in all parts of the country. Agnes was unable to check the feuds or to punish the offenders. Unable to form a plan of action, she fluttered from one counsellor to another, always dominated by the one who had advised her last. After enduring her helpless indecision for six years, Anno the archbishop of Cologne, Otto duke of Bavaria, and Count Ecbert of Brunswick determined to displace her. They decoyed the young king on board a boat on the Rhine and hastily set out for Cologne. Discovering their intention, Henry, fearing for his life, leaped overboard and would have drowned but for the heroic efforts of Ecbert. Agnes complained of this act of violence, but helplessly resigned her regency.

Henry IV and His Regent.

R., 107.

Unfortunately Henry soon fell under the influence of Adalbert, the ambitious and scheming archbishop of Bremen-Hamburg. To the ill advice of Adalbert can be traced the worst misfortunes of his reign. It was due to the archbishop that Henry became involved in a quarrel with Otto duke of Bavaria, and with Magnus duke of Saxony. And out of this quarrel came the long and disastrous wars with the people of those duchies. The Saxons were already in a rebellious frame of mind, because (1) Henry IV had built a palace in Goslar, a Saxon city, in which

Evil Influence of Adalbert.

Wrongs of the Saxons.

he spent much of his time. His constant presence there was obnoxious to the Saxons because of the heavy demands which he made on them for the support of his household. (2) Henry had also built a number of fortresses in Saxony, in order, as the Saxons declared, to reduce them to slavery. (3) The Saxons were offended because Henry had garrisoned his fortresses, and even the chief fortresses of the Saxon ducal family, with his ministerials,* who treated the Saxons with wanton violence and insolence. Added to all these grievances was the harsh treatment given their duke, which so enraged them that they rebelled.

The rebellion began in 1073, and as Henry's vassals refused to come at his call, the Saxons quickly compelled him to submit to their terms. They demanded that their duke be restored to his duchy, that the king's fortresses in Saxony be destroyed, that all who had taken part in the rebellion be pardoned, and that Otto of Nordheim be restored to the duchy of Bavaria. The Saxons proceeded to destroy the fortresses, the most hated of which was the Harzburg, a powerful fortress which Henry had built on a northern spur of the Harz Mountains. The peasants of the neighborhood, in venting their rage on this, burned the church and desecrated the graves of the brother and infant son of Henry by scattering their bones on the ground. Enraged at this, Henry renewed the war and called on the pope to punish all who were guilty of this sacrilege. In this war Henry was successful, and the Saxons, though more bitter than ever, were compelled to submit. Unfortunately Henry had not learned

The Saxons Rebel.

* The king, as well as all the great nobles, in need of household servants and attendants, had chosen the best of their young serfs, brought them into their palaces, and trained them for their new duties. These servants came to form a class by themselves and were called ministerials. Some of them, equipped with weapons and mounted on horseback, served their lord as a body-guard. Because they fought on horseback they came to form a lower rank of nobility. The kings made use of their ministerials also to assist them in the administration of the government. The proud Saxons were indignant that the king put his ministerials, men of unfree condition, over them. See S. B., 296, 297, for an account of the ministerials.

moderation, but added to the humiliation and resentment of the Saxons by ostentatiously rebuilding the destroyed fortresses. The Saxons therefore eagerly sought an opportunity to renew their rebellion. This they found when Henry became involved in a quarrel with the pope, Gregory VII.

The Issue between Empire and Papacy.

The question at issue in this struggle between empire and papacy, which began with Henry IV and continued at intervals and under various forms during the Middle Age, must first of all be made clear. The emperor, as we have seen, regarded himself as the divinely appointed possessor of universal political sovereignty, which necessarily included the control of the church. Gregory VII (1073-1085) entered the lists with the counterclaim that he was the divinely appointed possessor of universal ecclesiastical sovereignty, which necessarily included the control of all states and governments. This, the question of sovereignty, was and remained the fundamental question; all other questions were merely symptoms of it.

Gregory's Claims.

Dictatus Papæ.

S. B., 65.
O., 45.
R., 109.

The papal claims to sovereignty are expressed in the famous *Dictatus papæ*, which, although not written by Gregory, contains his fundamental principles. According to this document the pope is the only bishop who may be called universal and apostolic (paragraphs 2, 11). He is the supreme lawgiver of the church, having exclusive right to call councils and to ratify their actions (paragraphs 7, 16, 17, 18). He is the supreme judge in the church, to whom all cases may be appealed (paragraphs 19, 20, 21). He has also the supreme executive power, having the right to depose, to reinstate, and to transfer all clergymen as he will, and to erect new bishoprics as seems best to him (paragraphs 3, 5, 7, 13, 25). As universal bishop he has the whole world for his diocese, in which he may perform all episcopal functions without any regard to the local bishop. That is, his authority in every diocese is superior to that of the local bishop (paragraphs 14, 15). Nor are his political powers less sweeping. He is the possessor of all temporal power, for he alone has the right to use the imperial *insignia* (crown, sceptre, ornaments of dress; *cf.* the Donation of Constantine). That is, he has the right, by conferring these *insignia*, to appoint the emperor and, by withdrawing them, to depose him (paragraphs 8, 12). All temporal rulers and princes must acknowledge his supremacy by kissing his foot—an act symbolic of complete subjection (paragraph 9). He has the right to absolve subjects from the oath of fidelity which they have sworn to their lord, and to command them to make formal charges against their rulers (paragraphs 24, 27). His decrees are binding on all alike, and neither emperor nor king may annul them (paragraph 18). These powers are based on three things: (1) the divine origin of the church of Rome, by which is meant the papacy (paragraph 1); (2) the infallibility of the same, since it has never erred and never will err (paragraph 22); and (3) the holy character of each individual pope, which is conferred on him by his ordination (paragraph 23).

There is no doubt that Gregory VII acted according to the principles expressed in the *Dictatus*. Probably no other pope has done so much as he to realize the papal headship of the church and of the world. In ecclesiastical matters he acted with an amazing mastery and assurance. Yet in attempting to exercise the ecclesiastical authority which he claimed, he met with considerable opposition. Especially the bishops, few of whom had ever been made to feel the power of the bishop of Rome, resented what they considered Gregory's usurpation of their powers. He soon perceived that he must have a set of officials to act as a check on the distant clergy. So, as he said, because he could "not be everywhere present in person to attend to matters," he sent out his representatives, or legates, to all parts of the church. Through these legates, who acted in his name and by his authority, he was able to control the church. He compelled all bishops to take an oath of obedience and fidelity to him, and thus built up a universal ecclesiastical power, or state, in opposition to the imperial and royal governments.

Gregory and the Bishops.

Papal Legates.

S. B., 66.
S. B., 67.

The political power which Gregory claimed he also attempted

in the most energetic manner to exercise. He missed no opportunity to enter into relations with the temporal rulers of Europe, either openly asserting or covertly implying his political authority over them. More than once he declared that "our Lord Jesus Christ has made St. Peter ruler over all the kingdoms of this world, and has subjected to him principalities, and powers, and all the great ones of the world." * He was in part successful in this policy, especially with the rulers of the smaller countries, but in others he met with determined resistance. The kings of England, of France, and of Denmark, and the German emperor stubbornly refused to admit his claims, and resented what seemed to them his usurpation of temporal power. Gregory showed discretion in refraining from pushing his claims in all countries at once. He did not seek to force the issue with England and France, but concentrated all his energy on his struggle with the emperor.

Gregory and the Governments.

S. B., 68-73.

With the election of Gregory VII (1073) the spirit of Cluny took possession of the papal throne. It manifested itself immediately in certain reforms which he proclaimed: (1) The clergy everywhere should cease to marry; (2) church offices should no longer be bought and sold but should be filled in a canonical way; and (3) those who had been canonically elected should be invested with their office not by laymen but by the church. That is, his reforms included the prohibition of the marriage of the clergy, of simony, and of lay investiture.

Influence of Cluny.

S. B., 60-64. R., 108.

In regard to the celibacy of the clergy, it is certain that the church early favored it, in the belief that those who were unmarried, being less involved in the affairs and affections of this world, were better able to serve God and to attain a higher degree of holiness. The celibate life, being regarded from the

* In addition to the general statement that Christ had made St. Peter the lord of all the kingdoms of this world, Gregory claimed in specific terms the proprietorship of southern Italy, Sicily, Dalmatia, Germany, Bohemia, Poland, Hungary, Russia, all Spain, Provence, Corsica, and Ireland, but veiled somewhat his pretensions to France, England, Denmark, Norway, and Sweden.

tain statements already made. (1) From the first the Romans believed that the state had supreme authority over all religious matters. In accordance with this view Constantine and his successors assumed the same attitude toward Christianity as they had held toward the pagan religions. Consequently, they naturally regarded the Christian clergy as officials of the state, and, whenever occasion arose, used them in administering secular affairs. Thus they frequently gave bishops oversight of the administration of justice and the election of local officials. (2) Moreover, during the invasions of the barbarians, when the machinery of the imperial government was destroyed, the bishops naturally, because of their office and character, stood for law, order, and justice and they were more and more called on to perform the functions which had always been exercised by the government. (3) Furthermore, the German bishops, because of their learning, became the chief advisers of the king and were indeed indispensable to him in the management of the affairs of his court and government. Everywhere they were in the king's council, and all bishops were officials of the king, whether regularly taking part in his council or not. This council of the king was the germ from which the parliamentary body was developed, and so we find bishops having permanent seats in the parliamentary bodies of those countries which grew out of Germanic kingdoms. The clergy were so essentially a part of the state that they came to be called the "first estate," outranking the nobility, or "second estate," and the commons, or "third estate." (4) Finally, the high clergy had also become bound to the crown in another important way. Bishops and abbots had, in the course of centuries, acquired immense landed possessions. They were, in fact, among the largest landholders, and, like other great landlords, had certain duties to perform for the crown. That is, they had become vassals of the crown, and sustained the same relations to it as did the higher lay nobility. Thus it had come about in a natural way that rulers, whether kings or emperors, exercised a commanding authority over the clergy.

Relation between Church and State.

The office of a bishop had, therefore, become complex. (1) As bishop he had the administration of all ecclesiastical matters in his diocese; he controlled the clergy and was responsible for the spiritual welfare of all in his bishopric. Besides this spiritual side of his office he had also the management of all the temporal interests and possessions of his church—no small task, since the bishops were large landholders. And (2) he was an official and vassal of the king, holding office and lands from him as a fief. He had, in fact, the position of a duke or count, owing the king the same military service as they. He administered justice in his diocese and frequently possessed other *regalia*, such as the right to coin money and to establish markets. The bishop had, therefore, two sets of functions, the one spiritual, the other secular. His authority for exercising the one was in theory derived from the church; for exercising the other, from the king. But as a matter of fact no clear distinction had been made between these, and his investiture by the king was thought to confer on him the right to exercise his spiritual as well as his secular functions.

The Office of Bishop Twofold.

If we turn now to Germany we find that all that has been said about the relation of the clergy to the state applies with especial force to the German bishops, because they had been brought into peculiarly close relations with the emperor. All the German kings, whether crowned emperor or not, made constant use of bishops and abbots in the administration of the government and rewarded them with large gifts of land. As the government was feudalized, the high clergy, as great landlords, were drawn into the feudal relation. That is, they became both officials and vassals of the crown. Some of the bishops even had the title of duke. A peculiarly strong bond attached them to the emperor, who relied on them and used them as a countercheck to the turbulent lay nobility. Since the relation between the emperor and his high clergy was so intimate, he would of course wish to control their election. And in fact we find that from Charlemagne to Henry III all the emperors had

Close Relation of Bishops to Emperor.

S. B., 111, 112.

exercised the right of naming, appointing, or confirming bishops and abbots, and of solemnly investing them with their office. The bishop or abbot to be invested first took an oath of homage and fidelity to the emperor, and received from him the symbols of his office—a ring, a staff (the shepherd's crook, or crozier), and a sceptre.

Such was the situation when Gregory VII published his decrees concerning free ecclesiastical elections and investiture. A struggle was inevitable, for it was inconceivable that the emperor would tamely submit. First of all at stake was his imperial supremacy, and the emperor believed that he was emperor by divine right, with supreme power over the empire and the church. Although the imperial authority over the church had not been exactly defined, it was an undoubted fact, for emperors had even appointed and deposed popes. With a long line of precedents in his favor the emperor was by no means willing to yield his authority at the first demand. Besides the question of supremacy he had at stake large interests. As a feudal lord he was dependent on the undivided loyalty of his vassals, chief of whom were the bishops and abbots. If he could not control their election and investiture, he would be deprived of his rights as feudal lord, and be left without authority over many of his chief officials and vassals. If he could not command the service which they owed him for their fiefs, his power would be materially diminished. The loss of their military service alone would have been ruinous to him, for probably half of his available troops were furnished by them. To the emperor it must have seemed a struggle for existence.

The Struggle Inevitable.

R., 110.

When Gregory VII published his prohibition of simony and the marriage of the clergy (1074), he met with bitter opposition in Germany. Quite undaunted by this, he proceeded to excommunicate five of the king's councillors (1075) because they were guilty of simony. To this the king paid not the slightest attention, but retained his excommunicated councillors at court and continued to offend the pope by openly selling church

Beginning of the Struggle.

S. B., 74.
O., 46.
R., 111.

offices and appointing and investing bishops. Gregory then wrote him a vigorous letter (December, 1075), rebuking him for his disobedience and informing him that the decrees against simony and the marriage of the clergy would be strictly enforced. He further gave the bearers of the letter an oral message for Henry to the effect that if he did not mend his life and send away his excommunicated councillors, Gregory would not only excommunicate but also depose him. The letter and message raised a storm of indignation at the German court, for never before had so presumptuous a threat been heard there. Henry's answer was prompt. At a council held at Worms (January 24, 1076) he deposed Gregory and informed him of his deposition in a letter remarkable for its plain speech and direct charges. At the same time the German bishops wrote Gregory a letter in which they set forth his crimes, and justified their action in deposing him. Gregory immediately answered by deposing Henry and excommunicating him. In his letter of excommunication, after denying all the charges that had been made against him, he proceeds:

S. B., 75, 76.

Confident of my integrity and authority, I now declare in the name of omnipotent God the Father, Son, and Holy Spirit, that Henry, son of the emperor Henry, is deprived of his kingdom of Germany and Italy. I do this by thy (St. Peter's) authority and in defense of the honor of thy church, because he has rebelled against it. He who attempts to destroy the honor of the church should be deprived of such honor as he may have held. He has refused to obey as a Christian should, he has not returned to God from whom he wandered, he has had dealings with excommunicated persons, he has done many iniquities, he has despised the warnings which, as thou art witness, I sent to him for his salvation, he has cut himself off from thy church, and has attempted to rend it asunder; therefore by thy authority I place him under the curse. It is in thy name that I curse him, that all people may know that thou art Peter, and upon thy rock the Son of the living God has built his church, and the gates of hell shall not prevail against it.

Deposition had been answered by deposition, and the struggle was on. The situation would have been somewhat less trying for Henry if the Saxons had not renewed their rebellion. Using the excommunication as a pretext, they eagerly supported the cause of the pope. Moreover, in Germany the immediate effect of the excommunication was great. All who were in any way dissatisfied with the king—and they were many—accepted the excommunication with malicious satisfaction and withdrew their allegiance from him. Even Henry's friends deserted him, and when the Saxons took the field against him he found himself without troops. The rebellious princes determined, if possible, to make his deposition permanent. For this purpose they called a council to be held at Tribur (October 16, 1076). They refused to admit the king to the council, and he was forced to remain, for the sake of safety, at the little town of Oppenheim on the other side of the Rhine. They wrung the most humiliating concessions from him (the Oppenheim agreement); he annulled his decrees against Gregory, and agreed to submit to him in all things; he recognized the validity of the papal deposition and excommunication and promised to present himself for trial at a national council, which was to be held in the following February and over which Gregory was to come to Germany to preside; in the meantime he was to remain in Speier, and, laying aside every mark of royalty, live strictly as one under the ban of excommunication.

Deposition Answered by Deposition, 1076.

S. B., 77.
O., 48.
R., 113.

Saxons Rebel.

Henry IV Submits.

Oppenheim Agreement.

S. B., 78, 79.

Henry knew that his enemies, especially the Saxons, wished to make his deposition permanent, and were cloaking their rebellion with their devotion to the pope. He foresaw that, if Gregory should come to Germany, take up the cause of the Saxons, and sit in judgment on him, he would hardly be able to clear himself and retain his throne. He determined, therefore, by a clever stroke to prevent the pope from coming to Germany, to deprive his rebellious subjects of their pretext, and to destroy the alliance between them and Gregory. To this end he resolved to escape into Italy and to secure the removal of the ban by humbling himself

Henry IV Escapes to Italy.

before the pope. Accordingly he broke his royal word by secretly leaving Speier and setting out for Italy. Fortune favored him, for he safely made the dangerous journey over the Alps in the dead of winter. In the meantime Gregory, after waiting in vain on the border of Lombardy for the escort which the Saxon princes had promised him, had turned back. Not trusting the pacific intentions of Henry, Gregory thought it more prudent to retire to a place of safety. He

Canossa.

S. B., 80, 81. O., 49.

hastened to take refuge in the strong fortress of Canossa, which is situated on a spur of the chalk hills of northern Tuscany, commanding a wide view of the Lombard plain. Thither Henry followed him, only to find that the pope obdurately refused to receive him. Gregory demanded that he return to Germany, keep his agreement with the princes, and await the papal decision, which was to be rendered at the national council in February. For three days Henry presented himself in the garb of a penitent at the castle-gate before he succeeded in softening the papal resentment. Finally, at the earnest entreaties of those who were about him, Gregory yielded and admitted Henry to his presence. The king seemed so penitent and obedient that the pope could not hold out; so he removed the ban of excommunication and absolved him. The final settlement of the affair, however, was postponed to the national council, at which Gregory still expected to be present.

In absolving Henry Gregory had not kept his agreement with the Saxons, who were thereby offended. Gregory wrote them a letter in which he adroitly excused himself for what he had done and assured them that, in spite of the

R., 114.

The Tide Turns.

fact that he had removed the ban, nothing had been settled. Nevertheless, something had been settled. The affair at Canossa had the effect of turning the tide in favor of Henry. It turned out that the pope did not go to Germany, and the national council was not held. Since Henry had been freed from the ban, his friends came back to him and he began to make war on the Saxons, who, although deprived of their pretext, still persisted in their rebellion. They met and, after deposing Henry, elected an anti-king, Rudolf of Rheinfelden. Neither king could gain a decisive advantage in battle, and the war dragged along for some years. Each appealed to Gregory, but he refused to decide between them until he should come to Germany and hold a council. In 1080, however, seeing that the possibility of his going to Germany was very remote, Gregory again decided against Henry, and excommunicated and deposed him, calling on St. Peter and St. Paul to "inform all the world that they could take kingdoms from the unworthy and give them to the worthy"—another way of asserting the papal supremacy.

An Anti-King.

The Second Excommunication.

The excommunication of 1080 did not seriously affect Henry's position. His friends remained true to him and supported him more vigorously than ever. In answer to it Henry again deposed Gregory and set up an antipope. In the field, however, fortune never favored Henry. Time after time he was defeated, and, although the anti-king was slain in battle (October, 1080), the Saxons immediately elected another. The war was then carried into Italy. Matilda, the great countess of Tuscany, had become an ardent supporter of the pope, but many of her vassals were true to the king. These joined the strong imperial party in Lombardy and made war on all who supported the pope. At the call of his friends in Italy Henry crossed the Alps (1081–1082), and, after ravaging the lands of Matilda, went on to Rome. The Romans, however, refused to admit him. Not till 1084 was he admitted to the city. There the antipope crowned him emperor and held a synod, in which he excommunicated and deposed Gregory. Meanwhile Gregory had been besieged in the castle Sant' Angelo, anxiously awaiting the coming of his vassal, Robert Guiscard. Henry retired from the city as the Normans entered it. For having made terms with Henry they took vengeance on the Romans by burning some quarters of the city. At this the Romans were so enraged that Gregory did not dare remain there.

An Antipope.

S. B., 82.

Henry IV in Italy, 1081–1084.

Gregory VII Dies in Exile.

When the Normans withdrew to the south Gregory accompanied them. Age and the burdens of his office had broken him, and he died soon afterward (1085).

Henry's success seemed complete. He had been crowned emperor and had obtained the support of a large part of Italy; he had established his antipope in Rome and driven Gregory into exile; and he had thrown the church into such confusion that no successor to Gregory could be elected for nearly a year. In fact, it was almost three years before a worthy successor of Gregory was chosen. This was Urban II (1087-1099), a Frenchman and a monk of Cluny, thoroughly imbued with Gregory's ideas, whose programme he adopted and carried out so wisely and diplomatically that Henry's success was soon undone.

Saxon Wars.

S. B., 82.

Fortune Deserts Henry IV in Italy.

When Henry withdrew from Rome (1084), he returned to Germany where he spent the next six years in reducing the Saxons. He then again went to Italy to recover the lands of Matilda, which she had already given as a legacy to the papacy. There fortune deserted him. He could not conquer the forces of Matilda; his wife fled to Matilda and made grave charges against him; some of the Lombard cities joined the pope and made a league against him; his son Conrad, who had been made king of Italy, rebelled against him and joined the pope; and Urban II gradually won about all of Italy to his side. In 1097 Henry found it advisable to return to Germany, where great disorder was again prevailing. He was kept busy there for a few years restoring order and seemed to have succeeded when the pope renewed the old struggle by again excommunicating him (1102). Henry tried to outwit the pope by taking the cross and making the crusader's vow, which was supposed to dissolve the ban of excommunication. The pope, however, refused to accept his vow, and many of the princes, wanting only an excuse to rebel, again used the papal ban as a pretext. Their chief ground of complaint was that Henry did not punish his ministerials, who, relying on royal protection, committed with impunity many acts of violence. To make matters worse for Henry, his son, Henry V, who had been chosen as his successor, out of sheer ambition and in the most dastardly manner, rebelled against his father. With consummate hypocrisy he feigned adherence to the pope, and declared that he could have nothing to do with his father until he had secured his release from the ban. The Bavarians and Saxons joined Henry V, and Germany was again rent by civil war. In the midst of it Henry IV died, heart-broken by the shameless treatment which he had received at the hands of his son, Henry V, who succeeded to the throne.

Henry V Follows His Father's Policy.

S. B., 83.
R., 116.
S. B., 84.

That ambition had been the mainspring in the conduct of Henry V was shown by his change in policy. Once established in power, he adopted his father's position and continued the struggle against the papacy with the same unscrupulousness that had characterized his conduct toward his father. In 1110 he went to Italy and forced the issue with such vigor that the pope, Paschal II, made a complete surrender. In 1111 Paschal, in order to retain the right to invest bishops, agreed that all the bishops of the empire should surrender their lands and secular office to the emperor, and should live on the tithes and free-will offerings of their congregations. This, of course, would have ended the whole difficulty. Unfortunately, Paschal had reckoned without the bishops who were concerned. They refused to give up their great wealth and their influential position in the state, and brought such a storm down on the head of Paschal that he cancelled his agreement with Henry. The king, however, was not to be put off, and Paschal, yielding to force, surrendered to him the full right to invest bishops and abbots with all their lands, office, and power, both spiritual and temporal. Thereupon Paschal crowned him and solemnly promised never to put him under the ban.

Henry's victory, however, was of short duration. The clergy refused to abide by the pope's action, and Paschal was forced to annul this agreement also. Consequently the struggle was begun anew. For eleven years it was waged with as much bitterness as ever. Force, however, was of no avail against the unyielding sentiment of the church, and Henry's victories brought him no enduring advantages. The pope again put him under the ban and obdurately refused to treat with him. At length Henry was convinced of the futility of his efforts, and at the same time the new pope, Calixtus II (1119–1124), was a little less inflexible than his predecessors had been. Accordingly they were able to reach an agreement in the concordat of Worms (1122). The victory was with the church, for Henry made perpetual and fundamental concessions to it, while the concessions which he received were made to him personally and were not extended to his successors. He granted "to God, his holy apostles Peter and Paul, and to the whole catholic church . . . canonical election, free consecration, and the investiture with the ring and the staff (crozier)." In return for this perpetual grant, Calixtus made certain temporary concessions to Henry: in Germany bishops and abbots should be elected in Henry's presence, and, before they were consecrated, he should invest them with their *regalia* by means of the sceptre; in case of disputed elections Henry should, in accordance with the advice and judgment of the archbishop and bishops concerned, give his assent and support to the "wiser" party; outside of Germany investiture should take place within six months after consecration; and all should render Henry the services due him from their fiefs.

Concordat of Worms, 1122.

S. B., 85–86. O., 50. R., 117.

Under existing conditions this compromise was sensible, and, inasmuch as it protected the interests of both sides, it was as fair as any compromise was likely to be. Unfortunately, it was not a perpetual agreement. The concessions which Henry made to the church were for all time, but those which Calixtus made to him were secured to him alone, and not to his successors. By the concordat the papacy secured forever the principle of free elections and the right to invest with the ring and the staff. As the concordat was granted to Henry alone, his death (1125) annulled it. His successor did not ask to have it renewed, and in the disputes which later arose about elections

A Lull in the Struggle.

Cf. S. B., 94. S. B., 87.

neither side appealed to it. Later emperors, it should be added, refused to be bound by Henry's concessions to the church. In fact, Frederick Barbarossa and his successors exercised almost as much influence over the election of bishops as did the emperors in the days before the struggle over investiture began. So the concordat, contrary to the commonly accepted view, contributed very little to the solution of the question at issue between empire and papacy. Nevertheless, for the next thirty years a kind of truce was observed, and, although there were a few quarrels about the elections of bishops and abbots, neither party resorted to violence. The reason of this was found in the character of the men who were chosen emperor and in the difficulties which beset the popes.

Lothar III, 1125–1137, Yields to Pope.

S. B., 89.
S. B., 90, 91.

In the imperial election which followed the death of Henry V the extreme papal party scored a success. At the time the leader of that party was the archbishop of Mainz. In summoning the princes to a diet to elect a king he asked them to "bear in mind the oppression of the church in these days and to pray earnestly that in the providence of God this election may result in the freeing of the church from its yoke of servitude." Evidently this party regarded the limited control which the concordat gave to Henry V as "oppression" and as a "yoke of servitude." The diet was a stormy one, and it was a long time uncertain which party should win. In the end, however, the papal party, largely through the cleverness of the archbishop of Mainz, who presided over the meetings, elected its candidate, Lothar III (1125–1137). Although possessing considerable ability and conscious of the justice of the imperial claims, Lothar was nevertheless so subservient to the papacy that in all the most important matters he yielded to it. Pliant and timid, he never dared resort to extreme measures to defend the rights of the crown. Twice he ventured to ask the pope to restore to him the right of investiture as his predecessors had exercised it, but each time he was easily rebuffed. In regard to the lands of Matilda, he surrendered the imperial claim to them on the condition that the pope invest him with them. He thus became the pope's vassal for them. He made a vigorous campaign against the Normans in southern Italy, but, as it was unsuccessful, he did not succeed in advancing the imperial claims.

Quite as subservient to the pope was Lothar's successor, Conrad III (1138-1152). Although a member of the great Hohenstaufen family, he was a man of no ability and had neither the time nor the inclination to renew the struggle. Nor can he be said to have governed Germany well. That unfortunate country was distracted with feuds, which he was powerless to quell. Neglecting his duty to Germany, he spent some years on an ill-fated crusade. He wished to make war on the Normans in southern Italy, but his plans miscarried.

So also Conrad III, 1138-1152.

S. B., 92-93.

Nor was the papacy in a better position than the empire, since it was rent asunder by a disputed papal election. In 1130 the college of cardinals was divided into two parties, each of which uncompromisingly supported its candidate. At that time the law governing papal elections was defective, providing merely that the candidate who received the votes of the "wiser party" should be pope, without telling how to determine which was the "wiser" party. The simple expedient of requiring the successful candidate to receive a majority of the votes was not practised. Indeed, every one who received votes, no matter how few, might claim to be the true pope, on the ground that the party which supported him was the "wiser" one. Consequently disputed papal elections had to be settled by force. One of the candidates, Anaclete II (1130-1138), was supported by the Romans and the people of southern Italy. He bought the recognition of Roger, the Norman duke, by conferring on him the title of king and raising his duchy to the rank of a kingdom. The other, Innocent II (1130-1143), fled to France, where he won the support of Bernard of Clairvaux, and through him that of the kings of France and of Germany. It was chiefly through the efforts of Lothar III that Innocent overcame his rival, al-

Disputed Papal Election, 1130.

S. B., 88.

Innocent II, 1130-1143, Wins.

though the contest lasted for nearly ten years. Innocent finally brought Roger to his side by recognizing him as king of Sicily, thereby offending Conrad III, who regarded Sicily as a part of the empire and Roger as a usurper. Roger and his successors, however, were turbulent and aggressive subjects, who did not hesitate to make war on their feudal lord, even though he were the pope. The peace which Innocent made with Roger was of short duration, and during the next twenty-five years the kings of Sicily were generally in rebellion, and more than once invaded the papal lands in the effort to seize them and to add them to their kingdom. Against these Normans the pope could look only to the German emperor for help.

Scarcely had the troubles of the disputed papal election been settled when the papacy was beset by another danger, this time in Rome itself. The great communal movement, of which the episode in Rome was a part, will be described in a later chapter. For the present purpose it will suffice to say that in the tenth century the cities in Europe were governed in an autocratic way by lords; that in cities in which there was a bishop he was generally the lord, in others the lord was a layman; and that in the eleventh century the inhabitants of the cities began to rebel against their lords, and after driving them out they set up governments of their own. The communal movement was therefore to a certain extent an experiment in democracy. As in other cities, so also in Rome, its bishop had become its lord, governing it in an autocratic way. The movement in Rome differed from that in other cities, chiefly in the fact that there the chimerical attempt was made to restore Rome to her ancient position as mistress of the world, and to that end many of the ancient offices were restored in name.

The Romans Rebel against Papal Rule.

Rome again to Rule the World.

As through the political chaos in the west there still lived on the idea of the universal empire, so at Rome the memory of her greatness was still fresh, and the people had some idea of the power they had exercised in the time of the republic. Restive under all control, they had frequently rebelled against the growing absolutism of the pope. In 1143 they made a determined effort to put an end to papal domination. They drove the pope out of the city, removed all his officials from office, re-created the senate, and intrusted the government of the city to it. Two years later (1145) Arnold of Brescia came and soon obtained a dominating influence in the city. Born and reared in northern Italy, the home of the communal movement, he was thoroughly imbued with its spirit, and supported it with all his might. It was to him, however, merely a corollary of a more important principle. In the struggle about investitures he had come to the radical belief that the clergy should have nothing whatever to do in secular matters, but should devote themselves entirely to the religious duties of their office. Consequently, he held that bishops should resign their lands and their secular office to the emperor, thus ending forever the question about investitures. Furthermore, he was possessed with the idea of the sinfulness of property, an idea that had cropped out in the church at various times, and which was soon to become a central reforming principle of St. Francis. It is not quite clear how far he wished to apply this principle, but it is certain that he wished the clergy to live by it. He is credited with saying that "clergymen with property, bishops with *regalia*, and monks with possessions could not be saved." He himself exemplified his principles by a life of poverty and austere morality. Still another idea took possession of him after he came to Rome; fired by the memory of the city's greatness, he sought to make it again the head of the world. To accomplish this he attempted a complete restoration of its ancient government as well as of its ancient organization of society; he proposed to reform the senate and to invest it with all its ancient authority, to reorganize the knightly, or equestrian, order (the *equites*), and to fix the authority of the people (the *plebs*), to rebuild the capitol, and to restore the ancient offices exactly. The people of Rome, thus reorganized, were again to rule the world; even the emperor, who was to be chosen by them, was to be their official, and the

Arnold of Brescia and His Ideas.

pope was to have no authority, except in ecclesiastical and religious matters.

A moment's consideration will show that all such restorations are impossible. Nevertheless, the commune of Rome, although not at all the ancient Rome which it pretended to be, was an important factor in the politics of the next years. Popes condemned it and fought it, but were compelled to recognize it and to make peace with it. For months at a time it kept the pope out of the city. It confiscated his property, withheld his revenues, seized his strongholds, and made war on him. Eugene III (1145-1153), despairing of overcoming it, finally appealed to Conrad III and begged him to come and punish the rebellious city. Conrad, however, was engrossed with the difficulties which beset him in his realm, and was therefore unable to give the pope the desired aid.

Power of the Commune of Rome.

Still another danger threatened the papacy. The Greek emperor, remembering that all the west had once been a part of his empire, and wishing for commercial reasons to possess some Italian ports, made vigorous efforts for some years to get a foothold in Italy. He troubled the coast with his navy and landed his troops in various places. By force, bribery, and intrigue he seemed likely to accomplish his desire. This, of course, the pope opposed with all his might. So for many years the popes, in need of the emperor's help to restore them to their place in Rome, to protect them against the Norman king of Sicily, and to prevent the Greeks from reconquering a part of Italy, were more tractable, and settled their differences with the emperors without resorting to extreme measures. Nevertheless, during the last years of this period the papal pretensions to supremacy tended to become more firmly established, and to present themselves with greater assurance. The growing boldness of the papal claim was well illustrated by Innocent II, who, probably because Lothar III had become his vassal for the lands of Matilda, caused the wall of his palace to be decorated with a picture representing

The Greeks Threaten Italy.

Bold Claims of the Pope.

Lothar kneeling at the pope's feet, doing him homage, and receiving from him the imperial crown. The picture meant to say that the empire was a papal fief, as is evident from the following inscription, with which it was provided:

> "Rex venit ante fores jurans prius urbis honores,
> Post homo fit papæ recepit quo dante coronam."

That is, "The king comes before the gates of the city, first swearing to observe its rights; then he becomes the pope's vassal and receives from him the crown."

Results.

In the seventy-five years of struggle the pope had won certain solid advantages: he had a charter from the emperor, granting the free canonical election of bishops and abbots, and the right to invest them with the ring and the staff; he had got possession of the disputed lands of Matilda; by conferring on the duke the title of king he had assumed the feudal proprietorship of Sicily and southern Italy; and he had in a pictorial way asserted that the empire was a papal fief. The emperor, on the other hand, had gained nothing. Both Lothar and Conrad had served the papacy rather than the empire, admitting in many ways the supremacy of the pope. Consequently, under them the imperial pretensions to supremacy faded out and lost the aggressiveness which had characterized them under Henry IV. If we compare the position of the empire and papacy in 1075 with their position in 1152, there can be no doubt that the first period of the struggle had turned decidedly to the advantage of the papacy.

CHAPTER XII

THE STRUGGLE BETWEEN PAPACY AND EMPIRE. THE SECOND PERIOD (1152–1198)

Frederick Barbarossa, 1152–1190, Renews Ancient Imperial Claims.

S. B., 95, 96.

LOTHAR III and Conrad III had, as we have seen, subordinated the empire to the papacy. It was inevitable, however, that the struggle should be renewed as soon as there should come to the imperial throne an able and determined man. Such a one was Frederick Barbarossa (1152–1190),* and consequently he spent the best years of his long reign in a persistent effort to recover what his predecessors had surrendered. Thoroughly impressed with the dignity of the imperial office, he was filled with the ambition to restore the empire to its former greatness. Regarding himself as the successor and heir of the great emperors, he determined to rule in the same grand way as he imagined they had governed. At the time of his election Frederick announced to the pope that he was going to restore the empire to its former strength, and at the same time to honor and obey the clergy. Evidently he did not then perceive the irreconcilable conflict between the papal and imperial claims. His ideas, though large, were indefinite until he came into contact with professors of law in the university of Bologna, who expounded to him the imperial theory as they found it expressed in the code of Justinian. Thereafter his programme or policy was definitely and plainly formulated, and it brought him into conflict with the papacy and also with the Italian cities.

Basing his right to the German crown on the action of the

* From their ancestral castle in southern Germany (a few miles east of Stuttgart) he and his family are called the Hohenstaufen, or the Staufer; *cf.* genealogical tables.

princes, Frederick merely informed the pope of his election without asking him to confirm it. With a vigor unknown to that generation he set himself to the task of ending the feuds which were ruining Germany. The country was in a wretched state because the people would not resort to courts for justice against those who wronged them, but, taking the law into their own hands, made war on all their enemies. Consequently, petty and ruinous private warfare was raging from one end of Germany to the other. During Frederick's whole reign one of his chief interests was the maintenance of order. He more than once issued stringent laws, and threatened with severe punishment all who should disturb the peace. Passing through one province after another, he also compelled the people to take an oath that they would commit no act of violence.*

Vigorous Rule in Germany.

S. B., 247, 248.

At first Frederick thought only of working harmoniously with the pope. To govern the world was a task which had been committed jointly to the church and to the empire, and he informed the pope that he intended to do his whole duty as the character of his office demanded. Pope Eugene III was, as we have seen, in grave need of help. The Romans were in rebellion against him; his vassal, the king of Sicily, was at war with him; and the Greek emperor was trying to get possession of a part of the Italian mainland. Since Frederick's first ambition was to acquire the imperial crown, and since he could obtain this only from the pope, it was natural that he should espouse the papal cause. Accordingly, in 1153, Frederick and the pope concluded a treaty, in which the papal diplomatic skill took advantage of Frederick's eagerness to possess the imperial crown. Frederick promised in specific terms that without the consent of the pope he would not make peace with the Romans or with the king of Sicily, but that he would use all his power to re-

Treaty of Constance, 1153.

S. B., 97.

* Furthermore, he sought to diminish such warfare by reviving an ancient punishment which was extremely humiliating: he sentenced every noble who disturbed the peace to carry a dog in his arms a German mile (probably three or four English miles).

duce the Romans to papal subjection, and to defend the pope and his possessions against all who attacked them (meaning the king of Sicily). He further promised to do all he could to keep the Greek emperor from obtaining land in Italy. On the other hand, the pope promised merely to give him the imperial crown, and to aid him in "maintaining and increasing the honor of his realm," a phrase about the interpretation of which there could easily be a wide difference of opinion.

Frederick hastened the work of establishing peace in Germany in order to go as soon as possible to Rome to receive the imperial crown. This, however, was not the only reason of his haste. The smaller Lombard cities, oppressed by their more powerful neighbors, besought his aid, and the commune of Rome, still resisting the pope, appealed to him and wished to make terms with him. In the autumn of 1154, he crossed the Alps, and after spending some months in a fruitless attempt to settle the quarrels of the Italian cities, he proceeded to Rome. Just then the pope was Adrian IV, the only Englishman who has ever occupied the throne of St. Peter. As his situation had not changed, he renewed the treaty of Constance and looked to Frederick for help against all his enemies. When Frederick approached the city Adrian joined him. Their first meeting was marred by a dispute over a matter of etiquette, which did not augur well for their harmonious relations in the future. When the pope arrived at the king's camp, Frederick neither went out to meet him, nor led his horse, nor held his stirrup for him to dismount. Adrian was deeply offended at this lack of respect, and refused to enter into friendly relations with him and "to give him the kiss of peace." Frederick declared that it was beneath his dignity to render the pope such a service, and that it was not his duty to do so because none of his predecessors had ever done such a thing. For two days they argued the question with great bitterness. Finally Frederick was convinced by some of the older princes in his following that Lothar III had rendered the pope

Frederick in Italy.

The Stirrup Episode.

S. B., 98.

this service; consequently he submitted and did so too.* They then proceeded to Rome, where Adrian crowned him emperor. This offended the people of Rome, who, having restored, as they thought, the ancient republic of Rome, claimed the right to name and crown the emperor. Scarcely had the coronation ceremony been performed when the Romans attacked Frederick's troops in the streets. A bloody battle ensued, in which Frederick repulsed them, but for the sake of safety he withdrew from the city, taking Adrian IV with him. He still intended to make a campaign against the king of Sicily, but his vassals, fearing the great heat and the Italian fever, insisted on returning to Germany at once. He accordingly set out for the north without having in any way fulfilled the terms of the treaty of Constance. In fact he had rendered the situation of Adrian worse, for, because of his coronation and the battle in the streets, the Romans were more embittered against him than ever, and for some months refused to permit him to enter the city.

Coronation.

The pope, thwarted by the emperor's failure to keep his promise, was thrown on his own resources. In regard to the policy to be pursued the college of cardinals was divided. A large majority of them still contended that all hope was to be placed on the emperor, and that the pope should remain true to him and wait until he could return to Italy with an army sufficient to reduce all the enemies of the church. A small minority, however, was hostile to the emperor and urged Adrian to act independently of him and to make peace with William, who in the meantime had succeeded his father Roger as king of Sicily. After some months of deliberation Adrian decided to act on the advice of the minority. He accordingly came to an understanding with the people of Rome, and also concluded a favorable treaty with the king of Sicily without asking Frederick's consent. In making

The Cardinals Divided.

Adrian IV Makes Peace with Romans and Normans.

S. B., 99.

* In fact several German kings had done so; among them were Pippin, Ludwig the Pious, and Ludwig II.

this treaty Adrian assumed that he was feudal lord of Sicily, thus offending Frederick, who regarded Sicily as a part of the empire and William as a usurper. Furthermore, Frederick believed that Adrian was bound by the treaty of Constance not to make peace with the king of Sicily without his consent.

The Besançon Episode, 1157.

S. B., 100–102.

Frederick's anger soon found expression. A Danish bishop, while passing through the empire on his return from Rome, was seized by some barons and held as a prisoner. In spite of the pope's urgent appeals, Frederick made no attempt to have him released. Adrian finally wrote a sharp letter of remonstrance, which his legates delivered to Frederick at Besançon (1157). When this letter was translated into German in the presence of Frederick and his court, it produced the deepest indignation. For Adrian, after reminding Frederick that he had conferred the imperial crown on him, added that he did not regret this, but would gladly, if it were possible, confer on him even greater *beneficia*—which might mean either fiefs or kindnesses. The translator of the letter rendered it "fiefs," thus making it appear that the pope boldly claimed the empire as a papal fief. An angry discussion followed, during which some of the hotheaded nobles became so enraged that they drew their swords, rushed on the legates, and would have slain them but for the intervention of the emperor. Frederick seized all the papers of the legates, among which he found many copies of the pope's letter addressed to the bishops and abbots of Germany, and a large number of blank forms bearing the pope's seal and signature. These blanks, when filled out by the ambassadors, had the force of papal commands and were to be used for the purpose of levying assessments on the churches of Germany whenever and wherever the legates should see fit. At this Frederick's anger was deeply stirred. This feature of the episode is important, because it is one of the earliest evidences we possess that the papal taxation was becoming burdensome and creating dissatisfaction with the church. Frederick ordered the legates to return to Rome immediately on the same road by which they had come, turning neither to the right nor to the left. A spirited correspondence ensued, in which Adrian finally explained the objectionable phrases: by "conferring" the imperial crown he meant merely that he had placed it on Frederick's head, and by "*beneficia*" he had meant kindnesses.

Thus the incident was closed, but, as Adrian had not frankly declared that the empire was not a papal fief, nothing had been done to define the relation between empire and papacy. The deeper question at issue had therefore not been settled, and the quarrel was soon renewed. Many acts of the one offended the other, because each was acting in the belief that his authority was superior to that of the other. Adrian finally sent ambassadors to Frederick to state the papal demands: the emperor should not send his officials to Rome without the pope's consent, because the pope possessed independent sovereignty in the city; the emperor should not collect the *fodrum* (a tax in provisions for the support of himself and his army when passing through the territory) from papal lands except when he came to Rome for the imperial crown; bishops in Italy should take only the oath of fidelity to the emperor and not the oath of homage; this they should render only to the pope; the bishops should not be required to entertain (free of charge) the imperial ambassadors; and, finally, certain lands which were then in the emperor's hands should be restored to the pope because they belonged to him.* In reply to these demands Frederick presented a long list of his grievances against the pope, only a few of which are known: Adrian had broken the treaty of Constance, in which he had promised not to make peace with the Greeks, the Sicilians, or the Romans, without Frederick's consent; papal ambassadors came and went through Germany without the king's permission, and, while doing so, lived at the expense of the bishops; and the pope intrenched on the royal

The Quarrel Renewed.

S. B., 104.

* These were Tivoli, Ferrara, Massa, Fiscaglia, all the lands of the Countess Matilda, all the territory from Aquapendente to Rome, the duchy of Spoleto, and the islands of Sardinia and Corsica.

and imperial prerogatives by hearing appeals from Frederick's subjects. Frederick declared that he was willing to submit each point to investigation and trial, but the pope, regarding his own demands as an ultimatum, stubbornly refused to discuss them. He was about to put Frederick under the ban when he was suddenly cut off by death (1159).

This quarrel between pope and emperor led to a contested papal election. The anti-German party in the college of cardinals had grown, and by this time numbered among its adherents nearly all the cardinals. This party elected as pope Alexander III (1159–1181), a man who was known to be a determined opponent of Frederick. A small group of cardinals, believing that the emperor was in the right, and appealing to him for aid and protection, elected as antipope a man who was an ardent supporter of the imperial cause. Frederick supported this antipope and entered into a conflict with Alexander III which was to last for seventeen years. Frederick would probably have had little difficulty in overcoming the pope if he had not at the same time had other foes to contend with. These were his unruly German vassals and the cities of northern Italy.

Disputed Papal Election, 1159.

S. B., 105–107, 113.

We have already seen that the cities of Italy had rebelled against their lords, driven them out, and set up a government of their own, which we call communal. Although these cities still regarded themselves as a part of the empire and subject to the emperor, they each formed, in fact, a little city-state, exercising complete sovereignty within its walls and over the territory about it. They had been able to develop this sovereignty because the emperor's journeys into Italy had been relatively infrequent and of short duration. It was inevitable that there would be trouble if Frederick should attempt to recover sovereignty over them, and it was equally inevitable that he would make the attempt.

When Frederick went to Italy for the second time (1158), he held a diet on the Roncaglian plain (in the valley of the Po), to which he summoned representatives of all the cities and certain professors of the law school of Bologna. In a meeting of the diet Frederick set forth his claims to the rights of the crown (*regalia*) and, in order that there might be no misunderstanding in the matter, asked for a definition of them. Thereupon the diet unanimously decided that the emperor had the feudal sovereignty over the cities, and his *regalia* were defined as the right "to appoint dukes, marquises, counts, consuls (that is, the officials in the cities), to coin money, to levy tolls, to collect the *fodrum*, to collect customs and harbor dues, to furnish safe-conducts, to control mills, fisheries, bridges, and all the waterways, and to demand an annual tax not only from the land but also from each person."

The Emperor's Rights Defined.

S. B., 103.

After this clear decision had been reached it seemed that Frederick was on the point of realizing his high dream of restoring imperial sovereignty in Italy. He sent his officials through all the towns and even through Sardinia and Corsica to assume the authority which had been unanimously accorded him. Everywhere, however, difficulties beset them. The people, accustomed to elect their officials, were enraged that the ambassadors insisted on appointing them. Worse even than this was the imperial command to destroy the walls and towers with which every city had surrounded itself. Popular indignation increased daily against the men who had represented the cities in the diet as well as against the emperor. Everywhere rebellions broke out. Some of the imperial officials were maltreated, and others escaped the violence of the mob only by fleeing in the night. Frederick prepared to put down the rebellions and to chastise the offenders. Crema and Milan were the first to feel his anger. He took the little city of Crema after a desperate resistance of eight months, and Milan after a heroic defense of nearly three years. Both cities he completely destroyed and drove their inhabitants into exile. In these efforts, however, his forces were exhausted, and he was unable to continue the war. He was compelled to return to Germany, and, as he withdrew, the cities were left to restore their communal governments and to resume their course, which had been interrupted by his coming.

The Cities Rebel.

Three times after this Frederick returned to Italy to renew the struggle (1163, 1167, and 1174), but with ever-diminishing success. The opposition to him grew stronger, until the whole country was united to resist him. The pope, Alexander III, with great ability and untiring efforts, established against him the Lombard League, which included the king of Sicily, the papal states, and the Italian cities. Frederick's successes were temporary, and the few advantages which he won he could not retain, while the league constantly increased in power. At the critical moment some of Frederick's chief German vassals refused to come to his support. The end of the struggle was reached in the battle of Legnano (1176), in which Frederick was utterly defeated and his army destroyed. He was compelled to conclude a six years' truce, at the end of which, by the peace of Constance (1183), the relations between the emperor and the Lombard cities were defined and peace fully restored. Frederick surrendered his claims as they had been defined in the Roncaglian diet (1158), and granted the cities free self-government with the right to elect their own officials, and all the *regalia* and other rights which they had been accustomed to exercise. For Frederick very little was left: if there were any regalian rights which the cities had not exercised, he should have them; the consuls (chief officials) of each city should, before taking office, give him an oath of allegiance and swear to protect all his possessions and rights, and Frederick should invest them with their office; every time he came to Italy the cities should repair the roads and bridges, pay the *fodrum*, and furnish him and his troops with a market (that is, bring provisions to them to sell); the cities recognized Frederick as the highest judicial instance by according him the right to hear appeals and to establish his appellate judges in each city.

The Lombard League.

S. B., 112.

Defeat of Frederick.

Peace of Constance, 1183.

S. B., 108, 109. O., 70.

What Frederick had failed to acquire by force he set himself to get by peaceful and diplomatic means. Toward the cities he pursued a policy of conciliation which won him the love of the citizens, and during the last years of his reign nothing arose to disturb the peace established in 1183. With Alexander III Frederick made peace, but not all the points at issue between them were settled, and consequently their relations could not be entirely harmonious. In fact, Frederick continued to assert the imperial claims almost as if he had been victorious at Legnano. Having failed to wrest Sicily from the pope and from the Norman, he determined to secure it in a peaceable way. He married his son, Henry VI, to Constance, the heiress of the Sicilian crown. The pope, who foresaw the danger which this marriage threatened, opposed it, but in vain. The relations between Frederick and the pope grew constantly more strained. The grounds of offense were various: the quarrel about the lands of Matilda was renewed; the pope complained because in Germany tithes were sometimes paid to laymen instead of to the clergy; bishops and abbots were compelled to have laymen to represent them in secular affairs, and these advocates, as such representatives were called, had acquired so powerful a position that they often oppressed those whom their office bound them to protect; this evil, the pope said, Frederick did nothing to correct; at the death of a bishop Frederick was accustomed to seize all his possessions (*spolia*), and also to appropriate all the income of a bishopric as long as it was vacant. To these practices the pope vigorously objected; and some disputed episcopal elections, in which the pope favored one candidate and Frederick another, added to the bitterness between them.

Frederick's Diplomacy.

Grounds of Offense.

More than once a complete rupture seemed unavoidable. The papal policy, however, was frequently interrupted by death; there were four papal elections within the space of six years. And, at an opportune moment, the news that Saladin had taken Jerusalem came and filled all Europe with a new and overpowering interest. Jerusalem must be recovered at any cost. The death of the pope occurred a few days later, and the cardinals, determined that peace should be restored between papacy and empire, unanimously elected as pope a man who was known to be a

Death of Frederick, 1190.

warm friend of Frederick. The new pope was willing to concede to the emperor everything that rightfully belonged to him if only he would take the cross. This Frederick did, and so peace was made on terms favorable to him. He was not permitted, however, to enjoy the fruits of this peace, for on the way to Jerusalem he met his death by drowning (1190).

One of Frederick's dearest ambitions had been to secure his family in the possession of both the German and the imperial crowns. In 1169 he had persuaded the German princes to elect as king his son Henry VI, then only four years old. More than once he tried to procure the imperial crown for Henry, but this the pope steadily refused, declaring that from the nature of things there could be but one emperor. Henry VI had been intrusted with the government of Germany when his father set out on the crusade, and consequently when the news of Frederick's death reached Germany there was no break in the government. Shortly before this William II, the last of the Norman kings of Sicily, had died (1189), and Henry made all possible haste to go and take possession of that kingdom. On his way he stopped at Rome and was crowned emperor by the pope. Sicily, however, was not to be his without a struggle. A large party in that country, opposed to having a foreigner for their king, disregarded the claim of Constance to the throne, and elected as king one of their own number, Tancred, count of Lecce. The pope had already recognized Tancred, and was supporting him with his influence. Henry, however, was not to be turned back by this, and, although he knew that he would thereby incur the anger of the pope, he proceeded against Tancred. His first campaign ended disastrously, and he was compelled to return to Germany, where he was for some time engaged in overcoming rebellions and in settling feuds. At no time did his ability as a statesman manifest itself more clearly than in these first years of his reign. He had been brought up in the imperial idea, and it is not strange that his ambition should have outstripped that of his father. Henry VI already entertained the hope and the well-defined plan of re-establishing

Henry VI, 1190–1197.

the empire in its widest extent. To accomplish this he must have peace at home. Consequently he exerted himself to the utmost to establish peaceful relations among all his subjects. By nature he possessed a conciliatory and winning manner, and this had been developed by the training in diplomacy which he had received. Everywhere he showed that he was a successful peacemaker. He not only ended the feuds but also united those who had been engaged in them in an enthusiastic devotion to himself.

Establishes Peace in Germany.

Fortune for a while favored Henry VI in the realization of his imperial plans. Richard Lionheart, king of England, had been the centre of a league against him, allying himself with some of the rebellious nobles of Germany and with Tancred of Sicily. Richard, while returning from his crusade, attempted to pass through Germany, but was seized and delivered into Henry's hands. Richard could free himself only by paying a ransom, by agreeing to break his alliance with all who were Henry's enemies, to furnish Henry with troops for his campaign against Tancred, and, most important of all in Henry's eyes, by acknowledging that England was an imperial fief, doing homage to Henry, and receiving the crown of England from his hands (1194). In this way Henry accomplished the first great step toward the realization of his imperial dream.*

Makes Richard of England His Vassal.

On France Henry watchfully gazed, but in vain, for no opportunity to make the king of France his vassal presented itself. Sicily was still in rebellion; so in 1194 he recrossed the Alps. The Italian cities were once more involved in strife and were divided into two hostile parties. Henry cleverly conciliated them all and soon had them at peace with one another and devoted to himself. Regardless of the pope's claims to sovereignty, he established imperial officials throughout Italy. In the mean-

Establishes Imperial Government in Italy and Sicily.

* This subjection of England to the empire, which to Henry seemed so important, was of course merely nominal. The English paid no attention to it. In this the futility of all Henry's efforts may be seen. The imperial sovereignty of the world was but a will-o'-the-wisp.

time both Tancred and his only son, who was to succeed him, had died (1194), and Henry found little difficulty in taking possession of the Sicilian kingdom.

Plans to "Restore" the Empire.

Lord of a large part of the west, Henry was now in a position to turn his attention to the east. That he had not long before this been excommunicated was due to the fact that the ruling pope, Cœlestine III (1191-1198), was a weak and decrepit old man, who lacked the courage to proceed to extreme measures. At the same time he was so eager to bring about a crusade that he was willing to make almost any concessions. Accordingly, when Henry VI announced his intention of going on a crusade, Cœlestine III willingly forgave all and made peace with him. Henry was, of course, not in the least interested in a crusade as such, but it fitted well into his great plan of restoring the empire to its ancient boundaries. His crusade had for its object not merely the acquisition of Palestine but also the conquest of the Greek empire. For this, however, he needed a pretext to justify himself in the eyes of the Christian world.

The Pretext for Attacking the Greek Empire.

And just at that moment a plausible pretext presented itself. Irene, the daughter of the Greek emperor, Isaac Angelus, had been married to the son of Tancred and had fallen into the hands of Henry VI when he took possession of Palermo. This young widow he married to his brother, Philip, duke of Suabia, in the hope that through her his family might acquire a claim to the Greek throne. Isaac was a weak and inefficient ruler, and his position was daily becoming more insecure. In his need he appealed to Henry for help. This Henry promised, and at the same time sent his ambassadors to Constantinople to demand a large tribute, the cession of nearly all the Balkan peninsula, and a Greek fleet to aid him in the crusade he was about to make. If his demands were not granted Henry threatened to attack the Greek empire. A sudden change gave Henry a still better pretext. In an insurrection (1195) Isaac was dethroned and his brother Alexius made emperor in his place. With characteristic cruelty Alexius blinded Isaac and imprisoned him and his young son, who was afterward known as Alexius IV. Henry VI made preparations to invade the Greek empire, in order, as he said, to avenge Isaac and restore him to the throne, but in reality to seize the crown for himself.

Cyprus and Armenia Submit to Him.

During all this time Henry was busily engaged in enrolling crusaders, and as fast as possible sending them to the east. He himself found much to do in the west, and continually put off his departure. He carefully laid his plans for the extension of his power in the east. The kings of Cyprus and of Armenia became his vassals and promised to aid him not only against the Mohammedans but also against the Greeks. Although his plan was so great as to be chimerical, yet success seemed within his grasp when a brief illness cut him off (1197).

His Death.

His death put an end to his gigantic undertaking, and all that he had accomplished was quickly undone, because he left no one able to continue his policy. He had but one son, not quite three years old, afterward famous as Frederick II. The advantages which he had gained for the empire over the papacy were lost. Although Henry had already persuaded the nobles to elect his infant son king, a contest arose over the crown, which for some years involved Germany in civil war. The papacy, on the other hand, grew incomparably stronger. Cœlestine III was succeeded by Innocent III (1198-1216), one of the greatest of all popes. So this period, like the first one, ended with the papacy in the ascendancy.

CHAPTER XIII

THE STRUGGLE BETWEEN PAPACY AND EMPIRE. THE THIRD PERIOD (1198–1254)

WITH the pontificate of Innocent III (1198–1216) the papacy became, in fact, what it had long aspired to be, the supernational power of Europe, disposing of crowns and dignities, deposing emperors and kings, settling international disputes, and with supreme assurance controlling the internal affairs of all countries. Innocent might well be called the arbiter of Europe, for there was no one able successfully to resist him. The universal monarchy which Gregory VII tried to erect, Innocent completed, and he also rounded out the theory on which it was based. His writings, especially his letters, are rich in passages to prove (1) that the pope is the absolute governor of the church, with unlimited power over it; (2) that the pope is superior to all secular powers; and (3) that they must obey him in all things, temporal as well as spiritual. "As God, the creator of the universe, set two great lights in the firmament of the heaven, the greater light to rule the day, and the lesser light to rule the night (Gen. 1 : 15–16), so He set two great dignities in the firmament of the universal church, . . . the greater to rule the day, that is, souls, and the lesser to rule the night, that is, bodies. These dignities are the papal authority and the royal power. And just as the moon gets her light from the sun, and is inferior to the sun in quality, quantity, position, and effect, so the royal power gets the splendor of its dignity from the papal authority." "The hand of the Lord has raised us from the dust and set us upon the throne that we may sit in judgment not only with the rulers of the world, but over them." "There is a king set over each kingdom, but St. Peter and his successors are set over the whole world." "The church is free only where she possesses complete sovereignty in both spiritual

Supremacy of Innocent III, 1198–1216.

S. B., 114–115.

His Ideas.

and temporal affairs." The government of the whole world in both spiritual and temporal matters—a colossal task—rested upon the shoulders of the pope.

This task Innocent III set himself with great zeal and practical wisdom to perform. In a long and stubborn contest with John of England, during which he put England under the interdict* (1208) and excommunicated the king (1209), he obtained one of his greatest successes. He humbled John and forced him to admit that England was a papal fief and to accept the crown at his hands (1213). Upon England he levied a feudal tax of one thousand silver marks, which John promised should be paid annually.

Innocent III and England.

S. B., 126, 129.

With France Innocent's success was not so decisive. He attempted to interfere in the quarrel between Philip II and John of England, but Philip luckily evaded recognizing him as his feudal lord. In a moral question, however, Philip was compelled to submit to Innocent's judgment. In 1193 he had married a Danish princess, Ingeborg, in the hope that he would thereby secure Denmark's aid in his war against England. He immediately divorced her, and she appealed to the pope. When Innocent came to the papal throne he espoused her cause and ordered Philip to restore her to her rightful position as wife and queen. Philip refused to do so, and a long struggle ensued. Innocent put France under the interdict (1200), and threatened the king with excommunication. Not, however, until 1213 did Philip entirely submit to the will of the pope and receive Ingeborg as his wife.

France.

O., 66.

The kings of Spain, Denmark, and Norway, submitted to his claims; his authority was recognized in Bohemia and Poland; and by the success of the fourth crusade he became the feudal lord of the so-called Latin empire established in Constantinople. In fact, under Innocent III the papacy was at the height of its political power.

Other Countries.

S. B., 123-128.

* That is, he forbade all church services, sacraments, and Christian burial.

We are interested here chiefly in his relations with the empire. Henry VI had, as we have seen, set up an imperial government throughout Italy. His authority was established even in Rome, for the prefect (mayor) of the city was his official, receiving the investiture of his office from him (contrary to the terms of the peace of Constance). Innocent's first work was to destroy this imperial government and to put a papal government in its place. The day after his coronation he compelled the prefect of Rome to take an oath of allegiance to him and to do him liege homage. Thus he proceeded until in central and southern Italy not an imperial official was left. The situation in Sicily made his victory there easy. Constance, the widow of Henry VI, disliked the Germans and tried to drive them out of the kingdom. Many of them refused to go and, fortifying themselves in their castles, made war on her. In her extremity she turned to the pope, and, although Henry VI had never admitted that Sicily was a papal fief, she begged Innocent to invest her little son, Frederick II, with it. She agreed that the kingdom should pay the pope annually one thousand gold coins as feudal dues. Constance died in 1198, after appointing Innocent both guardian and regent for her son. Nothing could have fitted more perfectly into the plans of Innocent than this arrangement.

Innocent and the Empire.

Establishes a "Papal" Government in Italy and Sicily.

S. B., 123-125.

In Germany also the course of events favored Innocent, for the death of Henry VI was followed by a contested royal election which plunged that unfortunate country into civil war. Henry had obtained from the German princes the election of his infant son as king, but, on the death of Henry, the Guelf* party refused to recognize the child and eagerly sought a suitable candidate from their own party. Henry had intrusted his interests to his brother Philip, duke of Suabia, who hastened to Germany to secure that country for his nephew. Many princes, although wishing to maintain their fidelity to

Disputed Royal Election in Germany.

S. B., 130.

* The Hohenstaufen were commonly called the Ghibellines, and their opponents were known as the Guelfs.

the Hohenstaufen, were unwilling to subject Germany to the ills that would certainly attend the rule of a boy king, and they fairly forced the crown upon Philip. Seeing that the cause of his nephew was hopeless, Philip finally yielded and accepted the election (March, 1198). The Guelf party, having renewed the alliance with Richard Lionheart, and having come to an agreement with Innocent, elected as anti-king, Otto IV, the youngest son of Henry the Lion, the deposed duke of Saxony.* The rival kings prepared to fight, but at the same time both appealed to the pope for recognition and confirmation, not only as king of Germany but also as emperor. Innocent declared that it was his duty to decide in such cases, because the empire was a papal fief, deriving its origin and authority from the papacy; he also declared that the pope alone could create an emperor, crown him, and invest him with the empire. He put off his decision, however, as long as he could, because he was taking advantage of the situation to destroy the imperial government in Italy. Not till 1201 did he publish his decision. It was a foregone conclusion, however, that he would support Otto, who had already promised to concede all the papal demands. In a remarkable document he most ingeniously discussed the claims of the three candidates (Frederick II, Philip of Suabia, and Otto IV), examining the legality of the election of each, the fitness of each for the position, and the expediency from the point of view of the church of recognizing him.

The Decision of Innocent.

S. B., 130.

This decision of the pope had, of course, not the slightest effect. Philip made an alliance with Philip II of France, and Otto sought help of John of England. As Philip began to lose ground he tried to win Innocent's support by offering him large concessions. Innocent, however, refused, and the war was continued. Finally, in 1206, the fortune of war changed; Philip drove his

The Struggle.

S. B., 131, 133, 134.

* Henry the Lion, duke of Saxony, had refused to bring his army into Italy to aid Frederick Barbarossa; so after the battle of Legnano (1176), Frederick deposed him and drove him out of the country. *Cf.* S. B., 112.

rival from the field, and Innocent, a practical man, who reckoned with facts and made the best of them, recognized him as king. Peace was virtually concluded between them and Philip was firmly established in power, when he was basely murdered by his vassal, the palatine count, Otto of Wittelsbach. It was an act of personal vengeance, because Philip had broken his promise to give his daughter to Otto in marriage.

All Germany was shocked by the news of this tragic event, which left the field clear for Otto IV. In a short time he succeeded in conciliating the German princes, and the pope joyfully confirmed him as king and promised him the imperial crown. To receive this he went to Rome (1209). A bitter disappointment was in store for Innocent. For after the coronation Otto IV, with remarkable firmness, adopted the policy of the Hohenstaufen; he demanded of the pope all the land and rights which Henry VI had possessed at the time of his death; he appointed imperial officials in all the papal territory; he compelled the prefect of Rome to do him homage; and finally, disregarding the rights of Frederick II, in 1210 he invaded the kingdom of Sicily with the intention of adding it to his possessions. For these offenses Innocent deposed and excommunicated him (1210) and sought to raise up enemies against him in Germany. In this he succeeded beyond expectation, because the German princes were opposed to Otto's attempt to seize Sicily. A large number of them accordingly turned to Frederick II and elected him king (1211). Innocent had some misgivings about confirming the action of the princes, because he did not wish Sicily and Germany to be held by one and the same person, lest the papal claim to the feudal lordship of Sicily should thereby be weakened. Nevertheless, no other possible candidate was to be found. Consequently Innocent determined to support Frederick.

Otto IV Turns against the Pope.

Frederick II.

To prevent complications, Frederick had his son, then only a year old, crowned king of Sicily. He again acknowledged that he held Sicily as a papal fief, and for it he renewed his homage to Innocent. Without any reservation he conceded everything that Innocent demanded. Putting the regency of Sicily in the hands of his wife, he boldly set out to win the crown which his great ancestors had worn. Cleverly avoiding the guards which Otto IV had placed at the passes of the Alps to intercept him, he reached Germany, where he was re-elected and crowned (1212). He renewed the alliance with Philip II of France, who was at war with England and with some of his great vassals in the Netherlands. As neither Otto IV nor Frederick could gain a decisive victory in Germany, Otto determined to carry the war into France, and with King John planned a double invasion of that country. Both of them were unsuccessful; John met with so vigorous a resistance in Poitou that he could make no progress, and Philip II administered a crushing defeat to Otto and his allies* (1214, at Bouvines, a village in Belgium, near Lille). By this defeat Otto's power was broken, and he withdrew to his estates in Saxony, where

S. B., 134, 135.

Battle at Bouvines, 1214.

* It must be regarded as a sign of progress that we find here, for the first time during the Middle Age, something like international politics and alliances. The Guelfs in their contest with the Hohenstaufen had made an alliance with the lower Rhine provinces and with the king of England, while the Hohenstaufen were leagued with the king of France. There was enmity between France and England because the English king held a large part of French territory, and the French king was trying to wrest it from him. Cologne and the provinces about the mouth of the Rhine already carried on a considerable commerce with England, on account of which they preferred the friendship of England to that of their French or German neighbors on the continent. There was also a political reason why the lower Rhine provinces allied themselves with the enemies of France: possessing a large measure of independence, they feared the French king because he was trying to get possession of them and subject them to the French crown. This international alliance, having been joined by Sicily, had caused the emperor, Henry VI, much anxiety. It was not so dangerous, however, as it seemed, since its members were so far apart that they were not able to render efficient aid to one another. Henry VI was successful in conquering Sicily, and by a piece of good fortune Richard, king of England, fell into his hands as a prisoner. Against Henry VI the alliance was thus rendered powerless. The coalition was renewed against Frederick II and promised to be more effective. It was their troops, however, that the king of France overcame in the battle of Bouvines.

International Alliances.

S. B., 131, 132.

he spent the rest of his life, without, however, submitting to his victorious rival. He died in 1218.

Frederick II Becomes Emperor.

Meeting with no further effective opposition, Frederick II was soon accepted throughout Germany as king. His success meant the success of Innocent, for Frederick had already made the broadest concessions to him, yielding all the points at issue between the empire and the papacy. Frederick's next desire was the acquisition of the imperial crown. This Innocent was willing to grant. He first, however, secured from Frederick the promise that as soon as he should be crowned emperor he would resign the Sicilian crown to his son and release him from all paternal authority. Frederick declared that he made this promise because, "if we should become emperor and at the same time be king of Sicily, it might be inferred that the kingdom of Sicily belonged to the empire, and such an inference would do injury to the Roman church."

Innocent III and Heresy.

S. B., 116–118.

In ecclesiastical affairs Innocent's success and mastery were as complete as in political matters. He developed an astonishing activity, sending his legates everywhere and through them controlling everything with a master hand. One of his most difficult tasks was the suppression of heresy. The twelfth century is noted for the development and spread of heretical sects. Ancient heresies were revived and fused with new ones. Various were the ideas advanced: most common perhaps was the gnostic or Manichæan belief in the existence of two Gods, the one good, the other evil, and the corollary of this, that matter itself is evil; it was widely believed that the marriage relation was sinful; the Old Testament was rejected, and the sacraments of the church were the object of bitter attacks. Often ascetic in temperament, these heretics railed at the worldliness of the clergy; some declared that the priests were Pharisees and the pope the successor not of Christ but of Constantine. Many of them rejected all the ritual of the church and made one of their own; instead of baptism with water some believed in a baptism with the spirit alone; some practised the laying on of hands, and rejected the use of images, fasting, purgatory, the taking of oaths, and the death penalty. They were known by many names, some of which were derived from local leaders: Manichæans, Cathari, Petrobrussians, Henricians, Bogomiles, Patareni, Waldensians, Albigensians, and others. The great wealth of the bishops and their immersion in secular affairs had led to the belief in the sinfulness of property and the corresponding holiness of poverty (*cf.* the Poor Men of Lyons, and the Arnoldists, named from Arnold of Brescia). Differing as these sects did, one from another, they were alike in their opposition to the church and in their criticism of the pope and of the clergy. They had, as Gregory IX said, "different faces, but their tails were bound together."

Legates.

The Friars.

Against these heretics Innocent III took vigorous measures. He sent his legates to combat them and ordered all in authority to do their utmost to crush them. He directed that heretics should be exiled or put to death, and gave those who prosecuted them the right to confiscate their property. The Dominican order was established by St. Dominic for the special purpose of reclaiming heretics. One of the main principles on which the Franciscan order was founded was the sinfulness of property, but the pope was wise enough to render this feature of the order harmless, and to prevent it from becoming hostile to the church. These two orders became the most efficient papal aids in suppressing heresy.

The Inquisition.

In this connection a word may be said about the inquisition. So wide-spread was heresy that it was soon found that papal legates could by no means do all that was necessary. The next step was to put the matter into the hands of the bishops, thus forming an episcopal inquisition. In 1184 Pope Lucius III ordered each archbishop and bishop to inquire (hence inquisition) at least once a year of three or more men of good reputation in the diocese whether they knew of any who were guilty of heresy, and to compel them on oath to reveal the names of all such. This action was repeated by Innocent III in the Lateran council (1215). The council of Toulouse (1229) renewed it, and ordered each bishop to appoint one priest and two or three laymen in each parish to seek out the heretics. The bishops, however, were, as Gregory IX thought, entirely too mild in their treatment of heretics, and so in 1232 and 1233 he created the papal inquisition by intrusting the Dominican order with the duty of seeking out and punishing heresy. Punishment was to be inflicted according to the degree of guilt, and consisted in fasting, pilgrimages, payments of money, imprisonment, maiming, or death. As the clergy were not permitted because of their sacerdotal character to shed blood, secular officials were called on to inflict the severer punishments. To us, accustomed as we are to the idea of religious liberty—the right of each one to believe what he will—the inquisition seems especially cruel, and the men who used it, as well as those who invented it, as peculiarly bloodthirsty and inhuman. Such, however, was not necessarily the case. The church punished heresy for exactly the same reason, and, according to the ideas of the time, with exactly the same justice, that a modern state punishes treason in its subjects. In those times the church quite naturally regarded heresy as treason.

Innocent III and Dogma.

Innocent III was not merely a statesman. He was not submerged in his efforts to build up a colossal institution which should exercise supreme authority over both the church and political governments. He was also a theologian: he defended the doctrines of the church against the attacks of heretics, defined more clearly the dogma of the Trinity, and developed the dogma of transubstantiation and made it a part of the official creed of the church.

Reforms.

S. B., 119–122.

He was also a sane and earnest reformer, with an eye open to all the abuses and wrongs which needed reforming. He possessed a consuming zeal for clean morals and holy living. While engaged in political plans which embraced all Europe and parts of Asia and Africa —in fact all the world that was known to him—he labored with equal energy to improve the spiritual condition of both the clergy and the laity. He ordered bishops carefully to oversee the morals of their clergy and severely to punish all who were guilty of improper conduct. In the Middle Age preaching was not regarded as an essential part of church services; consequently it was not necessarily a part of the education of the clergy, many of whom seldom or never attempted to preach. Innocent, however, recognizing the educational and devotional value of it, commanded the bishops to preach and to appoint clergy throughout their dioceses who were able and fitted to do the same. He directed that at least two teachers should be connected with every cathedral and with every church which had a sufficient endowment to pay them. One of these was to instruct the clergy of the neighborhood in secular branches, the other in theology and in the duties of the clerical office. He prescribed rules for the dress and conduct of the clergy; he ordered them to devote themselves seriously to the duties of their office and regularly to attend the daily and nightly services, and he forbade them to engage in business, to be present at theatrical performances, to play dice, to frequent inns and public places, to drink to excess, to wear costly or showy ornaments and gaudy and gay clothing. Since, as he said, the care of souls is "the art of arts," he directed the bishops to exercise the greatest care to ordain as priests only those who were in every way qualified for the office, and to instruct them thoroughly in divine things; they should reject all candidates who were ignorant or who did not lead holy lives. He also forbade the clergy to hold more than one office or living. He forbade the practice of simony, especially in monasteries, and condemned usury, a term then used to denote the taking of interest, without regard to whether the rate was excessive or not. He manifested a humane spirit in forbidding the molestation or persecution of Jews. He ordained that every Christian should at least once a year confess his sins to his parish priest and seek absolution of them.

S. B., 119.

The dearest wish of his heart—a great and successful crusade—he did not live to see fulfilled. From the beginning of his pontificate to its very end he labored day and night for it. It grieved him beyond measure that the fourth crusade was turned from its original purpose and directed against Constantinople, but after it was an accomplished fact he endeavored to make the best and the most of it. In 1213 he called a universal council for the purpose of making arrangements to recover the holy land and to reform the whole church. He directed all bishops to exercise great care in noting everything that needed reform that the council might do its work intelligently and thoroughly.

S. B., 286-288.

Desires a Crusade.

The Fourth Lateran Council, 1215.

It met in 1215 in the Lateran church in Rome (hence called the fourth Lateran council). More than twelve hundred bishops and abbots were present besides the representatives of many others. With astonishing speed (only three sessions were held) the council examined into the condition of the church and passed about seventy acts, most of them reformatory in character. Under the presidency of Innocent it defined dogmas, condemned heresies, and ordained reforms. It crowned its labors with a comprehensive plan for a crusade. Europe, it seemed, was about to respond to this imperative call: Frederick II took the crusader's vow, and all the west began to equip itself for a supreme effort, when the death of Innocent (1216) put an end to the preparations.

Frederick II Changes Policy.

The death of Innocent had another important effect. He had been the guardian of Frederick II, had made him king of Sicily and protected his rights there, had made him king of Germany, and had promised him the imperial crown. Frederick recognized his obligations to Innocent and showed his gratitude by obeying him implicitly. The death of Innocent, however, produced a marked change in him. He was no doubt conscious of the imperial ideal and of the inherent contradiction between the imperial and papal theories. True to the tradition of his family, he now developed a policy which led him more and more into opposition to the pope. The crown of Sicily was the first point of contention. Papal interest demanded that Sicily should never be held by an emperor, lest he should renew the imperial claim to it. The Lateran council decreed that Frederick II should not be crowned emperor until he had made his little son, Henry [VII], king of Sicily and had resigned the kingdom to him. In 1216 Frederick had promised that as soon as he had been made emperor he would free his son from all paternal control and permit him to hold Sicily as a papal fief, entirely independent of the empire. In spite of his promise, however, Frederick was determined to retain Sicily in his own hands, not only because he loved it better than any other country, but also and chiefly because of the large revenues which he derived from it. After crowning his son king of Sicily he sent him off to Germany and carefully laid his plans to have him elected king of that country also. These plans he brought to a successful issue in 1220, when Henry [VII] was elected and crowned king of Germany. The pope, Honorius III (1216-1227), whose great age and ill health increased the natural mildness of his character, was displeased with this, but under the influence of Frederick's promise to go on a crusade and to protect the possessions of the church, he yielded to the inevitable. He not only crowned Frederick emperor (1220), but even permitted him to retain the title of king of Sicily and to exercise the functions of that office.

Henry [VII], 1220-1242.

In the contention about Sicily Frederick scored a victory over the pope and yet retained his friendship. In other matters he was not so fortunate. These were (1) the re-establishment of the imperial administration in Italy, which had been destroyed by Innocent III, and (2) the development of a strong royal government in Sicily. Immediately after his coronation he set about both these tasks. In one province of Italy after another he established his imperial officials, and in Sicily he took steps to diminish the power of the pope and of the nobility. That Honorius III did not excommunicate him at once was due to the fact that his heart was set on a crusade and for this he needed the support of the emperor—Frederick had taken the cross at the Lateran council (1215) and had renewed his vow in 1220. In spite, however, of papal commands and threats he continually put off the day of his departure, because his presence in the west was neces-

Grounds of Quarrel.

sary for the realization of his plans there. In 1223 he married Iolanthe, the daughter and heiress of the king of Jerusalem, thus acquiring a right to that kingdom (which was, however, almost entirely in the hands of the Mohammedans). After the marriage he assumed the title of king of Jerusalem. Finally, in 1225, he yielded to the papal demands and agreed to go on his crusade in 1227: if he should for any cause fail to keep his promise he should by that very act be excommunicated. When the time came he did indeed set sail, but because of illness and the death of one of his advisers he returned two days later. For this the new pope, Gregory IX (1227–1241), excommunicated him. Frederick tried in vain to have the ban removed. The pope was obdurate; so Frederick sailed with the ban still upon him (1228). Although the pope's emissaries everywhere intrigued against him, he nevertheless obtained by diplomacy the surrender of Jerusalem to the Christians.

"King of Jerusalem."

Frederick II Acquires Jerusalem.

In the meantime Gregory IX, in order to resist the encroachments of Frederick's officials, had raised three armies: one of these he employed in northern Italy, the second in central Italy, and the third he despatched against the kingdom of Sicily. In the midst of the pope's military successes Frederick returned to Italy (1229). In the field the pope's forces were no match for him and a series of victories made him master of the situation. Nevertheless, he offered most favorable terms to the pope. Peace was accordingly re-established between them by the treaty of San Germano (1230), in which Frederick made generous concessions.

Gregory IX Appeals to Arms.

San Germano, 1230.

S. B., 140–142.

The peace of San Germano, however, did not prevent Frederick from continuing his efforts to build up a strong royal power in Sicily and to re-establish the imperial administration throughout Italy. In 1231 he remodelled the government of Sicily and published a new body of laws for it (the constitutions of Sicily). His chief object in this was to make his own authority as nearly absolute

Frederick II Pursues His Policy.

as possible. He reduced the power of the vassals as well as of the high clergy and of the pope. In the administration of justice and of the finances he introduced systems that were in many respects modern. He established royal judges and courts to displace the baronial courts, and he imposed direct (land and poll taxes) and indirect taxes (tolls, state monopolies in salt, steel, copper, raw silk, and the like, and a tariff on imports and exports). By these methods Frederick acquired an immense income. This, it has been said, was the first modern government in Europe.

The Lombard Cities.

Gregory IX was highly displeased with what Frederick did in Sicily, but, if that had been all, would probably have contented himself with a protest. There was in addition, however, Frederick's persistent encroachment upon the pope's sovereignty in Italy. The situation was further complicated by Frederick's quarrel with the Lombard cities. Since the death of Henry VI (1197) those cities had been left to themselves, and they had taken advantage of the opportunity to increase their independence at the expense of the imperial rights which had been fixed by the peace of Constance (1183). Soon after his coronation as emperor (1220) Frederick II had attempted to exercise the powers which that treaty guaranteed to the emperor, but met with armed resistance. Through the intervention of the pope and others war was averted until 1236, when Frederick began to prosecute his claims with greater vigor. During the next two years his military operations were entirely successful. One after another of the cities surrendered or was taken by force, and at Cortenuova (1237) he gained a remarkable victory over the cities, killing about ten thousand of their troops. He then prepared to reorganize the government of all Italy and to make it thoroughly imperial.

The Pope Resists.

S B., 143, 144.

He began to displace the local (civil) as well as the papal officials with his own. He made his son, Enzio, king of Sardinia and married him to the heiress of its crown. The pope could restrain himself no longer, for Sardinia was a papal fief. A heated controversy ensued, in which each made charges and counter-charges, until the original question was lost sight of. In 1239 Gregory excommunicated Frederick and anathematized him on sixteen different counts, such as seizing papal lands, taxing, robbing, and destroying churches, preventing the free election of bishops, refusing to permit vacant bishoprics to be filled, and proscribing and killing the clergy.

It was inevitable that a bitter struggle should follow. The pope united the Italian cities against Frederick, and Italy was again ravaged by war. Frederick's arms were victorious. In 1241 he encamped before Rome, prepared to besiege it, when the death of Gregory put an end to the hostilities. After electing a pope who died in about two weeks the cardinals fled from Rome. For nearly two years the chair of St. Peter remained vacant, apparently because the cardinals could not agree upon any one. Finally they elected Innocent IV, who, after a year of parleying, began a war of extermination against the emperor and his family. He infused new life into the struggle by stirring up the Italian cities to renewed efforts. He fled to France and sought to enlist the French king in his service. He also fomented a rebellion in Germany and brought about the election of an anti-king, first, Henry Raspe of Thuringia (1246–1247), and then William of Holland (1247–1256). The death of Frederick, in 1250, turned the scale definitely in favor of the pope. Frederick's son, Conrad IV, died (1254) in a heroic effort to maintain himself as king in Germany. His death was followed by the period known as the interregnum (1254–1273), during which there was no recognized king of Germany. In Sicily Manfred, an illegitimate son of Frederick II, was recognized as king. He possessed in a high degree the ability to govern which characterized his family. Under his wise sway Sicily recovered its prosperity and enjoyed peace. The pope, however, was determined to destroy the Hohenstaufen family, and in order to drive out the last members of it (Manfred and Conradino, the son of Conrad IV) he called in Charles

Frederick's successes.

Death of Frederick II, 1250.

S. B., 145. O., 71.

The Interregnum, 1254–1273.

of Anjou, a brother of Louis IX, king of France. The price which he paid Charles was the crown of Sicily. Charles was successful in battle, and Manfred was slain (1266).* Conradino, whose youth had been spent in Germany, went to Italy to try to recover Sicily, but through the treachery of his troops was defeated. A few days later he was taken prisoner and beheaded (1268).

Charles of Anjou Gets Sicily.

End of the Hohenstaufen.

This struggle was an important milestone in the history of the world. It was a contest between two great institutions, both of which claimed universal authority. For centuries the Roman empire had pursued a lofty and alluring ideal: it had endeavored to destroy all national individualism, to obliterate all local and racial differences, and to make all peoples alike, to weld all nations into one people and into one political unit. It is needless to say that at times all the subjected peoples felt this rule to be tyranny. For about two centuries the papacy had pursued an ideal not less lofty and alluring: it had sought to make the world of one religious faith. That means, however, that it had sought to force the world to accept a creed made to order and to deprive the individual of his right to make his own creed. It sought unity in place of the living variety which is the result of individual thought. The victory was with the papacy. For the empire as for the Hohenstaufen family, the struggle was fatal. To be sure, the empire continued to exist for some centuries (to 1806), but only in name. Few of the later kings of Germany took the trouble to go to Rome for the imperial crown. Most

The Struggle between Two "Universal" Institutions.

Change in the Empire.

* Nothing more clearly shows the bitterness of the hatred engendered by this long strife than the savage treatment of the members of Manfred's family. Death set free his wife after five years of imprisonment, and a daughter after eighteen years of close imprisonment. One of his sons lived to endure the tortures of a prison for more than fifty years. Another son escaped from prison, and after begging from the court of one country to another throughout Europe, died at last in Egypt, a guest of the sultan, who gave him the alms denied him by Christian rulers.

of them saw that it was impossible to unite the two countries, and consequently resigned all pretension to authority over Italy and Sicily. To accomplish this result the papacy sought to exercise a political sovereignty not less complete than that of the empire. It is also needless to say that the rule of the church would be felt by many to be both a political and a religious tyranny. The world was growing away from the universal and toward the individual. The papacy, with its universal creed and its universal political power, had gained a victory, but this victory was to be brief. At the very threshold of his triumph the pope recognized, but underrated, the powers of the new enemy that was about to take up the struggle.

Nations and Individuals Prepare to Resist the "Universal" Power of the Pope.

S. B., 145.

"Some asserted that the pope [Gregory IX] desired above all else utterly to crush Frederick, whom he called the great dragon, in order that he might then destroy the kings of England and of France and the other Christian kings, whom he called kinglets and little serpents." For the moment the pope's cause was victorious, but over against the growing individualism of nations and persons, the pope was supporting a losing cause. The empire had been universal in name only. This nominal universal was displaced by another which really tried to be universal. Its efforts, however, merely hastened its own overthrow and the victory of the individual nation and of the individual man.

CHAPTER XIV

MOHAMMED AND MOHAMMEDANISM

The Arabic population of Arabia was divided into many tribes which were further subdivided into groups called clans or families, each of which consisted of all those who were related by blood through the male line. Their government was patriarchal: the oldest member of the family (clan) was generally its patriarch, to whom all the other members were subject. In all family affairs the patriarch's will was law. Each tribe had also its patriarch, who was assisted by the patriarchs of the families which composed it. The tribe, through its patriarch and chief men, managed its affairs, governed and controlled its members, and administered justice among them. Even in the largest cities, which were inhabited by many tribes, centralized government was practically unknown, although the leading men of all the tribes represented in the city acted together as a kind of city council to decide the few questions which were of general public concern. The tribes were so jealous of their independence that little progress toward the formation of a state could be made. The patriarchal form of government was to them adequate because many of the tribes were still nomadic; only a few of them had fixed abodes, and these chiefly in towns and villages. The primitive, vigorous sons of the desert preferred the unencumbered freedom of tent-dwellers.

The Arabs.

Patriarchal Organization.

The intertribal relations of the Arabs were such as are commonly found among primitive peoples, being controlled by the law of retaliation or blood vengeance. That is, each tribe was bound to avenge an insult or injury to any of its members, and consequently bloody feuds were of frequent occurrence. Since community of descent was to them the only conceivable bond of social union, blood relationship was of fundamental importance. Each family

Blood Vengeance

was, in fact, a little state in which citizenship was determined by blood relationship. A man without a family was without a country; he was common prey because there was no state to protect him and to avenge a wrong done to him. The low stage of civilization among the Arabs made protection a matter of chief importance. Treachery, vindictiveness, and cruelty were prominent traits of their character.*

Religion.

Mixture of Religious Ideas.

The religion of the Arabs was quite as primitive as their government, ranging from fetich to star worship. They peopled the earth, air, and sky with a host of malicious and capricious as well as friendly spirits, such as genii (djins), ogres, and demons, all of which played a great part in their literature (*cf. The Arabian Nights' Tales*). They had learned of fire-worship from the Persians, of Judaism from the Jews, and of Christianity from the people of Egypt and Abyssinia. Their religion, besides being powerless to improve their morals, lacked also those inspiring elements which would tend to raise them in the scale of civilization. For some centuries the Arabs had made but little progress. Yet their religion had not been entirely without effect upon them, for it forbade all acts of violence everywhere during certain holy months and seasons and prohibited them altogether in the neighborhood of temples and altars.

Commerce.

Under the protection which religion thus furnished, commerce flourished. During these holy seasons caravans moved unmolested across the country, and, in the security which the holy places gave them, merchants exposed their wares for sale. Important fairs or markets grew up about the temples, and people, drawn by the double attraction of security and trade, settled near them, thus forming cities and towns. The situation of Arabia was favorable to the development of commerce, lying, as it does, on the boundary between Asia and Africa and having the double advantage

* In the northern part of the peninsula and along the coast there was a numerous Jewish population living for the most part in separate colonies or villages; in their government they did not differ materially from the Arab tribes about them.

of trade by sea and by land. Caravan routes were established, connecting all parts of Arabia with the rest of Asia and with northern Africa. Moreover, by sea the Arabs carried on an extensive trade with India, with the far east, and with Africa.

Of all the cities of Arabia, Mecca held the first place, both in commerce and in religion. Its markets or fairs were famous and were visited by throngs of merchants from distant cities, and its streets were crowded with the nomadic hordes which inhabited the uplands of central Arabia. Its temple, called from its shape the Caaba (cube), had become a national sanctuary, the holiest spot of all Arabia. To the solid commercial advantages to be derived from a visit to Mecca the Caaba added another, more attractive, perhaps, though less substantial—the opportunity to appease the gods and to win their favor.

Mecca.

The Caaba.

Such was the state of Arabic society when Mohammed was born at Mecca, about 569. Of his early life little is known with certainty. His family was poor and he was compelled to perform menial labor, but his marriage with a rich widow, Khadijeh, whom he had served as camel-driver, raised him to a position of ease and influence. When about forty years old he developed an absorbing interest in religion and received, as he came to believe, divine revelations, which he felt obliged to preach to the people of Mecca. The substance of these revelations, put into the briefest form possible, is that there is but one God, Allah; he commands all men to practise certain virtues; those who obey him he will reward with eternal life and happiness in a paradise of delights, but he will punish in a hell of torments all who despise his commands. In consequence of the mockery with which he was met, Mohammed attempted to secure a respectful hearing by constantly reasserting his official position as the prophet of God. Opposition forced him to emphasize his relation to God and to put his own person more and more emphatically into the foreground, and soon he demanded from all the confession: "There is no God but Allah and Mohammed is his prophet."

Mohammed.

Mohammed's success was slow but substantial. Although the Meccans generally mocked him, laughed at his announcement of a day of divine judgment, and scorned his claim to be a prophet of God, he won, in the course of a dozen years or more, some 300 persons to his faith. Many of these were of the humblest rank, but a few of them were choice souls who were to be Mohammed's chief supporters and the most zealous propagators of his religion. Although his converts came from all the tribes which inhabited Mecca, they formed a little congregation closely bound to Allah, to Mohammed, and to each other; each one took an oath faithfully to obey Allah and his prophet, to pray at the regularly appointed times, and for the support of the poor to contribute a small sum which was regarded as an offering or atonement for his sins.

His Success.

To the Meccans this new society seemed to be revolutionary and dangerous because it was established not on the bond of blood relationship—of community of descent—but on that of community of religious belief; for Mohammed declared that if a believer was injured for God's cause, all other believers were his blood avengers. The Meccans were alarmed at the success of Mohammed in establishing such a new society. They accordingly resorted to persecution. Many of his followers, being forced to flee, went to Abyssinia, where they found freedom from persecution. The condition of those who remained in Mecca grew worse, and at length Mohammed foresaw that he and all his followers must seek safety elsewhere. He began to fear even for himself, for although his family had thus far protected him against all violence, its patriarch was no longer well disposed toward him and might at any moment withdraw his protecting favor and expel him from the family. After vainly appealing to several tribes for admission and protection, he finally persuaded some men from Medina to accept his faith, and they invited him and all his faithful to come and live in their city. The invitation was gladly accepted and the society withdrew to Medina (622). This "flight" (Hegira) of Mohammed was an event of such importance in his ca-

Persecution of His Followers.

The Flight (Hegira), 622.

reer that his followers reckoned time from it; and not unjustly, for it does indeed mark an era in Mohammed's development.

Mohammed and the Jews.

Mohammed had acquired nearly all his religious ideas from the Jews. From the first he had believed that he was preaching the true religion of Abraham and he labored with as much zeal to win the approbation of the Jews as to reform the Arabs. Nothing shows more conclusively his shallow theological knowledge and his simple religious enthusiasm than the fact that he believed himself in harmony with both Jews and Christians. "Believers (Mohammedans), Jews, and Christians . . . if they believe in God and the judgment day and do good, receive their reward (life in paradise) from their Lord" (Koran, surah 2 : 58). Their religions and his were revelations from the same God and therefore could not conflict. Whenever the Jews disagreed with him he naïvely declared that they had corrupted their religion and no longer held to the truth as it had originally been revealed to them. Although he held the Caaba at Mecca in high reverence, he honored Jerusalem still more by adopting the Jewish custom of turning the face toward it in prayer (*cf.* Daniel 6 : 10).

Turns to the Arabs.

On reaching Medina Mohammed redoubled his efforts to win the Jews, many colonies of whom were established in and about the city. For about a year he labored with them, but on all hands met only with insolent rebuffs. Angered at their persistent hardness of heart, and convinced that further efforts with them would be wasted, he denounced them and turned from them to his own people. Islam (submission to the will of God), as he called his new religion, was thereafter to be the national religion of the Arabs. He was shrewd enough to perceive that, if he would win them, he must start from a common standing-ground. To this end he determined to make Mecca his holy city and the Caaba the seat of his religion. Accordingly he deposed Jerusalem from its place of honor and began to turn his face toward Mecca in prayer. He commanded all believers to honor the

Caaba and to visit it in pilgrimages, although the city was at that time in the hands of his enemies and no Mohammedan was permitted to enter it.

In order to justify this change from Jerusalem to the Caaba, Mohammed resorted to an invention. He enlarged the tradition about Abraham and made him an Arab and the father of the Arabs, the builder of the Caaba, and the founder of Islam. According to this tale, God had made a covenant with Abraham in Mecca, had helped him build the Caaba, had instituted religious ceremonies in it, and had commanded pilgrimages to be made to it; Ishmael and not Isaac was Abraham's favored son and helper; and Abraham had foretold in prophecy the advent of the great prophet, Mohammed.

Inventions about Abraham.

The invention was successful and served a purpose which had been ripening in Mohammed's mind ever since his expulsion from Mecca. Being an Arab, Mohammed was vindictive, and his desire to take vengeance on the Meccans had grown till it had now completely taken possession of him. Up to that time Mohammed had preached peace, and had apparently never thought of propagating his religion by force. He now began, as he stoutly declared, to receive revelations from God, justifying war in general and war on Mecca in particular. "If God did not permit his people to fight, their enemies would destroy monasteries, churches, synagogues, and mosques, in which God's name is proclaimed. Permission to fight is given to those who fight because they have been unjustly treated and to those who have been driven from their home simply because they said 'Allah is our God'; Allah is able to help all such" (surah 22:40–41). Like many another, Mohammed identified God's cause with his own and discovered a way of satisfying his feelings of revenge while making it appear that it was God's will that the Meccans should be destroyed. "Fight for Allah's cause against those who fight you; kill them wherever you find them and drive them from the place from which they have driven you (Mecca); it is worse to tolerate their offense

Resorts to Force.

(idolatry) than to kill them; do not fight them near the consecrated temple of God (the Caaba) unless they first attack you there; but if they attack you there, kill them, for that is the reward of those who do not believe; make war on them till there is no more offense and all men worship Allah alone" (surah 2 : 186–189).

A Moral Retrogression in Mohammed.

The changes in Mohammed during the first two years after the flight were undoubtedly for the worse, for they led him into a course of ever-increasing deception and violence. Out of pique and shrewd calculation he had changed from Jerusalem to the Caaba; he had justified this change by forgeries about Abraham; yielding to the desire for revenge, he pretended to receive revelations from God at first justifying war in general, and then commanding war to be waged on the Meccans. From a war of vengeance to one of conquest was but an easy step, and Mohammed, once a man of peace and a preacher of righteousness, was now rapidly becoming a man of war and violence. As this change in him proceeded, his interests and activities were revolutionized. He began to receive revelations which bear every evidence of having been made to order; they accorded so perfectly with his desires and were so opportune that we are forced to believe that he fraudulently used the form of revelation in order to forestall criticism and opposition. When he did anything that gave offense to his followers, he promptly received a revelation in justification of what he had done. With these *ex post facto* revelations he was able to silence all except a few persistent critics, and these he put to death. He no longer occupied himself exclusively with the high moral and religious ideas, with zeal for which he had been consumed during the earliest years of his mission, but busied himself with political intrigues, marauding excursions, wars, and the acquisition of temporal power. Mohammed was no longer an enthusiastic religious reformer, nor the founder of a new religion; he was rather the unscrupulous maker of a state, ready to commit any act of violence or injustice that promised to advance his power.

As soon as Mohammed had safely established his people at Medina he began to seek an opportunity to take vengeance on the Meccans. With his men he scoured the country in all directions, hoping to catch some Meccan caravan at a disadvantage and plunder it. But the Meccans took such precautions that he found no favorable opportunity to fall upon them. Finally he determined to take advantage of the holy month to attack them, because at such a time they would not be on their guard. A handful of his men, having been ordered to make the treacherous onset, succeeded beyond expectation. They killed one Meccan, took some prisoners and a large amount of booty, and returned in safety to Medina. In support of this sacrilegious act Mohammed received a timely revelation. "They ask thee about fighting in the holy month; say: 'Fighting in the holy month is bad, but declension from the way of God, and unbelief, and the expulsion of his people from the holy temple at Mecca are worse; and to give offense (by idolatry) is worse.' And besides, they would not cease from fighting you until they had deprived you of your religion" (surah 2: 214).

Attacks the Meccans.

A few weeks later Mohammed achieved a notable victory at the village of Badr. While lying in wait for a caravan he fell in with the Meccans, who were anxious to avenge their recent injury. With only about 300 men he took an advantageous position on a hill and awaited the attack of the enemy, who numbered about 1,000. The superior numbers of the Meccans gave them no advantage, because they fought after the ancient Arabic manner, a few of them going out at a time to meet an equal number of the enemy in single combat. Mohammed, on the other hand, introduced a tactical change which was of the greatest consequence. He drew his forces up in a compact body and forbade them to leave their places without his consent. This, he said, was God's way of fighting. "God loves those who fight in his way in compact ranks" (surah 61: 4). The Mohammedans slew about seventy Meccans, took forty-three prisoners and much booty, consisting of camels, horses,

Battle of Badr, 624.

Cf. I Sam. 17.

and weapons. After the Meccans had paid a heavy ransom for the prisoners, Mohammed made the final disposition of the spoil. One-fifth of it he took for "God and his prophet and his family, for orphans, the poor, and travellers," some of it he gave as special rewards to those who had distinguished themselves for bravery, and all the rest of it he distributed equally among those who had taken part in the battle. This plan of division, which appealed so powerfully to the cupidity of the Arabs, was a masterly stroke of shrewdness on his part. His followers were affected by it as a lion's cub by the first taste of blood; to their zeal for the spread of their faith was added a still more powerful incentive, the desire of spoils. Neighboring tribes, which had hesitated to join him, were chagrined that they had missed a golden opportunity, and thereafter were eager to assist him in his marauding expeditions.

Division of the Booty.

For about a year after the battle of Badr Mohammed was successful in his raids, which were directed chiefly against prosperous Jewish colonies to the north of Medina. Unprepared for attack, they were easily conquered, and Mohammed enriched his people with ill-gotten wealth. Consequently his prestige grew and many Arabs, eager to share the prosperity of his followers, accepted his faith. He met, however, with one serious defeat. In a battle with the Meccans at Mt. Uhud, in 625, he was struck with a stone and almost killed, and his troops put to flight. In 627 the Meccans, with an army of about 10,000 men, laid siege to Medina, but were unable to take it. Their failure was equivalent to a victory for Mohammed, and his power continued to grow. The next year (628) he took steps to encourage the formation of a body of cavalry. In distributing the booty after a successful raid, he gave to each of the mounted men three times as much as to the foot-soldiers. The effect was magical; all strove to equip themselves with horses and Mohammed was soon in possession of a magnificent body of cavalry.

Plunders the Jews.

Battle of Uhud, 625.

Siege of Medina, 627.

In 630 Mohammed felt strong enough to attack Mecca, and

marched against it with a large force. He met with little resistance, however, for many of the inhabitants of Mecca were willing to submit to him, now that he was successful, and to accept his religion since it promised to enrich them. After the city surrendered to him he treated its inhabitants with surprising leniency, and endeavored to win their friendship and support by an exhibition of noble traits of character. His revenge spent itself in the execution of about a dozen persons, most of whom were his bitter personal enemies. He took possession of the Caaba and dedicated it wholly to the worship of Allah.

Takes Mecca, 630.

In the conquest of Mecca Mohammed attained the goal for which he had labored for eight years. Then, during the next two years, which were also his last, he developed his political ideas and created the form of government which characterized the Mohammedans for centuries. Faithful to his early belief that Jews and Christians worshipped the true God, he did not insist on their conversion, but he demanded of them political submission and the annual payment of a heavy poll tax. Toward the heathen, however, his attitude was entirely different; he gave them the choice between conversion and the sword. All Mohammedans were bound to pay a part of their income (generally a tenth) as alms, or a sin offering. "Take alms of their possessions, through which thou purifiest them and coverest their sins" (surah 9:104). Mohammed created a kind of central government (1) by acting as supreme judge in all litigation, (2) by levying a tax on all, and (3) by appointing a governor (emir) and tax-collectors for every tribe that had submitted to him. At his death (632) he was the acknowledged lord of Arabia, and was still sending out his troops to extend his power by further conquests.

Organization of the State.

Such is the simple story of Mohammed's life. He had, however, produced a book which was to exercise a remarkable influence over the millions of his followers. His religion is preeminently the religion of a book, and to this we must now give our attention. For some time before Mohammed began

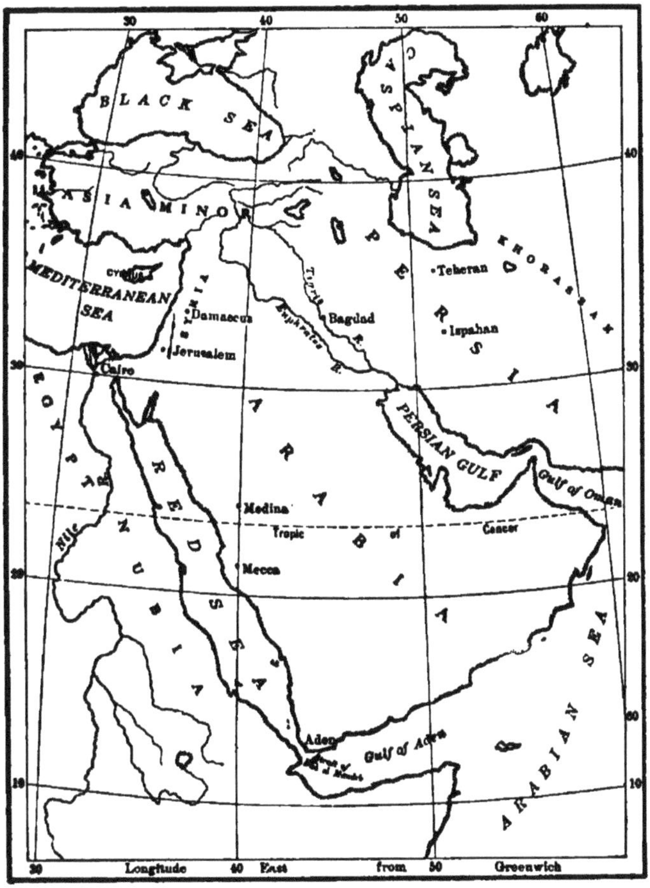

X

ARABIA

Note to Map X.—This map shows (1) Arabia and the adjacent countries, and (2) the chief cities connected with the religion or government of the Mohammedans. After 622 Mohammed lived at Medina, although Mecca became the seat of his religion. From 655 to 750 Damascus was the residence of the caliphs and the seat of the Mohammedan government. In 750 the caliphs removed to Bagdad. In the tenth century a rival caliphate was established in Egypt, the caliph of which had his residence at Cairo. A third independent caliphate was established in Spain with its capital at Cordova.

to receive revelations he is said to have been afflicted with a strange kind of nervous attack, which resembled epilepsy; he fell to the ground and became almost unconscious; he uttered inarticulate sounds; his eyes were fixed in a stony stare; and he heard a confused sound as of voices. At first he was alarmed because he feared that these attacks were the evidence of demoniacal possession, but in time he became convinced that they were caused by Allah, who was speaking to him in this way. He soon became able to tell what Allah had said to him while he was in this ecstatic state.* This interpretation of Mohammed's attacks is strikingly confirmed by the earliest surahs (chapters) of the Koran. They are merely broken ejaculations and exclamations, obscure in meaning, and they give evidence of having been uttered under the strongest nervous and religious excitement. After a while Mohammed became calmer, these nervous attacks seem to have ceased, and his revelations assumed a different character; they became clearer and show evidence of deliberation and calculation.

Mohammed Suffered from Nervous Attacks.

* Without attempting to explain the attacks from which Mohammed suffered, it is instructive to compare them with the mysterious phenomena which are produced under strong religious excitement, and which accompany the utterance of prophecy, especially among people on a low plane of civilization. A classic example of prophecy while in an ecstatic state, as this half-conscious state is called, is furnished by the account of Balaam, who three times tried in vain to curse Israel. Each time he lost power over himself, fell to the ground in a trance-like condition, and uttered a blessing instead of a curse (Num. 24: 4 *ff.*). Apparently akin to this was the "speaking with tongues," which accompanied St. Paul's preaching in Corinth (I Cor. 14: 2 *ff.*) and which was successfully reproduced for a while by the Irvingites in London in the early part of the nineteenth century. It is neither frivolous nor far-fetched in this connection to mention, for the sake of comparison, the extreme cases of nervous attack which often accompany great religious revivals, especially among negroes. Of the many interesting examples that might be cited from the heathen world, that of the Pythia, the prophetess of the god Apollo, at Delphi in Greece, is instructive. When any one came to Delphi to consult the god, a kind of incense was burned about his prophetess, and, as she inhaled the smoke of it, she either assumed a frenzy or actually became frenzied, and whatever she said while in this ecstatic state was regarded as the answer of the god to the question that had been propounded to him.

The Koran consists of these revelations, which are generally cast in the form of a dialogue between Allah and Mohammed. It is probable that Mohammed ceased to fall into the ecstatic state during his later years, although he retained the form of the dialogue and did not hesitate to put into the mouth of Allah his own ideas and desires. Even if he had been conscious of fraud in this procedure he would no doubt have justified it on the ground that he was sure of the truth of what he said, and that the end justified the means. It is a strong man indeed, who, believing that he has the truth, does not feel justified in lying for it and in using force to insure its success. Whether in this Mohammed consciously practised deception or was only self-deceived may be left to the psychologist or to the casuist.

The Koran.

O., 13.
R., 48.

The Koran has to a considerable extent an esoteric character; that is, it was intended primarily for those who already believed; it was meant for the instruction, direction, and comfort of Mohammed and his followers. To convince others, Mohammed preached, argued, and talked, quoting the Koran whenever it served his purpose. Neither his sermons nor his conversations were put into the Koran; it contains only his revelations. Some of these were written at the time they were revealed, while others were committed to memory by his followers. Although cherished as the word of God, they were not at once put together in an orderly way to form a book. So long as Mohammed lived the necessity of collecting his revelations in book form was not felt, because he could always be appealed to, and besides he more than once changed them to suit a new situation. But after his death there was nothing but the Koran to take his place. Accordingly, every effort was made to collect all the koranic utterances, and they were arranged in surahs or chapters without any regard to their chronological order. When these surahs are rearranged in their chronological order—a very difficult task—they enable us to follow Mohammed in his development and to trace the growth in his ideas. Mohammedans regard the Koran with idolatrous reverence. Blind to the numerous inconsistencies it contains, they see in it the final and highest authority in all matters, religious as well as secular.

Mohammed, as has been said, derived most of his doctrines from the Jews, but added enough to them to cause us to respect his ability. He had a high conception of the unity of God, and, at the first, felt religious truth in a direct way. His originality consisted not so much in new ideas as in the directness, vigor, and certainty of his religious perceptions. The idea of the unity of God was not new; two great religions had already been established on that as their basis. In the intensity of Mohammed's feeling, however, it became a new doctrine, filled with a quickening power sufficient to produce a great religious movement and to establish a third world religion on a monotheistic basis.

Mohammed's Originality.

In apparent imitation of the decalogue of the Jews Mohammed made a summary of his teachings in the following twelve commandments:

His Twelve Commandments.

"(1) Have no other God besides Allah, that thou mayst not be condemned and sit helpless. (2) Thy Lord has commanded thee to serve him alone. (3) Show kindness to thy parents whether one or both of them attain old age in thy house. . . . (4) Give thy kinsman his due, and the beggar, and the traveller, but not wastefully; for those that waste their possessions are brothers of the devil. . . . God gives daily bread to whom He will, and provides; for He knows his servants. (5) Do not kill your children out of fear that you will be brought to want; for we provide for them and for you. For to slay them is a great sin. (6) Draw not near unto fornication, for it is wickedness, and evil is the way thereof. (7) Kill not, except for just cause. (8) Touch not the possessions of orphans, except to improve them, until he becomes of age. (9) Keep your contract with Allah, for an account of it will be demanded. (10) Give full measure when you measure, and weigh with a true balance. . . . (11) Pursue [*i. e.*, repeat] nothing unless you know it to be true; for you must give an account of your eye, ear, and heart. (12) Walk not proudly on the earth, for you can neither split the earth nor equal the mountains in size" (surah 17 : 23-40).

Mohammed has been aptly compared to King David, in whom vindictiveness, cruelty, lust, and deceit were found side by side with the noblest qualities. Nothing can be said

Character of Mohammed.

derogatory to his character up to the time of his flight. After that he yielded to the ignoble desire

His Vices.

for revenge and to the corroding ambition for political power; and these, cloaked under a burning zeal for God's cause, corrupted the sources of his life. From the time he yielded to them there began a moral and religious retrogression in him, which increased to the day of his death. He became so impatient of all opposition that he was occasionally guilty of foul murder in order to rid himself of troublesome critics. He was guilty of wanton cruelty and murderous cupidity in attacking the Jews and seizing their property. At first a model in conduct to his followers, in the later years of his life he strove to exempt himself from all moral restrictions, and to create for himself a position in which, free from all restraints, he should be governed only by his desires. When an old man he fell under the dominion of lust, and, although he had limited his followers to four wives, he pretended to receive revelations from Allah ordering him to take as many wives and concubines as he wished—a command which he was not slow to obey. With consummate treachery he broke his oaths and alliances whenever it promised to be to his advantage. Under the opposition and persecution with which he met in Mecca the noblest traits of his character had developed, but in the freedom of Medina these began to fade and the vicious elements in his character won the upper hand. Mohammed no longer strove to be the moral pattern for his followers, or to exemplify his doctrines with his life.

Yet, if we study Mohammed in a comparative way from the point of view of his age and of his people and surroundings, we find that he possessed qualities and virtues which command our respect and admiration. Even in the days of his greatest success he remained simple in his tastes and in the manner of his life; refusing the service of slaves, he mended his own clothes and attended to his own wants. He was free from luxury in food and in his surroundings. He was true in his friendships and deeply grateful for any kindness shown him. He was not haughty, but associated freely with men of every rank. Although he put to death a few who opposed him and refused to believe in him, yet, for an Arab of the seventh century, he was remarkably mild and conciliatory. He showed considerable moderation in the manner in which he exercised his absolute power. In many respects he compares favorably with rulers who belonged to a superior race and who were on a much higher plane of civilization. Whatever his faults and vices, he will always hold a unique place in history. For he began his remarkable career as a camel-driver and ended it as the founder of a great religion and the autocratic head of a vigorous state, with powers as great as those of pope and emperor combined.

His Virtues.

Mohammedanism was from the first a missionary religion: that is, Mohammed made it the sacred duty of believers to labor for the spread of the faith and the conversion of unbelievers. In regard to the means of propagating the faith the Koran is inconsistent. During his early years Mohammed declared over and over again that there should be no compulsion in religion; that his whole duty consisted in persuasion and preaching; that the acceptance of his faith was left to the free choice of each individual. On the other hand, he later gave explicit commands to use force to compel its acceptance. Yet he certainly excepted Jews and Christians, and Mohammedans have generally followed the principle laid down by him in that they have forced their religion only upon heathen peoples, permitting Jews and Christians to retain their faith. But it must not be supposed that Mohammedanism has been spread only by the sword. It has been, and still is, spread by an army of missionaries, who, for their zeal and devotion to their work, for their fiery eloquence and power of persuasive preaching, for their perseverance in the

A Missionary Religion.

Force.

Persuasion.

face of apparently insurmountable obstacles, for their endurance of persecution, and for their heroic martyrdoms, are worthy to be set side by side with the great martyr missionaries of Christianity.

Spread of Mohammedanism.

Mohammed's death accelerated rather than checked the spread of his religion. Like a whirlwind his armies overran Palestine, Syria, Persia, and Egypt. And this was but the beginning. Within a hundred years after his death Armenia had been subjugated; the peoples of central Asia as far as the frontier of China had been conquered and converted; India had been invaded and the Punjaub occupied; and Asia Minor had been invaded. Then for years Mohammedan armies tried to force their way into eastern Europe, they took some of the Greek islands and attacked Constantinople, but were beaten off after memorable sieges (672 and 717). In Africa they were not less successful than in the east. By the year 711 they had taken North Africa and passed over into Spain. There they quickly put an end to the kingdom of the west Goths, and then crossed the Pyrenees and attacked the Franks. But here, after some successes, their power was broken in battle near Poitiers (732) by the forces of Charles Martel, and shortly thereafter they were compelled to withdraw beyond the Pyrenees. They took kindly to the sea and became intrepid seamen. They attacked the islands of the Mediterranean, and gradually conquered them (Sicily, 827–860). They invaded Italy and overran the southern part of it even to the gates of Rome. For some years it seemed that they would be able to establish a great Mohammedan state there. Although this danger passed away, they continued to hold various places till far into the eleventh century, when the Normans drove them out and took possession of both the mainland and Sicily.

Various factors had contributed to make the Mohammedan armies invincible. Mohammed's message concerning the one true God had acted as a life-bringing truth and had welded the scattered and contentious Arab tribes into a nation. A fierce national pride was the first product of their new national life. And this pride, together with their zeal for the spread of their faith and their desire for booty, both of which amounted to a passion with them, gave them an impetuous courage which swept everything before it. But other things must be taken into account too. Devastating wars and excessive taxation had destroyed the resisting power of the whole civilized world. Rome and Persia had been engaged for centuries in long and bloody wars, which had left both empires exhausted. Heavy taxation had oppressed and impoverished them. Moreover, many of the inhabitants of the empire in western Asia and Egypt, being heretical, were deeply disaffected because the government at Constantinople annoyed and persecuted them for religion's sake. Consequently they were glad to change their political masters, because they had greater religious liberty under a Mohammedan government than under the rule of orthodox emperors. But, after all, the real cause of their success is to be found in the fact that the genius of Mohammed had powerfully wrought upon them, revolutionized their minds, and started in them a tremendous impulse to achievement. And in this we have one measure of the personality of Mohammed.

Factors in the Success of the Armies.

Mohammed died in 632 without having made any provision for the government, either of his state or of his religion. Many of his followers thought that a prophet should be succeeded by a prophet, and in fact several prophets appeared immediately and sought recognition as his successor. Others thought that the office should be hereditary in the family of Mohammed and proposed that his son-in-law, Ali, should succeed him. Even before Mohammed's death there were two powerful factions intriguing to gain influence in the direction of affairs; one consisted of those who had fled with Mohammed from Mecca, and who regarded themselves as a kind of aristocracy of the faith; the other was composed of more recent converts, especially of the Meccans. The unexpected death of Mohammed and the presence of factions and conflicting opinions prevented the proper consideration of what should be done and led to hasty action. A few of the

Mohammed's Caliphs or "Successors."

more intimate companions of Mohammed, members of the faction first named, met and hastily elected Abu Bekr as his caliph or successor. This choice caused great dissatisfaction, and there were many uprisings and rebellions in various parts of Arabia. But Abu Bekr vigorously suppressed them and established his authority over all Arabia.

The rule of the first four caliphs (Abu Bekr 632–634, Omar 634–644, Othman 644–655, and Ali 655–661) is called the period of the undivided caliphate, although under Othman and Ali, both of whom were murdered, there were many rebellions and much civil strife. The high offices in both state and army had powerful attractions which awakened the ambitions of many. Consequently it is not strange that rival caliphs arose, one in Damascus, the other in Arabia, 661. After devastating wars the caliph at Damascus was victorious, and the office of caliph became hereditary in his family. He and his descendants are known as the Ommeiades. In spite of numerous rebellions and plots against them they reigned in Damascus to 750, when the Abbassides, the descendants of Abbas, an uncle of Mohammed, rebelled against them, destroyed them, seized the caliphate, and removed its seat to Bagdad.

The Undivided Caliphate, 632–661.

The Caliphate of Damascus, 661–750.

Of Bagdad, 750–1258.

The caliphate of Bagdad reached its height about 800 under the famous caliph, Haroun-al-Raschid, and began to decline soon afterward. Its political dismemberment was caused by the emirs or governors of the provinces, who made themselves independent of the caliph and ruled virtually as kings. In the eleventh century Turks from central Asia, who were still half barbarous, overran all western Asia. In 1058 the caliph invited their chief, Togrul Beg, to Bagdad and resigned into his hand all temporal authority and made him sultan of the Mohammedan world. The caliph retained only religious authority, but even this was merely nominal. This changed caliphate continued till 1258, when the son of the great conqueror, Ghengis Khan, put to death the last caliph.

End of Caliphate of Bagdad.

Besides that of Bagdad two other caliphates deserving a word were established, one in Spain, the other in Egypt. When the Ommeiades were destroyed (750) only one of them, Abd-er-Rahman, escaped. After long wanderings he finally reached Spain, where the Mohammedans acknowledged him as ruler (755). He and his descendants were called emirs, sultans, or sons of the caliphs. Although their territory was called the caliphate of Cordova it was not till 929 that Abd-er-Rahman III assumed the title of caliph. This caliphate was weakened by constant wars with the Christians and by internal rebellions. About 1031 the caliph was deposed, and the caliphate of Cordova soon dissolved into several independent states (Toledo, Seville, Cordova, etc.). By 1300 the Christians had conquered all of these except the little principality of Granada, which remained in the hands of Mohammedans to 1492.

Caliphate of Cordova.

Early in the tenth century a clever impostor, claiming to be a descendant of Fatima, a daughter of Mohammed, acquired considerable authority in Africa. He and his descendants, called the Fatimites, got possession of Egypt, and in 969 founded Cairo and made it the seat of their government. Their caliphate consisted of a large part of northern Africa and Sicily, and for a while they held Jerusalem and Syria. Their power began to wane in the eleventh century, when the Normans wrested Sicily from them (1060–1080). The decline of their power was hastened by revolts. In 1171 Saladin, who ruled western Asia (1169–1193), conquered their caliph, put an end to their caliphate, and took possession of their territory.

Caliphate of Cairo, 969–1171.

Islam is divided over speculative theological questions into as many sects as is Christianity. Inconsistent statements in the Koran have given rise to various interpretations, which have been accentuated and perpetuated by the formation of sects. A fierce theological battle was waged among their teachers over the formulation of the doctrines concerning God and his attributes. The question of foreordination and free will split the Mohammedan

Many Mohammedan Sects.

world into two great hostile camps. There was no mysticism in Mohammed's religion, yet Islam has produced schools of mystics quite as remarkable as those connected with Christianity. Neither was Mohammed ascetic nor is there anything in the Koran in favor of celibacy or monasticism, yet within Islam there has been developed an ascetic monastic movement of large proportions.

Mohammedan Civilization.

If for no other reason, Mohammed should awaken a sympathetic interest because of the marvellously stimulating effect of his personality on his followers; for it must be attributed to him that so many peoples, among them half-barbarous tribes, were suddenly welded together into a great and ambitious nation, and that during the first three or four centuries after his death they produced a civilization which was far in advance of that of Europe at the same time. The elements of this civilization they derived from Greece, Persia, and India, but they modified them and improved them, and the resulting civilization they spread from Spain far into central Asia. This civilization reached its height about 800 and rapidly declined in all those lands which came under the domination of the Turks. The Mohammedans* excelled in agriculture and horticulture, and practised them in a scientific way. They delighted in landscape-gardening, and, by grafting, produced new kinds of flowers and fruits. They knew the value of fertilizers and irrigation, by means of which they made the mountainous and rainless regions of their empire into gardens of delight. In manufactures and in the industrial arts they surpassed the world in perfection of workmanship and in the variety and beauty of design. They worked in metals—gold, silver, copper, bronze, iron, and steel. In the production of textile fabrics they have never been surpassed. They made glass and pottery and knew the secrets of dyeing. They excelled in dressing leather, as the terms "cordovan" and "morocco" testify. In order to prevent idolatry, Mohammed for-

* Saracen, originally the name of some nomadic Arabic tribes, came to be applied to all Mohammedans. The Mohammedans of North Africa and of Spain are commonly called Moors.

bade his people to make the likeness of man or beast in stone or in color. Consequently they have never excelled in sculpture or in painting. In architecture, however, they developed a beautiful style, which was characterized by the round and horseshoe arch, by the dome, by the tall and graceful minaret, and by richness of ornamentation, especially of their interiors. Their buildings were comparatively simple in construction, but marvels of perfection and of richness in detail and decoration. Their architectural remains, consisting chiefly of mosques and palaces, are still the wonder and admiration of the world.

Commerce.

Their commerce attained vast proportions, extending from Spain to China, and from Scandinavia to the interior of Africa. They were the middlemen between Europe and the east. Some of their fairs or markets were famous. Their commerce, industries, and manufactures made them rich, and wealth enabled them to indulge in luxuries and to procure everything that would gratify their senses. The *Arabian Nights*, although perhaps not an exact picture of actual conditions among them, at least portrays their mind and ideals. Although luxury-loving and sensual, they cultivated also the mind. Much of their learning was expended on the Koran. Numberless commentaries on it were written, and from it they derived their theology, law, ethics, and, nominally, their philosophy. In fact, however, they drew their philosophy from the Greek philosophers, chiefly Aristotle. Through them and their translations mediæval Europe obtained its first knowledge of Aristotle. They learned medicine and surgery from the Greeks (Galen, Hippocrates), but added materially to the stock of medical knowledge thus obtained. Chemistry they pursued rather as alchemy, in search of the secret of eternal youth (elixir of life) and of the philosopher's stone, which was supposed to have the power of changing base metals into gold. While doing so, however, they discovered new elements and produced new and valuable compounds, such as potash, alcohol, corrosive sublimate, nitrate of silver, and nitric and sulphuric acids.

They excelled in mathematics. In the twelfth century an Arab mathematician invented the zero, which is of fundamental importance because it created the decimal system by giving to the nine digits the value of position. Algebra is their creation. About 820 an Arab composed a treatise on algebra which contained equations of the second degree. It was later introduced into Europe, where it served as the text-book on that subject down to the sixteenth century. They developed spherical trigonometry. They made considerable progress in physics and in astronomy, and constructed various astronomical instruments; they calculated the angle of the ecliptic and the precession of the equinoxes. They were acquainted with the Ptolemaic system of astronomy, knew the shape of the earth, and taught geography by the use of globes. Much of their learning was carried into Europe in the twelfth and thirteenth centuries and hastened there the general awakening which is called the Renaissance.

Mathematics.

CHAPTER XV

THE CRUSADES

THE most picturesque and romantic movement of the Middle Age was the crusades, which had for one of their objects the reconquest of the land hallowed by the life and death of Jesus.

The "Holy Land."

Cf. R., 130.

To understand the origin of this movement we must follow the growth of the passionate affection which the people of the west had come to feel for the Holy Land, and particularly for Jerusalem. The emperor Hadrian (118–138) destroyed the city, and for about two hundred years it was a small town of no importance. Jews were forbidden to enter it, and Christians had not yet begun to show it special honor. The eyes of the world were again directed toward it in 326, when Helena, the mother of the emperor Constantine, made her famous pilgrimage to it. Her example found imitators in ever-increasing numbers, and the idea prevailed more and more that without visiting the places hallowed by the presence of Jesus while on earth no one could attain the highest degree of holiness; prayer in those places was regarded as more effectual, and God's grace was thought to be more easily and richly obtained there than elsewhere. So century by century the number of pilgrims to Jerusalem grew larger. Occasional protests against the custom, and against the belief on which it was based were made. "The way to heaven is neither longer nor more difficult from Britain than from Jerusalem, for the kingdom of God is within you," said St. Jerome; but his words were contradicted by his example, for he spent the last thirty-four years of his life as a monk in Bethlehem, attracted thither by the cradle of Christ. The Mohammedan conquest of Palestine scarcely affected its Christian population, nor did it interfere with the custom of making pilgrimages to the holy places, nor diminish the number of pilgrims. The Mohammedans left the Christians in undisturbed possession of their churches, with few exceptions, and permitted them to exercise their religion freely. Christian pilgrims came and went without molestation. Up to the eleventh century Christians suffered so little inconvenience from the Mohammedan occupation of Palestine that no one thought of making war to recover the holy places.

The advent of the Seljuk Turks, a people from central Asia, in the eleventh century changed this. Although they were Mohammedans, their coming was almost as disastrous to the Mohammedan population of the country as to the Christian. Being half-barbarous and fiercely fanatical, they had no appreciation of the civilization of the one, nor regard for the religion of the other. Under the weight of their barbarism the arts and industries languished, learning deteriorated, and the whole civilization retrograded. They were fanatically attached to the letter of the Koran and had, therefore, a low, formal type of Mohammedanism which accorded with their ignorance. They destroyed the liberal type of Mohammedanism which had prevailed for some three hundred years. During the last half of the eleventh century they overran much of Asia Minor and Syria and got possession of nearly all the cities, which they garrisoned without destroying the Christian population. After they took Jerusalem (1071) Christians had no peace there. The Turks defiled the churches and holy places, and oppressed the Christians in order to compel them to seek protection by accepting Mohammedanism. They were especially violent toward pilgrims; some they beat and robbed, some they killed, and others they seized and sold into slavery. Returning pilgrims recited these horrors as they passed through Europe, everywhere throughout the west exciting a strong desire to take vengeance on the infidels.

Turks Take Palestine.

The Turks advanced also into Asia Minor and the Greek emperor was unable to prevent them from conquering almost all his Asiatic provinces. For under a series of weak rulers the empire had been brought low, and owing to the peculation of officials, the army and navy were in a wretched condition and quite unable to offer effective resistance to a determined enemy. The treasury was empty and the people burdened with taxes. When Alexius I (1081–1118) came to the throne he found the empire threatened on all sides; the Turks were on the opposite shore of the Bosporus, seeking to attack Constantinople; other barbarous peoples were crossing the Danube and laying waste the empire to the very gates of Constantinople; and the Normans from southern Italy were landing on the Adriatic coast and making a bold and determined effort to conquer the whole Balkan peninsula (1081–1085). Alexius was a man of no mean ability. With the most heroic efforts he drove the Normans out of the empire and overwhelmed the barbarians on the Danube frontier; but, worn out by these labors, he was powerless to drive back the Turks. In his extremity he appealed to the pope for help (winter 1094–1095).

Attack the Greek Empire.

This was not the first appeal of the sort, for ever since the appearance of the Turks in Asia Minor the successive emperors had appealed, though in vain, to the pope for aid. Gregory VII (1073–1085) had indeed undertaken to raise an army for the succor of the emperor, but, after bringing together about 50,000 men for that purpose, was unable to lead or send them to the east. Alexius had already made frequent appeals to the pope, who, owing to his struggle with the western emperor, was unable to send troops to his relief. Alexius had, however, made Urban II (1088–1099) his friend, and in spite of the schism between the Greek and Latin churches, Urban had given him absolution and treated him as a faithful and orthodox son of the church. The political situation was favorable, for the emperor, Henry IV, had been compelled to withdraw to Germany, leaving the pope undisputed master in Italy. Urban II, in order to secure the fruits of his victory, was making a grand tour which should take him through northern Italy and even beyond the Alps into France. The messengers of Alexius came to him at Piacenza, where he held a council which was numerously attended (4,000 clergymen and 30,000 laymen). Urban

Alexius Appeals to the Pope for Help.

S. B., 278.

made an urgent and successful appeal to the assembled multitude, and the messengers of Alexius were able to return to Constantinople with the encouraging report that the pope had interested himself in the matter and that thousands in the west had promised to come to his aid.

Urban II continued his journey to France and held a great council at Clermont (November 18–28, 1095) which was attended by 14 archbishops, 250 bishops, 400 abbots, and thousands of priests and laymen. In a public square of the city on the 27th of November, Urban addressed the multitudes, renewing the appeal which he had made at Piacenza, and somewhat widening its scope. Beginning with a statement of the defeats and losses of the Greeks, and of their sufferings at the hands of the Turks, he described the unhappy condition of the Christians in Asia Minor, Syria, and Palestine, who were under Mohammedan rule, and aroused his hearers by a harrowing account of the atrocities inflicted upon them by the Turks. He then urged all who were present to go to the aid of the Greeks and to "destroy that vile race from the land of our friends." As if he had not already said enough to stir his hearers to action he continued: "You should be moved especially by the holy grave of our Lord and Saviour, which is now held by unclean peoples, and by the holy places which are treated with dishonor and irreverently befouled with their uncleanness." From a simple relief expedition in aid of the Greek emperor, such as Urban had announced at Piacenza, he had enlarged it to a united effort on the part of all Christians to destroy the Turks and to recover the holy places. Although Urban still put the emphasis on the aid which was to be given the Greeks, his hearers, who had no special interest in the Greek empire, thought principally of recovering the holy places to which they were deeply attached. And so the movement, in its very inception, was partially turned from what in the mind of Urban had been its original purpose.

Urban II at Clermont Asked Help for the Greeks and the Holy Places.

S. B., 279, 280. O., 282. R., 123.

The People Think Mostly of the Holy Places.

As further inducements Urban offered large spiritual rewards, announcing that "all who die by the way, whether by land or by sea, or in battle against the pagans, shall have immediate remission of sins." And in the council he enacted that "if any one out of devotion alone, and not for honor or gain, sets out for Jerusalem to free the church of God, the journey shall be regarded as the equivalent of all penance." Such action was not an innovation, for in the ninth century two popes had promised forgiveness of sins to all who should die in battle with Mohammedans, probably because such a death was regarded as akin to martyrdom.*

Spiritual Inducements.

S. B., 179, 281.
S. B., 274-277.

The effect of Urban's speech at Clermont was far greater

* Urban's successors went much further and offered other advantages of a secular character. In 1145 Eugene III enlarged on the promise of Urban as follows:

"Wishing, therefore, to provide for your welfare as well as to relieve the church in the east, we grant to those who, in a spirit of devotion, shall determine to accomplish this holy and necessary work, by the authority of God conferred on us, the same remission of sins as our predecessor, Pope Urban, granted. And we decree that their wives and children, their goods and possessions, shall be under the protection of the holy church, of ourselves, and of the archbishops, bishops, and other prelates of the church of God. And until they return, or their death is known, we forbid by our apostolic authority any lawsuit to be brought against them about any of the property of which they were in peaceful possession when they took the cross. . . . If any are in debt, but with a pure intention set out on this holy journey, they shall not pay the interest already due; and if they or others are pledged to pay the interest, by our apostolic authority we absolve them from their oath or pledge. If their relations or the lords on whose fiefs they live can not or will not lend them the money (necessary for the journey), they may pawn their lands and other possessions to churches, to clergymen, or to others, without the consent of the lords of their fiefs." *Cf.* the moratorium and similar protective measures for soldiers during the recent Great War.

S. B., 284.
R., 131.

Innocent III (1215) was still more liberal:

"Now, because it is only just that those who devote themselves to the service of the heavenly ruler should enjoy some special prerogative, and since it is a little more than a year until the time set for going, we decree that all who have taken the cross shall be free from all exactions, taxes, and other burdens. . . . We order the secular authorities to compel the Jews to remit the interest to all crusaders, and until they do remit it they shall have no association with Christians."

S. B., 288.
R., 132.

than he could have expected. Even while he spoke the great throng interrupted him with a mighty shout, "It is the will of God, it is the will of God," and thousands of them pressed forward, made a vow to go on the expedition, and received a cross of cloth which was fastened on their breast or arm. At the close of the council the thousands who had been in attendance scattered in all directions announcing the new movement and repeating the pope's appeal as they went. Urban commissioned various persons specially to preach the crusade, and he himself spent the next nine months travelling through France, holding councils, and persuading people to take the cross. In this, he, as well as those whom he sent out, met with an astonishing success.

Success of the Pope's Appeal.

The west seemed ripe for such a movement. The Cluniac reform which had been growing for nearly two hundred years had now reached its height. Under its influence the ascetic spirit had enveloped all Europe and had manifested itself in the establishment of several new monastic orders and in a burning desire to make the pilgrimage to Jerusalem—a desire which had become almost a passion when the Turkish occupation of Palestine made its realization impossible. Returning pilgrims, as has been said already, had excited the gaping crowds who gathered to listen to them by a harrowing account of the inhuman treatment which the Christians received at the hands of the Turks, and had awakened in them a strong desire to avenge the wrongs of their fellow Christians. The peasants were ready for anything, because they had been brought to despair by famine, caused by a series of disasters, such as floods and drouth, which had ruined the crops for some ten years (1085–1095). They felt that, no matter where they went or what they undertook, they could encounter nothing worse than the hunger and pestilence which were destroying them at home. Nor were the turbulent nobles less inclined to hear the call. Trained to arms and knowing no recreation but feuds and war, many of them were eager to engage in an expedition which promised such excitements. At the same time, owing to the combined

The West was Ripe for a Crusade.

efforts of the church and of the governments, society in Europe was becoming more stable. For more than a century the church had been striving to put an end to feuds and private warfare and the truce of God had no doubt had some effect in diminishing the violence of the nobility. The numerous checks put upon fighting seemed to the nobles like limitations on the exercise of their profession, and, since they were repeatedly compelled to take an oath not to engage in feuds or private warfare, they felt that they were without an occupation and were willing to go anywhere, provided they could find unhindered and profitable exercise of arms. Since, according to feudal custom, fiefs passed to the eldest son, the younger sons, left generally with little besides their swords, and having small opportunity to rise in the world, were strongly attracted by an expedition which had for its avowed object the destruction of the Turks and the partition of their lands and possessions. So it is not strange that the prospect of novel experiences and thrilling adventures in a strange land, the probable acquisition of temporal gain and honor, and the certitude of eternal reward, should have caused thousands to take the cross.

Crusading Mobs.

S. B., 282.

The beginning of the crusade was both disappointing and disgraceful, for the first bands that were collected were composed, for the most part, of unarmed peasants, vagabonds, thieves, and marauders of every description, who were a scourge to the country wherever they passed. Urban had named the middle of August (1096) as the time for the journey to begin, but this seemed too far away for the peasants. Early in the spring immense numbers of them put their meagre possessions on two-wheeled carts and, all unconscious of the hard fate that awaited them, set out with their wives and children, hopeful and eager "to be in at the death" of the Turk and to secure a large share of the spoils. As they passed through village and town they were joined by disreputable women and worthless men, who hoped, under the cover of a holy warfare and in the general turmoil and confusion, to ply their evil trades and arts without detection. Some of them, ambitious to attract attention and to gain a reputation for holiness which would enable them to prey upon the unsuspecting, burned a cross on their bodies with red-hot irons and shamelessly asserted that this had been done in a miraculous manner. They were gathered under various leaders, who won an evil distinction because of the unhappy outcome of their undertaking. Chief of these were Fulcher,* Gottschalk, Emicho, Walter Senzavoir ("Without possessions"), and Peter the Hermit.

The fanatical zeal of these marauders increased with their numbers, and everywhere they turned, as with one accord, against the Jews.† Like wild beasts they fell upon that helpless and defenseless people and put them to death with the most barbarous cruelty. In many cities of northern France and of the Rhine they almost destroyed the Jewish population, either forcing them into exile or slaying them. Of the Jews who fell into their hands hardly

The Jews Attacked.

* Fulcher, probably a priest of Orléans, reached Cologne with about 12,000 persons, mostly peasants with their wives and children, and from there set out on the journey (April 23, 1096). They passed through Saxony, Bohemia, and Hungary, robbing and plundering as they went. Everywhere they sought out the Jews and robbed, tortured, and killed all who refused to accept Christian baptism. In Hungary they took forcible possession of a small town, Neutra, established themselves there, and began the systematic plundering of the surrounding country. But the Hungarians collected an army, attacked and defeated them, and permitted only a few of them to escape.

The same fate overtook Gottschalk, a priest, and his army of 15,000, who, leaving Mainz (April 30, 1096), passed through Bavaria and the east mark into Hungary, living chiefly by plundering. At Wieselburg some of them engaged in a drunken brawl and killed a young Hungarian, and then the whole band began to rob and plunder the town. The Hungarians soon attacked them in force, surrounded them, and compelled them to surrender. After they had laid down their arms the Hungarians fell upon them and cut them to pieces, and only Gottschalk and a mere handful of his followers escaped.

† In explanation of the position of the Jews in the Middle Age and of the persecutions which they suffered, it may be said that they were not under the law of the land, but were in the hand of the king. He was their only protection and they had to look to him to redress their wrongs. In return for his protection, which was often of little value to them, he had the right to tax them as often and as heavily as he pleased (S. B., 120, 299, 300). Up to about 1000 the Jews in the west were traders and peddlers, thus performing a service that was very accepta-

one escaped death except by denying his religion and accepting Christian baptism. Some thousands of them remained true to their faith and suffered heroic martyrdom.*

Peter the Hermit.

S. B., 283.

The most famous of all these marauding bands was that led by Peter the Hermit and Walter Senzavoir, known as Walter the Penniless. It is not certain that Peter was at the council of Clermont, but, immediately after its close, according to the first authentic information that we have of him, he began to preach the crusade in the county of Berry. He then moved toward the north, visiting the chief cities, everywhere attracting the peasants and the most turbulent and worthless elements of society. He reached Cologne (April 12, 1096) with 20,000 or more in his train. Through his fiery preaching he won about as many more in and about Cologne. Many of them grew tired of waiting, and so about the middle of April, Walter set out with about 20,000 of them, of whom it is said only eight were knights. They seem to have had no difficulty until they reached Semlin

ble to the Christians. About that time, however, the Christians, who were engaging more extensively in commerce, began to try to monopolize it, and so they came to dislike the Jews because they were competitors in business. Moreover, the business of lending money had been in the hands of bishops and abbots, the only persons in the west who had money, but in consequence of the Cluniac reform the church forbade all Christians to lend money at interest (S. B., 119). The Jews, forced, to a certain extent, out of commerce, took up money-lending and were hated also on that account. The mob justified its barbarity against the Jews by charging them with having crucified Christ.

* Count William of Melun and Count Emicho of Leiningen, two barbarously cruel noblemen, were perhaps the worst offenders of all, and their bands were composed of those numerous small bands which had been most violent against the Jews. After committing unspeakable atrocities in Cologne, Mainz, Speier, Worms, Metz, Treves, and other cities, they marched by different routes through Bavaria and the east mark into Hungary. By the union of several of these bands about 30,000 were collected near Wieselburg, whose inhabitants, remembering the character of Gottschalk and his followers, closed the gates of the city and refused to supply them with food. The crusaders laid siege to the city and were on the point of taking it by storm, when, for some unknown reason, they became frightened, gave up the siege, and fled. So panic-stricken were they that the Hungarians had no difficulty in destroying them.

in Hungary, where, being denied market privileges, some of them began to plunder. When the Hungarians attacked them, Walter refused to fight and hastened on. He reached Constantinople about the 20th of July, where he waited for the arrival of Peter the Hermit.

Peter, with some 20,000, only a few of whom were properly armed, left Cologne April 19, 1096. When they reached Semlin they learned of the losses which the Hungarians had inflicted on Walter's followers and, in the desire of avenging them, stormed and sacked the city. When a Hungarian army approached they hastily fled from Hungary into Bulgaria. Near Nisch some of his German followers, believing that they had been cheated in the purchase of food, began to burn and plunder. The Bulgarians attacked them and put them to flight. Peter collected his scattered forces and finally (August 1) reached Constantinople, where he was joined by Walter. The emperor Alexius received them kindly, but his disappointment was great; for instead of an army of warriors he saw only helpless, unarmed, and undisciplined men, women, and children, who were a charge rather than a help to him. Worse than that, they despised the Greeks and immediately began to steal, plunder, and burn, as if they were in an enemy's country. In order to protect the city Alexius hastily sent them across the Bosporus and warned them not to proceed into the interior, but to wait until the main army of the crusaders should arrive. They disregarded his advice, however, and began the march toward Nicæa, stopping to plunder wherever they found an opportunity. Peter, having lost all control over them, had returned to Constantinople and they were wholly without discipline. Before reaching Nicæa they were attacked by the Turks and cut to pieces, only a few hundreds of them escaping to Constantinople. Some of these waited there with Peter for the main army which was then on its way, but most of them were so frightened that they hastily set out for home.

France and Germany, after the disappearance of these murderous bands beyond the frontier, again had peace, although the excitement was unabated; for thousands of nobles were arming themselves for the journey, and, accompanied by great numbers of knights, foot-soldiers, and pilgrims, were collecting at various places to be ready to begin the march at the appointed time. Count Hugo of Vermandois, brother of the French king, Philip I, was among the first to leave. With a numerous retinue of knights he passed rapidly through Italy and crossed from Bari to Durazzo, where the emperor's officials met him and conducted him to Constantinople. Alexius honorably received him and hospitably entertained him. Since the emperor had appealed to the pope for help and had been assured that the crusaders were coming to his aid, it is not strange that he should have tried from the very first to fix the conditions upon which they were to fight for him. He could not safely permit thousands of armed men to enter his realm without a clear understanding of their intentions, nor could he undertake a campaign with their aid without defining the relations which should exist between him and them. He therefore asked all the leaders of the crusaders to take an oath not to injure him or his realm, but to be faithful to him and to surrender to him any territory which they might wrest from the Turks, provided it had once been a part of the Greek empire. This oath was not in reality an oath of feudal vassalage, although the westerners, interpreting it in the light of conditions existing at home, generally regarded it as such. It is difficult to see how Alexius could have asked less. Unfortunately, however, he was wrong in supposing that the crusaders had come to help him. For the leaders had come with the fixed intention of securing territory and establishing themselves as independent princes, indifferent, for the most part, whether at the expense of Greek or Turk. The knights who accompanied them, being soldiers of fortune, were willing to fight where it would be most profitable to them, and the rank and file of the crusaders were interested chiefly in the recovery of the holy places from the Mohammedans. Hugo took the oath apparently without any misgiving or objection.

Crusaders Set Out, 1096.

O., 52. R., 124.

Reasonable Demands of Alexius.

Motives of the Leaders.

Godfrey of Bouillon, duke of lower Lotharingia, began the journey at the appointed time with 10,000 knights, 30,000 foot-soldiers, and a host of pilgrims. He was accompanied by a number of noblemen, among them his brother Baldwin (I) and his nephew Baldwin (II), both of whom were to win renown as kings of Jerusalem. Godfrey strictly forbade his men to steal or to commit any violence whatever, and, passing through the east mark and Hungary, entered the Greek empire without opposition from the natives. In obedience to the orders of Alexius, the Greeks supplied them with food and treated them with the highest consideration. When within a few miles of Constantinople, however, Godfrey heard that Alexius had taken Hugo and his retinue prisoners, and, to avenge the insult, he plundered and devastated the country far and wide, clear up to Constantinople, which he reached December 23. Count Hugo can hardly have been held as a prisoner, for he visited Godfrey, and, far from holding any resentment against Alexius, besought Godfrey to take the oath which the emperor demanded. This Godfrey stubbornly refused to do, but permitted his troops to plunder and steal as much as they chose. Alexius was forced to send his troops against him, and, after some severe fighting, Godfrey yielded and took the oath (January 20, 1097). He was unable, however, to compel his followers to keep the peace, and Alexius soon forced him to move his army across the Bosporus and encamp in Asia Minor (February 20, 1097).

Godfrey of Bouillon.

Cf. R., 125.

Raymond, count of Toulouse, the first nobleman of importance to take the cross, led his army, which was somewhat smaller than that of Godfrey, through north Italy and down the eastern shore of the Adriatic to Durazzo, and thence across the Balkan Peninsula to Constantinople. His troops helped themselves to what they needed, and, in consequence, were frequently attacked by the inhabitants of the countries through which they passed. After stubbornly refusing to take the oath, he finally yielded and soon became the fast friend of Alexius.

Raymond of Toulouse.

The most capable of all the leaders was Bohemond of Tarento, the oldest son of Robert Guiscard, who had disinherited him in favor of his second son, Roger, to whom he gave his duchy (Apulia, Calabria, and Sicily). Bohemond, fretted by the narrowness of his possessions, and feeling himself fitted for greater things, eagerly took the cross in the hope of acquiring a territory commensurate with his ability and ambition. Although poor, he succeeded in enlisting a few thousand knights, many of them, like himself, Normans and soldiers of fortune. Among them was his nephew, Tancred. Bohemond led his little army across the Adriatic and the Balkan Peninsula. Leaving Tancred in charge of his army, Bohemond hastened on to Constantinople. Alexius, remembering that Bohemond had been the chief assistant of Robert Guiscard when he invaded the empire (1081–1085), was filled with distrust toward him, and his distrust was changed into fear when Bohemond plainly declared that he had come to make his fortune and that he hoped to obtain territory where he could establish himself as an independent ruler, and asked to be put at the head of a large force of imperial troops. Alexius dissembled his feelings under a cloak of friendship and Bohemond took the oath with the utmost readiness. No sooner was Tancred left in charge of the army than trouble began; for he hated the Greeks so deeply that Bohemond only by the most stringent measures had restrained him from acts of wanton violence against them. Now that Bohemond was no longer present Tancred set his troops to pillaging the country. When they reached Constantinople Tancred disguised himself and crossed the Bosporus in order to escape taking the oath to the emperor.

Bohemond.

The last to reach Constantinople (middle of May, 1097) were Count Robert of Normandy, son of William the Conqueror, his brother-in-law, Count Stephen of Blois, and Count Robert of Flanders, each with a considerable following. The crusaders, accompanied by a detachment of the Greek army, had already left Constantinople and were on their way to Nicæa. There was hardly a semblance of organization in the army, which was

O., 53.
R., 126.

No Organization.

composed of probably 100,000 fighting men and perhaps as many more unarmed men, priests, women, and children. Each leader provided as best he could for the needs of those who had joined him, and led them forward with no regard to the movements of the other divisions. The vanguard reached Nicæa May 6, while the rear-guard did not arrive until June 3. The siege was conducted with great vigor, but with little prospect of success, until the Greeks hauled some boats overland on wagons and launched them on the small lake which washed the west walls of the city. On the morning of June 18 the Greeks and crusaders made a united attack by sea and land. The besieged, well knowing what they would suffer at the hands of the crusaders, who were eager to pillage the place, surrendered to the Greeks, who promptly closed the gates of the city against the crusaders. Alexius, delighted to recover the rich city almost undamaged by the siege, called all the leaders to him and placated them with valuable gifts. He directed them to proceed through Asia Minor as they had begun, while he would take a route farther north, but parallel to theirs. For in this way he calculated that the two armies would be more easily provisioned and would wrest more territory from the Turks. The leaders were pleased with his generous treatment of them and renewed their oaths to him. The army and the pilgrims, however, although he distributed a large sum of money among them, were enraged that he had not permitted them to sack Nicæa and cursed him for what they were pleased to call his treachery.

Siege of Nicæa, 1097.

The crusaders occupied the summer of 1097 with their march through Asia Minor. They suffered somewhat from the attacks of the Turks, but hunger, thirst, heat, and disease were their deadliest foes, cutting them down by the thousands. After they passed Iconium they suffered less from thirst and the Christian inhabitants supplied their wants. At Heraclea (Eregli) Tancred, who, in his eagerness to secure the best of the booty, had always kept as far as possible in advance of the army, determined to strike out for himself. He was joined by a number of knights who

The March through Asia Minor, 1097.

were of the same mind as he, and set out over the mountains to Tarsus. Baldwin I, who was jealous of Tancred and bent on having a share of any spoil he might take, followed him with a still larger force. Tancred reached Tarsus first. The Turkish garrison promptly fled, and the inhabitants, who were Christians, were on the point of surrendering to him, when Baldwin arrived and proposed that they sack the city in common. Tancred refused and, as his troops were outnumbered by those of Baldwin, withdrew and continued his march.

Fight over Spoils.

Again Baldwin followed him, and a pitched battle over spoils ensued between their forces. After both sides had suffered some loss they came to their senses and made peace. While Tancred moved eastward to rejoin the main army, Baldwin accepted an invitation to come to Edessa, a Christian (Armenian) city beyond the Euphrates. With about two hundred knights he reached the city and was so successful in a bold campaign against the Turks that the people of Edessa killed their prince and chose Baldwin to rule over them.

Baldwin I Goes to Edessa.

From Heraclius the main army turned sharply to the northeast till they reached Cæsarea, and then marched south to Antioch, which they reached October 21, 1097. Antioch was a prosperous city in the midst of a fertile territory, and therefore it appealed strongly to the ambition of the leaders, who determined to get possession of it. With the shortsightedness which had characterized their conduct from the beginning, the crusaders wasted the provisions, grain, and cattle which they found in the neighborhood so that they soon began to suffer from hunger. While some of them engaged in daily skirmishes with the enemy, others foraged, putting the country for miles around under contribution. Sickness broke out in the camp and many, losing courage, deserted and tried to return to Europe. The outlook of the crusaders was so hopeless that the detachment of Greek troops which, in accordance with the emperor's promise, had accompanied them, withdrew from the siege and returned to the emperor. In the spring of 1098, however, the crusaders re-

Siege of Antioch, 1097–1098.

newed the siege with greater energy, because they learned that a large Turkish army was coming to the relief of the city. It seems surprising that the crusaders were able to reach Syria without encountering more opposition and that they should have spent seven months before Antioch, in the very heart of the enemy's country, without having been attacked by overwhelming numbers. The emirs, however, were in rebellion against the central government and were so mutually jealous that they were unwilling to do anything in aid of one another. But for this political disruption the Turks could easily have destroyed the crusaders. The emir of Mosul was now bringing an army to the relief of Antioch, but he was marching at his leisure, and his forces were weakened by disunion and were ready to desert him.

The City Betrayed.

Some time before this Bohemond had secretly bribed a Turkish emir who had charge of the defense of some of the towers to betray the city to him. Bohemond asked the leaders first to swear that the city should belong to the one who had most to do with its capture. This they all refused to do, because of their oath to Alexius. Bohemond replied that, as the emperor had not kept his promise to them, they were released from their oath to him. This they denied, and declared that as the dangers and labors of all had been equal, they should all have an equal share in the spoils. Bohemond bided his time and when the Turkish army was within a few days' march of Antioch he told the leaders that he would take the city if they would give him the oath which he demanded. As the danger was pressing they yielded and agreed that Bohemond should have the city, but should surrender it to Alexius if the latter should fulfil all his former agreements. The following night the treacherous emir admitted Bohemond and a number of his men to one of the towers. The next morning (June 3, 1098) the crusaders made a united attack, and, as Bohemond opened the gates from the inside, they were soon in possession of all the city except the citadel. Two days later the emir of Mosul arrived and the crusaders were in turn besieged; their cour-

The Crusaders Besieged in Antioch.

age sank from day to day as the certainty of their capture increased. They were saved, however, by the successful execution of a pious fraud—the discovery of the "holy" lance with which the side of Jesus had been pierced—which so rekindled their enthusiasm and fanaticism that they defeated the Turks and caused them to raise the siege.

The way was now open to Jerusalem, but as a quarrel arose among the leaders as to what should be done with Antioch, they determined to spend the summer there. Raymond of Toulouse had broken his oath, seized a part of the city and fortified it, and refused to surrender it to Bohemond. While waiting for the quarrel to be ended, and also to escape the plague which had just broken out in Antioch, the crusaders, in the hope of making other conquests, scattered in all directions. Bohemond led a large force into Cilicia to assist the Armenians and make them his friends, since they were to be his neighbors; Tancred skirmished through northern Syria; Godfrey went to Edessa to visit his brother Baldwin; and the other leaders sought fame and fortune by trying to wrest other provinces from the Turks. So intent were the leaders in pursuing their private ends that they seemed to forget Jerusalem entirely. Not till November did they return to Antioch. They were then as far as ever from an agreement as to what should be done with the city. The pilgrims and common men now made themselves heard. They declared that if the leaders did not cease from their strife and proceed at once to Jerusalem they would burn Antioch and choose other commanders. The leaders were thus forced to set out, leaving Bohemond in possession of Antioch. Raymond of Toulouse made a show of starting, but stopped to lay siege to every town by the way. Bohemond, now that he had what he sought—a principality—had no intention of going on to Jerusalem. Nevertheless he followed Raymond for the purpose of keeping him from establishing himself in any city near Antioch. In this he was successful, and after Raymond had gone a sufficient distance Bohemond returned to Antioch. Raymond continued to waste the time

Quarrels among the Leaders.

The People Burn the Tents and Go to Jerusalem.

of the crusaders in fruitless and unnecessary sieges until they lost all patience, set fire to their tents, and began a mad race which did not end until they reached Jerusalem. At the sight of his burning tents and the disobedience and desertion of his men, Raymond wept with rage, but was powerless further to retard the progress of the crusade.

They reached Jerusalem, June 7, 1099, and in spite of their sufferings from heat and thirst prosecuted the siege with great energy. Their fanatical zeal was stirred as never before and, although the city was surrounded by high walls and was strongly garrisoned, they stormed and took it July 15 (1099). Scenes of indescribable barbarity ensued. They murdered the Mohammedan inhabitants, men, women, and children, without mercy, and sacked and plundered till they were exhausted. Covered with blood and laden with spoils they ended the day with a great procession to the Church of the Holy Sepulchre, where, in the midst of hysterical rejoicings, they gave thanks to God for their victory. The next day they renewed their search for booty, and completed the bloody work which had been interrupted by darkness. Eight days later, when they met to decide what disposition they should make of the city, some of the clergy wished the highest authority to be vested in a clerical head (presumably a patriarch), under whom a layman should be chosen to administer secular affairs. The leaders objected to this, and although they were all bitter against Raymond of Toulouse, they offered him the city. He refused it for various reasons. Jerusalem was neither on the sea nor on an important caravan route; it was without industries and commerce, and because of its situation it could never become the seat of a powerful principality. Jerusalem was too remote from Antioch to serve his purpose, for he had determined to devote the rest of his life, if necessary, to the destruction of Bohemond, so deep had his hatred and resentment become; so he wished to acquire territory in the north of Syria, where he could more easily lie in wait to destroy him. They then chose Godfrey of Bouil-

Siege of Jerusalem, 1099.

The Leaders Quarrel about the City.

Cf. R., 127.

lon, who accepted it, but, refusing the title of king, called himself prince, duke, or advocate (protector) of the holy grave. A few days later the crusaders were called out to repulse an army that was approaching from Egypt. The battle took place before the walls of Ascalon and the Christians were completely victorious (August 12). They would even have taken Ascalon but for a quarrel that arose between Godfrey and Raymond of Toulouse about who should have it. Raymond had no intention of remaining there, but he was unwilling to cede the city to Godfrey, who would have been greatly strengthened by the possession of it.

Fail to Take Ascalon.

The first crusade was now at an end. Of all the hosts that had begun it, not more than 20,000 were left to return home. Laden with relics and booty they marched to the north along the Mediterranean coast until they reached Laodicæa, whence most of them sailed for some Italian port. Raymond of Toulouse, however, remained in Laodicæa, and by the help of the Greek emperor soon got possession of several towns, among them Tripolis, which came to serve as the capital of his principality. As count of Tripolis he spent the brief remainder of his life (d. 1105) in a struggle to build up his own power. Selfish, ambitious, and incapable of working in harmony with others, he was to the end a troublesome neighbor to the rulers of the other crusader states.

Return of the Crusaders.

The material success of the first crusade was small indeed. Alexius had recovered a small part of Asia Minor; the Armenians had received some aid in their struggle with the Turks; Baldwin I had got possession of an Armenian city, Edessa, which, it must be remembered, was already Christian; Bohemond had obtained a small principality with Antioch as its capital; Raymond of Toulouse had Laodicæa, the beginning of a small state; and Godfrey of Bouillon had Jerusalem. Such was the meagre outcome of this great expedition which had begun with high promise. But that which counted for the most glorious success was the recovery of the Holy Sepulchre, the news of which gave Europe

Results of the First Crusade.

a paroxysm of joy. Thousands reproached themselves as laggards for having missed the opportunity to have a share in so glorious a work, and now, in a fit of the wildest enthusiasm, they hastened to the east in the hope of still achieving greatness. Puffed up with the ambition to do greater things than had been accomplished by the first crusade, they determined to attack the Mohammedan power in its principal seat, and so set out for Bagdad. The army, which was proceeding in three divisions and numbered probably more than 100,000, was cut to pieces by the Turks in Asia Minor, and the Mohammedan slave markets were glutted with the Christians who were taken prisoners.

Petty Character of the Crusader States.

The history of these petty crusader states (they are sometimes called Latin states) is quite unimportant. It is difficult for us to realize how insignificant they were. Godfrey was left with only a few fighting men and his kingdom at first hardly extended beyond the walls of Jerusalem. But the pious imagination of the west pictured him as a powerful king living in unparalleled splendor and magnificence. Nor were the rulers of the other crusader states much more powerful. Nothing could be more wearisome than a detailed account of their history, for it is full of petty jealousy, ambitious intrigue, unsavory scandal, civil strife, and treacherous murder. They fought against one another quite as much as against the Turks, and more than once allied themselves with the Turks to destroy one another. The inhabitants seemed to acquire the vices of both Mohammedans and Christians and to practise the virtues of neither.

Commerce.

The chief interest in these states is in the fact that they developed an extensive and important commerce with Europe which had a quickening and civilizing influence on the west. For by this means a part of what was best in the Mohammedan civilization was introduced into Europe.

This commerce was in the hands of the Italian cities, chief of which were Venice and Genoa, although many others had no small part in it. It was conducted in a peculiar way. A quarter in an eastern city, consisting of a number of squares (blocks) was granted to any western city that might ask for it. The western city, or, as we may call it, the home city, then peopled this quarter with its colonists. The quarter was surrounded with a wall and quite cut off from the rest of the city, its gates being closed in the evening and opened in the morning. These colonists acted as the agents of the merchants of the home city, buying the articles with which the ships were to be loaded on their return voyage and selling to the natives those which made up the cargoes of the incoming ships. The government of the quarter was controlled by the home city, which sent out an official for this purpose. He was expected to make frequent reports on the state of the colony, the articles for which there was a demand, and to give any other information that might be of service to the government as well as to the merchants of the home city. This was the origin of the office of the modern consul, who now plays so important a part in the commercial interests in all civilized countries. Among the numerous articles which through this commerce were carried from the orient into Europe may be mentioned sugar, incense, perfumes, a great variety of spices, glassware, precious stones, and all kinds of textile fabrics, such as silk, cloths, linen, muslin, rugs, and carpets.

"Consul."

Almost every year saw small bands of adventurous knights on the road to Jerusalem, where they hoped to "make their fortune." These, however, are of no interest to us, and even the later crusades may be dismissed with few words, for, although some of them caused a great commotion in Europe, they accomplished nothing in the east. The capture of Edessa by the Mohammedans (1144) led to the second crusade. Louis VII of France, already feeling that he ought to go on a crusade because of the unfulfilled vow of his brother, whose crown he had inherited, responded to the first call and took the cross. The pope approved his action and commissioned St. Bernard of Clairvaux to preach and organize the expedition. As he passed through France, thousands, at his appeal, took the cross. He then

Fall of Edessa, 1144, Leads to Second Crusade, 1147–1149.

S. B., 284.

Louis VII.

R., 128, 129.

went to Germany, where he had the same phenomenal success.

Conrad III.

After several fiery appeals he finally persuaded even the king, Conrad III (1133–1152), to take upon himself the crusader's vow. Fanatical enthusiasm ran high in both France and Germany, and again expressed itself in the most inhuman persecution of the Jews. Conrad, as well as Louis, collected an immense army, the efficiency of which was greatly diminished by the lack of organization, and by the presence of a great number of unarmed pilgrims and worthless and vicious camp-followers, who had been encouraged by the high promises of St. Bernard to join the expedition. St. Bernard looked upon the crusade not as a military expedition, which should be conducted in a sensible way, but rather as a religious demonstration, the success of which depended on numbers rather than on the fighting qualities of the crusaders. Both armies were destroyed in Asia Minor, and only a few thousand of them reached Jerusalem. Then, instead of attacking those emirs who were threatening the Christians, they committed the serious blunder of laying siege to Damascus, whose emir was friendly to them. The siege was unsuccessful and the crusaders, angry with the people of Jerusalem, to whose stupidity and short-sighted policy this mistake was due, returned to Europe with the feeling that the Christians in the east were of such a character that they were not worthy of the great efforts which the west had made to relieve them.

Make-up of the Army.

Destroyed in Asia Minor.

Blunders in Palestine.

The news of the conquest of Jerusalem by Saladin, in 1187, stirred the west profoundly and led the three chief sovereigns of Europe to join in the third crusade. Frederick Barbarossa, profiting by the experience which he had had as a youth in the second crusade, refused to permit any one to join his expedition who was not well armed and supplied with enough money to pay his expenses. In this way he collected an army of perhaps more than a hundred thousand fighting men. He met with determined opposition from the Greek emperor, who had made an alliance with the Mohammedans to prevent

The Third Crusade, 1189–1192.

Frederick Barbarossa.

S. B., 285.

Note to Map XI.—This map shows (1) the routes followed by the crusaders on the first four crusades; (2) the crusader states established in Syria and Palestine; (3) the two hostile caliphates of Bagdad and Cairo; (4) the Turkish possessions in Asia Minor, and (5) the Christian kingdom of Armenia, many cities of which were held by Turkish garrisons, a fact which could not be indicated on the map.

THE EMPIRE
ADRIATIC SEA
HUNGARY
SERVIA
BYZANTINE
Danube
Philippopolis
Naples
Richard
Brindisi
Otranto
Robert of Flanders
Thessalonica
Bohemond
Philip Augustus
CALABRIA
SICILY
THESSALY
MALTA
Philip Augustus and Richard
MEDITERRANEAN
AFRICA
L. L. POATES CO., N.Y.
Longitude
East
15
20
25
45
40
35
30

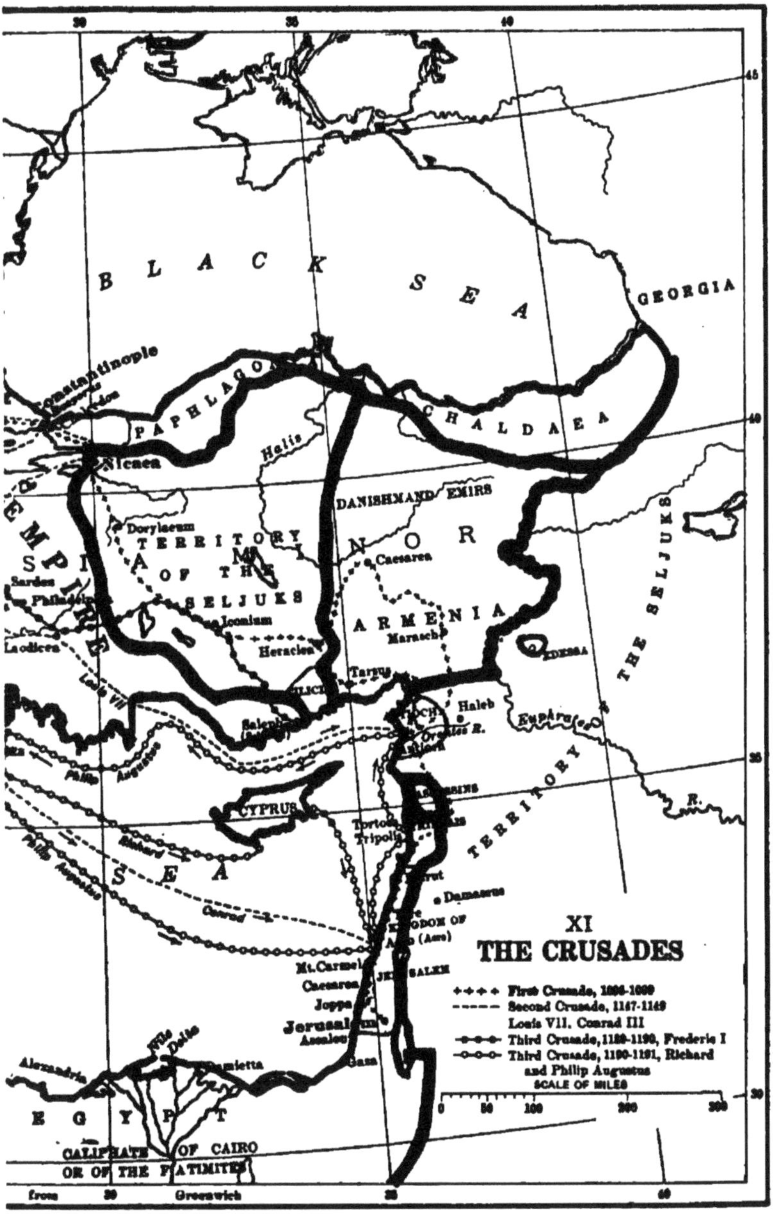

BLACK SEA
GEORGIA
Constantinople
PAPHLAGONIA
CHALDAEA
Halis
Nicaea
DANISHMAND EMIRS
Dorylaeum
TERRITORY OF THE SELJUKS
Caesarea
Sardes
Iconium
ARMENIA
Laodicea
Heraclea
Marasch
EDESSA
THE SELJUKS
Tarsus
Louis VII
Haleb
Orontes R.
Antioch
Euphrates
Philip Augustus
TERRITORY OF THE SELJUKS
CYPRUS
Tortosa
Tripolis
Richard
Philip Augustus
SEA
Damascus
Conrad
Mt. Carmel
Caesarea
Joppa
Jerusalem
Ascalon
Gaza
Alexandria
Nile Delta
Damietta
EGYPT
CALIPHATE OF CAIRO
OR OF THE FATIMITES
Greenwich
XI
THE CRUSADES
First Crusade, 1096-1099
Second Crusade, 1147-1149
Louis VII. Conrad III
Third Crusade, 1189-1190, Frederic I
Third Crusade, 1190-1191, Richard
and Philip Augustus
SCALE OF MILES
0
50
100
200
300

the crusading army from reaching the east. But Frederick was successful in passing Constantinople and in leading his army through Asia Minor. On the march thousands of his men perished of thirst, heat, and disease, but the worst of the journey was passed when, to the dismay of all, Frederick was drowned (June 10, 1190) while trying to ford the Saleph River (a few miles west of Tarsus). His soldiers were so overwhelmed by this misfortune that a large majority of them hastened to return to Europe; of the others, some, losing all faith in the Christian religion, deserted and adopted the Mohammedan faith, and only a few thousand of them proceeded to Palestine.

Philip II of France and Richard Lionheart of England, fearing the dangers of the journey by land, sailed with more than 100,000 men from different Mediterranean ports. They landed at Messina in Sicily, where they determined to spend the winter (1190–1191). They were joined there by a fleet of more than a hundred large transports and an immense number of smaller craft, which, loaded with men, had sailed from England. The kings soon quarrelled, being separated by jealousy and mutually conflicting interests. When they finally reached Palestine (1191, spring) they found two men contending for the title of king of Jerusalem. To make matters worse, Richard supported one of these and Philip the other. One of these claimants had, in his own interests and without any consideration of the general welfare, begun the siege of Acre (or Acco, August, 1189). The armies of the two kings might have accomplished something if they had made a united campaign into the interior. But they gathered at Acre to assist in the siege, which was made famous by the feats of valor and chivalry that were performed on both sides. But besides being decimated, the army lost valuable time there. They finally took Acre (July, 1191), but its capture hardly improved the situation of the Christians in the east.

Philip II and Richard Lionheart.

Quarrels.

Rival Kings.

Siege of Acco, 1189–1191.

Philip II immediately sailed home, but Richard remained

more than a year in Palestine. In all that time, however, he accomplished nothing of importance. With the greatest vacillation he planned campaigns only to give them up at the very moment when they promised to be successful. Without the least appreciation of the responsibilities that rested upon him, he wasted his time in the quest of knightly adventures. More than once he could, by a little diplomacy, have secured almost the whole kingdom of Jerusalem, but from sheer lack of practical common sense failed to take advantage of the opportunities. He was in most respects a model knight—the perfection of romantic chivalry. But this very fact rendered him incapable of conducting a crusade in a sensible manner. The third crusade ended in a deep and humiliating failure when he sailed away from Palestine (September, 1192). At a very conservative estimate it had cost 300,000 lives and had accomplished nothing but the capture of Acre. It was the last great effort to destroy the Mohammedan power. The popes continued to make frantic appeals to all Europe to make a crusade, and thousands of people took the crusader's vow upon them, but for various reasons no great expedition was ever again made. The political situation in the west had a good deal to do with this; in England the people were engaged in a great struggle with the king for the preservation of their rights; in France the king was occupied with the task of increasing his power at the expense of the feudal nobility; and in Germany and Italy the emperor was involved in a life-and-death struggle with the pope for supremacy. The natural leaders of a crusade being thus engaged at home with pressing personal interests, all Europe could never again be united to undertake a crusade. Nevertheless the east still offered attractions of many kinds to the restless, ambitious nobles of Europe, and for nearly a century almost every year saw the departure of one or more companies of knights who went to the east to try the fortune of arms against the Mohammedans.

Failure of the Crusade.

The Last Crusade on a Large Scale.

The West had Other Interests.

The emperor, Henry VI, was led by force of circumstances

to undertake a crusade. When a new king was chosen for the kingdom of Jerusalem, which existed now only in name, he determined to become the vassal of Henry VI and thus receive the royal title from an emperor. Henry VI received the feudal oath of the new king through ambassadors and promised to come to Cyprus to crown him. At the same time Leo, king of Armenia, wishing to free himself from the claims which the Greek emperor had over him, also offered to become the vassal of Henry VI. In the hope of extending his power in the east, Henry took the cross (1195) and began to make extensive preparations for the expedition. He had already sent several thousand crusaders in advance when his death (September, 1197) put an end to the preparations.

Plan of Henry VI, 1190–1197.

The expedition which is called the fourth crusade (1202–1204) did not proceed against the Mohammedans. It was a freebooting sort of undertaking by a few thousand French knights, soldiers of fortune, who, while serving the crusading cause, hoped to acquire fame, wealth, and territory in the east. They went to Venice expecting to hire Venetian boats to transport them to Egypt, against which they had planned to proceed, but when the time of sailing arrived they were not able to pay the passage money. Venice was at that time eager to increase its possessions on the east shore of the Adriatic and now fitted out an expedition for this purpose. The city offered to take the crusaders into its pay and, with a great show of disinterestedness, pointed out that this would give them an excellent opportunity to pay for their passage and thus enable them to complete their projected crusade. The crusaders accepted, the expedition sailed promptly, and they were successful in taking Triest, Muglia, and Zara (autumn, 1202). The crusaders were then turned from their original purpose of attacking Egypt and directed against Constantinople. The emperor, Isaac Angelus, had been dethroned (1195) by his brother, Alexius III, blinded, and imprisoned with his son, Alexius Angelus. The son, however, escaped from prison and fled to the court of

The Fourth Crusade Attacks the Greek Empire, 1202–1204.

his brother-in-law, Philip, king of Germany, who was married to his sister, the Greek princess, Irene.

It chanced that the leader of the crusade, Boniface of Montferrat, was at that time also at the court of Philip, and, being a soldier of fortune, eagerly listened to the rich inducements which Alexius Angelus offered to him, and to the crusaders, if they would assist him to recover the throne of his father. Alexius promised that, if they were successful in restoring him and his father to the throne, he would subject the Greek church to the pope, keep the crusading army supplied with provisions, pay them 200,000 marks, maintain 500 knights in Palestine as long as he should live, and either go with them in person on a campaign against Egypt, or send 10,000 soldiers in his place for one year. He also promised the Venetians 30,000 marks for their assistance. This served the interests of the Venetians very well, for, in the first place, they had friendly commercial relations with the Mohammedans in Egypt, and, in the second place, they were bitterly hostile to the people of Constantinople because of the commercial rivalry existing between them. Constantinople had a monopoly in the rich commerce of the Black Sea and would not permit Venetian vessels to pass through the Bosporus. By aiding the emperor Alexius and his father to recover their throne, the Venetians might hope to secure large commercial privileges and concessions in the east. They persuaded the crusaders that the Greeks were in the way of the success of a crusade and appealed to the deep hatred which the west had cherished against the Greeks ever since the first crusade. The crusaders finally closed the bargain, and sailed against Constantinople. They took it (July, 1203), restored the old emperor, Isaac Angelus, and his son to the throne as they had agreed to do, and demanded the immediate fulfilment of the promises which the son had made them. But he had promised more than he could perform. In the quarrel that followed, the crusaders stormed and sacked Constantinople. The emperor fled and established himself in Asia Minor, while the crusaders carved that part of the Greek empire which they had taken into several small

Takes Constantinople, 1203.

principalities, which were then given to westerners. Venice received three-eighths of the empire as its share of the spoils and Constantinople became the seat of a so-called Latin empire which existed to 1261, when the Greeks reconquered the city and re-established the Greek empire. The chief effect of the fourth crusade was to increase the power, wealth, and commerce of Venice.

The Empire Partitioned.

Europe was now thoroughly disgusted with the manner in which the crusades had been conducted, as well as with their failure. Devout minds declared that the sins of the crusaders were the cause of the disasters which had wrecked all the crusades; that God would not deign to work miracles and deliver the holy places when the crusaders themselves were so wicked. They asserted that, if an army of truly good and innocent persons, who were seeking not their own selfish and ambitious end sbut the redemption of the holy land, were sent to the east, God would deliver the Mohammedans into their hands. Out of such considerations and the deep yearning for the possession of the holy places sprang the preposterous idea of sending an army of unarmed children to the east to do battle with the Turks. Not that the children would be able to destroy them, but God, moved by their innocence and faith, would come to their aid in a series of mighty miracles, overwhelm the enemy, and restore the holy land to them. So, in June, 1212, near Vendôme in France, a shepherd boy named Stephen began to preach a crusade of children, declaring that Christ had appeared to him and commissioned him to lead an army of children to the sure recovery of the holy land; that, as the children of Israel had once passed through the Red Sea, so the Lord would make a way for them through the Mediterranean that they might pass through it dry-shod. Nothing is more characteristic of the Middle Age than the fact that this statement met with instant and enthusiastic acceptance. The news of the movement spread with unprecedented rapidity through France and western Germany. In a short time more than 30,000 French children were gathered about Stephen who led them to Marseilles

The Children's Crusade, 1212.

The French Children.

in the confident expectation that the sea would open and give them an easy passage to Palestine. When they had waited for some time in vain for this, some slave-traders, with cruel calculation, offered to transport them in vessels free of charge. They filled seven ships with children and sailed away only to deliver them, unsuspecting and helpless, into the hands of Mohammedan slave-dealers in Africa.

The German Children.

Along the Rhine a boy named Nicolas preached the crusade. He gathered about 20,000 German children at Cologne and led them over the Alps into Italy. Some of them reached Brindisi, but since the sea did not open for them, and there were no boats to transport them, they finally turned back. Only a few of them reached their homes.

S. B., 286–288.

The Fifth Crusade, 1217–1222, against Egypt.

Innocent III (1198–1216) devoted much energy and effort to bring about another great crusade, but his death suddenly checked the monster preparations which he was making. King Andrew of Hungary, however, had taken the vow and he finally sailed. His crusade, numbered the fifth (1217–1222), captured Damietta in Egypt (1219) after a memorable siege and gave promise of still greater successes. However, the crusaders fought over the division of the booty which they took in the city, and those who were in charge of the expedition quarrelled with one another constantly, and conducted it in such a blundering way that the Mohammedans finally retook the city, and the crusade ended in a complete failure. The sixth crusade (1228–1229) was remarkable in that, without fighting, it resulted in the acquisition of Jerusalem, Bethlehem, Nazareth, and a considerable strip of land lying along the sea and connecting all the places still in the hands of the Christians. This success was due to the diplomacy of Frederick II, who took advantage of the civil wars which were distracting the Mohammedans. The last two crusades are connected with the name of Louis IX, king of France. In 1248 he made an unsuccessful invasion of Egypt and spent some time in Palestine without, however, accomplishing anything. In 1270 he again set out on a crusade against Egypt, but while on the way changed the destination of his expedition. The bey of Tunis, it was said, wished to become a Christian, but, because of the fanaticism of his subjects, did not dare accept Christianity except under the appearance of compulsion. Deceived by this report the crusaders sailed to Tunis, where Louis died of the plague (August 25, 1270). His brother, Charles of Anjou, then king of Sicily, arrived about the same time and assumed charge of the siege. After the crusaders had obtained some advantages the bey offered to make terms. He was compelled to pay a large sum to the crusaders to raise the siege, and also a heavy annual tribute to Charles of Anjou.

The fate of the crusader states, which had long been foreseen, could no longer be postponed. The later crusades had brought them no relief, and their outlook became darker and darker. To the very end the insane rivalry between the various principalities and cities grew worse, and the two orders, the Templars and the Knights of St. John, fought each other with increasing fury. They were more hostile to each other than to the Mohammedans, and their constant feuds worked great injury to the cause which they had been organized to protect. Since the Christians were so faithless, so divided, and so hostile to one another, it seems strange that they should have held out as long as they did. Only the great fortresses which the orders had built and a few of the cities were still in their hands. In the thirteenth century the Turks reconquered all the places which the Christians still held. In 1244 they took Jerusalem and held it, it may be said, till 1917, when the English recovered it. Foot by foot they won their way to the coast, and in 1291 they retook Acre, Sidon, Beirut, Chaifa, Tortosa, and, last of all, Athlith (*castrum peregrinorum*), a fortress of the Templars, which had been regarded as impregnable, and Syria was again wholly in the possession of Mohammedans.

Conditions in the Crusader States.

Their End.

The Middle Age had two ideals, the soldier and the monk.

The monk was the spiritual, the soldier the military hero. The peculiar conditions existing on the border-land between Christians and Mohammedans, that is, in Palestine and in Spain, caused a fusion of these two ideals in the creation of military-monkish orders, whose members were both monks and soldiers. Three of these orders gained great renown: the Templars, established in 1119, the Hospitalers, or Knights of St. John, established a few years later, and the German order, founded in 1190. With the failure of the crusades they were driven out of the east. The Templars withdrew to Europe where they found no work to do. Their lazy and purposeless existence was brought to an end early in the fourteenth century by the king of France and the pope. The Hospitalers established themselves at first in the island of Rhodes and continued the war with the Turks, but were eventually dislodged. Malta then received them, from which they came to be known as the Knights of Malta. Early in the thirteenth century the German order settled among the Slavs of Prussia and conquered, Christianized, and Germanized them. It took possession of a large Slavic territory and became a real state. In the sixteenth century, however, the order was dissolved and its territory passed into the possession of the elector of Brandenburg.*

Military-Monkish Orders.

S. B., 265a, 266.

The Templars.

The Hospitalers.

The German Order.

We come now, at the end, to consider the most important question of all: How did the crusades affect the peoples of Europe? From the nature of the case it is impossible to weigh such matters accurately and so it is quite as easy to underrate their effects as it is to overrate them. We can, however, make a few definite statements in answer to the question.

Effects of the Crusades.

1. It is certain that the crusades increased commerce and the carrying trade immensely, and so did much to increase the wealth of Europe. Of course, it

Increased Commerce.

* Similar orders, that achieved a considerable local reputation, were established in Spain during the twelfth century for the purpose of fighting the Moors.

was the cities along the coast of the Mediterranean that profited most in this way, but the interior of Europe also shared in the commerce and derived great profit from it.

2. Europe also benefited immensely from the introduction of many new articles, some of luxury, many of common use, and all adding to the knowledge and well-being of the people. We can hardly estimate the civilizing effect of the introduction of such articles as all kinds of textile fabrics —silks, cloths, linen, muslin, rugs, carpets—glassware, sugar, spices, precious stones, perfumes, incense, and the culture of many kinds of fruits and flowers. Damascus blades and Morocco leather betray their origin by their names. We might easily extend the following list of words which indicate, to a certain extent, the influence of the Mohammedan civilization on Europe, although we cannot always affirm that their introduction was due directly to the crusades. But either the words themselves or the articles for which they stand, in many cases both, were derived from the Mohammedans. They are: sugar, citron, rice, pomegranate, peach, watermelon, muskmelon, apricot, artichoke, alfalfa, cotton, muslin, damask, damson, cordovan, cordwain, saffron, henna, borax, nitre, hashish, assassin, alchemy, alcohol, alkali, azimuth, elixir, alembic, amalgam, nadir, zenith, kermes, bazaar, algebra, zero, hazard, almanac, lute, talisman, alcove, and gazelle.

Gave Europe Many New Articles.

3. There is no question that the crusaders learned from the Mohammedans much in the art of war. They were impressed with the effectiveness of swift, light cavalry, they observed the scientific skill with which cities and fortresses were fortified, and for the first time they saw instruments cleverly adapted for besieging and defending such strongholds. The knowledge which they thus acquired in the east led to the modification of European methods of fortifying and besieging.

Improved the Art of War.

4. More important still was their effect in quickening the intellect and widening the mental horizon of Europe. In every village returning crusaders delighted in pouring into the ears of eager and gaping crowds the story of their wanderings, of

what they had seen and experienced. In this way the crusades largely increased the meagre stock of geographical knowledge which Europeans possessed, and awakened in them an interest in foreign lands. They not only ushered in, they also helped create, the period of voyage and discovery. A study of the intellectual life of Europe in the period during the crusades and immediately following them shows that the people were rapidly growing in intelligence and knowledge. This growth was accelerated by the learned and scientific books which they derived from the Mohammedans. Among them were many of the writings of Plato and Aristotle. These had been translated from Greek into Arabic and then into Latin. In this Latin form they passed into the hands of Europeans, on whose minds they had a vigorous, stimulating effect. In their quickening effect on the mind of Europe the crusades prepared the way for, and hastened, that stirring period which we call the Renaissance.

Quickened the Intellect.

New Scientific Knowledge.

5. Although in most respects the crusades had a beneficial effect on Europe, we must single out the fourth crusade especially and point out the evil which it did. For centuries the Greek empire had been an effective bulwark against the invasions of the Turks and had kept them from gaining a foothold in eastern Europe. For this service Europe owed the empire a debt of gratitude. As we have seen, the Venetians used the fourth crusade to ruin the empire; they took Constantinople and virtually all the empire that lay in Europe, together with the islands, and in the place of the emperor they put a western man. For more than fifty years the Greeks fought these invaders and eventually (1261) drove them out and recovered their empire. But no breathing space was given them to regain their lost strength and prosperity, for they had to face their old enemy, the Turks, who were relentlessly pressing on to the west. Weakened as the Greeks were with their long struggle with the crusaders, they nevertheless made a brave resistance. They were unable, however, to withstand the persistent attacks of the Turks,

Weakened the Greek Empire.

who took possession, one by one, of the provinces of the empire. Finally they laid siege to Constantinople, the capital of the empire and its last stronghold, and with its surrender (1453) the Greek empire came to an end. Since then the Turks have had a large empire in Europe, which has been a blight and a curse to the Christians under their rule. And for this misfortune the fourth crusade and the Venetians are no doubt largely responsible because they so thoroughly weakened the defensive power of the Greek empire.

CHAPTER XVI

THE GROWTH OF THE FRENCH NATION

Origin of the National Idea.

THE empire of Charlemagne was in a sense the continuation of the Roman empire. It was an attempt to perpetuate the "imperial" ideal of government—the organization of the civilized world in one great state, with a single head, a common law, and a government maintaining peace and order throughout its whole extent. This attempt of Charlemagne to revive the Roman empire failed, and his empire broke up into large sections, corresponding roughly to geographical and racial divisions. From these and from the territories outside of Charlemagne's empire, such as Spain and England, were to develop, during the long centuries of the Middle Age, the separate nations of Europe. The future of the political history of Europe was bound up with the principle of nationality, although it was a long time before that principle was to emerge clear-cut from the confusion of feudal conditions. The idea of the Roman empire survived as a vision to haunt the dreams of the German successors of Charlemagne, such as Otto the Great and Frederick Barbarossa, and of great conquerors like Napoleon, but it was never to be realized again.

Development of National Governments

A common racial element in the population and the occupation of a distinct geographical division—these are the latent or potential forces in the creation of a nation. The active force is the growth of a single central government; in the nations of western Europe the growth of national life and national feeling has depended very directly upon the growth of the national government. Such national governments, however, did not spring full-grown into being on the disappearance of the imperial system. During three centuries after the collapse of the Carolingian empire (roughly 900 to 1200) the prevailing political system was feudalism, and the prevalence of feudalism meant the absence of any effective public government.

Applying these general considerations to our problem of tracing the development of the French nation, it is apparent that we must consider (1) the natural elements of nationality in race and geography; (2) the feudal organization of France; (3) the growth of the French national monarchy.

One of the large divisions of Charlemagne's empire was the West Frankish territory, comprising most of old Roman Gaul. This was the portion of Charles the Bald in the division of 843.

Origin of "France."

R., I, 91.

As a separate state it came to be known as France. The century after the treaty of Verdun was the period of the decline of Carolingian government and the growth of that feudal society which we studied in a preceding chapter. Near the end of the tenth century (987) the direct Carolingian line came to an end in France, and the great nobles, into whose hands the actual power had passed, chose as their overlord Hugh Capet, count of Paris and duke of Francia, whom we may reckon the first feudal king of France and the founder of the national line of French monarchs. As

Origin of the National French Monarchy.

a matter of fact, the change of dynasty was not a revolutionary event; the later Carolingians were as much "Frenchmen" as Hugh Capet, and their power, like his, depended upon the support of the great lords. Since, however, he was the founder of a long line of kings under whom the French nation came into being, we may take the accession of Hugh as the beginning of French national history. His ancestors for more than a century had been hereditary counts of Paris and lords of a considerable territory in northern France. He belonged, therefore, to that class of feudal princes the formation of which we studied in the chapter on feudalism.

Geographically France formed a fairly distinct division. The ocean, the Pyrenees, and the Mediterranean bounded three sides. The eastern frontier had no natural barrier to serve as a boundary; at its northern end the political frontier, which ran along the western side of the Rhine valley, corresponded pretty closely, however, to the line between the Germanic and the Latin population. The absence of an effective barrier and the natural rivalry of the two races has made this region a cause of dispute between the French and German nations from that time to the present day. On the southern end of the eastern frontier France was cut off from the natural boundary of the Alps by the kingdom of Burgundy, occupying the valley of the Rhône River; this was destined eventually to become part of France.

Boundaries of France.

The most general fact about the French is that they are a Latin people. By the fifth century the Gauls had become completely Romanized; the Germanic tribes which settled in southern Gaul, the West Goths and Burgundians, had been pretty thoroughly absorbed in the Romanized population by the end of the tenth century; in a less degree this was true also of the Franks as far north as the political boundary of France. An external evidence of this is the fact that the language spoken in France in medieval and modern times is derived directly from the popular Latin spoken by the inhabitants of Gaul when it was part of the Roman empire.* The French are a Latin people in more than their language, however; deep-seated habits of social and intellectual life appear in their later history which were evidently acquired during the centuries of Roman rule, and which the Germanic invasions only disturbed and did not uproot.

The French a "Latin" People.

At the end of the tenth century France was far from constituting a nation politically, since there was no effective central government. Local government was in the hands not of public officials but of private landlords who controlled the serfs and peasants living on their lands. The powerful nobles, intrenched in their castles, were in the main a law unto themselves. The only authority they recognized was the personal authority of the greater lord to whom they owed allegiance. During the tenth century, in France as elsewhere, the feudal organization had progressed

Feudal Condition of France.

* This point is developed further in the chapter on "Medieval Civilization."

Note to Map XII.—This map shows the formation of the feudal principalities of France in the tenth century, when the power of the Carolingian kings had virtually disappeared. In each of the large divisions of the West Frankish kingdom, the actual direction of affairs had passed into the hands of the duke, the overlord of the counts and nobles of the region (see p. 309). The counts of Paris had become dukes of Francia, which included most of northern France. In 987, Hugh "Capet," duke of Francia, was recognized as king of France; his duchy of Francia, however, was reduced in size by the creation out of it of independent feudal principalities, such as the county of Flanders, the county of Champagne (with Chartres and Blois), and the county of Anjou (with Maine and Touraine). Thus the royal lands controlled directly by the Capetian kings were limited to the "Isle of France" as shown on Map XIII. Similarly the county of Toulouse later split off from the great duchy of Aquitaine and became one of the separate feudal principalities; it absorbed eventually the duchy of Septimania or Gothia. The county of Barcelona represents the old Spanish mark; for a time it was reckoned as a part of France and its count did homage to the king of France. Lying beyond the Pyrenees, however, its destiny was naturally connected with the history of the Spanish peninsula; it was to expand and become the kingdom of Aragon, one of the important parts of the Spanish state.

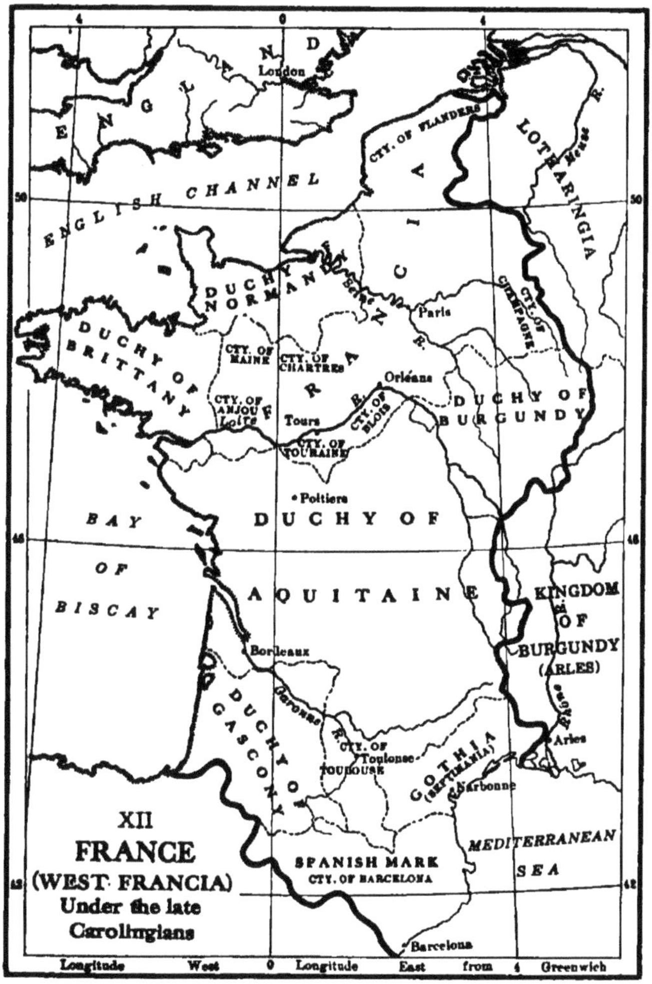
XII
FRANCE
(WEST FRANCIA)
Under the late
Carolingians
ENGLAND
London
ENGLISH CHANNEL
CTY. OF FLANDERS
LOTHARINGIA
Meuse R.
FRANCIA
DUCHY NORMANDY
Seine R.
Paris
CTY. OF CHAMPAGNE
DUCHY OF BRITTANY
CTY. OF MAINE
CTY. OF CHARTRES
Orléans
CTY. OF ANJOU
Loire R.
Tours
CTY. OF BLOIS
CTY. OF TOURAINE
DUCHY OF BURGUNDY
Poitiers
BAY OF BISCAY
DUCHY OF AQUITAINE
KINGDOM OF BURGUNDY (ARLES)
Bordeaux
Garonne R.
DUCHY OF GASCONY
CTY. OF TOULOUSE
Toulouse
GOTHIA (SEPTIMANIA)
Narbonne
Rhône
Arles
MEDITERRANEAN SEA
SPANISH MARK
CTY. OF BARCELONA
Barcelona
Longitude West 0 Longitude East from 4 Greenwich

so far as to produce the great feudal princes, lords of whole provinces. Since the power of these princes was to be the chief obstacle to the growth of royal power, we must notice their position.

Let us consider first the geographical location of these principalities. In the extreme north of France was the county of Flanders, corresponding pretty closely to modern Belgium.

Feudal Principalities.

Flanders. Normandy.

South of Flanders was the duchy of Normandy, occupying the lower valley of the Seine River. The line of dukes of Normandy had its origin in the grant of this province by one of the late Carolingian kings to the leader of a band of marauding Northmen, on the condition that he and his followers hold the territory against other Northmen, for the protection of Paris. These Northmen, living in the midst of a French population, rapidly assimilated French ways and became a part of the French people.

Brittany.

Southwest of Normandy lay the peninsula of Brittany, occupied by a Celtic population that had never been thoroughly Romanized, and that long retained their Celtic speech and characteristics. The duke of Brittany, while a vassal of the king of France, had also something of the position of tribal ruler of a separate little nation. South of Normandy, between the Seine and the Loire Rivers, was the county of Anjou, the counts of which were lords of a large district including Maine and Touraine as well as Anjou. In the centre of northern France about Paris was the duchy of Francia, which had grown out of the county of Paris. Hugh Capet was duke of Francia when he was chosen king of France, so that this principality became the crown land; since it was the only territory over which the kings of France in the early period exercised any effective control, it was the real basis of royal power. To the east of Paris lay the county of Champagne; south of Champagne the duchy of Burgundy. The south of France was divided between three great feudal territories. In the southeast the counts of Toulouse had made themselves overlords of a large principality. South of the Loire the great duchy

Anjou, Francia (Crown Land), Champagne, Burgundy. Toulouse, Aquitaine, Gascony.

of Aquitaine extended to the Garonne River. In the triangle made by the Garonne and the Pyrenees lay the duchy of Gascony; in the eleventh century this was absorbed in the duchy of Aquitaine, which then included all of southwestern France.

Position of the Feudal Princes.

The lords of these principalities—dukes of Normandy, Brittany, Burgundy, Aquitaine, counts of Flanders, Anjou, Champagne, Toulouse—were virtually independent of any superior authority. To be sure, they were vassals of the king of France, from whom they held their lands and powers and to whom they did homage, but the authority of the king was a personal one and did not give him the right to control the lands and subjects of his great vassals. The authority of these great lords over their own provinces was limited, of course, by the independent power of their own vassals, lesser counts and barons; allowing for this, however, we may say that they exercised whatever of sovereign powers had survived the disintegration of public government which followed the decline of the Carolingian empire. It is certain, in any event, that their sovereign powers were not restricted by any effective control from above. From this point of view, France was a loose confederation of princes owing personal allegiance to a nominal overlord, the king.

Weak Position of the King in the Feudal Age.

This situation explains the weakness of royalty in the feudal age. The king of France had the powers of a feudal lord over his own domain, the crown land, but over the rest of France he possessed none of the attributes of a real ruler. There was no system of public taxes; the old taxes of Carolingian and Roman times had been transformed into rents and dues paid to local lords. The king, therefore, had only the resources common to the other great lords, that is, the rents from the serfs in his own villages and the customary feudal dues paid by his own vassals. There was no national army raised and commanded by the king; he had only the services of his own private retainers and the military obligations of his vassals to rely upon for this purpose, and any one of the great feudal princes was about as powerful in a military way as the king. There was no administrative system centralized in the king; that is, he had no body of officials whom he could send out to govern parts of the country in his name; for local government was either exercised by the local landlord over his tenants in the manors or maintained by the greater lords for their provinces. Each one of the greater lords exercised sovereign powers (rights of justice, coinage, and control of roads) within his own fief, and therefore these powers were exercised by the king only on the crown land.

This, however, is not the whole story. There was latent in the position of the king a superior authority which was certain to emerge as society progressed in order and organization.

Non-Feudal Elements in the Monarchy.

Even in the early feudal age the king had a sanctity which distinguished him from the counts and dukes, no matter how powerful they might be. He was regarded in a vague way as the head of his people, responsible to God for their welfare—as the "fountain of justice," the protector of the poor, and the defender of the church. This notion of kingship was an inheritance from Charlemagne's empire, and it was cultivated in the French monarchy especially by the clergy. It was expressed in the anointing and consecration of the king at the time of his coronation. Later on we shall find the monarchy appealing to a still older tradition of sovereignty, in the revived study of Roman law, in which the supremacy of the central government over the whole state is an essential feature. Still later the natural tendency of the country to rally to the central government, once that government had proven itself strong enough to enforce law and order, was to produce the conception of the king as the embodiment of French national interests and feeling.

The realization of all this, however, was far in the future. At the time of Hugh Capet, the monarchy gave little evidence

Louis the Fat, 1108–1137, Reduces the Crown Land to Order.

of becoming the rallying point of national life. And the first four kings (Hugh Capet, Robert, Henry I, and Philip I) did little more than make the crown strictly hereditary in the Capetian line. Louis VI (Louis the Fat; 1108–1137) spent his active life in making himself master of the crown land. To do this he had to wage continual war on the turbulent barons who had erected their great stone towers in the country around Paris. They were direct vassals of the king, but they held the royal power in light esteem; from these strongholds they menaced the roads which led from one royal town to another, as from Paris to Orléans; they held up convoys of merchants, browbeat peasants and monks, and waged their own private wars with insolent disregard of their royal overlord. Louis VI set his hand to the necessary but troublesome task of reducing them to obedience. Time after time he led his little army of retainers against their castles and took them by siege or assault, hazarding with delight his own person in the fray. It was a purely local policy and on a small scale compared with the whole territory of France of which he was nominally king, but it laid the real foundations for the future greatness of the Capetian monarchy. Henceforth the king was master on his own domain, and could undertake the larger task of making himself respected by the greater feudal princes.

R., I, 93.

Louis VII, 1137–1180; His Bad Policy.

His son, Louis VII (1137–1180), did little to advance the royal power. He went on the second crusade, thus neglecting his immediate task in France and wasting needed resources in men and money. Before his accession his father had arranged a politic marriage for him with Eleanor, heiress of the great duchy of Aquitaine; this was a step toward the acquisition of that fief for the crown. It would have meant also a great advance in the extension of royal influence into the south of France. Louis VII, however, after he came back from the crusade, secured a divorce from Eleanor. This was probably justified by her light conduct, but it was an unfortunate act politically. Not only did he lose the opportunity of adding Aquitaine to the crown lands; what made it worse was that Eleanor then married the young count of Anjou, who was to become Henry II of England. This marriage brought Aquitaine, along with Normandy and Anjou, under the control of a foreign monarch, and was the source of great difficulty for later French kings.

Divorce of Eleanor of Aquitaine; Its Consequences.

At the end of the twelfth century, with the accession of Philip Augustus (Philip II, 1180–1223), the monarchy entered upon a period of rapid growth, the character of which we must study. The lines of growth were conditioned by the feudal state of society. The monarchs had first to increase their actual power and resources by increasing the extent of the royal land; this they did by absorbing into the crown land one after another of the great fiefs held by the feudal princes. The royal authority having by this means been made more effective, it was possible for the king to develop a machinery of government centering in his court and carried out by his agents; this in time became a real national public government for all of France.

Philip Augustus, 1180–1223.

Growth of the Monarchy.

The first great increase in the extent of the crown land was made when Philip Augustus seized some of the French lands held by the kings of England. From the time when William, duke of Normandy, in 1066, won the English crown, the kings of England had held Normandy as a family possession, doing homage to the king of France for it. Henry II, who became king of England in 1154, held other fiefs in France in addition to Normandy, which came to him, along with the English crown, through his mother, a granddaughter of the Conqueror. He was the son of the count of Anjou, and had married the heiress of the great duchy of Aquitaine. Thus he was lord of three great French territories—Normandy, Anjou, and Aquitaine—which together constituted over half of France; and while, of course, he did homage to the king of France for these, the possession of them made him a formidable rival to the French monarch.

First Increase in Crown Lands.

Origin of English Holdings in France.

During the first part of his long reign Philip Augustus devoted his efforts to the task of breaking this dangerous power. This involved him in constant intrigues and struggles against the English kings, Henry II, Richard Lionheart, and John. Philip was not troubled by scruples in this undertaking. He first conspired with the sons of Henry II in their revolts against their father. Henry II had invested three

Philip's Intrigues.

of his sons with the French fiefs of Normandy, Brittany, and Aquitaine. One after another they rose in rebellion against him, encouraged and aided in every case by Philip. After the death of Henry II, Philip intrigued against Henry's son, Richard I, his former ally. His opportunity came at the time of the third crusade. Richard and Philip had taken the vow and gone on the crusade together; Philip, however, suddenly abandoned the enterprise, returned to France, and began intriguing with Richard's brother John. Richard on his way back from the crusade was taken prisoner and held for ransom by his enemy, the emperor Henry VI. Philip and John tried to induce the emperor to keep him in captivity or to hand him over to them. Richard, however, was released by the emperor on payment of a heavy ransom, and returned to England to bring his brother to terms; he then undertook a war against Philip in France in the midst of which he died, in 1199. John succeeded as king of England, and Philip immediately turned against him. He first espoused the cause of John's nephew, Arthur of Brittany, who laid claim to the English throne. Arthur, however, fell into his uncle's hands and was put out of the way. In the meantime, Philip had summoned John as his vassal to appear before the royal court to answer charges brought against him by his enemies. On John's failure to appear the French court declared his fiefs forfeited, and Philip proceeded to conquer them. John made no serious effort to defend his possessions, and Philip took Normandy, Anjou, and part of the duchy of Aquitaine, and added them to the crown lands.

Against Henry II.

Against Richard I.

Against John.

R., I, 94a.

Philip Takes Most of the French Fiefs from John.

These acquisitions more than doubled the extent of the royal lands and the actual resources of the monarch. It raised him in actual strength far above any of the feudal princes. Henceforth the king was able to take a higher tone in dealing with his vassals, and was able to compel them to recognize his authority.

Effect on the Position of the King.

This was only the first in a series of additions to the crown land by the inheritance or confiscation of the fiefs of the great

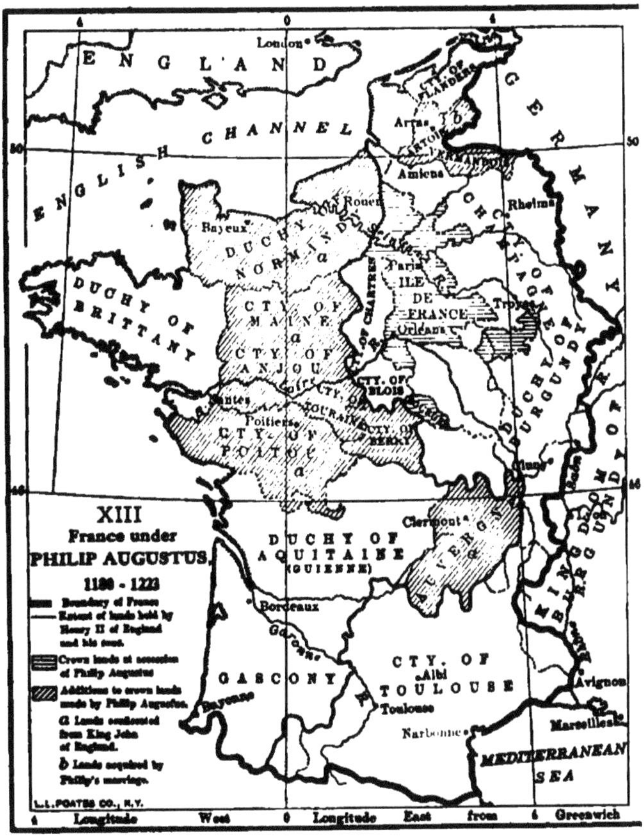

Note to Map XIII.—This map shows (1) the extent of lands held as fiefs by the Angevin kings of England (Henry II and his sons) before the confiscations which Philip Augustus made from John of England; (2) the extent of the crown lands at the accession of Philip Augustus; (3) the increase in the crown lands made by Philip (a), the lands confiscated from John (b), the counties of Artois and Vermandois acquired by Philip through his marriage with the daughter of the count of Flanders. The rest of France consisted of fiefs held by direct vassals of the king of France. Most of these were to fall one by one into the possession of the crown; Toulouse in 1272, Champagne in 1285, Burgundy in 1361, Guienne as the result of the Hundred Years' War, etc. On the other hand, the crown land was reduced in extent later by the grants of fiefs to younger sons of the royal line, who established new lines of feudal princes (see p. 322).

lords; we shall notice the others in the order of their occurrence. In Philip's reign the first step was taken in the process which was to bring into the crown land the important county of Toulouse. This was the "Albigensian crusade," inspired by Pope Innocent III against the count of Toulouse because of his support of the Albigensian heretics. Its political importance lay in the fact that the count of Toulouse was later able to make his peace only by ceding part of the county to the king of France and by agreeing to a marriage of his daughter with a member of the royal line, as a result of which eventually the whole county fell to the crown.

Other Additions to the Crown Lands.

From Philip's reign dates also the first important advance in the development of a royal administration, both central and local. The central government grew out of the king's court. This court comprised occasional assemblies of the great lords, who as vassals of the king came at his summons to give him advice or to act as a feudal court of justice. Its permanent element, however, was made up of the retainers and the officials and servants of the king. It conducted its business wherever the king might be staying—at Paris, at Orléans, or at any of the numerous castles which the king owned on the royal domain; there was, therefore, no fixed capital of the kingdom. The business which came before this court in the early period of the monarchy was more private than public; that is, it had to do with the management of the king's household, the administration of his private estates and the revenues derived from them, and the control of his own vassals and retainers.

Growth of Royal Government.

(1) Central.

In the time of Philip Augustus this court took on more of the character of a central government for France. The increased power of the king caused even the greater nobles to respect his summons and to recognize his authority. A body of officials, forming a class that found its interest in working for the king, developed around him, and the larger affairs that came under their control gave them something of the character of public officials rather than private servants.

The local government instituted by the king was at first, of course, confined to the royal land. The royal domain, or crown land, was composed of small fiefs held by local nobles as direct vassals of the king, and of villages (manors) under his immediate control. Louis VI had reduced the nobles on the crown land to obedience to the monarch, after which they became for the most part stanch supporters of the monarchy and furnished many members of the growing class of royal officials at the court. The royal villages were the most immediate source of the king's revenue in the feudal age; they were managed for him by local agents (*prévôts*), who collected the rents and dues from the peasants and administered justice to the inhabitants in the village courts. The prévôts were difficult to control, since they held their offices as hereditary charges and paid themselves out of the revenues which they collected. In order to improve the oversight over them, Philip divided the crown land into districts and appointed over each district an official, known as *bailli*, whose duty it was to watch the administration of the prévôts of his district and hold them to stricter account. The baillis held courts in their districts, and were given authority over the lesser nobles as well as over the prévôts. Drawn from the class of royal officials devoted to the king's service and his interests, their administration made a beginning of centralized government in the hands of the king, which was extended in scope with the growth of the crown lands.

(2) Local.

Prévôts and Baillis.

By this time also there had been accomplished a noticeable advance in national feeling and national life. The isolation and independence which had kept the provinces separated from one another were breaking down before the general increase in intercourse and advance in order and civilization. The crusades had brought together nobles from all parts of France, and in the second and third crusades they had followed the French king. The Albigensian crusade had caused the ruin of the culture in the south of France, and, while this was a sad loss, it lessened the divergence between north and south and hastened the extension of a single French culture. A type of

Growth of National Feeling.

In Noble Society.

literature had developed in the north which reflected the ideals and interests of the noble class and which acquired something of the vogue of a national literature. The form of Old French spoken in and about Paris came to be accepted as the standard literary form, an important step in the formation of a single national language.

This tendency toward unity affected not only the noble class. With the increase of commerce and industry and the growth of cities in the twelfth century, a middle class between noble and serf came into existence, composed of merchants, traders, and professional men. Commerce and trade required good and safe roads, and a simpler system of tolls and coinage. At first the cities had to make such arrangements for safe intercourse as they could, often at the cost of actual war with the nobles and robber barons. In the twelfth century, however, the king and the great nobles recognized the advantage of having wealthy and prosperous towns on their lands, and encouraged the holding of fairs and gave charters to the cities, securing them rights of self-government and protection and freedom of trade. This furthered the intercourse of city with city and accelerated the amalgamation of the diverse local elements into a single French people.

In the Merchant Class.

This advance must not be exaggerated, however. The earlier elements of disunity had not vanished. The great princes still ruled their provinces without any serious interference from the royal government. The barons were still a warlike and independent class. The mass of the population was still subject mainly to the control of their local landlords. The roads were still unsafe, and private wars were still frequent. These conditions, however, were passing; the future was with the growth of the central power of the king and the disappearance of feudal anarchy.

The fact that the monarchy was not yet beyond the period of struggle was made apparent in the next generation. Philip Augustus was succeeded by his son, Louis VIII, who reigned only three years (1223–1226) and left a young son of eleven years to succeed him. This was Louis IX, the greatest and best of the mediæval kings of France. During his minority his mother, Blanche of Castile, acted as regent. The great nobles, who had begun to feel the reins of royal power tightening upon them, took this opportunity to revolt. The queen-mother had to face several coalitions of nobles. To add to her troubles Henry III of England invaded the country in an attempt to recover the French lands lost by his father, King John. These difficulties still confronted Louis IX when he came of age in 1236. He got the better of them, however; the revolts of the nobles were crushed, and Henry III defeated and forced to make peace. In this settlement Louis IX recognized the title of Henry III to Guienne, the central part of the old duchy of Aquitaine, which Henry was to hold as a fief of the French crown; Henry, on his side, abandoned his claim to the rest of the lands once held by the kings of England in France.

Louis IX (1226–1270) Encounters Feudal Revolts.

But Gets the Better of Them.

The progress of royal power was very rapid under this wise and good king. He brought the rebellious count of Toulouse to terms, making him cede half of the county to the crown, and arranging the marriage between the daughter of the count and the brother of the king whereby the rest of the county later reverted to the crown. A notable improvement was made in the central government. The officials at the king's court were organized into separate and permanent bodies for the management of different kinds of business. The judicial affairs which came before the king had greatly increased in number and importance. For this very important business Louis IX created a special judicial body, made up of lawyers and judges; this was known as the *parlement*. The financial interests of the monarchy were intrusted to a special branch of the royal court, called the *chambre des comptes* (chamber of accounts). This body received and kept record of the revenues coming from the different sources of royal income. A third body comprised the official advisers of the king,

Growth of Royal Power under Louis IX.

Improvement of the Central Government.

who aided him in matters of general policy and administration; it bore the name of the *grand conseil* (great council). These departments were given permanent quarters in Paris, which thus became the capital of France.

Louis IX was not only the greatest of the mediæval kings of France; he was also one of the finest and most attractive figures of the Middle Age. We have an intimate picture of him in the memoirs of the Sire de Joinville, his faithful and devoted follower, who spent the active part of his life in attendance upon him. Joinville's examples are chosen mainly to illustrate the virtues of St. Louis, his piety, gentleness, modesty, and sense of justice. We get from this the impression of a man too virtuous to be a strong ruler; this must be corrected from what we know of his public acts. He put down the revolts of the nobles with a strong hand, and drove Henry III out of the kingdom. He strengthened the royal government and compelled obedience to it. He was reproached for not confiscating all the lands of Henry III after defeating him, but the peace which he made was a fair and sensible one. In spite of his piety and asceticism, which seemed excessive to the nobles of the time, he had the virtues of a knight: bravery, strength, and skill in arms. Nor was he subservient to the church; he knew how to keep the French clergy from encroaching on royal powers, and he refused to aid the pope in the struggle against the emperor, Frederick II.* His devotion, however, did lead him into the mistaken policy of trying to revive the crusades; in the middle of his reign he led an expedition to Egypt and Palestine, which kept him out of France for six years, and he met his death on another futile crusade against the Mohammedan power in Tunis, in northern Africa (1270). A generation after his death the church recognized his merits by declaring him a saint (1297), and he is known among the French kings as St. Louis.

Personality of St. Louis.

Joinville's Memoirs.

R., I, 95.

* He did, however, allow his younger brother, Charles of Anjou, to accept the crown of Sicily from the pope, in the latter's effort to oust the Hohenstaufen family. This was the beginning of French intervention in Italian affairs, which was to be very costly to France.

After the death of Louis IX the French monarchy continued to increase in strength and organization until the outbreak of the Hundred Years' War with England, which interrupted the growth. This period is covered by the reigns of Philip III, Philip IV, and the three sons of Philip IV (Louis X, Philip V, Charles IV). The crown lands were increased by the acquisition of the rest of the county of Toulouse and of the county of Champagne, which Philip IV acquired by marrying the heiress. For a time he had his hands also on the county of Flanders, but later restored it to the count.

At this point we must notice a practice adopted by the kings which had the effect of undoing to a certain extent this work of enlarging the royal domain. From the time of Louis VIII it became usual for the king to grant parts of the domain to younger sons, in order to endow them with estates and revenues adequate to their princely rank; these were held as fiefs from the crown. So the three younger brothers of Louis IX were made, respectively, counts of Anjou, Poitou, and Artois, lands which had been added to the crown domain by earlier kings. Louis IX did the same for his younger sons, and the practice was continued by succeeding kings. These fiefs, called "appanages," reduced the amount of land held immediately by the king, and the general result was to create a new feudal aristocracy, sprung, to be sure, from the royal line, but tending, like the older feudal princes, to seek their own interests and resist the extension of royal power. In the fourteenth and fifteenth centuries the kings were to have to face revolts and coalitions from this class of powerful lords, who could trace their origin to younger sons of former kings.*

"Appanages" Granted from the Crown Lands to Younger Sons.

An important feature of this period is the development of a theory of absolute government. While this was, in a way, the natural result of the growth of royal power, it drew its principles directly from Roman law, a knowledge of which was just becoming general in the thirteenth century. This movement is important and characteristic enough

Theory of Absolutism.

* See pp. 391–394 for illustration of this fact.

to justify our studying it for itself. The twelfth century was a period of intellectual revival, the essence of which was the recovery of a completer knowledge of the culture of the classical world than had been available to the early Middle Age. In the schools literature was studied from the great Latin writers, such as Vergil, Cicero, Terence, and Horace; mathematical studies included the geometry of Euclid and the astronomy of Ptolemy. The recovery of the works of Aristotle not only enabled the church scholars to construct a more scientific theology but also to study and teach philosophy as a separate science. The results appeared in the thirteenth century, in the growth of universities where the higher learning could be pursued, and in the growth of that complete synthesis of logic, philosophy, and theology which we know as the "scholastic system."

Twelfth-Century Revival.

An important feature of this revival was the recovery of a knowledge of Roman law in the systematic form which it had received in the codification of Justinian (the *Corpus iuris civilis*, or body of civil law). This body of logical, systematic, and withal humane legislation impressed the mediæval lawyers and administrators much as the works of Aristotle impressed the mediæval theologians and philosophers; they regarded it with reverence, treated it as a final authority in the field, and applied it as far as possible to their own problems. Now, one fundamental concept of the Roman law was the supremacy of the state; all individuals and all private interests in the empire were subject to the will of the state as expressed in the public law. By the time of Justinian the authority of the state was conceived of as embodied in the person of the emperor, not as a capricious despot but as the personification of the state and the head of the administrative system through which the authority of the state over individuals was carried out. The royal lawyers and royal officials (not only in France, but in all countries where a national monarchy was developing) found, therefore, in the code of Justinian a theory and a body of precedents upon which they could draw in trying to assert

Recovery of the Code of Justinian.

Theory of Roman Law.

the superiority of the royal authority over the private authority of feudal lords or church or communes.

This theory (which may be stated in the form that sovereign powers can be exercised only by the king or by the officials to whom he delegates them) had already been applied in the legislation of Louis IX, but the great age of its use was the reign of Philip IV (Philip the Fair, 1285–1314). It was given expression over and over in the royal ordinances of this monarch. This did not result in the sudden emergence of an absolute government; in fact, the great feudal lords continued for a long time to exercise sovereign powers, and the lesser landlords to possess private jurisdiction; but the theory of absolutism was given definite expression, and a beginning was made in withdrawing certain sovereign powers, such as control of coinage and keeping peace on the highways, from the lords, and putting them in the hands of the king.

Application of the Theory by the Royal Lawyers.

To Philip IV is also usually attributed the creation of a new organ of the central government which came later to be known as the States General, although similar assemblies had been held earlier. This was a national representative body, somewhat like the "Model Parliament" of Edward I, in England. It was composed of representatives of the three "estates" or classes, clergy, nobles, and the merchant class of the cities. It was called by Philip in 1302, when he was in the midst of his quarrel with Pope Boniface VIII, because he wished to assure himself of the support of the country in that struggle. On later occasions the king sometimes submitted his need for money to the States General, because authorization by this body would facilitate the collection of new taxes. Thus the States General had much the same reason for existence as the English Parliament; but, for reasons that will appear later, it never acquired the permanent and important position in the government that Parliament did in England.

Philip IV Summons the "States General," 1302.

The conflict of Philip IV with the pope, Boniface VIII, was an illustration of a fact that we shall have frequently to notice

—namely, that as soon as the national monarchy grew strong it was bound to enter into a contest with the church, which exercised such large powers in every country. The details of this contest are told in another chapter,* and we need notice here only the general outlines. The conflict began over the vital question of taxation. Philip IV, like other monarchs, was in the habit of securing grants of money from the clergy of his kingdom, which amounted to levying taxes on them. Pope Boniface, in the bull *Clericis Laicos*, forbade the practice, and threatened to excommunicate rulers who levied taxes on the church and to deprive of their offices clergy who paid them. In France the king had the better of the contest, and Boniface gave way, virtually admitting the right of the king to demand contributions from the clergy of France. After the death of Boniface VIII and the brief pontificate of Benedict XI, Philip IV was able to secure the election of a French prelate to the papacy; the new pope, Clement V, moved the papal court from Rome to Avignon, on the border of French territory, where it remained for seventy years. During this period the papacy was completely subservient to French influence.

Conflict of Philip and Pope Boniface VIII.

Papal Court at Avignon.

France under Philip IV occupied a leading position in Europe. The relations between states had not yet taken that form of acute rivalry which characterizes the whole course of modern history; for no government had as yet sufficiently mastered its own resources to be able to engage in an active foreign policy. This sort of rivalry was beginning to make its appearance at the end of the thirteenth century, however. Philip IV inherited a standing quarrel with the king of England, who still held lands in France. Philip tried to dispossess Edward I of these lands (the duchy of Guienne), and both monarchs sought allies, Philip in the Scotch, who were engaged then in a struggle with the English king, and Edward in the count of Flanders, who had revolted against the French king. The alliance of France and Scotland remained a traditional feature

Foreign Affairs.

England.

* See pp. 404, 405.

of French foreign policy well into the modern period. The struggle between Philip IV and Edward I was ended before it came to open war; Philip restored to Edward the duchy of Guienne, which he had seized; but this was one of a chain of incidents which was to lead, in the generation after Philip IV, to the Hundred Years' War between England and France.

The eastern frontier of France, along its whole length from the mouths of the Rhine to the Mediterranean, was bounded by the territories of the empire. The principal territories from north to south were: the Netherland territories of Hainault, Brabant, Luxemburg, the duchy of Lorraine, the free county of Burgundy (Franche Comté), Savoy, Dauphiné, and Provence. The decline of the imperial government after the death of Frederick II, in 1250, weakened the ties which bound these outlying territories to the empire and they tended to gravitate toward France. Philip IV was able to secure the recognition of his overlordship from several of the princes holding lands in this region; this was the first step in that advance of the French frontier eastward toward the Rhine River and the Alps which was to be one of the most important movements of modern history.

The Empire and the Eastern Frontier of France.

A characteristic feature of French national life which deserves attention is the position attained by the city of Paris as the centre of the nation. Paris is the heart and head of France to an extent that is not true of any other European capital. It had not, to be sure, acquired that quality within the limits of our period; in fact, it was the stirring events of the French revolution and the nineteenth century which completed the process. Nevertheless, the early stages in the process form an important part of the story. The nucleus of the city was the largest of a group of small islands in the Seine River. This, as Cæsar tell us, was the site of the fortified camp of the Gallic tribe of the Parisii. It was an important centre for the administration of northern Gaul in Roman and Frankish times, but its real importance in French history dates from the time when the local family of lords, the counts of Paris, became the royal line

Paris in the Middle Age.

Origins.

of France with the accession of Hugh Capet. As the kings built up a really national government during the twelfth and thirteenth centuries, Paris attracted to itself various elements of population, which settled in ever-expanding quarters on both banks of the river up and down the stream from the island. To-day the original town is lost in the immensity of the modern city, but the island still bears a name (la Cité) which recalls its ancient importance.

Growth.

The process of accretions by which the city grew is so characteristic of mediæval life that we can afford to analyze it. The most important step was the growth of Paris as a national capital through the permanent location there of the organs of royal government. From the beginning of the twelfth century Paris was the favorite, and in a way the official residence of the kings. The royal palace was built on the southern end of the island, and was continually enlarged by successive kings. The household of the king with the numerous private officials and servants and retainers was housed here; here also the king usually held his court, which would be attended on important occasions by the great feudal lords. The royal court of justice, the *parlement*, created under Louis IX, had its great hall and chambers in a quarter of the palace buildings. The department of the treasury (the chamber of accounts) was located in another part of the city, on the north bank, in the palace of the Templars; for that wealthy organization served the king somewhat as a modern national bank, and the royal treasurer was usually a member of the order.

As a Political Capital.

In the midst of the palace grounds Louis IX built, soon after 1240, the exquisite little Gothic church (la Sainte Chapelle), which still stands there. This was erected to serve as a shrine for the precious relic, the cross of thorns, which the pious king secured from Baldwin, emperor of Constantinople. By great good fortune the chapel has escaped the ravages of time and revolutions, to be preserved for us as one of the most perfect examples of Gothic architecture.

The "Sainte Chapelle."

Paris also contained that element which in most towns of the Middle Age was the chief cause of growth, the merchant class. The city, however, was too much of a royal town to become a self-governing commune, and during the mediæval period the chief official was the royal prévôt, who governed in the name of the king. In fact, the city government was a curious medley of jurisdictions, owing to the fact that various corporations were exempted by special charter or customary privilege from the authority of the royal prévôt. Ecclesiastical jurisdictions included not only that of the bishop of Paris, whose cathedral church was Notre Dame, but also many abbeys and convents. After the completion of its organization the university of Paris possessed jurisdiction over the students and masters which composed it. Among these jurisdictions must be reckoned the limited rights of self-government granted to the merchants.

Government of Paris.

Prévôt of the Merchants.

The bourgeois (citizens) had their own organization, with a "prévôt of the merchants" at its head. This organization had its own courts and customary law. The region of the merchants was on the north bank, east of the island, a region still marked by the present Hôtel de Ville, or city hall. In the troubled times of the Hundred Years' War the bourgeois, acting through the prévôt of the merchants, were to exercise considerable influence on the course of events.

Churches and Abbeys of Paris.

The ecclesiastical element in the growth of Paris was very considerable. Paris had its patron saints, more or less legendary, of whom the chief were St. Denis (Dionysius), missionary and martyr about 250, and Ste. Geneviève, who saved the city from Attila and his Huns. The abbey and church of St. Denis were held in special reverence by the kings of France; the royal standard in the Middle Age was the "oriflamme" (pennant) of St. Denis, and the kings were buried in the abbey church. Paris was the seat of a bishop, whose cathedral church was located at the northern end of the island. In the late twelfth and thirteenth century a splendid Gothic cathedral was erected in place of the older church, and dedicated to Notre Dame.* In addition to the cathedral and the parish churches, there were many rich monasteries located in Paris, which also built fine churches. In the middle of the twelfth century the Templars were granted a tract of land by the king and built their great castle, which was known as the Temple. One of the most famous trials of the Middle Age was the trial instituted by Philip IV against this order, which resulted in its dissolution and the confiscation of its wealth. In the thirteenth century both Dominican and Franciscan friars established convents and schools in Paris.

There were many schools in Paris, maintained at the cathedral and in the larger monasteries, and these schools played a very important part in the twelfth-century revival. In the first part of the twelfth century Abelard, the forerunner of the great philosophers and theologians of the thirteenth century, studied at the cathedral school of Notre Dame and the school of the abbey of Ste. Geneviève, and at the latter school began his lectures on theology in which he drew to an unprecedented extent upon the logic and philosophy of Aristotle, just then being introduced in full to western Europe. The university of Paris had its origin in the cathedral school in the cloisters of Notre Dame; it soon outgrew these quarters and was transferred to the south bank of the river. From the river south to the church of Ste. Geneviève, now the Panthéon, were built in the thirteenth and succeeding centuries the various schools and colleges, supported by the pious legacies of kings and wealthy men, which were incorporated into the university of Paris. The region of the schools bore (and still bears) the name of the Latin Quarter. Like all great universities it offered advanced instruction in the higher courses: the liberal arts, theology, philosophy, law, and medicine; but its pre-eminence in Europe rested especially upon the courses in theology and philosophy. In fact, the university of Paris took the lead in that movement which repre-

University of Paris.

* The special reverence for the Virgin Mary, which flourished in the thirteenth century, led to the rededication of many cathedrals to her under the title of "Our Lady."

sents the highest intellectual achievement of the Middle Age, the formation of the scholastic system, which attempted to make a complete system of theology on the basis of the logical method and metaphysical principles of Aristotle.

CHAPTER XVII

THE ORIGINS OF THE ENGLISH NATION

In the chapter on France we discussed the general question of the origin of nationality and noted the fundamental importance of that development for the history of Europe. In this and the following chapter on England our attention will be occupied mainly with the development of the English nation, and especially with the principal active factor in that development, the national government. For the beginning of this nation, however, we have to start farther back than in the case of France. The important mediæval nations on the continent grew out of the fragments of the empire of Charlemagne; the English people never formed a part of that empire, and their history runs back without a break to the coming of the original tribes of Angles and Saxons to Roman Britain. In contrast to the Franks, Burgundians, Lombards, and other German tribes that settled in Gaul or Italy and came under Roman influence, the Angles and Saxons continued in the new abode their native life, speaking their German dialects, worshipping their old gods, and keeping up their tribal organization. Although Britain had been part of the Roman empire for more than three centuries, the British inhabitants had never been Romanized in anything like the degree that the Gauls had been. This is shown by the fact that the descendants of the British, the Welsh, speak a Celtic language; the old Britons had apparently never adopted Latin as their popular speech. The Angles and Saxons, therefore, did not come into contact with Roman influences to any great extent when they settled in Britain. Certainly there is little evidence of Roman institutions and ideas in their early history.

Origins of the English.

During the fourth century, while Britain was still a part of the Roman empire, the eastern shores of the island were occasionally raided by bands of sea-robbers, whom the Romans called Saxons. At the end of that century (about 400) the Roman military forces were withdrawn from the island to defend the frontiers of the Rhine and Danube. The native Britons, long accustomed to depending on the Roman government for protection, were powerless to defend themselves. The raids became more frequent and the invaders established permanent footholds on the coast. Then whole tribes, with women and children, migrated to occupy the land thus won. By 500 most of the eastern and southern coast was in the hands of the newcomers; step by step they pushed inland, until by 600 they had won most of what is now England. The Britons, retreating before the invaders, were crowded back into the western part of the island, the peninsula of Cornwall and the mountainous region of Wales; here they held out, jealously guarding their own language and their Christian faith, and having as little intercourse as possible with their conquerors.

Beginning of the Invasions.

The invaders were Angles, Saxons, and a few Jutes, coming from their homeland in northern Germany and the Danish peninsula. The Angles occupied most of the eastern shore, north of the Thames River; the Saxons settled in the Thames valley, and all the region south as far west as Cornwall. The southeastern peninsula, known as Kent, was occupied by the Jutes.

The Invaders.

While they were engaged in the process of conquering the land the invaders had undergone a change that marked a decided advance in political organization. They had come to the island in many small tribes each under its own chief, but the need of combining to win the territory had brought about the formation of larger units. By the beginning of the seventh century we find them organized into a number of territorial kingdoms: Wessex, Essex, Sussex, Kent, East Anglia, Mercia, and Northumbria. These names are geographical for the most part; Wessex, Sussex, and Essex are the kingdoms of the west, south and east Saxons;

Formation of the English Kingdoms.

East Anglia the kingdom of the eastern Angles; Mercia, the "mark" or frontier kingdom; Northumbria the kingdom north of the Humber River.

Some of the tribal laws of these kingdoms, written down in the seventh and eighth centuries,* have been preserved to our own day, and they reveal to us the state of society among these early Englishmen. Each kingdom had its own tribal law and its own king. The kingdoms were divided into political divisions, called shires in Wessex; these divisions probably represent in most cases the original small tribes which united to form the larger territorial kingdoms. The shires, which correspond to the Frankish counties, were, like them, divided into hundreds. The free political life of tribal times was continued in the assemblies of all the freemen in the hundred-court and the shire-court, meeting under elected leaders. The government, of course, was very simple and primitive.†

Political Organization.

The first steps in English history had been taken, therefore, by 600: the invasion, conquest, and settlement of the territory, and the organization of social and political institutions in the new land. The next two centuries, 600 to 800, were to see the beginnings of important movements for the later history of the English. One of these was a tendency toward unification of all the English people into one state. One after another of the warlike kings sought to make himself supreme over his neighboring kings. About 600 Ethelbert of Kent is said to have been overlord of all the kingdoms south of the Humber. After his death Edwin king of Northumbria succeeded to the leadership. During most of the eighth century Mercia was the leading state, and one of

Tendency toward Unification.

* These laws were written in the Germanic dialects of the Angles and Saxons; whereas the similar laws of the Franks, Burgundians, Lombards, and other German tribes on the continent were written in Latin. This is a further evidence of the absence of Roman influence on the invaders.

† See pp. 24, 25 for a description of the tribal organization of the Germans before the invasion. The social structure of the Angles and Saxons in Britain in the seventh century was not much more developed than that.

its kings, Offa, a contemporary of Charlemagne, was overlord of most of the English kingdoms. At the beginning of the ninth century the southern kingdom of Wessex gained the supremacy under its king, Egbert. This sort of overlordship did not in itself constitute a single English government; the defeated kings became for a time dependent, but the subject kingdoms retained their own laws and separate governments. These were, however, tentative steps in the process of unification. From the time of Egbert the supremacy remained permanently in the line of the kings of Wessex.

Wessex Becomes the Leading State.

Another event of capital importance in English history was the conversion of the Angles and Saxons to Christianity. This movement did not start from the Christian church of the Britons, which had been established during the Roman period. The remnants of the British regarded their conquerors with fear and dislike, and made no serious attempt to convert them to the Christian faith. Down to the end of the sixth century the Angles and Saxons were still heathen. At this point (in 597) the pope, Gregory I, sent a band of Roman monks under Augustine to the English kingdom of Kent to carry the gospel to the heathen there, and bring them into the Roman Catholic fold. Ethelbert, king of Kent, had married a Christian princess of the Merovingian Frankish line. He received the Roman missionaries hospitably and soon he and his people adopted the Christian faith. It spread northward from Kent very slowly, however, being resisted especially by the heathen kings of Mercia. Moreover, some thirty years after the conversion of Kent missionaries from the older British church, which had spread to the north by the way of Ireland and Scotland, had established themselves in Northumbria, and had begun the work of converting the Angles of that region to their own form of Christianity.* The turning-

Conversion of the Angles and Saxons.

Sending of St. Augustine.

L., 24.
Ch., 31–34.

* Christianity had appeared among the Britons while they were under Roman rule in the third century. After the invasion of the Angles and Saxons it had been crowded back with the Britons to the western

point came when the king of Northumbria and his council decided in favor of the Roman church (664).

Conflict between the Roman and the Celtic Churches.

The story of this council, as told by Bede, the chronicler of the next century, is characteristic. The representatives of the Celtic church defended its claims by appealing to its antiquity and to the pious lives and deeds of the missionary saints who had established it. The Roman monks appealed to the familiar argument of the papacy—that St. Peter, the founder of the Roman church, had been given supreme authority over the church as the "rock" and the "keeper of the keys," and that he had handed on this power to his successors, the Roman bishops. When, in answer to the inquiry of the king, the Celtic monks had to admit the authority of St. Peter, the king, speaking for the council, declared for the Roman church, lest when he came to die the doorkeeper of heaven should refuse to admit him. We need not take Bede's account as necessarily authentic, for it is just the sort of popular story which a mediæval chronicler would use to illustrate his point, without concerning himself very much with the critical question of its origin, but it is an interesting illustration of the use made by the Roman emissaries of the "Petrine theory," in their efforts to establish the unity of the church in the west under the pope.

After this event the Christian church was rapidly established in all of the English kingdoms. A few years later (668), the pope sent one of his most able men, Theodore of Tarsus, to organize it as a part of the great Roman church of western

edge of Britain, and was cut off from the main body of the western church during the very time when the papacy was developing as the central authority; therefore the Celtic church developed apart from the Roman church and differed from it in some particulars. It continued to have a vigorous life, however. In the fifth century St. Patrick converted the Irish, and soon the Irish monks became famous for their learning, piety, and missionary zeal. They labored to convert not only the neighboring Scots, and the heathen Angles in Northumbria, but also went as missionaries among the heathen Germans on the continent. In the seventh and eighth centuries they founded monasteries in Gaul, Germany, and Italy; later, however, these monasteries were taken over and absorbed by the Roman church.

Europe. The English territory was divided into bishoprics, and these were grouped in two ecclesiastical provinces, under the archbishop of Canterbury in the south and the archbishop of York in the north. As we have seen, the missionary work had been done by monks, and monasteries sprang up wherever the church was planted. These became in England, as everywhere, centres not only of religious life but of civilization and learning as well. We have noticed elsewhere the great services performed by the monks in establishing schools in the monasteries where at least the elements of a Latin education could be obtained. In England this was especially true of the monasteries of Northumbria. At the monasteries of Wearmouth and Jarrow and the cathedral of York there were schools and libraries in the eighth century which were better than any in western Europe, with the possible exception of some of the Italian monasteries. The learned Bede, abbot of Jarrow, was the greatest scholar of the age, and when Charlemagne, in the eighth century, sought out a scholar to organize the monastic education in his empire, he sent to Northumbria and secured Alcuin.

Organization of the Roman Church in England.

Monastic Education in England.

The monastery schools of the eighth century were primarily concerned with religious teaching, and the amount of classical learning was very meagre. Still something of the general education of the Roman world survived in these schools, to throw a slender bridge across the dark ages from the fall of the Roman empire to the revival of the twelfth century.

It was by the establishment of the Roman church more than by anything else that the history of England became in this early period a part of the general history of western Europe. The intellectual and cultural development thenceforth followed the line that was to prevail in Europe generally; that is, the transmission by the church of an amount of classical culture which was constantly being increased by the recovery and application of Latin works that had been lost to sight in the first centuries of violence and disorder. On becoming a part of the Roman

Importance of the Church for English Civilization.

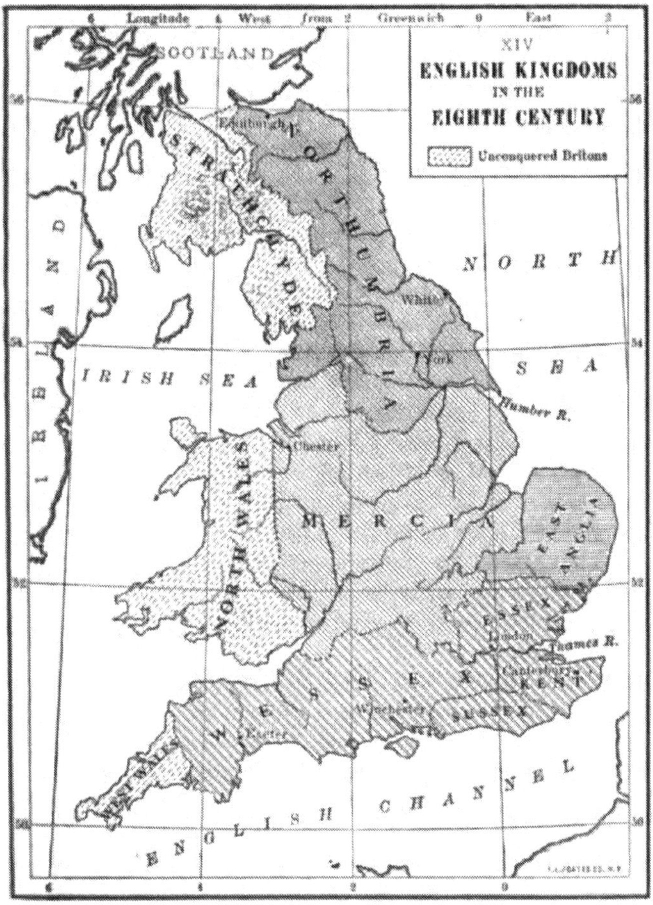

Note to Map XIV.—This map shows the formation of territorial kingdoms by the expansion westward of the Anglo and Saxon tribes. The West Saxons, Mercians, and Northumbrians were the leaders in this expansion; their growth cut off the eastern tribes, Jutes in Kent, East Saxons, South Saxons, and East Angles, and these kingdoms remained small. In the seventh and eighth centuries there were constant conflicts between the kings of the larger kingdoms for supremacy; early in the ninth century the supremacy passed permanently into the hands of the West Saxon kings.

church England was admitted to participation not only in the religious life common to all of western Europe but also to the inheritance of law and order and administration which had to such a large extent fallen to the church from the Roman imperial system.

The development of the English people, which we have now traced to the end of the eighth century, was at this point interrupted by a serious disaster. About this time the shores of England began to be visited by bands of pirates from the Scandinavian countries, whom the English called indiscriminately Danes. It was much like the movement which had brought the Angles and Saxons themselves to the island. The Danes would swoop down on the coast, make a landing and sack a town or a monastery, and escape to their boats before the inefficient local forces could gather. Finding an easy prey, they came in increasing numbers, and soon began to make permanent settlements on the coast, from which they advanced inland, conquering the country. Before long the northern kingdoms of Northumbria, Mercia, and East Anglia fell wholly or in part under Danish chiefs.

Invasion of the Danes.

The successors of Egbert of Wessex had to battle desperately to defend their own kingdom from the Danes. Alfred, grandson of Egbert, beat them off, but was forced to make a peace with them which left them in control of most of England north and east of the Thames valley. This Alfred (871–899) is known in English history as Alfred the Great. Later generations attributed to him the invention of most English institutions; although this is an exaggeration, his rule marks an important advance. After he had made peace with the Danes he devoted himself to the task of restoring order and prosperity in the land that had been disturbed by fifty years of Danish raids. This work, which included administrative reforms, military reforms, and the restoration of churches, was done not only for Wessex but for all of the smaller kingdoms in the centre and south that had become subject to Wessex. In this way all of

Alfred the Great, 871–899.

His Work.

the English who were not ruled by Danish chiefs were brought as never before under a single law and government; and this was the real basis of the political unification of the English.

Alfred, like Charlemagne, was concerned with the spiritual and intellectual welfare of his kingdom; and, like him, he began with a reform of education among the clergy. One interesting phase of this was the translation of Latin works undertaken by Alfred and the scholars he gathered about him, into Old English, the Germanic dialect of Wessex. These works were: Boëthius's *Consolations of Philosophy*, Pope Gregory's *Pastoral Care*, Orosius's *History of the World*, and Bede's *Ecclesiastical History of the English*. All of these works are religious in tone and all of them lie in the period between 400 and 800. The fact that they were regarded as the Latin works most worth preserving and studying gives us some measure of the meagre knowledge which the age of Alfred possessed of the great world of Roman culture.

L., 96.

Education.

The Danish occupation of northern England was not permanent. The vigorous successors of Alfred in the tenth century made war on the Danish rulers, defeated them, and brought all of England under their rule. Since the older lines of local English kings had disappeared during the Danish period, the way was open for the extension of Alfred's system to the reconquered territory. In this way all the English were brought not only under a single king but under a single system of government. The period of reconquest was followed by the peaceful and prosperous reign of King Edgar (959–975), which marks the highest point of the Anglo-Saxon period. It is a point at which we may pause to examine the form of government and society, since this will give us an idea of those deeply rooted English institutions which were to survive the Norman conquest and become a part of the England of later times.

Recovery of Danish Territory.

England under Edgar, 959–975.

England was now ruled by a single king, who bore the title of "king of the English"; he was also recognized as overlord by the Welsh and Scottish princes. The central government

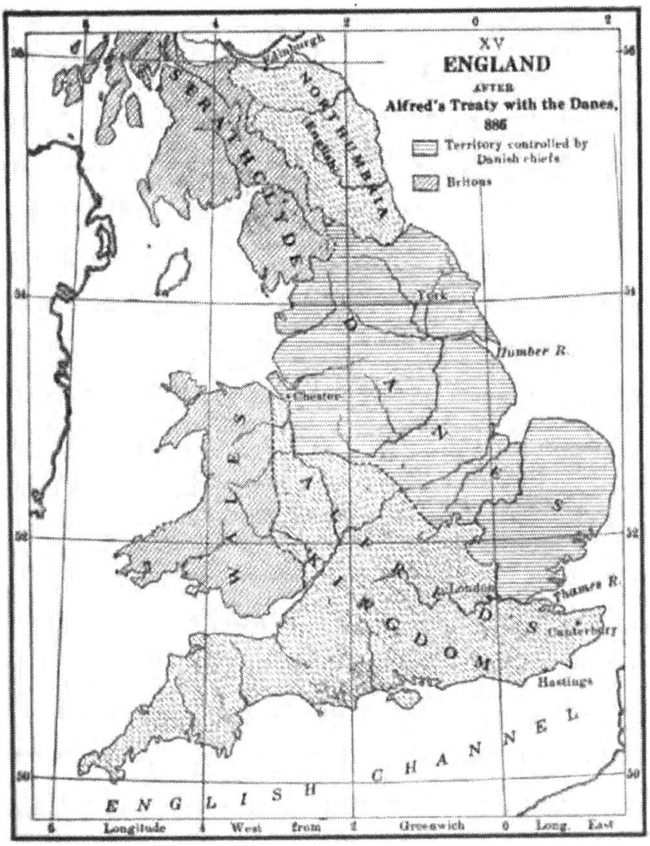

Note to Map XV.—This map shows the division arranged in 886 by King Alfred the Great and the chief leader of the Danes, Guthrum. The line from the Thames valley to Chester delimited their respective territories. In the far north a part of the Northumbrians retained their independence also. All of southern England formed a single state under King Alfred (871–899). Under Alfred's successors the Danish territory was reconquered and thus a single English kingdom was formed.

included the king's court and chief officials and a national council of leading lords and officials and clergy; this was called in Old English the *Witenagemot*, or "assembly of the wise." The kingdom was divided into shires, in each of which was a local assembly or shire-court. The shire-court was no longer the general assembly of all the freemen of the shire; its important members were the large landholders, but it included also representatives elected in the villages. The shire-court was under the direction, not of the old elected leader but of a royal agent known as the sheriff or shire-reeve, an official like the Frankish count. The shires were divided into hundreds, in each of which was a hundred-court, which served as an ordinary court of justice.

English Institutions.

Central Government.

Local: Shire-Courts.

An important change had taken place in the social structure. As among the Franks and other Germans on the continent, after the settlement a class of large landholders had developed, and the common freemen who had originally been free landowners were tending to become dependent on this upper class as serfs and tenants on their large estates. The former free institutions of tribal times became aristocratic, since the landlord class acquired political control of the local government. They also exercised to a considerable degree the rights of private jurisdiction over their dependents, although the local public courts of the shire and the hundred did not lose all of their power. Thus the manorial system grew up in England, though not as completely as on the continent. The relations of the landlords to one another and to the king had something of the private nature of allegiance which existed in feudalism, but not to the same extent. Moreover, military service was not a necessary feature of this relation. We may say, therefore, that the essential elements of the feudal and manorial systems were present in an incomplete and unsystematic form in England.

Social Structure.

Landed Nobles.

Dependent Tenants.

A distinctive feature of English life was the existence of a rich written literature in the native tongue. The dialects spoken by the Angles and Saxons were closely related; after the formation of a single kingdom the dialect of Wessex became the recognized standard and the basis of a single national language. This is known as Old English or Anglo-Saxon. Like all the Germans, the Angles and Saxons had from early times a popular literature dealing with the legendary history of the tribe and the heroic deeds of famous chiefs. This literature was produced by minstrels or bards attached to the courts of tribal kings and chieftains. In older times these tales in verse were recited and sung; in the eighth century they were put into written form. Out of this has come down to us one epic, or long narrative poem, the "Beowulf," reciting the heroic deeds and death of a legendary hero of that name, and a number of shorter poems. This poetry had its origin in the heathen age, but was continued for a time in the eighth century after the introduction of Christianity. There was also a considerable poetic literature in Old English of a religious sort. Old English prose begins with Alfred's translations and the compiling in his time of the *Anglo-Saxon Chronicle*, a history of the English from the time of the invasions, made up in its earlier parts from popular traditions, from Bede's history, and from local annals, and continued from Alfred's time on by contemporary entries.

Old English Language.

Old English Literature.

National Epic, the "Beowulf."

Religious Poetry.

Prose.

Such was the political, social, and intellectual condition of the English in the later tenth century. The hundred years from that point to the Norman conquest can be covered very briefly. After Edgar's time the kingdom fell on evil times. Under the weak rule of Ethelred "the Redeless" (or ill-advised), the Danes renewed their attacks. Sven "Forkbeard," king of Denmark, about the year 1000, invaded England and conquered it; Ethelred took refuge in Normandy with his family. Cnut, son of Sven, became king of England in 1016, and for a generation England was ruled by Danish kings. This made no great change, however, since Cnut and his sons governed by English law and as English kings. On the death

New Invasions of the Danes.

Cnut the Dane, King of England, 1016–1035.

of the last of these, in 1042, the line of Ethelred was restored in the person of his son Edward, known as Edward the Confessor, or St. Edward.

The principal importance of Edward the Confessor's reign was that it served as an introduction to the Norman conquest of England. Edward had been brought up from his childhood in Normandy. When he became king of England he brought with him a large number of Normans whom he placed in the chief positions in church and state. This led to a reaction on the part of an English party headed by the chief noble of the land, Godwin, earl of Wessex. After a civil struggle the Normans were expelled and Edward came completely under the control of Godwin's son, Harold. As Edward had no son to succeed him, he recognized Harold as his heir, and the national council, the *Witenagemot*, confirmed this by electing Harold as king, on Edward's death in 1066.

Edward the Confessor, 1042–1066.

Harold.

William, duke of Normandy, had hoped to secure the succession for himself. He now put forward a claim to the throne, alleging that Edward had designated him as his successor. In the fall of 1066 he sailed across the channel with an army of Normans and other French adventurers and landed in England. Harold, who had been occupied with a revolt in the north, hurried south to meet him. The great English earls, however, jealous perhaps of Harold's new title of king, failed to support him, and in the battle of Hastings Harold was defeated and slain. The national council, which had been hastily summoned by Harold, now submitted to the victor and recognized him as king. On Christmas day, 1066, William "the Conqueror" was crowned king of England. This ended the Anglo-Saxon period and began a new era in English history to which we must devote a separate chapter.

William of Normandy Invades England, 1066; Battle of Hastings.

Ch., 52, 53, 54.

CHAPTER XVIII

THE FORMATION OF THE ENGLISH NATION

THE Norman conquest proved to be a turning-point in English history. This was true especially in regard to the development of government. The political institutions of England have been produced by the combination of Old English or Anglo-Saxon elements with Norman elements brought in by the conquest. It is important, therefore, before beginning the study of the effects of the Norman conquest, to review the features of Anglo-Saxon life which had been developed during six centuries, for these constitute the deeper elements in the national character. One thing that distinguished England in the eleventh century from the countries on the continent was the existence of local institutions of self-government. The shire-court and the hundred-court were derived from the popular local assemblies of tribal times, in which the freemen themselves, under elected officials, administered justice according to the tribal law and managed local affairs. By the tenth century these assemblies had become more aristocratic, and their principal members were the local landlords; the ordinary freemen, however, were still represented in the assemblies and their cases were tried there by common law, although to a large extent they were subject also to the manorial justice of their own landlords. The survival of these courts is in marked contrast to the situation on the continent, where manorial and feudal justice had so completely usurped the field as to cause the older popular courts to disappear entirely.

Importance of the Norman Conquest.

Survival of Local Government in Shire and Hundred Courts.

It is in connection with these local courts that we should notice another important factor of English political and social life. This was the survival and development of the English common law. As we have seen in our chapter on feudalism, law in the feudal age was local custom, and the authority back of it was the personal authority of the lord. The Franks and other Germans on the continent had had tribal laws, applied in popular courts, but this system had vanished with the complete feudalizing of government. In England, however, the Anglo-Saxon kings, from the time of Alfred, had carried on the development of the tribal laws as laws of the united kingdom. This was the body of law that was administered in the shire and hundred courts. It constituted one of the elements which were later combined to form the English common law.

Common Law.

It is noteworthy also that the Anglo-Saxon kings, from the time of Alfred, had developed a government that was more nearly national than any to be found on the continent in the tenth or eleventh century. The Franks and other German tribes on the continent had been absorbed in the empire of Charlemagne, which, as we have noticed, was an attempt to revive the Roman imperial system; when that failed and the empire broke up into natural divisions, the work of developing national governments in those divisions was slow in beginning and had to be carried out with great difficulty in the face of the feudal system. In England, on the contrary, there had been steady progress toward unified government from the time of the invasions. The small tribes had united to form territorial kingdoms (Wessex, East Anglia, Northumbria, and so on) and these had united to form the one English kingdom. This had been accompanied by a corresponding unification of government. The tribal chieftains had been replaced by the territorial kings, and these by the king of all the English. The small tribes became divisions of the several kingdoms and were taken over as divisions of the single kingdom. The authority of the king was exercised through a national government. At the centre was the king and his court, and a national council; throughout the country the king was represented in the shires by the royal agents, the sheriffs. The king and the council legislated for the whole country. There was

National Monarchy.

even a suggestion of a national tax in the "Danegeld," a contribution levied by the central government on all land, originally instituted by Ethelred to buy off the Danes and kept up by his successors. This is not to say that the Anglo-Saxon government was strong, effective, and well-organized; but only that it was composed of native elements which had developed naturally, and that it was national in its scope.

Danegeld.

There is another general fact that must be taken into account in the subsequent development of English history. The English constituted only one of several elements in the British isles. In addition, there were the descendants of the older British inhabitants, many of whom continued to live a separate life in the west of Britain and developed into the Welsh. In Ireland and Scotland were numerous independent clans, mostly of Celtic blood like the Britons, but who had never come under Roman influence. During the Anglo-Saxon period, occasionally a strong English king had been able to assert an overlordship over some of the Welsh and Scottish princes; this was to be carried much farther after the Norman conquest, and eventually English influence and English rule became dominant in the whole of the British isles. The relation of the English government to the more or less subject Welsh, Scotch, and Irish constitutes one of the standing problems of English history.

Relation to Other Parts of British Isles.

In a political way the most obvious effect of the Norman conquest was the introduction into England of the feudal system, although the essential elements were to some extent already developed there. For several years after the battle of Hastings William the Conqueror was occupied in putting down local revolts of the English lords; the crushing of these revolts was the real conquest of England. This gave him an opportunity to confiscate the lands of the English nobility and confer them upon his Norman followers; in the space of a few years the great estates almost completely changed hands and became the fiefs of Norman lords. The terms on which they were held from the king

Norman Conquest Brings in the Feudal System.

were the familiar terms of the feudal system—personal allegiance and military service. The greater Norman lords in turn gave out parts of their lands to their own followers and retainers on the same terms, and compelled the smaller English landlords to enter into the same relation of vassalage. Thus the feudal relations were established throughout the landholding class.

In respect to the position of the king, however, the English government did not become feudal; in fact, the Norman period is marked by the establishment of a strong monarchy. This fact is so important for later history as to deserve a somewhat extended analysis.

In the first place, William occupied a much stronger position in relation to the feudal lords than did the contemporary king of France. The Norman lords in England received their lands in scattered portions, as one district after another was conquered and the lands confiscated and given out. Thus they were great and powerful landlords, but they were not semi-independent princes of distinct provinces, as were the French dukes and counts. Moreover, William was determined to be the personal ruler of all of the landed and military nobility, and not merely the overlord of the great lords. In 1086 he held a review of the military forces of the kingdom and compelled every holder of land by military tenure, whether he were a direct vassal of the king or the vassal of one of the great lords, to take an oath of allegiance to the king and swear fidelity to him before any other. This broke through the mediate or indirect character of the feudal bond, which was its weakest feature from the point of view of the monarchy. William also made it a rule that no noble could build a castle on his lands without authorization from the king.

Norman Kings Stronger than Other Feudal Kings.

William Controls Feudal Lords.

In the second place, William regarded himself as the successor of the old English kings and the heir to whatever national powers they had possessed. These powers he revived and strengthened, where they had, under the weaker rule of Edward the Confessor, fallen into disuse. He had a survey made of the landed wealth of the king-

Maintains Rule as English King.

dom,* and made this the basis for a stricter enforcement of the land-tax. The old *Witenagemot* transmitted to the Norman feudal council something of its character of a national council. William revived the use of the sheriffs as agents of the king in the shires. Thus he had in his hands a machinery of royal administration, both central and local, which was more effective than any to be found elsewhere in feudal states in the eleventh century.

A. and S., 4. Ch., 69.

And finally he preserved the old local government in the shires and hundreds. These assemblies enabled the king to keep a hand on local affairs through his sheriffs. Their preservation, however, served also to keep alive the Anglo-Saxon institutions of local self-government, and prevented the barons from absorbing all local powers. The shire-courts especially entered upon a more active political life; under later kings they were to become an important part in the development of a national government.

Preserves Local Government.

Before we take up what must be our main theme, the development of the government under the new line of kings, we should notice the effects of the conquest on other than political matters in English life. One of the most important consequences was the introduction of Norman-French language and literature. After the conquest the ruling class (higher clergy, nobles, royal officials) became almost exclusively Norman; the language used in public business and in polite society, therefore, was Norman-French. This was a dialect of Old French, the language spoken in northern France, which, as we have noticed elsewhere, was derived from the spoken Latin. The literature composed by poets for noble patrons in England in the twelfth and thirteenth centuries was essentially a branch of French romantic literature, dealing in the main with the same subjects: Charlemagne and his heroes, King Arthur and his knights. Old

Effects of Norman Conquest:

Norman-French Language.

And Literature.

* The returns were collected in the famous Domesday Book, which gives us a detailed picture of the economic and social conditions of England in the eleventh century.

English ceased almost entirely to be used as a literary language, although it continued to be spoken by the great body of the people.

Church Education.

The closer connection with the continent and especially with France opened the way for the rapid introduction into England of other forms of culture in respect to which Anglo-Saxon England had been backward. This was true especially of the culture fostered by the church. Under William and his successors for a long time the great churchmen were all Normans. The English church schools were thus brought into line with that intellectual awakening which is known as the "twelfth-century renaissance." This movement consisted in the recovery of the larger and more original Latin works which had been lost to sight during the centuries of violence and confusion; the result was that it was now possible to teach the ordinary subjects in an advanced form: to study grammar from more scientific Latin grammars and from the writings of Roman authors like Vergil; to study logic from translations of Aristotle; to study geometry from the great work of Euclid. This advance prepared the way for the development of special branches of study which were later to be taught in the universities. Although these developments are later than the conquest itself, it was that event which brought English education into the general current.

Lanfranc and Anselm.

The first Norman archbishop of Canterbury, Lanfranc, was a learned Italian who had been abbot of one of the chief Norman monasteries; he began the work of reforming and improving the English schools. This was carried on by his successor, the learned Anselm. The work of Anselm was really of European importance, since he was virtually the first mediæval theologian; the first to apply to religious questions, such as the existence and the nature of God, the logical and philosophical ideas which the Middle Age inherited from classical times. In this most important intellectual development England was to have an important part.

The Normans also brought with them the greatest of mediæval

arts, that of architecture; for they were great builders, of churches as well as of castles. The Anglo-Saxon churches were mostly wooden structures. In the Norman period was begun the construction of large stone churches. These were at first of the heavy Romanesque type; in the later twelfth century the lighter and more graceful Gothic type* developed in northern France and spread to England.

Norman Architecture.

So the Norman conquest is seen to be the beginning of a new life in every way for the English nation. The period of nearly a century, from the conquest to the accession of Henry II in 1154, is known as the "Norman period," since it is the time in which the Norman rule was established and men of the Norman race controlled virtually everything.

William the Conqueror reigned from 1066 to 1087. These twenty years were filled to the full with the most exacting duties. We shall meet with few monarchs of mediæval times as active and vigorous and intelligent as William I. He was strong-willed, and ruthless to his enemies, but in the main his rule was firm and just. The measures which he carried through laid the foundations of the strong national monarchy of England and they deserve to be analyzed.

William I, the Conqueror, 1066–1087.

(1) His first problem was the reduction of the English to obedience. The battle of Hastings was only the opening of this campaign. For five years (from 1066 to 1071) he was engaged in crushing revolts. Fortunately for him, these revolts occurred one after another in different parts of the country and under leaders who failed to act together. Had they united, the Normans might have been expelled. William's strength lay in the warlike character of his Norman followers, who had their fortunes to make in England from the confiscated estates of the English rebels. The Normans were greatly superior to the English in fighting, especially in the building of castles and the besieging of castles. The resistance to William came from various quarters. The

Crushing of English Revolts.

* For the description of these two types see pp. 491–494.

sons of Harold headed a revolt in the southwest. The great earls of Edward's time, fearing to lose the semi-royal position they had enjoyed, engaged in several revolts. In the north the English rose in behalf of Prince Edgar, a descendant of Ethelred, who claimed the throne. This rising was aided by the king of the Scots, who invaded England. William got the better of all of these revolts, but it required almost constant taking the field. We have already noted the fact that the crushing of these revolts resulted in the transfer of the great estates from English to Norman lords, and in the introduction of the feudal system of landholding.

Results.

(2) No sooner was William well finished with the English resistance than he had to fight against his own Norman followers. They were willing to aid him in conquering the English, since this was the way to make their own fortunes. They had no sympathy, however, for William's idea of a strong and orderly government. They expected to hold their lands on the loose feudal terms and rule them in the semi-independent manner familiar to French feudal lords. When they found William's hand strong to hold them in order some of the greater lords revolted. In this they were aided by William's eldest son, Robert. The revolts in Normandy were also aided by the French king, Philip I. William succeeded in putting down these revolts and punishing the leaders, but the Norman barons in England and Normandy were long to be a source of trouble to the kings.

Subduing Rebellious Norman Barons.

(3) The administrative policy and measures of William we have already noticed in the general discussion of the Norman period. He broke up the earldoms of the Anglo-Saxon system, which had comprised large sections of the kingdom. Henceforth the title of earl meant the chief lord of a single shire. He used the sheriffs to control the local government. He made a census of the lands and possessions of his subjects (the Domesday Book) to serve as the basis for the collection of taxes. He compelled all the landholding nobility to swear an oath of allegiance to him directly.

Establishing a Strong Government.

(4) His ecclesiastical policy had important results for the future. He worked with his Norman archbishop, Lanfranc, to reform the English church and bring it into closer connection with the general church of western Europe. The Cluniac reforms were introduced; the clergy were forbidden to marry and simony was condemned. William refused, however, to surrender his right to invest and control the bishops. Gregory VII put forth a claim to the overlordship of England and demanded that William do homage to him for the kingdom. William refused on the ground that former English kings had never done so, and Gregory VII was too much occupied with his struggle with the emperor Henry IV to press the matter.

Ecclesiastical Policy.

(5) William continued the policy of the strong English kings who had tried to establish some sort of overlordship over the Welsh and Scotch. The help given by the king of the Scots to the rebellious English gave William an excuse for invading Scotland and forcing the king of the Scots to do him homage. He kept the Welsh under by establishing powerful Norman lords on the frontier of Wales and encouraging them to encroach on the lands of the small Welsh chieftains.

Dealings with Welsh and Scotch.

(6) He was engaged in frequent quarrels with the king of France, Philip I. The relations of the feudal king with his great vassals were usually hostile, and William, as duke of Normandy, had fought against his overlord. After the conquest, however, the conflict took on a different aspect. William was both duke of Normandy and king of England; as duke of Normandy he was still a French lord and a vassal of the king of France. Philip constantly intrigued with the Norman barons in England and in Normandy and with William's son Robert, with the object of getting Normandy away from the king of England. It was in war against the king of France that William met his death, in 1087.

Conflict with the King of France.

On his death William I left Normandy to his oldest son Robert, but willed the English crown to his next son William. It was evidently his intention to separate the two possessions, but this was not the ultimate outcome. William II succeeded his father as king of England without difficulty. Robert, the older brother, accepted the duchy of Normandy; later, when he determined to go on the first crusade, he pledged it to William II for the money to make the expedition. The reign of William II (known as "William Rufus," from his red hair) was much harsher than that of his father. Where the Conqueror had used stern measures to establish order, William II had recourse to harsh and oppressive measures, merely to increase his own revenues without regard to justice or good government. He used his rights as feudal overlord to despoil the barons by collecting excessive feudal dues; he levied heavy taxes; he kept church offices vacant in order to collect the revenues from the estates attached to them. His treatment of the clergy brought on a conflict with the aged and pious archbishop Anselm, who had succeeded Lanfranc in 1093 after a four years' vacancy in the office. Anselm rebuked the king for his evil life and remonstrated against his abuse of the church. After a prolonged struggle Anselm was driven into exile. In spite of general discontent William Rufus ruled with a strong hand until his sudden death in 1100.*

William II, "Rufus," 1087–1100.

His Harsh Rule.

Conflict with Archbishop Anselm.

The evil reign of William II had one important result on the reign of his younger brother, Henry, who succeeded him: in order to win the support of the nobles and clergy, Henry I issued a charter in which he pledged himself to rule well, to abandon the evil customs of his brother, and to restore the laws of Edward the Confessor. This Charter of Liberties is the forerunner of the Great Charter (Magna Carta); it amounts to an admission

Henry I, 1100–1135.

L., 55. A. and S., 7. Ch., 73.

* The king was hunting in one of the royal forests when he was shot to death by an arrow from an unknown hand. His contemporaries regarded this violent death as an act of divine judgment because of his oppressive deeds. In popular minds it was associated with the harsh forest laws enforced by the Norman kings. William the Conqueror had made laws inflicting heavy penalties and even death upon any who should kill game in the hunting preserves claimed by the king.

that English subjects have rights under ancient law which may not be violated by the monarch.

Henry I also got the duchy of Normandy into his hands, although he had to fight against his older brother, Robert, and the French king, Louis VI, to do so. In this war English and Normans fought side by side in France. Henry sought in many ways to reconcile the older English population with his rule; among other things he married an English princess of the line of Alfred. Under him also there was an important advance in the organization of the government. The king's court became a real central government. Two special departments were created: the royal court of justice, whose judges tried the cases that came before the king, and also exercised supervision over the administration of justice in the shire-courts; and the exchequer or treasury, which systematized the collection of the revenue.

Government of Henry I.

The strong and just rule of Henry I was followed by a period of civil struggle between his daughter Matilda and another claimant for the throne, Stephen, count of Blois, a grandson of the Conqueror. This was the opportunity of the great barons, who had been held in check by the firm hands of former kings. They occupied royal lands, built castles without authorization, and made themselves virtually independent lords in their districts. The dispute over the throne was settled by an arrangement between Stephen and the son of Matilda, Henry of Anjou, whereby Henry was recognized as Stephen's heir. In 1154, on the death of Stephen, he succeeded to the throne as Henry II.

Civil War between Stephen and Matilda, 1135-1154.

The accession of Henry II is the beginning of a new period. The century and a half from then to the death of Edward I, in 1307, is the constructive period in the formation of the English constitution. This is the line which we must follow mainly, although we must notice other interesting movements also. In this movement three important phases are to be noted: (1) the administrative measures of Henry II, which connected the central with the local government and made a really national administrative system; (2) the enforced concession of the Great Charter by John, which guaranteed to English subjects justice and individual rights and is justly regarded as the foundation of English liberties; (3) the development of a new organ of government, the Parliament, which was composed partly of elected representatives, and which, possessing independent powers, acted as a check on the king and made the English monarchy a limited or constitutional monarchy.

French Lands of Henry II.

Henry II* was not only king of England, but also lord of a large part of France. Through his mother, Matilda, he was descended from William the Conqueror and inherited the English crown and the duchy of Normandy; his father was count of Anjou, one of the largest of the French principalities, which also fell to Henry; Henry had married Eleanor, heiress of the great duchy of Aquitaine, which brought that land into his control. Thus he was overlord of more than half of France, although, of course, he held these lands as a vassal of the king of France and did homage to him for them. These possessions involved Henry II and his successors in conflicts with the kings of France †; for this was the period in which the French monarchs, such as Philip Augustus, were working to make their authority real over all of France.

Administrative Measures.

Circuit Judges.

L., 62. Ch., 90.

Our chief interest, however, is with the administrative measures of Henry II as king of England. Building on the improvements made by Henry I, he sought to make his authority effective throughout the country, by linking up the local organs of government with the central government. Such a link already existed in the sheriffs, who collected revenues from the shires and reported to the exchequer. Henry strengthened this organization, and also established a national administration of justice by connecting the shire-courts with the royal court of justice. He divided the country into

* Henry II is the first of the "Plantagenet" or "Angevin" line of kings. These names were taken from his father's family of the counts of Anjou, whose badge was a sprig of broom (*planta genista*).

† See pp. 315-316 for the story of this struggle.

circuits, and appointed royal judges, whose duty it was to travel through their circuit and visit each shire to try the more important cases. A committee of the shire-court was to be appointed in each shire to report to the royal judges the local cases; this committee was called a jury, and is the forerunner of our modern grand jury.

Grand Jury.

These travelling judges were connected with the royal court of justice, which we mentioned as developing in the time of Henry I. It consisted now of two divisions, the court of King's Bench, which was concerned with important criminal cases and with crown cases, and the court of Common Pleas, to which private suits were appealed. The travelling judges put into effect the legislation of Henry II in their control of local justice in the shire-courts. Thus the old English common law was amalgamated with the new royal statutes and administrative law, making a single body of law for the whole kingdom. The private jurisdictions of landlords and the feudal customary law continued to exist, but became more and more exceptional.

In connection with this important judicial reform, we should notice the introduction of trial by jury, which was of Norman origin. In Anglo-Saxon as in other Germanic tribal courts, the fact of guilt or innocence was established by oaths or by the ordeal. The Normans had for some time employed the method of inquest: the determination of the facts by the testimony of a number of men sworn to tell the truth. This was first extended to legal cases where criminal charges were involved; during the reign of Henry II it came into general use in the trials before royal judges for civil as well as criminal cases. The jury was at this time not a real jury as we use the word, but rather a body of sworn witnesses, on whose testimony the royal judges decided the case. Much later it became what it is now, a sworn body of men who determine the fact of guilt or innocence according to the testimony of witnesses.

Trial by Jury.

Henry's efforts to bring the judicial system entirely under the royal court brought him into conflict with the church, in the famous case of Thomas Becket. Becket had been chancellor of the kingdom and one of Henry's trusted officials. Henry had made him archbishop of Canterbury, in the expectation that he would help to bring the church courts also under the royal control. Becket, however, devoted his energy rather to defending the independence of the ecclesiastical courts. When the king issued a law putting the clergy under the royal courts Becket resisted and retired from the country. A few years later he was induced to return, but the quarrel broke out again, and Becket was murdered by some of Henry's retainers. The pope made good political use of this evil deed; he declared Becket a martyr and saint,* and threatened the king with excommunication. Henry made peace only by withdrawing his obnoxious law and doing penance at the tomb of Becket. The case is significant as an early illustration of the fact that the national government was bound to run counter to the church as soon as it strove to bring sovereign authority completely into its hands; for the church exercised large powers in every country.

Conflict with the Church; Thomas Becket.

Murder of Becket.

The increased importance and activities of the shire-courts, owing to their connection in a functional way with the central government, had an interesting effect upon the local landed nobility. They found in the shire-courts opportunities for more peaceful and constructive work than fighting with their neighbors; they could serve on committees to deal with the sheriffs or on juries to meet with the royal judges. Another practice, developed at this time, worked in the same direction. It had become customary for the king to accept a money payment in lieu of military service from the lesser nobility. This payment, known as *scutage* (shield money) became a regular tax levied upon the landholding class. It freed the local landlords from the necessity of following the king in war, which was the obligation they owed for their lands, and left them to devote themselves to their local affairs. From feudal

Activity of Local Nobles in Shire-Courts.

Scutage.

* This is St. Thomas, of Canterbury, to whose tomb the pilgrims in Chaucer's *Canterbury Tales* were going.

warriors they became "country gentlemen" and developed into that conservative class which furnished the most solid element in the local government and the stanchest opponents of royal tyranny.

The extension of English rule over other parts of the British isles was greatly advanced during the reign of Henry II. Ireland was composed of numerous small clans; here in Henry's time some of the Norman lords found an outlet for their adventurous spirits by taking a hand in the petty wars that were constantly going on among these clans, and winning lands for themselves. Henry II forced these Norman lords and the native Irish chiefs to recognize him as overlord. Henceforth the English kings included among their titles the title of "Lord of Ireland." English rule, however, did not amount to much in Ireland during the Middle Age.

Henry II and Ireland.

Wales during the Norman period had been coming under English influence. Powerful Norman lords had been granted lands along the Welsh border and had increased their lands by encroaching on the native Welsh territory. In Henry's time there was little left of the independent kingdom of Wales except the outer shell along the coast. The native Welsh princes in this region were forced to do homage to Henry, so that all of Wales was in one way or the other subject to his government. The king of Scotland invaded England and was made prisoner; Henry released him only after he had done homage to the king of England for his Scotch throne.

Wales.

Scotland.

Henry's latter days were embittered by almost constant quarrels in his own family. He imprisoned his wife, Eleanor of Aquitaine, because she stirred up their sons to revolt. Philip Augustus of France took advantage of these quarrels in the English royal family and aided the sons of Henry as a means of embarrassing him in his French possessions. It was on an expedition against such a revolt in France, in which his sons were allied with the king of France, that Henry II met his death in 1189.

Henry's Sons Revolt.

The reign of Henry's son Richard Lionheart was spent mostly out of England, on the third crusade, in captivity in Germany on the way home from that crusade, and in wars in France against Philip Augustus. His reign, therefore, has little importance in the development of the English constitution. His prolonged absence put the governmental machinery of Henry II to a test which it stood very well.

Richard I, "Lionheart," 1189–1199.

Richard was succeeded in 1199 by his younger brother John. In the history of the English government the most important event of this reign was the granting of the Great Charter (Magna Carta). This charter was wrested from the king by the barons; the barons, however, acted as representatives of all the important classes of the kingdom, and they demanded, not that the royal power should be destroyed but that the king should rule in accordance with the law. In order to understand this we must recur to the peculiar situation in England. In strictly feudal countries political development necessarily took the form of a conflict between the great nobles trying to maintain their sovereign powers and the king striving to make himself the sole sovereign. The choice, therefore, was virtually between feudal disunion and absolute government. Germany developed in one way, France in the other. In England there was an element which stood between these two extremes and which was destined to develop at the expense of both. This was the Anglo-Saxon government which had developed from tribal times and which contained the seeds of free institutions. It was to this that Henry I referred when he promised, in the Charter of Liberties, to rule in accordance with the laws of Edward the Confessor; it was this element which Henry II connected with the central government in his administrative measures, which aimed at making the royal power supreme over the great lords. The old English institutions could be appealed to by the king against the feudal independence of the barons, and by the barons against the tyranny and misrule of a bad king. This latter use was now to be applied against King John.

John, 1199–1216.

Peculiar Feature of English Monarchy.

John succeeded in the course of his reign in turning against him all the important elements in the kingdom: clergy, great barons, landed nobles, and merchants of the cities. In the first place he allowed a large part of his French inheritance to slip from his hands. The shrewd and able Philip Augustus, who had sided with Richard and John in their revolts against their father Henry II, and had intrigued with John against Richard, now continued his machinations against John. The folly and incapacity of John furthered his schemes. Declaring John's French fiefs forfeited, Philip occupied Normandy and Anjou in force and added them to his own crown lands. John made half-hearted attempts to recover them, but the futility of his efforts only added to his humiliation. This was enough to turn against him the warlike barons of England who had been used to the leadership of strong men like Henry II and Richard; they were outraged also by John's demand for military service and military taxes for a war that was never seriously undertaken. As a matter of fact, in the long run the loss of Normandy and Anjou was a good thing for the nation, since it forced the nobles to abandon their foreign holdings and settle down as Englishmen. Nevertheless, it was felt as a humiliation by the baronage.

Discontent with John.

Loss of French Lands.

In the second place, John became involved in a quarrel with the great pope, Innocent III. A dispute had arisen over the election of the archbishop of Canterbury, and Innocent III, appealed to by one party, took the case into his own hands and appointed Stephen Langton, an Englishman attached to the papal court. John refused to accept him or to allow him to land in England. To bring the king to terms, the pope placed England under an interdict, which suspended the ordinary religious services and aroused great popular ill-will against the king. John disregarded the interdict and the pope excommunicated him. An excommunication had the effect of freeing his subjects and followers from their oaths of allegiance. John was aware that he had enemies enough who would gladly take

Conflict with Innocent III.

Humiliation of John.

this opportunity; the excommunication, therefore, brought him to his knees. Innocent drove a hard bargain: John had not only to sue for pardon and accept the archbishop; he had also to do homage to the pope as a vassal for the English crown and pay an annual tribute, which did not increase the respect of the barons for their king.

Finally, the government of John was tyrannical and capricious. He allowed foreign favorites to rule him and enrich themselves. He demanded excessive taxes from the nobles and the cities. He had bitterly oppressed the clergy during his quarrel with the pope. He allowed the strong administrative system of Henry II to fall to pieces, so that no man was sure of justice and peace. The great nobles at last rebelled. Under the leadership of the archbishop, Stephen Langton, they drew up a programme of reforms, based on the Charter of Liberties of Henry I, and presented it to John with their weapons in their hands. The meeting took place in an open meadow near London, known as Runnymede, on June 15, 1215. John was forced to yield and the Great Charter was issued in the form of a grant of liberties by the king.

His Arbitrary Rule.

R., I, 99. L., 75-79.

Magna Carta, 1215.

As was to be expected, the charter confirmed in detail the rights and privileges of the ruling class, the great barons and the clergy. It contained, however, more general provisions as well. To no one would the king deny, or delay, or sell justice; no freeman should be deprived of his liberty or his property except by trial before a jury of his peers. The king would not levy any tax or feudal aid without the consent of the Great Council. The charter was a recognition of the principle that the English nation had the right to government according to law, and that the earlier achievements in the way of liberties and orderly government were binding on succeeding kings. In this way the Great Charter is the foundation of English liberties.

R., I, 100. L., 80. A. and S., 29. O., 54, 55. Ch., 110.

Provisions.

Significance.

The next stage in the development of the English constitution was the growth of Parliament. This occurred in the reigns of the next two kings, Henry III and Edward I. The term Parliament was applied in the thirteenth century to meetings of the Great Council. This body was the successor of the old English *Witenagemot;* in the Norman period it had taken on a feudal character and was composed of the great barons who held their lands and titles directly from the king, including the higher clergy. It was customary occasionally to summon also representatives of the lesser nobility; this was done by sending out summonses through the sheriffs to the shire-courts to elect members to attend the meeting of the Great Council. Now, at the end of the thirteenth century, an important innovation was made, consisting of the summoning of representatives from the cities as well; this gave a still more representative character to Parliament. We must notice the circumstances which brought about this change.

Growth of Parliament.

Origin in the Great Council.

Henry III, son of John, succeeded in 1216 as a mere child. During his minority a regency of high officials and great barons ruled for him in accordance with the principles of the Great Charter. When he came of age, however, he turned out to be a weak and unwise ruler. He was personally a better man than his father; he was a brave knight and a pious man. This did not prevent him from ruling badly: he was governed by unworthy foreign favorites, he violated the principles of the Charter, and constantly demanded aids and taxes the proceeds of which were wasted. His foreign policy was no better. Twice he invaded France in attempts to recover the lands taken from John, and both enterprises were wretched failures.* Moreover, his piety caused him to take seriously his obligations as a vassal of the pope; he paid the annual tribute promised by John and aided the papacy with men and money in the struggle with the Emperor Frederick II, an affair that had no connection with the national interests of England. Several times the barons, in

Henry III, 1216–1272.

His unwise rule.

* They resulted, however, in a treaty which settled the matter for a time. Henry III abandoned his claims to the lands actually taken from John, and Louis IX invested him with the duchy of Guienne, which included part of the old duchy of Aquitaine.

meetings of the Great Council (or Parliaments), protested and made the king promise to abandon his excessive taxes and disregard of laws, but Henry had no difficulty in getting the pope to absolve him from these promises. Finally a party of the barons under the lead of Simon de Montfort, took arms and defeated the king's mercenary troops and made him prisoner.

Revolt of Simon de Montfort.

Parliament of Simon de Montfort, 1265.

In order to secure the backing of the nation for the permanent reforms which he aimed to make, de Montfort called a Parliament to which he summoned not only representatives from the landed gentry in the shires but also representatives of the merchant class in the cities. This was the first time that both sorts of representatives had met with the Great Council to form a Parliament; and the precedent is of great significance. It was not, to be sure, immediately followed up. Simon de Montfort was defeated and slain the same year and the king restored to his independence; for the next thirty years Parliament continued to mean a meeting of the prelates and barons.

Importance of the Precedent.

The permanent establishment of Parliament as a representative body came in the reign of Henry III's son and successor, Edward I (1272–1307). In 1295 he was confronted with a situation in which he needed the support of the whole nation, being threatened with war by the king of France and with revolts in Wales and Scotland. So he called a Parliament which included the Great Council (the higher clergy and great barons), representatives of the lower clergy, two knights from each shire, and two citizens (burgesses) from each important city (borough).

Edward I, 1272–1307.

"Model Parliament," 1295.

This body was truly representative; for it included members of all the important elements in the nation. Hence it is usually called the "Model Parliament."

Two Permanent Elements in Parliament: Peers and Commoners.

In later Parliaments the lower clergy were not included, since the church had its own representative councils and preferred to deal with the king as a separate corporation; the higher clergy continued to attend Parliament because they were members of the Great Council. This left two essential elements in the Parliaments: the "peers" or lords (both clerical and secular), who had formed the old Great Council; and the elected representatives of country and city districts. These two elements developed later into the House of Lords and the House of Commons.

Powers Acquired by Parliament.

The most important fact about Parliament was that it came to acquire certain defined powers. If Edward I and his successors called frequent meetings of Parliament, it was because they needed its support, especially in the raising of revenue to run the government. The practice of securing the needed revenues by general taxes had not developed in the thirteenth century. The chief sources of revenue were the personal estates of the king, and certain customary payments, such as feudal aids from the barons, "free gifts" from the church, and contributions from the cities. These were no longer adequate to the expenses of a governmental machinery that had since the time of Henry II become very complicated, and of a government that was about to embark in that most costly of national enterprises, foreign war.

Its Consent Required for the Levy of Taxes.

The old revenues, since they rested on ancient custom, could not be increased by the king without the consent of those who paid. In Parliament all the propertied classes were represented, and what the king sought from Parliament mainly was its authorization for the levying of contributions.

This Contains Germs of Later Powers.

This did not mean that Parliament levied taxes; it meant that it became a recognized principle that the king could not levy a new tax without the consent of Parliament. This contained the germs of all the later powers of Parliament; for if it had the right to grant taxes it also had the right to refuse to grant taxes, or at least to bargain with the king about granting taxes. These powers developed later than our period, but the fact that they were latent in the very reason for calling Parliament is what gives that body its chief significance.

Edward I was the greatest lawmaker among mediæval English kings. His laws were not innovations, but were aimed at putting into legal form the powers which the central government had acquired since the time of Henry II. An important feature of this legislation was his attempt to bring the independent jurisdiction exercised by the baronial courts and the church courts under the control of the royal judicial system. His more important laws were brought out as statutes, that is, laws enacted by the king with the advice and approval of Parliament. After Parliament became a permanently representative body, it continued to possess this right of being consulted in regard to the making of laws, and this was a source of the final control over legislation which it was eventually to acquire.

Edward I a Great Law-maker.

Statutes.

It was inevitable that this assertion of the supremacy of the national government should bring about a conflict with the church. The church, with its wealth and power, its strong organization, its own body of law and system of courts, already, even before the growth of national governments, occupied a large part of the field of authority over which the national government was attempting to establish its control. Since the time of Gregory VII the popes had maintained that the authority of the church was superior to that of the state. In the time of Edward I the difference arose over a matter of the greatest importance to the government, its right to tax the income and property of churchmen. Boniface VIII forbade this in the papal bull *Clericis Laicos*, as we noticed in the history of France. Edward I answered, with a lawyer's logic, that if the English clergy were not to contribute to the maintenance of the government, they need not expect protection from the English law. In the end the pope gave way; the clergy were to be allowed to pay taxes, but these were to be known as "free gifts."

Edward I and the Church.

Quarrel with Boniface VIII.

Clericis Laicos.

Edward I sought to extend the authority of the English government over Wales and Scotland. In Wales a native prince, Llewelyn, had brought the remnants of Welsh territory under his rule, and had even recovered a good deal of the lands formerly taken from the Welsh by the Norman lords. He had been able to do this because of the troubles in England at the time of the revolt of Simon de Montfort. On the accession of Edward I, Llewelyn refused to do him homage. Edward invaded Wales and brought him to terms, but later risings broke out and it was some time before Wales was entirely subdued. Edward then divided the Welsh lands into shires and introduced English government. The territory possessed a form of independent existence, since it was erected into a principality, to be held by the son of the king of England. "Prince of Wales" is the title still used by the heir to the English crown.

Edward I and Wales.

The "Prince of Wales."

Edward's attempt upon the independence of Scotland was not successful. In fact, it produced a national awakening in Scotland and a brief heroic period in Scotch history, connected with the names of Robert Bruce, Sir William Wallace, and the battle of Bannockburn. The affair began with a disputed succession to the Scotch throne, which was referred to Edward as arbitrator. The two principal claimants were Robert Bruce and John Balliol. Edward agreed to decide the case on the condition that the new king would do homage to him for the Scotch throne. He decided in favor of John Balliol, who then performed the act of homage. Later, however, when Edward I undertook to interfere in Scotch affairs, the Scotch forced Balliol to lead them in revolt, and the French king, Philip IV, sent them help. This was the occasion of the summoning of the Model Parliament by Edward I.

Scotland.

Scotch Succession.

Edward invaded Scotland, made Balliol prisoner, and proceeded to rule Scotland by his agents as if it were his personal possession. The harsh rule of the English agents led to a new rising, this time under a simple knight, Sir William Wallace.* He was successful in driving the English out of Scotland, but was defeated when Edward himself came to Scotland with an army.

First Invasion of Scotland.

Wallace's Revolt.

Second Invasion.

* This rising is the subject of the famous popular romance, *The Scottish Chiefs*, by Jane Porter.

Yet a third time the Scotch revolted. The leader in this was Robert Bruce, grandson of the Bruce who had been a candidate for the throne. After slaying an English agent Bruce took to the hills, gathered a following about him, and proclaimed himself king. Edward I again set out for Scotland, but died on the way. Under the weak rule of his incompetent son Edward II, Bruce succeeded in driving out the English garrisons and bringing all of Scotland under his rule. The decisive battle was that of Bannockburn in 1314.* In 1328 the English government recognized the independence of Scotland by the treaty of Northampton.

Rising of Robert Bruce.

Battle of Bannockburn, 1314; Scotch Independence 1328.

Edward I also had trouble with France in the latter part of his reign. Philip IV tried to take from him what was left of the English possessions in France; this was his motive in supporting the Scotch revolt. Edward I made ready for war and Philip gave way. To cement the peace, Prince Edward, later Edward II, married Isabella, daughter of Philip IV, a marriage from which later English kings derived their claim to the French throne.

Trouble with France.

The reign of Edward II showed a sad decline from the greatness of his father's rule. As has been noticed, he virtually abandoned the Scotch war, and allowed Robert Bruce to reconquer the kingdom from the English. All his life he was ruled by favorites, whom he allowed to govern for him and to enrich themselves at the expense of the country. At one time the great lords revolted and compelled the king to accept the control of a committee of the nobles. At the end of his reign his own wife, Isabella of France, sided with the discontented nobles in an attack upon him. He was defeated and compelled to abdicate in favor of his young son, Edward III, who was to rule under the regency of the queen and her paramour, Roger Mortimer (1377). The next year

Edward II, 1307–1327, Dethroned.

* Robert Burns's poem, "Bannockburn," purports to represent Bruce's address to the soldiers:

"Scots wha hae' wi' Wallace bled,
Scots wham Bruce hae' aften led," etc.

Edward II was brutally murdered in prison by the agents of Isabella and Mortimer. With the reign of Edward III we come to the period of the Hundred Years' War, which lies beyond the limits of this chapter.

CHAPTER XIX

THE HUNDRED YEARS' WAR—FIRST PART

In preceding chapters we have studied the history of England and of France to the end of the thirteenth century. By this time each may be said to have become a nation. We have now to study the history of the prolonged series of wars between these two countries, known as the "Hundred Years' War." This was really the culmination of a conflict that had been going on since the Norman conquest. The underlying cause was the fact that the king of England held lands in France as a vassal of the French king. This meant that the king of England was virtually ruler over a part of France, for the holding of a fief carried with it the exercise of a considerable measure of sovereign authority over the land and people which composed it. The inconsistency became more glaring after the king of France had developed a national government; he was not master in his kingdom as long as a foreign monarch ruled over part of it. We have noticed earlier phases of the conflict in the struggle of Philip Augustus against Henry II, Richard I, and John of England; in the wars of Louis IX and Henry III, and the threatened war between Philip IV and Edward I. By the beginning of the fourteenth century both countries had progressed so far in the development of national government and national feeling that the conflict took the form of national wars.

The Hundred Years' War; Real Cause.

The deeper cause of the war, therefore, was the long-standing hostility between the French government, determined to complete the unification of French territory under the king, and the English government, equally determined to retain possession of the French lands. The reason for the outbreak of war at this particular time, however, was another matter, the interference of France in Scotch affairs, which was regarded by the English government as a menace to English interests. T Scotch had won their independence under Robert Bruce, will be remembered, and the regents of Edward had recognized this in the treaty of 1328. Rob Bruce died in 1329, leaving an infant son, Da to succeed him. At this point the English g ernment encouraged another claimant, Edward B liol (son of that John Balliol who had been king of Scotl for a time under Edward I), to revive his claims to the Sco throne, and gave him help, on the condition that he would homage to England if he were successful. Balliol succeeded first, but the party of Bruce received help from France and stored their young king. The English answer was to decl war on France in 1337.

Immediate Occasion: French Interference in Scotch Affairs.

In declaring war Parliament asserted as its reason the rig of Edward III to the French throne.* As we have seen, he the son of a daughter of Philip IV of France. Charles IV, last of the sons of Philip IV, had died without le ing a son to succeed him, in 1328. At that ti the regents of Edward III had presented his clai but the French court had decided against him, claring that the French throne descended through the m

Claim of Edward III to the French Throne.

*Genealogy of French kings in first part of Hundred Years' War:

Philip III
- Philip IV
  - Louis X
  - Philip V
  - Charles IV, d. 1328
  - Isabella, m. Edward II of England
    - Edward III of England
- Charles of Valoi
  - Philip VI, 1328–1350
    - John, 1350–1364
      - Charles V, 1364–1380
        - Charles VI, 1380–1422

line and could not be transmitted by a woman.* The nearest heir by male descent was the son of a brother of Philip IV, who was recognized as Philip VI. In 1329 Edward III did homage to Philip VI for the duchy of Guienne. This amounted to a recognition of the new king. Now, some years later, the English revived the claims of Edward III, but it was evidently more of a pretext for war than a cause.

Flemish Towns.

Their Relations with England.

Another occasion for hostility between England and France was found in the situation of the Flemish towns. The cities of Flanders, such as Ghent, Bruges, and Ypres, were great trading and industrial centres. Their location on or near the mouths of the Rhine made them natural distributing points for northern Europe. The Baltic trade reached them through northern Germany; the Rhine brought to their docks goods from central and southern Germany, from Italy, and the eastern markets reached by the Italian traders; England sent them not only wool fleeces but also Bordeaux wine from the duchy of Guienne. The English trade was especially important to the Flemish towns; for their chief industry was weaving cloth from the English wool, and they exchanged their cloths and tapestries for the products which they received from other lands.

O., 74.

Edward III Makes an Alliance with the Flemish Towns.

It was quite in keeping with the character of the feudal age that there should be a standing quarrel between the cities and the count of Flanders. Just about this time the differences had led to actual war, in which the king of France had aided the count. The Flemish cities thereupon formed a league and sought the alliance of Edward III, who gladly accorded it. In the first years of the war Flanders constituted the English base for operations in northern France, until the capture of Calais in 1347 gave them a still nearer port.

Few sections of mediæval history are as familiar to the gen-

* This principle of succession came to be known as the "Salic law," because the French lawyers cited among other precedents the old law of the Salian Franks in regard to inheritance of land.

eral reader as the first part of the Hundred Years' War. Jean Froissart, a Flemish knight, who was attached to the English court and who took part in the events, wrote a chronicle of the times which has been a popular story-book ever since. Froissart was a court poet; it was the romantic, the adventurous, and the picturesque which caught his eye. It is he who tells the familiar stories of the exploits of the Black Prince, King Edward's son, and of the brave English knight, Sir John Chandos, and of the French hero, Bertrand du Guesclin. From him we get the interesting details of the battle of Crécy: how the French knights charged without order and were shot down by the stout English archers; how the blind king of Bohemia demanded to be led into the thick of the fight and was found after the battle in a heap of the slain; how King Edward refused to send reinforcements to the Black Prince when he was hard pressed, in order that the young warrior might win his spurs. His also is the familiar tale of the burghers of Calais who came out with ropes around their necks, to offer themselves as victims to the wrath of Edward, in order to save the rest of the citizens of the besieged city, and how they were spared through the pleading of the queen. The chronicle of Froissart was one of the earliest books to be printed. It was early translated into English and has been a source of interest and entertainment to every succeeding generation.

The Chronicle of Froissart.

Character.

Incidents.

War was declared in 1337, but for several years there was no serious fighting. Edward made two or three raids into northern France, starting from Flanders, but withdrew each time before encountering the French forces. In 1340 the English won a naval battle off Sluys on the Flemish coast which gave them control of the channel. The first real battle was fought in 1346. In the summer of that year Edward III landed with a considerable force in Normandy and advanced to the lower Seine. Moving up that river toward Paris he found the way blocked by a much larger French force and was compelled to retreat. Unable to go back through Normandy, he crossed the Seine and re-

Crécy, 1346.

Ch., 138.
R., I, 197.
O., 76.

treated north toward the coast. The French, hurrying after, came up with the English near the town of Crécy. A battle occurred here in which the English defeated a greatly superior French army, largely because of the skill of the English archers. The one important result of the battle of Crécy was the capture of the coast town of Calais. Edward III invested the city and after a siege of nearly a year it surrendered (1347). This was the nearest French port to England, and the English used it henceforth as the basis of their operations in northern France. Calais remained in English hands for over two centuries, long after they had lost the rest of their French lands.

Capture of Calais, 1347.

After the fall of Calais, hostilities were interrupted by a truce, which was prolonged for several years by the great plague known as the Black Death. In 1355 Edward's son, the Black Prince, made a raid from Bordeaux through the southern provinces of France. The next year he set out again from Bordeaux and marched north toward the Loire with the intention of joining another English army invading from the north. A larger French force intercepted his march, however, and forced him to fight near Poitiers (September, 1356). Once again, as at Crécy, the undisciplined feudal array of the French was beaten by the small organized English army. The day was disastrous for the French; a great many nobles fell on the field and King John of France (who had succeeded his father, Philip VI, in 1350) fell a prisoner into the hands of the Black Prince. The victor retired to Bordeaux and returned to England with his valuable captive.

Poitiers, 1356.

R., I, 198.

The defeat at Poitiers and the captivity of their king compelled the French to ask for a truce. The dauphin Charles, oldest son of King John, acted as regent during his father's absence, and his government encountered stormy times. The "free companies," bands of hired soldiers out of an occupation because of the truce, settled down on the land and devoured it. The peasants in the north, goaded to madness by their misery and by this added

Troubles of French Government.

plague, armed themselves and murdered their landlords. The States General, meeting at Paris, hampered the government of the regent by demanding reforms and a share in the administration. Etienne Marcel, the prévôt of the merchants (the chief official of the city) headed a popular rising in Paris and supported the demands of the States General. The government finally got the upper hand of these disturbances; the nobles crushed the peasant rising with great brutality, Marcel was abandoned by his partisans and assassinated in the streets of Paris, and the States General were pacified with vague promises and sent home. These disorders had so weakened the French government, however, that it had to make peace.

Treaty of Calais (or Brétigny), 1360.

Terms were agreed on in the treaty of Calais, better known as the treaty of Brétigny (1360). By this treaty Edward III acquired the land south of the Loire that had once formed the duchy of Aquitaine, and also the city of Calais and the territory around it. He was to hold these in full sovereignty and not as a vassal of the king of France; thus the French surrendered about one-fifth of their land. In return Edward abandoned his pretensions to the French crown as well as the old claims to Normandy and other fiefs lost in the thirteenth century.*

Charles V of France.

The dauphin Charles became King Charles V on the death of his father, in 1364. He is known among French kings as Charles the Wise, a title which he earned by his ability in mastering the disorders of the kingdom and in outwitting the English. He strengthened the royal government, kept the States General under control, and built up the finances and the army. He put an end to the dispute in Flanders, which had given the English such an advantage during the first years of the war; he cleared the country of the "free companies," enrolling some of them in the

* King John of France, who had been captured at the battle of Poitiers and taken to England as a prisoner, was released on the signing of the treaty. He left hostages in England as security for the payment of his ransom; one of these was his son John, who later broke his pledge and fled from England. King John thereupon returned to England and gave himself up as a prisoner, remaining there in honorable captivity until his death, in 1364.

royal army and forcing the rest to seek employment elsewhere. Then, when he felt himself ready, he found an excuse for provoking the English to a renewal of the war. When the nobles of Aquitaine protested to him against the administration of the Black Prince (who had been invested with the duchy by his father), Charles V summoned the prince to come to his court and answer the charges. This was clearly a repudiation of the treaty of Brétigny, which had recognized the complete sovereignty of the English over Aquitaine, and Edward III replied by declaring war (1369).

The Black Prince in Aquitaine.

Renewal of War, 1369.

The fortunes of war were completely reversed in this part of the struggle. The important towns of Limoges, Rochelle, and Poitiers, in Aquitaine, revolted against the English and opened their gates to the French. Relieving forces from England wasted their men in futile invasions through a hostile country. Edward the Black Prince retired, worn out and ill, to England, where he died in 1376. By the end of the reign of Edward III, 1377, the French had recovered most of the land, the English holding out only in certain strong towns on the coast, such as Bordeaux and Calais. The war virtually ceased with things in this state; for during the next forty years both countries were occupied with internal disturbances.

French Successes.

End of First Period.

One reason for the success of the French was the decline of the government of Edward III, who had sunk into his dotage and had allowed the government to be run by selfish nobles and unworthy favorites. Edward's son John of Gaunt, duke of Lancaster, was the head of the clique that governed the aged monarch. The older son, Edward the Black Prince, took the lead in a movement to reform the court, in which he was backed by Parliament. But the Black Prince was failing in health; he died in 1376, the year before the death of his father. In 1377 Edward III passed away, to be succeeded by his grandson Richard, the ten-year-old son of the Black Prince.

Decline of English Government.

The reign of Richard II (1377–1399) was full of disturbances. During his minority a council of regency ruled for him; the principal event of these years was the peasants' rising of 1381, which is discussed later. After he came of age he ruled unwisely and the great nobles made this a pretext for attacking him. In 1387 five of the leading nobles, including Richard's uncle, the duke of Gloucester, and his cousin Henry, son of John of Gaunt, made formal charges against him in Parliament. These lords are known as the "Lords Appellant." Parliament was under their control and did their bidding. The friends of Richard were banished or executed, and Richard was put under the control of a council composed of his accusers and enemies. He submitted for a time, and after two years was allowed to resume his independence. Richard never forgave the outrage visited on him by the Lords Appellant and Parliament, but for several years he bided his time. In 1397 he struck; he had his uncle, the duke of Gloucester, arrested and secretly put out of the way, and banished the other Lords Appellant. He dissolved Parliament after compelling it to transfer its powers to a standing committee which he could control. His despotic rule was brief, however; in 1399 his cousin Henry of Lancaster returned from exile to head a revolt, and Richard was defeated and forced to abdicate.*

Richard II, 1377–1399.

Quarrels with Great Nobles.

* Genealogy of the English kings in the first part of the Hundred Years' War:

Edward III, 1327–1377

Edward, the Black Prince	Lionel	Thomas, duke of Gloucester	John of Gaunt	Edmund, duke of York
Richard II, 1377–1399	Philippa, m. Edmund Mortimer, earl of March		Henry IV 1399–1413, first king of Lancastrian line	
	Roger Mortimer			
	Edmund Mortimer (representative of the older line, passed over in 1399)			

The victorious faction called a Parliament which accepted the abdication of Richard and recognized Henry as king. This Henry IV is the first of the Lancastrian line of kings. It should be noted, however, that he was not the nearest heir to the throne after Richard, for there was a young prince descended from an older son of Edward III; this flaw in the Lancastrian title was to lead to civil war later.

Henry of Lancaster Seizes Throne, 1399.

The century which ended with the abdication of Richard II and the accession of Henry IV was an important one in English history. Outwardly it appears as a period of unrest and violence, but these disturbances are symptoms of the changes that everywhere in Europe were bringing in the new age.

Growth of Parliament under Edward III.

The powers of Parliament developed rapidly during the forty years from the beginning of the war in 1337 to the death of Edward III in 1377. Its control over taxation had become a real power. The expenses of the war caused Edward III to ask Parliament for money nearly every year. This brought about a series of bargainings between the king and the representatives of the nation. Parliament would grant the king the right to collect an income tax (a tenth or a fifteenth) or to levy indirect taxes on imports and exports, and in return it would suggest changes in the laws and reforms in the administration, which the king would graciously promise to take up with his council. Thus it acquired a direct influence over legislation. During this time also it acquired an influence over the policy of the king; for Edward III often discussed with it the plans for war and other important matters, in order to assure himself of its support, and in later times Parliament considered that it had a right to be consulted. Finally Parliament acquired the right to call the king's officials to account for bad government. In 1376, when Edward III was in his dotage and the government had fallen into evil hands, the "Good Parliament," under the lead of the Black Prince, brought charges against the king's ministers and favorites, condemned them, and had them punished. This was the beginning of impeachments by Parliament. So in the reign of Edward III Parliament began to exercise those extensive powers which in their final form were to make it the controlling organ of the English government.

The fourteenth century was a time of economic unrest, due to changes in agriculture and industry which upset traditional relations. The most striking movements were the peasants' risings, which occurred in many parts of Europe in this and the following century. In England this movement culminated in the great peasants' revolt of 1381. The deeper causes are to be found in the transition from the manorial system, in which the relations of landlord and farm laborer were fixed by custom, to the wage system, in which the relations rested on a contract of hire. In the manorial system, which was virtually universal in the feudal age, the peasants were in the main serfs, born into a status or condition according to which they held a small piece of land on the payment of customary dues and the performance of a certain amount of labor for the lord. The serfs were not free to leave their land nor to dispose of their own labor. This system was breaking down in the fourteenth century, because of changes in methods of agriculture and the increase in the amount of currency. The lord found it to his advantage to hire laborers for a money wage and for a definite period; the serfs were allowed to free themselves from their customary services and restrictions by paying a money rent. Two results followed: serfdom tended to disappear, and a class of free laborers came into existence.

Peasants' Revolts.

Causes.

Passing away of Serfdom.

In the middle of the fourteenth century (1348) the Black Death swept over England and carried off from one-third to one-half of the working population. Herds and flocks roamed untended and crops rotted ungathered in the fields. When the landlords were ready to bid against one another for labor, wages automatically advanced; but to the landlord class it seemed that the laborers were taking inhuman advantage of the misery of the country. Since the landlords controlled the

Effects of the Black Death.

L., 94. Ch., 146.

L., 95.

government, they tried to meet the demands of the laborers with legal compulsion. In 1351 the king and Parliament enacted the first Statute of Laborers, which gave the landlords the right to compel laborers to work for them at the wages current before the Black Death. It was impossible to enforce this sort of law, and the attempts of the landlords to do so drove the laborers to form associations or unions to resist.

Conflict between Landlords and Laborers.

The Black Death also checked the movement which was causing serfdom to disappear. The scarcity of labor and the high wages demanded by the free laborers led the landlords to refuse to release their serfs from their customary obligation to labor on the lords' land. The serfs, on the other hand, were made more eager for freedom because of the high wages. Many of them fled from their lands, to turn up in other parts of the country as free laborers; the landlords secured legislation allowing them to pursue their runaway serfs and bring them back by force.

This conflict between the landholding and the working classes continued for many years, until it came to an outbreak in 1381. Other causes of discontent combined with this conflict to precipitate the revolt. The democratic and critical spirit, which had originated in the towns, was permeating all society in the fourteenth century.* Popular preaching by the friars and the "poor priests" of Wyclif called attention to the luxury and worldliness of the wealthy clergy and to the virtues of the simple folk. A sort of crude democracy appeared among peasant agitators, as expressed in the couplet:

Revolt of 1381.

"When Adam delved and Eve span,
Who was then the gentleman?"

There was political discontent as well; the great nobles who governed the country during the decline of Edward III

* This spirit is admirably shown in the poem of William Langland, *The Vision of Piers Plowman*, which pictures the misery of the poor laborers, the heartlessness of the nobles, and the corruption and worldliness of the clergy.

and the minority of Richard II ruled corruptly and extravagantly. A feeling was abroad among the peasants that they were being taxed heavily for a vicious and incompetent government, and this feeling was cultivated by popular ballads and satires. The crisis came in 1381, when the officials tried to collect a new poll tax levied by Parliament on all classes. Local resistance to tax-collectors swelled into a revolt against the ruling class and the government. In many districts there were local riots, in which the peasant sacked and burned manor houses and murdered agents and landlords, but the striking feature of the revolt was the march of an army of peasants and townsmen on London. For several days they held and terrorized the city, burning and sacking palaces and murdering hated officials.

Ch., 151.

Rebels Seize London.

Richard II, a youth of fifteen, showed at this crisis a courage and good sense that make his later failure even more tragic. He rode out to meet the rebels with a small following, listened to their demands for relief from oppressive laws, and promised to see to it that their grievances should be righted. A quarrel arose, however, and one of the kings' followers struck down Wat Tyler, the popular leader of the peasants. The young king averted the danger of a fight by riding forward among the angry peasants and declaring himself their leader and friend. Pacified by his promises, most of the peasants left London and returned to their homes. Richard's regents, however, failed to carry out his promises of redress and pardon. The rebels were hunted down and executed, and the objectionable laws were enforced as before. Serfdom, however, was dying a natural death, because of changed social and economic conditions, and before many years it had virtually disappeared in England.

Richard II and the Rebels.

Outcome.

Another mark of the new age was the emergence of a national language and a national literature. As we have noticed already, the Norman conquest had brought in a foreign language, French, which was for a long time the language of literature, of the ruling class, and of public affairs. English continued to be spoken by the mass of the people, but very little literature appeared in it. By the end of the thirteenth century, after more than two hundred years of common life, the two races had amalgamated to form a single English people; this process was favored especially by the growth of a national government under Henry II and Edward I. As a result there grew up a single national language, the basis of which was the old English speech, but which contained a large element of Norman-French. Since the decline of Anglo-Saxon literature, the native speech, unrestrained by a standard literary form, had changed very rapidly. It was not the old literary language of Wessex, but the popular dialect of the midland or old Mercian region, which emerged as the national language of England, with a considerable proportion of words adopted from the Norman French. This language is known as Middle English, to characterize its position between Old English, or Anglo-Saxon, and Modern English, the language since the age of Shakespeare. Its position as a literary language was fixed at the end of the fourteenth century by its use in certain writings such as the poetry of Geoffroy Chaucer and the translation of the Bible by John Wyclif.

Development of Language.

Middle English.

The religious movement connected with the name of Wyclif is a further evidence of the change from mediæval conditions that was making itself felt in the fourteenth century. In fact, the position taken by Wyclif was essentially that of the Protestant leaders, like Luther and Calvin, who headed the revolt from the church in the sixteenth century. Wyclif began by writing in defense of the national government against the pretensions of the papacy. This was the period of the "Babylonian Captivity," the time when the papal court, located at Avignon, was under French influence. This fact, coupled with the abuses in papal administration, had led to wide-spread criticism of the papacy. This was especially strong in England, where it was felt that the large sums of money raised for the popes by the selling of indulgences

Religious Revolt of John Wyclif, d. 1384.

Attacks Papal Abuses.

and other methods were being used against England. Under Edward III the government had enacted the statute of Provisors, forbidding the pope to appoint churchmen to rich offices in the English church, and the statute of Præmunire, forbidding the carrying of appeals from the English church courts to the papal court.

In defense of national government Wyclif denied the superior authority of the pope, and declared that civil governments derived their powers as directly from God as did the ecclesiastical. From this he was led to deny the right of the church to exercise secular powers and to question the right of the clergy to own land and property. Then he went further to attack abuses in the church and to reject certain fundamental doctrines. Finally he took the position that the Scriptures constituted the only authority for doctrines and church government. Nor was he content to stop with a criticism of the papacy and the church; he sought to institute a new religious movement in line with these ideas. He translated the Bible into English and wrote many tracts in English to appeal to public opinion; he founded an order of popular preachers, known as "poor priests," to spread his ideas among the common people. It seems strange that he could carry his attack on the church so far without being suppressed as a heretic; but the papacy was in trouble everywhere at this time, Wyclif had powerful supporters at court, and national feeling in England was for the moment hostile to the papacy. In any event, Wyclif continued his work to the end of his life, in 1384.

Wyclif Attacks Secular Powers of the Pope.

His Appeal to Scriptures.

Translates the Bible into English.

Thus the end of the fourteenth century in England, as everywhere, was marked by the stirrings of a new age. Mediæval institutions and conditions were beginning to break down and to give way to newer forms in every field: political, social, religious, and intellectual. Feudalism was passing away before the growth of a strong national monarchy, serfdom was disappearing, freedom of thought was beginning. It was to be a long time yet before these tendencies

Middle Age Passing Away.

triumphed; but the events we have noted—the growth of Parliament, the peasants' revolt, the new national language and literature, and Wyclif's movement—are prophetic of the future.

CHAPTER XX

THE HUNDRED YEARS' WAR—SECOND PART

As we saw in the preceding chapter, the first period of the Hundred Years' War came to an end with the virtual expulsion of the English from French soil. An English force still held Calais, but of the great duchy of Aquitaine which had been ceded to England in the treaty of Brétigny there remained in her hands only a narrow strip of land on the coast, with the important city of Bordeaux.

Situation at the End of the First Period, 1377.

The victory of France had been due directly to a revival of national force under the vigorous rule of Charles the Wise (Charles V, 1364–1380). It had been due partly, of course, to the weakness of the English government during the declining years of Edward III. For nearly forty years after his death, in 1377, the English government was prevented from undertaking seriously a foreign war by continued disturbances at home. The minority of Richard II had been troubled by popular discontent and agitation, which culminated in the peasants' revolt of 1381. As soon as he came of age he became involved in conflicts with the powerful barons and with Parliament; and his reign ended in civil war and his deposition, in 1399. Henry IV (1399–1413), the first of the Lancastrian kings, had to face several revolts, which threatened to unseat him. In 1400 he defeated a conspiracy to kill him and restore Richard II; the only result of this was to cause the disappearance of that unhappy monarch, who was secretly executed in prison. Then the Welsh rose under a native prince, Owen Glendower, and for years in their mountainous districts maintained a stubborn resistance to the armies of Henry IV. The Welsh were joined by a power-

Domestic Troubles in England, 1377–1413.

Richard II, 1377–1399.

Henry IV, 1399–1413.

ful faction of the nobles, headed by the great families of Percy (earls of Northumberland) and Mortimer (earls of March), who professed to be fighting for the rightful heir to the crown, the young Edmund Mortimer, earl of March.* Henry IV finally got the better of these revolts and conspiracies, and spent the last few years of his reign in comparative peace, but he died still in the prime of life, in 1413.

It was his son and successor, Henry V (1413–1422), who renewed the war with France. A young man, eager for military glory and rightly reckoning that a successful foreign war would put an end to factional opposition to the Lancastrian rule, he immediately made known his intention of reviving the claim to the French crown and making war on France. Parliament met him half-way, asserting his title to the throne of France and voting him a large grant of money for the war.

Henry V (1413–1422) Declares War on France.

The eagerness of the English to renew the war with France was prompted by the unhappy state of that kingdom. Since the death of Charles the Wise in 1380 the government had fallen on evil times. His son Charles VI was a mere child when he succeeded, and his minority was the occasion for quarrels among the princes of the royal family as to who should control the government. To make matters worse, Charles VI, after he grew up, developed fits of insanity which periodically incapacitated

Disorders in France under Charles VI, 1380–1422.

* The following genealogy shows the title of the earl of March and the connections of the Mortimers, Percys, and Owen Glendower:

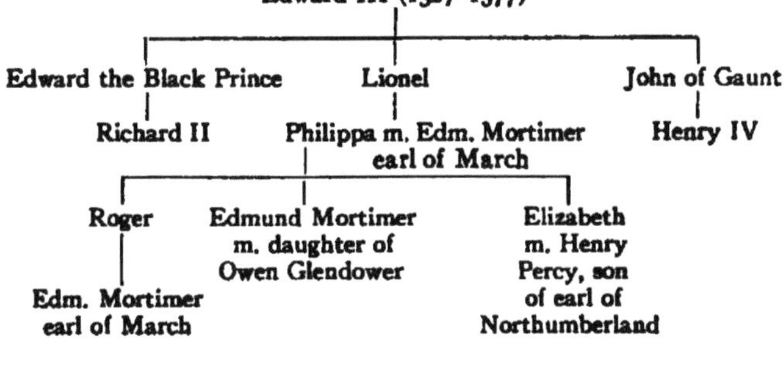

him for ruling. The factional struggles in the court were thus prolonged until they developed into civil war. These factions had formed around the king's brother, Louis, duke of Orléans, and the king's cousin, John, duke of Burgundy. In 1407 the duke of Orléans had been murdered at the instigation of the duke of Burgundy, and the son of the murdered man took up the quarrel more bitterly than ever. The party of the young duke of Orléans was led by his father-in-law, the count of Armagnac, a powerful noble of the south of France; from him the party received the name of the Armagnacs. Not only the court, but the country at large was divided between Burgundians and Armagnacs, and France was torn by civil war at the very moment when the king of England was preparing to invade the country.

Burgundians and Armagnacs.

In the summer of 1415 Henry V sailed from England with a considerable force and landed in Normandy. The siege of Harfleur at the mouth of the Seine detained him for several weeks, and the gathering of the French forces compelled him to strike north by the shortest route along the coast for the English stronghold of Calais. He found his way blocked by a greatly superior French army at the town of Agincourt, not far from the battlefield of Crécy. Once again, as at Crécy and Poitiers, the English proved their superiority in the field. The large French army was defeated and routed, and the English made good their withdrawal to Calais.

Henry V Invades France, 1415.

Battle of Agincourt.

In 1417 Henry V made a second expedition into France. Landing again in Normandy, he set out deliberately to conquer the province. For two years he was engaged in this task, until the surrender of its chief town, Rouen, in 1419, put the whole of Normandy in his hands. In the meantime the struggle between the Burgundians and Armagnacs continued unabated. The Burgundians had entered Paris in force, seizing the king and massacring the Armagnac nobles. The dauphin (the oldest son of the king) now became the leader of the Armagnac forces, which prepared to revenge their defeat.

Second Invasion, 1417; Conquest of Normandy, 1419.

Civil War in France.

XVI

FRANCE DURING THE HUNDRED YEARS' WAR

Note to Map XVI.—This shows the extent of the lands ceded to Edward III in the treaty of Calais (or Brétigny), 1360. Notice the two small territories in the north which were ceded also. In the later part of the war, these were all recovered by the French, except Calais. Note the advance into the Rhône valley by the acquisition of Dauphiné (1349); this was carried further by the acquisition of Provence under Louis XI (see Map XVII). Use this map for locating the events of the Hundred Years' War; the dates given on the map are those of events (treaties, battles, etc.) occurring at these places.

If France were not to fall an easy prey to the foreign invader, the war of the factions must be ended. At the solicitation of the leading clergy and officials, the duke of Burgundy and the dauphin consented to a conference. They met, each attended by a few followers, on a bridge at the town of Monterey near Paris, but the upshot of the interview was the murder of the duke of Burgundy by the followers of the dauphin.

Murder of the Duke of Burgundy, 1419.

This murder completed the disruption of France. The new duke of Burgundy, Philip the Good, son of the murdered man, openly joined the English with all his lands and forces. This gave Henry V possession of the person of the king and of the city of Paris, with a large part of northern France. The helpless, half-mad king, Charles VI, was induced to sign the treaty of Troyes (1420), which disinherited his son and recognized Henry V as regent of France and heir to the French throne. Two years later both of these kings were dead, Charles VI old and imbecile, Henry V in the prime of his age and vigor. Henry VI, an infant son of Henry V, less than a year old, was left to inherit the two crowns of England and France.

The Burgundian Party Joins the English.

Treaty of Troyes, 1420.

Death of Charles VI and of Henry V, 1422.

The struggle continued between the followers of the dauphin, who was recognized by them as the rightful heir to the throne, and the English and Burgundians, supporting the claims of Henry VI. In time French national feeling would of necessity rally about the dauphin, but in 1422 his prospects were not bright. The parlement of Paris had accepted the infant Henry VI as king of France, and English rule was being established over northern France by the wise and vigorous measures of his uncle and guardian, the duke of Bedford. By 1428 the English had control of all of the land north of the Loire except the city of Orléans and they were already besieging that stronghold.

Situation of the Dauphin.

English Successes; Siege of Orléans, 1428.

It was at this juncture, when things looked darkest for the dauphin and the national interests of France, that the French found a leader and an inspiration. This was the young peasant girl of Lorraine, Jeanne d'Arc (Joan of Arc, as the English called her). The forces which inspired her remarkable career were a simple popular faith and a sorrow for the sufferings of the country. She had waking visions, which we need not doubt were realities to her, of the saints, St. Michael the archangel and St. Catherine, and heard voices commanding her to lead the dauphin to Rheims to be crowned. Rheims was by long tradition the place of the consecration and coronation of the kings of France; at this time it was in the hands of the English. The voices became so insistent that she had to obey. Leaving her home secretly, she made her way to the court of the dauphin at Chinon, where he and his counsellors were awaiting in uncertainty and indecision the fate of Orléans. There she convinced the dauphin and the sceptical courtiers of the supernatural character of her call. They intrusted her with a small force of soldiers with which she succeeded in making her entry into the besieged city. Her confidence inspired the despairing forces within the town. On horseback and in armor she led them in sallies against the English and forced them to abandon the siege. Then she took the field at the head of her troops and cleared the English out of the eastern lands and opened the way to Rheims. There, in July, 1429, the dauphin was crowned as Charles VII.

Jeanne d'Arc.

Her Visions and Her Mission.

She Relieves Orléans.

And Leads the Dauphin to Rheims.

The mission of the maid was accomplished, but the king persuaded her to remain with the army. The French now advanced on Paris; at Compiègne, in a battle with the Burgundian forces, Jeanne d'Arc was cut off from the main body and made prisoner. The Burgundians turned her over to the English, who had her tried as a witch before an ecclesiastical court. Even under torture her testimony revealed only her simple faith in her mission and her devotion to France. She was condemned and burned at the stake in May, 1431.*

Jeanne Made Prisoner.

Ch., 176.

And Burned as a Witch, 1431.

* Some years later, in 1456, the sentence of witchcraft and heresy was revoked by an ecclesiastical court held in France with the consent of the pope. The French have always revered her memory as that of

Her larger mission, the rousing of France, was also accomplished. From the time of her appearance, the tide ran steadily against the English. In 1435 the duke of Burgundy returned to his allegiance, and the same year the English duke of Bedford died, leaving the conduct of the war to less skilful hands. In 1436 the city of Paris was recovered from the English. The English still held Normandy, won by Henry V, and their old possessions in the south around Bordeaux. In the next few years these also were wrested from their grasp. In 1450 Normandy was regained, and in 1453 a desperate attempt of the English to recover Bordeaux, which had revolted, was defeated in the battle of Castillon and the south passed definitely out of their hands. During these later years of the war the factional struggle in England known as the War of the Roses was beginning to distract the government and prevent it from carrying on the foreign war. The war ended without a formal treaty; in the modern period the kings of England were still to use the title of king of France and for a time in the sixteenth century were even to make occasional efforts to recover some of the lands in France. In effect, however, the issue was settled for good and all; of all their extensive holdings in France the English retained only the city of Calais and the Channel Islands.

French Successes.

The End of the War, 1453.

The Final Settlement.

The fourteenth and fifteenth centuries constitute a period of transition from the mediæval to the modern age. In political history this transition is marked by the sharper definition of national outlines and the growth of national rivalries. The Hundred Years' War is an important phase of this movement. At bottom it had been produced by that confusion between private possession and public government which was of the essence of feudal-

Significance of the Hundred Years' War.

a national heroine and martyr; the English, however, long continued to regard her as a witch, as is shown by Shakespeare's characterization in *Henry VI, Part I.* In the nineteenth century the French clergy began an active campaign in favor of her canonization. This has resulted in the pope issuing in 1908 the decree of beatification which gave her the title of Blessed, and in 1920 the decree of canonization which places her among the saints of the church.

ism as a political system. The kings of England had held lands in France as family possessions, but, since the possession of land carried with it in the feudal age a large measure of sovereign authority over the land and the people on it, the kings of England had been virtual rulers of a considerable part of France. The outcome of the Hundred Years' War put an end to this confused situation. Henceforth the king of France, with no equal rival in his own land, was in a position to extend his authority as a national monarch over the national territory.

England and France Become National States.

The kings of England, on the other hand, were released from the distraction of their feudal lordship in France and the contests with the French monarchs which it had entailed, and became more definitely and clearly national monarchs of England. During the generation following the war, in both countries, acute internal struggles occurred which resulted in the clearing up to a considerable degree of the confusion left over from the feudal stage of government and which prepared for the emergence at the end of the century of strong national states.

Decline of Royal Authority in France during the War.

In France the development of a strong national government followed necessarily, given the state of government and society in the fifteenth century, two main lines: (1) the concentration of authority in the hands of the king, and (2) the reduction of the great feudal princes. As we have seen in a former chapter, there had been constant progress in the former line during the two centuries from the accession of Louis VI, in 1108, to the death of Philip IV, in 1314. After that, however, more than a century of foreign war and civil strife had not only checked that progress but had caused actual retrogression. When, therefore, French successes enabled Charles VII, about 1440, to turn his attention to the work of building up the royal authority, he found serious obstacles in his way.

Aside from the independence of the feudal princes, which we shall consider by itself later, the principal obstacle to royal power was the authority which had been acquired by the States General, and by similar representative bodies in the local provinces. The States General was the name given to a general assembly of representatives of the three principal "estates," or classes—clergy, nobles, and citizens. It had been summoned first, it will be remembered, by Philip IV, in 1302, when he wished to assure himself of the support of the nation in his quarrel with the pope. During the Hundred Years' War the States General had been summoned frequently because the government needed its assent to the levying of taxes and subsidies for the heavy expenses of the war. Thus it had acquired a measure of control over the national revenues. In the frequent political crises of the fourteenth and fifteenth centuries the States General often sided with the parties of opposition and protested against the royal policy and demanded reforms.

Constitutional Limitations.

The States General.

Its Powers.

In appearance, therefore, the States General occupied a position like that of the English Parliament. For obvious reasons, however, it was destined to have a very different history. In the first place, it rested upon no such solid foundation as the English Parliament possessed in the self-governing shire-courts.* In the second place, the States General did not have the support of the nation. When the fortunes of France were at their lowest in both periods of the war, after 1360 and after 1420, the revival of national feeling had shown itself in a rallying of the nation about the king, while the States General had seemed to hamper rather than to help in that revival by its opposition to the king. The policy of Charles VII, therefore, in virtually dispensing with the States General after 1439 was not really revolutionary and met no serious opposition.

Decline of the States General; Reasons.

The decisive factor in the decline of the powers of the States General was its loss of control over the royal finances. The main sources of revenue (aside from the royal lands) were the general direct tax, known as the *taille*, indirect taxes called *aides*, and the salt monopoly, or *gabelle*. For the levying of the *taille* and the *aides* the govern-

Loses Control over Finances.

* See p. 360 above.

ment had usually (but not always) asked the assent of the States General. After the meeting of 1439, which was the last time it was summoned during his reign, Charles VII continued to collect these taxes on his own authority, basing his demands on the need of revenues to complete the conquest of French territory from the enemy. In its enthusiasm for the war the nation paid without protest. From that time on the king and his council determined how much revenue was needed and levied taxes accordingly without other authorization.

The legislative powers of the States General were irregular and spasmodic in their exercise. On occasions the government had asked its authorization for new measures and laws. On other occasions the States General had demanded reforms or the redress of grievances. It did not participate regularly in the making of laws, as the English Parliament did in the fashioning of the statutes. With its loss of financial powers and the greater infrequency of its meetings, the States General lost even its occasional control over legislation. Henceforth legislation in France took the form of the issuing of edicts by the king with the advice of his officials and council.

Loses Its Legislative Influence.

In many of the provinces of France there were local assemblies of the three estates, which had also acquired considerable powers during the period of the war. In some cases they met annually to apportion the share of the taxes among the classes and communities of the province, and even ventured occasionally to refuse to pay as much as had been assigned to the province. They also petitioned the king in regard to the bad administration of his officials or demanded reforms in the laws. In some provinces the estates exercised a certain measure of local authority, levying taxes for local needs and controlling certain local affairs. The provincial estates, however, declined very rapidly after 1450. In many provinces they simply ceased to meet. Where they did persist they were shorn of their independence; their powers were confined to the formal assenting to the levy of taxes de-

Provincial Estates; Their Powers.

manded from the province by the royal council and to the apportioning of this to the subdivisions.

Thus the constitutional limitations upon the power of the king disappeared in France after the middle of the fifteenth century. The government of France in principle was an absolute monarchy; to make it such in fact required the development of an effective centralized administration, and that development was not to occur for a long time yet. The actual power exercised by the king, therefore, depended to a considerable extent upon the personal qualities of the monarch; under Charles VII it was much less than under his shrewd, active, and unscrupulous son, Louis XI.

Government of France Absolute but not Strongly Centralized.

The monarchy had still to fight a hard battle with the great feudal nobles. The weakness of the government during long periods of the war had enabled the princes to acquire great independence. As we have seen, the older lines of feudal princes had for the most part disappeared before the beginning of the war, through the absorption of the great fiefs by the crown; of these there were left only the duke of Brittany and a few nobles of southern France, such as the counts of Foix and of Armagnac. The powerful lords with whom Charles VII and Louis XI had to struggle in order to establish royal authority were of later origin; they were descendants of younger sons and brothers of former kings, who had been endowed with fiefs (appanages) by the reigning monarchs from the crown lands. The greatest of these princes at this time was the duke of Burgundy, holding from the king of France not only that duchy but also the counties of Flanders and Artois, and from the emperor the "free county" of Burgundy (Franche Comté) and the Netherlands. Other powerful lords were: the duke of Bourbon, the duke of Orléans, the duke of Anjou, and the duke of Alençon. During the first part of the fifteenth century, when the central government was powerless, these lords acted almost as sovereign

Wars of Charles VII and Louis XI with the Feudal Princes.

Origin of the Feudal Princes from the Royal Line.

princes and each family sought its own aggrandizement at the expense of the royal power.*

The revival of the monarchy threatened the independence of these great princes and produced a series of coalitions and revolts against Charles VII and Louis XI. These coalitions lacked solidarity; each prince was seeking his own advantage. Moreover, the national forces were on the side of the monarchy and the kings eventually triumphed. Charles VII had to face three or four such coalitions between 1437 and 1442; he got the better of them, but his last years were embittered by the rebellion of his son and heir, the dauphin Louis, who acted as if he could not wait for his father's death to enter upon authority.

Feudal Coalitions against Charles VII.

Louis XI came to the throne on the death of his father in 1461. The feudal princes, who, because of his earlier acts,

* The following table shows diagrammatically the origin of the feudal princes of the age of Charles VII and Louis XI:

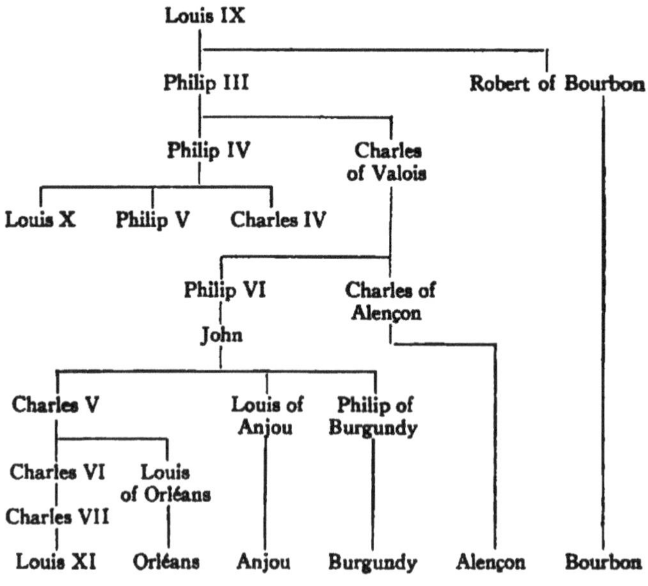

counted on finding an easy master in him, were soon undeceived. No monarch more greedy of power ever occupied the throne of France, and none more tireless in his efforts to encompass it. A contemporary ballad gave him the name of the "universal spider," a fitting title, with its suggestion of slyness, rapacity, and calculating patience. He succeeded in his enterprises not by armies and violence, but by intrigue, treachery, and cunning.

Louis XI, 1461–1483, "the Universal Spider."

Early in his reign Louis XI had to face a formidable coalition of the princes, which included his own brother, the duke of Berry, the dukes of Brittany, Alençon, and Bourbon, and the son of the duke of Burgundy. The forces of the coalition were stronger than any the king could muster, and he was defeated and forced to make concessions. These concessions show what the nobles were fighting for. They had taken up arms under the name of the "League of Public Welfare" and professed to be fighting for reforms and freedom of the people from oppression. Nothing of this appeared in the demands of the nobles, which were for pensions, privileges, offices, and fiefs for themselves. Once determined to make peace, Louis XI conceded all that they asked with a free hand, and then set about breaking up the coalition and preparing to take away again what he had given.

The "League of Public Welfare."

The conflict with the feudal princes took on a new character after Charles the Bold succeeded to the title of duke of Burgundy. In 1467 Philip the Good died; he was that duke of Burgundy who had gone over to the English in 1419 and had returned to his allegiance to Charles VII in 1435. He was succeeded by his son Charles, who bears the title of Charles the Bold. The duke of Burgundy was the lord of territories constituting almost an independent kingdom. In addition to the duchy of Burgundy, he held from the king of France the county of Flanders and other fiefs in the north, and from the emperor the "free county" of Burgundy (Franche Comté) and

Conflict with Charles the Bold, Duke of Burgundy.

The Burgundian Territories.

a whole group of territories just north of the French frontier in the region known as the Netherlands (modern Holland and Belgium).

Ambitious Projects of Charles the Bold.

His Schemes.

With these great resources the dukes of Burgundy had been able to treat with the kings of France almost as equals; it was the ambition of Charles the Bold to achieve complete independence and equality by erecting his territories into a separate kingdom. This lofty ambition involved him in wide-reaching negotiations of international scope. To prevent Louis XI from interfering with his plans he tried to keep alive the feudal revolts, and made an alliance with Edward IV of England, who agreed to make war on France. To secure the intervening lands between the two Burgundies and the Netherlands he bought up the rights of the Hapsburg lords to the county of Alsace and tried to induce the duke of Lorraine to put the control of that duchy into his hands. To secure the title of king he tried to draw the emperor Frederick III into his schemes. These negotiations were too complicated for the hasty and impolitic temperament of Charles the Bold; moreover, he had in Louis XI an antagonist of immensely superior skill in the game of diplomacy.

Louis XI Foils His Attempts.

Louis XI easily triumphed over the later feudal revolts. He kept Edward IV of England occupied by supporting the earl of Warwick in his revolt and helping to restore the Lancastrian party. When Edward finally, in 1475, invaded France, Charles the Bold was engaged in a futile campaign among the Rhine princes, and Louis had little difficulty in persuading the English monarch to withdraw for a round sum of money. The projects of Charles in Alsace and Lorraine aroused the apprehensions of the lesser German princes and of the Swiss Confederation, and Louis encouraged them to form a league for defense. This brought about the ruin of Charles the Bold. In 1477, in battle with the Swiss and the other allies at Nancy, in Lorraine, he met defeat and death.

Death of Charles the Bold, 1477.

Louis was not able to gather in, as he had hoped, all of the

Note to Map XVII.—This shows the possessions of Charles the Bold, duke of Burgundy. They are in two groups: a southern group consisting of the duchy of Burgundy in France and the county of Burgundy (Franche Comté) in the empire; a northern group composed of Flanders and other fiefs, partly in France and partly in the empire. It was the aim of Charles to unite his possessions by acquiring Alsace and the duchy of Lorraine, and to have them recognized by the emperor as an independent kingdom. Note the further expansion of France in the Rhône valley by the acquisition of the county of Provence.

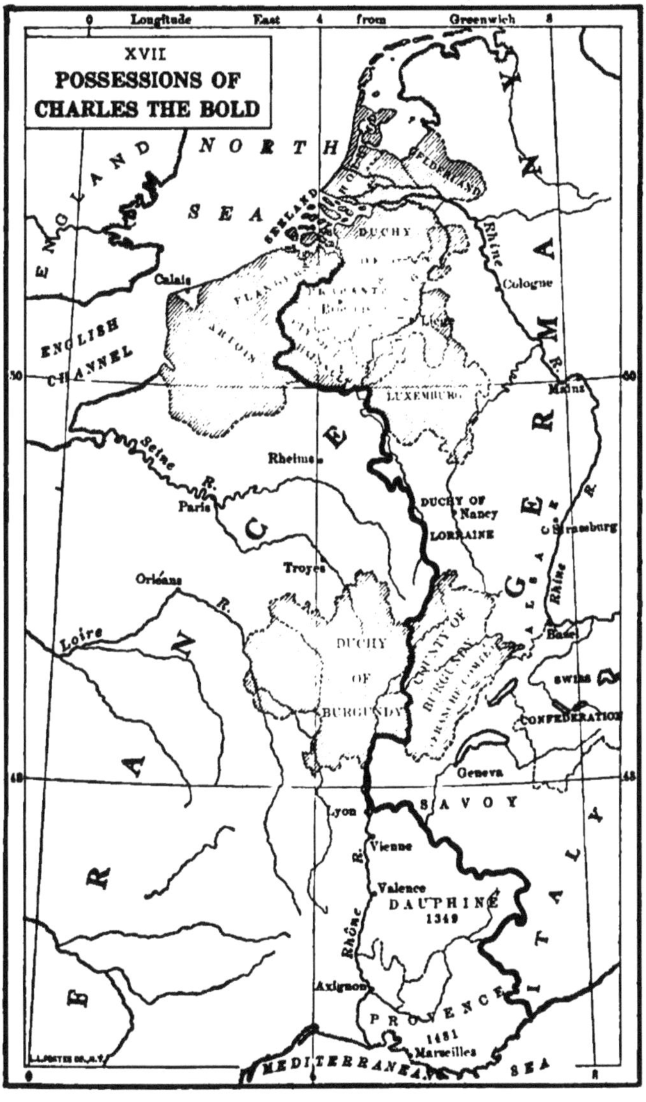
XVII
POSSESSIONS OF
CHARLES THE BOLD
Longitude East from Greenwich
ENGLAND
NORTH SEA
ENGLISH CHANNEL
Calais
ZEELAND
GELDERLAND
DUCHY OF
LUXEMBURG
ARTOIS
Rhine
Cologne
Mainz
Rheims
Seine R.
Paris
DUCHY OF
Nancy
LORRAINE
Strasburg
ALSACE
Rhine
Troyes
Orléans
Loire
DUCHY OF BURGUNDY
COUNTY OF BURGUNDY
Basel
SWISS CONFEDERATION
Geneva
SAVOY
Lyon
Vienne
Valence
DAUPHINÉ
1349
Rhône R.
Avignon
PROVENCE
1481
Marseilles
MEDITERRANEAN SEA
FRANCE
GERMANY
ITALY

rich inheritance of the dukes of Burgundy. Mary of Burgundy, daughter of Charles the Bold, had married Maximilian, archduke of Austria, of the Hapsburg family, heir of the emperor Frederick III. Maximilian defended the interests of his wife and, after some years of struggle, Louis was forced to recognize his right to the Netherlands, Franche Comté, and other fiefs lying outside of France. Louis acquired for the crown, however, the duchy of Burgundy and certain other French fiefs. The Netherlands became part of the vast family empire of the Hapsburgs, which came, in the generation after Louis XI, into the hands of the emperor Charles V; they were to be a constant source of conflict between France and the Hapsburg powers of Spain and Austria.

The Burgundian Inheritance.

The Hapsburgs Acquire the Netherlands.

Louis XI Acquires the Duchy of Burgundy.

The defeat of Charles the Bold marked the final triumph of Louis XI over the feudal princes. Fortune and cunning enabled him to reap a rich harvest of fiefs made vacant by death or confiscation. In addition to Burgundy he added to the crown land the fiefs of his brother the duke of Berry, of the duke of Alençon, and of the duke of Anjou. The latter included not only Anjou and Maine in France, but also the county of Provence, which belonged nominally to the empire. Adding this to the crown land meant virtually incorporating it into the territory of France. In this connection we must pause to notice the process by which French influence and control were being extended beyond the mediæval frontiers of France.

Other Acquisitions of Louis XI.

Provence.

France was bounded on the east along its whole extent by lands belonging to the empire. Geographically these constituted three groups: the lower Rhine lands, comprising the Netherlands, the middle Rhine territories of Lorraine and Alsace, and the Rhône valley. In the later Middle Age the ties which bound these lands to the empire were of the loosest sort, and they tended to gravitate toward the stronger and more compact nation of France. The external evidence of this drift toward France was the way

French Expansion Eastward.

in which French noble families acquired fiefs in these regions; we have seen illustrations of this in the cases of the Netherlands, Lorraine, Franche Comté, and Provence. This was a step toward their incorporation into the French nation.

The Rhône Valley.

Within the limits of the Middle Age this process had already gone very far in the case of the Rhône valley. In the early period this region had constituted the independent kingdom of Arles or Burgundy, lying between France, Germany, and Italy. It had been added to the empire in the eleventh century, but the failure of the imperial government had resulted in this region breaking up into virtually independent little principalities. The chief of these were the county of Provence, the county of Vienne, or Dauphiné, the county of Burgundy, or Franche Comté, and the duchy of Savoy. Dauphiné had been left by the will of the last count, in 1349, to the oldest son of the king of France, and since that time the heir to the French throne had regularly borne the title of dauphin and held this fief. Franche Comté had come into the possession of the French dukes of Burgundy, but, as we have just seen, it escaped the grasp of Louis XI by being drawn into the Hapsburg possession. Provence was acquired by Louis XI as part of the inheritance of the house of Anjou. The dukes of Savoy were related by marriage to the French royal line, but their future was bound to Italy rather than to France. By the acquisition of Dauphiné and Provence the Rhône became a French river. The extension of French political influence over Franche Comté, Alsace and Lorraine, which would bring the French frontier up to the Rhine, was the great aim of ambitious French rulers in the modern period.

Dauphiné.

Franche Comté.

Provence.

Savoy.

Death of Louis XI, 1483.

Louis XI died in 1483, leaving the French monarchy stronger than it had been at any time since the beginning of French national history. It was far from being a well-organized state in the modern sense, but the tireless activities of the king had made his authority felt everywhere. He called the States General but once during his reign. His personal agents, of high or low degree, lorded it over feudal nobles, provincial estates, and city governments.

Character of His Rule.

Triumph of the French Monarchy.

The spirit of resistance in the great feudal princes was broken. Of the lines that were left, that of Brittany was absorbed in the royal line by the marriage of the next king, Charles VIII, with the heiress of the dukes of Brittany, and that of Orléans came to the throne, after the death of Charles VIII, in the person of Louis XII. At the opening of the modern period the king of France was undisputed head of the government and lord of the country.

The "War of the Roses," 1455-1485.

Origin of the Dispute over the Crown.

In England the generation after the Hundred Years' War was a period of civil struggle, known as the "War of the Roses."* This was a struggle for the throne between two branches of the royal line, the Lancastrian and the Yorkist. As we have seen, the Lancastrian title was defective from the point of strict heredity. Henry IV had seized the throne and had then secured the complacent acquiescence of Parliament. In doing so, however, he had passed over the claims of an older line, represented by the young earl of March, who was descended from an older son of Edward III. These claims had now (by the middle of the fifteenth century) fallen by marriage to another branch of the royal line, that of the dukes of York. The popularity of Henry V and the national enthusiasm aroused by his successful war in France prevented the bringing forward of these claims; it was certain, however, that they would be revived if the Lancastrian rule should become unpopular. This situation was produced by the minority and the weak rule of Henry VI.

Lancastrians and Yorkists.

* This name was invented by later chroniclers of the Tudor period, based on the supposition that the Yorkist and Lancastrian families used as emblems respectively the white and the red rose. The use of the red rose as a Lancastrian badge comes in with the Tudor family; the idea of the opposition of the roses seems to have been derived from the practice of the Tudor monarchs in adopting a double rose, red and white, to indicate that they had inherited both Yorkist and Lancastrian claims.

There is another aspect to the War of the Roses which needs to be considered. It may be regarded as the last struggle of the great nobles against the growing power of the national government, and it corresponds in that respect to the contemporaneous movement in France. Everywhere in western Europe feudalism as a system of government was disappearing; the great lords retained their social pre-eminence, their economic advantages in the ownership of land, and to a considerable extent their private jurisdiction over tenants and retainers; their political rôle was disappearing before the encroachments of the national royal government. In England there were a few great families, raised far above the ranks of the ordinary nobility by their possession of vast estates. This was the result of a concentration of lands and titles through intermarriage and inheritance that had been going on among the upper ranks since the middle of the fourteenth century. As in France, most of these families were connected with the royal line; their power, however, rested not upon the overlordship of whole provinces, but upon their landed wealth and the maintenance of armed bands of retainers, who wore the livery or badge of their lord and fought in his private quarrels. The battles of the War of the Roses were fought mainly by these forces, and the devastation in their ranks and the extinction of great families in the course of this bloody struggle broke the power of the higher nobility. In this sense, then, the War of the Roses is the last gasp of the feudal nobility in England.

The War of the Roses as a Feudal Struggle.

The Great Barons in England.

The Last Struggle of the Baronage.

We may pass rather rapidly over the incidents in the struggle. Henry VI was less than a year old when in 1422 he succeeded to the claims of his father to the thrones of England and of France. For a time his father's brother, the wise duke of Bedford, carried on the war in France with success and maintained good government in England. On his death in 1435, however, the English policy was unsuccessful in both directions: the French were steadily winning back their

Incidents of the War of the Roses.

territory, and the government at home was disturbed by factional quarrels of the great nobles. When Henry VI came of age, therefore, the Lancastrian rule had already lost its popularity, and was the object of popular discontent and of factional opposition. The party in power in the court had advocated peace with France, as a means of saving something of the English possessions there, and had negotiated the marriage of Henry VI with a French princess, Margaret of Anjou. This gave the factious nobles an opportunity to appeal to national feeling against the government, and to lay the blame of the French losses on the king and his French wife. Added to this was the discontent and restlessness in the country at large, due to the inefficient government and to heavy taxes.

Decline of the Lancastrian Rule.

The French Marriage.

All these forces of opposition, the selfish clique of the great nobles, the outraged national feeling, and the demands for better government, naturally found a leader in the Yorkist claimant to the throne. This was Richard, duke of York, representative, as we have seen, of an older line than that of the Lancastrians. The situation was made worse by the intermittent madness of Henry VI, which began to afflict him after 1453. Parliament and the nobles insisted that Richard of York be made regent, the queen resisted because she feared his pretensions to the crown. The conflict went on in this form until 1460, when Richard of York formally asserted his right to the throne, and Parliament recognized him as regent for Henry VI and as heir to the throne on his death. Henry VI and Margaret had a son, Edward, prince of Wales, and the high-spirited queen refused to submit to his disinheritance. She took up arms and defeated the Yorkists in a battle in which Richard of York was slain and his younger son murdered in cold blood after the battle. The next year (1461), however, the older son of Richard, Edward, who had become duke of York on his father's death, defeated

Richard, Duke of York, Leader of the Opposition.

Richard of York Claims the Throne, 1460.

Defeated and Slain, 1461.

His Son Edward Becomes King, 1461.

Edward IV, 1461–1483.

the Lancastrian forces, occupied London, secured from a hastily summoned Parliament the title of Edward IV, and then met and destroyed the main Lancastrian force. Soon after he got his hands on the unhappy Henry VI and held him prisoner in the Tower of London. Margaret of Anjou, with her young son, escaped to the continent and took refuge at the court of the French king, Louis XI.

The reign of Edward IV was interrupted by a new civil war, caused by the unsatisfied ambition of his chief supporter. Richard Neville, earl of Warwick, was the most powerful of the great nobles; the Neville connection could raise a whole army of retainers, and it was largely by their help that the Yorkists had triumphed over the Lancastrian forces. Warwick naturally expected to have the leading place in the government of the young king, but Edward IV was determined to rule in his own person. Disappointed in his ambition, Warwick began to plot against the king; Edward IV turned on him and drove him and his supporters out of the kingdom. Warwick took refuge in France, where the wily Louis XI succeeded in bringing about an alliance between him and Margaret of Anjou, with the object of restoring the Lancastrian line. In 1470 Warwick returned to England, raised an army from his own retainers and from the Lancastrian party, and in turn drove Edward from England. Warwick then took the half-mad Henry VI from his imprisonment and restored him to the throne.

The Earl of Warwick, "the King-maker."

Warwick Restores Henry VI, 1470.

The restored Lancastrian rule was very brief. Edward IV had found refuge with Louis XI's bitter enemy, the duke of Burgundy; the next year (1471) he came back to England, defeated Warwick in battle, in which the earl himself was slain, and recovered the crown. In the battle of Tewksbury he defeated the forces which Margaret of Anjou was bringing to the support of Warwick, and after the battle the young prince of Wales, the hope of the Lancastrian line, was slain in cold blood. The unhappy Henry VI

Defeated and Slain, 1471.

was returned to his prison, and there shortly disappeared, murdered, it is supposed, by the agents of Edward IV. The rest of the reign of Edward IV was troubled only by the plotting of his brother George, duke of Clarence; Edward had him condemned by Parliament and secretly executed.* Edward IV died in 1483, leaving a young son to succeed him as Edward V.

Death of Henry VI.

This youth never reigned. His uncle, Richard, duke of Gloucester, seized control of the government, put the young king and his still younger brother, the little duke of York, into the Tower, where they were murdered, and induced the subservient Parliament to acknowledge him as King Richard III. In spite, however, of his efforts to win favor and popularity, the country turned against him. The direct Lancastrian line had been killed off, but the revolt found a leader in a member of a collateral branch, Henry Tudor, earl of Richmond, a descendant of John of Gaunt. In 1485 Richard III was defeated and slain in the last battle of the war of the Roses, the battle of Bosworth. The earl of Richmond became Henry VII, first of the Tudor line of monarchs.

Edward V Murdered, 1483.

Richard III, 1483–1485.

Henry VII, First of the Tudor Monarchs.

The outcome of thirty years of revolution, civil war, and assassination was the Tudor despotism. The extinction of families and the confiscation of lands had broken the power of the great nobles. Parliament had become the subservient tool of the faction in power. The country, as represented by the substantial classes of the local landlords and the merchants of the cities, was heartily sick of violence and disorder and ready to accept a strong government. The Tudors were able to establish and maintain a strong personal rule without arousing any general protest. The older constitutional checks on the power of the

War of the Roses Leads to the Tudor Despotism.

* All of these crimes—the slaying of Edward, prince of Wales, after the battle of Tewksbury, the murder of Henry VI and of George, duke of Clarence—were attributed in later times to Richard III, but without good warrant.

monarch, consisting of legal limitations in the charters and statutes, and of the active participation of Parliament in the government, fell into abeyance, and for more than a century the English government was virtually an absolutism.

CHAPTER XXI

THE DECLINE OF THE TEMPORAL POWER OF THE PAPACY (1250–1500)

AT the beginning of the Middle Age it was the common belief that God had foreordained that the empire should never pass away, and that he had appointed the emperor to rule the world, giving him supreme authority over it. The emperor, therefore, based his authority on "divine right." In opposition to this imperial theory the pope, Gregory VII, formulated the papal theory, by which he claimed supreme temporal authority over the whole world; in place of the empire, the church was to be eternal; in place of the emperor, the pope was by divine right the ruler of the world, having the power to make and depose emperors and kings. A few popes, such as Gregory VII, Alexander III, and Innocent III, were able to realize approximately their ideal of temporal supremacy.

World Empire and World Church.

After the middle of the thirteenth century, however, the temporal power of the papacy declined. The pope was no longer the unchallenged arbiter, the "supernational" power of Europe. He ceased to dictate in the internal affairs of the countries, and to exercise a dominating influence in international matters. Both kings and peoples began to resent all papal interference in their political affairs. There were many indications that the pope was losing his hard-won position as temporal sovereign of the world.

Decline of the Papacy.

The chief cause of this decline in the temporal power of the pope is found in a corresponding increase in the power of secular rulers. (1) Feudalism broke down and the power passed into the hands of the king, who thereby became so much more powerful than his vassals that he was able to rule them and all his people without the aid of the pope. (2) International relations became clearer, being dominated by political and commercial interests, which permitted no papal interference. (3) There had grown up a national pride, a national spirit, which united king and people and made them quick and strong to resist any attempt which a foreigner might make to control them. Kings, no longer hampered by the rebellious resistance of their great vassals, found a strong support in their people. This newly developed sense of nationality served the kings as a basis for ambitious schemes and wars (for example, the wars which England waged with Ireland, with Scotland, and with France).

The Kings Become Strong, Do Not Need the Pope's Aid.

Cf. S. B., 175.

The first clear evidence that a new order of things had begun was furnished by the contest which Philip IV (1285–1314) of France had with the pope, Boniface VIII (1294–1303), and his successors. In France the particular question at issue was the right of the king to tax the property of the clergy for the support of the general government. In theory all ecclesiastical persons and possessions were exempt from secular taxation, but the pope frequently permitted temporal rulers to levy a tax on them for the aid of the state in times of public necessity. With the consent of the pope such taxes had been assessed to carry on the crusades, to make war on Frederick II, to put down heresy, and for various other purposes. It frequently happened, however, that the large sums raised in this way for the crusades went into the king's treasury and were spent in other ways. Toward the end of the thirteenth century Philip IV of France made heavy assessments on the French clergy for secular purposes. Boniface VIII, recognizing that the immunities and liberties of the church were thereby being destroyed, issued the famous bull *Clericis Laicos* (1296), strictly forbidding laymen to tax the possessions of the church for any purpose whatsoever. Philip retaliated by forbidding money to be carried out of France, thus cutting off the pope's income from that country.

Philip IV Humbles the Papacy.

"*Clericis Laicos*," 1296.

S. B., 162.

A bitter struggle involving the question of supremacy ensued. Boniface went so far as to summon the French clergy to a council at Rome for the purpose of dictating a settlement of all the disorders in France. In reply to this Philip first assembled his States General and assured himself of the support of his people against the pope, and then sent an embassy to Rome with a refusal and a warning. The pope was not disconcerted by this, but plied the ambassadors with the most extravagant statements of his secular power. On the heels of this he published the noted bull *Unam Sanctam* (1302), which is the classic mediæval expression of the papal claims to universal temporal sovereignty. In this bull Boniface declared that submission to the pope in temporal matters was necessary for salvation. Quite undaunted by this, Philip preferred a number of charges against Boniface and called for a general council to settle the quarrel. Boniface then published the ban against Philip and declared him deposed, but a month later (1303) Boniface was besieged in Anagni by the king's supporters and taken prisoner. He was personally maltreated, but a few days later set free. He died, however, the next month, probably from chagrin and anger caused by the indignities which had been heaped upon him. The victory of Philip was complete. Not only was Boniface humbled; his successors came so thoroughly under the control of Philip that the papal seat was removed to Avignon, on the borderland of France, where for about seventy years (1309–1377) the popes were under the influence of the French kings. As the duration of the papal residence at Avignon was about the same as that of the captivity of the Jews in Babylon, these seventy years are known in the history of the papacy as the "Babylonian captivity."

S. B., 164.
O., 67.
R., 134.

The Papacy at Avignon, 1309–1377, under French Influence.

In England also there were many indications that the opposition to papal domination was growing. In 1351 Parliament passed the "statute of provisors," forbidding the pope to appoint any one to a benefice or living in England during the life of the holder of the benefice. In 1353 Parliament also passed the "statute of præ-

English Opposition to Papacy.

munire," forbidding Englishmen to carry their cases before a foreign judge. This was meant to put a stop to the custom of appealing cases to the pope. Further proofs of the increasing resistance of the English are found in the refusal of Parliament to pay tribute to the pope, and in the support which Wyclif's attacks on the papacy found among the people.

In Germany also the pope met with a severe check. Heretofore the popes had resorted to force, and their contests with the emperors had been settled by an appeal to arms. But the long quarrel of the pope John XXII (1316–1335) with the emperor Ludwig of Bavaria (1314–1347) was a battle of books. The interesting and significant fact is that during this struggle a new theory of the sovereignty of the state and of its relation to the church was proposed. In a book called the *Defensor Pacis* ("Defender of Peace"), written about 1324, Marsilius of Padua declared that the people are the state and hence may decide on the form of government which they wish; the church is subject to the state in all things; the bishop of Rome has no more authority than any other bishop; and the controlling power in the church is a general council composed of the whole body of Christians. The failure of Boniface VIII to defeat Philip IV of France showed that the papacy lacked the power to enforce its claims; the aim of Marsilius was to destroy the theory on which those claims were based.

Opposition in Germany.

S. B., 157.

Marsilius of Padua.

Defensor Pacis.

S. B., 165, 166.

The residence of the popes at Avignon and their consequent subservience to the interests of the French king diminished the papal prestige. Throughout the Hundred Years' War the English regarded the popes as the allies of France, and likewise the Germans during the struggle of Ludwig of Bavaria with John XXII identified the papacy with France. As a matter of fact, the popes of the period were all Frenchmen, and French in their sympathies, and instead of impartially aiding all governments alike they seemed to be in the service of the French kings. Furthermore, at Avignon the papal income was not so great as it had been at

"French" Popes.

R., 210.

Rome, while the erection of suitable buildings and the maintenance of the papal court necessitated the expenditure of greater sums than ever before. All Christendom began to grumble loudly at the heavy taxes of various kinds which the popes now levied. This taxation called forth the severest criticisms of the papal court, which was charged with luxury and avarice. Protests and legislation were, however, all in vain, for the pope continued to levy larger sums on all Christian countries.

Papal Taxation.

Cf. S. B., 163. R., 212, 213.

The "Babylonian captivity" was followed by the great schism. In 1377 Gregory XI was induced to move his court back to Rome, where he died the next year. During the absence of the popes Rome had decayed rapidly. The cardinals, a majority of whom were French, were dissatisfied with the city and wished to return to Avignon, where life had been far more comfortable. The new pope, Urban VI, refused to leave Rome and showed scant courtesy to the French cardinals, who finally seceded from him and elected a new pope, Clement VII, who returned to Avignon. The seceding cardinals alleged that the election of Urban VI was invalid because the papal palace, in which they had met in conclave, had been surrounded by a Roman mob, some of whom had even forced their way into the conclave and threatened the cardinals with death, unless they should immediately elect a Roman or at least an Italian as pope; in terror for their lives and in order to quiet the mob they had hastily gone through the form of electing Urban VI, thinking that he would be honest enough to recognize the invalidity of his election.

The Great Schism, 1388–1417.

S. B., 167. O., 68. R., 211.

Whatever the facts in the case were, the result was deplorable. For the next twenty-nine years there were always two men (a part of the time even three) claiming to be pope, exercising the papal functions and prerogatives, and demanding obedience from all the Christian world. Each of the popes claimed the right to create cardinals and to confirm archbishops, bishops, and abbots, so that there were two colleges of cardinals, one in Rome, the other in Avignon, and for

Two Popes.

most of the high positions in the church there were two claimants—two men contesting for the same bishopric or monastery. Each pope attempted to collect all the ecclesiastical dues, and each excommunicated and anathematized the other with all his followers and supporters. France naturally supported Clement VII, and England, because of the Hundred Years' War, quite as naturally favored Urban VI.

No Legal Way of Ending the Schism.

S. B., 168.

Such a state of affairs was unendurable, but there was no legal way of bringing it to an end. For some years the matter was discussed, but so long as the pope's headship of the church was held there was no way out of the difficulty. People began, however, to examine the grounds on which the papal claims were based, and this examination led to a denial of the papal headship. It was asserted that the whole church was superior to the pope, and that therefore a general council of the church was qualified to act as a court, to call the two claimants before it, and to decide between them. There were many who refused to accept such a solution and doggedly stood by the papal theory that the pope was supreme and could be judged by no one. But, as the situation grew worse, and no other way seemed possible, the two colleges of cardinals finally agreed to call a general council. It met in Pisa in 1409, and was largely attended. After solemnly declaring its competency to try the two popes, it summoned them to appear before it for trial. Neither of the popes recognized its authority, and neither obeyed its summons. The council then deposed them and elected another, Alexander V (1409–1410). This action only increased the scandal and confusion and made the schism worse, for, as neither of the deposed popes yielded, there were now three popes.

Council of Pisa, 1409.

S. B., 169, 170.

Council of Constance, 1414.

This situation led to the calling of another council, this time at Constance, in 1414. It was attended by hundreds of persons from all parts of Europe and was a truly international assemblage. Although called for the purpose of ending the schism, there were two other important matters to come before it. It was expected to deal with the heresy of John Huss in Bohemia, and to reform the church "in its head and in its members." It soon disposed of the question of heresy by condemning Huss and handing him over to the state to be burned (1415). The council was then divided over the programme to be pursued. The reform party demanded that the church should first be reformed, after which the pope should be elected. The opposing party insisted that the church should first have a head in order that he might direct the reforms.* The latter party won and the council determined to end the schism by electing a pope. This council was more cautious than the council at Pisa had been, and planned to clear the way for the new election by first assuring itself of the removal of the three existing popes. Pope John XXIII, who had called the council, was frightened at its tone, and, fearing that he would be deposed, fled in disguise. Fortunately for the council, he was overtaken, brought back to Constance, and imprisoned. The leadership then passed definitely into the hands of the council. A long list of charges was made against John and he was tried and deposed. As he was a prisoner in the hands of the council, he was unable to offer any resistance to it and soon submitted. Negotiations were

S. B., 171. R., 213, 214.

Heresy.

Question of Reforms.

* The following is a list of the popes and antipopes during the schism. The names of those who are recognized by the church as true popes are in italics.

Roman Popes	Antipopes at Avignon
Gregory XI (1370–1378) returned to Rome, 1377.	Clement VII (1378–1394).
Urban VI (1378–1389).	
Boniface IX (1389–1404).	Benedict XIII (1394–1417) deposed in 1417.
Innocent VIII (1404–1406).	
Gregory XII (1406–1415) resigned in 1415, but the church reckons his resignation from 1409.	

The Line of the Council of Pisa

Alexander V (1409–1410).
John XXIII (1410–1416).

The Line of the Council of Constance

Martin V (1417–1431), whose election ended the schism.

begun with Gregory XII, the Roman pope, who was induced to resign. Benedict XIII, the pope at Avignon, however, stubbornly refused to yield, and, as he still had a numerous following, especially in Spain, nothing could be done. Finally, in 1417, the Spaniards were induced to desert his cause. The council then deposed him and ended the schism by electing Martin V (1417–1431).

Martin V.

The council was then free to address itself to the question of reform. It was immediately apparent, however, that no thoroughgoing reforms would be made. There was no agreement in the council as to whether the council or the pope should conduct the reforms, nor was there agreement as to what reforms should be undertaken. The cardinals and bishops generally did not wish to be "reformed," because nearly all the reforms proposed had for their aim the diminution of the income of the clergy. At length, after much discussion, the reform party had to content itself (1) with a decree that general councils should be held every ten years, and (2) with enumerating certain matters in which reforms were desirable. These matters were nearly all of a financial character, concerning chiefly the pope's power to dispose of ecclesiastical offices and benefices, his use of the income and property of the churches, the sale of indulgences, and, in general, the papal custom of getting all the money possible out of the churches. The list of reforms demanded shows conclusively that the wide-spread dissatisfaction with the church was due chiefly to the financial burdens which the clergy placed on the people. The whole matter of reform was left to the discretion of the pope, and the council was dissolved without having done anything but end the schism.

Reforms.

S. B., 172, 173.

Martin V, after some hesitation, eventually called another general council, to meet at Basel, in 1431. The chief business to come before it was the question of the heresy in Bohemia, a matter which it finally settled by making a very sensible compromise with the conservative Bohemian party. The council then engaged in a quarrel with the pope over the question of authority. It lost the

Council of Basel, 1431–1449.

Cf. O., 69.

favor of Europe when it deposed him and renewed the schism by electing an antipope. Such ill-advised action was fatal to the prestige which it had gained by its promise of reforms. The pope cleverly made separate agreements with the chief governments, granting them certain advantages, and in this way he deprived the council of all support. It dragged its aimless and idle existence along until 1449, when it yielded to the pope and dissolved itself. This ended the period which is commonly called the "conciliar epoch," for thereafter people had very little confidence in the efficiency of a general council. Appeals for a new council were fruitless, because the popes always refused to call another. In 1459 Pius II forbade all appeals to a general council, and even condemned them as heretical. The idea, however, did not die out. Luther renewed the appeal, and the great council of Trent (1545–1563) was summoned as a last resort with the purpose originally of effecting a compromise with the Lutherans and of putting an end to the schism begun by Luther. Protestantism, it may be said, accepted the conciliar theory, while the Roman Catholic church finally rejected it, promulgating in 1870 the decree of papal infallibility, according to which the pope is the supreme authority in the church, in no way amenable to any power on earth.

Appeals to a Council Forbidden.

S. B., 174.

After its victory over the conciliar idea the papacy entered on a new period, during which it was animated by the spirit of the Renaissance. The popes were drawn into the political struggles of Italy and devoted themselves to the task of increasing their territory and power. In this they were so absorbed that they seemed to be temporal princes rather than the head of the church. They kept a standing army and were frequently engaged in war with their political enemies. They achieved undying fame by becoming munificent patrons of art and learning, and by gathering about them a host of artists and literary men. They spent incredible sums in the erection of buildings, and for manuscripts, pictures, statues, precious stones, and all kinds of works of art. Their court was brilliant and they lived in magnificent

Renaissance Popes.

splendor. It became the custom for each pope to enrich the members of his family, conferring on them titles and providing them with incomes from the possessions of the church (nepotism). To the loud demands for reform and retrenchment the popes replied by multiplying their expenditures. They put the world under contribution, by levying taxes of various kinds and under different names, so that gold flowed in streams from all lands to Rome. For this, however, they paid a ruinous price; they lost not only the affection but even the confidence and respect of a large part of Europe.

S. B., 177, 178.

Nothing more clearly shows the ill-repute into which the papacy sank during this period than the biting epigrams and stories—whether true or not—which were circulated to the disparagement of the popes. Innocent VIII (1484–1493) was popularly charged with selling safe-conducts to robbers, and his treasurer ironically commended him for doing so by saying: "Your Holiness does well, for God willeth not the death of any sinner, but rather that all should *pay* and live." A Roman wit declared that it was quite proper to call this same Innocent VIII "father" (pope means father) because he had eight sons and as many daughters. A keen epigram was coined about Alexander VI: "Alexander sells the keys, the altars, and Christ; well, he has the right to sell them, because he bought them." It was reported of Leo X that after his election he said, "I mean to enjoy my pontificate," and that he later spoke of Christianity as a very lucrative fable. The popes derived a large income from the sale of offices and indulgences, and Sixtus IV was credited with saying: "A pope needs only pen and ink to get all the money he wants."

Epigrams about the Popes.

S. B., 179.

Although we are grateful to the popes of that period for their patronage of arts and learning, their artistic triumphs did not reconcile the people who had to pay for them. On the contrary, the people everywhere began to ask why they should furnish the money to support the pope, his family, and his court in luxury, and to

Rising Discontent with the Papacy.

pay for his buildings and works of art. This discontent increased and produced bitter and revolutionary criticism of the church. The grounds for dissatisfaction were various, yet the chief one was, without doubt, the papal taxation. Almost all the complaints against the church—and they were many—were essentially financial in character. Threatening voices were heard: "The time is coming when your possessions will be seized and divided as if they were the possessions of an enemy." In Germany especially the burdens of papal taxation caused such deep and wide-spread dissatisfaction that the revolt of Luther was promptly popular and successful.

Papal Taxation.

S. B., 177, 178.

We began our study of the Middle Age with an empire that claimed to be universal. No limits in time or space were set to the Roman empire. Its aim was to make the world one politically. It strove to destroy nations and nationality. But the task was too great for it. In the long struggle that ensued nationality won and the peoples of Europe grouped themselves together as nations and kingdoms. In the same way the church claimed to be universal. Its aim was to make the whole world one in religion. It strove to crush out all independent thought and to confine the individual, in his thinking, to prescribed limits. At the cost of much bloodshed and persecution the church was able during the Middle Age to suppress heresy, as all independent thinking was called. But at the very threshold of the Modern Period the individual, in the person of Martin Luther, asserted his right to interpret the Bible for himself. The course of events in the Middle Age showed that a world empire, whether of bodies or souls, was impossible of realization.

CHAPTER XXII

GERMANY FROM 1250 TO 1500

In the contest for supremacy between the empire and the papacy the empire, as we already know, was ruined. After the death of Frederick II (1250) it existed merely in name.

The Empire Ruined.

S. B., 147.

The kings of Germany saw that the union of Germany and Italy was impossible, and, for the most part, wisely remained at home and permitted Italy to go its own way. Rudolf of Hapsburg (1273–1291), recognizing that Italy had caused the ruin of his predecessors, compared it with a lion's cave, "all the tracks going in and none coming out." He made peace with the pope and with Charles of Anjou, king of Sicily, and acknowledged the papal claims, thus surrendering all for which the emperors for two hundred years had fought. A few of his successors did indeed attempt to renew the imperial claims in Italy, but their efforts were lamentably weak.

The "Idea" Still Existed.

S. B., 158, 159.

Nevertheless the idea of a world-wide empire did live on, and men who were otherwise sane and sensible appealed to the magic of its name as if it were still the great power that it had once been. Thus, in 1338, Edward III of England sought the aid of the emperor Ludwig of Bavaria (1313–1347). At the diet of Coblenz (1338) Ludwig was seated on a lofty throne with the princes of Germany and the king of England below him. Edward III, who, you will remember, had just laid claim to the French crown, appealed to Ludwig against the king of France. Thereupon Ludwig pompously "proclaimed to all the crimes, disobedience, and wickedness of the king of France. And after he had declared that the king of France had broken his oath to the emperor, he published a decree of forfeiture against him and his followers." He then adjudged the crown of France to Edward III of England. To us the whole performance seems a huge farce, for the emperors had long since ceased to exercise any authority over the nations of France and England, and even in Germany they had become mere figureheads, without authority or force. Ludwig himself was absurdly weak, cowardly, and ineffectual. Unable to chastise his unruly subjects, he could not control even his own duchy. The mere thought of his disposing of the French crown or of interfering effectually in the affairs of France was absurd. This action of Ludwig had of course not the slightest effect on the course of events.

Although the idea of the empire still lived on, we may without loss omit further discussion of it and confine our attention entirely to the kingdom of Germany.* Instead of tracing the history of each king, however, it will be more profitable to describe certain movements and events which were of lasting importance. These were (1) the dissolution of Germany into a few hundred little sovereign principalities and a corresponding decline of the royal power, (2) the rise and growth of the Hapsburg family through the acquisition of extensive lands, (3) the selfish power of the seven electors, (4) the expansion of Germany to the east, (5) the development of the cities and the formation of leagues among them, (6) the founding of the power of the Hohenzollern family, and (7) the beginning of Switzerland.

Matters of Chief Interest.

During the last centuries of the Middle Age the political development in Germany was exactly the opposite of that in England and France. While the kings of those countries were destroying the power of their great vassals and building up a strong central government, the kings of Germany were losing more and more of their power, and their vassals were acquiring more and more sovereignty in their fiefs. That is, their fiefs were growing into sovereign principalities. This dissolution of Germany into a large number of small independent principalities was due in large

Royal Power Grows Weaker.

* S. B., Nos. 231–233 and 245–250, throw many interesting sidelights on the life of this period.

measure to a mistaken policy of the German kings—a policy with which we are already familiar. To carry out their imperial plans in Italy they needed more aid from their German vassals than feudal custom permitted them to demand. They were therefore reduced to the necessity of buying the military service of their vassals, who, taking advantage of the situation, demanded in return for their support of the imperial schemes a large increase in their power and independence. This price, although ruinous to the royal power, the kings of Germany felt constrained to pay. Time after time they bought the support of their vassals by surrendering to them some of their regalian rights.

Cause.

S. B., 136–139.

The rights most commonly demanded were the supreme judicial power, coinage, the establishment of markets, tolls, and the exemption from military service and from attendance upon the diet. Thus, in 1156, in order to obtain the support of his uncle, Henry "Ja-so-mir-Gott," and to smooth the way for his approaching expedition into Italy, Frederick I raised the mark of Austria to the rank of a duchy and gave it to his uncle and his wife, declaring "that (1) they and their children after them, whether sons or daughters, shall hold and possess it by hereditary right. If our uncle and his wife should die without children, they may leave the duchy by will to whomsoever they desire. (2) We decree also that no person, great or small, shall presume to exercise any of the rights of justice within the duchy without the consent and permission of the duke. (3) The duke of Austria does not owe any service to the empire except to attend, when summoned, such diets as may be held in Bavaria. (4) He is not bound to join the emperor on any campaign except such as may be directed against parts of the empire neighboring to Austria." Such broad concessions left the king with little authority in the duchy of Austria.

Duchy of Austria, 1156.

S. B., 110.

Unfortunately this policy of surrendering crown rights for support and aid strengthened the feudal tendencies which were just then powerful in Germany. Feudalism, a century and a half slower in its development in Germany than elsewhere, was in fact just reaching the point of domination there. During the reign of Frederick I the feudalization of the government of Germany was completed. From the days of Charlemagne to about 1180 all the royal officials (dukes, margraves, landgraves, palatine counts, and counts, the counts forming by far the most numerous class) ranked as princes of the realm and were by virtue of their office members of the diet. Frederick I, however, changed this about 1180. From that time not the holding of an office but the holding of an important fief directly from the king made a man a member of the diet. Thereafter the diet was composed not of the king's officials but of his tenants-in-chief. In this way the lay princes of the realm were reduced from a few hundreds to sixteen (nine dukes, two palatine counts, three margraves, one landgrave, and one count). The king, however, had the power to increase this number by creating new fiefs and conferring them upon whom he would. The ecclesiastical princes (archbishops, bishops, abbots, and abbesses) numbered more than sixty, and by virtue of their numbers had a preponderating influence in the diet.

The Government Feudalized, about 1180.

Make-up of the Diet.

Frederick II was even more prodigal of the crown rights than his predecessors had been. In 1220, wishing to make his son king of Germany, he bought the support of the ecclesiastical princes by granting them such extensive regalian rights as to make them little kings, in fact if not in name, and in 1232 he granted similar rights to the secular princes also. The time soon came when the princes could pillage the crown with impunity, for after the death of Frederick II (1250) there was a period, called the interregnum, during which there were several kings, although none of them was everywhere recognized. The death of Otto IV (1254) gave his rival, William of Holland, a clear field, and William was slowly winning recognition when he was killed by some Dutch peasants with whom he was at war. Rival kings were

Frederick II Gave away Crown Rights.

S. B., 136–139.

The Interregnum.

then elected, Richard of Cornwall, brother of Henry III of England, and Alfonso of Castile. Neither of them really exercised any authority in Germany. In fact, Richard spent very little time in Germany and Alfonso never even visited that country at all. Taking advantage of the situation, the nobles, both lay and clerical, seized all the crown lands they could, as well as the crown rights. Consequently, when a king was finally elected (1273), he found that his new honor brought with it little income. For three reasons the acquisition of land in his own name and not in the name of the crown became his chief interest. (1) He was compelled to defray the expenses of his government out of his private income; he would therefore wish to increase his income as much as possible. (2) Some of the princes of Germany had become possessed of so large a measure of sovereignty that the king had very little authority. So, if he wished to be more than a mere figurehead in German affairs, he must have enough force to impose his will on the princes. This he saw he could do only by making himself more powerful than they. (3) The German crown was elective. In order that his son might follow him in the kingship he must make his family so powerful that the electors could not refuse to choose his son. Accordingly we find that after 1273 all the kings of Germany have the same policy: each one of them attempted to enrich his family by getting possession of all the territory he could. Whenever it was possible he did this at the expense of the crown. That is, he gave the crown lands to his own family, thus impoverishing the crown still more. So long as his family held the crown, that would make little difference, but a king chosen from another family would find the crown's resources diminished. To justify himself in this policy he could say that the crown was already hopelessly weak, and that a strong family would eventually make the crown strong.

Nobles Seize Lands and Rights of the Crown.

Rudolf of Hapsburg Gives Lands to his family.

S. B., 150.

Policy of the Kings toward Their Families.

The most conspicuous example of this policy is furnished by the house of Hapsburg. When Rudolf, count of Hapsburg,

Note to Map XVIII.—The heavy black line is the boundary of the Holy Roman Empire, which still existed theoretically, although it had ceased to have meaning as a political organization. Already by the end of the fifteenth century the outlying parts were drifting away from it. The Netherlands with Luxemburg had come into the possession of the French dukes of Burgundy (later into the hands of the Hapsburgs), and formed virtually a distinct territory. Lorraine and Franche Comté (largely French in population) were being drawn into the circle of French political influence. The Swiss Confederation was virtually a separate state. The parts of northern Italy which were reckoned as belonging to the empire (Milan, Florence, etc.) were in fact independent states. On the east, Bohemia was to come under the control of the Austrian Hapsburgs and form part of the Austria-Hungary of later times. Thus the empire was being reduced to the territory corresponding to modern Germany; even within the German part there was no real political unity, but each prince and each free city was virtually independent of control from the nominal head, the emperor.

The splitting up of Germany into virtually independent states had gone so far by 1500 that it would be impossible in a small map to show all the divisions (Shepard, *Atlas*, pp. 86, 87, gives a good impression of this condition). Note the seven electoral principalities (underlined): namely, the three archbishoprics of Mainz, Trier, and Cologne; and the four secular states, the kingdom of Bohemia, the Palatinate of the Rhine, the electorate of Saxony, and the mark of Brandenburg. Other principalities of considerable size were: the duchy of Bavaria, the duchy of Saxony, the duchy of Brunswick, the county of Nassau, etc. There were a great many other counties and lordships of smaller extent, and in addition the ecclesiastical lords, archbishops, bishops, and abbots ruled as princes over the fiefs attached to their office. Note the large number of free or imperial cities, which were virtually self-governing city republics: Basel, Strassburg, Worms, Frankfort, Cologne, Bremen, Hamburg, Lübeck, Augsburg, Nuremberg, etc.

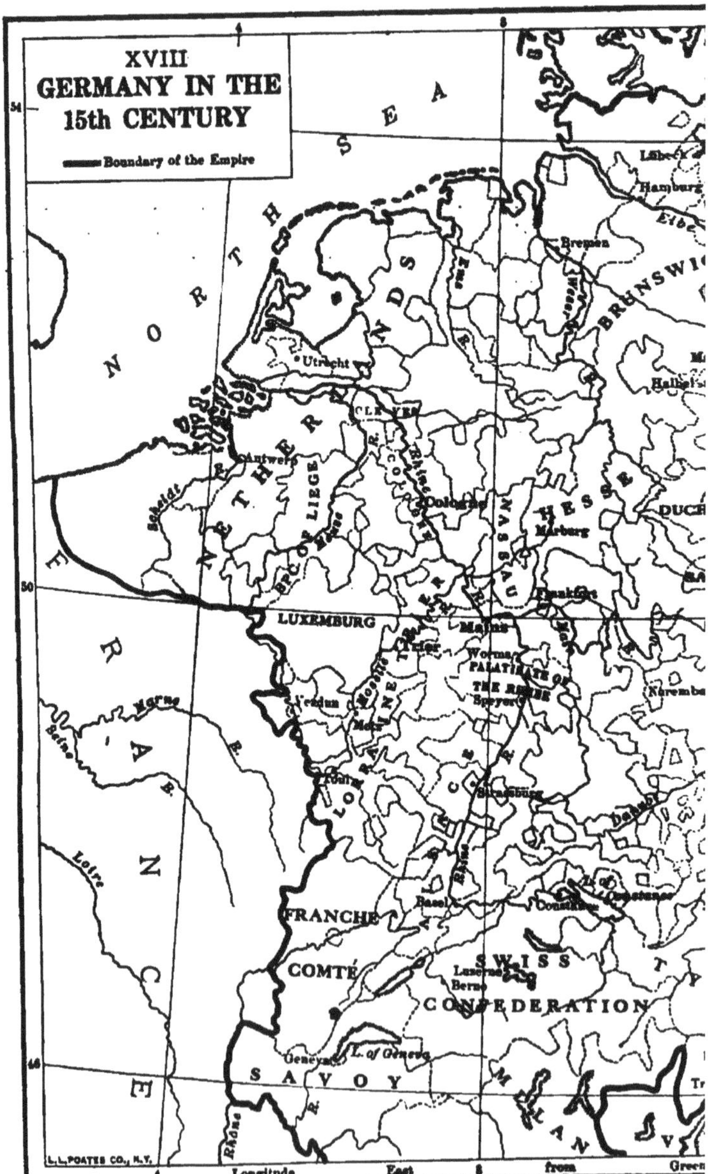

XVIII
GERMANY IN THE
15th CENTURY
Boundary of the Empire
NORTH SEA
NETHERLANDS
Utrecht
Antwerp
CLEVES
BPC OF LIEGE
Cologne
NASSAU
HESSE
Marburg
Frankfort
Bremen
Hamburg
Lübeck
Elbe
Weser
Ems
BRUNSWIC
Halbe
DUCH
Scheldt
Meuse
Rhine
LUXEMBURG
Mainz
Trier
Worms
PALATINATE OF THE RHINE
Speyer
Moselle
Verdun
Metz
LORRAINE
Strassburg
ALSACE
Danube
Nuremb
FRANCE
Marne
Seine
Loire
Basel
Constance
L. of Constance
FRANCHE COMTÉ
SWISS CONFEDERATION
Lucerne
Berne
Geneva
L. of Geneva
SAVOY
MILAN
Rhône
Longitude East from Green
L. L. POATES CO., N.Y.

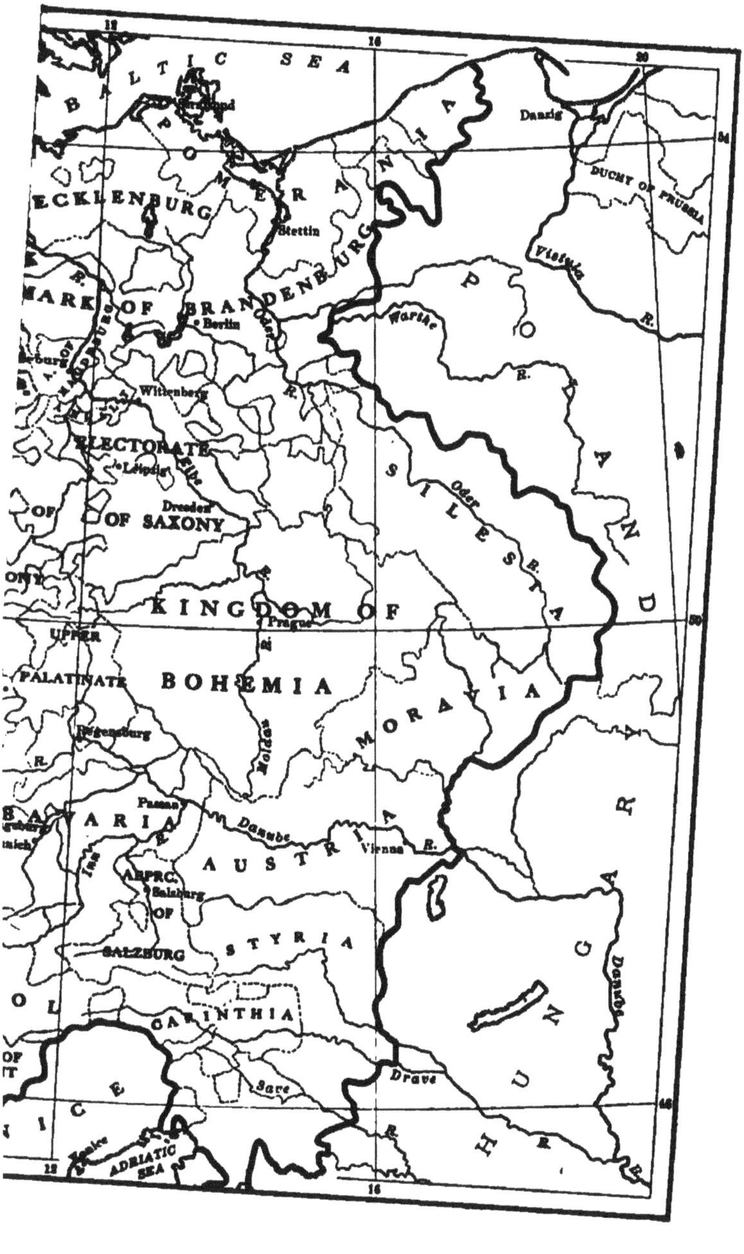

12
16
20
54
50
46
BALTIC SEA
Stralsund
POMERANIA
Stettin
Danzig
DUCHY OF PRUSSIA
Vistula
R.
POLAND
MARK OF BRANDENBURG
Berlin
Oder
R.
Warthe
R.
Wittenberg
ELECTORATE
Leipzig
Elbe
Dresden
OF SAXONY
SILESIA
Oder
R.
KINGDOM OF
BOHEMIA
Prague
UPPER
PALATINATE
Regensburg
Moldau
MORAVIA
Passau
Danube
R.
Vienna
AUSTRIA
Inn
Salzburg
SALZBURG
STYRIA
CARINTHIA
Drave
Save
R.
HUNGARY
Danube
R.
Venice
ADRIATIC
SEA

was made king of Germany (1273–1291) his family,* although not obscure, was by no means powerful. He was confronted with a difficult task. Many parts of Germany were infested with robber barons, the roads were insecure, the coinage was debased, and the crown lands and rights had been appropriated by the nobles. To recover these he made strenuous efforts. Although the princes, in solemn diet, awarded them to him and told him it was his right and duty to recover them, they stubbornly refused to surrender those which they themselves had seized. Nevertheless, by cleverness and a series of lucky events he acquired possession of some of the largest principalities in Germany. Among these were the duchies of Austria, Styria, Carinthia, and Tyrol, and the kingdoms of Bohemia, Poland, and Hungary. Although not all of these remained in continuous possession of the Hapsburgs, the family nevertheless became so powerful that it practically acquired hereditary possession of the German crown, for after 1438 it furnished all the German kings except two.

Growth of the Hapsburgs.

S. B., 146, 148, 151.

S. B., 150.

Although the Hapsburg family became rich and powerful, it could not make the crown strong. It was not able to arrest the process of disintegration which the German kings, especially Frederick Barbarossa and Frederick II had done so much to advance. The nobles continued to increase their sovereign powers until German unity was destroyed. After 1250 Germany disintegrated rapidly, and

Germany Dismembered.

* His ancestors had been active in acquiring land, and their possessions were scattered over northern Switzerland and southern Germany. Rudolf was so notorious a "grabber" that it was a common saying that if God should vacate his throne for a few minutes Rudolf would carry if off. And the bishop of Basel, on hearing of the election of Rudolf, exclaimed: "Sit tight on your throne, O Lord, or Rudolf will crowd you off." The result of this land-grabbing policy, which has characterized the Hapsburgs ever since, is to be seen in the motley make-up of the realm of the Hapsburgs, the empire of Austria-Hungary, which was composed of about a dozen different nationalities that have been subjected during the last six hundred years. And it was this same land-grabbing policy of the Hapsburgs—the seizure of little states in the Balkans, Bosnia, and Herzegovina in 1908, and the determination to seize Servia—that led directly to the Great War in 1914.

at the close of the Middle Age (*i. e.*, 1500) it consisted of about 350 little states, each enjoying a large measure of sovereignty.

Golden Bull, 1356.

S. B., 160.

In 1356 Charles IV published the golden bull, in which he attempted to fix as in a constitution the rights and status of the princes. He saw that Germany was no longer a monarchy but a federation of sovereign states. This document shows in the clearest manner possible that sovereignty had passed from the crown to the princes. It deals chiefly not with the important elements of a government, but with matters of etiquette. It confirms the sovereign rights of the princes, but passes in silence over the rights of the crown, which were, in fact, almost negligible.

The Seven Electors.

S. B., 153–156.
S. B., 149.

Although all the princes of Germany were virtually sovereign in their lands, there were seven of them who quite overtopped all the others. These were the archbishops of Mainz, Cologne, and Treves, the king of Bohemia, the margrave of Brandenburg, the duke of Saxony, and the count palatine on the Rhine. They owed their high distinction to the fact that, about the middle of the thirteenth century, in some way—no one knows exactly how—they had acquired the sole right of voting for the king. Hence they were called the seven electors. They took advantage of their position to sell their votes outright and to squeeze out of the candidate all the advantages they could. No elector would cast his vote until he had reached an agreement with the candidate as to the price to be paid for it. Some of these agreements have been preserved for us and show the shameless manner in which all the electors, ecclesiastical as well as lay, trafficked in their votes. They also secured for themselves a controlling voice in the management of affairs by binding the king not to take any important action without first obtaining their consent, for which, of course, they always demanded some kind of pay. It was due largely to this selfish policy of the electors that the crown remained weak and unable to build up a strong royal power.

If we should look only at the political history of Germany

during the period from 1250 to 1500 we should find it trivial and dull. All, from the king down, were absorbed in a narrow, selfish policy, to the complete ruin of the central power. But there were certain things being accomplished in a quiet way which were to be of lasting benefit to Germany. The first of these was the expansion of Germany to the east. Since the days of Charlemagne the German frontier had been steadily advanced to the east at the cost of the independence of many Slavic tribes, who occupied all of what is now Germany east of the Elbe. The princes who held lands along the frontier endeavored to conquer and germanize the neighboring Slavs, and the church eagerly devoted itself to the task of Christianizing them. Merchants, colonists, and monks did their share of the work. The German order, having failed to obtain a permanent place in Palestine, saved itself for a while from degenerating and from the fate of the Templars by establishing itself among the Slavs on the east Baltic. The order became a little state, extended its boundaries by conquest, and ruled over the conquered peoples with an iron hand. Weakened, however, by a long and unsuccessful conflict with Poland, it came to an end in the sixteenth century, and the margrave of Brandenburg (a member of the Hohenzollern family) inherited its lands.

Expansion of Germany to the East.

S. B., 298.
O., 58.

The political disunion in Germany had at least one compensation, for it fostered the development of a large number of cities. These cities were governed by their lord (archbishop, bishop, abbot, duke, count), but from the twelfth century many of them succeeded in freeing themselves from this arbitrary rule and acquired the right to govern themselves. All cities which governed themselves were called "free cities." In all of them the government was much the same in form, consisting of a mayor, or burgomaster, and a board of aldermen. In Germany, as elsewhere in Europe, the towns represent the new and modern element, which was rapidly changing feudal society and institutions. Before the growing power of the cities feudalism was disappearing, but not without a hard

German Cities.

S. B., 301–325.
R., 118, 119.

The Form of City Government.

struggle. The lords resented the increasing wealth and independence of the towns and often made war on them. Although the nobles won all the battles in the open field, they could not take the cities. The increasing wealth of the citizens gave them an advantage over the nobility, and their power grew while that of the nobles declined. Of course these German cities did not claim to be independent states as the cities in Italy did. They recognized that they were a part of Germany and that they were under a lord, but they were intent on reducing the extent of their obligations to him as much as possible. From the fact that some of the cities had the emperor for their lord they were called "imperial cities," while those which had another lord (duke, bishop, etc.) were called "provincial cities." Imperial cities enjoyed the distinction of being invited to send representatives to the diet to assist in its deliberations.

Imperial Cities.
S. B., 310, 311.

As the cities were engaged chiefly in industry and commerce it was of the greatest importance to them that the land should have peace. The weakness of the central government and the spirit of violence which animated the nobility, many of whom were "robber barons," forced the cities to take measures to protect themselves. The Rhine league was formed (1254) to clear the Rhine of robbers and to make it safe for the merchants with their goods to pass from one city to another. The Hanseatic league was formed by the cities around the Baltic for a similar purpose. It had its origin in a local agreement between Lubeck and Hamburg for the mutual protection of their merchants (1241). Fortunately for these cities, there were no great princes in northern Germany to hamper their growth and development. The league served its purpose so well that all the towns of the north were soon glad to become members of it. Under its protection an extensive commerce was developed, from which the cities grew rich. Although at first the league's only object was the protection of commerce, it soon became necessary for it to interfere in political matters. It was strong enough to carry on a success-

Rhine League, 1254.
S. B. 318, 319. O., 59.
The Hanseatic League, 1241.
S. B., 320–325.

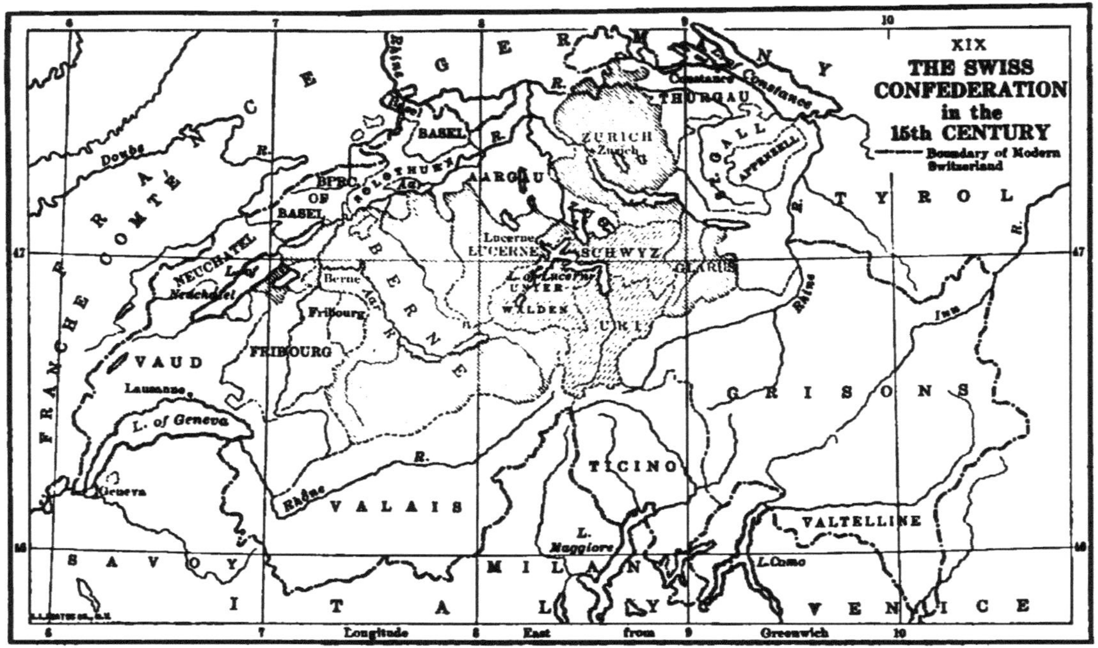

Note to Map XIX.—This shows the growth of the Swiss Confederation in its early stages. The first union was that of Uri, Schwyz, and Unterwalden in 1315;-about 1350 this was joined by the five cantons of Berne, Luzerne, Zurich, Glarus,

ful war with Denmark, and for some years it was the undisdisputed master of the whole north. In the fifteenth century the league began to decline in power. The Baltic cities had been fortunate in being near the rich herring fisheries along the coast of Sweden. But in the first half of the fifteenth century the herring ceased to enter the Baltic and were to be found in large numbers only along the coast of Holland. The commercial importance of the league declined still further when new and more important trade routes were discovered and developed. The cities gradually lost also their political independence and importance, and in the course of time were absorbed by the governments of the countries in which they were situated.

The Hohenzollerns Acquire Brandenburg, 1411.

S. B., 160a, 160b.

We have yet to record a fact, which, without particular importance at the time, was destined later to lead to the political regeneration and unification of Germany. The mark of Brandenburg, being flat, sandy, and marshy, was not a valuable possession. Its chief attraction was the political influence which it conferred on its possessor, who thereby became one of the seven electors. When the electoral family died out, in 1411, the mark was granted to Frederick of Hohenzollern, burgrave of Nuremberg, who now became an elector. He and his successors built up a political power in the mark which, in the nineteenth century, became the ruling power (Prussia) in Germany.

Beginning of Switzerland.

The Forest Cantons.

S. B., 152, 152a

In the southern part of the empire we find the beginnings of another movement which was to lead to the establishment of a separate and independent state, subsequently known as Switzerland. The troubles and violence of the times led the communities of the three forest cantons (counties) Schwyz, Uri, and Unterwalden, to renew and enlarge a former agreement to aid one another against all enemies and lawbreakers. The special point for which they contended was that they belonged directly to the crown and had no lord but the emperor. In the course of time they were joined by other cantons and their power began to be felt. They had to contend against two families which tried to get possession of them. The Hapsburgs tried it first, but in three famous battles the Swiss peasants were more than a match for the best armies that the duke could bring into the field. Then their hard-earned independence was threatened by Charles the Bold of Burgundy, but, with the aid of their allies, they cut his army to pieces (1477, battle of Nancy) and Charles himself was slain. They remained nominally a part of the empire to the peace of Westphalia (1648), when their neutral independence was recognized.

CHAPTER XXIII

THE REMAINING COUNTRIES OF EUROPE

We have given a somewhat detailed account of England, France, and Germany, because during the Middle Age they were the leading powers of Europe. For the sake of completeness there is added here a brief account of the minor countries also.

1. Bohemia.—Since the days of Charlemagne the German kings had regarded Bohemia as a part of their kingdom. In 1204 Philip of Suabia honored its duke by conferring on him the title of king, a title which Innocent III afterward confirmed. When this royal family became extinct there was a long struggle over the possession of the crown, but the Hapsburg family finally got it, and Bohemia remained a part of the Hapsburg's empire until its dissolution in 1919.

The Hapsburgs Acquire Bohemia.

On Bohemia, at the beginning of the fifteenth century, the eyes of all Europe were fixed because of the appearance there of the teachings of Wyclif under a slightly different form. As the wife of Richard II was a Bohemian princess, there was a good deal of intercourse between England and Bohemia. Among others, Bohemian students found their way to Oxford, imbibed the doctrines of Wyclif, and carried his writings back to Bohemia. Some of these writings fell into the hands of John Huss. After studying them he adopted their doctrines and began to teach them to his students in the university of Prague. He was soon charged with heresy, and the university, the city, and even the whole country were divided into two hostile camps, the one in support of him, the other against him. The Germans, of whom there were many in Bohemia, generally opposed him, while the Bohemians, who, in the flush of a growing national pride, had come to hate the Germans as foreigners, regarded Huss as a national hero and sup-

John Huss.

ported him with all the intensity of ardor born of race hatred. Under the influence of Germans, the Bohemians, like all the other Slavs lying along the eastern frontier of Germany, had been losing their nationality and becoming Germanized, but all Bohemia was now aroused in a vigorous reaction against this German influence, and supported Huss. The bitterness increased until Germans were no longer safe in Prague, and consequently both professors and students withdrew from Bohemia into Germany, where they gave a new impetus to learning.

The great council of Constance (1414–1417) then took the matter in hand. It summoned Huss into its presence, tried him, convicted him of heresy, and had him burned. His death caused an uprising in Bohemia. After he had been condemned as a heretic, many of the Bohemians, unwilling to support his cause further, remained faithful to the church. But others clung fanatically to his doctrines and took up arms to defend them. Civil war followed between these two parties, and Sigismund, the German king, who had inherited the crown of Bohemia, made several unsuccessful attempts to pacify the country. Finally the Hussites quarrelled among themselves, separated into two parties, and made war on each other. The more conservative of them were victorious in battle and then became reconciled to the church. The extremists, after being utterly defeated in battle, changed in character completely. They lost all their fanatical violence and preached and practised non-resistance to the state. Bitter persecutions failed to destroy them, and they spread through Moravia and Poland. Finally they were exiled from Bohemia. They settled in Saxony, where they established schools which became famous. The Moravian, or Bohemian Brethren in America (there is a large settlement of them at Bethlehem, Pennsylvania) are some of the remains of this sect, whose romantic history and educational activities we cannot follow here in their interesting details.

Burned as a Heretic, 1415.

Civil War.

Moravian or United Brethren.

2. Poland.—Besides Bohemia there were, east of Germany, several other Slavic states, chief of which were Poland and

Lithuania. The archbishop of Magdeburg regarded it as his special duty to Christianize and Germanize all these Slavs. In the year 1000 an effective check was given to the German influence among them by the establishment of a Polish archbishop at Gnesen; and, as we have already seen, this independent ecclesiastical organization was a means of preserving their nationality. In the eleventh century Poland was small, consisting chiefly of the territory lying in the valley of the river Wartha. In the next century, by conquering and annexing Pomerania, Poland acquired a seaboard. Then, by the marriage of a Polish princess to Prince Jagello of Lithuania, the two countries were united. Poland made a successful war on the German order and took a large part of its land. At the close of the Middle Age Poland occupied a large belt of territory east of the Germans, extending from the Baltic to the Black Sea, and gave promise of becoming one of the powerful states of Europe. But its situation exposed it to the attacks of its powerful and covetous neighbors, Russia on the east, and Prussia and Austria on the west; and the dissensions among its nobility and the lack of a native royal family were to cause its ruin and, in the eighteenth century, to lead to its dismemberment.

Poland.

3. RUSSIA.—The early history of Russia is somewhat legendary, but it is probable that the Norsemen made some settlements among the Slavs east of the Baltic, and one of the Norse leaders, Rurik, is credited with having united all the tribes of Slavs about Novgorod under his rule (862). Other tribes were conquered, and the young kingdom expanded to the south and soon included Kiev on the Dnieper. Norse settlements were scattered along the rivers to the Black Sea, and through them the country was brought into connection with Constantinople rather than with Rome. In the tenth century Russia adopted the Greek form of Christianity, to which it still adheres. In the thirteenth century Russia, which had broken up into several little principalities, was overwhelmed by the Mongols, and for about two hundred years was subject to the great khan, paying him

Russia.

Rurik the Swede.

Accepts the Greek Church.

The Mongols.

tribute. Toward the end of the fifteenth century the prince of Moscow, feeling strong enough to rebel, killed the khan's representatives who came to demand the annual tribute, and made himself independent of the Mongol rule. He and his successors, however, remained oriental in customs, manners, and dress, and Russia had no relations with the rest of Europe until Peter the Great (1689–1725) made it a European power, and brought his people into contact with European culture.

4. HUNGARY.—The Magyars, or Hungarians, when defeated by Otto I in 955, settled in the territory which they still occupy. Christianity was soon afterward introduced among them, and in the year 1000 Hungary became a Christian kingdom and papal fief, their ruler receiving from the pope the title of king. The direct line of their native royal family died out in 1301, and the crown passed to a collateral line. There ensued, however, a long contest over the crown, in which the Hapsburg family was finally successful. Hungary was a part of the Hapsburgs' possessions until 1919. In the fifteenth century the Turks invaded the country and completed its conquest in 1526, destroying the Hungarian army in the battle of Mohacs. The history of the heroic struggle of the people against the Turks and their final victory over them belongs to the modern period.

Hungary, 955.

5. THE GREEK EMPIRE AND THE TURKS.—During a part of the Middle Age the Greek empire, through Constantinople, dominated the eastern Mediterranean commercially and grew rich through this supremacy. Constantinople, however, encountered strong competition from the Italian cities, and the fourth crusade broke its power for more than fifty years. The Mohammedans pressed on the empire from the east and the emperors were generally so occupied with the struggle for existence against them and the barbarians north of the Danube that they were never able to take any important part in the affairs of the west. About the middle of the fourteenth century the Osman Turks came from central Asia and began a brilliant period of conquest which made them masters of western

The Greek Empire.

The Osman Turks.

Asia. They then attacked the Greek empire and encroached steadily on its territory. They invaded the Balkan peninsula and extended their sway far north of the Danube. The Greeks made a long but ineffectual resistance to their progress. Constantinople held out for some time after all the territory of the empire had been taken, but with its fall, in 1453, the Greek empire came to an end, and a Mohammedan state was established in Europe with its capital at Constantinople. The Turks pushed far up into central Europe and conquered Hungary (1526). They did not cease to be a danger to Christian Europe until the end of the seventeenth century. The story of their successes, of their siege of Vienna where their power was finally broken, of their gradual withdrawal, and of the heroic rebellion of various Christian provinces (Greece, Bulgaria, Roumania, Servia, and others) belongs to the history of the modern period.

Fall of Constantinople, 1453.

6. Denmark, Norway, and Sweden.—The Germanic peoples (commonly called Northmen) who inhabited Denmark, Norway, and Sweden were divided into many independent tribes, much as the Germans were in the days of Tacitus. During the ninth and tenth centuries a process of consolidation took place, the little tribes of each country being united to form a kingdom. For nearly four centuries, while these countries were slowly emerging from barbarism, their history is a confused succession of international wars and civil strife caused chiefly by the ambitions of their rulers. In 1397 both their international and civil wars were brought to an end by the union of Calmar, an agreement by which the three countries were united under one ruler, Queen Margaret. In theory the three countries were equal, but, as a matter of fact, Denmark, being the strongest, was the leading power and dominated the other two. The Swedes resented this and after several attempts to revolt finally succeeded in gaining their independence (1523, Gustavus Vasa).

Scandinavia.

Union of Calmar, 1397.

During the ninth and tenth centuries it seems that many of the tribal chiefs were unwilling to yield to the movement of unification and so took to the sea and lived by plundering the countries which lay along it. Eventually they settled in the countries which they had first visited as marauders. They settled in the islands north of Scotland, in Iceland, and Greenland, and even visited the coast of North America. Their conquest and settlement of England in the ninth and tenth centuries have already been mentioned. They planted colonies also in Ireland and in Russia. The most important of all their settlements was in the valley of the Seine (911), which came to be called Normandy. Their fundamental character was not changed by emigration, for these Normans were one of the most ambitious and restless peoples of Europe. Their duke, William, in 1066 conquered England and became its king. In the eleventh century Norman nobles went as adventurers to southern Italy, where they succeeded in building up a kingdom (Sicily). From there they more than once tried to conquer the Greek empire, and Bohemond, the greatest of the leaders of the first crusade, was a Norman.

Settlements of Northmen.

"Normandy."

7. Spain.—Spain was occupied by Mohammedans early in the eighth century (711), but some of the population withdrew before the invaders into the southern slopes of the Pyrenees, where they were able to hold out against all Mohammedan attacks. Charlemagne went to their aid and organized the territory as far south as the Ebro into the Spanish march. This march gradually broke up and little kingdoms were formed in the north, such as Catalonia, Aragon, Navarre, Castile, and Leon. These kingdoms kept up an incessant struggle against the Mohammedans and were increasingly successful. The Mohammedan power grew weaker, and the result was the dissolution of the caliphate of Cordova and the establishment of several small Mohammedan states (Toledo, Seville, Cordova, Saragossa, and others). By 1300 these Mohammedan states had all been conquered and absorbed by the Christian kingdoms, and only the little principality of Granada was left in the hands of Mo-

Spain.

Little Kingdoms.

hammedans. Then these Christian kingdoms were gradually united. Castile and Aragon, the leading states, having absorbed all the others, were themselves united in 1474 by the marriage of Isabella, queen of Castile, to Ferdinand, king of Aragon. They completed the unification of Spain by expelling the Moors from Granada (1492), and under their vigorous rule Spain became one of the leading powers of Europe.

Spain United, 1474.

Granada, 1492.

8. PORTUGAL.—Geographically and racially Portugal belongs to Spain, but, by a curious freak of fortune, escaped being absorbed by Castile, as the other neighboring kingdoms were. In 1095 the county of Portugal consisted only of a small territory on the Douro River. In that year Alfonso, king of Castile, invested his son-in-law, Henry of Burgundy, with it. In consequence of a famous victory over the Moors, in 1139, its count was made a king. Fortune favored his family, and successive kings not only maintained their independence against the growing power of Castile, but within one hundred years they had, by a series of successful campaigns against the Mohammedans, increased their kingdom to its present size.

Portugal.

1095.

1139.

9. THE LEADING POWERS OF ITALY.—The city-states of Italy, which had for some time been governing themselves, eventually fell into the hands of usurpers, so that this period of Italian history may be called the age of the despots. No attempt will be made to give a history of all the little states into which Italy had been broken up, but a word may be said about the five most important of them. These are the kingdoms of Sicily and of Naples, and the republics of Florence, Venice, and Genoa. The papal state was not less important than these, but an account of it is given elsewhere. In 1266 the pope gave the kingdom of Sicily (which, it will be remembered, included both Sicily and southern Italy) to Charles of Anjou, the brother of the king of France. In 1282, however, Sicily rebelled, drove Charles out, and conferred the crown on Pedro II, king of Aragon.

Italy.

Sicily.

Pedro II, of Aragon.

Pedro's wife was the daughter of Manfred, and consequently the Sicilians regarded him as the heir of the Hohenstaufen claims. Sicily remained in the possession of the royal family of Aragon during the rest of the Middle Age. The crown of Naples passed from one branch of the Angevin family to another, and for a while (during the middle of the fifteenth century) it was reunited to the kingdom of Sicily. Eventually the Angevin claim passed to Charles VIII of France, who in 1494 was persuaded to invade Italy with the hope of acquiring the crown of Naples. The kingdoms of both Sicily and Naples suffered much from the incompetence and violence of their rulers, and neither of them shared to any extent in the Renaissance which made the same period so glorious in all the rest of Italy.

Naples and the Angevins.

In Florence, after about three centuries of democratic rule, the Medici family got possession of the government and ruled the city in an autocratic way. In this respect the history of Florence is typical of that of all the Italian cities (except Venice), in every one of which the democratic form of government was overthrown and replaced by an autocratic one. In each case it was some local family that made itself master of the city. In Milan first the Visconti family (1312) and then the Sforza family (1450) obtained the government. A quarrel arose between two members of the latter family, and one of them, hoping to improve his position, urged Charles VIII of France to come to Italy to make good his claim to the throne of Naples.

Florence.

Cities Seized by "Despots."

When the Greek empire was divided among the crusaders (1204) Venice received as its share of the spoils nearly all the Greek islands, besides some ports on the mainland. Through these possessions its power was so increased that for some time it dominated the Mediterranean commercially. A bitter and senseless commercial rivalry arose between Venice and Genoa which involved them in a war for more than a hundred years. In the battle of Chioggia (1381) Venice broke Genoa's power

Venice Acquires Land in the East.

War between Venice and Genoa.

by destroying its fleet. Genoa then lost its importance as well as its independence and became subject in turn to Milan and to France. Venice did not long enjoy the fruits of its victory over Genoa. While the two cities were wearing each other out in this ill-advised and suicidal war, a new enemy, the Turk, was slowly extending his power to the west, conquering foot by foot the Greek empire, and one by one depriving Venice of its islands. The two cities, blinded by their ill-timed jealousy, were so intent on destroying each other that they paid no attention to the successes of the Turks. There was enough commerce to make both cities rich, and they should have joined their forces to resist the common enemy. It was due in large measure to this blind and stupid jealousy between Venice and Genoa that the Turks were able to conquer so much of Europe. Venice saw its mistake when it was too late. Down to about 1400 the city had played no part in Italian affairs, but when it discovered that it was losing all its lands in the east to the Turks, it turned its face to the west and began to make conquests on the Italian mainland. During the fifteenth century it was one of the "great powers" in Italy.

Chioggia, 1381.

The Turks Advance.

10. The Mongols.—While pope and emperor were engaged in their uncompromising struggle for supremacy, the Mongols threatened to deluge Europe with heathenism. This strange, half-barbarous people, whose home was in the neighborhood of Lake Baikal, became a great power during the latter half of the twelfth century. The founder of their power, Temujin, better known as Genghis Khan (the great khan, 1155-1227), overran and subjected an immense territory which extended from the Pacific to central Europe, and included Corea, northern China, central and western Asia, southern Russia, and the valley of the lower Danube. At his death, in 1227, his great empire was divided among his sons, who continued his aggressive policy. Southern Russia, Poland, Hungary, Croatia, Dalmatia, Servia, and Bulgaria, were almost ruined by their devastating armies.

Mongols.

Of all their conquests in Europe they retained possession only of Russia, which remained subject to the great khan until about 1480, when the prince of Moscow threw off the Mongol yoke and successfully maintained his independence.

CHAPTER XXIV

THE CITIES AND CITY LIFE; INDUSTRIAL LIFE AND COMMERCE; WAYFARING LIFE

A HISTORY of Europe in the Middle Age would not be complete if it did not tell us something about how the people lived. In the chapter on feudalism we had a glimpse of the life of the peasants and of the nobility. Let us now consider the rise and life of the middle class—the people who lived in the cities. We shall find that the cities furnish a romantic and picturesque element in the history of the period, and in their government they made an interesting experiment in democracy, which merits our attention.

Cf. S. B., 289-293.

Decline of Roman Cities.

In the Roman empire at its height there were many prosperous cities, varying, of course, in size. Generally they had a vigorous industrial life. There was, in fact, a kind of factory system, for slaves, working side by side with free artisans in factories, produced various articles of commerce. Their prosperity had its source in their flourishing industries and commerce. The formation of great estates (*latifundia*), however, had a most disastrous effect on them, because as the people lost their economic independence and freedom and sank into the position of *coloni* (perpetual renters), they lost their powers of production and consequently also their purchasing power. Under those conditions commerce and industry dwindled and the prosperity of the cities declined. Their ruin was made complete by the heavy taxes imposed on them by the emperors and by the invasions of the barbarians. Some cities were even deserted by their inhabitants and fell into decay. Others, though not entirely ruined, suffered a great loss in their population and sank into insignificance. Industries ceased, factories went out of existence, and there was a rapid decline in technical skill. People returned to primitive conditions, for, since they were unable to buy, each one was compelled to make in a crude way his tools and clothing. The cities of Italy suffered less than those in other parts of the west and they were also the first to begin to recover from the general ruin. As the invasions ceased and order was somewhat restored, commerce gradually revived, and the condition of the cities improved.

New Cities Founded.

S. B., 292, 293.

New cities also arose, growing out of settlements made about a church, or monastery, or market, or in the neighborhood of a castle, or in some convenient spot on a river or on the coast. Nobles, seeing the advantages to be derived from having a city on their lands, frequently founded a new city and offered special favors to all who would come and settle in it. The population of the cities was increased by the number of serfs who ran away from their lords and sought to hide themselves in the cities. Of course their lords frequently tried to recover them, but the inhabitants of the cities sheltered them and it became an established principle that if a serf should remain in a city unmolested for a year and a day he thereby acquired his freedom. The growth of a city was generally dependent on the growth of its commerce, and with the great increase in commerce after the eleventh century many cities entered on a period of rapid growth and prosperity. Naturally, the greater the commercial advantages of a city, the more rapid was its growth.

Groups.

Cf. S. B., 296.
O., 57
Cf. R., 169, 170.

We must at the outset try to get an idea of the make-up of the population of a mediæval town or city. It seldom happened that all the people of a town possessed the same degree of freedom, or belonged to the same lord, or lived according to the same law. If the city was the seat of a bishop, there would be a large number of people there who were dependent wholly or in part on him and subject to his jurisdiction. This group would consist of serfs, or unfree, of common freemen, and possibly even of nobles. If the king or emperor had a palace or fortress in the city, there would also be a similar group of people dependent on him and governed by his official called the "burgrave." A rich church or monastery within the city would also have a similar group, and if a great baron had his castle in or near the city there would also be a similar group dependent on him. There might also be a number of freemen as well as of nobles within the city's walls. This diversity in the population added complexity to every movement within the city and made it impossible for a mediæval town to have the unity which we find in the cities of modern times.

In the time of Charlemagne each town formed a part of the county in which it was situated, and, like the rest of the county, was governed by the king's official, a count, who might be either an ecclesiastic or a layman. Almost every bishop was also a count and performed the duties of that office. Local self-government was unknown, the inhabitants having no voice in the management of public affairs. Now, as feudalism developed, the count naturally became the lord of the town as he did of the county. The inhabitants of the towns, or at least a large part of them, lost a certain degree of their personal freedom and came to be regarded as having much the same relation to their lord as did the serfs in the country. That is, as the serf was attached to the soil, so the inhabitants of the town had no right to move from one town to another without the consent of their lord. Gradually, in the administration of affairs, the town was separated from the rest of the county, and the town with its inhabitants was set in contrast with the country and its inhabitants. The latter were known as peasants and serfs, and the former, from the fact that they lived in cities, we may call "citizens."

Counts Govern the Cities.

Cf. S. B., 7: 11.

The inhabitants of the cities, after submitting for a century or two to the arbitrary rule of their lords, began to resist it. Generally the lord insisted on his customary rights, and the people rose in arms and expelled him and his officials from the city. The following account of what took place in Cologne in the year 1074 will give some idea of the extraordinary rights of the lord of the city and of the manner in which the people rebelled.

The Communal Movement.

The Cities Rebel.

Cologne, 1074.

S. B., 308, 309.

The archbishop spent Easter in Cologne with his friend, the bishop of Münster, whom he had invited to celebrate the festival with him. When the bishop was ready to go home, the archbishop ordered his servants to get a suitable boat ready for him. They looked all about, and finally found a good boat which belonged to a rich merchant of the city, and demanded it for the archbishop's use. They ordered it to be got ready at once, and threw out all the merchandise, with which it was loaded. The merchant's servants, who had charge of the boat, resisted, but the archbishop's men threatened them with violence, unless they immediately obeyed. The merchant's servants hastily ran to their lord and told him what had happened to the boat, and asked him what they should do. The merchant had a son who was both bold and strong. He was related to the great families of the city, and, because of his character, was very popular. He hastily collected his servants and as many of the young men of the city as he could, rushed to the boat, ordered the archbishop's servants to get out of it, and violently ejected them from it. The advocate of the city was called in, but his arrival only increased the tumult, and the merchant's son drove him off and put him to flight. The friends of both parties seized arms and came to their aid, and it looked as if a great battle was going to be fought in the city. The news of the struggle was carried to the archbishop, who immediately sent men to quell the riot, and being very angry, he threatened the young men with dire punishment in the next session of court. . . . The riot in the city was finally quieted a little, but the young man, who was very angry as well as elated over his success, kept on making all the disturbance he could. He went about the city making speeches to the people about the harsh government of the archbishop, whom he accused of laying unjust burdens on the people, of depriving innocent persons of their property, and of insulting honorable citizens with his violent and offensive words. . . . It was not difficult for him to raise a mob. . . . Besides, the inhabitants of Cologne all regarded it as a great and glorious deed on the part of the people of Worms that they had driven out their bishop because he was governing them too rigidly. And since they were more numerous and wealthy than the people of Worms, and had arms, they disliked to have it thought that they were not equal to the people of Worms in courage, and it seemed to them a disgrace to submit like women to the rule of the archbishop, who was governing them in a tyrannical manner.

As soon as the government of the feudal lord in a city was thus overthrown the people set up one of their own. Although there were many variations in details, in general outline these local governments (called communal, republican, democratic) were much the same everywhere, consisting generally of a mayor, or burgomaster, and a city council, or board of aldermen. Not all the inhabitants of a town had the right to vote for these officials, the franchise being generally limited to the members of the most important guilds. This limited citizenship led to long and riotous disturbances in the cities, because the lower guilds of artisans demanded a share in the government, but were refused. They then resorted to force, and eventually, often after years of civil strife in the city, generally succeeded in obtaining a voice and share in the government.

Form of Government.

S. B., 316, 317

Limited Suffrage.

In addition to these disturbances over the right to a share in the government there were many others, arising from the problems of city government, such as are connected with finance, police, the administration of justice, and partisanship in elections and in the management of affairs. There were many dishonest officials who were guilty of theft, fraud, and peculation. Party feeling was so intense that riotous disorder and violence in the streets were common. With these conditions the city police was never able to cope. And when a party was successful in the elections and got control of the city government, instead of giving all its attention to an effort to provide good government, it began to scheme to retain its power and offices and to keep its opponents out. It is apparent, therefore, that this experiment in communal government was not a success.

Failure of Communal Government.

The fate of the cities was different in different countries. In Italy, where there was no central government, the cities maintained their complete independence and sovereignty, and remained city-states. But the democratic government gradually broke down in them, and the power was usurped by some local family (as the Scala family in Verona, the Visconti and Sforza families in Milan, the Medici family in Florence). These new govern-

Fate of the Cities in Italy.

ments, although often tyrannical, were in some respects better than the democratic governments which they displaced. At any rate the change made the government more stable and put an end to the violent factions within the walls.

In France, as the central government grew strong, the king took advantage of the disorder in the cities to seize their government and to deprive them of all the liberties which they possessed. As the king's officials displaced those elected by the citizens, the cities lost their independence and came completely under the king's control (about 1300), thereby adding to the power and resources of the crown.

In France.

In Germany there was much greater variation in the status of the cities, and it is difficult to make a general statement about them. But it may be said that they acquired a greater degree of local independence and self-government, and retained them longer than did the cities of France. Yet they never attained that degree of sovereignty which was reached by the cities of Italy. For in Germany all the cities, even the most independent, acknowledged the emperor as their lord. In some cases, however, this was a mere form and they really governed themselves like free republics. A few of the imperial cities became sovereign states, and two of them at least, Hamburg and Bremen, were little city-republics and sovereign members of the German empire.

In Germany.

S. B., 301–307, 310–313.

The city walls and the style of architecture of the houses gave the mediæval city a unique and interesting appearance. Barbarian invasions and constant feuds between the cities and their neighbors made it necessary for the city to protect itself by means of walls. These were further strengthened by moats, towers, and fortresses, and were decorated with battlements which also offered protection to those who fought from the top of the wall. As it was necessary to economize space, the streets were generally narrow, and the houses tall, often having five or six stories. The houses were usually con-

City Walls.

Narrow Streets.

Houses.

structed in a curious way, each upper story jutting out for some distance beyond the one below it, so that the highest stories almost met over the street. Space within the walls was so valuable that no provision could be made for parks and pleasure-grounds, except outside the gates. There was usually, however, a small open space or square, in front of the city hall, which served as the meeting-place for the people, for public entertainments, and for a market. Walls and narrow streets diminished the comfort and cramped the life of the inhabitants.

The Square.

It is difficult for us to imagine the filthy and unsanitary condition of the streets. There were no sewers. If a stream flowed through the town, it served as a sewer. The streets were generally unpaved and in wet weather were no doubt almost impassable with mud and filth. The following quotation from the contract between the mayor of Siena and the man who had bought the right to clean the market-place (nothing is said of cleaning the streets) will give some idea of the character and efficiency of the "street cleaning department" of that city. Probably the condition of the market-place of Siena was neither better nor worse than that of the market place of other cities.

Lack of Sanitation.

In the year 1296, October the ninth, I, Segnalini, mayor of Siena, . . . in the name of the government of Siena, sell, give, and grant to you, John Vetture, of the ward which is called St. Martin's, all the sweepings, garbage, and waste stuff [that is, scattered grain, vegetables, etc., left in the market place] which you can get by sweeping the market place and the paved spaces around it, from now to the twenty-eighth day of next September. . . . Likewise, and for the same length of time, I give and grant to you the right to keep a sow and four pigs in the market place to eat up the waste stuff left there. . . . And I give and grant you the full permission and authority to sweep and clean the said market place and the paved spaces around it, and to have all the sweepings . . . and the waste stuff, and all that goes with the sweepings of the said market place,* etc.

* Translation of the original document in Latin, which is printed in L. Zdekauer, *La Vita Pubblica dei Senesi nel dugento*, conferenza tenuta, 10 Aprile, 1897, pp. 116 *ff*.

The endless variety of "ready-made" articles for all sorts of purposes, and the ease with which we can secure them, make it difficult for us to realize that the mediæval man lacked all such things. In our great stores we can find hundreds of articles which we think are necessary to us, but which were entirely unknown to him. For we must remember that the industrial life that had flourished in the Greek and Roman cities had ceased when the people lost their economic freedom and had become impoverished. Everything was "home-made" and "hand-made." There were no great factories and no manufacturing machinery, and the only source of power was that of water and wind, and these were used chiefly in mills for grinding. The peasant grew flax and hemp and his wife spun and wove them into linen, and the wool from his sheep she wove into yarn or cloth. Skins of animals, either wild or domestic, he fashioned into clothing and covering for the feet. The tools which he needed in his daily work he made himself. In fact, he made everything that he used. Consequently we can be sure that most of his tools were of wood, because it was difficult to work in iron.

"Home-Made"; "Hand-Made."

There were two kinds of work that were extremely important, yet difficult, requiring more or less training and practice: the art of pottery-making and blacksmithing, or working in iron. Because of their difficult character and their importance it is probable that some villages or communities hired a "village" blacksmith and a "village" potter, and, in return for the meagre salary which they paid him, the smith did all their iron work, which was no doubt simple in character, and the potter made their earthenware, for which there was, of course, a large and constant demand.

Village Blacksmith and Potter.

In the monasteries and on the estates of the great landlords there were probably more and better tools, because the large number of monks and serfs made it possible to have some men devote themselves exclusively to the work of making the required tools and implements. We learn this from an interesting document of Charlemagne, about 800, in which he gave minute directions to the men whom he set as stewards over his lands. He ordered the stewards to have, each in his own district, blacksmiths, goldsmiths, silversmiths, shoemakers, tailors, saddlers, lathe workers, carpenters, makers of shields and coats of mail, fishermen, fowlers, soapmakers, beer-brewers, makers of apple cider and pear cider, bakers who knew how to bake rolls, makers of nets for trapping wild animals and catching fish and birds, "and many other kinds of workmen too numerous to mention." Here it is evident that the process of specialization was well begun again, and certain kinds of work were developing into trades. It is also quite clear that each district, just as each peasant, was to be entirely self-sufficient, since its inhabitants supplied all their own needs.

Specialization on Big Estates.

Gradually, as villages were established and increased in population, the process of specialization was necessarily quickened. In the villages and cities there grew up for the first time during the Middle Age a class of free working men who, since they had no connection with the soil, had to make a living with their hands. These became the industrial class. It became necessary for the members of a family to produce more than they needed for their own personal use, and to produce articles for which there would be a demand more or less general. The first difficulty which such a class met was in finding purchasers for the products of their labor. There was no storekeeping class to act as middlemen, buying the products of the labor of others and selling them to the consumer. Hence, those who made articles for sale were compelled also to sell them. The workshop became also the salesroom. In order to bring maker and consumer together markets, or "fairs," were held, and after about 1000 A. D. these rapidly increased in number and importance. Better facilities of selling naturally enlarged the profits of this sort of production, and so the industrial, or artisan, class increased in numbers. At the same time not only the agricultural class was growing in numbers, but the amount of land under cultivation was constantly increasing, and better methods of agricul-

The Industrial Class.

ture were developed. Consequently, the agricultural class, having more farm products for sale or exchange, were able to buy many better articles and more cheaply than they could themselves make them. So specialization tended to become more and more the rule, and the articles improved in quality.

It was not probable that the artisans would ever be able to glut the market with their home-made articles, because the method of making everything by hand was slow and raw materials were expensive. We are told that in the fourteenth century a ton of iron in England cost about $500; a thousand weavers, working a whole year, could produce about five thousand bolts of cloth, the monthly output of a good modern woollen-mill; and toward the end of the fifteenth century a master locksmith required two weeks to make a good lock. So, no matter how clever the workmen were, their output would necessarily be small. Not content with the natural protection which the existing conditions afforded them, the industrial class sought to improve their situation by artificial means. They organized themselves into associations, called guilds, the chief purposes of which were to secure a monopoly both in the manufacture and in the sale of their products, and to obtain freedom from tolls. In the Middle Age free trade was unknown, and tolls were heavy and burdensome, for each town and market sought to tax every article that was brought in and offered for sale.

High Cost, Small Output.

These guilds had a profound influence on mediæval life because they included in their membership nearly all the inhabitants of a town.

The aristocracy, that is, the merchants and bankers, belonged to merchant guilds; the laborers and artisans, who sold the product of their labors, belonged to craft guilds. The merchant guilds tried to secure a monopoly of trade in the town and in its neighborhood. They refused to permit a travelling merchant to sell his wares in the town, because, as they said, the public could not be protected against deception in the quality of the goods; for when such a foreigner had left the town it would be almost impossible to punish him

Guilds.

for having misrepresented his wares. For the same reason craft guilds were organized to secure a monopoly in the trades and industries of the town. Thus only the members of the guild of shoemakers were permitted to make and sell shoes.

Apprentice, Journeyman, Master.

When a boy had chosen the trade which he wished to follow, he was apprenticed to a master in it. After he had finished his apprenticeship, which lasted from two to ten years, according to the character of the trade, he became a journeyman, and was permitted to work at his trade, not independently but in the shop of a master. After serving as a skilled laborer for a number of years, if he gave evidence of having the proper character, he might, by a vote of the masters in his guild, establish himself as a master with a business of his own. In order to prevent competition the guild strictly limited and regulated the number of apprentices and masters.

Industries.

In the early Middle Age there was little commerce, and consequently each city had to supply its own wants by means of its local manufactures and industries. Gradually, however, commerce increased, and it became possible for a city to sell a part of its products and to buy articles which it could not produce. Each city then developed those industries which it could practise most advantageously. Thus, fishing became the chief occupation of the inhabitants of the towns along the seashore and on the great inland seas; some of the Baltic cities had an important trade in amber; the Flemish cities grew rich from weaving; other cities became famous for their leathers and furs; and still others for their work in metals.

Articles of Commerce.

We have seen that commerce was ruined when the people lost their economic freedom and became *coloni*. Then for some centuries the invasions of the barbarians, heavy taxation, bad roads, robbers, the lack of police protection, the lack of money as a medium of exchange, and the heavy tolls collected in harbors, at bridges, at city gates and at innumerable points along the roads, made commerce on a large scale impossible. The immediate effect of this was, as we have seen, that each community, often indeed each family, had to produce enough to supply all its wants. Such was the condition of affairs until after the year 1000, when commerce began to increase rapidly. During this early period of the Middle Age we must not suppose, however, that there was no commerce at all. Silks and other textile fabrics, perfumes, incense, spices, nutmegs, cloves, pepper, jewels, pearls, precious stones, and other articles from southern and eastern Asia, were brought by adventurous merchants to the west and found their way into remote parts of Europe. In return, the Europeans gave many kinds of fur, amber, slaves, hunting falcons, woollen cloth, and other articles.

Commercial Routes.

There were several well-defined routes of travel which this commerce followed. From the Baltic one route led by way of Lake Ladoga and the Volga River to the Caspian, and thence to China. Another followed the Dnieper to the Black Sea, thence to the east, passing either north or south of the Caucasus, or to the southeast through Asia Minor. From central Germany merchants could go by way of the Danube and the Black Sea to Constantinople, and from that point they had a choice of routes, either by way of the Black Sea, or through Asia Minor, or by boat to any of the Mediterranean ports. From France, Spain, Italy, and northern Africa the Mediterranean furnished the safest and most convenient routes, with a wide range of ports to choose from, according to the character of the merchant's wares. The routes to India and the East Indies went either overland to the Euphrates and on through Persia, or by the Red Sea and the Indian Ocean. From the Mediterranean to England and northwest Europe a merchant could go by way of one of the passes in the Alps, or by the Rhône, or by boat through the strait of Gibraltar. It was not customary for merchants to make the whole journey from the far east to the far west, but the merchandise was carried by one merchant over the territory with which he was familiar and then sold to another merchant, who continued the journey. In this way the Mohammedan peoples of central and western Asia acted as

Note to Map XX.—This map shows the locations of the chief towns of the later Middle Age, the more important connections by land routes, and the sea routes around Europe and to the east. The dotted lines surround groups of cities which were bound together in leagues at different times. Venice and Genoa virtually monopolized the trade through the Mediterranean to the east; their vessels picked up cargoes at Constantinople, Antioch, Alexandria, and other eastern Mediterranean ports, and carried them back to northern Italy; from here the goods were transported across the Alps to the upper waters of the German rivers or to southern France, and so were passed on to all parts of Europe. Each important town on the way was a distributing centre for its region; such were Milan, Augsburg, Cologne, Troyes (the fairs of Champagne), Paris, Bruges, London, etc. The Hanseatic towns of northern Germany controlled the trade with the Baltic regions, the Scandinavian peninsula, and the interior of Russia, exchanging manufactured goods and products of the south and east for the raw materials of these northern lands (fish, furs, lumber, grain). Manufacturing industries naturally sprang up in towns along the trade routes. The factors in the growth of commercial towns, therefore, were: location on a main trade route, position as a distributing centre, and development of industries.

XX
CITY GROUPS AND
CONNECTING TRADE ROUTES
CHIEF CITY LEAGUES:
I The Hanseatic League
II The Flemish Towns
III The Rhine League
IV The Lombard League
ATLANTIC OCEAN
NORTH SEA
Bay of Biscay
English Channel
Str. of Gibraltar
London
Hamburg
Lübeck
Bremen
Berlin
Magdeburg
Cologne
Frankfort
Worms
Nuremberg
Augsburg
Paris
Chartres
Orléans
Tours
Poitiers
Limoges
Bordeaux
Bayonne
Toulouse
Avignon
Narbonne
Marseilles
Burgos
Pampeluna
Barcelona
Valencia
Verona
Ravenna
Ancona
Rome
Berwick
Carlisle
York
Chester
Rheims
Longitude 5 West 0 Longitude 5 East 10 from 15

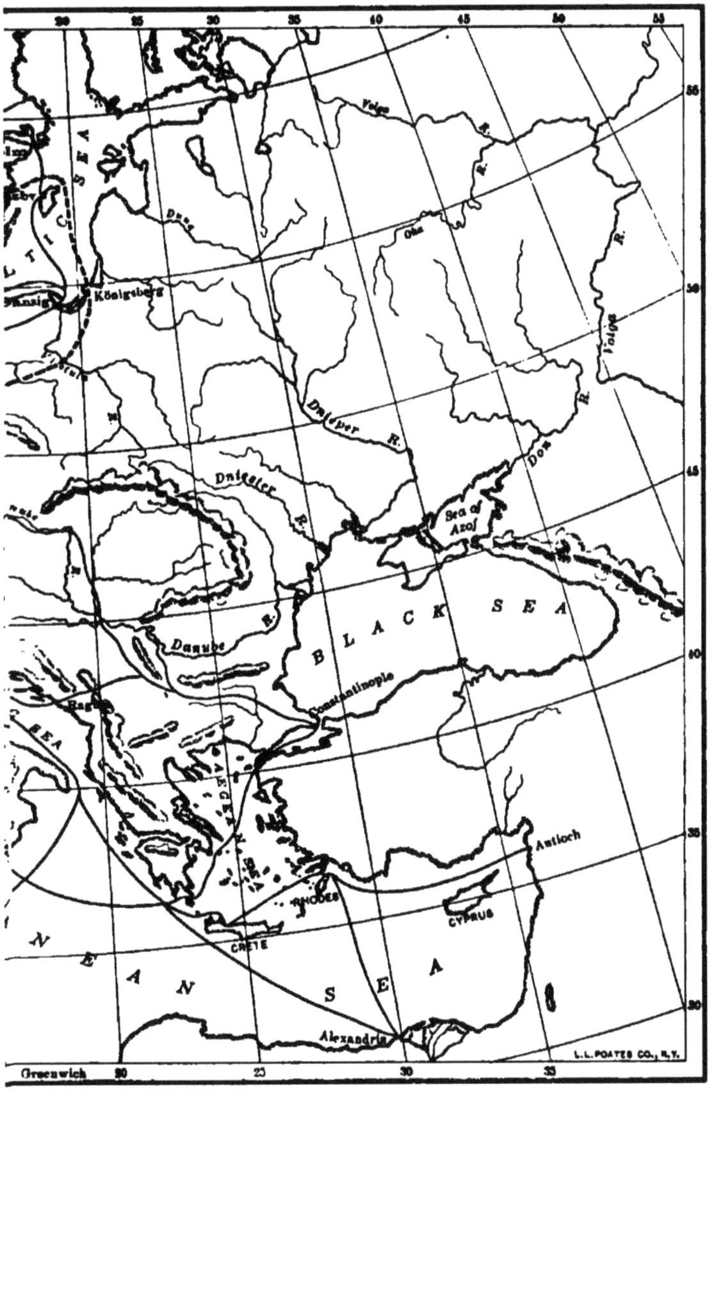
Königsberg
Volga R.
Duna
Oka
Dnieper R.
Dniester R.
Don R.
Sea of Azof
Danube R.
BLACK SEA
Constantinople
Antioch
RHODES
CYPRUS
CRETE
Alexandria
Greenwich
L.L. POATES CO., N.Y.

middlemen between the east and the west. The Greeks, with Constantinople as their chief city, had a sharp rivalry with the Italian cities for the carrying trade.

In this commerce the Jews not only had a very extensive part; they were also pioneers in it. They possessed great ability for merchandising; they were adventurous travellers; and, through their widely scattered kinship and their faithfulness and helpfulness to others of their race, they were able to establish business connections from the east to the west. By pack and by horse they carried their wares throughout western Europe and so became an important commercial factor. A city that admitted Jews as residents immediately acquired importance as a commercial centre.

Jews in Commerce.

In the eleventh century commerce began to increase, and, after the crusaders had established their principalities in the east, it assumed large proportions. Although the northern route from the Baltic to the east was closed about the same time by the invasions of hostile tribes, commerce along all the other routes constantly grew in volume and importance. In this increasing commerce the cities on the Mediterranean naturally had exceptional opportunities to share. The cities of Italy especially made the most of their fortunate situation and rapidly grew rich. Not only did this commerce increase in volume; it also opened up many new routes and new markets, and came to embrace many new articles. This commerce led to the period of voyage and discovery, and hence to the discovery of America.

Growth of Commerce.

There was some opposition to this commerce, however, for various popes, regarding all traffic with Mohammedans as injurious to the cause of the crusades, frequently prohibited it, although their prohibitions had little effect. In 1198 Innocent III wrote a letter to the Venetians as follows:

Papal Opposition.

In support of the eastern province (that is, the crusader states) . . . we have renewed that decree of the Lateran council (held under Alexander III, 1179), which excommunicated those Christians who shall furnish the Saracens with weapons, iron, or timbers for their galleys, and those who serve the Saracens as helmsmen or in any other way on their galleys and piratical craft, and which furthermore ordered that their property be confiscated by the secular princes and the consuls of the cities, and that, if any such persons should be taken prisoner, they should be the slaves of those who capture them. We furthermore excommunicated all those Christians who shall hereafter have anything to do with the Saracens either directly or indirectly, or shall attempt to give them aid in any way so long as the war between them and us shall last. But recently our beloved sons, Andrew Donatus, and Benedict Grilion, your messengers, came and explained to us that your city was suffering great loss by this our decree, because Venice does not engage in agriculture, but in shipping and commerce. Nevertheless, we are led by the paternal love which we have for you to forbid you to aid the Saracens by selling them, giving them, or exchanging with them, iron, flax (oakum), pitch, edged tools, rope, weapons, galleys, ships and timbers, whether hewn or in the rough. But for the present and till we order to the contrary, we permit those who are going to Egypt to carry other kinds of merchandise whenever it shall be necessary.

The desire for gain, however, was so strong, that all other considerations had little or no influence.

The immediate effect of this commerce was a great increase in wealth. The cities which engaged in it grew rich and proud and entered on a period of great prosperity. The people seem to have known how to enjoy, for they spent their money lavishly on fine buildings, artistic furniture and household equipment, on works of art, magnificent dress, and brilliant private and public social functions. In accordance with their wealth the cities began to play an important rôle in public affairs. To clear the roads of robbers, the sea of pirates, and to secure adequate police protection, the cities of Germany and of all northwestern Europe entered into an alliance, which, called the Hanseatic league, became a great political as well as a civilizing power.

Wealth and Luxury.

The economic and civilizing work of the Italian cities was materially limited by the bitter and senseless rivalry in which they indulged. The mediæval city and the mediæval merchant had no conception of free and honorable competition. If they met a competitor in the field, they thought only of destroying him. So, when the merchants of two cities came into competition for trade, they resorted to arms. In this way one after another of the Italian cities was conquered by its more powerful neighbor and rival and its commerce diminished or ruined. Finally Venice and Genoa engaged in a deadly rivalry for commercial supremacy. For more than a hundred years they were engaged in a more or less desultory warfare, which was profitable to neither and ruinous to both. But in 1380 the Venetians destroyed the Genoese fleet and from that time Venice was without a rival in the west. In the meantime, however, the Osman Turks had been extending their conquests westward and when Venice had destroyed her last western rival she found herself face to face with them —a stronger, more relentless foe. The Turks not only took her eastern lands from her, but also successfully closed the eastern markets against her merchants, and so put an end to her prosperity. Turkish domination of the eastern Mediterranean markets meant Turkish monopoly in the handling of all Asiatic products and this had a far-reaching effect on the world's history. It broke the power of Venice and from the commercial ruin that gradually overtook her she never recovered; and it also awakened in the minds of sailors the idea and the desire of finding a new route to the markets of India, the East Indies, and China, and thus led the Portuguese to find the route to India by way of the Cape of Good Hope and Columbus to discover America.

Rivalry Leads to War.

Markets, or fairs, as they were called, had an important place in mediæval commerce because they brought together those who wished to sell and those who wished to buy, and they no doubt added much to the life of a town. At first they were held on holidays (Sundays and saints' days). *Feriæ*, from which the word "fair" is derived, meant originally "holidays," but came to mean the fairs or markets which were held on those days. Since on such days the churches were the natural meeting-places of the people, markets were held in the church squares, and some-

Markets.

S. B., 301–305.

times even in the churches themselves. Some towns held fairs once a week, others once a month, others twice a year, and still others once a year. Some of the annual fairs continued for two months and were attended by thousands of merchants and people who came from hundreds of miles around. In fact, some merchants spent their time travelling from one fair to another. The value of such fairs in the development of the economic and intellectual life of the Middle Age was in part offset by the fact that they served to spread all sorts of contagious diseases, including the plague.

Many of these fairs preserved their fame until well into the nineteenth century. Better shipping facilities and improved means of travel and communication (railroads, steamboats, and the postal system) finally destroyed their importance. In Europe they have diminished in numbers, till now only three great annual fairs are held there; one at Beaucaire in France, another at Leipzig in Germany, and the third at Nijni-Novgorod in Russia. Of these the largest as well as the most picturesque is at Nijni-Novgorod, its sales amounting each year to more than $100,000,000. In Asia and in Africa, where railroads and steamboats are almost unknown, such fairs are still held and have lost none of their economic importance.

In mediæval life there were present certain social elements and features which added immensely to the picturesqueness of it. In the first place, the church had a large number of holy days, most of which were holidays, and all of them were utilized for processions and joyous gatherings and celebrations. In the spring the priest headed an interested and eager procession throughout all the countryside to bless the fields and to pray for a rich harvest. And every city had a patron saint whose day all the citizens celebrated as a holiday with processions and festivities made gay with song and dance. Civic pride brought out all the citizenship, and the guilds and other associations vied with one another in the brilliance and magnitude of their display. Every guild had its patron saint, too, and when his day came it was given up to a celebration that was characterized by feasting,

Picturesque Processions.

dancing, and general hilarity. Brilliantly colored robes and banners made all such processions attractive to the eye. We may be sure that the streets in those days were far richer in picturesque and entertaining sights than are those of to-day. And in one respect we may really envy the inhabitants of a mediæval city: they were not so overwhelmed with business that they did not have leisure to enjoy the pleasures which the days brought them.*

Means of Travel.

Waterways.

Means of travel and communication have always been an important factor in civilization. In the Middle Age, in the absence of a regular, efficient postal system, of the telephone and telegraph, and of what we now call rapid transit, it is evident that travel and travellers were almost the only means of disseminating news and ideas. In the streams and rivers of Europe there was a ready-made system of highways. An important part of this system was composed of the small streams, which now play no part in travel. For boats were generally small, since, for the most part, they had to be either rowed or "poled." Only on the larger streams sails might be used when the winds were favorable. Travel by boat might be, on the whole, less expensive, less laborious, and less dangerous than travel by land, and so no doubt every stream that could float a boat comfortably was made to serve the travelling public. So extensively were all streams used in this way that it became a matter of public concern that they should be kept open for travel, and generally it was assumed that the king or ruler had the right to control the building of dams, mills, and anything else that might obstruct the free passage of boats. Endless was the litigation and innumerable the appeals to the king over the construction and removal of such obstructions in the streams.

Roads.

The roads were hardly worthy of the name. They were mere trails, ungraded and unpaved, with the exception of the old Roman roads, which in the course of time wore out. They became impassable in time of heavy

* Religious processions are now uncommon in Protestant countries, but they are still an interesting feature in Catholic lands.

and continuous rains. They were full of stones, mudholes, ruts, and washes, and only a strongly built vehicle could stand the strain of travelling them. There was constant danger that a wagon would upset or stick fast in the mud.

Crossing the streams was a serious problem. Some of the smaller ones could be forded. Over others ferries were maintained, and over others bridges were built. Probably out of common pity for the traveller because of the notorious hardships which he must undergo on the road, the building of bridges came to be regarded as a pious work, in which the clergy and monks had a special interest. On the continent there was even a monkish order which had for its object the building and care of bridges and ferries. In England there were guilds formed for the same purpose. The pious character of the work is further seen in the fact that a chapel was nearly always erected either on the bridge or at one end of it, which was dedicated to some saint, who was then regarded as the patron saint and guardian of the bridge. Frequently some hermit or friar took up his residence on the bridge, collected tolls, and was supposed to keep it in repair.

Bridges.

Bridges were built out of funds raised by a tax on the neighborhood, by tolls collected from passers-by and from boats that passed under it, and from gifts that came from many sources. Sometimes a monastery or a great lord in the neighborhood was charged with its construction, or the work was assumed by a bridge-building order or guild. They were supposed to be maintained in much the same way, but, as a matter of fact, the chronicles of the bridges show that the work of maintaining them was generally neglected. Although the funds and tolls were constantly collected, some one appropriated them to private ends, and they frequently became the subject of wearisome litigation.

Of all the examples of the bridge-builder's art probably the London Bridge was the most famous. It was begun in 1179 on the ruins of an old wooden structure, and was completed in 1209. An Englishman named Colechurch superintended its construction to 1201, when King John called a Frenchman named Isembert, a famous bridge-builder, to complete it. All

England was excited about the bridge, and gifts and legacies poured in on it. On either side of the roadway houses were built on the bridge itself, the rentals from which formed a part of the bridge's income. These houses were several stories in height and had cellars and storerooms in the masonry of the piers. In one of the arches was a drawbridge to let boats pass. The bridge was supplied with a chapel and with towers for defense. There are still standing and in use a considerable number of bridges built in the Middle Age. One of the finest of these is at Cahors, France, built in the thirteenth century.

London Bridge, 1179–1209.

Probably the commonest way of travelling was afoot. A majority of travellers had not the means to provide themselves with a horse. And in the case of a long journey, such as a crusade or a pilgrimage or a journey to Rome, it was less expensive and in many ways more convenient to go afoot. The other common way of travelling was on horseback. All who could afford this would supply themselves with horses and travel as did Chaucer's famous story-tellers. The king and the very wealthy had heavy, lumbering carriages, which in spite of the pains bestowed on them must have been uncomfortable. For hauling their produce strong carts were in common use.

On Foot and on Horseback.

Such were the roads. Who travelled them? First of all, the kings and their courts and messengers and all who were sent out on the king's business. We have seen that the kings had no fixed residence, but were constantly moving about their realms. This was due partly to the fact that one province after another required their presence, and partly to the fact that, since their living was derived in large measure from their lands, which were scattered all over the kingdom, it was easier for them to go to their provisions than to transport their provisions to them at some central place. They were generally accompanied by a large retinue, composed of their counsellors or chief advisers, judges, officials, their household attendants, and a considerable body-guard. They had the right to require the people living along the road to assist them with

Mediæval Travellers.

Kings and Their Retinues.

vehicles and horses. Since the king could not be present everywhere, it was necessary for him to employ a large number of messengers, whom he sent on his business to all parts of his kingdom.

The nobility also were to be met on the roads in considerable numbers. They travelled from one of their estates to another, to the king's court, to tournaments, as well as for many other purposes. An important contingent of the travelling public was composed of the high clergy, abbots, monks, and friars. The high clergy, as we have seen, had two sets of functions, the one secular, the other spiritual, and the interests of both together compelled them to do much travelling. Appeals to the pope were numerous, and representatives of both sides of a case were generally sent to Rome to try to secure the papal decision. During the last three centuries of the Middle Age the orders of friars were very active and numbers of them were to be met along the way. The rules of their order forbade them to ride on horseback, and, although they sometimes evaded the rule, they generally travelled afoot.

Nobles.

Clergy.

S. B., 271.

Merchants and peddlers were to be met with everywhere as they went from town to town and from market to market.

Merchants.

During the Middle Age pilgrimages were exceedingly common, either as a form of devotion or as penance. Consequently there were numerous pilgrims and penitents on the road, and the great shrines of Europe were visited yearly by thousands. A typical caravan of pilgrims was that which Chaucer has immortalized in his *Canterbury Tales*.

Pilgrims.

It is impossible to name all the classes of travellers which during the last centuries of the Middle Age made up the travelling public, but one more class deserves particular mention. This was the large and interesting class of those who lived by their wits. To this class belonged all those who gained a livelihood by furnishing some form of entertainment. Among them were musicians and strolling players, story-tellers, jugglers, tricksters of all sorts, dancers, acrobats, pardoners, dealers in relics and in

Minstrels, Jugglers, Vagabonds.

forged indulgences, petty thieves, and beggars and vagabonds of an infinite number of varieties. A dancing bear or a monkey was an attractive adjunct which enabled its owner to draw the pennies out of the pockets of the gaping crowds. Vagabonds were numerous and formed a kind of fraternity, much as do the tramps of to-day. By means of cabalistic signs which they chalked up along the way they conveyed to their fellows information in regard to the sort of reception which they were likely to receive at the next house or village. They were masters in the art of begging and of deception, and were able to simulate all sorts of bodily misfortunes and deformities which would make a sympathetic appeal to the purses of those whom they met.*

Danger of Travel.

We can hardly form an adequate conception of the dangers that beset the traveller from thieves and robbers. Acts of violence were common, and, when occasion offered, were frequently committed by those who did not gain their livelihood by such means. Besides the numerous thieves and robbers there were many robber barons who levied on all who passed their way. At the close of a war mercenary troops who had been engaged in it generally became robbers and lived by acts of violence at the expense of others.

Monasteries as Inns.

Of inns and hotels, such as they were, there was no lack. Most of them were extremely uncomfortable and innkeepers were notorious for their sharp practices. Every monastery also served as a hotel and generally provided a house outside the monastery walls in which travellers could pass the night. It is needless to say that their hospitality was often abused.

* In chapter LIII of *The Cloister and the Hearth* Charles Reade has given an interesting and truthful picture of some of the tricks of this wily class. Indeed, the whole book is worthy of careful reading, because it contains in an attractive form so much actual information about the roads, inns, the travelling public, and the dangers that beset the traveller.

CHAPTER XXV

CIVILIZATION AND CULTURE IN THE MIDDLE AGE

THERE were in the Middle Age so many movements and forces that were destructive in their effects that it seems, at the first glance, that there could have been very little civilization and culture. There were in the first place the invasions of barbarians, who throughout a large part of the period harried and ravaged the more civilized portions of Europe. Merely to mention them—the Huns, the Germans, the Slavs, the Hungarians, the Saracens, the Northmen, the Normans, the Turks, the Tatars and Mongols—calls up a series of pictures of wanton and wide-spread ruin. Scarcely less destructive were the numerous wars, private, civil, and international. Nation was set against nation, city against city, noble against noble, noble against city, class against class, as in the peasants' uprisings. The forces that made for protection and order in the feudal state were notoriously inadequate. Hunger and famine also did their deadly work. There was no intelligent treatment of the sick and epidemics and plagues raged incessantly.

Yet in spite of the desolation wrought by these destructive forces, the Middle Age produced a civilization that makes a strong appeal to us. Besides the civilizing forces which, as we have seen, were centred in the cities, there were others, such as the legacy of Rome, in the form of literature, law, and ideals; the church, with her great system of doctrines, practices, and ideals, and with her army of clergy, monks, and friars; the literature of the church and of feudalism; schools and universities; and the fine arts—architecture, sculpture, and painting. These will now engage our attention.

In discussing the civilization of the Middle Age we are confronted with serious difficulties. In the first place, the peoples of the different countries were not on the same plane of civilization, so that what was true of one of them might not be true of the others; and furthermore, the peoples were making progress all the time, so that what was true of a people in the early Middle Age would not be true of them in a later period. Perhaps it will be more satisfactory, therefore, for us to look at the forces which were operating to civilize the peoples rather than to attempt to describe in detail the successive stages of civilization to which the people of each country attained.

The Church.

First of all the civilizing agencies, we must consider the Christian church, because, in many ways, its influence was exerted for the betterment of the people. It developed a system of religious belief and practice which undoubtedly had a civilizing influence on the rude nations of Europe. Its system of morals and its standards of conduct, although not perfect, were nevertheless uplifting. The church was the guardian of learning and the promoter of all the arts, and many of the greatest men and women of the Middle Age—the men and women who appealed most strongly to the popular imagination and admiration, and who were therefore great civilizers—were living embodiments of the virtues which the church taught. Furthermore, the church regarded it as her duty to watch over every individual from the cradle to the grave, and she surrounded him with an ample machinery, or apparatus, for effecting his salvation. This machinery she put into the hands of the clergy, who were, by virtue of their ordination, given a peculiar power over the operation of it.

Its Organization.

At its height the church possessed a remarkable organization, which brought every individual into contact with the clergy. The whole land—including country, villages, and cities—was divided into parishes, over each of which was a priest, whose duty it was to minister to the spiritual needs of its inhabitants. A number of parishes were grouped together to form a diocese, or bishopric, over which a bishop presided, whose duty it was to oversee the parish clergy. In the same way dioceses or bishoprics were grouped together to form an archdiocese, or archbishopric, over which an archbishop presided, whose duty it was to oversee the bishops. Over the archbishops was the pope, with supreme authority over all. With such an organization the church extended her influence even to the most remote rural regions, and none could escape it.

In addition to the clergy, the church had at her disposal a great army of monks, who, in a way, re-enforced the clergy and materially aided in the work of Christianizing and civilizing Europe.

Monks as Civilizers.

Although monks were reckoned with the clergy and were spoken of as a part of the regular clergy, a large part of them were merely laymen who had taken the monastic vows. Only a small percentage of them became priests by receiving ordination. These monks were established on the dangerous frontier, where their monasteries were built like fortresses and were able to resist a severe attack of the hostile or rebellious barbarians. Monks were generally the first colonists to enter a conquered territory, carrying with them not only the gospel and learning but also the civilizing arts, trades, and vocations. They were leaders in agriculture and introduced the culture of many grains, fruits, and plants. They were the great builders and called all the fine and practical arts to their aid in beautifying their churches. They wrought in iron, silver, and gold. In their gardens grew all sorts of medicinal herbs as well as a great variety of vegetables. They spun and wove. In short, there was no existing art or craft which the monks did not make known to the barbarians among whom they settled. And, above all, although admitting the weaknesses and backslidings of the monks, we must not forget the moral and religious uplift which they communicated to the people about them.

In the course of some centuries the church had worked out and formulated a system of religious belief, or a creed, and a system of sacraments, and to the clergy were intrusted both the guardianship of the creed and the operation of the sacraments. It was the duty of the clergy to teach the creed and to prevent any one from entertaining a belief that was opposed to it. The salvation of the individual

Creed and Sacraments.

was closely bound up with his acceptance of the true faith and with the operation of the sacraments, of which there were seven.

Baptism was, in a way, the door into the church; it was performed on an adult when he professed his faith in Christ and on a new-born babe. The church taught that all the descendants of Adam shared in his sin, and that baptism washed away this sin as well as all that the individual had committed up to the time of baptism.

Baptism.

When the child came to years of understanding—about twelve years of age—he received the sacrament of confirmation, the purpose of which was to increase in him the sanctifying grace which would keep him from sinning and give him strength to believe and uphold the faith. In this sacrament the bishop, who alone could perform it, laid his hand on the head of the candidate for confirmation and anointed his head with oil.

Confirmation.

But baptism and confirmation, which could be performed on the same individual but once, were not able to prevent him from committing further sin. To cover this sin, there were two sacraments, penance and the eucharist. Penance is a sacrament by which those who have committed sins, by confessing them with true repentance and with a sincere purpose of making satisfaction to God, are absolved from their sins by the priest. As a sacrament it consists of four parts: the sinner must repent, or feel contrition for his sins, confess them to the priest, and make whatever satisfaction the priest may lay on him; the fourth part is performed by the priest, who absolves the penitent from his sins.

Penance.

The sacrament of the eucharist, or the mass, took the form of the consecration of the bread and wine into the body and blood of Christ and the offering them up to God as a sacrifice to secure grace and the pardon of sin. It was the central part of public worship.

Eucharist, or Mass.

Marriage.

By the sacrament of marriage husband and wife were united in the bonds of holy matrimony, which could never be sundered.

Extreme Unction.

In the sacrament of extreme (last) unction, which was administered only on the approach of death, and consisted in the application of holy oil, the soul was freed from sin and strengthened to undergo the ordeal of death.

Ordination.

Finally, there was the fundamental sacrament of ordination, by which the priests were consecrated to their sacred functions and received the sacerdotal, or priestly, character, which empowered them to perform the sacraments effectively. For it is a part of the sacramental system that the sacraments can be administered effectively only by those who, by ordination, have received the sacerdotal character. By ordination, therefore, priests were sharply separated from laymen and put into a special class. The gulf separating them from laymen was widened by the fact that to them was committed the guardianship of the doctrines of the church; for laymen were not expected or permitted to discuss or pass judgment on the creed or practices of the church, but such matters were left wholly to the clergy.

The church, however, undertook to control the whole progress of civilization. Its statements were to be accepted merely on its authority. It declared its system to be final. Great as its ideals were, its system permitted no growth except along its prescribed lines. And these lines were too limited to satisfy the human mind. Consequently, during the Middle Age there were many rebellions against the finalities and limitations of the ecclesiastical system. Numerous sects arose, but were stamped out as heretical. From the twelfth century on the popes were more and more engaged in fighting heresies. So compact was the ecclesiastical system that no thorough-going reform was possible. Nevertheless there arose many "reformers before the Reformation," chief of whom were Wyclif and Huss. Although they all failed to break through, the Modern Period begins with Luther's successful revolt against the authority of the church and the finality of its system.

The church was responsible for an immense literary activity throughout the whole Middle Age. In one edition (edited by

Migne) there have been published 165 large volumes of ecclesiastical writings in Greek and 217 volumes in Latin. All of these were written before 1216. In addition to these works there were many others, a good part of which has never been published; some of them have been lost. They were mostly theological and controversial; some dealt with history and biography, especially with the lives of the saints. There was a large body of hymns, some of which are still sung (in translation) even in Protestant churches.

Out of practical needs there grew in the thirteenth century two great movements which deeply influenced each other and at the same time enriched the life of the period. These movements were embodied in the Franciscan and Dominican orders, also called the mendicant or begging orders, because they lived by begging. It is difficult for us to imagine the wretched lot of those who fell ill during the Middle Age. Physicians were ignorant and inefficient, and of nurses and hospitals there were almost none. To this we must add the unsanitary condition of the houses and their total lack of comforts. From the point of view of the sick we can hardly overestimate the beneficent work of the Franciscans. That order was founded for the purpose of putting into practice the conception which St. Francis had of the imitation of Christ.

Franciscans.

The idea of the imitation of Christ has always been in the church, but, beginning with the twelfth century, it may be said to have been for a while one of the dominant ideas of Christendom. This may have been due to the fact that during the eleventh and twelfth centuries, because of the crusades, the attention of Europe was fixed as never before on the places where Christ's life had been spent. The idea found its classic literary expression a little later in the book entitled the *Imitation of Christ*, attributed to Thomas à Kempis (1380–1471), and its classic exemplification in the life of St. Francis of Assisi (1181–1222), the founder of the Franciscan order.

Francis of Assisi was a gay spendthrift until his twentieth year, when, in consequence of a dangerous illness, he became a serious, devout man. His one thought was to imitate Christ and his apostles in their poverty, in preaching, and in their service to others. Like Jesus, St. Francis wished only to "go about doing good." He devoted himself first to the most disagreeable work he could find, the care of lepers. He conquered the repugnance which he felt at their sight and contact, and thereafter his path was plain. His burning zeal soon won imitators and followers, and the idea of establishing an order took possession of him. In this he believed that he was inspired by God, for he says: "And afterward the Lord gave me brothers, and no one showed me what I ought to do, but the Lord himself revealed to me that I ought to live according to the holy gospel, and I caused it to be written in a few simple words, and the pope confirmed the rule." "The form of the holy gospel," according to St. Francis, was poverty and service.

St. Francis.

S. B., 269, 270. O., 63–65. R., 154–156. H., p. 344.

The Franciscans

He provided that his "brothers" should spend their lives on the highway, preaching and ministering to others whenever and wherever occasion offered; they should work for their bread if work could be found; if not, they might beg it; but they should never receive money under any circumstances, nor more food than was necessary for their wants for the day; all kinds of property or possession were forbidden; and, like Christ, they should not have even where to lay their heads. Our practical common sense tells us that such an ideal was impossible and unreasonable, but never before was an impossible and unreasonable ideal made so plausible and attractive as this one was by the sweet charm and gracious example of St. Francis. But, as the number of his "brothers" increased, the impossibility of his ideal became apparent. So large a body of men could not exist without some kind of home. In spite of the prohibition of St. Francis, the order began to accept the gifts of property which were offered them. Within a few years after his death the order was immensely wealthy, possessing a large number of rich monastic establishments. The rule of poverty, however, was observed tech-

His Ideal Impossible.

S. B., 271–273.

nically, for although the order became rich no member possessed anything.

The order of the preaching brothers, or Dominicans, was founded by St. Dominic, a Spaniard (1170–1221), for the express purpose of combating the heresies which were then appearing with alarming frequency in many parts of Europe. He provided that its members should be thoroughly trained in the doctrines of the church and fitted to instruct the people in them. In imitation of St. Francis he introduced the rule of poverty into his order and the Franciscans imitated the Dominicans in the education of their members for the purpose of teaching and preaching. While influencing each other, there was an intense rivalry between them. Both orders grew rapidly rich and powerful and spread to all parts of Christendom. Their popularity was great and they completely overshadowed all other orders in the thirteenth and fourteenth centuries. In the practical work of caring for the sick, in their high ideals of neighborly helpfulness, in preaching, in teaching, in learning, in building, and especially in the inspiring influence of the charming personality of St. Francis himself, these two orders contributed heavily to the civilizing influences of the thirteenth century.

The Dominicans.

S B., 116–118.

If we should judge of the civilization of the Middle Age by the degree of order and safety maintained, and by the difficulty and delays with which justice was administered, we should be compelled to put a very low estimate on it. The people, and especially the nobles, had little regard for law and order, and the government was unable to maintain peace and secure safety for the inhabitants. One of the worst features of the Middle Age was the prevalence of private warfare, for the nobles insisted on their right to fight out their own quarrels without appeal to law. Continuous warfare meant not only violence and oppression of the weaker members of society; it also hindered any advance in civilization for the whole society. Here, too, help came from the church, for she took the first steps to relieve this wretched condition. The first attempts took the form of the "peace of

Peace of God.

S. B., 240, 241.

God," proclaimed by a meeting of all the clergy of a province. Such proclamations, several of which appeared toward the end of the tenth century, forbade all violence and warfare, on the ground that they were contrary to the Christian spirit.

The peace of God, however, did not attain much success, because the turbulent nobles could not be made entirely to give up fighting. Then the church attempted at least to mitigate these evils by means of the "truce of God," in which all fighting was prohibited on certain days and in certain periods. The truce was to last from vespers, or sunset, on Wednesday evening to sunrise on the following Monday morning, and was also to be observed on holy days. The church regarded the keeping of the peace as a religious rather than a political duty. The only means which she had for enforcing the truce were ecclesiastical penalties, such as penance, excommunication, and anathema. In addition to supporting the truce, kings came to regard themselves as the guardians of the peace of the land, and attempted to secure peace and order by police regulations, enforcing them with severe punishments on offenders. But, in spite of the efforts of the church and kings, there was throughout the Middle Age much lawlessness and violence.

Truce of God.

S. B., 242–244.
S. B., 245–250.

In the organization as well as in the administration of justice governments were very weak. There was no system of courts, one rising above another from the lowest to the highest court of appeals, nor were the courts in any way co-ordinated. Merely to mention the most important ones, there were ecclesiastical courts, in which all ecclesiastical cases were heard and which, by an easy and gradual usurpation of authority, came to hear many cases that involved only secular matters. And, in accordance with the high claims of the papacy, the pope regarded himself as the highest judge on earth and openly invited the people of all nations to appeal to him. Toward the end of the Middle Age, however, kings generally forbade their subjects to appeal to the pope, and this was a frequent cause for a quarrel.

Ecclesiastical Courts.

Cf. S. B., 231, and Introduction

There were manorial courts, held generally not by the landlords in person but by their agents. Each manor, or village, had its own court, which heard and adjudicated the every-day affairs of the villagers and their relations to their landlord.

Manorial Courts.

Then there were feudal, or baronial, courts, in which every lord undertook to administer justice to his vassals according to feudal custom.

Baronial Courts.

Finally, there was in each country the royal court, with the king at its head, but presided over by his judges, which he strove to make superior to all other courts. By all possible means he tried to increase the number of "royal" cases, that is, cases that must from their nature come before his court. The most successful examples of this policy are furnished by the kings of England and France, who, by their travelling judges and other means, carried the "king's" justice to all parts of their realms.

Royal Courts.

We must note also that in the Middle Age there was not much lawmaking, as we understand the term, because the common conception was that custom was law. Thus when Frederick Barbarossa refused to hold the pope's stirrup he declared that he was not bound to do so because it had not been the custom for the king of Germany to perform such an act, and he yielded only when he learned that one of his predecessors had rendered the pope that service. The work of every court, therefore, was to determine what had been the custom. This the court did generally by asking the oldest men in the community what the practice in regard to any particular matter had been, and their testimony, when once established, was final.

Custom is Law.

When the regular rules of evidence were not sufficient, the court appealed to the ordeal, or judgment of God. It might be used either to determine which of two persons was in the wrong or to test the guilt of an accused person. The commonest forms of the ordeal were the ordeal of the cross, in which the two persons stood with outstretched arms in the form of a cross, and the one whose

Ordeals.

S. B., 234–239.

arms fell first lost his case; the ordeal by hot water, and the ordeal by hot iron, in which the accused either thrust his hand into boiling water, or carried a piece of hot iron in his hands a certain distance, or walked over pieces of hot iron; if after a certain time he showed no traces of having been burned, he was declared innocent; the ordeal by the suspended bread or psalter, in which the suspended object was expected to turn in one direction if the accused were guilty and in the opposite direction if he were innocent; the ordeal of the sacrament, in which the accused took the eucharist, the expectation being that if he were guilty the consequences would be fatal. The judicial combat, or the ordeal by arms, though opposed by the church, was in common practice among the nobility.

Municipal Schools in the Roman Empire.

During the Middle Age the common people, burdened with the struggle for existence, had neither the time nor the means to acquire culture, and the nobles, delighting in war and sports, sought their culture chiefly in the practice of arms. It is not strange, therefore, that during a large part of the period learning was to be found only among the clergy. In the first centuries of our era the larger towns in the Roman empire had municipal schools, the teachers in which were paid by the town. There were at the same time, no doubt, other teachers who conducted private schools. With the invasion of the Germans these municipal schools disappeared, and public instruction would have perished entirely had not the church assumed the task of instructing the people. The church was already engaged in giving religious instruction, having created in this way a kind of religious school system, in which the churches were the schoolhouses, the priests the teachers, and the children and even the adults of the parish the pupils.

Instruction by the Priest.

The priest instructed his parishioners in the principal doctrines of the church, in the Lord's prayer, the ten commandments, and in some form of the creed. All committed these to memory and some of them also learned to read. Probably every parish priest conducted a catechetical school of this sort in his parish. The church then adapted herself with rare skill to the new needs of the people, and enlarged the field of her activities, making use of her primitive educational machinery to instruct the people in secular branches as well as in religion. She established schools in connection with cathedral churches and in monasteries, and from the sixth to the twelfth century these were the only educational institutions.

The Church and Education.

The cathedral schools owed their existence to the good sense and insight of the bishops, who were accustomed to educate their own clergy. Although many bishops began such schools of their own accord and on their own authority, the church soon assumed control of them, and various councils passed suitable laws and regulations concerning them. Every bishop was expected to have such a school in connection with his cathedral and to see that it was supplied with a "master" fitted to teach his pupils as well as to train them in good morals. The work in such schools was quite elementary, consisting of the reading of the Bible and some of the works of the church fathers, the study of the simplest Christian doctrines, the creed, the Lord's prayer, and music, especially singing. The teacher was expected to train up a good choir for the cathedral, for singing was an important part of the church services.

Cathedral Schools.

R., 106.

From the beginning of monasticism in the west a certain emphasis had been laid on study, since without some education the monks could not read the Bible and the religious books which formed a part of their devotions. The rule of St. Benedict took this into account, and the practical needs of the monastery caused the monks to lay more and more stress on learning. In the monastic schools instruction was given to the monks, to the children who, having been devoted to the monastic life, lived in the monastery, and to all laymen who desired it. At first, instruction was free to all, but a present was expected from the laymen, and eventually demanded of them as a fee. The instruction in the monasteries was a little broader than in the cathedral schools, arithmetic being added and, in the larger monasteries, gram-

Monastic Schools.

mar, or Latin literature, and theology. The method of instruction was by lecture, discussion, question and answer, and the composition of letters, poems, and the like. But the incalculable service which the monks rendered to the cause of education was the copying and preserving of books. The need of books for their devotions as well as for their studies led the monks to expend a great deal of energy on this work. There was generally a room (*scriptorium*) in the monastery reserved for the copyists. Sometimes one monk read aloud the text which he was copying and other monks also wrote the words as he pronounced them. Thus several copies of the same work were produced at the same time. Generally, however, only one copyist was occupied in copying a manuscript. The copyists were instructed to take the greatest pains to copy word for word, but in spite of their efforts many errors crept into their work. Some abbots spared neither pains nor expense to secure manuscripts for their libraries, which were often the object of their deepest pride.

S. B., 10.

Manuscripts Copied.

Chronicles.

We are also indebted to the intellectual movement in the monasteries for a large number of the mediæval chronicles. One of the monks in each monastery was charged with the task of committing to writing all the important events and news of the day. Since the monasteries served as hotels, keeping a number of rooms for the accommodation of travellers, the chronicler of a monastery had exceptional opportunities for learning what was going on in the world. From guests as well as from local sources he was able to obtain materials for his narrative.

The fact that the church undertook to give instruction in common-school branches as well as in religion is of immense importance in the history of civilization; for it had the effect of preserving from the general ruin a certain amount of the learning and science which had flourished in the Roman empire and which might otherwise have been lost to humanity. Its importance justifies our studying the process in some detail.

The practical motive which impelled the church to this undertaking was the continued need of an educated and trained clergy. The church of the late Roman empire was a very elaborate structure. During its development from the simple congregations of the apostolic time it had grown up in the midst of a highly civilized society; as it widened its scope and took in larger and larger numbers from all ranks and classes, it inevitably absorbed more and more of the culture of the age. In the matter of creed and doctrines, for example, the church fathers found it necessary to explain the meaning of difficult ideas, or to defend the faith against the sneers and attacks of pagan critics, or to determine the correct and orthodox view in questions that were open to dispute. In this work they had, of course, to use the existing material for argument and exposition; that is, the logical methods and the metaphysical ideas of Greek philosophy. The form of service was elaborated and enriched from the art and literature of the time. The government of the church became more complicated, and the Roman law and Roman government were drawn upon for this purpose.

Need of an Educated Clergy.

It is evident that the officiating clergy of such a church would have to possess at least the general elements of the prevailing system of education; the simple evangelist of the apostolic type would no longer suffice. This minimum of education the clergy would acquire in the natural process of going to the Roman public schools, while the higher learning and training which would fit for leadership and commanding position in the church would be secured in the special schools maintained by the church in some of the great cities, and in the higher schools of rhetoric or philosophy which flourished in the empire.

The collapse of the Roman empire in the west in the fifth century and the ruin of Roman culture presented a very serious problem to the church. It became more and more difficult to recruit an educated clergy after the public schools ceased. Under these conditions leading churchmen undertook to develop a system of church education which would include the necessary secular studies no longer obtainable in the public schools. Previous to that time the attitude of the church toward pagan culture had been

Starting of Church School System.

largely hostile, although it had in fact taken up a good deal of that culture. St. Augustine, the greatest of the church fathers of the western church in this period, recognized the value not only of letters but also of history, rhetoric, and logic.

The best example of the actual incorporation of secular branches in church instruction is given by the work of Cassiodorus. This learned Roman had been the secretary of state for the Ostrogothic king of Italy, Theodoric. Late in life he retired from the world and founded a monastery (540). For the training of the monks who lived there he collected a library of secular as well as religious books, and himself composed a manual of the elementary branches of learning, based on the text-books and manuals current at the time. In the early seventh century the learned bishop of Seville, Isidore, composed a great encyclopædia intended to contain the elements of secular knowledge which would be of value to churchmen.

Cassiodorus.

Isidore of Seville.

When the churchmen of the seventh and eighth centuries undertook to compile text-books and collect manuscripts for the monastery schools, they had recourse, of course, to the material which had been used in the Roman public schools. This general education had already been reduced to order and system in the "seven liberal arts," namely: the literary studies (the *trivium*)—grammar, rhetoric, and dialectic, or logic; the mathematical studies (the *quadrivium*)—arithmetic, geometry, astronomy, and music. This was derived by the Romans from the elementary studies earlier developed among the Greeks. The amount of knowledge contained in the Roman text-books and manuals of the fourth century was not very great; it was easily supplemented by the larger text-books on particular studies and by the great classical works, such as those of Vergil, Cicero, and others, which were still read in the late Roman empire. Moreover, the studies of the public schools were regarded by the Romans as merely preparatory, either for practical life, or for advanced studies in higher schools. This larger background, however, tended to disappear from knowl-

The "Seven Liberal Arts."

Manuals and Text-books.

edge in the general decline of culture, and the church schools were left with little beyond the elementary texts and manuals which the churchmen had collected or had used in writing texts of their own. Since the churchmen were interested in preserving the elements of education for a practical purpose, and still regarded pagan culture as a thing to be guarded against, they neglected the larger works and the finer products of the classical intellectual development.

On one side, the Roman system itself was very meagre. In adapting Greek learning to the Latin world, the Romans had paid less attention to the abstract than to the practical side of education. They took over a very little of the theoretical part, of logic or arithmetic or geometry or astronomy; any one especially interested in those matters could go to the famous schools of Athens or Alexandria in the east. Hence, when the churchmen adapted the Latin text-books to their own use, they transmitted only this meagre amount of mathematical and logical material.

Charlemagne's Revival of Monastery Schools.

S. B., 7:25, 10, 11, 12.

The small and dwindling stream of learning was precariously preserved in certain monastery schools during the Dark Ages, especially in Italy and England; elsewhere in western Europe the ignorance was scarcely relieved. Hence, when Charlemagne sought to raise the clergy of his empire to a higher level in order to use them as a civilizing force, he sought out learned men from the few corners where learning survived: he brought to his court Alcuin (of York, in Northumbria), and Peter of Pisa, and Paul the Lombard from Italy. Alcuin was intrusted especially with the work of organizing the monastery schools of the empire; the monastery of Tours, of which he became abbot, was a sort of training-school for teachers, who then went to establish schools in other monasteries. The amount of learning which Alcuin and his contemporaries were able to communicate was very slight, because of the disappearance of so much that had been familiar to the educated world of the fourth century. Nevertheless, it presented the outlines of a general system of common-school education in the seven liberal arts, and these outlines were constantly being filled out in the later centuries.

The intellectual revival of the age of Charlemagne may be regarded as a second beginning of the system of church schools. From that point the amount of knowledge of Roman culture constantly increased and the quality of instruction constantly improved, until the movement culminated in the great university period of the thirteenth century. The general manner of the advance was the recovery of larger and finer works that had been forgotten but not destroyed. The Latin authorities and authors known to Alcuin in the eighth century merely as names were constantly being rediscovered in the tenth and eleventh centuries; copies were made and exchanged among the monasteries, and text-books were enlarged and improved.

Progress in Monastic Education during the Middle Age.

The mathematical studies were especially enriched by the rediscovery of their originals. We have already noticed that the more abstract side of these studies was not available in Latin works and had therefore not been carried over into the church system of learning. They were brought to the knowledge of the monastery schools by a curious and roundabout route. The Mohammedans had spread over the Greek world of the eastern Mediterranean and had occupied such centres of Greek culture as Alexandria in Egypt. They had taken into their Arabian culture a good deal more of Greek mathematics and science and philosophy than had been transmitted to the Latin schools of the west. The Moors in Spain had participated in this development, and the Spanish universities of Cordova and Seville were far in advance of the schools of Christian Europe. In the twelfth century monkish scholars from England, France, and Germany went to Spain to study and brought back translations of Greek works on mathematics and philosophy with their Arabian commentaries.

Mathematical Sciences among the Mohammedans.

What we have made out here will show the mistake of believing that there was no intellectual progress within the limits of the Middle Age. On the contrary, from the ninth century on, every generation saw an increase in the amount of knowledge and an improvement in the instruments for imparting it.

Meagre Amount of Learning in the Ninth Century.

A measure of this advance can be gained by comparing the monastic learning of the age of Charlemagne with that of the twelfth century. The education available in the schools founded by Alcuin and his co-workers in the empire of Charlemagne was very meagre. It was based mainly on the slight manuals and summaries which had been compiled by the church fathers of the sixth, seventh, and eighth centuries. To be sure, there were some copies of older and better works, but these were few and apparently the teachers of the ninth century were not competent to use them. Grammar, rhetoric, and logic were confined to the learning of formal rules and definitions; the larger technical works familiar to Roman scholars of the fourth century were not studied, and little use was made of the models of language, style, and ideas to be found in the masterpieces of Roman literature. Arithmetic included little more than the simple operations of computing, rendered more difficult by the clumsy Roman numerals. It embraced also the study of the mystic properties of numbers.* Geometry was largely composed of simple rules for land measurement and descriptions of the different parts of the world, or what we should call geography. Astronomy meant the study of the seasons, the phases of the moon, for the reckoning of the date of Easter, the names of the stars, and astrology (the notions about the influence of the stars on human fortunes).

Advance by the Twelfth Century.

The monastery schools of the ninth century, therefore, supplied a very thin diet of learning to its scholars, a curious compound made up of the elements of Roman studies, of misunderstood conceptions of higher knowledge, and of absurd and superstitious notions. By the end of the twelfth century the content of the studies was

* The mystic properties of numbers seem to us imaginary. Thus, six was regarded as the only perfect number because it equals the sum of all its divisors, and because it was a perfect number God created the world in six days. Three was supposed to have a mystic property because it is the only number whose square is greater than the cube of the number next below it.

immensely increased and improved. The literary studies of grammar and rhetoric included the larger technical grammars, the rhetorical works of learned Romans like Cicero and Quintilian, and the study of Roman literature from the classical writings of Vergil and other Roman authors. Logic was based on a knowledge of the complete logical works of Aristotle and of many Greek and Arabian commentaries, made available in Latin translations.

Literary Studies.

The mathematical studies were especially enriched. In arithmetic, the monastery schools had acquired from the Mohammedans the use of the so-called Arabic (really Hindu) numerals, including the zero, by means of which quantity could be indicated by the position of the digits. It also included the use of letters or symbols, that is, elementary algebra. The works of the Greek mathematician Euclid of Alexandria were secured also from Arabian translations current in Mohammedan Spain, and made possible a very fair course in plane geometry. Similarly for astronomy, the standard work of Greek learning in this science, the astronomy of Ptolemy, became familiar to the schools in the west in the twelfth century.

Mathematical Studies.

The result of all this advance was that the "seven liberal arts" could be pursued as higher studies. This was true, of course, mainly of the larger schools in favored situations, and especially of the cathedral or bishops' schools, which were usually located in the larger cities. There large libraries were collected and the means developed for higher instruction. All this was preparatory to the emergence of the universities, which grew out of cathedral rather than monastery schools, and in which an essential division was the "faculty of arts," the enlarged curriculum the evolution of which we have been tracing. This advance in learning may be regarded as the real origin of the universities. The advance was not confined to the general course in "arts"; technical studies like theology, law, and medicine developed in the same way to the point where they could be pursued as advanced subjects. The greater universi-

The "Faculty of Arts" in the Universities.

ties regularly included "faculties" of arts, medicine, law, and theology.

In the intellectual system of the Middle Age the highest study was theology, which in fact included philosophy also. The greatest intellectual achievement of the mediæval scholars was the thirteenth-century synthesis of the existing doctrines of the church and the existing ideas of philosophy and science and logic. This combination was in the form of a systematic theology, reconciling faith and reason, in which faith was represented by the teachings of the church resting on divine authority, and reason was represented by the philosophical system of Aristotle, enjoying an almost equal reverence of the theologians.

Theology, Including Philosophy.

The logical and metaphysical element in mediæval theology had been introduced in three stages. (1) The lowest and deepest stratum was that amount of Greek philosophy which had been imported into the Christian doctrines in the period of their formulation, down to about 400. Controversies had arisen in the early church over the difficulties and mysteries of the faith, in which both parties to the conflict took the weapons of argument at hand in the learning of the age. The incarnation, the Trinity, the relation of the Son to the Father, and similar questions, were settled by using the conceptions of Greek philosophy, and these conceptions were embodied in the creed and doctrines. (2) The early Middle Age had little knowledge of the philosophy upon which this original work rested, but it possessed, in the elementary treatises on logic which were studied in the monastery schools, some hints of the problems which Greek schools of philosophy had handled. An occasional scholar of the tenth or eleventh century made hesitating attempts to apply logical methods and philosophical conceptions to religious questions, but with very inadequate material and with modest results. (3) The twelfth century saw the introduction of the complete works of Aristotle to the knowledge of the church

Stages in Development of Philosophy.

(1) In the Early Formation of Christian Doctrines.

(2) In the Dark Ages.

(3) In the Revival of Aristotle.

schoolmen. This system of thinking, so completely organized, so comprehensive in its reach, so carefully grounded in logic and reason, made a tremendous impression on them. At first regarded by the church authorities with suspicion, because of its complete reliance on human reason and its complete ignoring of faith, it was eventually adopted by theologians and made the basis of a new and more systematic formulation of Catholic doctrine.

This evolution can be illustrated by noticing the prevailing tendencies in theology in successive periods. In the early Middle Age, to the eleventh century, theology was little more than the learning of what had been handed down by the early church fathers. In the eleventh century there arose a philosophical controversy over the question of the "universals" (whether the general ideas or concepts were real things, or whether reality inhered only in the particular objects or forms).* This problem, which was at the root of the conflict between the ancient Greek schools of Plato and Aristotle, was found in the text-books on logic which the churchmen studied in the schools. In that century the learned Anselm, archbishop of Canterbury, attempted to demonstrate the existence of God, the nature of Christ, and other fundamental propositions of the faith, by logic and reason, using what knowledge was then available of Greek philosophy.

Eleventh-Century Interest in Logic and Philosophy

* Those who held that general or abstract terms corresponded to realities having real existence, were known as "realists"; those who, on the contrary, held that reality was to be found only in individual things and that general or abstract terms were merely names, were known as "nominalists."

Roscelin, canon of the cathedral of Compiègne, about 1090, expounded the nominalist doctrine. He taught that genera, species, qualities were abstractions and not realities. He based his argument on the appeal to the senses. Who ever saw "humanity," or "wisdom," or "color"? Individual human beings are real things, but humanity as such has no independent existence. Color or wisdom does not exist by itself; on the other hand, a wise man or a colored object has real existence.

Obviously this teaching was sceptical and materialistic in its tendency; Roscelin himself had been led by it to cast doubt on the reality of the Trinity as one God. The teaching was therefore combated by the leading churchmen and theologians of the time. The contem-

Both the controversy over universals and the attempts of Anselm at constructing a systematic theology were seriously hampered by the incomplete knowledge and the mistaken interpretations which characterized the education of the time.

Abelard. R., I, 187, 188, 189.

In the early twelfth century a more complete knowledge of the logic of Aristotle led the great French scholar, Abelard, to criticise the accepted interpretations of theology and to submit the doctrines of the church to the test of reason. To the orthodox churchmen of the time his teachings seemed to be based entirely on human reason and logic, and to constitute a serious menace to faith. He was driven from one school to another, and finally compelled, under threat of excommunication, to abandon his teaching and to retract his opinions.

Systematic Theology of the Thirteenth Century.

The real valùe of Aristotle for the formulation and systematizing of theology was too great to permit his works to be neglected. The way of reconciling faith and reason, Christian doctrine and Greek philosophy, was found by the theologians of the thirteenth century. Accepting the whole body of faith as final and authoritative and beyond question, because they were divinely revealed, these schoolmen used the logic and metaphysics of Aristotle to demonstrate that they were reasonable also. This work was done largely by members of the Dominican order,

porary William of Champeaux, at the cathedral school of Paris, set forth the realist position. True reality belongs only to the genus or species: humanity (the human species) is a real thing; it is the substance which manifests itself in the accidental (or individual) form of the man Socrates or the man Plato. Anselm, the learned archbishop of Canterbury, gives a similar explanation in his theological works. The attributes (abstract qualities) are true substances and are the object of rational knowledge; they have an existence anterior to and more real than the objects of sense (the individual things). Humanity, wisdom, color, therefore, are realities, universal substances.

The realist doctrine was evidently the one more adapted to explaining the mysteries of the faith. It gave a metaphysical basis for comprehending the mystery of the Trinity (one God in three persons), the Incarnation, transubstantiation (the change of the substance of the bread and wine into the substance of the body and blood of Christ, while the accidents of material and shape remained the same).

which secured virtually a monopoly of the teaching of theology in the universities. The devotion of this order to the church made certain in advance that these studies would not lead to a weakening of the faith, and so a way was found for a fairly complete and independent study of philosophy, although it was always officially subordinate to theology.

Work of the Dominicans.

The greatest example of this work was the systematic theology of St. Thomas Aquinas (Thomas of Aquino, in Italy). He was a Dominican friar who studied and later taught at the university of Paris and at other centres of learning shortly after the middle of the thirteenth century. He was deeply versed in Aristotle, upon whose works he wrote several learned treatises. His great work, the *Summa Theologiæ*, well illustrates both the learning and the methods of the period. It was an attempt to construct a complete system of the doctrines and teachings and practices of the church, supported and demonstrated by the accepted principles of the logic and metaphysics of Aristotle and by all other sources of logic and reason available at the time. Beginning with the most fundamental problem (whether the existence of God is demonstrable or not) he proceeds step by step to examine and prove every particular point in Catholic faith. The result was intended, and was generally accepted, as the incontrovertible demonstration of the truth of Christian doctrine by both divine and human authority, by both faith and reason.

St. Thomas Aquinas.

R., I, 194.

The method of demonstration was characteristic of the age in its trust in formal logical rules. At each point he begins by stating the problem and first giving the reasons for denying what he expects to prove. Then he poses the authoritative statement upon which the accepted belief rests, usually from the Scriptures or from one of the orthodox fathers. Then he gives the reasons for accepting the belief, very largely based on the principles of Aristotle's metaphysics, and finally refutes the objections to the belief which he had first stated. Such a demonstration has the appearance of considering both sides of the problem and reaching the con-

Scholastic Method.

clusion on the grounds of logic and reason; in fact, of course, the conclusion had been reached in advance in the mind of the writer, on grounds of faith and the authority of the church.*

St. Thomas was only one (although the chief one) of a number of philosophical theologians, mostly members of the Dominican order. Their combined work in systematizing religious belief constitutes what is usually known as the "scholastic system" or "scholasticism." Its main features, as is apparent from what we have studied, were: (1) complete acceptance of the authority of the church in matters of belief and opinion; (2) reverence for Aristotle as the final authority in logic and reason, "the master of those who know," as the contemporary Dante calls him; and (3) a formal logical method of demonstration, which was more valuable for systematizing past knowledge than for acquiring new.

The "Scholastic System."

Its Characteristics.

Civil law was taught in many schools, sometimes as a part of grammar, sometimes as a part of rhetoric, but finally as an independent subject. The clergy and monks devoted themselves to its study with great zeal and practised it with financial profit. For some time they were the chief, if not the only, lawyers in many parts. Medicine was very little studied in the schools, its study and practice being confined chiefly to the clergy and monks. It is known that

Civil Law.

* To illustrate this subtle method, we may summarize the argument in the section on the existence of God. First the question is posed: "Whether God exists or not." Then the reasons for denying the existence of God: "It seems that God does not exist. For if one of two contradictions is infinite, the other is destroyed. But the name God means infinite good; therefore, if God exists there can be no evil. But there is evil; hence God does not exist." Then the authoritative word: "But against this is the word of God in Exodus 3:14; 'I am that I am.'" Then the reasons for believing that God exists, drawn from philosophical notions of the "prime mover," the "first cause," etc., with references to Aristotle. And finally the refutation of the argument from the existence of evil, on the authority of Augustine; namely, that it belongs to the infinite goodness of God to permit evil to exist in order that He may bring good out of it.

An excellent illustration of this method is the letter of Innocent III, in which he decides between the claimants of the imperial crown. The letter will be found in the Source Book, No. 130.

clergymen occasionally owed their advancement to high positions in the church (bishoprics) to their reputation as practising physicians. Whatever medical knowledge they possessed was obtained from translations of medical works by Greek authors.

During the twelfth century the monastery schools seem to have closed their doors to all except monks, and the cathedral schools then sprang into fame and began a development which resulted in the establishment of universities, which were fostered by both the pope and secular rulers. The name of a university in the Middle Age was *studium generale*, meaning a place of study which received students from everywhere. *Universitas* meant simply the "whole," or "all," and was a common name for a guild. In the twelfth century there were only four universities existing in Europe, namely, Paris, Oxford, Bologna (famous for its law), and Salerno (for its medicine). The university of Salerno seems to have had no influence on the development of universities and the university movement. The other three, however, served as models for the organization of other universities.

Rise of Universities.

S. B., 176. R., 190.

Bologna, a "Student" University.

The university of Bologna is called a "student" university, because its government and organization had their beginning in the guilds or associations of students. Bologna was the home of many professors, whose fame attracted students from all quarters. The professors were, however, merely private teachers, without organization, each one following his profession in an independent way. Many of the students at Bologna were foreigners, and, being without political rights there, they formed guilds for mutual protection and co-operation (a little before 1200). These student guilds elected a student as their head or rector to look after their interests. He made terms with the professors, hiring them and fixing the amount of their fees. The students proved to be rather hard masters and made stringent rules for the conduct of the professors. They fined a professor who failed to meet his class or who came late. No professor could leave the city without the consent of his pupils and of the rector; and, besides, he had to deposit a sum of money with the rector as a guarantee that he would return. The professor was at the mercy of the students, who found it easy to bring him to terms by boycotting him. In the same way the students were able to put great pressure on the tradesmen and landlords of the town. Of the city government the students demanded many favors, such as freedom from arrest and from taxation, and the right to be tried in a court of their own. They were generally able to secure what they demanded by threatening to secede and go to some other city. As the university had no buildings or property, but consisted merely of students and teachers, it could easily be removed from one place to another.

O., 62.

From the number and character of the students' songs that have come down to us we may form some idea of their gay, careless life.

Paris, a University of Professors.

O, 60. R, 191, 192.

The university of Paris grew out of the cathedral school of Paris and had its beginning in a guild of masters. The chancellor of the cathedral, who had charge of the cathedral schools, was bound to grant a license to teach to all who successfully passed the examination which he set them. All who were thus licensed were called masters. In the twelfth century the number of these masters increased rapidly and they formed a guild (about 1170) for mutual aid and protection, just as the students of Bologna had done. They put themselves under the protection of the pope and asked his aid. They often had quarrels with the people of the city, in which they were generally victorious. Their weapons were the boycott, strike, and secession. More than once they withdrew from Paris and refused to return until their demands were granted. The bishop of Paris, through the chancellor of his cathedral, retained a large measure of control over the university.

Oxford, a Third Type.

The university of Oxford furnishes us a slightly different type. It seems to have been founded by English masters and students, who, about 1167, for some unknown reason, withdrew from the university of Paris. In general, it resembled the university of Paris, being a university of masters. But as Oxford was not a cathedral town, its university had a development somewhat different from that of the university of Paris. The university of Oxford was able to free itself from the control of the bishop, who lived at Lincoln, some distance away, and to acquire greater powers of self-government. In fact, it was not long before the government of the town was largely in the hands of the officials of the university.

Growth of the Educational Movement.

O., 61

The educational movement grew, as may be seen from the fact that in the thirteenth century seventeen universities were founded, in the fourteenth twenty-one, and in the fifteenth not less than thirty-five. These were all founded on the model of one of the three universities which have just been described. Strikes and secessions on the part of the professors or students were common, and often resulted in the establishment of a university in a neighboring town. The great increase in the number of masters, who wished to gain a livelihood by teaching, also had some influence, and occasionally a town, being ambitious to have a *studium generale*, took the initiative and hired the professors of some university to come and establish a university among them. It was inevitable that in the interest of uniformity all masters should be required to have about the same attainments. Consequently, a standard curriculum, or course of study, was early established, certain subjects and a fixed number of years of residence being required before the candidate could obtain the license to teach (master's degree). The students then, losing sight of the broader aim of culture, unwisely confined themselves to the required subjects and neglected all branches which were not necessary for obtaining a degree. Under this scheme the study of the classics (Latin literature) declined, and education became sterile and stereotyped. This state of affairs lasted until the great educational reforms of the Renaissance, a prominent feature of which was the sympathetic study of the classics for their living beauty.

Much of the education in the Middle Age was what we should to-day call practical, or vocational. That is, it was planned for the express purpose of fitting men for their life-work: to be clergymen, teachers, and secretaries. Many pursued the course of study in an uninterested way, content to acquire the smallest possible amount of learning that would permit them to follow their profession. On the other hand, ambition led some of them to apply themselves with great zeal to their studies, in the hope that they might rise to the positions of highest honor open to them. There was, however, toward the end of the Middle Age an increasing number of men, who studied for the pleasure in acquiring knowledge, for the joy in knowing, and for the culture which comes only from an acquaintance with the best things that have been said and done.*

Practical Education.

S. B., 10.

One of the most characteristic features of the culture of the Middle Age was the literature produced by feudal society. The best of it was in the form of narrative poems of the "romantic" type, dealing with the adventures and deeds of heroes, and colored with all the picturesque life of the feudal age. Before we consider it, however, we must first notice briefly the development of the national languages in which it was written. The languages spoken in western Europe in the Middle Age, as now, were mainly of two groups, Romance and Germanic, or Teutonic. The Romance languages are those which developed out of the Latin spoken in the provinces of the Roman empire; they are to be found, therefore, in that part of Europe in which the population, even after the Germanic invasions, was still largely composed of the descendants of Roman provincials. The Germanic languages were those developed out of the dialects spoken by the German tribes. They are to be found in central Europe, which is the ancient home of the Germans; in that part of the Rhine valley which was occupied in great number by the Germans during the invasions; in the British isles, where the Angles

Mediæval Literature.

Popular Languages of the Middle Age.

The Romance Languages.

* Education not only enabled one to make a living; it was also held in such high repute that it supplied all the defects of birth, and made its possessor, although of common birth, the equal, in the social scale, of the nobleman. *Cf.* S. B., 294, 295.

and Saxons became the ruling part of the population, and in the Scandinavian countries to the far north.*

The Romance languages (French, Spanish, Italian, Portuguese, Roumanian, and Romansch) developed out of "spoken Latin," not out of the literary Latin which we study. We all recognize that there is a difference between the language of every-day speech and the language which we read in books and use in writing. The latter is more conventional and fixed in its forms. In every-day speech there are popular tendencies which, if allowed to develop freely, would change the language in successive generations, and produce wider and wider differences in different parts of the country. There are tendencies to neglect the rules of grammar in talking, to pronounce words differently in different parts of the country, and to use words and phrases not generally found or tolerated in the written language. What prevents our own language from changing in this way more rapidly than it does, is a common and wide-spread knowledge of the standard and fixed form, due to public education and general reading. The same thing was true of the Latin spoken in the empire. There was a high level of culture among the upper classes, and even the uneducated heard correct Latin in public speeches, in the theatre, and in public proclamations. Moreover, the natural tendency to speak differently in different parts of the empire was checked by the strong bonds which held the whole empire together; the language used in Rome itself was known throughout the whole empire because Roman officials and soldiers went everywhere, and because the one standard literary form was heard and read everywhere.

Their Evolution from Spoken Latin.

Now, it was just the failure of these bonds and the decline of this culture which produced the several distinct Romance languages. The shock of the invasions was followed by three

* Notice the "language frontier" established by the researches of recent scholars, as pictured on the accompanying map. It marks the limit of the actual occupation of Roman territory by the Germans west and south of the Rhine-Danube frontier. After the migrations the languages spoken south and west of that line were Latin, and those east and north were Germanic.

Note to Map XXI.—The dotted line represents the modern frontier between the Germanic and the Romance groups of languages. East and north of the line the people speak languages developed from the speech of the German tribes: Frisians, Franks, Saxons, Bavarians, Alemanni, etc.; south and west the people speak languages derived from the Latin speech of the Roman provincials. Flemish is spoken in northern Belgium; Dutch in Holland. The people of Germany use one standard literary language, but the popular speech is in two dialects, High German in the centre and south, Low German in the north. The "Walloons" are the people of southern Belgium, who speak a dialect of French. Switzerland also is divided by the language frontier; the southwestern part speaks French (around the Lake of Geneva); the northeastern part (Berne, Zurich, Luzerne, etc.) speaks High German; a small strip on the south contains Italian-speaking people. In this southern part there are also a few small districts in which a Romance language distinct from Italian is spoken; this is known as Rhæto-Romanic, a name derived from the old Roman province of Rhætia, in this region.

This is the language frontier of to-day; it corresponds pretty closely to that of the Middle Age. Note the advance south and west of the Germanic language, beyond the line of the Rhine and Danube, which must have been the language frontier in Roman times. This represents the limits of the actual germanizing of Roman lands by the invasions: the Germans who settled farther within the empire (such as the Western Franks, the Burgundians, the Lombards, etc.) were absorbed in the Roman population and their descendants speak Romance languages.

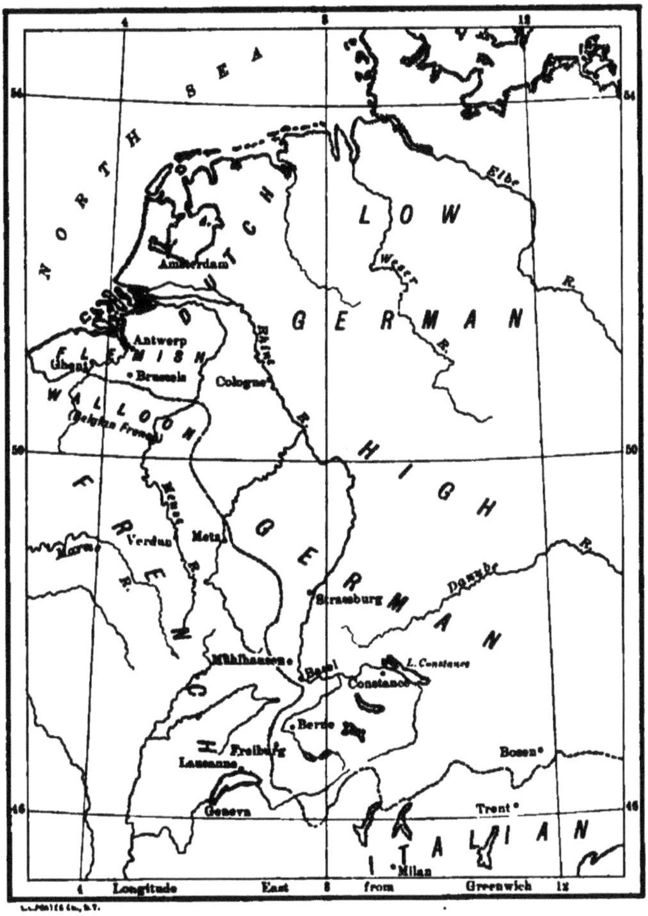

XXI

LANGUAGE FRONTIER BETWEEN THE ROMANCE AND GERMANIC PEOPLES

or four hundred years of violence and disorder. The Roman empire and its institutions fell to pieces; the schools ceased, the theatre and the forum fell into ruins. No longer confronted by a standard and conventionalized language, the popular speech developed its tendencies freely, changing in each generation farther and farther away from what had once been recognized as the correct Latin. Since the empire was no longer under one government, the speech of the different provinces tended to diverge more and more widely. The result was the formation of the distinct Romance languages, differing widely from the literary Latin we read in classical works, and differing widely also from one another, although their relationship both to Latin and to one another is easily recognized.

Germanic Languages.

The Germanic languages developed out of the dialects spoken by the German tribes before the invasions; the history of the languages therefore is directly related to the history of the tribes. Some of them migrated and settled far within the empire, and were absorbed in the Roman population; their speech disappeared entirely, except as it may have influenced somewhat the character of the Romance dialects of the regions in which they settled. Such was the fate of the speech of the Burgundians, Lombards, Goths, and Vandals. The small tribes of Angles and Saxons became the ruling element of the population in the British isles, and their speech furnished the basis of the great national literary language, English. East Franks, Bavarians, Alamanni, and Saxons united to form a single nation, the Germans, and a single national language, German, developed among them. The northern part of the Netherlands became an independent state, Holland, and the local dialect spoken there developed into the literary language known as Dutch.

Feudal Literature.

The principal literary languages of the Middle Age were Old French, the language of northern France; Provençal, the language of southern France; "Middle High German," the language of southern Germany in the twelfth and thirteenth centuries; and English. There were also important works written in Spanish, Italian, and the Scandinavian tongues, but these lie rather to one side of the main current of feudal literature. In the first place, we should notice that the literature of the feudal age is a direct product of feudal society. This literature could not develop until feudal society had progressed far enough in organizing its resources and its life to demand and support a literature expressing its ideals and appealing to its sentiments and interests. The hearth of this literature was, therefore, the feudal castle, and especially the great castle which was the court of a great feudal prince. Here the feudal poet found an appreciative audience and found also encouragement and patronage. The literature had to be in the form of exciting stories which would interest the feudal audience. The poets found their materials in the legends and traditions that had come down to the feudal age from various sources in the past: old Germanic traditions and myths, legendary stories of Charlemagne and his age, Celtic traditions of the great hero Arthur and his companions, and romantic tales from the later Roman empire, dealing with the siege of Troy and the famous exploits of Alexander and Cæsar. These stories they retold in the language of the feudal nobles whom they served, and in the spirit and manner of the feudal age, picturing Greek heroes, Charlemagne's followers, and Arthur's warriors, all alike, as feudal knights of the twelfth or thirteenth century.

Old French Literature.

"Chansons de Geste."

"Chanson de Roland."

The finest and most characteristic feudal literature is that in Old French. There are two distinct periods. The earlier poems, from the middle of the eleventh to the middle of the twelfth century, reflect the manners of the earlier rough feudal age; the later poems picture a society in which chivalry and courtesy had made a great advance. The earlier were called "chansons de geste," or "poems of heroic deeds." The poets took their themes from the traditions of the age of Charlemagne. Many of them deal with the defense of southern France against the Mohammedans in Spain; others are stories of brutal private war between feudal nobles. The most famous is the "Song of Roland" ("Chanson de Roland"). It is a long narrative poem of some 4,000 lines, and tells the familiar story of how Roland, a hero of Charlemagne's court, defended the rear-guard with 20,000 knights, against hundreds of thousands of Mohammedans.

In these poems the narrative consists, for the greater part, of the description of battles, told in the form of a series of single combats, with what would seem to us monotonous repetition of the same sort of incidents. They are brutal and bloody, but convey somehow an impression of grandeur. The ideals of the feudal knight as pictured in this literature are those of the rough and warlike period of feudalism: sheer physical strength and courage, pride and arrogance, fidelity of vassal and follower to his lord combined with a proud insistence on his own individual rights and dignity, and an unquestioning acceptance of the Christian faith, shown principally by a hatred of the infidel (the spirit of the first crusade). Women play almost no part in the stories; it is an age of fighters and heroes.

Character.

The literature of the later period, after the middle of the twelfth century, differs very greatly from this earlier, cruder form, both in its subjects and in its spirit. Feudal society had made great advances in organization and in refinement. The great courts of feudal princes had become the centres of polite society; manners and tastes had improved, and greater stress was laid on social intercourse and on courtesy. These changes brought about a change in the literary taste of the nobles; they preferred to hear tales of love, of marvellous adventures, of tournaments and festivals.* The professional poets of course produced a poetry to meet the new demands; in this sense the literature of this period may be called "court poetry." The poets had to seek new subjects, since the type of hero treated in the Charlemagne

Romances of Chivalry.

* This change was partly due to the influence of the south of France upon feudal society in the north. In the courts of Provence and Toulouse and Aquitaine a rich culture had developed earlier than in the north, and the ideals of chivalry and courtesy had been reflected in the local literature. This literature was in the form of short lyric love poems, composed by professional court poets known as "troubadours."

stories had become fixed. They found this material in the fabulous stories of Arthur and his heroes. These stories had grown up among the Celts in Brittany and Wales, centring around the legendary figure of an ancient tribal hero, who, they imagined, had defeated the Saxons, conquered the Romans, and ruled over the world. From Brittany directly, or from Wales through the Norman-English poets, the poets of northern France became acquainted with this legendary material and used it for the framework of their romances of chivalry.* In these later French poems the ideals of the knight were those of a more refined age. The chief motives which actuated the heroes of these tales were love of a lady and desire for adventure and fame. The knight was still brave and strong, but his prowess was shown in tournaments and in adventures encountered on the way, rather than in feudal warfare or fighting with the infidel. The stories are enlivened by descriptions of tournaments, of ceremonies such as knighting, of arms and armor, and of life in the castle, showing the more cultured, if less heroic, spirit of this age.

One branch of the Arthur stories received an elaborate treatment in the thirteenth and later centuries because it appealed to religious sentiment as well as to a taste for tales of chivalry.

Legends of the "Holy Grail."

This was the legend of the "Holy Grail," the cup of the Last Supper which caught the blood that flowed from the side of Jesus on the cross. The crusading age had developed in western Europe an intense interest in the relics of the life of Jesus, and many old traditions coming from early Christianity had grown into marvellous legends, such as stories of the true cross, the crown of thorns, the lance that pierced the side of Jesus, and the Holy Grail. The Grail story was combined with a Celtic fairy-story of a marvellous vessel, first told by a French poet at the end of the twelfth century (the story of "Perceval" by Christian of Troyes, about

* These are the stories which the Englishman Mallory translated in the fifteenth century, and which Tennyson retold in his "Idylls of the King"—the stories of Lancelot and Guinevere, of Tristan and Isolde, of Geraint and Enid.

1180). The tale was taken up and elaborated later by French and German poets, and became the centre of a whole group of romances, telling of a marvellous castle in which the Grail was guarded by an order of knights dedicated to that service, and of the adventures of Arthur's knights in trying to find it.

The feudal literature of other lands we can only mention briefly. That of Germany began with translations of French romances, but it included also poems dealing with ancient traditions. The most famous of these and the only one that has come down to us in a complete form is the "Song of the Nibelungs" (das "Nibelungenlied"). It is the famous story of Siegfried and Brunhilda, which Wagner took as the theme of his music dramas. The German court poets also produced a fine literature in the form of short lyrics, dealing mainly with love. This is known as the poetry of the Minnesingers, "Minne" being an old German word for love. It was inspired by the earlier lyric poetry of the troubadours of the south of France. In Spain, in Italy, and in England feudal poets were producing in this age a beautiful and abundant literature, not differing essentially, however, from that we have already described in the case of France.

Feudal Literature in Middle High German

"Nibelungenlied."

Minnesingers.

We cannot leave the subject of literature in native languages without noticing one very important form produced under the auspices of the church. The church in the Middle Age sought by every possible means to impress the people with the ideas of the faith and with the history of Christianity. One popular and successful method was found in the dramatizing of the incidents of the religious story. On great feast days, especially Christmas and Easter, the service was accompanied or followed by a representation of the incidents celebrated in the service. On Christmas, for example, the clergy would show the chorus of angels, the shepherds coming to the cradle of Jesus, the procession of the wise men of the east, and the group of Joseph and Mary with the child. On Easter they would show the empty tomb, and the women who came seeking the body of Jesus, and the angel who said: "He

Religious Drama.

is not here, but is risen." These little scenes were really amplified parts of the service, and the words of the actors were taken from the service itself or from the Scriptures. In the later centuries, after 1200, they became very popular and soon outgrew the limitations of the church setting. At first they had been short scenes composed in Latin by the clergy; later they became long and elaborate plays, written in the native languages and composed by professional writers. They were presented in the public squares on stages specially built for the purpose, and they came to include a great many elements that were not religious but intended simply to amuse or interest the audiences. Thus they passed from the control of the church and became popular entertainments, but they still retained something of their religious character, in that the plots were still drawn from religious stories. The later plays were not restricted, however, to tales from the Bible, but drew very largely from the legendary lives of the saints, and from stories of miracles performed by relics and statues, and from other popular tales.

The culture of a period may be estimated to a certain extent by its practice of the fine arts. It is important, therefore, to know something about the architecture, sculpture, and painting of the Middle Age. You will recall that the Roman empire had been expanded so that it included the territory west of the Rhine and also what is now called England. Within that territory the Roman art of building had flourished, and in the cities were to be found fine examples of temples, amphitheatres, and other buildings that compared favorably with those in Italy and other parts of the empire. After the German invasions, however, the Roman art of building almost ceased for some centuries and even many of the buildings that had been erected fell into decay. Of course the people in those lands from the fifth to the tenth century must have built some sort of structures, but very few of them have survived, so that we have scant information about them. They probably made most of their buildings of wood. They did, however, erect some buildings in stone, and

Roman Architecture Declined.

FAÇADE OF NOTRE-DAME-DE LA-GRANDE, AT POITIERS.

FAÇADE OF SAINT-PIERRE, AT ANGOULÊME.

FAÇADE OF NOTRE-DAME-DU-PUY.
Photo Neurdein.

EXAMPLES OF ROMANESQUE ARCHITECTURE.

CHURCH OF LA TRINITÉ, VENDÔME.

NAVE OF THE CATHEDRAL OF AMIENS.

CANTERBURY CATHEDRAL.

Photo by Spooner.

LINCOLN CATHEDRAL.

EXAMPLES OF GOTHIC ARCHITECTURE

BAS-RELIEF IN BAYEUX CATHEDRAL.

NAVE OF THE CATHEDRAL OF CHARTRES.

NATIVITY.
Fragment of the destroyed rood-screen of the Cathedral of Chartres.

FLYING BUTTRESSES OF STE. GUDULE, BRUSSELS.
(Reusens, Archéologie Chrétienne.)

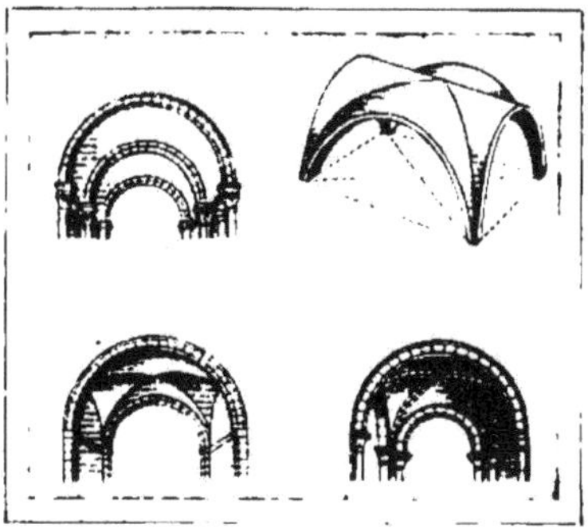

TYPES OF VAULTS.
1. Barrel vault. 2. Extrados of a groined vault. 3. Intrados of a Roman groined vault. 4. Intrados of a groined vault with salient ribs.
(Reusens, Archéologie Chrétienne.)

FRAGMENT OF STAINED GLASS OF NOTRE-DAME-DE-CHARTRES.
The Annunciation—The Annunciation to the Shepherds—The Nativity.

(Bibliothèque Nationale, Paris.)

SIEGE OF JERICHO.
History of the Jews, by Josephus.
JEAN FOUQUET.

(Bibliothèque Nationale. Paris.)
Photo Berthaud.

ST. JUSTINA.
MORETTO.
(Museum, Vienna.)

THE MARRIAGE AT CANA.
Ms. Lat. 919. JACQUEMART DE HESDIN.
(Bibliothèque Nationale, Paris.)

PROPHET, CHURCH OF SOUILLAC.

VIRGIN AND CHILD. FAÇADE OF THE CHURCH OF SAINTE-CROIX, AT LA CHARITÉ.

Photo Mieusement.

SAINT THEODORE, SOUTH PORCH OF THE CATHEDRAL OF CHARTRES.

STATUE OF SAINT FOY AT CONQUES.

VIRGIN AND CHILD.
(Louvre, Paris.)
Wood.

EXAMPLES OF EARLY DECORATIVE CHURCH SCULPTURE.

BUST OF NICCOLO DA UZZANO (?).
DONATELLO.
(Museum, Florence.)

THE ANNUNCIATION.
BENEDETTO DE MAJANO.
(Church of Monte Oliveto, Naples.)
Photo by Alinari.

MADONNA WITH SAINTS.
MINO DA FIESOLE.
(Cathedral, Fiesole.)

HEAD OF THE DAVID.
MICHELANGELO.
(Academy, Florence.)

EXAMPLES OF RENAISSANCE SCULPTURE.

RICCARDI (MEDICI) PALACE, FLORENCE.

FAÇADE OF THE CERTOSA, PAVIA.

COURT OF THE PALAZZO DELLA CANCELLARIA, ROME.

COURT OF THE PALAZZO MARINO, MILAN.

EXAMPLES OF RENAISSANCE ARCHITECTURE.

CARTOON FOR A HOLY FAMILY.
LEONARDO DA VINCI.
(Royal Academy, London.)

MONNA LISA GIOCONDA.
LEONARDO DA VINCI.
(The Louvre.)

THE VIRGIN AND CHILD WITH SAINTS AND ANGELS.
PERUGINO.
(The Louvre.)
Photo Neurdein.

THE LAST SUPPER. LEONARDO DA VINCI.
(Refectory of Santa Maria delle Grazie, Milan.) *From Raphael Morghen's engraving.*

VIRGIN AND CHILD.
GIOVANNI BELLINI.
(National Gallery, London.)

MOSES. MICHELANGELO.
(Church of St. Pietro in Vincoli, Rome.)

MADONNA DELLA CASA TEMPI.
RAPHAEL.
(Pinacothek, Munich.)
Photo by Hanfstaengl.

THE THREE SISTERS.
PALMA.
(Dresden Gallery.)

EXAMPLES OF RENAISSANCE PAINTING AND SCULPTURE (MOSES).

those which still exist show features of the Byzantine style, a name that is applied to the architecture of Constantinople and the eastern empire. We know that when Charlemagne wished to build his church at Aachen (Aix-la-Chapelle) he had a number of pillars brought for it from Ravenna, in Italy, and his architect adopted the plan of one of the churches of Ravenna. Now, Ravenna had been for many years the residence of the Greek governor of Italy and its churches were Byzantine in style.

Romanesque Architecture.

Early in the eleventh century, however, there began in the west a new period of building. Raoul Glaber, a Burgundian monk, who died in 1050, wrote in his chronicle: "It was as if the world, throwing off its old garments, desired to reclothe itself in the white robes of the church. . . . The Christian nations seemed to rival one another in magnificence, in order to erect the most elegant churches. . . . All the religious buildings, cathedrals, country churches, and village chapels, were rebuilt and transformed into something better" shortly after the year 1000. He referred to the new style of architecture that had just made its appearance and is called Romanesque. From the illustrations between pages 490–491, we may easily determine the chief characteristics of the Romanesque style. It is characterized by the use of round arches, many of which are used merely in a decorative way to enliven what would otherwise be a big expanse of vacant wall. Horizontal lines are a prominent feature, by which the buildings seem to rise by stories. The walls are comparatively thick. Consequently, Romanesque churches are inclined to be dark and gloomy. The churches seem low and depressed. Because of the apparent strength and majesty of the buildings, the general impression is one of heaviness.

The walls were made thick and heavy in order to meet a change in the construction and material of the ceilings. Instead of making the ceilings flat and of wood, as hitherto, architects began to arch them and to construct them of stone. Thus the ceilings assumed the form of the "barrel" vaulting which of course was known to the Romans. The great weight of the stones and the "thrust" (as the side, or outward, pressure is called), caused by the heavy arched ceiling, tended to make the walls spread apart. To resist this outward pressure, or thrust, the walls were made thick, and, at regular intervals, strengthened by buttresses.

The spread of the Romanesque style, which arose about the year 1000, was due to the Benedictine monks, who were then closely bound together under the leadership of the monastery of Cluny. Hundreds of monasteries vied with one another in erecting magnificent churches, all in the Romanesque style. Most of the noted abbey churches of Europe are in this style.

Gothic Architecture.

Early in the twelfth century there was developed a new style of architecture called Gothic. Architects learned that by using diagonal and transverse ribs following the lines of intersection of two Romanesque vaults, *thus substituting the groined for the barrel vault*, by the adjustments of the piers and thrusts of different arches operating in counterpoise, and by the use of the flying buttress, they could concentrate the outward pressure, or thrust, on certain points of the wall, leaving the rest of the wall comparatively free from the weight of the roof. It was therefore no longer necessary to make the whole wall so thick, reinforcement being required only at those points at which the weight of the roof was concentrated. At such points the walls were strengthened with buttresses. To transfer the thrust of the vaulting to the buttresses, which also they reinforced by weighting them with pinnacles, the architects invented the flying buttress. That is, from the top of the buttress they threw an arch, called a flying buttress, over to that point of the wall at which the weight of the ceiling was concentrated. Now, a flying buttress, owing to its arch structure, is very strong and thus capable of aiding in the support of an immense weight. Consequently the architects were able to erect buildings more lofty than ever before. The ceilings of many of the Gothic churches reach a height of from one hundred to one hundred and seventy-five feet.

The two great principles underlying Gothic were the substitution of the groined for the barrel vault and the balance of transmitted thrusts. The skeleton construction thus secured made possible the great windows and an abundance of light so characteristic of Gothic. Since the weight of the vaulting was concentrated at certain points of the wall, the intervening spaces could be used for windows without weakening it. Consequently, in place of the comparatively solid walls of the Romanesque churches, Gothic buildings have many windows. They are also richly decorated with pinnacles and beautiful tracery and many other forms cut in stone. Long perpendicular lines predominate, and, as compared with the Romanesque style, the general impression is one of loftiness and comparative lightness.

It took a long time to build a great cathedral and it frequently happened that the work was interrupted for many years. When it was resumed it was generally necessary to employ another architect, and he often changed the style of the building to suit the taste and fashion of the time. So it is not uncommon to find a building, some parts of which are Romanesque, others in successive styles of Gothic, and still others of a later style.

Spread of Gothic.

Gothic architecture,* which had its beginnings in the first quarter of the twelfth century, spread rapidly through France and England, where it became popular and displaced, to a great extent, the Romanesque style. It spread more slowly to Germany, where the first Gothic buildings were erected in the thirteenth century. Once established, however, it held sway till deep into the sixteenth century, when it was slowly replaced by the art of the Renaissance, an account of which will be given in the next chapter. The Gothic style was employed chiefly in the cities, many of which had then become large and rich. In a spirit of rivalry they sought to outdo each other in erecting enormous Gothic churches, and they employed the same style in many of their city halls and other public buildings. Art in general, after

* What has been said about architecture applies fully only to western Europe. It does not concern Russia, which, as we have seen, had little in common with the rest of Europe, and it touches Italy only remotely. The examples of Italian Gothic architecture generally have only a limited and formal rather than structural resemblance to the Gothic buildings of western Europe.

having been used for centuries almost exclusively in the service of the church and religion, began to be used by laymen to enrich and beautify their life. They not only built for themselves magnificent Gothic palaces but also filled them with a profusion of works of art.

The people of the Middle Age spared no pains to make their churches beautiful. They decorated the exterior walls and roof with statues and bas-reliefs, and the interior with wall-paintings, statues, stained-glass windows, crucifixes, and other objects of art and beauty. Every church had also a number of chapels and altars which were also lavishly decorated with paintings, costly holy vessels, and various precious objects. So the churches of Europe, besides being venerable as churches, also possess the charm and interest of great museums of art.

Sculpture.

Sculpture was extensively practised, especially for the decoration of churches and public buildings. Architects made a most lavish use of it on the inside as well as on the outside of their buildings. Wherever it was possible they made a niche or a pedestal for one or more statues. Some of the cathedrals are decorated with hundreds of them, and the Milan cathedral has on its exterior alone more than two thousand. For the decoration of churches and public buildings Biblical characters and scenes and national heroes were generally chosen. Reclining statues of kings and other great persons were frequently placed on their tombs. Crucifixes and statues of saints dotted the roadside, and innumerable statuettes in wood and ivory were made for the decoration of chapels and altars. From the illustrations shown between pages 490–491 you might readily infer that the statues were often made not by artists but by stonemasons and other common laborers who possessed very little technical skill in their trade. In fact, however, the skill of the workmen who carved the statues no doubt surpassed the artists' ability to design. The poor statuary of the early Middle Age is no doubt due to the low artistic standard that prevailed and to the small inventing and designing ability of the artists of that time. Although mediæval statues are in general technically imperfect, yet in spite of clumsy drapery, awkward postures, and defective modelling, many of them possess great charm, and some of them are of admirable merit, being cleverly modified in a structural sense to accord with the architecture they decorate.

Painting.

The art of painting was practised in the Middle Age chiefly for the decoration of churches and the illumination of manuscripts. Especially the broad spaces on the walls of the Romanesque churches invited the painter's brush, and it early became the custom to fill the windows with stained and painted glass. Painters knew nothing of drawing and painting from models or from nature, and their drawing was consequently very defective. They told their story in a conventional and often crude way. They had a stereotyped way of presenting Biblical characters and scenes, and no painter dared deviate very far from the traditional manner or type, until the freer spirit of the Renaissance began to make itself felt. Before Giotto only in the illumination of manuscripts did the painter's art show much personal originality. The monks delighted to illustrate and decorate their devotional books, choosing for their subjects events from the Bible and from the lives of the saints. Some of the illuminators possessed a marvellous fertility of design and excelled in decorative tracery, surrounding the picture with a perfect maze of graceful lines and figures, the whole in the most brilliant colors.

CHAPTER XXVI

THE RENAISSANCE

In order to complete our study of the Middle Age we have yet to discuss one very important question: What brought about the change from the Middle Age to the Modern period? The cause is, of course, a very complex one, and is, to a great extent, to be found in what is called the Renaissance, a brief account of which is now to be given.

First of all, however, as a general preparation for the change from Mediæval to Modern, we must consider the fact that the peoples of Europe had made great progress in wealth and in all that wealth brings with it, and were therefore rapidly outgrowing their mediæval conditions. In the cities there was developing a society that was in many essential respects new. It was based not on nobility of birth, but rather on the possession of wealth. And since the wealth had generally been made through the personal efforts of its possessors, we may add that this society was based on individual worth and ability as well as on wealth. It contrasted strongly with feudal society, which had had its seat in the castle, perched on some hill more or less inaccessible. The nobles had spent their time in fighting, hunting, hawking, holding tournaments, and in other unproductive amusements and occupations. In the early centuries of feudalism the castle itself was meagrely furnished with simple, almost primitive furniture, and articles of comfort, to say nothing of luxury, were unknown. In the fourteenth and fifteenth centuries, however, we find in the cities a new society composed of the common people who had grown rich through industry and commerce. Between the serfs of feudal days and the nobility there had appeared what we now call the great middle class, rich in resources, strong in the will to do, and keen in the power to reason and to know.

Progress of the Peoples.

This society in the cities was in many respects much like

modern society and practised the same forms of social intercourse and entertainment as are practised now. Dinner parties, dances, masked balls, picnics, birthday parties, and gay festivities in connection with marriages were some of the amusements which characterized this new society in the cities, very much as they characterize society to-day. Fortunes were spent in the lavish entertainment of guests. This society regarded social intercourse as a fine art and tried to express it in beautiful and appropriate forms. At the same time house-decorating became an art again, and large sums of money were expended by wealthy householders for objects of art and for luxurious and comfortable furniture and furnishings. It is evident, therefore, that the new society formed a good basis for the change to the Modern period and that a long step had already been taken away from the Mediæval. The peoples of Europe, who, as we have seen, were barbarian in the fourth century, had in the intervening centuries developed much as a boy develops into a young man, and they were rapidly reaching their full intellectual stature.

New Society.

The heart of the Renaissance was humanism, a name that is applied to the new learning of the time. It was characterized by an intense admiration of everything that was ancient Roman and the eager adoption and imitation of it. Primarily, it concerned itself with the Latin language and literature, but the humanists, as its representatives are called, devoted themselves with boundless enthusiasm to the study of every field of Roman antiquity. They sought to acquire the culture of ancient Rome by restoring her language, literature, ideas, and ideals. The Latin word, *humanitas*, "humanity," was used to express the highest and most harmonious culture of all the human faculties and powers. Hence the name humanism was applied to the new learning, because it was thought to be the best means for developing in each individual the true humanity, that is, the highest culture and refinement. And the separate branches of study, such as Latin grammar, literature, poetry, history, and philology, came to be called the humanities.

Humanism. Its Ideals

Let us look first at Italian humanism, because the new learning had its origin in that country.* Dante (1265–1321) is generally regarded as the great forerunner of humanism, and Petrarch (1304–1374) its first great representative.

Dante.

Although Dante was not really a humanist and was not able to write a fine, clear Latin, nevertheless by his writings he did much to turn the thoughts of men toward Rome and her marvellous history. Of all the Latin authors he especially admired Vergil, whom he called his "leader, master and lord." He gave himself up to the dream of restoring Rome to her ancient position as head of the world by making the city again the residence of the emperors with the same power and authority as the great emperors had once exercised. The world to-day, however, remembers him not for his efforts in that direction, but for his great poem, "The Divine Comedy," which he composed not in Latin, but in Italian.

Petrarch.

On the other hand, Petrarch was a master of Latin. He wrote it with great refinement of style and spoke it with fluency and accuracy. He regarded Cicero as the greatest master of style, and he had the distinction of discovering some of the forgotten letters and orations of that famous orator. He thereby gave a great impulse to the quest for manuscripts containing the works of Latin authors. He wrote many works in Latin, on which he based his hope of fame. These, however, are now forgotten, and his literary fame rests on the beautiful poems and sonnets in Italian which he composed in his youth before he had become enamoured of Latin.

Many Humanists.

The great popularity of Petrarch led to the rapid spread of humanistic studies in all parts of Italy, although the universities were for some time uninfluenced by them. Hundreds of young men imitated him, and there was soon a host of humanists seeking employment and preferment at the courts of the numerous little principalities

* Of course Latin had been studied in all the schools of Europe, and there had been a revival of learning in the ninth century as a result of the attention which Charlemagne had bestowed on education. And there was a still greater revival of learning in the twelfth century, a prominent feature of which was the renewed study of Roman law.

and republics into which Italy had become divided. Popes, princes, and the rich aristocracy in the cities vied with one another in surrounding themselves with humanists, whom they employed as secretaries, ambassadors, companions, and tutors, intrusting them especially with the education of their children. Throughout Italy these humanists developed a many-sided activity. They produced poems, histories, works of fancy, grammars, critical studies, and stories, or "novelettes," in the greatest profusion. Some of them extended the field of their studies to include mathematics, physics, and other sciences. Indeed, "humanist" came soon to be identical with "polyhistor," for his ideal was enlarged into the desire to know all that could be known and to excel in every field of endeavor.* It was, in fact, not uncommon for a humanist to achieve fame as a poet, a prose-writer, athlete, scientist, painter, sculptor, and architect. His ambition was to be complete in his many-sidedness.

Study of Greek.

The Greek language and literature shared in the general admiration which the humanists had for antiquity. Merely to possess a Greek manuscript was a coveted distinction; a large sum was paid for a manuscript of Homer, although the purchaser could not read a word of it. Greeks were eagerly sought as teachers of their language. The first Greek teacher of note in Italy was Chrysoloras (1355–1415), who, at the pressing invitation of the people of Florence, came to that city and accepted a professorship of Greek (1396). He met with immense success and many of the greatest men in Florence became his pupils. He travelled extensively in the west and was at various times engaged in many of the Italian cities as a teacher of Greek. Toward the middle of the fifteenth century many Greeks, attracted by the rewards offered, came into Italy, where they won fame and wealth as teachers of Greek and translators of Greek writings.

* Polyhistor, a universal scholar; *i. e.*, one who has a large knowledge of all the departments, or fields, of learning and endeavor. This was the ideal which many men in the Renaissance pursued and virtually attained.

Italy was the home of humanism and of the Renaissance in general. Rome, being the head of the Christian world, annually drew many thousands who came on business connected with the church. These and thousands of pilgrims and merchants no doubt helped spread the ideas of the Renaissance. Travelling scholars and professors and artists, however, probably did the larger part of the work of dissemination. Naturally it spread to the neighboring countries first. Early in the fifteenth century the new learning was enthusiastically adopted in France and in Germany, and somewhat later it spread to England. In those northern countries, however, it took on a more serious character, and many humanists devoted themselves to the study of the Bible. Erasmus, the greatest of all the humanists, employed his scholarship in making a critical edition of the New Testament in Greek—the first one ever published—with a corrected Latin translation and learned notes. He was a bitter critic of the ignorance that prevailed among the monks and clergy and hoped to bring about the desired reform in the church through the spread of the new learning. And Melanchthon, the greatest of the German humanists, was closely associated with Luther and his reform movement.

Spread of Humanism.

The revival of learning had an important effect on education. Universities and schools had deteriorated because the course of study and the methods of teaching had become stereotyped, and students thought only of acquiring sufficient training to enable them to fill the positions which they hoped to obtain. In becoming merely vocational, education had lost much of its power to enlarge and beautify life. Now, in the minds of the humanists that was the chief object of education. So they naturally sought to change the course of study in such a way as to acquire the broadest and most perfect culture. The dull text-books that had been in use they replaced with the great masterpieces of Rome and Greece. In the classroom they read the works of Cicero, Vergil, Plautus, Aristotle (in Latin translation), and other great authors, with an appreciation and enthusiasm that have never been sur-

Revival in Education.

passed. The humanists made the course of study more effective by their better method of teaching and enriched it by the introduction of new subjects. In the course of study were to be found Latin, Greek, Hebrew, philology, psychology, physics, mathematics, history, geography, astronomy, law, medicine, and theology. The chief reform, however, was in the new spirit and method of teaching and studying. The universities generally opposed the new learning and the reform in education, but humanists established some new universities and independent schools, and the old universities were eventually forced to join the new movement. The old learning had been entirely under the control of the church; it was theological and scholastic. That is, it sought to co-ordinate all knowledge into one great system that would be in harmony with the creed of the church. The new learning was secular; it resisted all ecclesiastical domination and interference. The humanists generally sought first of all the truth, regardless of whether it agreed with the creed or not. The church must be made to conform to the truth, not the truth to the creed of the church.

In the field of art the Renaissance brought in a radical change. Roman architecture also shared in the admiration which the humanists felt for antiquity. In Italy there were still many Roman buildings in existence, so it is only natural that they should have had a marked influence on the architects of the time. Discarding the features that had characterized the Byzantine, the Romanesque, and the Gothic, they revived the Roman, or classical, style, employing the three ancient orders of architecture, the Doric, the Ionic, and the Corinthian. The huge size of many of the buildings which they erected permitted them to use all these orders in the same building, the Doric in the first story, the Ionic in the second, and the Corinthian in the third. The existence of a rich class in the cities created a demand for immense palaces, some of which are still the admiration of the world. They were frequently built of massive stone blocks, which in the lower story were left rough-hewn to increase the impression of strength and solidity. In the upper stories the blocks were generally smoother and less massive. And the whole building was crowned with a cornice of great width, which both added dignity and beauty to the building and protected it to some extent against the sun's rays. The new art, like the new learning, had its origin in Italy, and from there it spread in the course of the fifteenth and sixteenth centuries to the other countries of western Europe and gradually displaced all other styles of architecture.

The artistic sense of the people, which for some centuries had kept step with their intellectual growth and improvement, was undoubtedly quickened by the study of the remains of ancient art. By chance some fine Roman sculpture was discovered by workmen who were making an excavation, and to those who saw it it was a revelation of the beauty of the human form. In this way the people of that time were led to see that the ideal of the ancient artists had been to express physical beauty, while artists in the Middle Age had in early periods treated sculpture in general as ecclesiastical symbolism, though occasionally giving their figures spiritual expression, and in Gothic times sculpture was remarkable for realism. Under the stimulus of the beauty of these newly found statues sculptors began to copy and to imitate them, and from this they were led to draw and model from nature and from the human figure. Painters followed their example and soon both painting and sculpture had become new arts. From the illustrations between pages 490–491, you can easily see that the Renaissance artists excelled in drawing and in technical skill in executing their works and that their object was to express beauty in the human form.

Influence of Roman Statuary.

The study of antiquity did not, however, absorb all the interest and energy of the people. They were no less active in exploring the earth and in learning its extent, its resources, and its peoples. Never before had there been manifested so much interest in exploration and discovery. The crusades (1096–1270) had awakened a strong curiosity about foreign lands and peoples, which was quickened and reinforced by the gain to be derived from commerce with them. The first great traveller was Marco Polo (1254–1325),

Exploration and Discovery.

a Venetian, who was led by a variety of interests to spend many years in travel and residence in Asia. While a prisoner of war in Genoa he was persuaded to tell about his travels and experiences and a fellow prisoner committed his story to writing. Polo's recognition as prince of mediæval travellers is due to his romantic story and to the vast compass of his travels. His book is a rich mine of information about Asia and the islands along its shores, and, although there are many passages that seemed incredible, yet further exploration and study have proved the general correctness of his narrative.

Marco Polo

The desire to make pilgrimages and the pure love of travel and adventure brought about a gradual increase in the number of travellers and led to the making of guide-books to assist them in finding their way. The most noted of these guide-books passes under the name of *The Travels of Sir John Mandeville*, and, although this is probably a fictitious name, there can be no doubt that these travels were widely read and that they had considerable influence in spreading geographical knowledge and in promoting the spirit of voyage and discovery in the fifteenth and sixteenth centuries.

Guide-books

Mercantile interests, however, furnished the chief motive for exploring the world. You will recall that in the fourteenth and fifteenth centuries the Turks conquered the eastern Mediterranean lands and thereby cut off the Italian cities from direct commerce with the orient. That not only diminished the business and profits of western merchants, but also raised the price of pepper and other spices, to the use of which the western nations had become addicted. The west was therefore forced to hunt for another route to the east. And this could be only by way of the ocean. Now, navigation was just then improved by the use of the compass, the invention of the astrolabe (an instrument used to determine the position of ships), and the building of ships with high decks to keep out the waves.

Mercantile Interests

In the quest for a water-route to the east Portugal led the way. A Portuguese prince, Henry the Navigator (1394–1460), devoted most of his life to this work. He established a school of navigation on the coast near Cape St. Vincent, in which he trained a number of men in the art of navigation. Every year he sent out exploring expeditions, some of which discovered the Madeira islands and explored a large part of the west coast of Africa. Finally his dream of reaching the Indies by sailing around Africa was realized when Vasco da Gama rounded the Cape of Good Hope and after some weeks cast anchor in the bay of Calcutta (1497).

Portugal.

Spaniards also were interested in reaching the Indies, and Columbus, believing that the earth was round, conceived the idea of sailing around it to the rich source of supplies in the east. After his discovery of land (1492) others followed in his wake. Ponce de Leon explored Florida in 1513; in the same year Balboa discovered the Pacific, and Cortes invaded Mexico in 1519. England and France also sent out many exploring expeditions which added to the world's geographical knowledge. The period of voyage and discovery reached its culmination in the journey around the world, which Magellan began in 1519. Although he met his death at the hands of the natives of the Philippines, some of his vessels safely reached the port in Spain from which they had sailed. It is difficult for us even to imagine how great was the stimulus which all these discoveries imparted to the peoples of western Europe.

Spain.

It is impossible to calculate the effect on the general course of history and civilization of a few great inventions which came into common use during the period of the Renaissance. First of these was the compass. Without it mariners had been forced to sail continually in sight of land or to guide their course by the sun by day and the stars by night. But the heavenly bodies could not be depended on because they were often hidden by clouds, and shoals and rocks and sudden winds made it dangerous to keep near the coast. Navigation was thus hampered until the mariner's compass came into use. It is certain that the Chinese, probably as early as the Christian era, used the magnetic

The Compass

needle to guide their boats. From China the knowledge and use of it eventually spread into western Asia and from there the Arabs introduced it into Europe. Mention was made of it by a Mohammedan poet of Spain in 853 A. D., and by Christian writers about three centuries later. In the thirteenth century it came into common use by sailors, who were thereby made independent of all landmarks as well as of the heavenly bodies. Needless to say, the introduction of the compass into Europe made possible the brilliant achievements of the new man in his work of exploring the world.

Gunpowder.

Gunpowder, too, like the mariner's compass, was invented in China, although it was first used in firearms on a large scale and in an effective way after it was introduced into Europe. The weapons in which it was used at first lacked precision and were consequently somewhat ineffective, but in time they were so improved that, with the use of gunpowder, the art and practice of war and of defense were completely revolutionized. The castle of the mediæval baron, which had been impregnable because of its lofty position, was no longer secure against artillery attacks. Coats of mail, which had offered sufficient resistance to arrows, soon ceased to be worn, because they gave little or no protection against bullets. The longbow, the crossbow, and the pike disappeared, being displaced by more deadly weapons possessing a longer range and greater power of penetration. Cities no longer enjoyed complete protection and safety, because their walls and buildings could be battered down by cannon. The high stone walls of the mediæval city, being no longer a protection, were supplemented and eventually displaced by a series of fortresses which surrounded the city and barred the way against an invading army. And gunpowder also helped the king increase his power over his subjects, for his greater wealth enabled him to hire and keep in the field a larger standing army and to equip it with more and better artillery than his vassals possessed. With such advantages in his favor the king was able to destroy the independence of his great vassals and to make himself absolute master of his realm. The kings of Spain, of France, and of England owed their great power in the sixteenth century chiefly to gunpowder. So it may fairly be said that the use of gunpowder hastened the destruction of feudalism and the centralization of power in the king's hands.

Not less important than the invention of gunpowder was that of paper. A most serious hindrance to the spread of knowledge during the Middle Age was the cost of books. They were written by hand on parchment or vellum, which was prepared in a laborious manner from the skins of animals, chiefly of sheep, goats, and calves. The cost of such parchments made books very expensive, and it was impossible to produce them rapidly and cheaply until some less expensive material for them should be found and a faster way of reproducing them than by hand. Again it was China to which Europe was indebted for an important invention, the process of making paper. More than eighteen hundred years ago the Chinese made paper by reducing rags, linen, hemp, cotton, rice-straw, and the inner bark of the mulberry-tree, to a pulp in water, and then spreading it out in a thin layer to dry. From China the art of making paper spread to the west by way of India and Persia. The Mohammedans practised it throughout their empire. From the Mohammedans in Spain it passed to the Christians, and, before 1500, paper was extensively made in every country of Europe. The invention of movable type, which made printing easy and rapid, created a great demand for it, and its manufacture soon became an important industry.

Paper.

This invention of movable type, about the middle of the fifteenth century, revolutionized the making of books. Printing was not unknown, for small books had already been printed from blocks, each block printing a whole page. The important thing here was the invention of movable type, each type representing a letter. In spite of some uncertainty in the matter, it is generally believed that John Gutenberg, a resident of Mainz,

Movable Type.

Gutenberg.

in Germany, deserves the credit for this invention. At any rate, he excelled all others in his improved way of making type and hence may properly be regarded as the inventor. He melted metal and cast the single letters in moulds, thus making them all of the same size or font. For some years the secret of his invention was known only to the printers of Mainz and of the neighboring cities. But when Mainz was sacked in 1462 (in a war against its archbishop), the printers of the city were scattered, the art became public property, and printing-presses were soon established in nearly all the cities of Europe. There is great uncertainty, it may be said, about the date of publication of the first book. We know, however, that in 1448 Gutenberg was engaged in printing in Mainz, where he probably first produced a few small books or pamphlets. He printed the Bible as early as 1456, although some believe that he may have printed it several years earlier. The first printed book bearing a date is from the year 1457.

The Blight of War.

At the end of the fifteenth century Europe was all astir with new ideas and interests. Art, learning, literature, industry, commerce, and all that goes to make up civilization were flourishing as never before, and everything indicated that Europe was entering on a period of rapid development in civilization, which should surpass that of all previous ages. The Renaissance man, abounding with life, energy, and ambition, justified the hope that he was about to master the world and its secrets and to inaugurate a golden age of progress in all the fields of his activity. This high promise, however, was, for various reasons, not entirely fulfilled. In the first place, the various powers that engaged in discovering the new lands began to fight for the possession of them. Moreover, ambition—a common characteristic of the Renaissance man—led many rulers to covet the lands of neighboring states, and so there was inaugurated a long period of international wars for conquest. And, finally, the general situation was complicated and embittered by the fact that the freer religious movement met with stubborn resistance and led to gigantic and ruinous civil struggles. These wars, religious, civil, and international, involved all of western Europe, and effectively checked the course of civilization that had made so rapid progress during the Renaissance.

BIBLIOGRAPHY

No attempt is made to give a complete bibliography of the history of the Middle Age.

WORKS ON BIBLIOGRAPHY AND SOURCE MATERIAL

Langlois, *Manuel de Bibliographie Historique.* 2 vols.
Potthast, *Wegweiser durch die Geschichtswerke des Europäischen Mittelalters bis 1500.* 2 vols.
Dahlmann-Waitz, *Quellenkunde der deutschen Geschichte.*
Molinier, *Les Sources de l'Histoire de France des Origines aux Guerres d'Italie.* 3 vols.
Gross, *Sources of English History.*
Wattenbach, *Deutschlands Geschichtsquellen im Mittelalter.* 2 vols.
Early Chroniclers of Europe. 3 vols. England, Gairdner; France, Masson; Italy, Balzani.

HISTORICAL ATLASES

Droysen, Schrader, Putzger, Poole, Spruner-Menke, Dow, Shepard.

SOURCE BOOKS

Thatcher and McNeal, *Source Book for Mediæval History* (cited S. B.).
Ogg, *A Source Book of Medieval History* (cited O.).
Robinson, *Readings in European History,* vol. I (cited R.).
Munro and Sellery, *Medieval Civilization.*
Henderson, *Selected Documents of the Middle Ages.*
Translations and Reprints from the Original Sources of European History. (The University of Pennsylvania.)
Adams and Stephens, *Select Documents of English Constitutional History* (cited A. and S.).
Munro, *A Source Book for Roman History* (cited M.).
Lee, *Source Book of English history* (cited L.).
Cheyney, *Readings in English History drawn from the Original Sources* (cited Ch.).
Colby, *Selections from the Sources of English History.*
Bell, *English History Source Books.*

WORKS OF A MORE OR LESS GENERAL CHARACTER

Lavisse, *General View of the Political History of Europe.*
Lavisse et Rambaud, *Histoire générale du IVe Siècle à nos Jours.* (First four volumes deal with the Middle Age.)

The Cambridge Medieval History. 2 vols. have appeared.
The Cambridge Modern History, vol. I.
Assmann, *Geschichte des Mittelalters.* 2 vols.
C. R. L. Fletcher, *The Making of Western Europe*, 300 to 1190. 2 vols.
C. F. Young, *East and West through Fifteen Centuries.* 4 vols.
Masterman, *The Dawn of Medieval Europe*, 476–918.
Lee, *The Central Period of the Middle Age*, 918–1273.
Lodge, *The End of the Middle Age*, 1273–1453.
Oman, *The Dark Ages*, 476–918.
Tout, *The Empire and the Papacy*, 918–1273.
Lodge, *The Close of the Middle Ages*, 1273–1494.
Hallam, *View of the States of Europe in the Middle Ages.*
Stillé, *Studies in Medieval Europe.*
Emerton, *Introduction to the Middle Ages.*
Mediæval Europe.
Beginnings of Modern Europe.
Thorndike, *The History of Medieval Europe.*
Gibbon, *Decline and Fall of the Roman Empire*, edited by J. B. Bury.
H. O. Taylor, *The Medieval Mind.* 2 vols.
Maitland, *The Dark Ages.*
Adams, *Civilization during the Middle Ages.*
Guizot, *History of Civilization.*
Bryce, *The Holy Roman Empire.*
H. Fisher, *The Medieval Empire.* 2 vols.
Richter, *Annalen des deutschen Reiches.* 3 vols.
Jastrow-Winter, *Deutsche Geschichte im Zeitalter der Hohenstaufen.*
Loserth, *Geschichte des späteren Mittelalters.*
Henderson, *History of Germany in the Middle Ages.*
Lavisse, *Histoire de France.* 8 vols.
MacDonald, *History of France.* 3 vols.
Kitchin, *History of France.* 3 vols.
Traill, *Social England*, vols. 1, 2.
Newman, *Manual of Church History*, vol. 1.
Alzog, *Manual of Universal Church History.* 3 vols.
Milman, *History of Latin Christianity.*
Schaff, *History of the Christian Church*, vols. 1–4.

Works of Special Reference to Particular Chapters

Introduction

Thomas, *Source Book for Social Origins*, pp. 1–139, with bibliography.
Semple, *The Influence of Geographic Environment.*

Chapter I. The Roman Empire

Friedländer, *Darstellungen aus der Sittengeschichte Roms.* 2 vols.
Dill, *Roman Society in the Last Century of the Western Empire.*
Taylor, *The Classical Heritage of the Middle Ages.*

CHAPTER II. THE INVASIONS. CHAPTER III. JUSTINIAN

Hodgkin, *Italy and Her Invaders.* 8 vols.
The Dynasty of Theodosius.
Theodoric the Goth.
Bury, *History of the Later Roman Empire.* 2 vols.
Villari, *The Barbarian Invasions of Italy.* 2 vols.
Augustine, *City of God* (tr. by John Healey in the Temple Classics).

CHAPTER IV. THE FRANKS. CHAPTER V. THE HOUSE OF CHARLEMAGNE

Davis, *Charlemagne.*
Hodgkin, *Charles the Great.*
Mombert, *History of Charles the Great.*
Sergeant, *The Franks.*
Gregory of Tours, *History of the Franks* (tr. by Brehaut in *Records of Civilization*).
Einhard, *Life of Charlemagne* (tr. by Turner).
For the Northmen and the Normans, who are frequently mentioned:
Johnson, *The Normans.*
Haskins, *The Normans in European History.*
Keary, *The Vikings in Western Europe.*

CHAPTER VII. FEUDALISM

Seignobos, *The Feudal Régime.*
Luchaire, *Social France.*
Cornish, *Chivalry.*
Cheyney, *Documents Illustrative of Feudalism* (Translations and Reprints, vol. 4, no. 3).

CHAPTER VIII. THE DEVELOPMENT OF THE PAPACY

Hatch, *Growth of Church Institutions.*
Duchesne, *The Early Church.*
Wells, *The Age of Charlemagne* (Epochs of Church History).

CHAPTER IX. MONASTICISM

Rogers, *Students' History of Philosophy,* pp. 119–190.
Wishart, *A Short History of Monks and Monasticism.*
Montalembert, *The Monks of the West.*
Workman, *The Evolution of the Monastic Ideal.*
Harnack, *Monasticism.*

CHAPTER X. GERMANY AND THE EMPIRE

Stubbs, Germany in the Early Middle Ages.

CHAPTER XI. EMPIRE AND PAPACY. FIRST PERIOD

Mathew, *Life and Times of Hildebrand.*
Stephens, *Hildebrand and His Times* (Epochs of Church History).

CHAPTER XII, CHAPTER XIII. EMPIRE AND PAPACY. SECOND AND THIRD PERIODS

Balzani, *The Popes and the Hohenstaufen.*
Kingston-Oliphant, *History of Frederick II.* 2 vols.

CHAPTER XIV. MOHAMMED

Gilman, *The Saracens.*
Lane-Poole, *Speeches and Table-Talk of the Prophet Mohammed.*
Palmer, *Translation of the Koran.*
Margoliouth, *Mohammed* (Heroes of the Nations).

CHAPTER XV. THE CRUSADES

Archer and Kingford, *The Crusades.*
Neale, *The Story of the Crusades.*
von Sybel, *The History and Literature of the First Crusade* (tr. by Lady Duff Gordon).
Pears, *The Fall of Constantinople.*
Condor, *The Latin Kingdom of Jerusalem.*
Archer, *The Crusade of Richard I.*
Kugler, *Geschichte der Kreuzzüge.*
Röhricht, *Geschichte des ersten Kreuzzuges.*
Geschichte des Königreiches Jerusalem.
Gray, *The Children's Crusade.*

CHAPTER XVI. GROWTH OF THE FRENCH NATION

Adams, *Growth of the French Nation.*
Hutton, *Philip Augustus.*
Perry, *St. Louis.*
Joinville, *Life of St. Louis* (Chronicles of the Crusades, Everyman's Library).

CHAPTER XVII. THE ORIGINS OF THE ENGLISH NATION.

Oman, *England before the Norman Conquest.*
Hodgkin, *Political History of England to* 1066.
Plummer, *Life and Times of Alfred the Great.*
Bede and the Anglo-Saxon Chronicle (tr. by Giles in Bohn's Library).

CHAPTER XVIII. FORMATION OF THE ENGLISH NATION

Adams, *Political History of England*, 1066–1216.
Davis, *England under the Normans and Angevins.*
Tout, *Edward I.*
Medley, *English Constitutional History.*
Pollock and Maitland, *History of English Law through Edward I.*

CHAPTER XIX. THE HUNDRED YEARS' WAR. FIRST PART

Longman, *Life and Times of Edward III.* 2 vols.
Tout, *Political History of England*, 1216–1377.

Trevelyan, *England in the Age of Wyclif.*
Oman, *The Great Revolt of* 1381.
Froissart, *Chronicle* (Globe edition).

CHAPTER XX. THE HUNDRED YEARS' WAR. SECOND PART

Vickers, *England in the Later Middle Ages.*
Oman, *Political History of England,* 1377–1485.
Lowell, *Joan of Arc.*
James, *Joan of Arc.*
Lang, *The Maid of Orleans.*
Commines, *Memoirs* (Bohn Library, 2 vols.).

CHAPTER XXI. DECLINE OF THE PAPACY

Pastor, *History of the Popes,* vol. I.
Creighton, *History of the Papacy,* vol. I.
Van Dyke, *Age of the Renascence* (Epochs of Church History).
Lea, *History of the Inquisition.*

CHAPTER XXII. GERMANY, 1250–1500

Stubbs, *Germany in the Later Middle Ages.*

CHAPTER XXIV. CITIES AND CITY LIFE

Histories of Commerce: Gibbins, Heyd, Day.
Industrial Histories: Levasseur, Cunningham, Cheyney.
Jusserand, *English Wayfaring Life in the Middle Ages.*
Zimmern, *The Hansa Towns.*
Symonds, *The Age of the Despots.*

CHAPTER XXV. CIVILIZATION AND CULTURE

Rashdall, *History of the Universities of Europe in the Middle Ages.* 3 vols.
Laurie. *The Rise of the Universities* (Humboldt Library).
Sabatier, *St. Francis of Assisi.*
Jessopp, *Coming of the Friars.*
The Little Flowers of St. Francis (Temple Classics).
Literature of the Middle Age in translation:
  Butler, *The Song of Roland.*
  Newell, *King Arthur.* 2 vols. (From *Chrestien de Troyes.*)
  Nibelungenlied (Everyman's Library).
Cox and Jones, *Popular Romances of the Middle Ages.*
Moore, *Gothic Architecture.*

CHAPTER XXVI. THE RENAISSANCE

Symonds, *The Renaissance in Italy.*
Geiger, *Humanismus und Renaissance in Italien und Deutschland.*
Voigt, *Wiederbelebung des classischen Altertums.* 2 vols.
Armstrong, *Lorenzo de' Medici.*
Robinson and Rolfe, *Petrarch.*
Machiavelli, *The Prince* (Bohn Library).

Historical Novels

Hardy, *Passe-Rose* (the age of Charlemagne).
von Scheffel, *Ekkehard* (tenth century).
Scott, *Ivanhoe* (the crusades), *The Talisman* (the crusades), *Quentin Durward* (time of Louis XI).
Reade, *The Cloister and the Hearth* (fifteenth century).
Kingsley, *Hypatia* (fourth century), *Hereward the Wake* (England in the time of William the Conqueror).
Porter, *Scottish Chiefs* (Scotland in the time of Edward I).
Lytton, *The Last of the Barons* (time of the war of the Roses).

CHRONOLOGICAL TABLES

I

EMPERORS AND POPES

NOTE.—The table of Emperors is complete from Charlemagne on; the table of Popes contains only the more important names.

NOTE 2.—The names in italics are those of German kings who never made any claim to the imperial title. Those marked with an * were never actually crowned at Rome. Charles V. was crowned by the Pope, but at Bologna, not at Rome.

Year of Accession.	Popes.	Emperors.	Year of Accession.
A.D.			A.D.
314	Sylvester I. (d. 336).		
		Constantine (the Great), alone.	323
		Julian the Apostate.	361
		Theodosius I.	379
		Arcadius (in the East), Honorius (in the West).	395
		Theodosius II. (E.).	408
		Valentinian III. (W.).	424
440	Leo I. (the Great). (d. 461).		
		Romulus Augustulus (W.).	475
		(Western line ends with Romulus Augustulus, 476.)	
		[*Till 800, there are Emperors only at Constantinople.*]	
		Anastasius I.	491
		Justin I.	518
		Justinian.	527
		Justin II.	565
590	Gregory I. (the Great), d. 604.		
715	Gregory II.		

Year of Accession.	Popes.	Emperors.	Year of Accession.
A.D.			A.D.
		Leo III. (the Isaurian).	718
731	Gregory III.		
741	Zacharias.		
752	Stephen II.		
752	Stephen III.		
772	Hadrian I.		
		Constantine VI.	780
		(Deposition of Constantine VI. by Irene, 797.)	
		[The table gives henceforth only the Emperors of the new Western line.]	
795	Leo III.		
		Charlemagne.	800
		Ludwig I.	814
816	Stephen IV. (d. 817).		
		Lothar I.	840
		Ludwig II. (in Italy).	855
872	John VIII. (d. 882).		
		Charles II. (the Bald).	875
		Charles III. (the Fat).	881
885	Stephen V.		
891	Formosus.	Guido (in Italy).	891
		Lambert (in Italy).	894
896	Boniface VI.		
896	Stephen VI. (d. 897).	Arnulf.	896
		Ludwig the Child.	899
		Louis III. of Provence (in Italy).	901
		Conrad I.	911
		Berengar (in Italy).	915
		Henry I. (*the Fowler*).	918
955	John XII.		
		Otto I., *King*, 936; Emperor, 962.	962
963	Leo VIII. (d. 965).		
		Otto II.	973
		Otto III.	983
		Henry II. (the Holy).	1002
		Conrad II. (the Salic).	1024
		Henry III. (the Black).	1039
		Henry IV.	1056
1057	Stephen IX.		
1058	Benedict X.		
1059	Nicholas II.		
1061	Alexander II.		
1073	Gregory VII. (Hildebrand).		
		(Rudolph of Suabia, rival.)	1077
1080	(Clement, Anti-pope.)		
		(Hermann of Luxemburg, rival.)	1081

Year of Accession.	Popes.	Emperors.	Year of Accession.
A.D.			A.D.
1086	Victor III.		
1087	Urban II.		
		(Conrad of Franconia, rival.)	1093
1099	Paschal II.		
		Henry V.	1106
1118	Gelasius II.		
1119	Calixtus II. (d. 1124).		
		Lothar II.	1125
		*Conrad III.	1138
		Frederick I. (Barbarossa).	1152
1154	Hadrian IV.		
1159	Alexander III. (d. 1181).		
1159	(Victor Anti-pope).		
		Henry VI.	1190
		*Philip of Suabia, Otto IV. (rivals).	1197
1198	Innocent III.		
		Otto IV., alone.	1208
		Frederick II.	1212
1216	Honorius III.		
1227	Gregory IX.		
1241	Celestine IV.		
1243	Innocent IV. (d. 1254).		
		(Henry Raspe, rival.)	1246
		(William of Holland, rival.)	1246
		*Conrad IV.	1250
		Interregnum.	1254
		*Richard of Cornwall and *Alfonso of Castile, rivals.	1257
1271	Gregory X. (d. 1276).		
		*Rudolph I. of Hapsburg.	1273
1277	Nicholas III. (d. 1281).		
		*Adolph of Nassau.	1292
1294	Boniface VIII.		
		*Albrecht I. of Hapsburg.	1298
1303	Benedict XI.		
1305	Clement V. (who removes Papacy to Avignon).		
		Henry VII. of Luxemburg.	1308
		Louis IV. of Bavaria.	1314
		(Frederick of Austria, rival.)	
1316	John XXII. (d. 1334).		
		Charles IV. of Luxemburg.	1347
		(Günther of Schwarzburg, rival.)	
1352	Innocent VI.		

Year of Accession.	Popes.	Emperors.	Year of Accession.
A.D.			A.D.
1362	Urban V.		
1370	Gregory XI. (who brings Papacy back to Rome).		
1378	Urban VI. (Clement VI., Anti-pope.) [*Here begins the Great Schism.*]	*Wenzel of Luxemburg.	1378
		*Rupert of the Palatinate.	1400
		Sigismund of Luxemburg.	1410
1417	Martin V. [*Great Schism healed.*]		
1431	Eugene IV.		
		*Albert II. of Hapsburg.	1438
		Frederick III. of Hapsburg.	1440
1447	Nicholas V.		
1455	Calixtus IV.		
1458	Pius II. (Æneas Piccolomini).		
1464	Paul II.		
1471	Sixtus IV.		
1484	Innocent VIII.		
1492	Alexander VI. (Borgia), d. 1503.		
		*Maximilian I. of Hapsburg.	1493
		Charles V. of Hapsburg.	1519

This table has been compiled from Bryce's Holy Roman Empire, with the kind permission of the publishers, The Macmillan Company.

II.—THE MEROVINGIAN KINGS TO DAGOBERT I.

- Chlodovech I., 481–511.
  - Theuderic I., King of Metz (Austrasia), 511–34.
    - Theudebert, King of Austrasia, 534–48.
      - Theudebald, King of Austrasia, 548–55.
  - Chlodomer, King of Orleans, 511–54.
  - Childebert I., King of Paris, 511–58.
  - Chlothar I., King of Soissons, 511–61; sole King of the Franks, 558–61.
    - Charibert, King of Paris, 561–67.
      - Bertha, Queen of Kent.
    - Gontran, King of Orleans and Burgundy, 561–94.
    - Sigebert I., King of Austrasia, 561–75.
      - Childebert II., King of Austrasia, 575–96; and of Burgundy, 593–96.
        - Theudebert II., King of Austrasia, 596–612.
        - Theuderic II., King of Orleans and of Burgundy, 596–612; and of Austrasia, 612.
    - Chilperic I. King of Soissons, 561–84; King of Neustria, 567–84.
      - Chlothar II., King of Soissons, 584–628; sole King of the Franks, 613–28.
        - Dagobert I., sole king, 628–38.

NOTE.—After Dagobert come the Donothing Kings (rois faindants).

III.—THE DUKES OF AUSTRASIA (Ancestors of Karl the Great).

Pippin of Landen, 614–639–40 (?).
- Grimoald, + 656.
- Begga = Adalgisel, + 685 (son of Arnulf, bishop of Metz).
  - Plectrud = Pippin of Heristhal = Alpais (concubine). 685–714.
    - (by Plectrud) Drogo, + 708.
    - (by Plectrud) Grimoald, + 714.
    - (by Alpais) Charles Martel, 714–41.
      - Karlman, entered monastery, + 754.
      - Pippin the Short [Mayor, 741–51. King, 751–68.]
        - Charlemagne, 768–814.
        - Karlman, 768–72.

IV.—THE CAROLINGIAN HOUSE (THE KARLINGS).

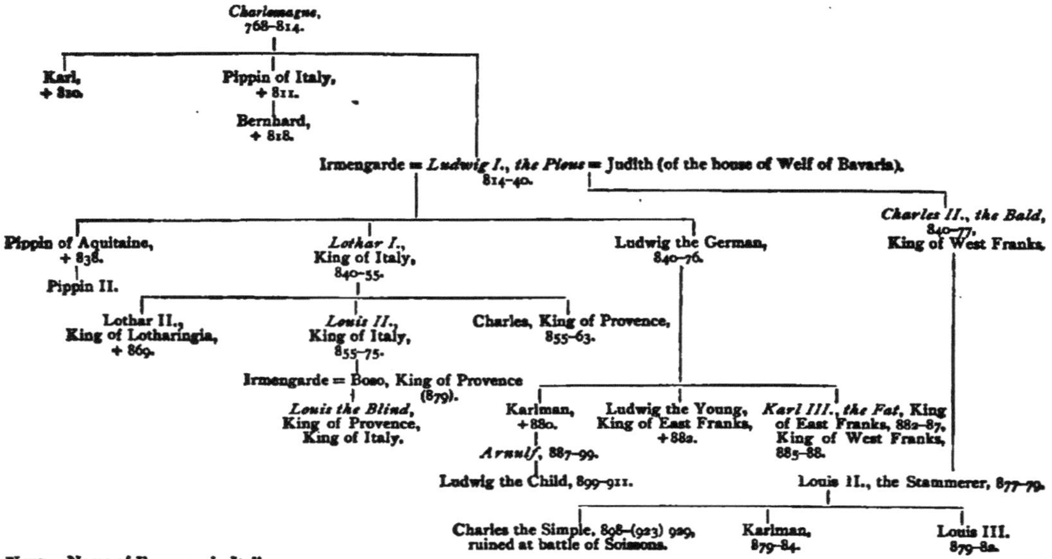

NOTE.—Name of Emperors in Italics.

V.—LATER CAROLINGIANS AND FIRST CAPETIANS (ROBERTINES), SHOWING THEIR CONNECTION AND RIVALRY.

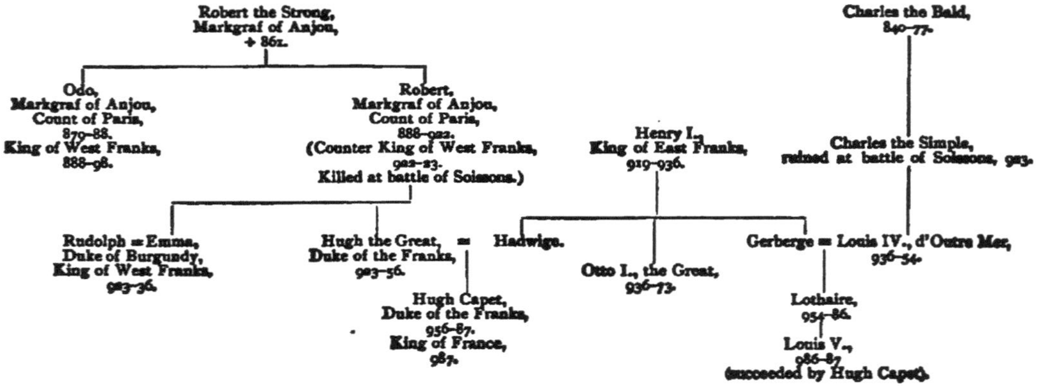

VI.—KINGS OF ENGLAND TO THE NORMAN CONQUEST.

SAXON KINGS OF ENGLAND.

- Egbert, 827–36.
  - Æthelwolf, 836–57.
    - Æthelbald, 857–60.
    - Æthelbert, 860–66.
    - Æthelred I., 866–71.
    - Ælfred, 871–901.
      - Eadward the Elder, 901–25.
        - Æthelstan, 925–41.
        - Eadmund I., 941–46.
          - Eadwy, 955–58.
          - Eadgar, 959–75.
            - Eadward the Martyr, 975–78.
            - Æthelred II., the Redeless, 978–1013, 1014–16. = Emma = *Knut*, 1016–35.
              - (Æthelred II.) Eadmund Ironsides, April–November, 1016.
              - (Æthelred II. and Emma) Eadward the Confessor, 1042–66.
              - (Knut) *Harold I.*, 1035–39.
              - (Knut) *Hardiknut*, 1039–42.
        - Eadred, 946–55.

DANISH KINGS OF ENGLAND.

- *Swein*, 1013–14.
  - *Knut*, 1016–35.

NORMAN DUKES.

- **Rolf.**
  - **William Longsword.**
    - **Richard the Fearless.**
      - Emma
      - **Richard the Good.**
        - **Robert the Devil.**
          - **William the Conqueror** (invaded and conquered England, 1066), 1066–87.

NOTE.—Norman Dukes in fullface type.
Danish Kings in *italics*.
Saxon Kings in roman.

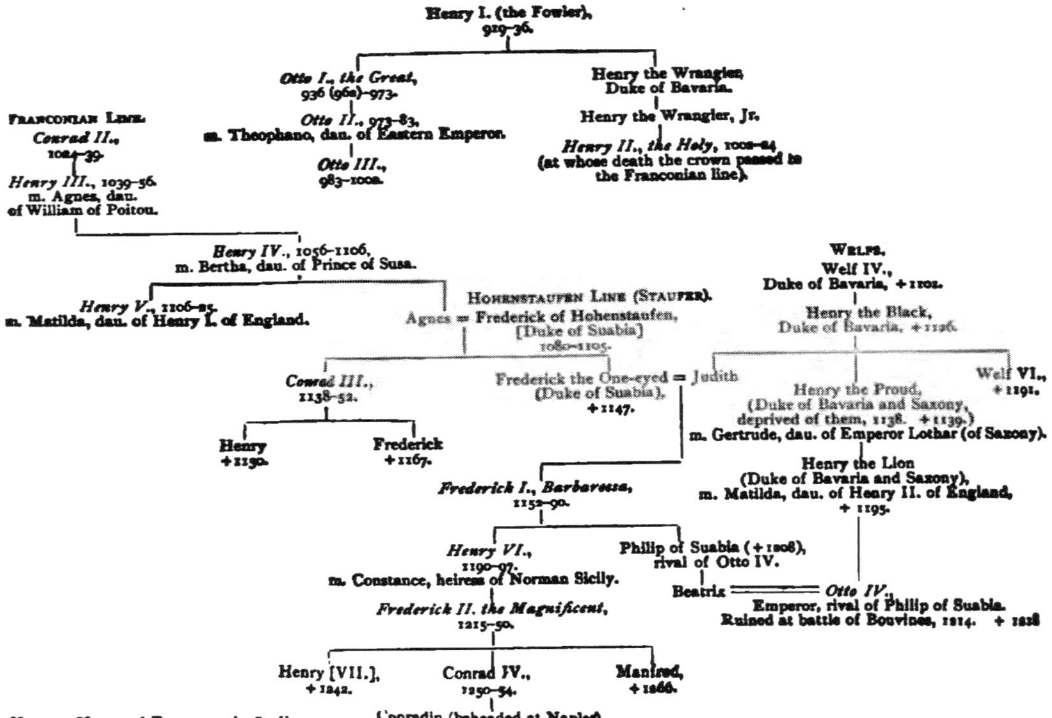

Note.— Name of Emperors in Italics.

VIII.—KINGS OF FRANCE AND COLLATERAL BRANCHES

CAPETIAN HOUSE.

- Hugh Capet, 987–96.
  - Robert the Pious, 996–1031.
    - Henry I., 1031–60.
      - Philip I., 1060–1108.
        - Louis VI., the Fat, 1108–37.
          - Louis VII., the Young, 1137–80.
            - Philip II., Augustus, 1180–1223.
              - Louis VIII., 1223–26.
                - Louis IX. (Saint Louis), 1226–70
                  - Philip III., the Rash, 1270–85.
                    - Philip IV., the Fair, 1285–1314.
                      - Isabel, m. Edward II., King of England.
                        - Edward III., King of England. (Claimed French crown, 1328.)
                      - Louis X., 1314–16.
                        - Jeanne of Navarre.
                          - Charles the Bad.
                      - Philip V., 1316–22.
                      - Charles IV., 1322–28.
                    - **VALOIS.** Charles of Valois.
                      - Philip VI., 1328–50.
                        - John II., 1350–64.
                          - **SECOND HOUSE OF ANJOU-NAPLES. (Only intermittently in possession.)** Louis, Duke of Anjou. Founder of Second House of Naples.
                            - Louis II., + 1417.
                              - Louis III., + 1434.
                              - René, + 1480.
                              - (Charles of Maine.)
                                - Charles, + 1481. Leaving Anjou and claims to Naples to Louis XI.
                          - Charles V., the Wise, 1364–80.
                            - Charles VI., 1380–1422.
                              - Charles VII., 1422–61.
                                - Louis XI., 1461–83.
                                  - Charles VIII., 1483–98.
                          - **BURGUNDY.** Philip, Duke of Burgundy, 1361–1404.
                            - John the Fearless, 1404–19.
                              - Philip the Good, 1419–67.
                                - Charles the Bold, 1467–77.
                                  - Mary = Maximilian of Austria.
                - **FIRST HOUSE OF ANJOU-NAPLES.** Charles of Anjou (who supplanted the Hohenstaufen in Norman Sicily or Naples), 1266–85.
                  - Charles II., + 1309.
                    - Robert, + 1343.
                      - (Charles.)
                        - Joan I., + 1382.

IX.—KINGS OF ENGLAND FROM THE NORMAN CONQUEST TO HENRY VII.

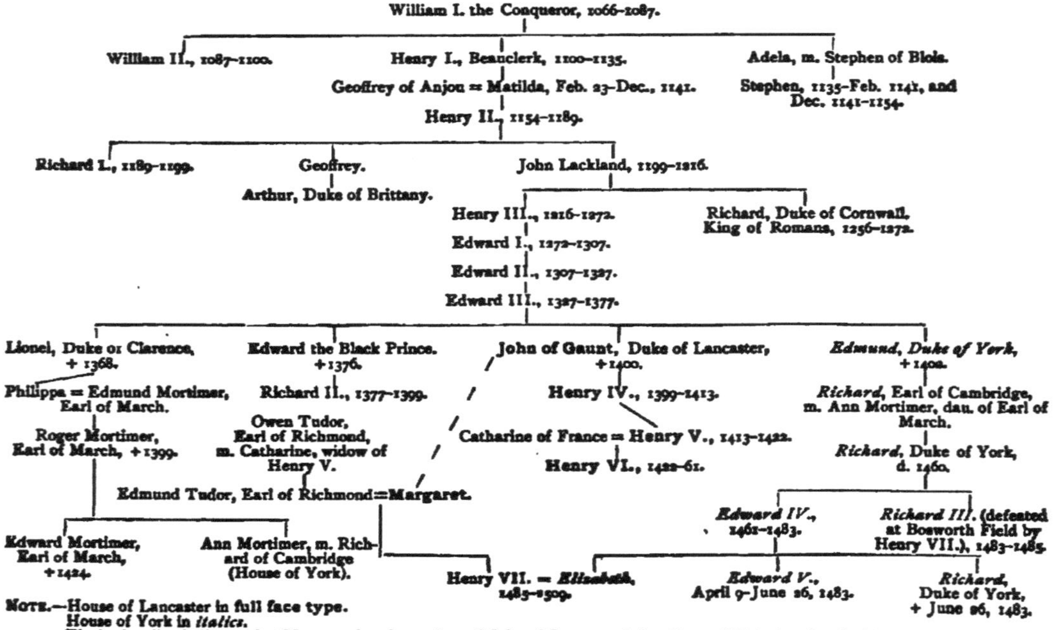

NOTE.—House of Lancaster in full face type.
House of York in *italics*.
The broken line indicates that Margaret is a descendant of John of Gaunt, and that Henry VII. is therefore by his mother a Lancastrian.

X.—THE HAPSBURG-BURGUNDIAN AND HAPSBURG-SPANISH MARRIAGES.

Maximilian I., d. 1519. = Mary of Burgundy, Daughter of Charles the Bold.

Ferdinand, King of Aragon, d. 1516. = Isabella, Queen of Castile, d. 1504.

Philip the Fair, Archduke of Austria. = Joanna the Insane, Queen of Aragon-Castile.

Charles I. (Spain), V. (Emperor), d. 1558.

INDEX